Wisdom of Communities

Wisdom of Communities

Volume 4
Communication in Community

Published by
The Fellowship for Intentional Community
Rutledge, Missouri

The Fellowship for Intentional Community, Rutledge, MO 63563

ISBN: 978-0-9995885-7-4
Printed by CreateSpace.

Cover design: Megan Cranford, www.megancranforddesign.com

Layout design: Marty Klaif

Project managers: Chris Roth, Christopher Kindig

SUSTAINABILITY IN COMMUNITY
(Wisdom of Communities, Volume 4)

CONTENTS

Introduction 1

I. FOOD, WATER, AND PERMACULTURE

Community Composting: A Transformative Practice 5
Communities 143, 48–51   Jason Grubb and Mason Vollmer
At Camphill Soltane, composting is both a metaphor for and essential element in the process of building community.

Water Is Life 9
Communities 143, 42–43   Leila Dregger
In southern Portugal, the Tamera community creates a model for reversing desertification and enhancing regional food autonomy.

Food Security in Community 11
Communities 144, 54–56, 79   Blake Cothron
In increasingly difficult times, growing our own food in community can be the best form of food security. Lessons learned from other groups can help our own gardens and communities bloom.

To Learn Sustainability Is To Learn Community: An Example from South Portugal 16
Communities 147, 26–29   Leila Dregger
Strained by difficult economic and ecological conditions, farmers Claudio and Fernando discover new avenues toward prosperity and land restoration through alliances with a peace community dedicated to regional renewal.

The Gift of Compost 20
Communities 152, 37   Jesse Harasta
To the Compostmeister at a collective house, the cycles of compost embody a new economics that focuses upon human needs and relationships.

Permaculture at The Farm: Climate Prophylaxis 22
Communities 153, 24–26   Albert Bates
Drawing on its long association with permaculture, The Farm in Tennessee institutes on-the-ground projects designed to provide resilience in times of climate change.

Hugelkultur on the Prairie, or Learning from Our Mistakes 25
Communities 153, 30–31   Alyson Ewald
Degraded slopes, crumbling logs, plenty of trench-digging, seven blueberry plants, and an unanticipated drought combine to teach some important lessons.

The Future of Water:
Halting desertification, restoring ecosystems, and nourishing communities 27
Communities 153, 32, 74   Jeff Anderson
Working with permaculturalist Sepp Holzer, Tamera Peace Research Center in Portugal dramatically increases the water in its landscape, restoring soil fertility and demonstrating techniques with worldwide application.

Permaculture on Low to No Budget **29**
Communities 153, 33–35   Elizabeth Barrette
By following basic principles, taking advantage of money-saving ideas, and involving the local
community, we can start functional permaculture landscapes with little or no money.

Permaculture as a Tool for Ecological Community Design **32**
Communities 153, 50–53   Ethan Hirsch-Tauber
A veteran of educational programs at Auroville in India and Sirius Community in Massachusetts applies
permaculture principles to the creation of dynamic, regenerative communities.

How Permaculture Stole My Community! **36**
Communities 153, 54–55   Arjuna da Silva
After a painful period stranded in "permaculture heaven," an Earthaven founder finds her community
finally moving back towards balance with its eco-spiritual roots.

Doing It, or Are We? **38**
Communities 153, 46–47   Tracy Matfin with Dona Willoughby
On Hawaii's Big Island, La'akea Community explores sustainability through myriad experiments—from
keeping wild pet pigs in the garden to eating 100 percent locally to mowing with sheep.

Southern Exposure Seed Exchange Wrestles with Growth **40**
Communities 163, 16–17   Irena Hollowell
For an income-sharing group in Virginia, economic success presents challenges and opportunities.

The Dirty Business of Growing a Cohousing Community Farm **43**
Communities 163, 29–33   Sandy Thomson
A farm is not a clod of dirt; it is more like mud that slips through your hands, gets on your boots, and is
tracked all through the community.

Recipe for Community **48**
Communities 167, 8   Chris Roth
Food is often at the center of our interdependence as human beings—a potent force in bringing us
together and in helping us understand and define who we are together.

How the Kitchen Is the Heart of a Community **49**
Communities 167, 10–11   Devon Bonady
A shared kitchen provides not just physical sustenance, but emotional benefits and greater connection to
our food and one another.

Cookin' Dinner for the Revolution **52**
Communities 167, 12–14   Jesika Feather
A vibrant, reliable, and nourishing home-base can provide activists with a much-needed feeling of
sustainability.

Hot Topic, Raw Emotion, and the Spice of Life: Chewing over Food Choice in Community **56**
Communities 167, 18–21   Tracy Matfin
At La'akea, members' various approaches to food reflect the quest for emotional as well as physical
sustainability.

My Journey with Food in Community: A Banquet, in Five Courses **60**
Communities 167, 22–25   Gigi Wahba
Whether among families, friends, communitarians, or neighbors, food has many roles and provides
critical context for community functioning.

Make Food, Make *Hygge*, Make Happy. 64
Communities 167, 26–27   Jane Moran
The art of creating intimacy, conviviality, and contentment is an essential ingredient in vibrant
community.

Discovering the Joy of Communal Food:
Camaraderie and Work at Maitreya Mountain Village 66
Communities 167, 28   Dan Schultz
A community pioneer finds greater satisfaction in becoming less independent.

The Community's Garden Orchestra. 67
Communities 167, 32–35   Chris Roth
Engaging in collective food-production is like making our own music together: it's both difficult and
rewarding, especially with diverse players involved.

How Do We Eat As If We Plan to Be Here for Another 10,000 Years?
Cultivating Food Culture in Stewardship of Place 72
Communities 167, 36–38   Olivia Rathbone
The Occidental Arts and Ecology Center suggests that in addressing the eco-crisis (or "crisis of home"),
the best place to start may be around the dinner table.

Fours Ways to Grow at Heartwood. 75
Communities 167, 39–41   Sandy Thomson
Small to large in scale, and solo to collective in orientation, a palette of gardening and farming options
helps feed this cohousing community.

Belfast Ecovillage Produces Farm. 78
Communities 167, 46   Sarah Lozanova
Twenty-two members in a 36-unit ecovillage contribute to maintaining a Community Supported
Agriculture farm on land that they own collectively.

The Balancing Act of Farming in Community 79
Communities 167, 47–51   Coleen O'Connell
Is Cobb Hill a model of how to do community and farming cooperatively, or a case study in their
challenges?

Cardboard, Control, and Catch-22s: Community and the Food Production Dilemma 84
Communities 167, 52–54   Moss Mulligan
Even our best-intentioned gardening and farming methods may be more a part of the problem than the
solution.

Glimpsing the Wild Within: the Sacred Violence of Eating 87
Communities 167, 55–57   Lindsay Hagamen
Embracing the eternal dance of Life transforming itself from one form to another also means accepting
our own sometimes-bloody struggle to survive.

Cool Pickles. 90
Communities 167, 60   Albert Bates
Good for the soil, the climate, and our digestive tracts, biochar often finds itself in a pickle at The Farm.

Small and Large Miracles: Food, Land, and Community at Kibbutz Lotan 91
Communities 167, 61–62   Alex Cicelsky
Food production, permaculture, and communal meals are at the heart and economic center of this
group's life.

Celebrating the Local, Shared Bounty at Groundswell Cohousing. 93
Communities 167, 63   Julia Jongkind
The love of food—growing it, eating it, sharing and preserving it—has been what holds these cohousers
together through thick and thin.

II. SHELTER AND ECO-BUILDING

Beyond Sustainability: Building for Health. 97
Communities 147, 60–64   Julie Genser
People with environmental intolerances could be a perfect match for intentional community living if
their needs were better understood and met there. Are communities willing to educate themselves and
perhaps stretch their definitions of "sustainability" in order to accommodate the environmentally ill?

Tiny Houses as Appropriate Technology 102
Communities 165, 54–59   Mary Murphy
Tiny houses are simple, homemade solutions that solve housing problems, increase our sustainability,
and add a little more beauty and fun to the world.

It Takes All Kinds to Raise a Village 108
Communities 168, 17–19   Melanie Rios
After an engaged local citizenry creates cultural shifts, a city endorses rather than prosecutes code-
bending strategies that promote resilient community.

My Struggle to Legalize Sustainable Living 111
Communities 168, 22–25   Graham Ellis
After nearly three decades of activity, a pioneering eco-community collapses under the weight of legal
attacks by a small group of neighbors.

Adventures of the Mini Moon:
Realities of building your own earthen house with reused materials and volunteer labor 115
Communities 179, 8–11   Jenny Leis
Becoming a general contractor for a project way beyond one's abilities can be a powerful, humbling,
community-building learning adventure, especially when the house is made of horse manure.

Building Collectively Is Greener, Easier, and Cheaper 120
Communities 179, 12–15   Jenny Pickerill
Eco-building in community offers both opportunities and challenges, benefits and potential drawbacks,
as compared to doing it alone.

Harmonious Homemade Habitat 124
Communities 179, 16–18   Laura Harris
Having built the strawbale house of her dreams, a Tolstoy Farm resident encourages others to use natural
building and eco-materials to construct durable, nontoxic, low-impact, energy-efficient, and creative
structures.

Building in an Ecovillage: Lessons Learned. 127
Communities 179, 19–21   Tony "Papa Bear" Barrett
Yes, you can build your own house; you don't have to do it alone; you don't have to do it all...and 18
more tips from a professional builder who learned his trade at Dancing Rabbit Ecovillage.

Ionia's Barn Project: Where Community and Natural Building Meet 130
Communities 179, 22–25   Eliza Eller
At this cooperative ecovillage, the barn is magical, a space that will make a liberating special meeting
area, meditation nook, reading loft, and more...once, after nine long years of building, it is done.

Building with Respect. **134**
Communities 179, 26–28   Alexis Zeigler
Green building could be our salvation or hasten our destruction, depending on what we pursue and
how. Here are a dozen suggestions to make the former more likely.

Eco-Building at the Ecovillage (I Have Built a Home) **137**
Communities 179, 29–31   Arjuna da Silva
At Earthaven Ecovillage, the experience of planning, building, working with others, and living in the
sensual, earthy "Leela"—part temple, part hideaway—proves to be a dream come true.

Good Neighbours with Earth:
Using natural building materials in community-scale construction **140**
Communities 179, 32–35   Robin Allison
Earthsong Eco-Neighbourhood offers their mistakes, successes, and learnings in the hope of encouraging
the wider use of natural building materials and systems in cohousing projects.

A High-Performance Building for Cohousing: From Vision to Move-In **145**
Communities 179, 36–41   Michael Mariano
So you want to design, build, and live in community in the most ecologically positive building that can
be built? After a decade-long pursuit of that goal, a co-creator of Capitol Hill Urban Cohousing recounts
lessons learned along the way.

From Blight to Beautiful: Renovating an Urban House By and For Community **151**
Communities 179, 42–45   Lindsay Speer
An overgrown lot with a dilapidated house transforms into an urban permaculture oasis thanks to the
efforts of the Bread and Roses Collective in Syracuse, New York.

III. ENERGY AND ECOLOGICAL FOOTPRINT

Sharing and Climate Change. **157**
Communities 143, 16–17   Bucket Von Harmony
A simple solution could drastically reduce the energy consumption and carbon emissions of the modern
citizen, and it does not require new technology or a drastic reduction in quality of life. We all learned
about it in Kindergarten, and statistics from Twin Oaks prove its effectiveness.

Revolutionary Communitarianism? **159**
Communities 143, 18–19   Alexis Zeigler
The author's activist friends in rural Virginia turn out to have *above* American average per-capita energy
use. Intentional communities, with shockingly lower energy footprints, are the sleeping giant of the
conservation movement.

Cars and Rabbits **161**
Communities 143, 20–21   Alline Anderson
What separates the men from the boys, the wheat from the chaff, the truly eco-concerned from the cotton-
headed ninny-muggins? Car use. Dancing Rabbit Ecovillage has honed the practice of car-sharing to an
art.

Ecovillages, How Ecological Are You? **163**
Communities 143, 22–24   Prudence-Elise Breton
The author finds that ecovillages can play powerful roles in the social transition to sustainability, but
need to pay attention to quantification and evaluation to match their results to their intentions and
become meaningful examples.

Findhorn's Incredible Shrinking Footprint **166**
Communities 143, 26–27, 71   Jonathan Dawson
With the lowest ecological footprint of any ever measured in the industrialized world, a Scottish
community finds it's time to re-invent itself once again in response to climate change.

Svanholm in Denmark Goes Carbon-Neutral **169**
Communities 144, 57   Christina Adler Jensen
Denmark's largest intentional community and ecovillage adopts innovative technologies to save energy
resources and become carbon-neutral.

Car-Reduced and Car-Free Rural Communities **170**
Communities 147, 58–59, 79   Greg Ramsey
In the quest to create eco-communities that can lead us toward a sustainable future, nothing is more
important than reducing car dependence—and fortunately, we already know how.

Community Makes Renewable Energy Work **173**
Communities 161, 8–11   Alexis Zeigler
Living Energy Farm embodies the promise of renewable energy used cooperatively.

Putting Our Lives on the Line **177**
Communities 161, 12–13   Josina Guess
Jubilee Partners' clothesline does more than dry clothes with solar power; it helps build community.

Generating Your Own Electricity: Why and How **179**
Communities 161, 24–25   Mary Wildfire
Every community can benefit from producing renewable power.

Going For the Grid: A Community Ditches Energy Independence to Get Greener. **181**
Communities 161, 26–29, 75   Sarah Stoner
After three decades off-grid in Washington state, Walker Creek members decide on-grid living is more
sustainable.

Burlington Cohousing's Excellent Solar Adventures **186**
Communities 161, 30–33   Don Schramm
When community members want to place "private" panels on "public" roofs, don't expect clear sailing.

Establishing and Incorporating Renewable Energy Technologies in Camphill Communities:
A Personal Journey **190**
Communities 161, 34–35   Martin Sturm
Introducing renewable power can require not only technical expertise, but group dynamics skills.

Energy Efficient Heating, Renewable Electricity, and Community Renaissance at ZEGG **192**
Communities 161, 36–37, 77   Achim Ecker
A German ecovillage derives new energy from a solar-assisted biogas plant, photovoltaic panels, and
holacracy.

Energy Efficiency in Cohousing **195**
Communities 161, 48–49   Charles Durrett
Sustainability is embedded in community—even without a minus-$88-per-year electric bill.

The Sun Touches Heartwood **197**
Communities 161, 50–51   Richard Grossman
A Colorado cohousing group learns and grows along with its renewable energy systems.

The Personal and the Planetary: Spiritual and Planetary Renewal at Lama Foundation **200**
Communities 161, 52–53   Scott Shuker
In northern New Mexico, active and passive solar meet almost all of a community's energy needs.

Loving Earth Sanctuary: Two Women's Quest for a Low-Tech Life 202
Communities 165, 38–41   Gloria Wilson
A forming community in the hills of California's Central Coast encounters both challenges and blessings
in the pursuit of radical simplicity.

Technology in Service of Community 207
Communities 165, 47–51   Lindsay Hagamen and Walt Patrick
Windward develops appropriate technology with the goal of creating a localized village-scale energy
system that can be replicated by rural communities around the world.

Life with the Solar Kitchen 212
Communities 165, 52–53, 75   Frederick Weihe
The Tamera Solar Village combines solar thermal and biogas technologies to create a kitchen that not
only promotes responsible relationships to the earth and sky, but also builds human community.

Living Energy Farm: An Answer for Climate Change 216
Communities 174, 12–15   Alexis Zeigler
A fossil-fuel-free community empowers its members to dramatically reduce their dependence on the
corporate economy.

Limiting the Damage of Climate Change: Lessons from Dancing Rabbit 220
Communities 174, 16–21   Ma'ikwe Ludwig
Committed communitarians cut their carbon emissions to around 10 percent of the American average.

Addressing Climate Change: Two Generations at Heart-Culture Farm Community 226
Communities 174, 25–27   Kara Huntermoon
For the next generation, planting trees, growing food, and living in community are only the start.

Eco-Energy at Heartwood Cohousing 229
Communities 179, 66–67   Richard Grossman and the Common Facilities Team
                                                                    of Heartwood Cohousing
Even if a person or community cannot afford the infrastructure to provide renewable energy at the time
of building, they can build in such a way that it is easy to add later.
• **Creating Budgetary Line Items for Ecological Upgrades** — Maraiah Lynn Nadeau

IV. ECOVILLAGE DESIGN AND IMPLEMENTATION

Triumphs and Struggles at Los Angeles Eco-Village 233
Communities 140, 16–20   Alison Rosenblatt and Lois Arkin
An urban community engages with its neighborhood to confront local issues.

Ecologically Speaking Communities 238
Communities 141, 55–57   Kate Reidel
Awakening to their society's environmental impacts, residents of Enright Ridge Urban Eco-Village build
community while fostering a sustainable urban neighborhood.

An Ecovillage Future 241
Communities 156, 11   Chris Roth
For the health of our species and the planet, we need ecovillages.

Off the Grid and Out of the Trash Can 242
Communities 156, 14–16   Arjuna da Silva
Earthaven members derive sustenance, energy, interconnection, and inspiration from Earth, Wind, Sun,
Water, and Fire.

Aspiring to the Working Class 245
Communities 156, 17–19   Lee Walker Warren
By learning necessary physical skills, these ecovillagers transcend the limitations of their middle-class
educations.

Ecovillage Infrastructure: The Skeleton of Community 248
Communities 156, 22–23, 74   Gwendolyn Hallsmith
Water supply, human waste treatment, zoning regulations, legal structure, homeownership models, and
other core technical issues are essential in ecovillage planning.

From Camp to Village 251
Communities 156, 24–25, 75   Andrew Heben
The ecovillage movement can assist organized tent villages to address homelessness and sustainability
together.

Good Neighbors: Top 10 Reasons to Live Next to an Ecovillage 254
Communities 156, 26–28   Alyson Ewald
A communitarian discovers the best place on Earth to live.

Getting Ecovillages Noticed. 257
Communities 156, 29–33   Alex Whitcroft
Minor cultural shifts, including overcoming fear of specialists and regulations, could help ecovillages
increase their public influence in major ways.

Creating eCohousing. 262
Communities 156, 34–35   Vivian Vaillant
The Yarrow Ecovillage uses the cohousing model to create ecological buildings that meet their occupants'
needs.

Coming of Age: 21 Years of EcoVillage Planning and Living 264
Communities 156, 36–40   Liz Walker
In Ithaca, New York, a pioneering project continues to break new ground in ecological design, education,
and community.

Growing Up in EcoVillage at Ithaca. 269
Communities 156, 41   Allegra Willett
A homeschooler appreciates her ecovillage childhood and the love of exploration it has nurtured in her.

Fifty Years On: Living Now in the Findhorn Foundation Community 270
Communities 156, 42–43, 76   Lisa Sutherland
This influential Scottish ecovillage pursues sustainability that is not just environmental, but also spiritual,
social, and economic.

Earthsong Eco-Neighbourhood— Rebuilding Community within the City 273
Communities 156, 44–46 Robin Allison
In a neighborhood outside Aukland, Australia, community and eco-living prove mutually reinforcing.

Dandelion Village: Building an Ecovillage in Town 276
Communities 156, 47–48, 77   Maggie Sullivan
Aspiring communitarians rally support and navigate the legal hoops to establish an ecovillage in
Bloomington, Indiana.

Living the Questions 279
Communities 156, 52–54   Coleen O'Connell
Belfast Cohousing & Ecovillage grapples with obstacles to create a visionary housing project in rural
Maine.

Nashira: An Ecovillage from the Grassroots. 282
Communities 156, 56–57   Giovanni Ciarlo
Founded and run by low-income women heads of households, an urban ecovillage in Colombia shows
the promise of cooperative local self-empowerment.

Ecovillages and the FIC. 284
Communities 171, 6–7   Sky Blue
Ecovillages embody one of the most contemporary and nuanced approaches to collective living.

Around the World in 80 Pages. 286
Communities 171, 8   Chris Roth
To understand the scope and the potential of the ecovillage movement, we need to look worldwide.

Overcoming Apartheid—the Global Ecovillage Network. 287
Communities 171, 10–12   Kosha Anja Joubert
Communities worldwide are exploring how to heal our separation from each other and the natural
world.

Ecovillages Worldwide—Local Solutions for Global Problems. 291
Communities 171, 18–20   Leila Dregger
A wide array of ecovillages throughout the Global North and South address our shared challenges.

Creating Carbon-Negative Communities:
Ecovillages and the UN's New Sustainable Development Goals 294
Communities 171, 24–27   Rob Wheeler
Diverse ecovillages are modeling how to create more just, equitable, and sustainable human societies.

Learning in Ecovillages AND Getting a College Degree. 298
Communities 171, 32–35. 76   Karen Stupski and Giovanni Ciarlo
Pursuing holistic education through ecovillage immersion experiences can be both challenging and
rewarding.

Yarrow Ecovillage: Cohousing as a Building Block to the Ecovillage. 303
Communities 171, 41–43, 77   Charles Durrett and Katie McCamant
A Canadian community pioneers ecovillage zoning while incorporating both intergenerational and
senior cohousing.

Want an Ecovillage? Stay Put! 307
Communities 171, 44   Abeja Hummel
How can we care for a place if we're not there, day after day, year after year, paying attention?

Land and Culture Collaboration. 309
Communities 171, 45–48   Tom Shaver
Emerald Earth Sanctuary explores how to engage constructively with its northern California ecosystem.

Cloughjordan Ecovillage:
Modeling the Transition to a Low-Carbon Society. 313
Communities 171, 49–53   Peadar Kirby
Irish ecovillagers achieve the smallest ecological footprints recorded in their country.

True Sustainability: Indigenous Pathways. 318
Communities 171, 54–55   Dan Schultz
At Maitreya Mountain Village, mainstream pragmatism meets radical idealism.

V. ECO-EDUCATION

Seeking an Alternative Education 323
Communities 143, 58–59   Alison Cole
What's a verb to do in a land of harsh nouns, industrial adjectives, and wasteful superlatives? Two
students look for answers in an Indian reforestation project.

Education for Sustainability 326
Communities 147, 14–15   Chris Roth
Eco-educational programs in community give us direct experience of a hopeful reality: one person at a
time, one step at a time, from the ground up, the world does change.

Live and Learn: O.U.R. Ecovillage Builds Learning Community 328
Communities 147, 16–17, 74   Elke Cole with Javan Kerby Bernakevitch
The residents of an eco-oriented, education-focused intentional community and demonstration site wear
many hats, both public and private.

Teaching Hands-On Workshops in Community 331
Communities 147, 18–25   Michael G. Smith
One-day workshops, two-week intensives, two-month apprenticeships, season-long internships, work
parties, work exchanges, and other hands-on learning programs all offer unique benefits and challenges
for both participants and intentional community members. A veteran teacher and natural builder shares
his experiences from Emerald Earth Sanctuary.

Seeing the Good in the World:
Connecting Communities and Students for Sustainability Education and Transformation 339
Communities 147, 30–31, 75   Joshua Lockyer
After several years teaching about community in the abstract, an anthropologist and environmental
studies teacher finds that direct student engagement with intentional communities provides the spark
needed for personal inspiration, connection, and the potential for social transformation.

Sustainability: Reflections from an Eco-Warrior 342
Communities 147, 32–33, 76   Bruce Davidson
A cofounder of Sirius Community traces his path to a broadened understanding of sustainability—one
which depends, more than anything else, on a change of consciousness.

Ecovillages and Academia 345
Communities 147, 34–37   Daniel Greenberg
Ecovillages offer ideal campuses for sustainability education, but cannot fulfill their potential if cloistered
from academia. Building bridges between the two is essential for the survival and relevance of both.

Leadership for Social Change: Living Routes in Action at Huehuecoyotl 350
Communities 147, 38–39   Giovanni Ciarlo
An action learning program at a Mexican ecovillage offers students real-world lessons in project
implementation and community service, while also benefiting residents and neighbors.

Olympic-Sized Community 352
Communities 147, 40–41   Satyama Dawn Lasby
The sustainability coordinator for the biggest event in the world realizes that catering with washable
dishware and eliminating bottled water from the green rooms, while laudable, are ultimately just drops
in the bucket.

Intentional "Colonies" and Tropical Sustainability 354
Communities 147, 42–44   Jon Kohl
Intentional communities in developing countries often seem like intentional colonies instead, appealing
to the rich and the mobile but inaccessible to local people. Effective sustainability education requires an
alternative model.

Towards a Seventh Generation 357
Communities 147, 45, 77   Understanding Israel, M.A. Education
Tracing results within her own community, a lifelong educator suggests that time spent teaching children
now to love and respect the earth will help us all move towards a sustainable future.

Busted, Almost Bludgeoned, Possibly Broke:
Hard Lessons from the Trenches of Sustainability Education 359
Communities 147, 52–55   Lee Icterus
Making your community a home base for sustainability education programs can bring unanticipated
challenges, potential pitfalls, and learning experiences no one thought they had signed up for. A survivor
shares cautionary tales and tips.

VI. FINDING RESILIENCE IN COOPERATIVE CULTURE

The Nature of Our Work 365
Communities 143, 28–29   Stacie Whitney
The path to sustainability involves not only technological solutions, but a willingness and ability to
continually evolve, adapt, and create—to break old patterns of behavior and attitude and accept that
change is not only inevitable, but it is also *good*.

How Ecology Led Me to Community 367
Communities 143, 30–33, 73   Chris Roth
The author recounts some of the off-beat marching orders he received from an eco-oriented "different
drummer"—and how, instead of becoming a hermit, he became a communitarian.

Environmental Activism: Securing Your Community's Quality of Life into the Future 372
Communities 143, 44–46, 75   Chant Thomas
With a long history of protecting the local watershed, Trillium Farm Community in southern Oregon
grows not only organic food, but ecological activists.

Software, Hardware, and Ecology at Ganas 377
Communities 143, 55–57   Tom Reichert with Peggy Wonder
Internal attitudes and willingness to change behaviors can be more powerful than simple technological
solutions in shifting a community toward sustainability.

The Transition Initiative Comes to Cohousing 380
Communities 144, 51–53   Sonja Eriksson
A cohousing group joins the Transition Town movement in response to peak oil and climate change, and
discovers many collateral benefits.

Work Less, Simplify More 384
Communities 152, 16–19   Kim Scheidt
By reducing our economic impact, we can shrink our ecological footprint, while freeing up time and
energy to contribute to community and a more sustainable world.

Social Permaculture 388
Communities 153, 14–16   Starhawk
While expert at understanding ecological connections, permaculturalists often founder in relating with
one another. Applying permaculture principles to group dynamics can help us work together more
effectively.

Self-Reliance, Right Livelihood, and Economic "Realities": Finding Peace in Compromise 392
Communities 158, 12–15   Abeja Hummel
Life in a small rural ecovillage can mean embracing complex choices while balancing idealism with
necessity.

Communities, Political Empowerment, and Collective Self-Sufficiency 396
Communities 158, 16–17   Mary Wildfire
In the face of huge problems, what's an activist to do? Community provides answers.

Climate Changes: Turn to Face the Strange 398
Communities 161, 14–18   Christopher Kindig
Intentional communities are in a unique position to respond to climate change.

Confessions of a Fallen Eco-Warrior 403
Communities 161, 38–42   Chris Roth
A communitarian stops counting nanowatts, and starts counting blessings.

Land Management and Lifesharing at Innisfree Village 408
Communities 161, 54–57   Rhonda Miska
Responsible stewardship of assets, meaningful engagement of community members, and financial
sustainability are all key to Innisfree's land efforts.

Technology, Nature, and Community 412
Communities 165, 8–9   Chris Roth
Technology may have a monopoly on modern attention, but its language is a young one compared to our
shared evolutionary roots in the natural world.

Back to Life: Returning from the Virtual to the Real 414
Communities 165, 14–19   Ethan Hughes
To shake our addiction to modern technology, we must understand its true costs. Stillwaters Sanctuary
works to create a culture of greater connection, where it is easier to live without industrial society.

Technology on the Path to Reality: Snapshots from the Pre-Post-Digital Age 421
Communities 165, 33–37   Chris Roth
Misadventures with a cell phone help the author dial into more enduring, meaningful adventures and
relationships not dependent on an electronic-communications hamster wheel.

Ridgewood Ranch: A Mecca For Adaptive Community 426
Communities 174, 30–33   Steve Hellman and Daniel Spiro
Numerous projects on a community's 5,000 acres contribute to climate-adaptive land stewardship.

Economy, Community, and Place 431
Communities 175, 31–33   Lindsay Hagamen
Economy and *stewarding our home* were once synonymous, and can be again.

Together Resilient:
Why This Book? Thoughts on Building Community in the Age of Climate Disruption 434
Communities 175, 76   Sky Blue
Collectively, humanity has the answers, tools, and pieces of the puzzle—we just have to put them
together.

The Virtues of Unsettling 435
Communities 176, 75   Nancy Roth
The Unsettlers: In Search of the Good Life in Today's America takes us on a rewarding adventure, both
without—from Northeast Missouri to Detroit to Montana—and within.

Introduction

Volumes 1 and 2 in this series address how to find your place in intentional community by either creating or joining one. But how can this experience—and communities themselves—last past the "honeymoon" phase? How can groups turn long-term ideals into reality within their lives together?

A combination of "soft" and "hard" skills and systems must be present for intentional communities and their members to endure, evolve, and thrive. Sustainability in both human and ecological relationships is key to developing a cooperative culture that lasts—and is the focus of *Wisdom of Communities Volumes* 3 and 4.

The stories in this final volume focus on the "hard," practical skills and approaches that allow communitarians to live more ecologically now while preparing for the future. Authors share experiences, tools, advice, and perspectives that will benefit anyone who wants to help their community endure through changing local and planetary conditions.

Articles explore the nuts and bolts of developing eco-resilience: food, water, and permaculture; shelter and eco-building; energy and ecological footprint; ecovillage design and implementation; eco-education; and finding resilience in cooperative culture. These areas will prove more and more essential in allowing communities to navigate changing circumstances on our planet while growing into new, regenerative ways of living. Learning about these "hard" sustainability skills from others engaged in similar work can help communities immeasurably.

All articles are drawn from the past decade of COMMUNITIES magazine. For this volume we drew heavily from our specifically eco-themed issues, of which we publish at least one a year. Some of these issues proved so popular that they are out of print and available (until now) only digitally.

Every issue of COMMUNITIES contains further treatments of these and similar themes, so we hope that you'll not only learn from these past stories, but also keep up with new ones by subscribing to the magazine (ic.org/subscribe).

Thanks for making use of these resources, and good luck on your community journey!

Chris Roth
Editor, COMMUNITIES
June 2018

I
FOOD, WATER, AND PERMACULTURE

Community Composting:
A Transformative Practice

By Jason Grubb and Mason Vollmer

Composting within an intentional community is a wonderful metaphor for the process of building community. It is an opportunity to transform ideals about the environment, held by many people, into real practice; and to transform waste, generated by many people, into a valuable material that nurtures the environment.

As you arrive at Camphill Soltane, set in the rolling countryside of southeast Pennsylvania, the land provides a first snapshot impression of the community. Even before you have met the people living, learning, and working here, seeing the land reflects how we, as a community, care for ourselves. As the environment around each and every one of us has an effect on our well-being, nurturing the land promotes the well-being of anyone living at—or visiting—Camphill Soltane.

Camphill Soltane is one of over 100 communities in the international Camphill movement, dedicated to community living that supports and values the contributions of all members and helps each achieve their fullest potential. Camphill Soltane provides a residential, college-like educational program for 25 young adults with developmental disabilities, and provides meaningful work opportunities and long-term residential living for about 20 older adults with developmental disabilities. Long-term residential volunteers from around the world come for a year or more of service as "coworkers," supporting people as needed, providing leadership and assistance for our many educational and vocational programs, and helping to create community life.

Besides being home to roughly 80 people, our 50-acre estate is also home to a 200-tree apple and peach tree orchard, blueberry, blackberry, and raspberry bushes, a vegetable garden, and 11 landscaped houses and buildings.

The art of composting imitates nature's method of enriching and renewing the earth's capacity for plant growth. Nature knows no waste: everything is recycled, and the foundation of life is, strangely enough, a triumph over decay.

Compost Making: The Foundation of Sustainability

Many intentional communities have as their goal to live on the earth more sustainably, and this desire runs deep at Camphill Soltane. We have a dedicated recycling group, try to get as much local produce as possible, carpool, and, of course, compost. For those of us who value that holy trinity of "Reduce, Reuse, and Recycle," composting makes absolute sense. It is our way of ensuring that we waste as little as possible while at the same time getting the most "bang for our buck." Composting is both simple and complex, and, we would say, underappreciated.

The art of composting is the gardeners' practice of mixing materials to imitate nature's method of enriching and renewing the earth's capacity for plant growth through the recycling of organic materials. Nature knows no waste: everything is recycled, and the foundation of life is, strangely enough, a triumph over decay. Fallen leaves build and nourish the soil on the forest floor, and the soil, in turn, sustains the trees.

Composting always begins with an appreciation for the role soil plays in our lives. As much as the soil provides the foundation for us to walk on the earth, it also provides the foundation for us to *live* on the earth. Soil anchors plants, which capture the sun's energy, transforming it into another energy form—food, by way of leaves, seeds, and fruit—upon which humans and other animals depend. Plants, in turn, are nourished by the soil—both the small portion of the soil that is made up of organic matter, called humus, and the larger portion of the soil that is made up of mineral particles.

In the soil live microbes, which do the actual work of transforming dead and decaying plant and animal matter into the building blocks of life—the nutrients that support plant growth and development. As it turns out, in the smallest handful of

Left: The re-purposed compost shed at Camphill Soltane, with kitty litter pails that households bring and exchange every day visible at the lower left. Right: The re-purposed compost shed at Camphill Soltane, with our tumbler (inside), and a season's supply of fall leaves stockpiled nearby to mix with kitchen waste and other green materials throughout the year.

compost, there are billions of microbes (or microorganisms), whose powerful role in the web of life is just beginning to be recognized. One recent study reported, "Beneficial soil bacteria confer immunity against a wide range of foliar diseases by activating plant defenses, thereby reducing a plant's susceptibility to pathogen attack." The study goes on to relate how plants, suffering from a leaf disease, can summon bacteria in the soil to their defense and successfully fend off diseases.[1] Of course, this hands-off approach to plant health is possible only when the soil plants are growing in is alive with a diverse array of these microorganisms, which are enhanced by the addition of compost.

Biodynamic Compost and the Agricultural Individuality

Rudolf Steiner (1861-1925) was a great innovator, teacher, and philosopher who encouraged farms to be self-sufficient in their biological needs. He suggested that forming an ecological entity embracing soil, pasture, and livestock could create a kind of agricultural individuality whose productive capacity would be a function of the careful management and conservation of its members. This approach came to be known as Biodynamic agriculture.

The Biodynamic approach to composting starts with the cow. The cow first takes plant matter in and "balls it up" in her rumen, then finds a quiet place to chew her cud. This re-chewing grinds up the material to get as much goodness out of the grass as possible and to create more surface area for microbial activity to continue what her own digestion cannot. Microorganisms, like bacteria, initiate enzymatic activity that helps release more nutrients to the cow. The manure thus produced is further ripened by more microorganisms, eventually creating a

A hands-off approach to plant health is possible only when the soil plants are growing in is alive with a diverse array of microorganisms, which are enhanced by the addition of compost. The smallest handful of compost contains billions of them.

compost rich in humus, with all its beneficial physical, chemical, and biological properties. Biodynamic growers add specially prepared compost activators during the final ripening phase of the compost.

Making Compost Without a Cow

• Gather as much organic matter as possible: kitchen scraps, fallen leaves, grass clippings, pulled weeds, shredded paper, etc.

• Grind these up to expose as much surface area as possible for the microbes to do their work (using a mower or shredder works well on leaves and grass).

• Mix these materials together, making sure you have a balance of carbonaceous materials ("brown" materials that do not tend to emit odors or change color when decaying, like fallen leaves, shredded paper, etc.), and nitrogenous materials ("green" materials that often emit odors and change color when decaying, like kitchen waste or grass clippings).

• Add a scoop of finished compost or soil to jump-start microbial activity. Granular lime can be added to help neutralize odors and balance acidity.

• Stack the mixed material in a pile at least three feet high and wide, where the initial heating and de-composition can take place. Leave the pile uncovered, so rains will keep it moist, and set it directly on top of the ground, so earthworms and soil organisms can access it.

• (Optional) Add the Biodynamic preparations, cover the pile, and let the compost cool down. (See sidebar.)

• Enjoy some time with your community while you wait for nature to take its course, usually four to eight months. The compost is finished when the original materials are no longer apparent, and the compost is dark black, crumbly, and has a

Left: Andrew Schwartz, a community resident and member of the Land Crew, brings a load of decomposing materials from the tumbler to our outdoor composting yard. Right: The outdoor compost yard at Camphill Soltane, with strawbale sides surrounded by chain link fence. Materials are added to this pile after first being mixed and initially decomposed in the compost tumbler. Here, the compost matures and "finishes."

sweet, earthy smell.

• Troubleshooting: Mix in more green matter, shred the pile, or turn the pile over if the material isn't decomposing, and mix in more brown matter if the pile is very goopy or smelly. If most of the pile looks finished, but you can still identify some parent materials, the compost may be put through a screen and any undecomposed materials can be added back to the pile.

This process mimics the transformative action of the cow, and produces fresh, living, wonderful compost. This compost can then be used to enrich the orchard, garden, or as the basis for soil mixes for raising seedlings and container plants. Accept no substitutes—this is far superior to anything you can buy.

The spirit of our times cries out: "Heal the Earth, Serve Humanity." Make a little compost today. It will nurture and beautify your environment, strengthen your community, and support your local food system.

The Practical Routine

In our community, where people have differing abilities, we wanted an approach where everyone could participate in the process of making compost.

Our work starts in the fall, when the land crew stockpiles enough leaves for a year's supply of carbonaceous material to mix with the kitchen scraps.

In each of the nine households in our community, we have at least two compost buckets—square kitty litter buckets that we got free at the recycling center, which fit well in our carts and shed. Each day, the household sends someone with the compost bucket to the compost shed, where they drop off the full bucket and pick up a new bucket half-filled with leaves and a small scoop (six ounce tuna can size) of granular lime to reduce odor and balance acidity. Our community café, which operates two days a week, gets extra buckets.

Twice a day, in the morning and after lunch, someone from the land crew checks on the compost shed and empties any buckets that have been dropped off into a compost tumbler and refills the bucket with leaves and lime. They may add a scoop of soil or finished compost to the tumbler to help get things going.

With a good mixture of nitrogenous and carbonaceous materials, the microbes go to work so vigorously that things start heating up in the tumbler, so that on cold mornings it's steaming. Twice a week, we remove about a wheelbarrow full of steaming compost from the tumbler and stack it in a pile. For this pile, we made a bin of old hay bales, and surrounded it with a recycled chain link fence to make an enclosure to discourage critters, which had become accustomed to feeding on our old unenclosed pile system.

The pile quickly heats up to around 120 degrees, and stays that warm for about three to four weeks, burning up any weed seeds, and purifying itself during its initial transformation. We add the Biodynamic preparations to the pile at this time.

Following this hot phase of composting, the secondary ripening or maturation occurs. It is to compost what aging is to wine after the original fermentation. Different microbes populate the pile now, and transform it into "woodsy-smelling humus." This is what distinguishes good compost and great compost.

So what do we do with our finished compost? Among our community garden, berry bushes, apple trees, and the gardens around each house, the compost is all used to nurture our environment.

These practices can be adapted to fit the resources available and the approaches that are appropriate for your community.

Co-Creating Together, Celebrating Together

Through the interaction of our land crew with the other members of the community, both through shared composting and other activities on the land, we are able to nurture our environment, and celebrate the fruits of our labor together.

On the land crew, our work on behalf of the community continues year-round. Within the group, we have been able to create a strong team where our strengths complement one another's nicely. The camaraderie of a shared victory (completion of our seasonal pruning, or finishing the berry harvest, for example) and seeing the literal fruits of our labor (such as apples and berries) are extremely gratifying. Moreover, we know that the rest of the community appreciates our efforts—there is nothing more uplifting than seeing someone's mood brightened from taking a stroll through the orchard or admiring the garden's bounty.

Many times throughout the year, the land crew invites the community to join in the work on the land. For the festival of Michaelmas, which occurs in prime apple harvest season on September 29th, we invite the entire community to collect, sort, and pare apples; the celebration culminates in a shared dinner replete with fresh apple pies and cider. During Holy Week, we also work together on shared projects on the land; this is a wonderful time to renew and deepen our relationships with each other.

Transforming Our Communities

When we enrich the soil through making compost from our own waste materials, we approach the ideal of sustainable production by integrating the soil, vegetation, and animal and human partnerships.

Today we live at a turning point: much of our agricultural production uses factory farming techniques, based on fossil fuel inputs that are not sustainable, ecologically or economically. There is a new surge in interest—from universities, government agencies, businesses, consumers, and particularly in intentional communities—towards developing sustainable, local, and environmentally sound food production systems.

As many pioneers in this movement have noted, the next step is to inspire, educate, and encourage a new generation to take up the art and practice of sustainable food production. As we transform the world, so too do we transform ourselves.

What will it take for us to restore our sense of sacredness for our dear earth, this hallowed ground of our ancestors and future home to our heirs? The spirit of our times cries out: "Heal the Earth, Serve Humanity." Make a little compost today. It will nurture and beautify your environment, strengthen your community, and support your local food system.

A wealth of composting and agricultural resources, including information on Biodynamics, is available at: www.attra.ncat.org. ❀

Jason Grubb has lived at Camphill Soltane for three and a half years. Over time, he discovered a love of getting dirty, and found himself at peace when working with a crew on the land. He is currently enrolled in the year-long, part-time Biodynamic Training Program at the Pfeiffer Center in Chestnut Ridge, New York.

Mason Vollmer was a gardening teacher for 18 years in two Waldorf schools, and has been a Biodynamic farmer and gardener since 1975. He helped to tend Soltane's orchard in its early years, and has been working with the land crew again since late summer 2008.

Tumblers and Sheds

Compost happens—anywhere and anytime a space is made for materials to decompose. However, here are a couple of items we've found helpful for our community:

Tumblers: We've come to really appreciate the value of a tumbler. First, it keeps the food scraps away from interested critters (skunks, raccoons, and rodents) and second, it mixes the material. This is a nice way to gather a big quantity of compost materials, in the right proportions, before putting everything on a pile outside. We don't empty the tumbler entirely at any one time, in order to keep the biological activity and the warmth it generates, since if it really gets cold and everything freezes, the biological activity necessary for composting gets put on hold.

A Shed: We re-purposed a small shed that was no longer used for livestock for a convenient place to store and exchange our kitchen compost buckets, to keep them out of the snow and rain.

We have an idea to move this whole set-up into a passive solar greenhouse, where the warmth of the greenhouse would stimulate the compost, and the warmth from the compost would help heat the greenhouse—an example of a positive greenhouse effect.

---

1. PLANT PHYSIOLOGY at www.plantphysiol.org: "Root Secreted Malic Acid Recruits Beneficial Soil Bacteria," www.plantphysiol.org/cgi/rapidpdf/pp.108.127613v1?eaf

Water Is Life!

Tamera Is Creating a Model for Reversing Desertification

By Leila Dregger

In southern Portugal, the Peace Research Center Tamera is creating a pilot model that will show how the desertification of threatened places in the world can be stopped. It is also a model for regional food autonomy.

Mother Earth lies brown and soft under my feet. Golden light shines through the leaves. Leaning against an old cork oak, I look into a little valley: the air is shimmering in the heat of a summer afternoon. The branches above give home to birds and beetles, and ferns are moving softly in the breeze.

This could be paradise. But in fact, it is not. The green of the little valley before me is created by rock roses—pioneer plants on devastated soils throughout the Mediterranean. Through their monotonous surface, the corpses of cork oaks arise here and there like sunken ships in a sandy bay. The opposite side of the valley is already clear: no oaks, no grass, not even rock roses—only grayish eucalyptus on top.

The cork oaks of southern Portugal are dying, and still no government or university has found a formula to stop it. Even the proud tree at my back shows the unavoidable signs of the coming death: brown stains in the bark from fungi. Old farmers here say that the tree is crying.

And I am crying as well. It is not only about the century-old traditional culture that shaped the look of the Alentejo that is coming to a close. Desert is also developing right before our eyes. Southern Europe is turning into a second Sahel Zone.

I wonder why nobody runs shouting through the towns, ringing a bell, sounding the alarm: Watch out, wake up—our land, our mother is dying! What will we eat tomorrow?

The Sahara is coming north. Portugal, Spain, Italy, and Greece all suffer under increasing summer droughts; forests are burning; and in Portugal every 20 minutes a farmer gives up his farm. More than 80 percent of the population lives in big cities and on the coast; 80 percent of the food is imported; and the "delicious garden," the fertile land of the Moors in the Middle Ages, is turning into dust.

"Who cares?" city people may say. "We get our food from the supermarket."

An incident in June of last year showed how weak this argument is and how thin the layers of peace and richness in Europe might be. A strike of fuel truck drivers hit Portugal. On the second day, the first gas stations had run out of gas; on the third day, the first supermarkets had empty shelves; and then two people working to block some fuel trucks that were trying to break the strike were run over deliberately.

If this kind of thing should happen more in the future, we have to ask: What will we eat? Where will our water come from? Our electricity? How will we survive? When the last fuel has been used, these questions will not be answered by global systems, but in our neighborhoods, our communities, and through our relationship to the land we live on.

What can we do—we as an intentional community? Pancho, Tamera member, nature walker, and ecologist, gives a surprisingly sober answer. "We have to heal the water balance."

In Tamera, we are working on peace—not only between people but with nature as well. On 350 acres, our ecologists develop local solutions for global problems.

"Droughts are not a natural law," according to Sepp Holzer. This Austrian mountain farmer is one of our ecological advisors. "They are the consequence of deforestation, monocultures, and overgrazing. After decades of wrong treatment, it´s not small steps that are needed, but bigger steps of correction."

*Top left: Construction site of the lake. Top middle: The lake is growing. Top right: Tibetan monks in Tamera in front of the lake.
Bottom left: Sepp Holzer demonstrating the edible landscape. Bottom middle: Carrots in the edible landscape and harvest in Tamera.
Bottom right: Fish in the water. Opposite page: The Lake is full.*

Consulting Sepp, we began two years ago to build the water landscape of Tamera.

The first water retention basin was started in August 2007.

Now, one and a half years later, the winter rain has turned the dry landscape into a shining water expanse. Even in summer, when in the Alentejo everything has turned brown and meadows are as dry as straw, we now can see a different world: Fresh green shoots are sprouting on the terraces. Fruit trees, berry bushes, and reeds are growing. The densely-growing leaves on the terraces are edible plants such as radishes, cabbage, turnips, lettuce, and old varieties of cereals which all grow here abundantly—not in straight lines and rows, but as Mother Nature would have sown them herself. Our visitors, who come on weekends, are allowed to eat from this abundance. This first impression of the new Tamera water landscape is convincing—and tasty.

It is part of a comprehensive concept for the retention and saving of the winter rain, for regeneration of the landscape, for reforestation with polycultures, and for food cultivation. The lake supplies the surroundings with water. A "Sunpulse"—a water pump which is run by solar energy—distributes the water from the lake to the gardens on the banks.

"Water is information. Water is life. Water is capital," Sepp Holzer says. The lake is indeed an elaborate system of self-purification and regulation of different temperatures. The flatter shorelines serve to clean the lake and to grow tropical plants. Natural marble stones are standing on the shore and in some shallow parts of the lake; they are useful giants functioning like a tiled fireplace. At night they radiate the heat to their surroundings.

Deeper zones of the lake create the differences in temperature leading to water movements which carry oxygen into the lake and help the fish thrive and prosper.

"Edible landscapes" is a term which makes mouths water. The mixed plant cultures which were sown earlier this year are growing now. As much as possible, native species are grown—plants which will later sow their own seeds. Sepp Holzer: "In nature it is the same as with human beings: community is better than solitude." This is something that we as human community can agree to easily.

One hundred thousand tons of soil were removed for the construction of the first water retention basin. The next two ponds were built in fall 2008—smaller, but directly in the former vegetable garden which has turned into a water garden. The design of the lakes incorporates a gently rising dam with an overflow and an outlet discharge structure that regulates the water level and makes the population of water plants and fish controllable.

Beyond its task of ecological regeneration, the water landscape can become an important economic factor. We think that in this way communities can produce their own food and take care of nature at the same time.

Together with the solar energy systems which we have been developing in Tamera for some years, this "lakescape" is a model for decentralized sustainability in times when the supermarkets can't take care of us any more.

Maybe this could be paradise after all. ❁

Leila Dregger, ecologist and international journalist, based in Tamera (www.tamera.org), gives classes in peace journalism. She is working on a science fiction novel about a comprehensive ecological, social, and sexual transformation.

FOOD SECURITY IN COMMUNITY

By Blake Cothron

The theme of this issue is "Hard Times in Community" and there's not much that's harder than going hungry. Not that I've ever known real hunger or food scarcity, having grown up in the privileged US, with grocery-store aisles perennially overflowing with food (albeit food of questionable quality, but rarely was there any shortage). Now things are changing and we need to change too.

In the US and many other countries, the systems we've relied on for over a century, including agriculture, energy, and transportation, are in serious question. Many complex challenges confront agriculture. We face the real dangers of genetically engineered food, terminator seed technology, irradiation, pesticides, and vast soil degradation turning once fertile land into deserts. Regular outbreaks of food poisoning due to contaminated industrial produce reinforce the need for solutions to our current food systems. We have relied on petroleum to transport our food great distances and to produce the fertilizer and pesticides necessary to industrial agriculture. With petroleum a source of constant warfare, vast pollution, and dwindling in supply, big questions loom. How can intentional communities respond to issues of food security? What are the options available and what routes can your community take to becoming more food secure and sustainable?

> *Growing your own food is the safest and most assured form of food security available. In my explorations I've seen it done extremely well and I've also seen it done poorly or completely abandoned.*

Throughout my community explorations in the US and much online research, I've noticed that almost every intentional community shares one strong desire the world over: the desire to grow food. When humans start forming groups and settling into communities, they seem naturally to gravitate towards agriculture. Nearly every community I come across expresses food production as a goal.

Being an organic gardener myself, I love growing food. I believe that growing your own food is the safest and most assured form of food security available. It's also the most affordable. Some intentional communities are richly agricultural, abundant places. In my explorations I've seen it done extremely well and I've also seen it done poorly or completely abandoned. What were the communities that were actively growing much of their own food doing right? What were some of the problems faced?

I believe that in these uncertain and increasingly difficult times, every intentional community and in fact every community everywhere needs to start growing food. Homegrown food makes sense from every angle: better nutrition, better taste, greater connection to nature, exercise and fresh air, safer and more secure food supply, less land plowed under by mega-farms, more money for other things, less reliance on industry and petroleum...the list goes on. If looked at in this way, com-

11

munity food production positively impacts nearly every major issue facing humans today.

Growing food is an art and an intricate science. To grow good food you must LOVE what you are doing. It doesn't take machinery, lots of tools, expensive seeds, ideal conditions, or back-breaking labor. I've noticed that the communities actively growing food have several things in common, and it's not ideal climate, perfect soil, or big tractors. What were the successful gardening communities doing?

First of all they had the INTENTION to grow food. They got together and decided they shared an interest in growing food— that it was important to them and something they valued. They did not conclude that their soil was too poor, the growing season too short, or that it was too much work. They believed they could do it and they had a strong interest.

Second, they PLANNED. They researched what species would grow well in their area. They identified leaders in the community who would take on responsibility and oversee things. They perhaps hired teachers and permaculture designers to give insight and direction. They planned things carefully in advance. Planning and site selection are crucial and are mapped out well by most of the successful gardeners. Permaculture design principles are highly recommended and popular in communities.

Third, they STARTED. They did whatever was necessary; they cleared land, mowed fields, acquired seeds, built greenhouses, plowed the soil, and built beds. Once you start, food starts rolling in quickly. There must be initiation and subsequent dedication to obtain production.

Here are some key elements to incorporate and questions to ask to assure that the planning and execution stages succeed:

Identifying *what your community will eat* is a very important and often overlooked aspect of growing food in community. I've heard of people planting communal gardens with 50-foot rows of arugula. Who can eat 50 feet of arugula? Not these folks, as I heard most of it went to waste, along with all the work and resources to grow it. Is anyone going to eat all those beets, or all those brussel sprouts? What veggies will the cooks utilize? What would the kids like to eat? What can be preserved if there is an excess? Will anyone do it?

Animals often play important roles in food production systems. Animals generally take much more care than plants, so be very realistic and plan for animals far in advance. Goats and cows can destroy entire gardens and orchards overnight, so make sure secure fencing is in place, or design pens for them. Do not rush introducing animals to your community. I once lived in a community with a woman who, out of her compassion, obtained several chickens, rescuing them from the frying pan when an industrial egg farm closed down. I tried to warn her about hastily getting these animals, but it went unheard and within a few days the chickens were here. She housed them in a dilapidated old shack that was hastily converted to a basic chicken coop. In a few days, she was horrified to find a bloody mess in the coop, and feathers everywhere. One of the chickens was dead. The next day: another. The day after that: another. A wily mongoose was easily getting into the inadequate structure and having chicken for dinner every night. She quickly rounded up the survivors and gave them all away, disappointed in herself and feeling a bit foolish. Proper planning beforehand and knowledge about the realities of raising animals could have prevented this, and grown productive happy animals. Planning can predict and reduce conflicts, possible problems, and incompatibilities (such as a loose goat in a young orchard).

Communities are utilizing tree crops more and more as crucial elements in their food systems. What tree crops grow well in your climate? What do people desire? Will people be around to prune the apple trees every single year? Will anyone collect all the walnuts and pecans before the squirrels do? Are the trees planted the correct distance apart and far enough away from any houses or power lines? Will they be watered correctly as they establish? Carefully consider these things before a major planting is done.

I always urge people to *start small!* Successful community farms and gardens were generally small at first (or shrunk later), and are equivalent to the stable work force. By small, I mean start with a modest but meaningful goal of around 10-20 percent of the community's diet, unless the community has very experienced and hard working gardeners. Many times I've heard people in community say, "We would just love to have a garden!"—without being realistic that a garden takes *gardeners*. Gardens and orchards are not static elements to be installed, like a new building or a road. They are dynamic, living systems that take much care and skill to flourish. Before a garden or orchard is built, realistically consider how many stable and dedicated people will be there to take care of it. Start small enough so

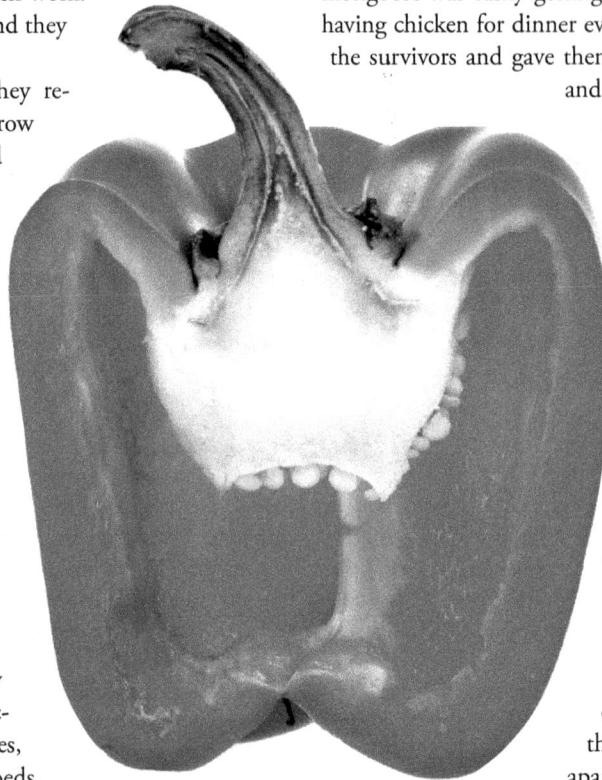

that taking care of the garden and orchard is a fun, life-enhancing, and productive event, and not an overwhelming burden or overgrown mess. If the work force is small or inexperienced, focus on perennial vegetables and easy-to-care-for fruit and nut trees, such as (depending on your location and climate zone) mulberry, figs, citrus, avocado, persimmon, and berry bushes. Plenty of wonderful perennial vegetables require little care and live for many years. Native edibles are always a fine choice, and very easy.

Many communities once had abundant beautiful gardens but then lost the crucial element: the gardeners. I believe it is not sustainable for a community to have one or two gardeners. These people will eventually not be around, and then what will happen to the gardens and community food supply? Relying on purely outside labor, such as WWOOF volunteers to work the garden, is equally unsustainable. There is also the very common occurrence that someone plants something or makes a garden and then leaves the community, and it disappears. Oftentimes as well, some great garden or planting someone did in the past is destroyed or damaged by a (hopefully) well-meaning newcomer. I've heard of abundant asparagus patches yielding 100 pounds a year being dug up and discarded by the new gardener, and of raspberry patches being leveled when all someone with a mower saw was a mess of thorny bushes. This is why it is crucial to have stable gardeners or at least detailed garden maps and community-wide knowledge about community food production.

All the work involved can seem intimidating, so start with what feels comfortable. There is no big rush (as of yet), and moving with haste is a big mistake I've seen many make. However, the time to start (small) is definitely now! Having the attitude "We'll start when we need to" is like saying you'll learn CPR when someone is choking or learn to swim when you're drowning.

Careful planning and in-depth knowledge about your land is necessary, and only truly gleaned from staying in one place for years of observation. Start small and fun. Permaculture design describes planting gardens close by the kitchen for easy access, as well as combining vegetables, herbs, and fruits together to make beautiful, fun, and easy-to-care-for mixed plantings. The "lasagna bed" method of gardening describes ways to make fertile gardens with no tilling or digging whatsoever.

The best way to make food production sustainable is to get everyone involved. If you're trying to get community gardens going, talk with everyone and see what people would like to grow. Have work parties to build garden beds and plant trees. Let everyone know what is ripening, and when a homegrown ingredient is featured in a meal. Get the children involved too; they can be picking berries and playing with worms while the adults dig and transplant. Make flower gardens that are inviting and places of peace. Put benches all around to invite people to sit and be with the gardens. Have everyone in the community plant a fruit tree.

A shining example of this happens weekly in a Zen Buddhist community in which I lived in California. Every single Wednesday morning, after the 4:45 a.m. meditation, *every single person in the community* would simultaneously walk out into their large organic farm together, hoes and rakes in hand. There we would all silently cultivate the rows of bright colorful lettuce, Swiss chard, broccoli, cabbage, and carrots. It was wonderful; the early morning fog rolling around the pines and redwoods, the only sounds being birds singing and the gentle clicking and clanging of the garden tools. I was so impressed by this weekly community event. It was a great way to get every single person out there, working together, watching the plants grow, and gaining a deeper connection with the food served to them straight from their fields.

I believe the only long-term sustainable form of food security in community is to get nearly everyone involved in some aspect. This includes people growing the food, cooking community meals, watering gardens, pulling weeds, discussing strategies, picking fruit; there's something that everyone can do. Some communities have shared gardens where each person gets a personal growing bed or two and the garden is tended individually, with most of the produce going to the shared kitchen. This works well for some groups and can be fun. Trees can also be planted as memorials for big events, such as births and deaths, community breakthroughs, and celebrations. This gives connection and meaning to the planting and gets people involved.

An intentional community can help the greater community through food production in many ways. Some communities give away excess production to local food banks and shelters. Through seed exchanges, which are free seed giveaways, communities can distribute regionally-adapted non-GMO seed to local people (and also obtain it). (We should utilize seed exchanges while we still can; I've heard that they are actually illegal in parts of Europe and that the Monsanto corporation is working hard to make it that way in the US.) Groups can offer classes and workshops on permaculture design, seed-saving, aquaculture systems, beekeeping, and raising animals, as outreach to the local communities and as a right-livelihood income source.

Buying locally also increases food security. Purchasing local organic food helps reweave the local food systems and support

(continued on p. 79)

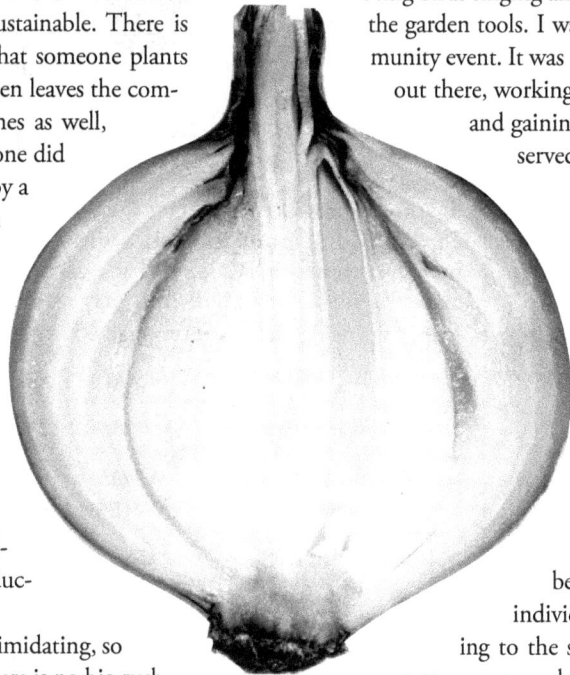

13

FOOD SECURITY IN COMMUNITY

(continued from p. 56)

organic food helps reweave the local food systems and support local farmers, while receiving much better quality produce and relying less on vast transportation systems and polluting petroleum-based agrichemicals. Even better, talk with local organic farms about obtaining CSA (community supported agriculture) shares. In fact, try to buy everything possible local, including honey, spices, wine, beer, meat, seafood, dairy, and any other items, including non-food items. Deeply question reliance on staple foods that are imported vast distances, such as bananas, coffee, chocolate, and tea. Most bananas are distributed by very unethical and polluting businesses operating in "banana republics" that destroy indigenous communities.

Making connections with other people and farms is another way to reweave the local food web and make friends. Inquire what items are available from your neighbors, and offer something valuable in exchange, including labor. Maybe they are beekeepers, grow mushrooms, or raise goats that produce milk. You could offer them veggies, fruits, or a helping hand for trade. Keep these connections going. Investigate what local options are available, and ask around. Keep in mind also that the wild rural places where many communities are located often abound with wild greens, nuts, and fruits. Urban locations often are surprising cornucopias of forgotten fruit trees, herbs, and edible landscaping. Many people in urban areas will gladly let you harvest their fruit trees—just ask.

The time is now to become more food secure. I wish for abundance and fertility in your community and every community in the world. ❀

Blake Cothron is an avid permaculturist, gardener, orchardist, and community visionary. He has been exploring intentional community life throughout the US for nearly 4 years. He is from Louisville, Kentucky and is 24 years old.

RELATED BACK ISSUES

Community in Hard Times

The following COMMUNITIES back issues speak to various aspects of our current "Community in Hard Times" theme, as do some others not listed here. See communities.ic.org/back_issues for a complete list of back issues and ordering information. You may also order back issues ($5 apiece plus shipping) using the form on page 65.

#141	Winter 2008	SCARCITY AND ABUNDANCE
#137	Winter 2007	COMMUNITIES MAKING A DIFFERENCE
#135	Summer 2007	WHAT DO YOU EAT? WHERE DOES IT COME FROM?
#133	Winter 2006	HELPING YOUR LOCAL ECONOMY THRIVE
#131	Summer 2006	GOOD WORKS IN COMMUNITY
#130	Spring 2006	PEAK OIL AND SUSTAINABILITY
#128	Fall 2005	RESOLVING CONFLICT IN COMMUNITY
#121	Winter 2003	THRIVING IN COMMUNITY
#119	Fall 2003	RIGHT LIVELIHOOD IN COMMUNITY
#116	Fall-Winter 2002	CAN WE AFFORD TO LIVE IN COMMUNITY?
#115	Summer 2002	THE HEART OF SUSTAINABILITY
#113	Winter 2001	COMMUNICATION & PROCESS
#105	Winter 1999	TRANSITION & CHANGE: THE HARD ROAD TO ACCOUNTABILITY
#101	Winter 1998	COMMUNITIES, THE MILLENNIUM, AND Y2K
#99	Summer 1998	SUSTAINABLE COMMUNITIES
#98	Spring 1998	VALUES, VISION, AND MONEY: MANIFESTING OUR DREAMS
#94	Spring 1997	MAKING A LIVING

We have the land, we have the vision
We have a co-working, co-living space

ARE YOU? the missing piece

8th Life PANAMA

HTTP://8THLIFEPANAMA.ORG @8thLifeAstoria

In 2003, "La Cité Écologique" was founded, in Colebrook New Hampshire, on 315 acres of beautiful land surrounded by forest and mountains. Our ecovillage gives priority to education, optimal living to its members, a cooperative culture with resilience in its development and social entrepreneurship. So far, we have built one single family building, two large community residences, where people live in a kind of condo arrangement, and one community building (all powered by solar). We are expanding new building projects, to give a home to growing families and/or new members. We've created businesses, non-profits, a nonprofit school, and an organic farm, that helps better serve ours, and the local community. Visitors are welcome to our annual Open House in June, and Harvest Celebration in September. Guided tours, and internship programs are also available from May through October.

Contact: Leonie Brien (603) 331-1669
www.citeecologiquenh.org

La Cité Écologique
of New Hampshire
An Ecovillage since 2005

To Learn Sustainability Is To Learn Community
An Example from South Portugal

By Leila Dregger

Walk 20 miles away from the ocean, and South Portugal becomes dry and dusty in summer and devoid of people in any season. What had been a lush landscape for centuries, with oak forests, white stucco villages, and vegetable gardens and pastures, was destroyed in the 1940s to create industrial cereal production for Spain during the civil war. Now the landscape seems slowly to be turning into a desert. Villages are dying. Food is imported. Only very few farmers continue their hard work under difficult economic and ecological conditions.

One of them is Claudio, a farmer in the Alto Alentejo. His 4000 hectare (10,000 acre) site, inherited from his father, includes beautiful nature reserves and extended cork oak and olive groves. Employing 20 workers, he started with the vision of reestablishing the original extensive cultivation of cork, pork, and Biodynamic vegetables. And he is doing just that. But to maintain the farm under tight economic conditions, he has developed intensive mass animal farming with thousands of pigs and turkeys. "If I didn't farm this way, I would have to fire my workers, and I feel responsible for them. What could I do?" His wife left him two years ago, taking their two daughters with her. Maybe this was not the only reason, but she could not stand the mass slaughters and the tension her husband is living under. Living alone in his big farm house, Claudio is urgently looking for an alternative and a new start in his life.

Fernando grew up in a little village in the Baixo Alentejo. Like all his classmates, he left for Lisbon to study and become an engineer. Before he finished the studies, his father died and Fernando had to return home. Now he runs the apiary with 2000 bee hives. He produces organic honey but has to sell it for a low price to the industry, as the market for organic products is still too small. Thus his income is limited, and after 12 hours of daily work he feels very tired. He is 38 years old, smart, good looking, and speaks several languages. However, living rurally with his mother makes it difficult for him to find friends and a mate: the average age in the village is 52.

Fernando's and Claudio's stories illustrate the situation in many similar places. Sustainability is a complex issue: it involves politics, economics, and ecology, and it definitely involves cultural, social, and human conditions. If living in the countryside does not become more interesting for young people, we can never hope to have nature and land maintained and cared for.

Tamera permaculture water landscape from above.

Tamera pilgrimage through Portugal.

Maria Soares

The peace community of Tamera did not come to the Alentejo originally to help this situation. In fact, it came because innovative and enthusiastic local authorities and the abundance of sun were good conditions for its aim of building a global peace model based on solar technology. However, 160 people living, working, and studying together make a difference—internationally by peace training, education, and nonviolent actions, and regionally by teaching ecological skills and creating a regional network for food and water sustainability.

The Tamera community decided that it would stop buying food from supermarkets by the end of 2010, and by then would also produce all its own electricity using solar energy. Why is this so important for a peace project? Because industrial production of food is a sort of war. Electricity comes from the plug, fuel from the petrol station, coffee from the supermarket, water from the tap, and steak from the butcher. Those who look a bit deeper than this will see the cruelty of today's industrial globalisation at the origin of our everyday consumer goods. Behind nearly every product you will find suffering, ignorance, and violence. Even those who are aware of it, and don't want to support it, find it difficult to become independent from these connections.

The need to find another strategy is not only a matter of ethics. An incident which happened two years ago in Portugal makes this clear. At a time of high oil prices, the drivers went on strike, and the fuel was no longer distributed. After one day, there was no petrol in many gas stations. After two days, the first supermarkets had empty shelves. After three days, two drivers who wanted to prevent strike-breakers from working were driven over. That quickly can the supply system collapse; and that thin is the layer of social peace.

An obvious solution for the insanity of globalisation is regionalisation: to reestablish the regional supply which global trade destroyed, and to do it with socially and ecologically friendly means. Every region of the world should be able to meet its basic needs for food, water, and energy. The special goods desired from further away could be bought or bartered from other countries.

The task of Tamera—building a model for a peace culture—includes showing that

Dia Aberto.

regional food and energy autonomy is possible without lowering quality of life. In order to do so, one team at Tamera is working on the permaculture water landscape, where a part of the food needed is grown. The community also produces olive oil, honey, and herbs. Another team develops a regional network for sustainability. Its aims are to share knowledge about ecological skills, share the supply and production of basic food, water, and energy needs, and cultivate social contacts.

Tamera started to meet local farmers and traders, and so we met Claudio. Very quickly, we agreed on a win-win-situation: starting in 2010, he will produce olive oil, rice, cereals, oat flakes, and vegetables especially for the needs of Tamera. Additionally he will give Tamera all the things he cannot sell and would have to destroy. This arrangement gives Claudio the possibility of producing independent of the market. Therefore he is not forced to throw away fruits that are too small or don't

have the normal shape. He will even earn much more than the market price, and Tamera will get valuable organic food at a reasonable cost.

Now, in the spring of 2010, we stand in the stable which last year held 3000 turkeys. Their shouts still seem to fill the air. But the stable is empty, and soon it will be a place to store cereals. Having seen the new economic possibilities in his cooperation with Tamera, Claudio has taken the risk to eliminate, step by step, his industrial livestock farming. Even more hopeful, on a visit to Tamera he saw the possibilities of permaculture. Now, two ecologists from Tamera will advise him on how to build a water landscape on a part of his land. Thus Claudio will join the movement to reforest the land and bring back the water. "My vision is to save this beautiful land and make a part of it a retreat and educational place for city people to learn natural cycles."

Maria Soares

The visitors also experience something which has been lost in the villages: a vital social life of different age groups.

Agreements like this could become the basis for cooperatively meeting basic needs in the future, with communities telling farmers what they need, and farmers growing it for them.

Not all the foods we commonly consume are produced in Portugal. For example, neither sugar cane nor sugar beets are cultivated in this country anymore. But there is something much better and healthier than sugar to provide sweetness: honey.

Twelve bee hives at Tamera are not enough for our needs, and so we got to know Fernando. Buying organic honey from Fernando is cheaper than buying honey in the supermarket, and still, by selling to Tamera, he earns nearly double what he would by producing for industry. Tamera coworkers also help to move the bee hives. As Silke from the ecology team says, "This is synergy: We help Fernando, but the bees in our permaculture landscape help us. They are the most important insects

for pollinating our fruit trees."

Four times a year, Tamera invites interested people for an open Saturday. Those are days to get to know some of our sustainable tools and methods. For most of our neighbours, permaculture, compost toilets, solar energy systems, and strawbale buildings are still very exotic. School classes and University students come to observe in practice the ecological systems they have studied. Local farmers, politicians, teachers, and journalists enjoy this day; they see the presence of water in every season, lunch cooked by solar energy, and an abundance of food growing without fertilizers. Representatives of the beautiful neighbouring village Amoreiras come to see a plant-based system for water purification to decide if they want to build it in their village too. At the same time, the visitors also experience something which has been lost in the villages: a vital social life of different age groups. This is what can bring life back to the villages.

Bringing back sustainability and saving the rural areas means reestablishing the regional circuits that have been cut down in the times of industrialisation. In order to bring back life to the countryside, the connections and synergies have to be reinvigorated on a new and modern level, such as between producers and consumers, between water and trees, between bees and trees, between young and old people. And even between men and women, as the example of Fernando shows: on one of the open Saturdays at Tamera, he met Ilona, an Italian woman. Now she is preparing to move to his farm. "Although I love him very much, I could not imagine following Fernando onto his remote farm without having a place like Tamera nearby. We can always go there and meet friends, get inspiration, have cultural life."

In the end, even an international community like Tamera has to face the fact that one day—maybe after peak oil, after the next financial crisis, or after climate change—it will not be global contacts that will help us to survive. Instead, it will be the surrounding region and the neighbourhood, with stable and trustful networks. Now is the time to develop them. ✳

Leila Dregger, 50, freelance journalist from Germany, former publisher of a women's magazine and book writer, joined Tamera in 2003. She works in Tamera's political network office especially to build a bridge to the Portuguese people. Her aim is to establish a school for peace journalism in Tamera. For more about Tamera, its visitor programs, and Summer University (July 25-August 5, 2010), see www.tamera.org.

The Gift of Compost

By Jesse Harasta

During the past three years while I have lived at the Bread and Roses Collective House in Syracuse, New York, my most frequent House Chore has been that of the "Compostmeister." Beyond dealing with the one to one-and-a-half buckets of compost generated weekly by myself and my nine housemates, I have also picked up buckets from a nearby coffeeshop and roaster as well as a Vegan cafe, totaling perhaps 30-35 15-liter buckets of compost a week. I also was involved in the searching out of pallets to construct our six composting bins, and the purchase and maintenance of our finicky woodchipper, which provides layers of "brown" compost for the pile. This yearly total of around 26 cubic meters of compost is being used by the House to create what we hope to be the largest organic garden in all of Syracuse, including 12 two-meter by 10-meter raised beds, three terraces, and a small orchard.

As I gather, spread, and layer compost (not to mention wash buckets) I tend not to think about the future uses of the material, but instead of the various people and organizations that these food remnants represent: the potlucks, midnight snacks, lunches out, coffee breaks, and pancake breakfasts. The food scraps are organic material which break down into nutrients which we then use to grow more food, but they cannot be summed up only by their physical nature, because they also both represent and make real human relationships.

I am an anthropologist and as I teach Anthropology 101, I am always faced with the challenge of teaching my students to understand "economics" as not simply the measurable transfer of currency, but as the ways in which human beings use their physical surroundings to continue their social, cultural, familial and, yes, physical lives. One of the classic works I always refer to is *The Gift* (1923) by Marcel Mauss. Mauss—and those who have worked with his ideas later—tell us that a gift is never "free" but is instead always couched within social relationships, and one gift is always meant to lead to another (though perhaps not directly back to the original giver). Everything about the giving of gifts, not just their worth, but the nature of the object (a dozen roses and a child's book may cost the same but mean different things), and the circumstances of the giving all shape the nature of the gift. Gifts can "make real" relationships between people, such as an underling giving tribute to a lord or a gift of an engagement ring. They are more than symbolic, as they often allow people to have the resources to do important tasks, such as the gifts given at baby showers and graduation parties.

The buckets of decomposing coffee grounds, potato peels, and lemon skins that I pour into a heap and cover with ground-up tree branches make real relationships: between our House and the people at the two local restaurants that we frequent, between housemates cooking for each other, between me—Compostmeister—and my housemates, and eventually between the gardeners and those who eat the food. Food is remarkably rich symbolically and it is perhaps the most common type of gift given by humans. The ability for us to grow and give it is a far more powerful ability than the mere weight of the nutrients collected.

My compost musings point to a new economics, one that focuses upon human needs and human relationships, but one that does not try to have us subsist off of good feelings and hugs, but instead off of a firm ground of well-fertilized soil. 🐛

Compostmeister Jesse Harasta lives at Bread and Roses Collective House in Syracuse, New York. He is an anthropologist at Syracuse University who studies minority language survival in Britain.

Photo courtesy of Yulia Z.

Communal Studies Association

Encouraging the study of
Intentional Community since 1975

Our Mission: * Provide a **forum** for the discussion of Intentional Community
* Help **preserve** America's Communal Sites
* To **communicate** the ssuccessful ideas and lessons learned from
Intentional Communities

We hold an **Annual Conference** each fall at an historic
communal site. We encourage all to come and
participate, learn and contribute to the discussion.

We also publish a **journal** and a **newsletter**, both
issued twice-yearly.

Special registration and **membership rates** are available
for community members.

For more information or to join us, visit our website
www.communalstudies.org

Permaculture at The Farm: Climate Prophylaxis

By Albert Bates

For the past 10 years or so, the land management decisions of The Farm (a 40-year-old intentional community on 1750 acres in rural Tennessee, pop. ~200) have been informed by permaculture. Permaculture was influential in the design and early curricula of The Farm's Ecovillage Training Center in 1994, and since many, if not all, of the community's residents have now been exposed to it, it is not surprising to learn that a number of people serving on various village committees, as well some in public office in the surrounding county, have Permaculture Design certificates.

Our relationship with permaculture traces back to our connection to Bill Mollison, one of permaculture's founders, who received the Right Livelihood Award, sometimes called the "Alternative Nobel Prize," in the year after we did. RLA winners are a gregarious lot and gather from time to time to swap tales, so we have been fortunate to share such meetings with Bill over the past 30 years. We are also fortunate to have had the influence of an erstwhile neighbor, Peter Bane, who for many years published the quarterly *Permaculture Activist* from his former home in Primm Springs, Tennessee.

Today, as a permaculture instructor, I travel to many of the convergences of the movement and have come to know many practitioners. Our Farm team has taught permaculture courses on six continents and in 27 countries now, so it would only be surprising if The Farm did *not* have permaculture going on.

A few years ago our Land Use Committee, which was redrafting The Farm's land management plan, began getting interested in preparing for climate change in the coming century. Of course there is really no preparing for what is now unfolding, other than to become more nimble, or perhaps to begin moving underground.

In 1990, my book, *Climate in Crisis: The Greenhouse Effect and What You Can Do*, painted two very different pathways forward. One was the way blazed by signatories to the Montreal Protocol: international cooperation; hard reduction targets; firm dates. The other was political impasse and social apathy, or even antipathy, auguring 500 to 600 ppm of CO_2-equivalent concentrations to the atmosphere, two to seven degrees of warming, and passing several known tipping points and likely some unknown ones. That second course risks Earth becoming as lifeless as Venus or Mars.

Sadly, we have not retraced our steps and turned up the path to safety for 20 years,

Photos by Albert Bates

now, making the Biblical quote on the frontispiece of my book especially poignant: "They have sown the wind; and they shall reap the whirlwind." That the food riots precipitating the Tunisian Spring and the Egyptian uprising of 2011 were the result of a fried wheat crop in Russia in 2010 seems still to elude most people.

Our generation doesn't need to beat itself up too much over its apathy. It is possible that what was already in the pipeline from the preceding 150 years of coal, oil, and gas is inexorably taking our species to extinction. If we have any cause for shame, it would only be because our generation has not done more to avert that uncertain demise while it is yet uncertain.

Two terms generally bandied about by climate negotiators, "mitigation" and "adaptation," are losing a lot of their luster now, as we come to recognize that if the worst comes, neither of those choices will be available to us. While many who write about climate change still offer long-odds solutions like carbon farming and tree-planting (including my own recent book, *The Biochar Solution*), we know that cultural inertia is not on our side. The Civil Rights movement of the 1950s and '60s had strong allies in the church and Northern media. Today the church is allied with advocates of unfettered population and the media has been subsumed into the climate-denier corporate world.

The Civil Rights movement also held the advantage of knowing, as an abiding article of faith, that in the end it would prevail. While the arc of the moral universe may be long and bend towards justice, as Martin Luther King said, climate scientists are quick to remind us that the arc of the physical universe is short and bends towards heat.

The goal of The Farm's Land Use Committee is to avoid the mistakes of the past, such as planting heirloom tree species from earlier centuries while climate isotherms are migrating poleward 70 miles per decade. We'd like to provide as much comfort for our coming generations, and those of our brethren

a segment on biochar and terra preta soils and Darren himself demonstrated keyline plowing.

The keyline method was developed by Australian stockman P.A. Yeomans in the 1950s. By studying the lay of the land, Yeomans noticed that in the usual flow of things, gravity takes water downhill by the shortest route, carrying water, topsoil, and soluble minerals from the ridges and concentrating rich deposits in the valleys. What is really needed is the opposite—to distribute soil moisture from the wetter valleys or field indentations out towards the drier ridgelines, and to cover the largest possible area with migrating minerals when it rains.

Yeomans' Keyline® Plow, a $55,000 piece of equipment made only in Australia, has a plow that resembles the secret

---

We asked Australian Darren Doherty for advice. "Don't put in the dams until you've keylined the place," he said.

---

species, as might reasonably be salvaged. Thinking about putting more ponds, lakes, and aquifer-recharge zones into our 4000-acre landholding, we asked Australian Darren Doherty for advice.

"Don't put in the dams until you've keylined the place," he said. So in 2009, we invited Darren and a group of distinguished co-teachers to give the first carbon-farming course in North America. We brought in Kurt Gadzia and Joel Salatin to teach holistic management, Brad Lancaster to teach water capture, Eric Toensmeyer to teach agroforestry, and Elaine Ingham to teach soil microbiology. I chipped in

"winged" keel shape that helped *Australia II* dethrone the USA in the America's Cup sailing regatta of 1983. Operating like a hydrofoil, it has "terro"dynamic horizontal fins at the subsoil bottom of a vertical shaft. Three to five of these rigid shanks are mounted on a heavy steel frame and dragged along behind

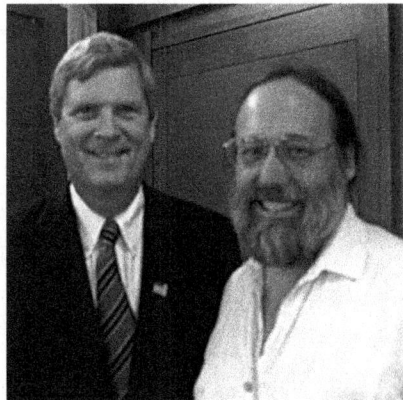

Left to right: 1. Keyline Cowboy at The Farm, keylining with Ford Tractor.
2. Former stockbroker Brian Bankston now calls himself the "Keyline Cowboy" after a carbon farming course at The Farm's Ecovillage Training Center transformed his life. He quit his job, bought a keyline plow and compost tea brewer, and moved to The Farm.
3. Nine months pregnant, Ann Marie Bankston lays out the contours for keylining, using a GSI laser level.
4. The Farm scene. 5. Agriculture Secretary Tom Vilsack with author, at first North American Biochar Conference, 2009.

Permaculture is the only way we can imagine our children still living here in another 50 or 75 years.

Scenes from The Farm.

the tractor. A coulter disc precedes the shanks, slicing open the upper soil layer to minimize surface disturbance and reduce the energy required to pull the device. The angle of action at the shares' leading edge is very slight—only eight percent compared to typically 25 percent in chisel plows and subsoilers.

During cultivation, the soil is gently raised and loosened without turning a furrow. Rain and air enter the soil and release the minerals that chelate and loosely attach themselves to clay particles and humic acid. The released minerals are not water-soluble and are readily available to roots. Immediate results are dramatic and magical. Water moves from valleys to ridges.

Every piece of land is unique and will be influenced by how water passes through it, irrespective of where the farm, cattle ranch, shopping mall, or four-lane highway gets put. By directing that water from valley to ridge, gravity and rain make the life of the farmer and rancher much easier. Keyline design combines cultivation, irrigation, and stock management techniques to greatly speed up the natural process of soil formation, and results of 400 to 600 tons of topsoil per acre each year are possible. Keylining can annually deepen topsoil four to six inches, and darken it a meter deep in less than a decade.

One of the students in our class was a former securities trader named Brian Bankston. He was so impressed with the keyline method that he went out and bought a keyline plow and took it to his farm in Arkansas. A year later, he relocated to The Farm and became one of the strongest weapons in our Land Use Committee's arsenal. Each year he has been reclaiming more and more of the pastures and croplands of The Farm, using a combination of keyline method, compost tea slurry application, rock dust, and biochar.

As Darren Doherty had told us when we first asked him, keylining is doing more to hold water in the landscape of The Farm and to protect its fields and forests than any number of dams could have. It is recharging both our aquifers and the water-retaining capacity of our soils. As The Farm gradually becomes more tropical, with just two seasons instead of the once-usual four, this capacity will be critical for keeping the rain that falls in the wet times of year, making water available for crops and animals when it is dry and temperatures climb well above 100°F.

Permaculture is the only way we can imagine our children still living here in another 50 or 75 years. Or the trees in our forests, the squirrels, and the butterflies, for that matter. 🐦

Albert Bates is author of The Financial Collapse Survival Guide and Cookbook *and 14 other books on energy, environment, and history, including* Climate in Crisis *(1990) and* The Post-Petroleum Survival Guide and Cookbook *(2006). A former environmental and civil rights lawyer, he has argued before the US Supreme Court and written a number of legislative acts. A cofounder and past president of the Global Ecovillage Network, he is presently GEN's representative to the UN climate talks. When not inventing fuel wringers for algae or pyrolizing cookstoves, he teaches permaculture, village design, and natural building, and is a special advisor for Gaia University. He wrote the chapter on agriculture for* State of the World 2010. *His latest book is* The Biochar Solution: Carbon Farming and Climate Change *(New Society 2010).*

Hugelkultur on the Prairie, or Learning from Our Mistakes

By Alyson Ewald

I'm a sheet-mulching, swale-digging, perennial-planting lunatic like most permies, but no matter what I do I can never seem to get enough organic matter down into our solid clay subsoil. So when I heard about hugelkultur—burying logs in the ground beneath your plants—I was instantly sold.

I began shopping around our homestead at Red Earth Farms in rural Missouri as if it were a vast open-air hugelkultur store. My partner was thrilled with my sudden interest in all his piles of wooden detritus, too rotten to become firewood or construction materials. It seemed like every bit of degraded slope on our place was crying out for trenches filled with old sticks. I roamed around with a shovel and a deranged glint in my eye until I found two perfect spots. My only question was what to plant.

Hugelkultur, German for "mound culture," may have roots in an ancient form of Eastern European sheet mulching. It has come to refer to a practice used by Austrian farmer Sepp Holzer and spread across the internet by permaculture maven Paul Wheaton and other bloggers. The idea is to build a raised bed by first digging a deep trench or pit and then filling it with woody stuff, adding some nitrogen-rich compost materials like grass clippings or manure if you have them, piling the soil back on top, mulching, and leaving it to break down. You can plant into it immediately or wait a while. You can also do it without the pit—just pile any soil or compost on top of a stack of logs.

The wood acts like a sponge, holding a tremendous amount of water and nutrients and feeding them slowly to your plants. The decomposing wood attracts earthworms deep into your subsoil, extends your growing season by adding warmth, creates air pockets for your plants' roots to enter, and encourages mycelia to join the party. Sounded like a win-win-win to me.

I'd read that potatoes and cucurbits had been shown to do well in hugelkultur beds, but I had already planted those in other places. I'd also heard that the moist, decomposing logs could tie up nitrogen and lower soil pH, like a bog. I wanted to experiment with hugelkultur on a crop that I knew would enjoy the low pH. Like...blueberries!

Shockingly, the internet turned up exactly zero people who had tried blueberries in a hugelkultur bed. Clearly someone would have to launch this experiment. Then I received two things: a strong-armed intern, and a phone call from a neighbor offering me as many mature blueberry plants as I wanted. The universe was sending me a message. So we began to dig.

In the sites I had chosen, the soil was already quite acidic (pH 5.1). We dug a trench a few feet wide and about a foot and a half deep and laid the sodden, already crumbling logs and sticks in the bottom. Then we piled the subsoil and topsoil around the logs, stuck in some 10-year-old blueberry plants that were still holding soil around their roots, and mulched them like crazy with mown hay from our fields.

The plants initially thrived in our moist springtime. Although they had been completely neglected and unpruned in their old home, they stood proudly atop their hugels and set a fair amount of large, sweet fruit. Our

First fruit ripens in hugelkultur bed closest to pond.

25

daughter rejoiced in the berries and we celebrated our success.

Then came the drought. Two of the seven plants suddenly blackened and turned brittle. And I realized I had failed to heed fully two great tenets of permaculture: that we must put things in the right place, and that important functions should be performed by multiple elements.

"Place the elements of your design in ways that create useful relationships and time-saving connections among all parts," says Toby Hemenway, author of *Gaia's Garden*. Well, of course I was aiming for a placement that would create those connections. That's why I'd planted them along a frequently traveled path, where my community members and I could observe and tend (and harvest) easily. And that's why I had chosen them to extend the "edge" of our orchard, where scything and leaf-fall would generate sufficient mulch nearby. I had placed them uphill of the rest of the orchard, so that any excess nutrients would run down to the fruit trees, and so that liming

Intern Teresa Rutten covers logs with soil to create a hugelkultur bed.

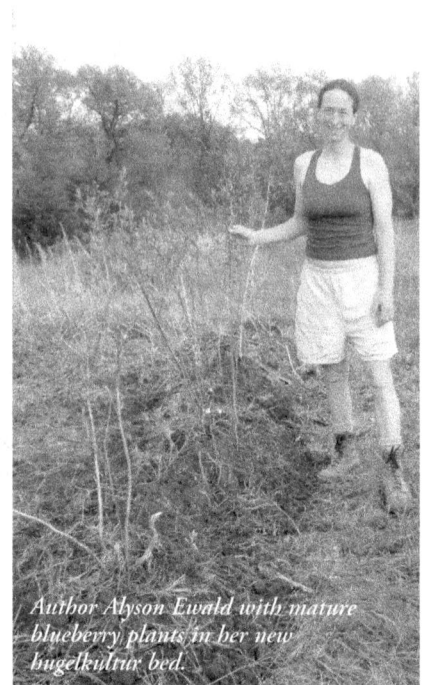

Author Alyson Ewald with mature blueberry plants in her new hugelkultur bed.

Photos courtesy of Alyson Ewald

only source of water—our pond. This was not a useful relationship or a time-saving connection. There was no element serving the all-important function of providing adequate water to saturate the logs, encourage them to compost, and fill the cavities between them and the soil. The poor plants were left literally high and dry, and I had little patience for hauling buckets of water up the hill in a cart.

The saving grace at this juncture turned out to be community. Thank God I do not live alone out here on the prairie. Family, friends, and neighbors have all helped me get adequate water and more mulch to the blueberries, and despite a continuing drought we have managed collectively to stave off the

> ## The saving grace turned out to be community. Thank God I do not live alone out here on the prairie.

the orchard would not raise the pH of the blueberry bed. I was stacking functions—the logs would hold water and build organic matter and soil health, the perennial plants would hold soil and provide food, wildlife cover, beauty, and mulch, and the mound and hedge as a whole would help buffer the orchard against prevailing winds. I was turning a problem (acidic soil, unsightly log piles) into a solution (tasty berries). I had even placed the mounds along a slope so they would catch and store water, reducing runoff and protecting against erosion. What had I done wrong?

As the hot, dry July days continued, the answer became painfully clear: I had placed them far uphill from the

death of the five remaining plants. Spring will tell whether the hugelkultur experiment has succeeded.

Interestingly, the blueberries closest to our house have shown no difficulty at all. I suspect they have received more attention, mulch, urine, and water than those farther away. Which reminds me of another principle I forgot—start close to home and work slowly outward. A friend just gave me a couple more young blueberry plants, which I'm planning to put near the surviving ones closest to the house (and pond).

Sometimes I think I learn more from my failures than from my successes. Hey, guess what? That's Toby Hemenway's Permaculture Principle #14: "Mistakes are tools for learning." At least there's one principle I'm following. I'm considering building my next hugelkultur beds right here below the house, downhill from the pond. I think I'll put in potatoes. ❧

Alyson Ewald is an organizer, fundraiser, baker, and founding member of Red Earth Farms, a 76-acre community land trust in Missouri. She and her partner Mark experiment with permaculture, natural building, and child-raising together, with varying degrees of success.

The Future of Water

Halting desertification, restoring ecosystems, and nourishing communities

By Jeff Anderson

In sharp contrast to the paradisiacal beauty of our planet Earth pictured from afar—blue, green, and white in its wealth of life-giving water—a growing proportion of the world's inhabitants face the harsh reality of water scarcity. The world faces a crisis concerning one of the most basic elements of life, with humanitarian and ecological consequences far beyond the economic shocks likely to result from the diminishing fossil energy supply.

In answer to this crisis and to the threat of desertification, the Tamera Peace Research Centre, an intentional community located on 331 acres in southern Portugal, has been establishing a permacultural water landscape on its land. Readers may recall the article "Water Is Life!" (COMMUNITIES #143, Summer 2009), which described the development of Tamera's water landscape since the vision was first presented to the community in 2007 by "Rebel Farmer" and permaculture expert Sepp Holzer. Within only two years, Tamera already seemed to have been transformed into a land blessed with an abundance of water—even at the height of its long, hot, and dry summers—providing a glimpse into an entirely different possibility for the dry landscape that stretches hundreds of miles east across the entire Iberian Peninsula.

Last year, another large water retention space was added, and after last winter's exceptionally high rainfall, all of Tamera's many lakes and ponds were filled to capacity. Maddy Harland, editor of the UK-based *Permaculture Magazine*, described her astonishment during a visit earlier this year, saying "It is almost unbelievable that in such an arid landscape, so much water can be collected." However, the existing retention spaces are still not sufficient to hold back all of the winter rains.

This summer, work began on what will become Tamera's largest retention space, enabling the land to retain the entire rainfall of an average winter—a true *Water Retention Landscape*. Bernd Müller, coordinator for Tamera's water landscape, describes how the only water then leaving the land will be fresh, clear, and vitalised spring-water. From this new retention space situated on the highest part of Tamera's land, water will flow continuously throughout the year. It will then also be possible to maintain the water level of all the other retention spaces, and the whole land can be irrigated (as long as still necessary) without needing any additional energy for pumping.

The fertility of the land is being restored by bringing back moisture to the earth-body, and

Building the water landscape.

Tamera Water Dia Aberto.

Photos courtesy of Jeff Anderson

(continued on p. 74)

THE FUTURE OF WATER

(continued from p. 32)

also through a process described by Thomas Lüdert, lead engineer for Tamera's water landscape, as "erosion in reverse." Large volumes of topsoil, which had been eroded from the hillsides over the previous decades, are excavated from the valley where the earth dam will be built. This rich, fertile soil is taken back to the hillsides onto new terraces that will stay moist in summer and well drained throughout the rest of the year.

With an increasingly moist earth-body, and a richer, deeper topsoil, artificial irrigation can be reduced and eventually dispensed with altogether. Plants and especially trees can then thrive on vitalised water provided naturally from below, as they are encouraged to root deep into the ground rather than becoming addicted to water dripped onto the surface from plastic piping above.

In the "edible landscape" that is cultivated around the retention spaces, nutritious organic produce provides not only for human communities but for all the wild creatures of nature that also belong there. "Nature is like a mother: treat her right and she'll give you everything you need!" says Holzer, summing up this way of permaculture, oriented towards full contact and cooperation with nature.

Both Holzer and Bernd Müller wish to see the model applied worldwide. "The principle of decentralised water landscapes is valid across many climate zones," says Bernd. "Even in the desert it is possible to collect rainwater so that it has time to slowly enter the earth-body and create life." Water landscapes can also be adapted to the humid tropics, where they can prevent fatal landslides and act in place of the fragile topsoil that is often completely washed away in a single rainy season after the clearance of the rainforests.

A world in which water—and consequently food—is freely available to all humankind is entirely feasible. Bringing this vision into reality, however, requires a revolutionary shift in human thinking. Instead of systems based on ideas of scarcity, mistrust, domination, and subjugation of nature, there must be a reorientation towards a life based on abundance, trust, mutual support, and cooperation with nature.

In this way, the new communities of the world can regain their healthy connection with the core power of life, and our hearts may open once again in the knowledge that we can heal the Earth. ❧

Jeff Anderson has been a permaculture trainee in the Tamera Peace Research Centre (founded 1995; current population about 200) since 2007.

The Fund for Democratic Communities is a Greensboro, North Carolina based foundation supporting community-centered initiatives and institutions that foster authentic democracy and make communities better places to live.

FUND 4 DEMOCRATIC COMMUNITIES

Permaculture on Low to No Budget

By Elizabeth Barrette

Permaculture as a horticultural approach creates a densely planted landscape with rich connections linking all its parts together. Books and courses on permaculture tend to view a landscape as a whole, which can imply a need to begin the whole permaculture all at once. This may work for people with a large landscaping budget, but many communities have less to work with in that regard. Happily, permaculture draws its inspiration from nature, and nature is the ultimate expert at making do.

You don't need large amounts of money to start practicing permaculture, although having at least a little will help. You also don't need to plan out the whole thing in advance. If you're new to permaculture, there are advantages to starting small, such as with a single rain garden to manage a soggy place or with a butterfly garden to attract beneficial insects. Many aspects of permaculture also lend themselves well to saving money.

Basic Principles

Permaculture looks quite different from conventional agriculture or landscaping; it looks more like wilderness. Yet permaculture is a system of order, not chaos. It grows out of a set of principles derived from careful observations of nature. Applying these principles creates a beautiful, functional, and frugal habitat. Below are just a handful of the fundamental ideas.

Start where you are; use what you have. Nature started with a dead bare rock and made the biosphere of the Earth. No matter how depleted your local environment may seem, you actually have quite a lot to build on. Identify the resources you have and take advantage of those before buying anything else. You may be surprised how much potential a close look reveals. Also, it is not necessary to landscape an entire area all at once. You can start small and grow from there.

Everything is connected. A natural ecosystem forms a dense web of resources and processes. Nothing is ever really wasted or lost. Permaculture uses that as inspiration to create tightly interlocking communities of plants and animals that suit human desires. One example is a "guild" of plants chosen to meet each other's needs. Closing the loop conserves resources and minimizes what you need to import.

Trees sweat so you don't have to. Nature does tremendous amounts of work all the time. Let it. Trees cool the air and retain moisture, reducing the need for air conditioning and supplemental watering. Miner plants ("dynamic accumulators") such as chicory draw trace elements from the subsoil so you don't need to add them. Nitrogen-fixing plants such as clover filter fertilizer out of the air, alleviating the need to buy it. Permaculture maximizes the work that nature does, reducing the need for human labor and extra materials.

Nature produces bounty. Everything has uses; learn what they are. Identify what you want and need from a landscape, then design your permaculture to provide that. Stack functions so that a single plant provides multiple benefits; for instance, an apple tree provides shade, fruit, wildlife habitat, and nice wood for carving or burning. By studying what different parts of the ecosystem do, you can fit them together snugly in ways that benefit both humans and nature.

Get out of the way. Far more environmental problems come from humans than from nature. Earth's biosphere is well prepared to repair damage. If you don't know how to fix a problem, and it came from human interference—such as clearcutting or stripping off the topsoil—then often the best approach is to watch how nature responds and look for ways to assist that process. Similarly, try to avoid causing problems; in a permaculture system, think in the long term and resist the temptation to micromanage. "Don't just do something, stand there."

Clover attracts butterflies and other beneficial insects to Fieldhaven's prairie garden.

Photos by Elizabeth Barrette

29

Ways to Save Money

Because permaculture draws much of its structure from nature, rather than human economic systems, it lends itself well to frugality. Some of these techniques overlap with related models, such as organic gardening, while others relate more closely to permaculture in particular. Look at your community's budget for gardening, landscaping, etc. and see if you can think of more ways to conserve funds.

Get seeds or plants for free. Many options exist for this. Join a seed swap or plant swap to gain new varieties. Choose open-pollinated heirloom cultivars that breed true, so that you can save seeds for replanting in the spring. Watch for opportunities to gather native plants or seeds—sometimes a nature reserve will have a seed-gathering day or a developer will let people dig up native plants prior to a construction project. To establish a row of brush and trees attractive to local birds, till up a line of soil and then string a wire above it. Birds perching on the wire will deposit seeds in their droppings. The Bradley method of habitat restoration involves, at its core, starting with a patch that includes some native plants and simply clearing out all the exotic competitors so that the natives can spread.

Divide and conquer. Many plants, both natives and desirable exotics, spread themselves by clumping, runners, or other nonsexual means. Spring and fall are good times to divide dense patches and move some of the plants to a new area. Instead of buying a large number of expensive plants, you can buy a smaller number and propagate them yourself to cover the desired area. Learn which plants multiply and divide well, and when to divide each plant.

Choose native species that need minimum support. Many garden flowers and vegetables are exotics that require lots of extra water, weeding, fertilizer, and fussing to stay alive. Native plants may need a little extra care when first introduced, but once established they can largely take care of themselves. Explore your local environment to discover what edible, decorative, or otherwise useful plants live nearby and how they fit themselves together. This doesn't mean you have to do without all your favorite cultivated plants, just that replacing some domesticated varieties with natives can save you both money and effort.

Favor perennials over annuals. Perennial plants return year after year, saving both time and money. Annuals require that you obtain new seeds or plants each spring. Some annuals, however, reseed themselves well enough that they function more like perennials in a permaculture context. You can still grow your favorite annuals, but the more perennials you can use, the better.

Buy just the right plants. Start by using free methods, as described above, to obtain as many plants or seeds as possible. Then fill in the gaps by buying the varieties you need to fill specific roles in your permaculture. You'll get better results by paying for a few ideal plants than by settling for something free that doesn't fit well or doing without. Look in heirloom seed catalogs or conservation catalogs for reasonably priced plants suited to permaculture. Ordinary gardening catalogs tend to stock mostly hybrids and exotics that are less useful for this purpose.

Harvest materials from the landscape for its own maintenance. For instance, when trimming excess brush out of a wooded area, save some branches for staking peas or tomatoes. Soaking comfrey leaves in water makes a good fertilizer spray. Wormwood, rue, pyrethrum, and pennyroyal are just a few herbs that produce insect repellent.

Keep a compost pile. This allows you to process not only dead weeds and other plant refuse from your permaculture project, but also kitchen scraps. A compost pile produces abundant amounts of dark, fluffy organic matter that enriches your soil and aids water retention. It's one more thing you don't have to buy.

Lower water bills with water conservation. Fill soggy areas with a rain garden. In dry areas, bury rotten logs or a quantity of wood chips to absorb and hold water underground. On slopes, dig swales (shallow ditches) to catch runoff. Use mulch around trees and between plants both for catching water as it arrives and preventing its loss via evaporation. Also, water is one area where a modest investment can really pay off: buy one or more rain barrels to catch the free water that falls on your roof. A hose or tap in the barrel makes it easy to water nearby plants directly from the rain barrel. Alternatively, you can route downspout water to a rain garden or water garden.

Close the money loop. Remember that permaculture is a cyclic system. When you buy plants, tools, or materials for it that means money flowing out. Find ways to make money flow in. Permaculture generates many useful—and marketable—resources including food, cut flowers, craft materials, and firewood. A well-planned

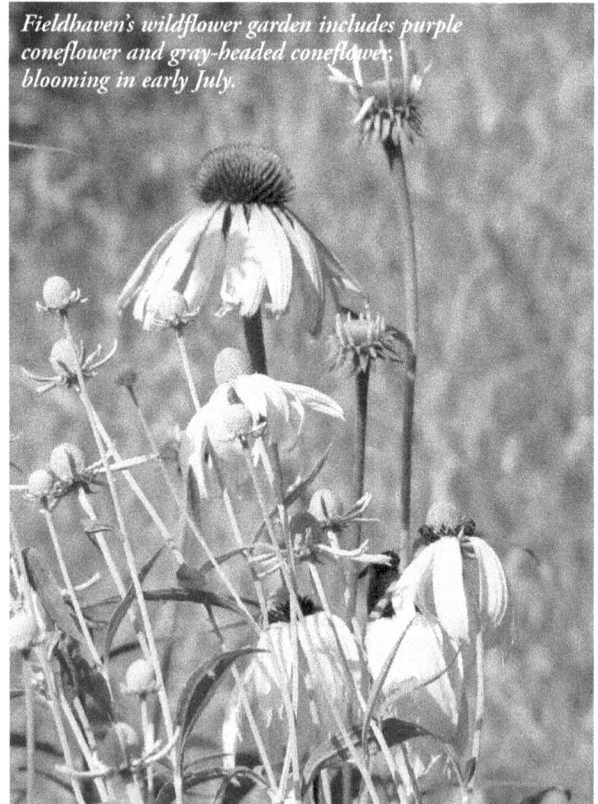

Fieldhaven's wildflower garden includes purple coneflower and gray-headed coneflower, blooming in early July.

permaculture can thus support its own modest budget through sale of surplus materials.

Permaculture in Community

Permaculture resembles intentional community in many ways. Its underlying structure creates stability and consistency over the long term. Within that context, things grow and change, allowing for diversity and adaptability. This helps make permaculture a good fit for the community context.

First, consider your human resources. The more members your community involves in its permaculture projects, the higher the chance of success. Encourage people to participate in all the stages—brainstorming, planning, planting, tending, and harvesting. Different folks might find that their talents apply to different stages or projects, and that's okay. In permaculture there are ways for everyone to contribute, depending on their interests and abilities.

Also, think about your community members and their needs. Look at your land with an eye toward its strengths and weaknesses. This will tell you what kind of permaculture projects might work best for you.

Do you have elderly and/or handicapped members in your community? They might appreciate wide, smooth walkways with comfortable resting places amidst a scenic garden filled with wildflowers and interesting shrubs.

Do you have active children and young adults? They may enjoy an "adventure garden" sturdy enough to withstand foot traffic as they learn about plants and animals. It also helps to keep a sizable patch of lawn—which most permaculture projects minimize— available as play space.

Are there many artists, writers, and other creative people? Consider designing some areas for inspiration, such as a flower garden for painting, a collection of plants that yield natural dyes, or tall grasses and willows for basket making.

Are people interested in environmental awareness? Plant a wildlife garden to attract birds, beneficial insects, and other animals. Include a restoration patch of plants native to your region. Grow plants that make fertilizers, insect repellents, cleansers, and other substances so that you need fewer chemicals.

Does your land include a barren patch that is too hot or cold, wet or dry, or somehow damaged to grow much of interest? Examine the "weeds" there and try to figure out what they're doing to survive and repair the earth. You can probably think of some native species that would suit the same conditions while also being more attractive and useful.

Does your community want to grow part or all of your own food? Permaculture offers many options such as a food forest, an orchard built from different fruit tree guilds, a vegetable polyculture, or a spiral garden full of herbs. You can enjoy many unusual flavors rarely found in supermarkets, such as mulberries, pawpaws, or elder-flower fritters.

Do you entertain a lot of guests? A dooryard garden at the guest house or community center looks inviting and helps start conversations. If the lodging is spread out, you might prefer a focal garden at your community entrance or some other highly visible location.

Ideally, permaculture is a long-term project. You might start with just one or two pieces, then connect them, and

> ## Permaculture is a lot like intentional community— many individuals living together for mutual benefit.

gradually expand to cover more area. As new people move into your community, the permaculture plan can grow and change accordingly to accommodate new interests. Connecting with other people or communities interested in permaculture can also give you fresh ideas. Over time, the increasing variety of plants will attract more types of birds, insects, and other wildlife for you to enjoy. Just remember that permaculture is a lot like intentional community—many individuals living together for mutual benefit. So get to know your plant neighbors. You'll be glad you did. ❧

Elizabeth Barrette writes and edits nonfiction, fiction, and poetry in diverse fields including speculative fiction, green living, community, and politics. Visit her blog The Wordsmith's Forge (ysabetwordsmith. livejournal.com).

Recommended Resources

The Basics of Permaculture Design by Ross Mars. Permanent Publications, 2005. Introduces theory and design principles of permaculture.

The Food Forest—A permaculture farm offering classes and information: www.foodforest.com.au.

Gaia's Garden: A Guide to Home-Scale Permaculture by Toby Hemenway. Chelsea Green Publishing, 2009. Explains the basic principles of permaculture and how to practice it in small to medium areas, with many practical examples.

Getting Started In Permaculture: 50 Practical Projects to Build and Design Productive Gardens by Ross Mars and Jenny Mars. Permanent Publications, 2007. Sample gardens designed on permaculture principles.

The Permaculture Institute—Website with information about permaculture classes, a blog, and articles on permaculture topics: www.permaculture.org.

Permaculture as a Tool for Ecological Community Design

By Ethan Hirsch-Tauber

At the moment, I feel pretty well-fed, physically, emotionally, intellectually, and spiritually. I've just spent the past three weeks at Sirius Community near Amherst in western Massachusetts, where I attended a Permaculture Design Certification course.[1] The program was organized by Living Routes, an educational nonprofit, which partners with the University of Massachusetts Amherst to offer college-level programs based in "ecovillages" around the world.[2]

Living in an intentional, ecologically-focused community while studying permaculture presented a double whammy of a learning opportunity: I was able to observe the same permaculture principles and techniques and concepts as they were put into practice at Sirius, and we utilized our new skills by working in the community. These activities ranged from manual labor projects, such as sheet-mulching a new garden, making a new pond, and lime-plastering a cob bench, to completing a permaculture site analysis and design process for a family's yard in the community. While I don't know what it's like to study permaculture in a standard classroom setting, I can't see how it could be any more holistic and integrative as a learning experience.

I've had exposure to various permaculture concepts and practices over the past few years, but I still consider myself in "beginner's mind" in this field of study. I went into the class with a very basic understanding of permaculture. What I learned was an entirely new, and in my opinion, brilliant lens with which to look at the world.

Permaculture as an ecological approach has evolved quite a bit over the past 30-plus years since it was first articulated by Australian ecologists Bill Mollison and David Holmgren in the '70s. Though commonly misperceived as merely a method for sustainable land and resource use, permaculture has a broader scope than just creating permanent *agriculture*; it works towards creating permanent *culture*, which includes agriculture, but also other facets of human habitation on the planet. "Permanent" in this context does not mean creating human settlements that are rigidly set in their structures and ways, but rather adaptable human settlements as dynamic and changeable as the world in which they exist.

What does permaculture tell us about existing communities, as well as how to create new ones? Ecovillages and other intentional communities with similar ecological worldviews are, by their very nature, adaptable. Over the past several years, I've been on an inspiring journey to visit

Dawn bonfire for Auroville's 40th birthday celebration.

Abbey Schoenfeld

and experience communities around the world that are loci of positive social and environmental change. I've seen how much diversity exists among these communities and have also noted that they tend to follow a set of ethics and principles modeled after those seen in nature.

Permaculture too holds at its core a set of guiding principles that model nature and generate adaptability. With my new permaculture hat on, I am able to see how much similarity lies between the goals and missions of ecovillages and those of permaculture. I am sure this is no accident. There has been a vast exchange of knowledge between these two movements over the years. Many communities even directly incorporate permaculture into their projects. But since I am just now realizing how deep this connection goes, I will consider just a few of these key permaculture principles and describe how they relate to the dynamic, regenerative communities many of us seek to create. The principles I reference here come primarily from David Holmgren, who outlines 12, though I have also integrated several concepts from other permaculturists, including Bill Mollison.

Observe and Interact;
Make Small and Slow Solutions
(Holmgren)

Observation, possibly the most important lesson of permaculture, can apply to virtually every aspect of life. When observation becomes an intentional aspect of planning, nature can more readily become the teacher, and inform decisions for community development. One of the major differences I have observed between intentional communities and other communities in the world is that the former often develop much more slowly, starting small, only gradually increasing in population size and land usage. While many factors may contribute to this, it seems that many ecologically-minded communities spend a great deal of time observing the environments in which they exist, and considering the potential impacts of their actions. This might not be said of many human settle-

Fire and people: Hundreds of people gather for a predawn bonfire for Auroville's 40th birthday celebration.

Abbey Schoenfeld

ments in the world today, where rapid development is paramount.

I also notice this concept within intentional methods of communication, which are increasingly used in community settings. Compassionate communication and other similar styles of interaction require first observing one's own thoughts and emotions in a conversation, prior to responding to another individual.[3] This simple step added to a heated discussion or other challenging social interaction can give the space to fully experience and understand one's reactions and then proceed without having a knee-jerk response that may cause more harm than good. Observation of communication can also add to the joy and gratitude within a community, as people create more space for these experiences to arise and be acknowledged.

"The Problem Is the Solution" (Mollison)

One of the most commonly quoted permaculture ideas during my course, this also seems to me one of the most crucial. As we enter an age where tremendous forces of change are spreading rapidly throughout the world—a transitional period which ecological philosopher Joanna Macy has titled "The Great Turning"—it is vital that we step back from the perceived "problems" that we face and reexamine them from a different angle (Macy). If we can learn to do so effectively, we will be able to view perceived negatives as opportunities. A great example is reuse of a perceived "waste" stream, like cardboard or newspaper, as a source for creating healthy soil through sheet mulching.

In Auroville, an international spiritual community in India where I have spent much of the past few years, this concept has been put into practice as Aurovilians have come into conflict with traditional Tamil villages over reforestation work, villager land use, and livestock grazing rights.[4] Previously-deforested land has been replanted over the last 40 years, allowing ecosystem restoration, including indigenous plant species with medicinal properties, to benefit everyone in the region. However, in the early years of the reforestation project, the Aurovilians' need to protect the young trees clashed with the needs of poor villagers who wanted to graze livestock and collect firewood. These confrontations occasionally even led to violence.

Over time, as the forests matured, there was enough dead wood for the villagers to use as fuel, and enough common land for cows and goats to graze on. The mature forest ecosystem could also withstand the effects of grazing far better than barren land. By solving the problem of environmental degradation through reforestation, both communities benefited. On other occasions, clashes were resolved through dialogue and creative thinking about sharing and dividing land, to the benefit of both sides. The perceived problem that both groups wanted to use the same land actually became a tool for strengthening relationships between the people of these very different communities, while allowing for regeneration of the bioregion. This process, clearly quite difficult, requires thought outside the box, and use of our inherent, though sometimes latent ingenuity, but the potential for shifting from a negative to a positive perspective is truly staggering.

Use and Value Diversity (Holmgren); Plan for Redundancy

In non-human ecosystems, diversity creates stability as a larger variety of organisms are able to fill various niches. Permaculture seeks to model this by increasing the diversity of biota through ecosystem design. It also seeks to create redundancy in meeting each essential need in a system in multiple ways. I have seen these ideas present in communities too: Findhorn Foundation in Scotland, for example, encourages members to gain experience in a variety of different jobs and types of work.[5] This not only allows for a greater sense of freedom for individuals, but also provides a stronger network of people with multiple skills to suit the various needs of the community.

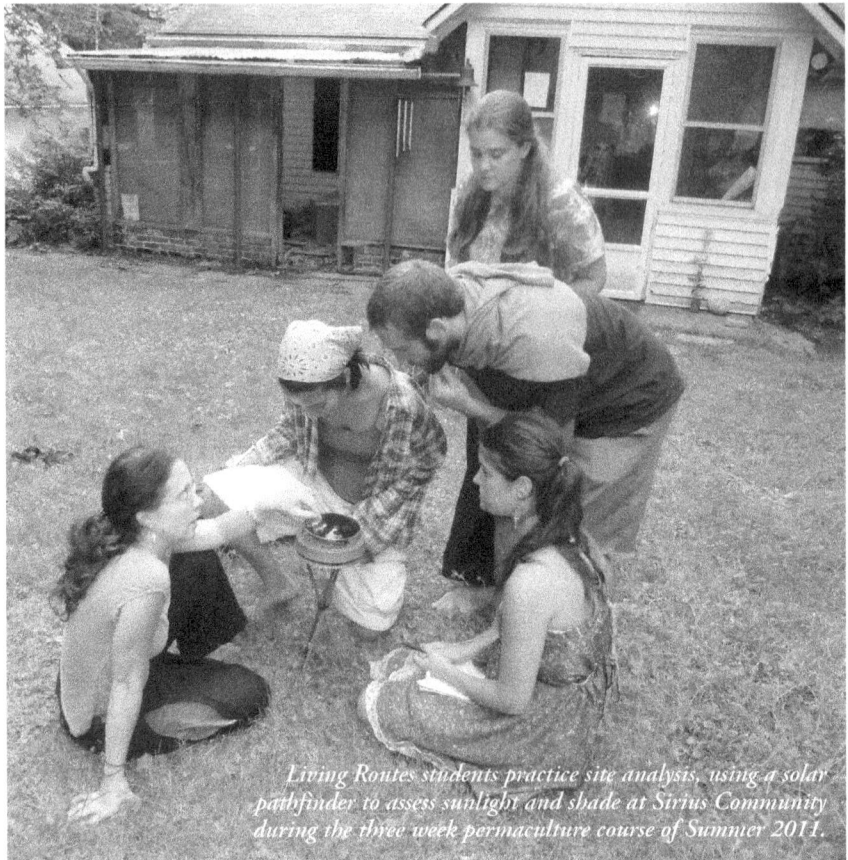

Living Routes students practice site analysis, using a solar pathfinder to assess sunlight and shade at Sirius Community during the three week permaculture course of Summer 2011.

On a larger scale, if we look at the diversity of intentional human settlements that exist throughout the world, the range of form and function of these communities— from urban ecovillages to traditional indigenous villages to rural homesteads— is also amazing. As we move into the Great Turning, this diversity can only provide a stronger web of support for one another.

Use Edges and Value the Marginal (Holmgren)

The edges between different ecosystems hold great potential for nutrient and energy exchange. For this reason, permaculturists frequently use zig-zag patterns and crenellated edges to maximize space and increase productivity. Emphasizing the marginal can help not only in growing ecosystems, but people in community too. In my experience of social interaction and group dynamics, the fringe and marginalized voices are also the most easily overlooked or ignored. However, these individuals are those who can most readily help a community learn and grow, as they tend to challenge the status quo and can encourage alternative solutions to group problems. This is why many communities

---

1. More information about Sirius Community can be found at www.siriuscommunity.org.

2. More information about Living Routes can be found at www.livingroutes.org. For information specifically about the Permaculture program at Sirius, go to www.livingroutes.org/programs/p_sirius.htm. And for course teacher contacts, refer to Sowing Solutions Permaculture Design and Education, Kay Cafasso, sowingsolutions.net, and Natalie Krueger, greenvoices@gmail.com.

3. More information on Compassionate and Nonviolent Communication can be found at www.cnvc.org.

4. More information about Auroville can be found at www.auroville.org.

5. More information about Findhorn Foundation can be found at www.findhorn.org.

6. More information about Tamera can be found at www.tamera.org.

7. As an example, the number 150, identified as "Dunbar's number," has been theorized as the "cognitive limit to the number of people with whom one can maintain stable social relationships." Of course the patterns of human social interaction are far more complex than just one number, and multiple other ranges exist. For more on these ideas go to en.wikipedia.org/wiki/Dunbar's_number and an interesting blog, www.lifewithalacrity.com/2004/03/the_dunbar_numb.html.

use consensus or similar decision-making models; at least in theory, these create space for marginal and edge voices, though in practice they can sometimes still be overlooked. Some communities, like Tamera in Portugal, use specific communication tools such as Forum, a creative, artistic form of communication used by groups to generate trust between members, to gain the most from all representative voices.[6]

Design from Patterns to Details (Holmgren)

Certain patterns found in nature have evolved and been selected for over possibly millions of years. Human design can and should utilize these patterns whenever possible, as they contain inherent wisdom for maximized functionality. Maximizing garden bed edge space using geometrical patterns, such as in spirals based on the Fibonacci sequence, is a good example of incorporating patterns into design. The principle of designing from patterns to details, however, builds even more on this idea: it suggests that we look at the bigger picture before planning out the finer details in a system. Thus, if we model the whole system based on observed natural patterns, it should be more functional and effective when individual elements are worked out.

In group dynamics, certain numbers of individuals and formations of organization seem to be the most effective for reaching decisions and living harmoniously.[7] Communities can design their living spaces and social organization to account for these seeming inherent patterns of human interaction. I've noticed that many intentional communities are building their living environments to account for these numbers. When numbers and social structures exceed these limits (as in Auroville, which at present has about 2,000 members), challenges come up in working out complex community dynamics. Auroville has at least partially addressed this issue by creating working groups which deal with specific areas such as forests, farming, new membership, or housing.

Expanding on the Principles

The above principles are just a few of the many seeds of wisdom contained within permaculture. Some others that deserve mention here are the concept of relative location (components of a system should be placed within logical relation to one another); functional interconnection (components in a system have mutually beneficial products); and catching and storing energy and resources (energy in a system should be circulated as many times as possible). All of these ideas could equally apply to communities. I believe one of the greatest strengths of permaculture is that it clearly defines and lays out these principles as critical pieces for creating functional sustainable systems. Many communities today may have some or even all of these principles as part of their mission statements or at work within their daily functioning. However, stating them clearly and directly, and thereby understanding in richer detail how they are being applied, is an important step in planning for the future.

Permaculture contains the seeds not just for ecosystem planning, but for a complete

societal overhaul towards finding a regenerative human habitation on this planet. While this may be some way off for the behemoth of Western consumer culture, it merges quite readily with the ecovillage movement and can inform decisions made by those of us living in these communities around the world. And while the going may be slow, our communities can act as role models for mainstream society in the coming years of predicted flux, manifesting permaculture principles of dynamic adaptation. I am grateful and excited to have a deeper understanding of this excellent tool for ecological communities to work with in the world. ❧

> ## Our communities can act as role models in the coming years of flux by manifesting permaculture principles of dynamic adaptation.

A self-titled "ecovillage educator," Ethan Hirsch-Tauber spent the past two years as a faculty member for the Living Routes Integral Sustainability semester in Auroville, India, and is on a mission to experience as many inspiring communities around the world as he can. His personal goal statement—distilled from the recent permaculture course—is: "I am connecting movements of inspired people to regenerate the world." He is grateful to everyone from his permaculture course, both the teachers (particularly Kay Cafasso and Natalie Krueger) and students, as well as to Living Routes and the whole of Sirius Community, for contributing so much to his learning. Contact him at ethan@ livingroutes.org.

Works Cited:

Holmgren, David. *Permaculture: Principles and pathways beyond sustainability.* Holmgren Design Services (publisher), 2001.

Macy, Joanna. "The Great Turning as Compass and Lens: What it means to be alive in a moment of global crisis and possibility." Yes! Magazine, May 2006. Online at www.yesmagazine.org/issues/5000-years-of-empire/the-great-turning-as-compass-and-lens

Mollison, Bill. *Permaculture: A Designer's Manual.* Tagari Publications, 1988.

How Permaculture Stole My Community!

By Arjuna da Silva

Permaculture stole my community—or perhaps just borrowed it.

To understand how that happened, you need to know the backstory...

Before Earthaven

Before joining the Earthaven founders in western North Carolina (where I now live with about 60 other members on 320 acres of land), I helped start several small, short-lived intentional communities around the country. Each one in its own way was a transformational social/spiritual/cultural endeavor. We lived closer to Earth than we had in our cities and suburbs, but we didn't make sustainability or food production our focus, and we'd never heard of permaculture In each case we fell apart, mostly because we weren't supporting ourselves from the land and couldn't find jobs in our local rural areas.

Later, in Gainesville, Florida, I was part of an extended community made of up to 10 households, with several collective businesses to keep everyone afloat, and with a shared commitment to a spiritual path. It was here that I first encountered the term "permaculture," and was intrigued, though I still knew nothing about it.

After the Gainesville group had scattered, I went land-searching with another group from that same spiritual path. Permaculture came up as the land use and design system we would need to put our social-cultural vision on the ground. By this time, it seemed to me that everyone knew about permaculture—unknown just a couple decades before, it had become the "happening thing" for communities, land-wise, just as consensus was the happening thing, governance-wise.

Earthaven: The Dream Evolves

When the dream of creating Earthaven first began, my two closest friends were involved. They kept me apprised of the visionary and land-search work going on, so a few yeas later when it came time for me to leave Florida, we showed up at the formal invitational meeting together. (The name Earthaven came later.)

That meeting and the subsequent first few years of Earthaven's existence (starting in 1994) were like magic. The people who gathered to take up the mission of establishing eco-spiritual community outside of Asheville, North Carolina became my best friends. It was also reassuring to discover that two of my cofounders were permaculture designers who would, from my perspective, be able to help us rubes

The main street through Earthaven Ecovillage is "Another Way." Quite fitting.

Photos by Dave Wheitner

get some important things right.

Little did I know that permaculture was more than a design system—it's a movement for recreating society in a practical and ethical way. It is so enthralling in its breadth and accessibility that many other more ephemeral goals wind up in the back row while the huge learning curves in land-based living (for us: clearing land, utilizing timber, building homes, developing basic infrastructure, learning to farm, raise animals, raise children in the woods, etc.) seem to take up all the available focus a person can muster.

Okay, I'm exaggerating. We have not abandoned commensurate skill development in communication and social contracts, interpersonal and inner work, but it has mostly gotten the energy left over from all the other more primary endeavors. And lately it gets a lot more attention than ever. But that's after a few long years of what now seems to have been a terrible imbalance, years when I wondered where I'd come to and how I'd gotten abandoned here!

The first decade or so developing property on a shoestring budget requires enormous focus on support systems for living a moderately modern lifestyle. Whereas our first few years getting to know each other while sketching out our dreams and plans (and living for the most part in town) were deeply infused with what I'll call higher-vibe activities like meditation, dancing, singing, and ceremony, as we became immersed in the ordeals of infrastructure development and land use our focus subtly but inexorably shifted. We were teaching each other as well as folks from around the world how to apply permaculture to a forested habitat; there were certification courses turning out dozens of new "permies" every year; we were learning and teaching natural building methods, gathering courage to begin some serious land clearing for agriculture. Meanwhile, the higher-vibe activities slipped into the background, while rest and relaxation and a bit of good ol' community socializing seemed to be all we could really muster to balance out the workload.

Stranded in Permaculture Heaven

One day, several years into the unexpectedly solo project of building an earth-and-straw house, I caught myself wondering how I could have gotten to the place where I'd traded in my normal conversations about subpersonalities and form-and-emptiness for a daily litany of plant, soil, weather, and energy data. Wah! Where did everyone go? How come they left me here in permaculture heaven? (Almost every one of my friends from Earthaven's founding stage never made it to the level of pioneer, and I'm still waiting to share my building site with others.)

If I didn't love this land, if I didn't love this lifestyle, if I didn't love this house, if I didn't feel close to a small circle of friends here, if I hadn't learned to enjoy the satisfaction of being a homesteader—I'd go start me another community and make sure permaculture just stayed in its place! I'd know to get all the founders to sign promissory notes giving the community the next 10 years of their lives. (How to do that? How about

A small neighborhood farm.

a deposit refundable after 10 years?) I'd know to write down all the visionary and spiritually woo-woo things we'd say in the beginning, even if that new group also thought they were so obvious and "transparent" there wouldn't ever be a need to know "what the founders meant."

Moving Toward Balance

It may be that Earthaven Ecovillage is the right model in the right place at the right time to help folks in this lunatic culture get hold of a replicable example of sane living in obedience to natural laws. Hopefully, it will also come to pass that my discontent will settle out and I'll make a graceful peace with the world of land use and permaculture gridlock, and find myself focusing at long last again on life on the inside of reality.

Things could be changing. New folks have stepped up in leadership and are holding forth with a more powerful spiritual presence. Tools for stronger connection are being presented and some are taking hold. Lately folks I've given tours to seem spiritually and socially quite wise as well as savvy about alternative technologies. Maybe I've just been unnecessarily impatient. Maybe Spirit just let permaculture borrow my community so it could set itself up on a large enough scale in the US to be noticed. Maybe balance is right around the corner.

As we celebrate our 17th year on the community road together, despite or perhaps integral with all the surprises, disappointments, and losses, I have come to see that the container—the crucible—of community still has given me opportunities only it can provide to see myself as others might see me, to encounter my foibles and flaws in stark relief and plenty of empathy, and to quietly, sometimes uproariously, etch my way home to stillness and the internal balance that is yearning to be seen and felt on the outside. ◆

Arjuna da Silva is an inveterate optimist, certified alchemical hypnotherapist, group facilitator, and visionary. She'll be spending the next year settling into her gorgeous new home and landscape at Earthaven, while beginning several book-length projects about life in the 21st century. Arjuna can be reached at arjuna@earthaven.org.

Doing It, or Are We?

By Tracy Matfin with Dona Willoughby

The corners of my mouth curl up in a contented smile and the warmth that started in my heart spreads throughout my body. I am lying in bed with my napping three-year-old listening to chomping and rustling sounds outside my window. Getting up, looking out, I see two small wild pigs. They're foraging for food in the purple sweet potatoes we use as ground cover. I am reminded of my wild pet pigs, Bear and Summer—among the many experiments that comprise my current life living in a permaculture community on the Big Island of Hawaii.

My life here is conscious participation in myriad experiments—some of which I am aware of right now and others which will be revealed as time moves on. This constant education program is evidence to me that we are "Doing it." Permaculture is the harmonious integration of landscape and people providing their food, shelter, energy, and other material and non-material needs in a sustainable way. On a daily basis, we immerse ourselves in the questions and actions it takes to need fewer and fewer inputs from the outside world.

Heart of palm salad, stewed wild boar with taro and beyjool seeds, baked orange squash, an enormous leafy green salad with kale, topped off with a banana cassava cake, scrumptiously fill stomachs with a local dinner. Food, a primary focus of our sustainability efforts, averages about 70 percent from our land. The leafy greens and the annual vegetables come from an organic garden with raised beds. The remainder comes from food forests which mimic natural ecosystems. Tall palm trees coexist with shorter fruit and nut trees and bananas, interplanted with spindly cassava plants, berry bushes, kava, coffee, and cacao. Vanilla orchids and air potatoes climb up the trees. Squash grows around the edge of the food forest.

Six years have passed since La'akea changed hands and became an intentional community. During this time, many of the members have taken and presented permaculture classes. We've obtained, planted, and given away plant cuttings, observed them for their possible applications, developed recipes.

Three years ago, several members dedicated a month to eating 100 percent locally, from the big island. While they were successful, one challenge was getting enough starch. What to eat if not rice, wheat, or other grains? Grains do not grow well in the tropics. So the fourth year we opened our eyes to alternative starches. We already had taro, and to this we added cassava, peach palm fruit, air potatoes, squash, and beyjool seeds. Year five, two of us went 100 percent local again. The diet nurtured us psychically and physically, producing very little non-compostable waste. After six years, we have enough food to survive. The land is not lacking. It is our taste buds and preferences for what is familiar that need to change. Harvesting and preparing foods from the land requires labor. Efficiency could be greatly increased if more members, including myself, were ready to make the switch.

Our members are a group of people who do not come from a sustainable culture. Most of us weren't breast-fed. We've been surrounded by plastics and disposable commodities for significant portions of our lives, and have had access to fossil fuels since birth. Difficulties arise as we challenge norms and habits acquired from our past. We encourage feelings to come to the surface. Repressed anger may give birth to loud voices and tears. Our local Kilauea volcano provides an excellent example of the benefits of not holding back. By constantly releasing small amounts of hot red lava, it avoids tumultuous explosions. Sitting together, every Thursday evening, sharing, listening, touching,

La'akea main house with taro

Chickens in the compost

at our "heart shares," we create space for emotional expression. Clearing the slate, through periodic emotional release, simplifies communication with oneself, other people, and other species. The often-neglected zone zero (emotional health), the home of personal growth, is vitally important to our permaculture system.

In addition to our heart shares, we have found a variety of "tools" to assist each other in creating a supportive environment. These include Compassionate Communication (NVC), Peer Counseling, Huna, parental support meetings, and daily check-ins. Every morning we meet to share 10 to 20 minutes over breakfast. During this time, individuals share their present emotional condition as well as their hopes for the day. This serves us both logistically and socially. At this time anyone may express a need or desire for additional support, whether it be with a physical activity or an emotional process. This daily meeting is not mandatory. We attend most of the time knowing how beneficial it is to our functioning as a cohesive family.

We all have areas of life for which we feel passion and that give us purpose. These passions bring forth individual talents which are offered to the community, and move us further toward sustainability. The use of our talents makes us better stewards of our piece of the Aina (land) and moves us toward more loving intimate relationships.

For instance, some of us are chicken folks. We have an 81-year-old and a three-year-old member who both seem to have a special affinity for those wonderful birds. The chickens keep our compost pile turned and produce eggs/fritatas aplenty for community members.

Several of our members are now sheep specialists. When we arrived at La'akea, the jungle was higher than the fruit trees in our orchards. Foliage in a rain forest grows very fast. Saws and weed whackers were wasteful and intensive not only of fossil fuel, but of human energy. So we partnered with sheep to keep the orchards mowed and fertilized, and the nitrogen-fixing trees under control. Maintaining just the right number of sheep so pastures are not overgrazed is a talent that one of our members has developed. This member also developed the spiritual and emotional capacity to part with beloved sheep, butcher them, and serve them to La'akea meat eaters.

Other talents required are repairing and construction. We could have continued living in the huts and several buildings available at La'akea when purchased. However, moldy clothing after a week of daily rain, sharing your hut with a rat (also seeking dryness), and getting into moist blankets at night all get old. We now live in spaces that can be kept dry when it's rainy, and rat-free. One such space is a beautiful octagon building recycled from a nearby subdivision. It was moved to La'akea piece by

> ## We have enough food to survive. The land is not lacking. It is our taste buds and preferences for what is familiar that need to change.

piece and reassembled by members and work traders, instead of ending up in landfill. Four other dry homes were constructed, some using rocks and trees off our land. Our homes are really just bedroom cabins, since the kitchen, office, yoga room, living spaces, shower, and toilets are communal.

So are we doing it? What is the measure of sustainability? If we look at the five garbage cans headed for the dump, or the contents of the recycling center, one could easily say we are not there yet.

It may be said that if we want to change our future we have to change the substrates of our culture—the food, the entertainment, the tools, the art, and much else. This is a process, one experiment after another, one small step after another. In this sense we are doing it.

While we do not have a common vision for where we are going, we are all clear that we want to be less dependent on non-sustainable, non-local products. While there is no clear structure for getting from here to there, we want to help one another be more conscious about what is going on—within ourselves, within our group, within the larger world—and support one another .

By the way, did you wonder how the pet pig experiment, mentioned in the first paragraph, ended? The plan was for them to be living rototillers. After their third break-in and rooting destruction of the garden beds in our greenhouse, we relocated them to Green Lake, a beautiful wild area. I missed giving them coconut oil massages, but my partner Biko and I created a beautiful human baby to nurture and love. 🌿

Inside a greenhouse.

Tracy Matfin and coauthor Dona Willoughby live, learn, teach, and grow at La'akea Community, currently comprised of nine adults and two children on 23 acres on Hawaii's Big Island (permaculture-hawaii.com).

Southern Exposure Seed Exchange Wrestles with Growth

By Irena Hollowell

At Southern Exposure Seed Exchange, we sell garden vegetable seed, mostly certified organic, with a focus on heirloom varieties that have been passed down through the generations. Our customers are home gardeners and small farmers. Our home is Acorn Community, an egalitarian, income-sharing group of about 28 members on 72 acres in Mineral, Virginia (www.southernexposure.com; www.acorncommunity.org).

We do remarkably little to promote ourselves. We encourage gardeners to save seed and reduce their dependence on companies like us. And yet we continue to grow. In the summer of 2013, in a community meeting focused on the size of the business, almost everyone in the community agreed that Southern Exposure was growing faster than would be best. In talking to Ira, who does most of our promotion and networking, I've argued more aggressively for slowing down the growth.

We agree that there is a lot to be said for growing the business. We want to help people grow more and bigger gardens, so that they can be more self-sufficient and eat healthier food. And money, though overvalued by mainstream culture, does have value. We'd like to have more of it rather than less.

In late December 2013 and early January 2014, we moved into the new office that we'd been building for two years. The new office has timber framing, a radiant floor, super-insulated blown-in cellulose walls, large south-facing windows, wide eaves to make it cool in summer, a loading dock, a small warehouse, and on the cool north side, an insulated, air-conditioned, dehumidified seed room with a strawbale wall. But in some ways, as of early March, the office is still under construction. It still has no running water. We're using space heaters while the wood furnace gets finished. One room still has more construction equipment than office space. One section of roof will be a living roof—but isn't yet. The move was very rushed due to a fire in the house where, until this winter, the business was located.

Even with all this haphazard finishing of the building, the new space fits our needs much better than the old, and makes growth of the business easier on us. When we ran the business out of our main house, up to three people could put seed orders together at once. Now seven or eight can. Before, there was one good, shared space for shipping orders and two mediocre spaces, plus whatever shipping spaces people set up in their personal rooms. Now we've had eight people shipping orders at once in our main office. People answering customer calls used to shush loud conversations in the office. A very recent step in our move into our new space was to separate the computers and phones from the shipping and seed packing areas. Now packers and shippers can listen to loud music at any time of day.

This new space is one solution in our search for a healthy kind of growth. We're also working on other solutions:

Having a more stable population

Historically, Acorn has had very high turnover, including lots of young travelers. This leads to lots of time spent training people on new jobs. Many factors, including better housing, are leading us to attract a more significant number of people who want to be more stable.

Developing efficient systems

I'll give two examples.

We have a new seed-packing machine. We're still learning how to use it. From what we hear from other seed companies, it will save us a lot of time.

We used to print out two copies of each order—one for the customer and one for our records—and a mailing label. We've very recently started using a system that allows us to print out only one copy of each order and put it in a little (recycled) pouch on the outside of the package so that it serves as the mailing label as well. This will save us time and resources.

Spreading out the core responsibility

Ken, my boyfriend, keeps track of the inventory, corresponds with farmers who grow seed for us, and makes sure all the germination tests get done. When I ask him where we get a particular one of our 750 or so varieties, he generally knows off the top of his head. When I ask how much seed we have on hand, he generally has a pretty good idea even before looking it up. So it's not surprising that delegating is harder for Ken than for most of us. This winter I've been using all the methods I can think of to convince him to let go of small portions of his work—and then figuring out who is willing and able to take those jobs on.

Developing cooperative models to grow the business beyond Acorn

This is the most exciting and also the most difficult of the various ways we can expand our capacity.

Currently, most of the work that is done here is still done by people who live here. Work is organized in such an ad-hoc fashion that it often astounds me that all the really necessary jobs get done. We don't use job titles within the company. No one comes here expecting to make a lot of money. We sign up for phone shifts on a weekly rota. We each take on the jobs that we consider worth our time. We each do our jobs when we choose to do them. If we feel we've taken on more than we should, we ask for help. Each Acorn member chooses whether or not to keep track of their hours. Some of us do most of our work in the business; some of us do most of our work in house and farm areas. No one here tells any other person that they must do any particular task or work at any particular time. Even our hourly workers could switch to different tasks or different times, generally with only a little effort.

Can we scale this model up? That's one of our main questions.

While we can hire people on an hourly basis, we'd rather not do a lot of that. To do so would be to become more like a conventional, capitalist, hierarchical business. Many of us feel very strongly that we want to retain the freedoms we have. We want to continue to be radical and egalitarian.

We're also interested in splitting off relatively discrete parts of the business. Already, several areas of work for Southern Exposure are being done by neighboring communities. One part of our business, seed racks, is run out of Twin Oaks Community—of which Acorn was originally an offshoot—though still with some help from Acorn. This branch of Southern Exposure sells larger quantities of seed packets to retail stores that then resell them to customers. Twin Oaks is also our biggest seed grower—we work with a network of almost 50 small farms that grow seed for us—and we sometimes also fund crop trials by the Twin Oaks seed-growing team. Sapling Community, a recent offshoot of Acorn, now owns and runs Garden Medicinals and Culinaries, a small herb seed business that was founded by the same person who founded Southern Exposure, and that was owned by Acorn for several years. Living Energy Farm is yet another community in our county, including dual members with Acorn and Twin Oaks. Living Energy Farm manages Southern Exposure's shipment of sweet potato slips in late spring.

These parts of the business haven't been too hard to split off. But it's unclear what else we hope other communities will do for Southern Exposure in the future. We're in the beginning stages of exploring ideas about an inter-community worker cooperative that would give other involved communities more stake in the business as a whole.

But however Southern Exposure continues to evolve, this is my main message: It is possible, at least in our current situation, to run a business without mandatory timesheets, and without anyone telling anyone else that they must do any particular task. ❧

Irena Hollowell has lived at Acorn Community in Mineral, Virginia since 2009 and previously at other communities; see www.acorncommunity.org.

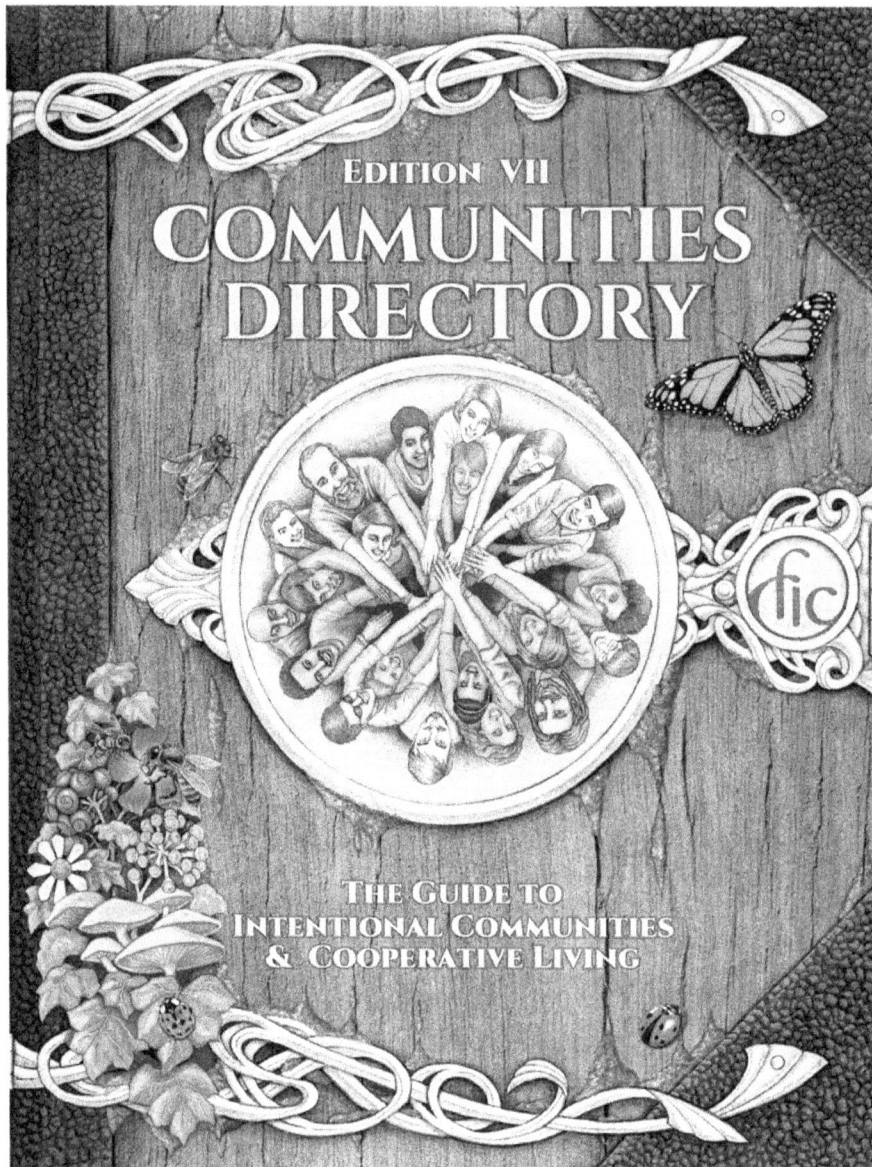

Communities Directory book!

In addition to profiling more than 1,000 communities, this new book includes full-page maps showing where communities are located, charts that compare communities by more than 30 qualities, and an easy index to find communities interested in specific pursuits. Also included are articles on how to start or join a community, the basics of group dynamics and decision-making, and countless additional resources and links to help your community thrive!

Order your book today: www.ic.org/New-Directory

The Dirty Business of Growing a Cohousing Community Farm

By Sandy Thomson

The idea of creating Heartwood Farms came about during a visioning retreat in 2007. You know the type, an all-day, community-wide retreat hosted in the common house with lots of positive energy, good food, and everyone in a good mood? Picture five or six smaller groups gathered around, on the floor, sitting on couches, hanging out around the kitchen island, all trying to come up with the perfect vision of what our community would look and feel like in 10 years!

We live on roughly 250 acres in rural southwestern Colorado. Seventy of those acres are irrigated and we as a community have agreed to steward them in the best way possible. Now we are basically a bunch of city kids wanting to experience the rural lifestyle...environmentally friendly with strawbale houses, kids collecting eggs as one of their chores, that sort of thing. So when the idea of growing our own food came up in numerous subgroups within the retreat, a group of us decided that of course we need to grow our own food. Let's do it! We produced collages, word boards, and pictures in our heads of beautiful vegetables and fruits grown organically on our land by people we love. We pictured days sitting in the grass while the children played with the baby goats and chased good-natured chickens around the pasture.

Simple, right? We had land and we had water, now all we needed were some seeds. We even had a whole community that eats organic and supports local food sources AND an experienced grower to grow that food living right here in the community. We have a word for this kind of idea at Heartwood; it is called a "no brainer." Only a "no brainer" at Heartwood is not what you think. A "no brainer" here means an idea that you think could not possibly have any opposition, that everyone will agree with, as in "duh, that's a no brainer," but in reality there are a thousand questions and almost as many concerns. This is a difficult dynamic ever-present in community; there is always a group raring to go and another group wanting to consider every possible thing that can go wrong. But what it ultimately comes down to is power and trust.

Our core identity statement *(see sidebar)* reads: "We cultivate a fertile ground in which members bring forth their gifts, talents, and passions to manifest a marvelous diversity of creations. We embrace, celebrate, and support those diverse manifestations that are consistent with our stated values."

Sounds wonderful, doesn't it? But many questions can come up when a business venture is proposed that operates within a community setting, especially if the members are creating the business primarily to meet the needs or desires of the community. Be forewarned it is not an easy process no matter how well your community functions. There are so many things to consider when resources are shared and

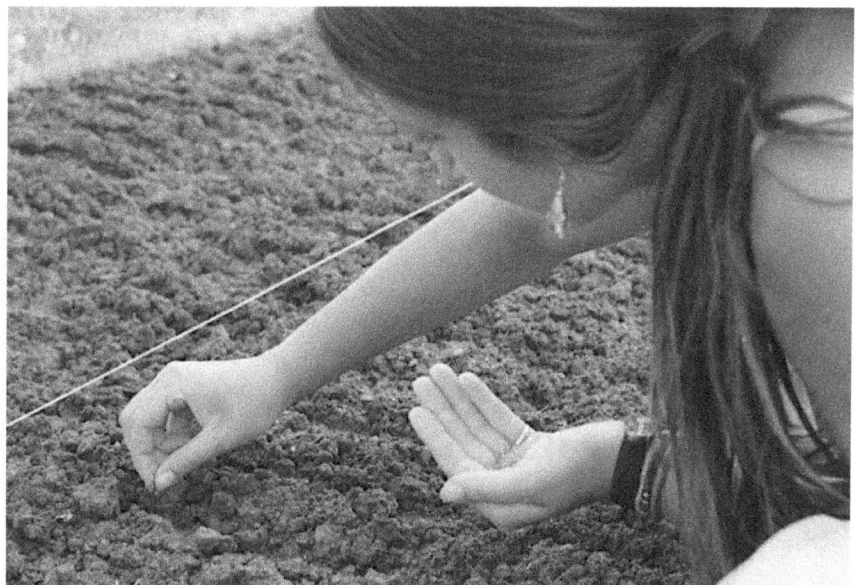

relationships are complicated and interdependent.

Community members might want to know:

• Who owns the business?

• What are the liability ramifications for the community?

• Should the community be compensated for the use of community resources? If so, how much? (This is a big one.)

• What kind of oversight is needed for the business entity? (We're all members here after all.)

Not to mention the complexities associated with hiring interns *(see sidebar)* to work on the business. Interns were an essential part of the farming operation and our goal of making the world a better place.

• Do they pay HOA dues?

• Where do they live?

• Who is responsible for their behavior or their use of community resources?

Well, we have a pretty amazing community. They were willing to jump right in and say go for it even though there were still so many unknowns.

The first few years were exciting and fun. We built thousands of dollars worth of infrastructure with seed money from individual community members, fund raisers, and veggie sales—not to mentions thousands of volunteer hours from interns and community members. As the farm grew and prospered, changing, growing organi-

Heartwood interns Claire, Rachel, Miguel, Sammy, Gina, Steve, Tony, Cameron, and Heartwood kids Gabe and Zander.

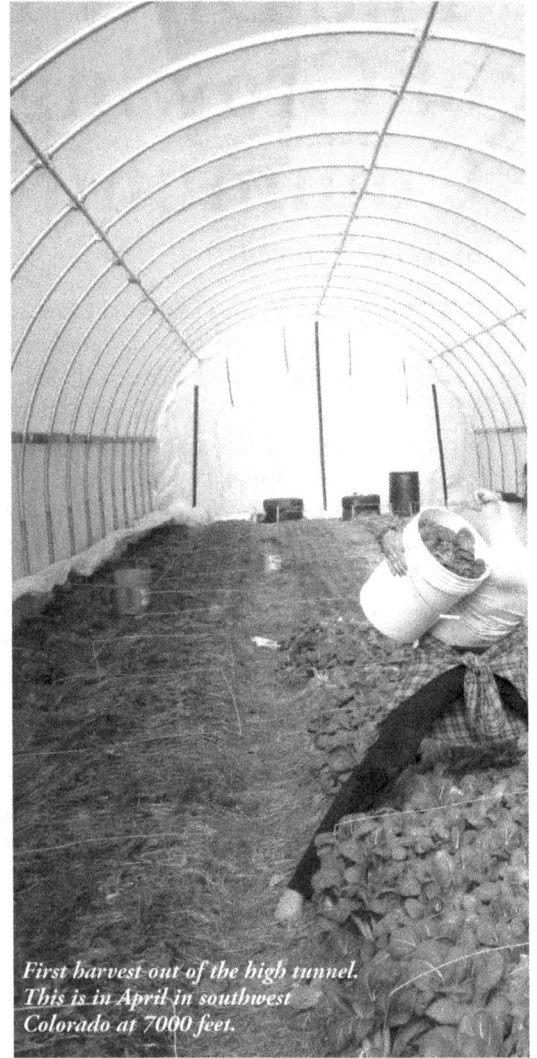

First harvest out of the high tunnel. This is in April in southwest Colorado at 7000 feet.

Photos courtesy of Sandy Thomson

Kids, interns, and farm manager plant squash on a beautiful spring day.

Interns: The Spice of Life

Interns are the spice of life in a cohousing community. You take the soup of families with kids of all ages, older single people, retired couples, dogs, cats, and you add the secret ingredient: that 18-25 age group that is notoriously missing from cohousing. They are upbeat, idealistic, friendly, hard working, and fun. They aren't afraid to get dirty and they dive right in. The kids and dogs love them because they are willing to look silly and come down to their level. The older set love them because they can hire them to do some of the backbreaking labor around their homes. The 40-50-year-olds love them because they wake up that often dormant feeling of hope and idealism that is so important at that time of life when we are questioning if it can be done and is it worth fighting for or not?

Our interns have added so much to the experience of living in cohousing that when members are asked, "What is the best part about the farm?," it is not the food, or the land stewardship, but the presence of interns that is often the answer. They answer it with a slight smile on their face as if they are remembering that time in their own lives—the time in their lives when anything was possible.

Intern energy! I wish I could bottle that and sell it. I bet I could get a lot more for it than the dollar a pound we get for potatoes.

Intern energy is like a litter of golden retrievers with powerful brains that are working all the time.

Some things that can be heard when eavesdropping on the interns at common meals:

"Hey let's try to do without money the rest of the season."

"I finally got the recipe for shampoo right—look, my hair actually looks clean. Now I don't have to buy into all those chemical corporations."

"Maybe we can just all live in trees and live off the land, wouldn't that be great?"

"Yeah and we can play music and make art and be happy."

"I want to learn how to be totally self-sufficient. I want to learn how to grow my own food, build my own house, and make anything that I might need."

You just don't get that kind of energy from the meat and potatoes of cohousing!

—S.T.

cally, some members of the community were getting uncomfortable with the still unanswered questions. But a business like a farm is hard to pin down. A farm is not a clod of dirt; it is more like mud that slips through your hands, gets on your boots, and is tracked all through the community. We wanted this to be an integrated farm and it was—deeply integrated with the community. Now a few members were asking for it to be separated out, put in a box, and defined. Some members didn't trust the farm because the members on the farm board couldn't answer all these complex questions.

Bad feelings developed on both sides. Some of the energy on the farm turned sour. The member who was the primary grower left for greener pastures or ones less bogged down in the manure of community process. This trying to define and pin down the farm has gone on now for the last two years. We have had meetings and more meetings. We formed a task force that did great work on trust, hurt feelings, and misunderstandings. We recently consensed on a new structure for the governance of the farm, but questions still persist. Our next retreat will be with a skilled outside facilitator who will help us see where the process went wrong. He will help us further untangle issues of power and trust that have been brought to light by this experience.

For those of us who have been part of the farm since the beginning it has been an exhausting two years—much more exhausting than all the physical labor that we put in during the first two years making the farm great. I am not sure where the farm will

Sweet Ally Baba loving fresh-picked Heartwood Beets.

Summer bounty from Heartwood Farms sold on the terrace of the common house.

Jessica, one of our interns last year, was passionate about bees. She helped us get our honey production up.

Community Vision and Values

These are Heartwood Cohousing's community vision and values:

Vision

To create and live in a community which fosters harmony with each other, the larger community, and Nature.

Values

Honesty and Trust: We act with openness and honesty because of the trust we have in each other. We have the courage and trust to speak up when we see contradictions or inconsistencies between our behavior and our stated values and goals.

Cooperation: Through tolerance, generosity, sharing, and compassion, we live cooperatively with one another. When appropriate, we place the interests of the community ahead of our own self-interests.

Interconnectedness: We recognize our interdependence with all life. To all that came before us, we offer our respect and remembrance. To all with whom we share this world, we seek mutual understanding and respect. And to all who will come after us, we strive to leave for you a better world.

Commitment: Though we know that the path may be rough at times, we are committed to our Vision for the long haul.

Participation: Knowing that our community is fueled by the energy we give it, we all actively participate in community life and work at Heartwood. Each of us chooses how to give his or her energy.

Support: Our community supports friendship and an extended family environment, thereby creating a sense of belonging. We support the growth of each other individually and the relationships amongst us. Each of us is willing to work on our own personal growth so that we can improve those relationships.

Respect: We respect the freedom of each person to live as he/she chooses, so long as that doesn't interfere with the freedom of others in the community to do the same. We respect personal privacy. We respect diversity in ideology, spirituality, interests, talents, beliefs, opinions, race, age, income, and so on. And we welcome expressions of that diversity.

Equality and Fairness: We value every member, including children, equally and treat them with fairness.

Stewardship: We live gently on the Earth. We are thankful for Nature's resources, being conscious to take good care of them and use them efficiently.

Safety: Our community is a safe place—emotionally, physically, and spiritually.

Balance: We maintain balance in our community life: between group and individual; between building for tomorrow and enjoyment of today; between heart, mind, and soul; etc.

Responsibility: Each of us, as well as all of us as a community, takes responsibility for our actions.

Education: We seek the exchange of knowledge, skills, and resources with each other and the larger community.

Flexibility: Creating community is an ongoing process. We remain flexible to change.

—S.T.

go from here. The constraints from the community and from the county have us bogged down. It feels heavy, like walking through the heavy clay soil we have to work with. Some see it as a new beginning, a chance to create something new with full community buy-in. I am worried that trying to do something like this in the confines of community is too exhausting and time-consuming to deal with. But I have hope. I have to.

What have I learned from this process?
• It is very difficult to run a business within a community setting.
• It is important for people to know how to follow as well as lead.
• Nothing polarizes a community faster than talking behind each other's backs.
• There is nothing cut and dried about farming.
• Sometimes a squeaky wheel is just a squeaky wheel.
• Being in community is about letting go but not giving up.

Really when it comes down to it, it has to do with trust. Trust in each other. Trust in the process. Trust that everything will turn out all right.

If I had it all to do over again, would I do it?

Yes. It is in alignment with my values and those of the community. *(See sidebar.)*

What would I do different?

I would follow our interpersonal agreements and insist that others do the same. *(See sidebar.)*

It seems easy when you look at it this way. Just follow your vision and values and every one of your interpersonal agreements. Anyone who lives in community knows these are ideals and hard to live up to all the time. It is the 20-somethings, those goofy interns, who continually remind us to keep striving for those ideals. It takes work and sometimes it's messy but in the end it is worth it.

If you want to start a business inside a community structure put your hat on, pull up your boot straps, and hang on. You are in for a wild ride. 🐦

Sandy Thomson is one of the founding members of Heartwood Cohousing in Bayfield, Colorado: www.heartwoodcohousing.com. She and her husband Mac have raised three children in their community. Sandy created and ran a homeschool co-op when her kids were little; now that they are in high school she has turned her attention to creating Heartwood Farms, a nonprofit foundation to support local agriculture and the education of our future farmers (www.heartwoodfarms.org).

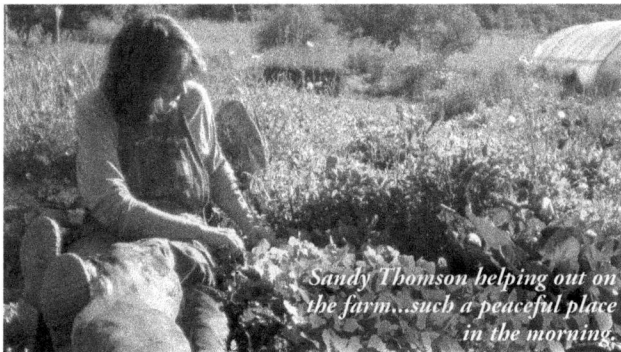

Sandy Thomson helping out on the farm...such a peaceful place in the morning.

Interpersonal Agreements

These are Heartwood's interpersonal agreements:

To Communicate with Integrity: I agree to tell my truth, with compassion for myself and others, and to trust that others are doing the same.

To Listen with My Heart: I agree to listen respectfully to the communications of others and attune to their deepest meaning.

To Own My Feelings: I agree to take responsibility for my feelings and how I react to the words and actions of others. And I agree to express those feelings in a spirit of openness and compassion.

To Honor Each Person's Process: I agree to acknowledge that everyone, including myself, is making the best possible choice or decision we are capable of at that moment.

To Express Appreciation: I agree to appreciate others and myself.

To Cooperate with Others: I agree to maintain a sense of cooperation and caring in my interactions with others.

To Honor Our Differences: I understand that goals are often the same even though methods for achieving them may differ.

To Be Aware of Conflict: I agree to look for the unresolved issues within me that create a disproportionate adverse reaction to another's behavior.

To Resolve Conflicts Constructively: I agree to take problems and complaints to the person(s) with whom I can resolve them, at the earliest opportunity. I agree not to criticize or complain to someone who cannot do something about my complaint, and I will redirect others to do the same. I will not say behind someone's back what I am not willing to say to their face.

To Maintain Harmony: I agree to take the time to establish rapport with others and then to reconnect with anyone with whom I feel out of harmony as soon as it is appropriate.

To Freely Participate: I agree to freely choose and re-choose to participate in the Heartwood Cohousing Community. It is my choice.

To Lighten Up!: I agree to allow fun and joy in my relationships, my work, and my life.

(Note: These Interpersonal Agreements are based in large part on those of Geneva Community.)

—S.T.

Core Identity

What makes the Heartwood community distinctive?

• We are a close-knit, multigenerational, rural cohousing neighborhood.

• We are committed to deeply knowing, supporting, respecting, and caring for each other and ourselves as distinctive individuals; as a result, deep interpersonal relationships are possible here.

• We share with each other the value of sustainable interactions with the planet, though our individual efforts and choices may vary. We steward our land to maintain or improve its viability and vitality over the long haul.

• We are interconnected with all of humanity. We welcome new ideas and interactions with the larger community and are open to associations and the sharing of resources with those who share our values.

• We cultivate a fertile ground in which members bring forth their gifts, talents, and passions to manifest a marvelous diversity of creations. We embrace, celebrate, and support those diverse manifestations that are consistent with our stated values.

All of these distinctive qualities are part of our enduring core identity, which does not change. What does change are the various manifestations themselves. These dynamic expressions that come and go over time add a rich flavor to our community culture.

—S.T.

Recipe for Community

Colin Doyle

A s editor of COMMUNITIES, I don't like to play favorites, but I've enjoyed assembling this issue on Food and Community at least as much as any other we've put out over the last seven years. The theme elicited a cornucopia of high-quality submissions—I think largely because its two elements lie at the heart of each of our lives. Among human beings, food and community are almost entirely interdependent.

A community of people with no ability to ingest food is called a cemetery; a living community can't exist without physical nourishment. Community absolutely depends on food—though there is endless variety in what that food is, how it is produced, how it is distributed or acquired, how it is prepared and shared. The stories that follow give a taste of that variety.

Likewise, at least for us in the modern world, food absolutely depends on community. An infinitesimally small portion of the world's population may be solo hermits subsisting exclusively on wild food, without help or participation from any other human being. Everyone else, even a "self-sufficient" farmer or gardener, depends on a network of other people to do everything from breed plants and manufacture tools to supply fuel or lend a hand with physical labor.

Closely examining either food or community will shatter any illusion that human beings are truly independent of each other. We depend on one another in more ways than we usually recognize, whether in meeting our most basic physical needs or in satisfying our requirements for emotional and spiritual connection and nourishment. Food is often at the center of our interdependence—it's no surprise that it's such a potent force in bringing us together and in helping us understand and define who we are together.

Whether in intentional communities, in neighborhoods, among networks of friends, or in any other form of community—at all scales up to the global—issues surrounding food provide a microcosm of the issues we confront in other areas as well. How we make decisions, how we relate to one another and to the earth, how we balance individual and collective needs and preferences, how we maintain health and well-being, how we reconcile ethics and economic exigencies, service and self-preservation, idealism and practicality—all of these come into play when we consider food. And like every aspect of our lives as social creatures, our relationship to food has unavoidable impacts and repercussions within the larger human community—whether those are understood and acknowledged, or not.

For all of these reasons and more (many of them both delicious and nutritious), food can be a pathway to greater consciousness and greater intentionality, both in our personal lives and in our lives together. Our authors suggest some of the ways this can happen.

Please enjoy this issue! 🐦

Chris Roth (editor@ic.org) edits COMMUNITIES.

How the Kitchen Is the Heart of a Community

By Devon Bonady

Purple and pink potatoes grown and enjoyed at Fern Hill Sanctuary.

The music switches from soothing vocals to an upbeat tune reminiscent of a place a thousand miles south. Suddenly, voices rise and two dancers take the floor. They dance lively salsa in front of the dining room door. This could be a scene from Cuba, lovers in an outdoor patio, dancing the night away. Guess again. It's happening in the middle of our modest community kitchen! The salsa dancing, joyful and energizing as it is, can be grating to those of us who are in the middle of cooking a meal for 50 people. We sneak around them, cookbooks and measuring cups in hand, shouting instructions over the music. Although I am responsible for the meal, I love the energy of dancing in the kitchen. The head cook, my friend and boss, as well as other community members who cook at night, can get disgruntled by this. Even so, the dancing can help the dish crew finish their task more quickly and happily.

Before the dancing became a meeting topic at our 40-member rural intentional community in Oregon, someone took it in their own hands to express their feeling creatively. A "No Salsa Dancing" sign, complete with a universal "no" red icon, was placed on both of the kitchen doors. At first, dancers did not heed the sign, but eventually, after a few meetings, dancing moved through the door and into the dining room. At that point, I even took advantage of the chance for a free lesson.

Salsa dancing was just one of the things that drew people to the community kitchen to socialize. Cooks on duty also played lovely music of their choice and often joined in singing. Music was one way that the kitchen served as a social and emotional outlet for community members. In community, I believe that the kitchen serves as a place for meeting social, emotional, and physical needs of community members as well as a spiritual connection to life cycles through the food that we eat and prepare.

Preparing fresh food is an essential piece in the middle of a greater cycle. Before food can be prepared we must engage in planting, cultivating, and harvesting plants and raising, nurturing, and killing animals. These plants and animals experience their entire life cycle before they enter the kitchen. After food preparation, we eat the food, nourish our bodies, and excrete the remains, which, combined with excess plant and animal parts, can be composted and turned into fertile soil. This soil is the essential ingredient needed for us to begin planting seeds once again. Even if we are not involved in each of these pieces, as someone who cooks and eats, we are connected to the entire cycle. In some communities, we even incorporate growing food, raising animals, composting waste, and building soil into our daily lives.

In my experience, the more that I am connected to growing food and participating in the different parts of the life cycle, the more I appreciate healthy food and feel physically nourished from it. I am a plant person, and when I lived in the community mentioned above, I participated in food plant growing, cooking, and composting. We also had many community members whose joy and gift lay in other aspects of community life such as management, building maintenance, or healing arts. For these people, the kitchen was the first point of connection to the physical nourishment of food. The large daily salad from our garden, served twice a day to all members, helped keep everyone healthy and appreciative of what we accomplished and how we valued health.

While physical nourishment may be an obvious need met by a community kitchen, some may overlook the emotional benefits of the kitchen in community. As it tends to be a social hub, it is a place where people may relax and chat while preparing, eating, or cleaning up a meal. In this community, we usually had three or four people preparing each meal. During weekend personal growth retreats, participants in the retreat workshops were assigned to assist in food preparation. They had a chance to switch their focus from intense interpersonal communication to voluntary labor. Some people, myself included, found kitchen time to be a great opportunity for deep discussion while hands are busy. More often than not, at this time, emotions ran high, and tears could fly, especially if onion chopping was involved. With the cooking and crying came connection in community. At times, the emotions grew out of the cooking experience, such as stress related to burnt food. Other times, the soothing music and quiet tone of the cooking team created a meditative environment.

When I lived in this community, all members were involved in food preparation and cleanup. It was the only task that was divided somewhat equally, with the exception of two people whose job was to work as a kitchen manager and assistant. The kitchen was the first place that I would go to find someone I was looking for. The kitchen is where we would plan to meet before our work crew headed to the garden, before a group went offsite on carpool, and on Friday mornings for chore time. It was in the kitchen that I would see members and guests that I rarely saw elsewhere. In this way, the kitchen was the central meeting place, the hub. I have yet to visit a community, be it a hundred members or one shared household, where the kitchen does not become the hub. At times, it may not seem to be the ideal physical location for a hub, but it is where people gather. For instance, my dear friends at Heart and Spoon (see article, page 12) bought a community house together, knowing that the kitchen would be their hub. And the kitchen happens to be the smallest room in the house (besides the bathroom), yet remains the community hub, even when you just can't get through the bodies to the other side.

I used to get frustrated when the kitchen was crowded and I found it difficult to get dinner ready on time. Why do people continue to enter the kitchen and leave another mess for me to clean? Why do people keep distracting me from keeping my eye on the oven? Yet more often than not, people came into the kitchen for some food and nourishment, and I could help them meet that need, and so they left me feeling helpful and fulfilled in my role as cook and nourisher. Before I became a mother, this was my chance to feel like a mother, caring for my family and friends by growing, preparing, and serving food.

Even though my community is different now, I still find much fulfillment from growing, preparing, and sharing food. Community and food are constantly connected. I find much joy in preparing meals for the folks who come to stay with us and help us on our farm, for friends and family who visit, and for friends to whom I travel. Dinner time, which happens close to the kitchen, is the one time of day when we are all together. In my community, local food and homesteading are encouraged and appreciated. Every meal we eat at home is full of connections that remind me of my community. For example, a recent meal included broccoli and potatoes from our garden, shiitake mushrooms that we grew on oak logs from our forest, cheese we made from the milk of our neighbors' cow that we milk when they are away, and pork sausage from our friends' pig that my son watched grow and graze. As I continue to strive towards creating community in my life, I have learned that one of the best ways for me to connect with others is through a shared appreciation for local food and a shared joy for growing food, and often that happens in a kitchen.

The kitchen is a place that we all need to go since we all need to eat. In some communities and families, it may be the only place where you see everyone at once or at all. The kitchen is a place where we can find social, physical, and emotional nourishment as well as a sense of connection to the greater biological life cycles on our planet. Even when the kitchen is mutable and changing, just as community changes, the place where food is prepared and served becomes the tie that keeps us together.

I was part of a portable and temporary community on wheels when I traveled with 40 "superheroes serving others" by bicycle through Arizona. I pulled a trailer behind my bike with up to 100 pounds of food, including a 40 pound bag of shredded coconut, generously donated to us. We set up our kitchen each day, in a new place, and proceeded to prepare three meals a day for our large group while also volunteering in the community and coming up with creative ways to add coconut to everything. At one point in our travels, we had a long day that included freeway riding. Five of our members who brought up the rear reached the freeway at dark and instead chose to camp alone, 20 miles from the rest of the group. This was the day that I had cooked beans in a pot and wrapped them tightly in my sleeping bag to cook as I pulled them in my trailer, so they would be ready at dinner. Luckily, they were ready, because we did not have much else for dinner, as the five folks in the rear had most of our ingredients. They did not have a stove, however, so they ate raw oats for dinner and breakfast. Thus, we had no breakfast but a few leftover beans, and we were in a food desert in the middle of the desert with only a gas station to feed us. Luckily, the food was reunited when those riders met us midday.

This experience reminded me that a kitchen, like community, when divided, cannot fully nourish us. When healthy and strong, kitchen is the heart of community. ◆

Devon Bonady is a gardener, mother, and teacher who loves to cook local food, eat local food, and share it with her community. She is especially excited about native edible plants from the Pacific Northwest and the past and present culture and community that surround them.

Abundant fall squash harvest.

Calzones made with love by friends in our cob pizza oven.

A bountiful garlic harvest.

Photos by Brian Basor

November, 1963. In the middle of the Pentagon's grey corridors, the inner courtyard is a green haven for civilians and military on their lunch break. On a crisp fall day, an attractive young matron waves to her navel lieutenant husband. It is 12:15 pm, and Kay has nothing on her mind except the small picnic basket she has brought. Along with the rest of the United States, she is oblivious to preparations in a Dallas office building, perhaps on a nearby grassy knoll, which at this moment remain suspended in time, subject to intervention and choice, if we only knew.

If we only knew then what we know now...

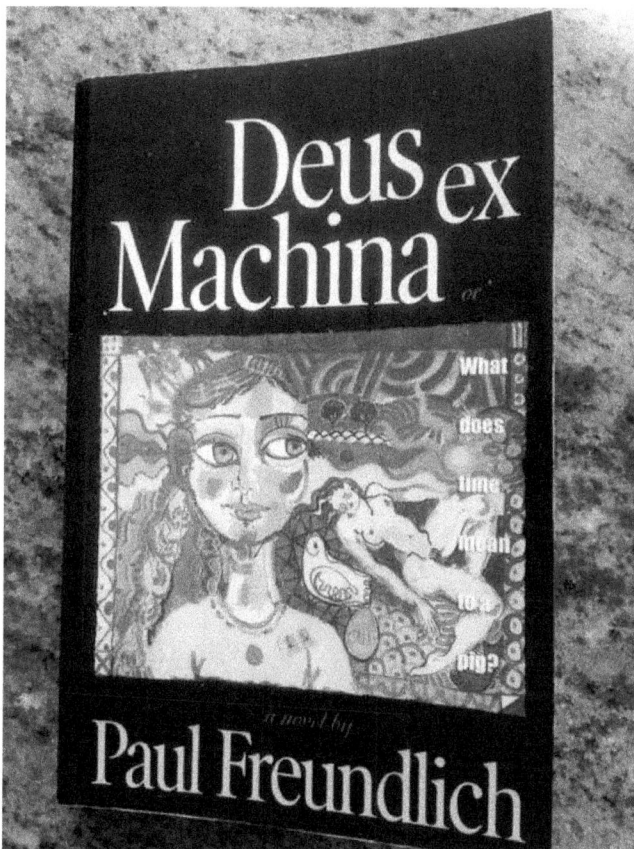

Plunked down in the middle of the 20th century, reverted to his childhood body, but his memory intact, Joshua Leyden takes a run at revising his own life, and changing a future that needs some tinkering.

"Held me every step of the way. A great read, challenging ideas, fascinating and seductive." – David Kahn, Harvard Faculty.

Consider two trains heading in opposite directions, but stopped in a station. While the trains wait, it is possible to change between them. Transferring passengers would then head down their own timelines, reviewing past images incrementally. So it is with memories. So it is with dreams.

"Wonderful, touching characters, reworking our fate." – Hazel Henderson, Economist.

...and the most outrageous, yet logical path for time travel ever.

Each night, the sun went down, Nora to bed, and Josh prowled around her soul, searching for a key to unlock their mystery. While Nora slept beyond a narrow wall, Josh fought the need to break on through to the other side – replaying every mistake he'd ever made in either life. Rising, hitting the brandy, writing in a notebook lest the typewriter wake the girl. He couldn't even feel sorry for himself when he knew Nora had it far worse.

It's about time: A love story, both provocative and playful...

Paul Freundlich, Founder of Green America and Dance New England; for a decade an Editor of "Communities"; filmmaker, essayist and activist has created a journey that transcends time and reworks reality. **Available from Amazon**.com [search: Paul Freundlich]

Cookin' Dinner for the Revolution

By Jesika Feather

Our community first began cooking together in Waveland, Mississippi in 2005 just after Hurricane Katrina. We made our separate ways to a disaster relief kitchen called The New Waveland Café, which was started by the Rainbow Family. We spent the next nine months living in a tent city while we cooked breakfast, lunch, and dinner daily for an average of 400 hurricane survivors and volunteers. That December we moved our kitchen to St. Bernard Parish, Louisiana, renamed it The Made with Love Café, and created a nonprofit, Emergency Communities.

We woke up each morning at 5:30 to crack eggs, fry bacon, mix pancake batter, and chop fruit salad. As we stood in our outdoor kitchen before dawn in January, our fingers throbbed and froze pealing boxes of oranges pre-soaked in bleach water to combat the post-Katrina toxins.

We cried together over vats of too-lumpy gravy, and prayed to about 17 higher powers that our spice cake (sans baking powder) might defy chemistry. We shared elated glances as we handed out fried chicken, bowls of cheesy grits, and mounds of fresh salad to people who'd eaten nothing but MREs and Vienna sausages for months.

It is true that we nourished thousands of survivors of Hurricane Katrina but, just as importantly, we created a safe space—inside a huge, dome-shaped dining room tent— where people could come together over red beans and rice or butterscotch pie to recreate their culture, ignite friendships, and rebuild faith in the idea that life could be worth living.

As we established that space for hurricane survivors, we inadvertently created a place for ourselves to become a family. Because each day was concentrated with intense experience, we built a rich history in only nine months. In that short time we grew to trust each so deeply that, when our kitchen closed, many of us moved forward as a team. We bought a house together in Eugene, Oregon and created The Heart and Spoon Community.

Nearly 10 years have stretched between our formation on the Gulf Coast and the present. A decade of new experiences has diluted those disaster relief memories so that they feel more like legends than reality. Most of the original founders of this community have moved out of the house and new people have become deeply invested in The Heart and Spoon. The overall personality of this community has mutated dramatically, though we've maintained one ongoing through-line: a combined commitment to human service and dinnertime.

Our full community is a rich blend of current household members, past housemates, and a general barrage of friends and family who feel comfortable showing up at any time, usually unannounced, and who frequently stay for dinner.

Right now our in-house community holds 12 people: four single adults, four parents, and four kids (two five-year-olds and two seven-year-olds). The adults range in age from 20 to 38. This variance in age and lifestyle is one of my favorite elements of The Heart and Spoon, though the practice of merging our diverse group in a way that keeps us feeling like a family requires a lot of work and communication.

Maintaining a consistent dinnertime for the whole community is the primary way we connect. Between planning, shopping, cooking, and cleaning, the entire routine can easily span from 4:30 until 9:00 every evening. Most of the time, we parents assume the responsibility of meal planning and preparation. Nearly everyone enjoys cooking, but the parents' demand for a solid schedule causes us to initiate before others are usually ready. We feel that a timely dinner is mandatory to help the kids feel stable in a household that is otherwise prone to fluctuation.

As a rule, we Heart and Spooners don't make a huge distinction between residents and regular guests. All visitors are encouraged to help out by cooking, cleaning, or playing with kids. Due to our eternally changing population of housemates and our ongoing stream of visitors, it's become almost instinctual to view The Heart and Spoon as a home to whoever happens to be present at the time, whether or not they pay for a bedroom. The kids have been known to ask our regular visitors, "Do you live here?"

Generally this "open home" philosophy has positive results. Our informal approach helps visitors feel more accepted and more invested in the community. It isn't uncommon for peo-

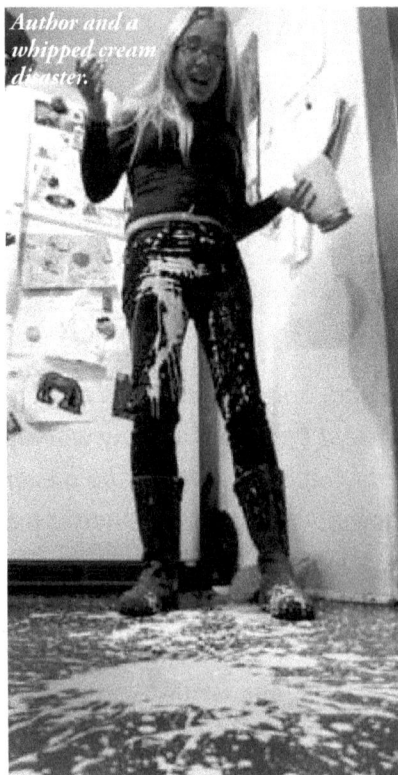

Author and a whipped cream disaster.

Photo credit: Tara Whitsitt

The Heart and Spoon *Together Hug.*

Frequently music accompanies dinner.

Photos by Valisa Higman

Heart and Spoon kids *on Pi(e) Day.*

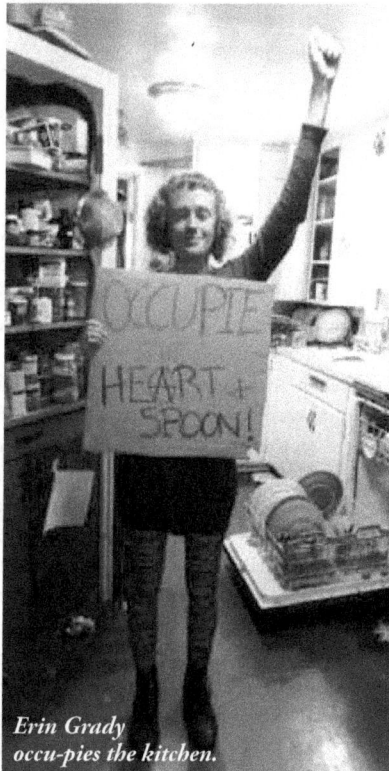

Erin Grady occu-pies the kitchen.

ple who don't actually live here to facilitate a meal, help with a household project, or host an event at our house.

White Bird is also a notable fixture in our community. White Bird is a 24-hour, collectively run crisis clinic in our town. Right now, half the adult population of our house works full-time at White Bird, and nearly everyone in our house has contributed to White Bird in some capacity. Because we're accustomed to feeding large numbers, our home has become a common dining stop for CAHOOTS. CAHOOTS is White Bird's mobile crisis unit. Their van is staffed by both a medic and a crisis worker. They respond, through police dispatch, to nonviolent 911 calls.

About three nights a week the CAHOOTS workers use our house as a dinner stop. Their presence in uniform, complete with police radio, is another regular reminder of our ongoing fusion of food and human service.

While it generally feels like an honor to live in a house that is home to so many, the responsibility can feel overwhelming. There are stints when our community is very aware that it's valued and cherished by an astonishing number people, but for those of us who keep it going, the daily maintenance can become staggering and downright stifling.

Our commitment to a daily communal dinner is a titanic assignment. Though the amount of food is minuscule compared to my disaster relief experience, this obligation is far more difficult. Cooking all day for hurricane victims under a circus tent with dozens of garishly dressed hippies and anarchist punks felt kind of glamorous and badass.

Dedicating large portions of each day to feeding one's own large family, along with the physical and emotional upkeep of the community, is not nearly as romantic and does not illicit a lot of recognition. It isn't uncommon for me to feel exhausted and wonder... *Why are we doing this?* Immediately followed by the next question... *What exactly are we doing?*

After nearly a decade of wondering whether I'm just working way too hard to get a bunch of hippies to eat together, I'm finally zoning in to the truth. The reason it's so taxing, and the reason we do it anyway, is because our dinners aren't only dedicated to creating "family time" for our household. This community is a hub for numerous, overlapping cooperatives dedicated to revolutionary social change.

Our job at The Heart and Spoon is to

hold a space that feels safe, fun, and nourishing for the people who work on the front lines of organized social transformation.

Though holding a space is a grueling process, the work is so subtle that we've spent years not even realizing that we're doing it. It is subtle because it is based in daily routine, and it is arduous because it requires relentless consistency.

Holding a space is actually a work of art, like writing or painting. When you do it well, it appears effortless. I'm sure there are people who visit The Heart and Spoon who imagine that all this dinner-making and family gathering flows as easily as the flatulence from your drunken uncle.

In reality there are uncomfortable house meetings regarding food cost, hours of accounting, and lots of time invested in respecting individual food preferences.

There are evenings when we expect 15 people for dinner, and then find only us parents and kids in front of two baked chickens and a stockpot full of mashed potatoes. After three hours of food prep, we're left to clean it all up ourselves, while also getting the kids ready for bed and packing their lunches for school the next day.

And of course there's the frequently awkward, occasionally contentious, but primarily incessant communication involved in blending parents, children, and single individuals into a stable, intimate family.

Holding this space is like a marriage. It requires ongoing effort even when the work feels unwanted or superfluous. This type of labor embodies every hippie and anarchist's greatest aversion: monotony. It

Kids table on sushi night.

means cleaning messes that come right back and cooking food that's about to be eaten. Consistency is vital. Without the monotony, the magic doesn't happen.

In February 2015 we were all given an unexpected, reality-based pop quiz, testing whether we could still work the magic.

We cook for holidays, birthdays, theme parties...any ol' reason to spice up our lives. These gatherings usually leave us feeling proud of our community and generally inspired. But it wasn't until we catered our first tragedy since Katrina that I felt my most solid reminder of our true purpose.

On February 14th, one of our solid, long-term community members disappeared while in a paranoid and delusional mental state.

Within 48 hours of Noah's disappearance dozens of his friends and family members began gathering at The Heart and Spoon. For two weeks we met each night to have dinner, discuss search methods, work on media outreach, and share information from the day. People who lived out of town stayed at our house. People who weren't available to search donated us boxes of food, coffee, and wine. We received letters, texts, Facebook messages, and financial contributions from people who couldn't travel. We had long, intimate conversa-

tions with Noah's childhood friends whom we'd previously never even heard of.

The weeks following his disappearance were surreal. Many evenings I sat at the table looking around at all the characters who'd woven the plot line of Noah's life. His sister sat next to his best friend from kindergarten, who sat beside his ex-girlfriend, who ladled soup for one of his journalist buddies from the college newspaper. Across the table, Noah's current sweetheart passed the salad bowl to his aunt and uncle.

People arrived from every nook and cranny of Noah's history, and the most healing thing any of us could think of to do was to bake three quiches, roll enchiladas, chop radishes, and simmer pots of soup.

More than at any other time since our community's formation, I've become acutely aware of the importance of a physical space where people can share ideas, make plans, and create a common culture. Life is unpredictable and it's important for people to have a few fundamentals they can depend on.

At The Heart and Spoon, dinner happens at 7:00 and we have one dinnertime ritual: The Together Hug. It's our non-dogmatic equivalent of a blessing. It doesn't happen at any specific point in the meal. We usually make the kid plates first, and then the adults serve themselves. We attempt to have a Together Hug sometime after the last adult is served, but before the kids escape. Really it happens whenever we remember. At that point we all reach out to "hug" the friend on either side and we sing "1...2...3...TOGETHER HUG!"

It takes only a few seconds, but it's a refreshing moment of solidarity. With all the ruckus of people retrieving condiments, filling last-minute water glasses, and cleaning spills, it's good to have a moment for pause and appreciation of the group who has gathered around the table.

Due to our number, our diversity, and the nature of the people we attract, maintaining consistency at The Heart and Spoon will always be a challenge, but finally learning to define the service that our community provides has helped me significantly. I hope we can help more activists recognize that a healthy, vibrant, reliable home-base bestows a feeling of sustainability to the general effort. Whether we're facing off tragedy, reveling in celebration, or scrubbing at the scum of the mundane, we're still gonna keep on makin' dinner. 🍃

Jesika Feather is a mother, writer, teacher, and community organizer who lives at The Heart and Spoon Community in Eugene, Oregon. She blogs about living communally and parenting at jesmamasmusings. blogspot.com.

In 2003, "La Cité Écologique" was founded, in Colebrook New Hampshire, on 315 acres of beautiful land surrounded by forest and mountains. Our ecovillage gives priority to education, optimal living to its members, a cooperative culture with resilience in its development and social entrepreneurship. So far, we have built one single family building, two large community residences, where people live in a kind of condo arrangement, and one community building (all powered by solar). We are expanding new building projects, to give a home to growing families and/or new members. We've created businesses, non-profits, a nonprofit school, and an organic farm, that helps better serve ours, and the local community. Visitors are welcome to our annual Open House in June, and Harvest Celebration in September. Guided tours, and internship programs are also available from May through October.

Contact: Leonie Brien (603) 331-1669
www.citeecologiquenh.org

La Cité Écologique
of New Hampshire
An Ecovillage since 2003

Hot Topic, Raw Emotion, and the Spice of Life:

Chewing over Food Choice in Community

By Tracy Matfin

Deep breath in, deep breath out. I sit on one of the twin beds in our upstairs meeting room, leaning against the wall, with a steaming cup of freshly harvested and brewed turmeric ginger tea, mildly sweetened with honey from the bees on the farm. A small smile of contentment and anticipation plays across my lips as the drumming of the rain on the roof fills the room and individuals start appearing at the top of the staircase. A wet morning rewards the choice to spend time with chosen family, discussing important issues and fostering our common vision.

I am a founding member of La'akea Community (Big Island, Hawaii), which, formed 10 years ago, has 11 adult members, two kids, and one trial member. Our years of success stem from a shared belief that people must continuously connect with one another and the land to live sustainably. A primary way we connect is around food.

Business meetings at La'akea follow a format designed to encourage the honest sharing of minds and hearts. We begin with "check-ins," then move on to "appreciations" and "withholds," followed by "announcements," "homework," and then finally the "agenda." Some of these processes I will describe further on.

At the meeting today, our facilitator starts by calling for check-ins. These are typically brief reports where individuals share their current emotional state and any plans for the day. One community member—a tall, dark-haired man, a strong presence on the land and loving father—speaks first. "I feel refreshed, well-rested, and happy the weather is complicit with our need to stay in this morning. I do not relish being soggy."

As others take turns sharing, I appreciate the wisdom and intelligence of our most senior members, the patience and joy of several of the women, and the peaceful energy of several others. Our group is diverse and eclectic, ranging in age from 32 to 84, in education from high school to Ph.D., and in financial status from enough-to-get-by to established-retirement-fund. We are all fit and healthy within our varying body types. More than half of the group initially connected through the Network for a New Culture.

I take a turn at checking in. I begin by sharing an appreciation: "I am incredibly grateful for our daily experiment in how to live together. I appreciate every one of us for our commitment and dedication to each other and the land we steward." I then share that I feel anxious that there are food-related items on the agenda. Food has been

La'akea Community Members 2015.

Photos courtesy of Tracy Matfin

Author Tracy Matfin brings in the harvest with her daughter Ai'ala.

Tropical fruit abundance.

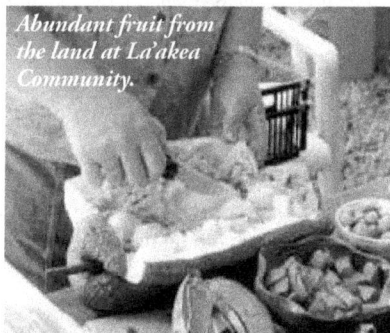

Abundant fruit from the land at La'akea Community.

Eating local, eating well: taro, sheep stew, green papaya salad, and a garden salad.

at the center of many energy-filled discussions throughout La'akea's history. I am going to share several episodes from that history to provide an insight into our community processes.

Since our inception, we have been a partial income-sharing community. We take in money through collective endeavors (like events and guest fees) as well as through monthly membership dues. We use that money for a variety of group needs—for example, for our truck and tractor, tools, garden amendments and supplies, household and office goods. We use that money to buy food.

Early in our history, members used La'akea money to buy whatever food they wanted, with the exception of: foods deemed "luxury items" (coffee, chocolate), fruit over $2.50/lb., and any other items over $8/lb. This system was too vague and had to be changed within a year and a half. We devised a "food list"—a list of items we agreed were OK to buy. We made this list by starting with basic staples that were always in the kitchen, then added items we each liked to eat regularly. Faced with the daunting project of getting everyone to agree on every item on the list, we agreed (through consensus) to scratch consensus in this instance and use a voting system instead. If at least three people wanted an item on the list, we kept it. About two hours later, we had our first "food list."

Moving forward in La'akea's history, the dance around food came to include not just what we bought with La'akea money but also what we didn't buy—what we chose to grow, harvest, prepare, and eat from the land.

"Did anyone harvest the cacao?" I heard this question within a year of the exultant cry, "The cacao is fruiting!" The answer: "Well, no. The last time I made a chocolate cake I used the cocoa powder from the store. It was sitting right there on the shelf and I chose what was easier."

"For dinner tonight we have wild pig and taro stew, taro with pesto, heart of palm salad, and a kale salad." Most of the items were grown on the farm, harvested and then prepared. This meal took most of a day to prepare, the reward being to eat food grown and harvested from the land.

"For dinner tonight we have tortillas, black beans, rice, grated cheese, avocado, and salsa." One, maybe two, of these items is from the land: the avocados and the salsa (if freshly made). Everything else was purchased. This meal took only a few hours to prepare, the reward being ease.

The tension around the foods we bought and foods we grew and harvested eventually, about two years ago, led the topic back to the business meeting. If the general idea was to grow our own food and eat locally, why was our "food list" so big? Time had arrived for revision. We began by airing our concerns through a go-around. Each person in turn shared their thoughts and feelings around food in our community. This time we shared a strong desire to motivate change in our eating. We removed from the list (to name just some of the items) cocoa powder, dates, cashews, yogurt, cheese, and mayonnaise. A new list was born.

We now return to the present day. The rain continues to patter against the roof as I take another sip of sweet, nourishing tea. "Food list" has made it to the agenda yet again.

"Does anyone wish to share a withhold?" our facilitator asks. A withhold is a feeling or judgment that someone has kept to themselves—something that they are holding on to—that keeps them from being present. They share to be more present, to connect with the person or people to whom their withhold is directed.

"Yes," hisses one of the members. She continues in an audibly irate tone, "this is for the whole group. Last night when I went to make dinner, I was disgusted by the mess on the counter. I went to put my collards down next to the sink and I saw a

spattering of blood. I know a pig was slaughtered yesterday morning and to find this was beyond tolerable." After hearing this withhold, we chose to make it a business item, to discuss raw meat and cleanliness in the kitchen at greater length.

Are you vegan? Vegetarian? Omnivore? Do you eat only raw food or prefer ayurvedically-prepared meals? La'akea's mission statement welcomes such diversity: "We embrace processes which work to bring us into unity, while respecting each person's autonomy." Take a poll at La'akea and you'll find one raw vegan, two vegetarians, four gluten-free, and several serious carnivores. Now let's share a kitchen and make community meals together.

We decided to address the issue of the bloody counter by using an abbreviated version of the Hawaiian ho'oponopono. Each member shared their story:

"I assisted in the harvesting of the pig. We were very careful to do most of the work out in the slaughterhouse. We only did the final packaging for the freezer in the kitchen."

"I remember wiping the counters very thoroughly."

Then each shared how they were responsible for the blood on the counter.

"I could have gone over all the counters once again after everything was put away."

"I could have been more careful to use only one area."

"I could have wiped up the blood when I saw it."

"I could have helped when I saw the process going on in the kitchen."

After everyone, including the angry community member, took responsibility for their actions and feelings, the ho'oponopono was complete. We decided to move forward with a renewed consciousness around meat: to be more thorough in cleaning up, to use only the red cutting board, and to use the counter to the left of the first sink.

As we go on to address the topic of the food list, it's obvious that food stirs our emotions. Culturally-influenced food choices, personal dietary needs, and sustainability ideals swirl together in a potential maelstrom. Every community, regardless of size, addresses these issues. Some communities come together around food. I've seen vegan communities, primal-diet communities, and 80-10-10 groups.

Sustainability is difficult to measure; there are many perspectives on what it is. From a land-based permaculture point of view, we could study the climate zone and research the crops historically grown in the area, especially those grown by the more indigenous cultures. Taro, breadfruit, turmeric, and sweet potato exist at the top of this list for Hawaii. Other tropically-oriented foods found here come from Central America, Brazil, Thailand, and the Philippines, such as cacao, palms, ginger, pumpkins, and spices. These plants grow well here and are easy to propagate; many are perennials that hardly ever succumb to insect or other plant pests; if you put them in the ground and walk away, these plants will do

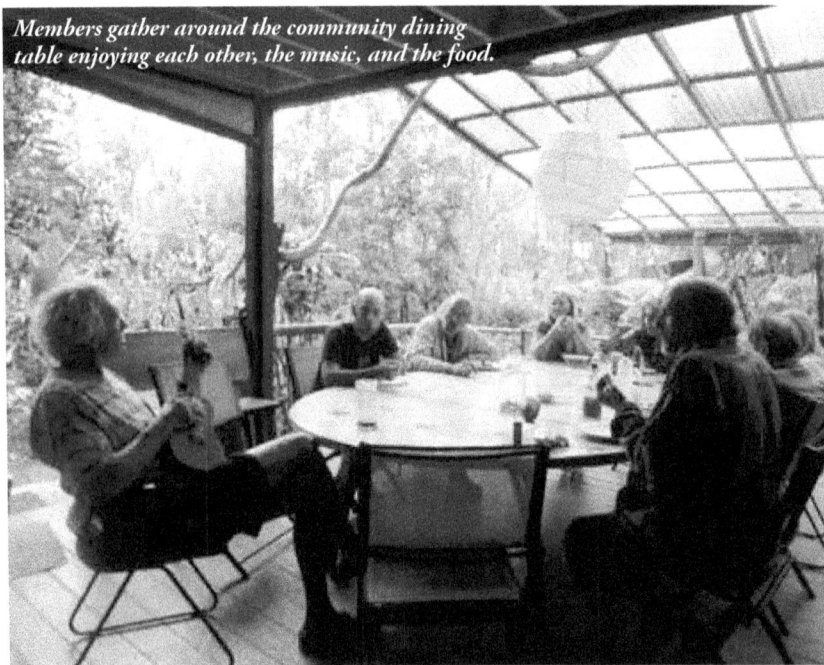

Members gather around the community dining table enjoying each other, the music, and the food.

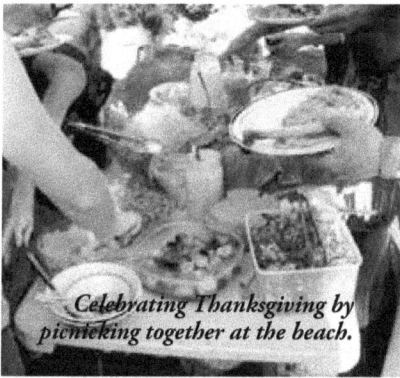
Celebrating Thanksgiving by picnicking together at the beach.

Putting love into the food as Dona makes community ferments.

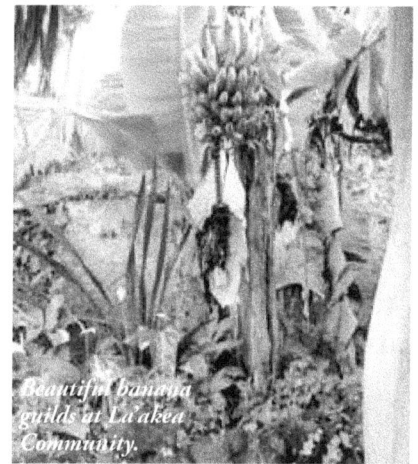
Beautiful banana guilds at La'akea Community.

Derek and Ruben in the La'akea kitchen, playing around during the preparation of a group meal.

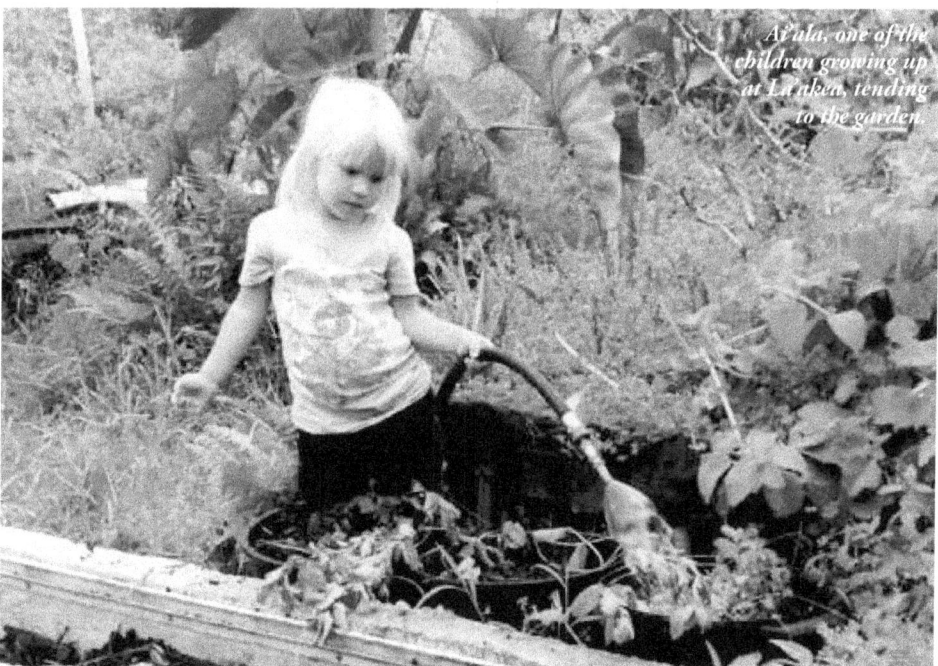
At'ala, one of the children growing up at La'akea, tending to the garden.

fine. Our need for ease will clearly be met by choosing these plants.

Yet there are other ways to view sustainability. Most of the members at La'akea did not grow up eating these foods, so..."What do we choose to eat?" "What do we choose to harvest?" This emotional angle asks, "Which foods bring us comfort? Which foods are linked to years of memories?" Our taste buds know these foods, as do our digestive systems. So we continue to grow the vegetables that need more care, more fertilizers, more protection from hungry insects, and require the purchase of seed shipped in from the continent. Balance, harmony, and sustainability are not just questions of physical reality.

I consider myself and many others at La'akea "opportunistic locavores." As we open to the opportunity, we eat locally. We grow and purchase foods we know and love and foods we are learning to love.

The anxiety I felt earlier fades away as I realize it's not all about the food list after all. It is about the connection that listening and understanding brings. Our community continues to thrive because we choose to take the time to connect with our chosen family. We choose to remember that to live sustainably we need to practice compassion, understanding, acceptance, and our consensus process. 🌿

Tracy Matfin is an educator turned farmer, mother, and permaculture instructor. Tracy cofounded La'akea Community (www.permaculture-hawaii.com). Sharing the community's living experiment through tours and internship programs brings her great pleasure. She loves sitting with trees, communing with the "weeds" she is removing from the garden, and laughing with her daughter, friends, and family.

My Journey with Food in Community: A Banquet, in Five Courses

By Gigi Wahba

Food has always occupied a revered place within the many communities of my life. I have come to appreciate that food isn't just about sustenance. Rather, it has many roles and provides a critical context for the functioning of a community.

I. Food = Identity

Like many people, I find my first community in my nuclear family, and having meals together is our most basic ritual. My parents were first-generation immigrants to America. They had grown up in Egypt, enjoying proximity to their extended family and a close-knit community. However, due to political unrest in the '40s and '50s, their family was forced to leave ("expelled" was the official term). Their property and assets were seized and they became scattered across the globe with the few possessions they were able to carry with them. My parents emigrated first to England and then, five years later, to America.

As a child, I quickly learned that our family identity and our heritage were intricately tied to the food we ate.

Unlike my American-born friends, we didn't have soda, ketchup, or TV dinners in our fridge. Instead, every meal was made from scratch and only reluctantly did my mother allow processed food such as cereal, pre-made cookies, and pop tarts. It was absolutely obligatory to be at the table for the dinner meals and we never skipped meals. In fact, we rarely skipped high tea. Sleepovers were seen as an odd practice, breaking up the family mealtime. My parents also had different patterns of shopping from other families; they had a personal relationship with every vendor and visited numerous grocers, butchers, and ethnic markets throughout the week.

Sunday afternoons we often ate stewed fava beans, affectionately called "fuul." These beans are a staple food from their homeland, packed with protein and a very satisfying flavor, especially in the traditional form—mashed together with olive oil, cumin, sea salt, freshly ground pepper, and boiled eggs. Often pita bread was available to scoop up the last of the mash. Other traditional dishes included hummus, chicken soup seasoned with melokhiya (an herb rich in calcium), and, of course, many desserts and appetizers made from filo dough layered with butter. We ate what has now become known as the "Mediterranean diet" with all its healthful and varied flavors.

On the somewhat rare occasions when relatives came from distant towns, the baking and cooking began days ahead with special dishes with French, Spanish, and Arabic names. For these events, my mom would often invite local friends who also came from Egypt or other Sephardic areas. I remember sitting on the top steps of our split-level home, looking down on the exotic faces, hearing unique accents of the three languages we spoke at home, and feeling the heat of the crowded living room rising. This, I could wistfully imagine, would have been the scene at my grandmother's home each Sunday were the politics different and my family able to stay in Egypt.

II. Food = Camaraderie

Fast forward to college, to eating on the "meal plan." I have to say, at first I felt a kind of liberation to be able to eat or not eat at any time and with whomever I chose. While my mom's food was gourmet by any standard, I was ready to drop all the fuss about cooking and eating. I savored the typical, buffet-style American food which included French fries, cream pies, pizzas, etc. This change of diet had a deeply sedating effect, contraindicated for intense study, but still satisfying to my quest of finally becoming a true American.

By my third year, when most of my friends were living off campus and out of proximity, we realized that we missed the social aspect of eating together. A friend of our household came up with the idea of a weekly potluck, late morning Sundays. We asked people to bring food or drink and help clean up. It was a fabulous success and soon people started asking other people to come. There was always something to enjoy—good food, animated conversation, a little music, a little gossip, etc.

Food was not so much about who we were but what we had to offer each other.

This same group of friends decided, one year, to stay in our college town for the Thanksgiving break. Again, we had a potluck for the festive meal but that year we had a couple who came and brought a curious casserole made with tofu. Most of that evening's conversation was about the environmental impact of food choices. We talked about how all that corn we saw in the fields was for animal consumption and that crowded stockyards were the norm. I remember noticing that while this information was disturbing and a call to action of some sort, learning about it in the context of a celebration made me feel hopeful.

Each week that we had the potlucks, the camaraderie offered by sharing meals was a great touchstone, helping ground everybody and providing opportunity to develop ideas. It also made clear the notion that the whole is greater than the sum of the parts. We always had a feast of food and ideas even though we were only students with limited resources.

III. Food = Love

After college I was without community for a while. I traveled, explored my new career, fell in and out of relationships. Eventually, I followed my passion for modern dance to study in Amsterdam for a summer. While the dance school was a community of sorts, I connected more with a sub-community interested in spiritual growth. At the close of the summer session, I was invited to travel to an "intentional community" in the northern part of the Netherlands—there, spiritual practice was developed in everyday farm life.

After a weeklong visit, I decided to return to this vegetarian, nonviolent community after my summer lease was over. Since I knew nothing about farming but did have experience growing produce in a community garden, I quickly volunteered to help out in the garden. It was late summer and the garden beds were brimming with greens, tomatoes, peppers, etc. The work was very peaceful and included taking care of three ewes who were living out their old age. By the next spring, I joined the woman who mentored me to become the garden team. We had three garden plots: one at home, two at locations about five kilometers away. We would commute by bicycle six days a week and spend full days

Gigi with giant cabbage from CSA.

Spring at Valentine CSA.

Photos courtesy of Gigi Wahba

at the gardens.

In that intentional community, as in my nuclear family, we would eat all three meals together. However, unlike at my childhood home, there was often some kind of sharing and discussion of personal-growth issues at mealtimes. With about 20 members sitting at three long tables arranged in a horseshoe pattern, there was one facilitated discussion at a time. While occasionally I would be a protagonist in a discussion for something I

> ## I rarely cooked the same meal twice because there were vast combinations of available homegrown foods throughout the year.

had done well (or not so well), I was mostly an observer, feeling that my life experiences thus far had given me little wisdom when it came to human dynamics. Still, I longed to contribute and appreciate fully what others were sharing.

After a while, I realized that my work in the gardens—bringing fresh food to the table—was what I could best offer while I learned the more subtle art of personal engagement. I have delightful memories of hauling our garden harvests in a bike trailer with the satisfaction that this produce was grown and delivered with love for all to enjoy.

In that almost monastic environment, I gave deep thanks to my mother for her many, many years of channeling her love through her cooking.

IV. Food = Place

After four years abroad in this remote farm and healing center (without internet!), I was ready to put my new skills and positive outlook to action back in my home country. I moved to Eugene, Oregon to join my sister and I found work at one of the natural food markets. I became the cheese specialist and enthusiastically learned and shared the intricate flavors and processes of making cheese around the world. I was fascinated by the importance of local yeasts, caves, dairy breeds, etc. Though we are a global culture, each society has its farmers and crafters who have been cultivating specific food and animal varieties for gen-

erations. For them, an intimate connection with place—land, water, microbes, climate, etc.—is what defines food.

All my discussions and research about "terroir" (the critical role of local conditions in the final outcome of a food product) got me wanting to get back on the land. When I was 34, I traveled through the Midwest and had the chance to visit Sandhill Farm, a well-established intentional community, having gotten its start in 1974. There the population ranges from four to nine members who grow most of their own food including vegetables and fruits, wheat and beans, maple syrup and sorghum, and some livestock. Everyone who visits is almost instantly awed by the product of this effort—root cellars chock full, many kinds of homebrew available, meat off the land in the freezer, and several bushels of produce available for the cook of the day to choose from.

As it turned out, I moved to this community and grew some very deep roots there both in lasting friendships and starting a family. Again I worked in the gardens but this time I learned the next level of food self-sufficiency—not only eating fresh during the growing season but also storing food for winter and early spring consumption. Food storage took the form of canning, freezing, dehydrating, wine making, and fermenting. Everyone played a role in the agriculture and we took turns preparing meals. I rarely cooked the same meal twice because there were vast combinations of available foods throughout the year.

Often too, we were busy with a food-related task such as shelling beans or cleaning herbs during our regular community meetings. While I was there we formalized our intern program to share what we were learning about food self-sufficiency and group dynamics. We, of course, also wanted to widen our social circle by opening up our home (also without internet at that time). I think it was fascinating for visitors to see how much food production defined our daily lives and our sense of well-being. For example, our biggest party of the year was a May Day celebration, complete with lots of food, a May Pole, live music, a sweat hut, games, and a full day of visiting with friends and neighbors too.

If one word could describe the feeling, it would be "abundance," as we welcomed in the new growing season and appreciated our land and our many connections with it.

At Sandhill Farm, we not only grew garden and field crops but we also cultivated pe-

Activism: instating a Health Ordinance.

Activism: public meeting on cafos.

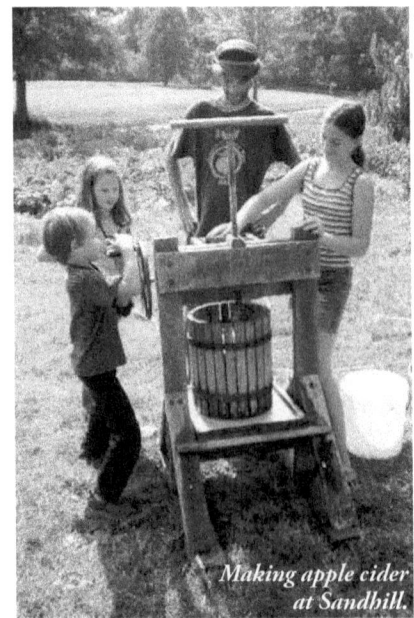
Making apple cider at Sandhill.

rennials, wildcrafted mushrooms, tapped maple trees, and got most of our meat from hunting deer from our land. These ties to the land all had their season and their rituals. It was always exciting to find the first morels or see the bluebells return for their brief spring show. Maple season required buckets and taps and driving the little tractor up and down icy paths.

We also took our farm products to local harvest fairs: handcrafted sorghum, salsa, garlic braids, beeswax candles, and other unique offerings. It was clear to me that these same products produced anywhere else would have different qualities. As an organic farm, we had been inputting wholesome nutrients onto the land for over 30 years. We also had been harvesting trees for our wood needs, planting new trees, and restoring prairie.

V. Food = Activism

To continue with my personal story, I did move away from communal living three years ago in favor of buying a house in the small town where my daughter is finishing up high school. I have continued to grow much of my food and have the only front yard garden and rainwater catchment system in town. (It's just what I do, but it turns out to be a pretty big statement in this conservative town.) Well, as long as I was making statements, I decided to write a monthly garden column in the local paper to talk about organic vegetable gardening and delve into some of the broader sustainability issues.

I had some earlier exposure to this town community. A few years back, we had an influx of confined animal feed operations (cafos) move into the surrounding farmland. Somehow I got pulled into the forefront of the confrontation with these operators and got involved with negotiations between them and the county. At the same time, I had been working with two other women to build up a farmers' market at our downtown, courthouse square. We did petition and win a countywide vote to instate a health ordinance to control the impacts of the feed operations. I'm glad I've been able to put my energies toward the farmers' market as a positive alternative to industrial agriculture.

The farmers' market, while still very small, is a sweet scene with five to eight vendors. About half the vendors are from the Mennonite community in our area. We have a few crafters as well. Sometimes friends come by to play music or one of the service groups in town will set up to promote an upcoming event. So we create opportunity for some mixing of social groups at the market and I get to socialize and sell a few vegetables from my garden.

Two years ago, I started the first Community Supported Agriculture (CSA) in our area as a way to do the work I love while also building the local food options. Each subscriber to my farm pays in advance for weekly delivery of fresh produce during the garden season. So far I have extended the shares to like-minded friends. This year I may get bold and

advertise to the general public.

It seems each year there is more that can be done to promote access and diversity in our food system. A few years ago, I connected our elementary school with FEDCO's seeds fundraiser and talked with the elementary kids about seed diversity, local economy, and the great feeling of fresh tomato squirt! Last year, I took up two plots at the community garden. We are lucky that one of the pastors in town is also an avid gardener and he converted a portion of hayfield to community gardens. I grew potatoes and green beans there as well as the lesser-known okra and celery, just because I thought it would be fun for other gardeners to see and wonder about—and it was. This year, I am helping organize a local seed swap and expect to continue to grow seed for the Southern Exposure Seed Exchange catalog. I will also need to drop my monthly columns and my work as farmers' market manager so that my life does not become unbalanced with food growing and activism.

When I think about it, all my activism around food issues is a sort of invitation to create community in my new town.

Gigi Wahba lives in Memphis, Missouri and maintains ties with the northeast Missouri intentional communities: Sandhill Farm, Dancing Rabbit Ecovillage, Red Earth Farms, and the Possibility Alliance. She also serves on the board of the Missouri Southern Iowa (MOSI) artists' guild.

Place: carrots grow here.

May Day at Sandhill.

Keren and Geoff: interns at Sandhill.

Make Food, Make *Hygge*, Make Happy

By Jane Moran

The hefty, six-burner, commercial-grade, propane-ready stove floats invisibly, glowing with promise, just above the newly laid kitchen tile.

"Just think of all the sunchokes we can cook!" exclaims Nick, laughing at the prospect of huge "fartichoke" spreads we can boil, simmer, and sautee—all at once!—on the giant new stove. (Giant relative to the two-burner camp stove we've been sharing for the last seven years!)

"And one person could stand on one side of the stove, and somebody else on the other side, and other people could be over here hanging out on this couch, and other people eating at the table!" Fantasy carries me into a not-so-distant future when the stove will be a real object—one that we're driving a few hundred miles to pick up this weekend, for a great price—and the couches and tables and chairs and counters will all take their places in the room, transforming this spot from a construction project into real infrastructure for community. Infrastructure designed, specifically, for *hygge*—a funny-sounding word that exemplifies, to us, one of the fundamental intentions of any community.

Hygge, pronounced "hyoogah," is a Danish word with no direct English translation. Helen Dyrbye in *Xenophobe's Guide to the Danes*, writes of hygge, "It is the art of creating intimacy: a sense of comradeship, conviviality and contentment rolled into one." Wikipedia explains: "hygge is a concept that evokes 'coziness,' particularly when relaxing with good friends or loved ones and while enjoying good food. Christmas time, when loved ones sit close together on a cold rainy night, is a true moment of *hygge*, as is grilling a *pølse* (Danish sausage) and drinking a beer on a long summer evening." To me, learning the word "hygge" was like discovering a name for my favorite color—I knew I liked all those things in the definition, but I had never been able to congeal them so succinctly into one spot-on, concrete label and say, "This. This is what I want. This is what we are doing."

In Denmark, tourism billboards advertise hygge as a basic tenet of the national culture. Danes claim that their value of hygge—which they consider more important than material wealth—explains the nation's top rankings in international happiness surveys. Many of us drawn to intentional community all over the world share this value; even when it seems at odds with aspects of American Consumerist Capitalism, in which we're meant to believe that money is the "bottom line." Naming our community's value of hygge feels empowering, as

Inside the Hygge Hall with woodstove blazin'!

Photos courtesy of Jane Moran

the word helps focus our intention on what we want to create. Even though our village is geographically remote—surrounded by wilderness on all sides and almost an hour's drive from the only incorporated city in our rural county—residents and visitors alike revel in the spirit of hygge that we cultivate by prioritizing human interaction and care. A lack of internet and cellphone reception also means that we're all forced to notice the people, plants, animals, and physical world around us instead of "connecting" to a virtual world. .

In our little community, we've finally reached a tipping point where we can shift our resources from the creation of basic survival infrastructure into focusing more directly on making space for hygge.

Seven years ago, our founding member, Dan, arrived in this undeveloped patch of forest and lived for a year in a tent with his dog, bathing in the cold river and clearing trees to make space for buildings and gardens, envisioning the village we live in today. Since then, dozens of others have come and gone, lending their energy to the project, building several small cabins and a bigger community center, creating and cultivating acres of gardens, and more recently completing a greenhouse and two ponds. The newest building, christened the "Hygge Hall," represents a lot of luxury for us, including an indoor storage area, kitchen, and living room.

It's hard to imagine that the village infrastructure might ever be "finished," since there's always something else that would be fun to add. But until this spring, all of the cabins where we live have shared a year-round outdoor kitchen—which is great when the weather is nice, but challenging in storms, snow, and even mosquito-clouded summer evenings. The Hygge Hall means a place to gather even in inclement weather, a place to prepare food and share meals, to enjoy each other's company without needing to retreat to private cabins. Nothing describes our intention better than the simple word, hygge.

I suppose a Hygge Hall by any other name would smell as sweet—whether it's a kitchen, a mess hall, or a fire pit, the place of food and sustenance tends to become the center of any home or community. It's a place of respite and nourishment, of heat and good smells and the sweet relief of a good meal after hard work; a place to share the rewards of being human.

To us, sharing the challenges and rewards of survival, from growing and preparing food to providing shelter, heat, and human connection, *is* the experience of community. We help keep each other alive, and we help keep each other nourished. When we grow our own food, our community consciously extends to include the land that we care for and from which we are fed. Tacking the final touches onto our beloved new Hall, with space for storing, processing, and sharing our precious bounty from the land, we reverently name and celebrate the value of hygge in our lives and community. ❧

Jane Moran is a member of Maitreya Mountain Village (www.maitreyamountainvillage.com), where she toils and eats communally in the Northern California wilderness. She is also an organizer for Transition Del Norte and the local timebank, Del Norte Hour Exchange, and sometimes writes for publications about experiments in community building.

Hygge Hall construction. Right top: Hygge Hall almost done outside! The old kitchen (a camping stove, picnic table, and sink) is in foreground.

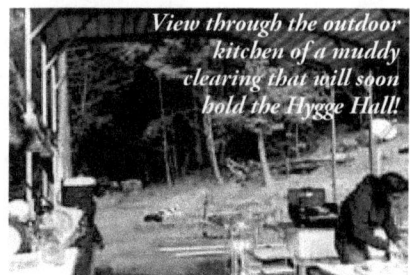

View through the outdoor kitchen of a muddy clearing that will soon hold the Hygge Hall!

Discovering the Joy of Communal Food:
Camaraderie and Work at Maitreya Mountain Village

By Dan Schultz

In 2008, when I began carving what is now Maitreya Mountain Village out of the raw, densely forested, rugged Siskiyou landscape, I brought my work ethic with me. I wrote the charter, posted the project online, and some really great people came to be a part of it. I found much to be learned from taking on this kind of vision, none more meaningful than the lessons I learned from the nourishing, even spiritual, relationship with food.

While our permaculture and sustainability aspects moved forward, I tended to want to work independently on separate tasks. It seemed more efficient, partly because multitasking had never come naturally to me and working *with* other people could be distracting, even frustrating at times. It slowed me down.

My dietary habits were similarly independent. I was set on listening to my body to take meals when and only when I was hungry. I ate to the beat of my own internal drum and had come to altogether ignore when others convened for their "meal times" (much to the chagrin of my family when Thanksgiving dinner was served). So it was the rule, with few exception, that I ate separately from our newfound community.

These initial community members were WWOOFers and volunteers who came from Vermont, Australia, Germany—all over the country and globe—along with a few locals. Mostly they were Millennial generation, hippie kids, for lack of a better general description: 18-25-year-olds imbued by culture that valued communal practices of all sorts. Unlike me, they tended to want to both work and break bread with one another. I think my ways threw them off a little. Sometimes I could see how I rubbed off on them—and then, sometimes, them on me.

In the first few years I was keen to observe certain patterns of

community morale, especially as it related to the pace of work. I was (and still am, to a degree) about getting the job done. I noticed that when meals were shared (by chance timing, convenience, or invitation) camaraderie went up. Increments of enthusiasm became more present. More consideration and creativity entered our project realm. My unfaltering internal work-o-meter told me so!

As the infrastructure and number of buildings grew, I more often engaged in communal gardening, food preparation, and the community ritual of meal sharing. I was raised with a dearth of such practices, but soon gained a deeper appreciation for the primal cohesiveness of gathering around something as elemental as food. Cooked or raw, food warmed the conversation. As we shared our sustenance, I felt the humanness we shared as well. It made nourishment more about thriving than surviving.

> **When meals were shared, enthusiasm increased, and more consideration and creativity entered our project realm.**

As I look back and currently appreciate it, discovering and embracing the joy of communal food allowed me to also find more joy in work. I slowed down (which actually often makes things go faster—what a concept!) and working in togetherness with others brought an alchemy to our projects overall, whereby 1+1+1+1 often equaled 20.

This has affected me deeply, in ways I will not expound upon in this writing, and I often take a reverent pause to give thanks for all the gifts that the living fruits of earth have brought me. 🐟

Dan Schultz is co-director of Maitreya Mountain Village (www. maitreyamountanvillage.com), which creates intentional, caring community and farming in an off-grid, wilderness setting. Dan hosts and produces a talk radio program called New Culture Radio focused on sustainability, and together with his partner Jane leads Transition Del Norte in Northwestern California.

Illustrations by Amelia Troyer

The Community's Garden Orchestra

By Chris Roth

In the modern world, many people generate music by flicking a switch, pressing a button, turning a dial, or tapping a keypad or touchscreen. And many of us obtain food by swiping a card or lightening a wallet.

Others, however, create music by picking up instruments or using their own voices. And some people grow at least a portion of their own food too, by participating intimately with its creation in a garden or on a farm.

Likewise, although the feeling of community may be instantly available to us by tuning into a sports game or visiting a Facebook page, we can also choose to take a deeper plunge into the process of growing more intimate real-world community with others.

When an intentional community—or group of committed friends or neighbors—*also* makes the choice to grow some of its own food together, it challenges both the culture of purchased food and the modern culture of individualism (a culture very much related to that in which the push of a button can bring someone with adequate credit almost anything, whether for entertainment or sustenance).

My own experience in community tells me that getting involved in food-production, especially in a group setting, is like making our own music: it's not necessarily the easier choice, but the ultimate results can nourish us and our communities in ways much more profound than a pre-packaged product ever could.

• • •

There are as many ways to grow food together as there are to create music together. My brother, a classical violinist, has performed both in conventionally-run orchestras and in an innovative conductorless orchestra called Orpheus, in which participants share in leadership and can find themselves simultaneously more individually empowered and more connected with each other. Collective gardening projects can adopt either approach or anything in between or even beyond this spectrum. While some groups emulate the hierarchical structure of a traditional orchestra, the more egalitarian, participant-run approach of Orpheus more closely matches what many communities engage in or aspire to.

In the diverse instruments of an orchestra, opportunities for cacophony abound—so too in a "garden orchestra" made up of diverse communitarians. Not every instrument belongs in every orchestra—some end up being simply incompatible, especially when their populations are not in proper proportion with one another. Whether in collective music-making or collective food-growing, optimal results come when players learn to cooperate, listen to one another, engage in give-and-take, achieve attunement, and find a balance of tension and harmony among the very different, potentially clashing voices and positions they bring to the endeavor.

This kind of creative alchemy isn't always easy, considering the wide variety of approaches, temperaments, and preferences quickly manifested in any group of do-it-yourselfers—yet it is necessary if you want to have any hope of producing your own music or food together. Listed below are some of the parts I've witnessed—individuals who may join, or wish to join, your community's garden orchestra (each assigned a vegetable or herb name, for the purpose of keeping their real-life doppelgangers anonymous). This list is incomplete—feel free to suggest additions:

Amaranth: First trained in the French-intensive biodynamic method of gardening, and then attracted by permaculture's more natural approach, Amaranth values a combination of order and wildness in the garden.

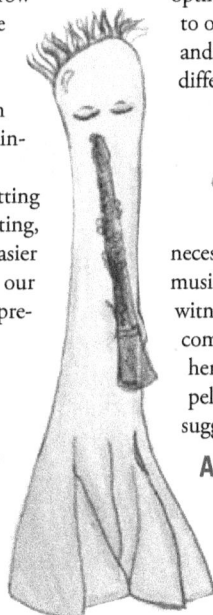

Amaranth leaves volunteer vegetables and edible or useful weeds to grow, while tenaciously removing less desirable plants. Amaranth likes to garden well in relatively smaller areas rather than garden sloppily in larger areas, and prefers to encourage the native ecosystem except in the focused high-production growing areas. Amaranth values both the process of growing—the experience—and the product—the food grown—and how those things are done matters a lot to Amaranth, who uses hand tools almost exclusively. Every choice expresses a value, either supporting or working against the kind of world that we want to live in and/or create, both in the garden and outside of it.

Artichoke: Artichoke is a strict utilitarian whose main goal is to maximize food production. Time and efficiency are central factors. Artichoke will happily use a rototiller, mower, or tractor for tillage or weed control, if that will save time over more labor-intensive methods. For Artichoke, gardening is less a spiritual, aesthetic, interpersonal, community-building, or natural-history experience than an economic one, intended to meet the needs of humans for physical nourishment.

Arugula: Arugula takes Artichoke's perspective a step further. Whereas Artichoke may hold the group's needs as the highest priority, Arugula is an entrepreneur who has learned, and brings to the garden, the philosophy that the priority for each individual must be to meet their own needs—and the results of the individual's success or prosperity will then ripple outward. Arugula will not think twice about enlisting leased garden space for the highest-income use, even if, for example, that is not growing food for consumption by the community, but instead growing vegetable starts for the local farmers' market.

Basil: Extensively read in permaculture before ever getting involved in a garden, Basil brings the perspective that growing food shouldn't be hard work—we can set up systems that will eventually feed us almost effortlessly. Basil resists getting sucked into work that appears to be monotonous or "drudgery," instead preferring to design food forests, plan swales, and create hugelkultur beds.

Bean: Bean, on the other hand, is acutely aware of the working conditions of most farmworkers around the world. Bean considers "let nature do the work" and "lazy gardener" approaches to be escapist, elitist fantasies of the privileged, and uses gardening as a way to become a "world citizen," aspiring to work as hard as any campesino. Bean will create extra work, even dig a bed twice, simply as a way of staying true to the vision of being an equal world citizen, allied with those who have no other choice but to work tirelessly to feed themselves and others.

Beet: For Beet, gardening is most importantly a way to get to know other people. Beet loves working alongside others, having conversations, singing, finding a common rhythm. Beet

would rather spend twice as long in the garden to achieve the same amount of physical work if it means having quality human connections while doing so.

Borage: Borage, on the other hand, thinks talk and socializing are distractions. For that reason, Borage prefers to work alone, and sees gardening almost as a workout, a sport in which the competition may be with self rather than others, but in which there is no room for lack of focus.

Broccoli: Broccoli also likes working alone, but as a form of meditation and spiritual attunement. Like Beet, Broccoli would rather spend twice as long in the garden to achieve the same amount of physical work—if it means that Broccoli's soul is nourished by slowing down to connect with the larger natural and spiritual worlds.

Brussel Sprout: Brussel Sprout is a spontaneous, intuitive gardener who prefers going to the garden each day and seeing what it is asking for rather than mapping out most activities in advance. A large number of variables, from current weather to soil moisture to recent plant growth to insect presence, can tip the scales in one direction or another. This can be either illuminating or frustrating to others working under Brussel Sprout's leadership or tutelage—illuminating if they are able to learn how Brussel Sprout does it, frustrating if they just want to know and prepare for what is going to happen that day in the garden.

Cabbage: Cabbage loves planning, scheduling, and record-keeping. No activity occurs in Cabbage's garden without first being written down and perhaps illustrated in the garden planner. Meticulous records of the history of every bed are a natural accompaniment to the crop labels adorning every planting. Those working under Cabbage's leadership will always know ahead of time what to look forward to—with excitement or not—in the garden that day.

Cardoon: Cardoon likes to keep things simple: one crop per bed. Interplanting complicates things. Any plant out of place is considered a weed—and, ideally, eliminated. Paths are scraped clean and/or mulched so as to prevent unwanted plant growth. Cardoon also likes to weigh every ounce of vegetable production, and record its place of origin within the garden—a process made easier by this "zero-tolerance" monocrop method.

Carrot: Carrot likes to "mix it up," and sees conventional rows and single-crop plantings as boring. Every gardening season Carrot seeks to expand the known horizons of companion planting and garden bed geometry, with (as expected) mixed results.

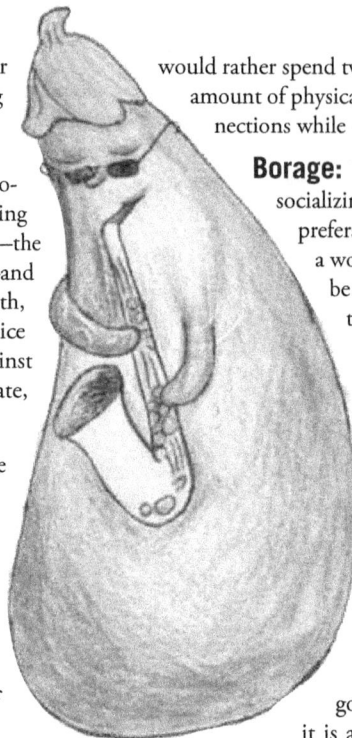

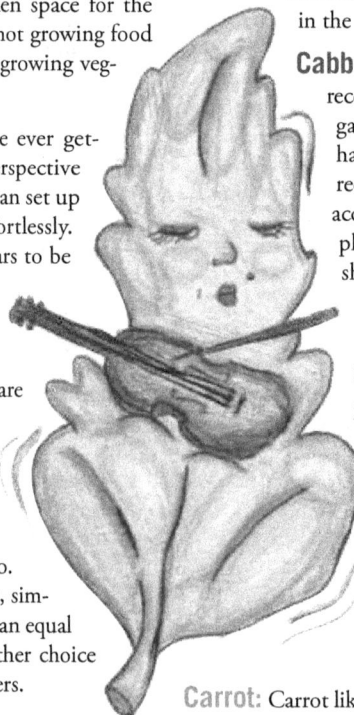

Cauliflower: Cauliflower saves seeds from almost everything. In fact, at any time at least half of Cauliflower's garden seems to have gone to seed. Paths become nonnavigable, and harvestable crops more difficult to find, but fellow gardeners also appreciate the savings in financial outlay and the flourishing of homegrown vegetable and herb varieties.

Celeriac: Celeriac can't tolerate plants gone to seed, and instead may crank out twice as many crops per year as Cauliflower does—all out of purchased seed packets. Pollinators prefer Cauliflower's garden, but Celeriac wins the prize for neatness and ease of harvest.

Celery: Celery believes that if some water is good for plants, more is better. Every day all garden beds receive several hours of water. Roots tend to stay near the surface, and mildew and disease can take hold, but at least the soil feels moist most of the time, and nothing dies of thirst.

Chard: Chard likes to dry-farm whenever possible. In fact, the only plants that survive in Chard's garden are ones that can tolerate dehydration. To be fair, Chard has developed several methods for conserving water in the soil that may come in very handy when irrigation is less available or when drought sets in.

Chicory: Chicory is a strict no-digger. Chicory encourages the soil ecosystem by never disturbing its layers, but instead only plucking from the surface and top-dressing with organic matter left to break down there.

Cilantro: Cilantro is a double- and even triple-digger, who likes nothing more than going deep down into the soil, loosening it up, and adding organic matter into it, while still attempting to maintain its previously-existing layers as much as possible.

Collard: Collard likes digging too—except Collard turns the soil upside down while doing so, to bury stuff that might have been growing on the surface and "give the other soil a chance."

Corn: Corn loves plastic, whether in the form of plant pots, seedling trays, row covers, or greenhouse plastic—citing its convenience and low cost.

Cress: Cress detests plastic on both environmental and aesthetic grounds, and uses alternatives whenever available (and whenever they will fly with other community members).

Cucumber: Cucumber gets up early every morning, and likes to "beat the heat" by working hard before taking a midday break.

Dill: Dill would by preference sleep until late morning, and start gardening no earlier than noon.

Eggplant: Eggplant is a novice gardener already disillusioned by the fact that we are growing almost exclusively crops from Europe and Asia, rather than native crops,

here on North American soil. (Ironically, Eggplant is a transplant from Eurasia as well.)

Endive: Endive is a new garden apprentice who is excited to try anything (be it digging a bed, weeding, sowing vegetable starts, thinning beets, building compost)—once. After that, the novelty usually wears off and it's drudgery.

Fennel: By contrast, fellow garden newcomer Fennel rarely voluntarily tries a new activity, once a groove is found on a now-familiar activity. Currently, Fennel seems unlikely to put down a shovel to learn how to save seeds unless the shovel is taken forcefully from co's tightly-clenched hands (an act which would violate community nonviolence agreements).

Garlic: Garlic is comfortable when it's clear who is in charge. Garlic can adapt to being on either end of a hierarchy—making decisions and giving direction, or following someone else's decisions and direction—but does not like group decision-making or lack of clear structure.

Kale: Kale doesn't like it when *anybody* is in charge. Period.

Kohlrabi: Kohlrabi grew up rurally, and was made to do farm chores throughout childhood by parents with a deeply-ingrained Protestant work ethic. Kohlrabi doesn't want to do any more gardening, ever.

Lambsquarter: Lambsquarter, on the other hand, appreciates the back-to-the-land childhood that has made gardening and farming as comfortable and familiar as eating and sleeping. Lambsquarter may or may not feel discouraged by the apparent cluelessness that some fellow communitarians possess about basic rural living skills.

Leek: Leek also has a lot of background in physical labor—perhaps too much. Leek now suffers from chronic injuries and conditions which impede the ability to perform many gardening tasks.

Lettuce: Lettuce has no background in physical labor, but leaps into a full-time gardening apprenticeship wholeheartedly, only to discover that a lifetime of sitting at desks in climate-controlled environments proves ill preparation for spending anything more than an hour or two a day doing physical work outside.

Melon: New gardener Melon has read a lot about gardening—including so much contradictory information that doing it the "right" way now seems like an insoluble puzzle. Melon is thinking about switching to the construction crew, or perhaps getting into bookkeeping.

Mustard: Mustard is a photographer, writer, and blogger. A little actual gardening goes a long way on a typical gardening day—especially when Mustard has a

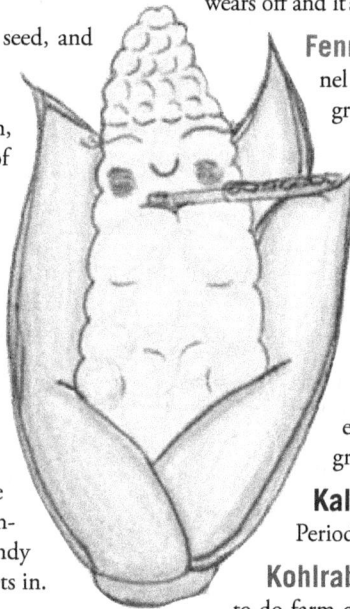

Sustainability in Community: Wisdom of Communities, Volume 4

macro-lens-equipped digital camera, a notebook, and/or a smart phone in hand.

Onion: Onion loves gardening, but hates kids...or at least kids in the garden. "One step forward, two steps back" is Onion's wry comment every time one appears to lend a hand.

Orach: Orach loves both gardening and children, believing that, together, they're our only hopes for the future. To Orach, a little backwards progress is a small price to pay for helping raise the next generation of gardeners.

Oregano: Oregano is rarely seen without earbuds—either listening to internet radio or having cell phone chats with friends or family. This lends itself better to peaceful coexistence with other gardeners than did Oregano's previous practice of toting around a blaring boombox—but communicating with Oregano in "real space" can still present challenges.

Parsley: Parsley is a strict vegan, and carries that philosophy into the garden. Parsley avoids the use both of animals and of animal manures in the garden, relying instead on the vegetable and mineral realms to return nutrients to the soil.

Parsnip: Parsnip believes the cycle of life is not complete without including animals in the gardening mix, and happily makes use of both trucked-in manures (for nutrients and organic matter) and on-farm animals (for soil improvement, pest control, egg and meat production, entertainment, etc.).

Pea: Pea is an ex-gardener, now massage therapist, attending to the needs of the current gardeners (future massage therapists) still active in the field.

Pepper: Pepper starts every day in the garden with a ritual attunement, and usually asks permission of vegetables before harvesting them. Pepper also blesses seeds while planting, praying for improved germination and growth.

Potato: Potato is skeptical of everything Pepper holds sacred—and in fact of anything that can't be proven scientifically. In a side-by-side trial initiated by Potato, seeds that Potato had cursed actually outperformed seeds that Pepper had blessed—not only in germination but in growth rates and in harvest produced. Third parties were left to wonder, "Is Potato's curse actually a blessing?"

Pumpkin: Pumpkin is the ultimate taste-tester. In the same way that grazing deer leave unmistakable marks on the landscape, Pumpkin's trail through the garden is easily spotted.

Purslane: Purslane, by contrast, never snacks in the garden at all. "I just brushed my teeth" is Purslane's most common explanation, but an irrational slug-slime phobia may be at the root.

Radish: Radish's main reason for being in the garden is that it's a socially-approved form of incessant nature-study. Hearing

40 different bird species' songs and calls in a morning will excite Radish much more than an unexpectedly doubled yield of, for example, radishes.

Rhubarb: Rhubarb grew up believing that the outdoors is boring, and that physical work and rural life are to be avoided at all costs. Unfortunately, despite Rhubarb's best efforts to overcome prejudice through total immersion, these deeply ingrained beliefs are proving hard to shake.

Rutabaga: Rutabaga is about public service. Any excess garden production goes to the local soup kitchen. Public tours and education are a central part of the gardening activity. Volunteers from the local community, and even from within the criminal justice system, are welcomed into Rutabaga's garden.

Spinach: Spinach resents Rutabaga's exporting of organic matter (excess produce) from the community's gardens, since it could be used to create compost to grow next year's crops. Spinach is not eager to have paroled prisoners hanging out in the gardens either.

Squash: Squash is one of the community's kitchen managers. Having gardened for many years, Squash welcomes anything the gardens produce and encourages cooks to incorporate it in meals, even if it is blemished, irregularly shaped, more difficult to clean, or more unusual than purchased produce would be. Why order broccoli from off-site when various brassica plants in our own gardens are sending up many smaller broccoli-like flower bud clusters?

Sunchoke: Sometime-kitchen-manager Sunchoke, by contrast, prefers to order more standard produce from off-site—especially for meals served to visitors and outside groups—rather than mess with what seem like sub-optimal crops from the community's gardens. Why use random brassica flower buds from the garden when big, familiar, *actual* broccoli is available from the local organic wholesaler?

Tomato: Tomato arrives at the community ready to help heal the relationship between people, food, and the land. What will Tomato learn?

Turnip: Turnip recognizes that there are many possible parts to play in a garden and in a community, but that the single most important thing is simply to be there—to engage—and to see what unfolds. Something beautiful and nourishing, Turnip knows, will eventually grow out of it, despite and even because of the hardships and challenges.

Chris Roth edits Communities, *and, in another lifetime, was a garden coordinator and organic gardening teacher whose* Beetless' Gardening Book: An Organic Gardening Songbook/Guidebook *(Carrotseed Press) formed a unique entry into the 1997 garden-book canon. Please send garden orchestra member additions to editor@ic.org.*

70

CREATING THE IDEAL INTENTIONAL COMMUNITY
(OR REVITALIZING AN EXISTING ONE)

I, Sahmat, grew up in intentional communities and have lived in 10 of them. I have been so dedicated to Community with both humans and Nature that I've been called "The Community Guy". The communities I grew up in shared a fairly strong "sense of community". I call this deep and sustained sense of community "Common-unity" because it's a state of unity we share in common, with the unique individuality of each human and each species still honored. It's this state of Common-unity that I've found most valuable in life and to me it's the main reason for living in an intentional community. When a group is deep in Common-unity together, there's a shared sense of love, joy, and peace that tops any other group experience.

However, I've found that in all the communities I've lived in, the sense of community is not nearly as deep and sustained as it could be. It's precisely this lack of Common-unity that is the root cause of the catastrophic global suffering of racism, wars, child abuse, abuse of women, environmental and species destruction, etc. So the ultimate goal is ending global suffering through "Global Common-unity": the spreading of Common-unity throughout the world by forming a global network of Common-unity-dedicated Communities.

So I've spent my life learning how to create Common-unity-dedicated communities that share true Common-unity: a deeper and more sustained sense of community. There are two keys to starting a Common-unity community (or moving an existing community into deeper Common-unity):

1. The first key to Common-unity is for everyone to be "Common-unity-dedicated" as their top common priority. This doesn't seem to be the case in any existing community, which results in focus and energies being bled off into other priorities. So maintenance of Common-unity doesn't get enough time and energy.

2. The second key to Common-unity is to learn "Common-unity Skills", skills that must be practiced to maintain Common-unity: Speaking from the Heart, Empathetic Listening, Emptying of Ego-attachments, Conflict Resolution, Consensus, Heart Wound Healing, Cooperative Housing, and Cooperative Economics. Modern culture does not teach us these skills.

We at the Alliance for Global Community have developed free workshops that train you in these Common-unity Skills. The workshops contain the Sharing Circle process developed by M. Scott Peck, a Nature connection exercise developed by John Seed and Joanna Macy, healing exercises developed by Byron Katie and Richard Moss, and exercises in creating Cooperative Housing and Cooperative Economics. We've tested various versions of these Common-unity Skill Building workshops over the past 25 years, and we've found them to be quite effective in teaching Common-unity skills that can help maintain Common-unity. If you'd like to start a Common-unity-dedicated community, or if you'd like to bring more Common-unity into an existing community (perhaps through a Common-unity sub-community or "pod"), you need to learn or improve these Common-unity skills as soon as possible.

To find out how to sign up for a free public Common-unity Skills workshop or schedule a free workshop for an existing group or community, please go to my website thecommunityguy.org There you can also find out how to get a free copy of the book "Skill Building for Global Common-unity". You can contact Sahmat directly at info@thecommunityguy.org or at 434-305-4770.

COMMON-UNITY WITH HUMANITY AND NATURE

How Do We Eat As If We Plan to Be Here for Another 10,000 Years?
Cultivating Food Culture in Stewardship of Place

By Olivia Rathbone

More than anything, food brings us together. The eco-crisis, or the "crisis of home," can and must be addressed at home, and what better place to start than around the dinner table?

The Occidental Arts and Ecology Center (Occidental, California) has been cultivating food culture since 1994; and our farm, which we call the Mother Garden, provides the foods around which we build and sustain our community.

Food is an expression of the land that we steward, and truly vibrant food is proof that the more closely we can understand and emulate nature, the more abundant our lives become. We are the direct beneficiaries of the ecological services that a living, breathing ecosystem such as the Mother Garden provides.

The Mother Garden has been on the forefront of the organic agriculture movement and has served as a renowned demonstration farm, nonprofit educational retreat center, intentional community, and eco-think-tank since the early 1970s, first as the Farallones Institute, next as the Center for Seven Generations, and now in its current incarnation as the Occidental Arts and Ecology Center and Sowing Circle Community. The Mother Garden was one of the first farms to be certified organic in California, and in 1994, forged one of the first organic agriculture easements in the US, preserving the land's status as an organic garden into perpetuity. The legacy lives on

today as the Mother Garden continues to feed and inspire activists, biologists, educators, and artists seeking innovative and practical approaches to the pressing environmental, cultural, and economic crises of our day—all while having fun and eating well.

Since the beginning of the 20th century, much of the genetic diversity of our food crops —the backbone of ecological resilience—has been lost and continues to be threatened by industrialized agribusiness. A main goal at OAEC is to educate visitors about sustainable food production and the array of plant species, particularly food crops, thankfully still available to us. OAEC's Biodiversity Program focuses on curating and propagating a plant and seed collection of more than 3000 varieties of heirloom, open-pollinated annuals and more than 1000 varieties of edible, medicinal, and ornamental habitat-friendly perennials. Over time, the garden has become something of a cradle of plant and animal diversity. We have collected and evaluated thousands of varieties, chosen our favorites, planted those that do well here again and again, and shared them with others. Sometime in the late '80s this land's stewards started calling its gardens the "Mother Garden," referring, even at its relatively young age, to the fact that the garden was providing a wealth of seeds, plant material, and wisdom to other gardens and gardeners and figuratively giving birth to daughter gardens.

The happy byproduct of this endeavor, of course, is that the Mother Garden and orchard provide organic fruit, vegetables, herbs, and flowers for thousands of meals prepared on-site each year.

In our workshops, the lessons taught in the classroom and out in the garden come together on the plate. Food becomes both a centerpiece for meaningful conversation and an unspoken, cellular avenue for learning. So much of our mission and work is tied into the promotion of eco-literacy through gardening, and our guests get to experience on a gut level, "Oh,

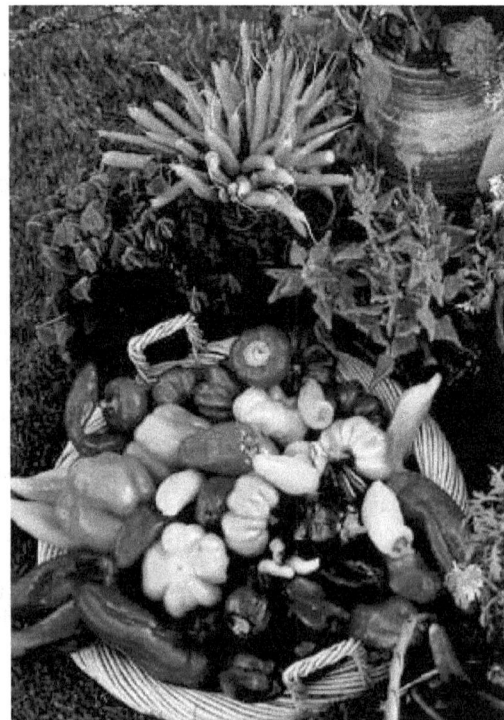

Photos courtesy of Occidental Arts and Ecology Center

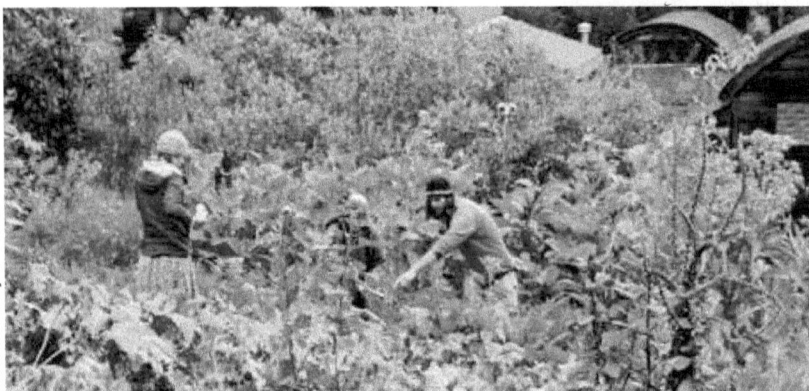

THIS is what sustainability TASTES like! Food grown in healthy soil from locally adapted seed in a biodiverse ecosystem prepared by happy people tastes great!" Class dismissed.

As an intentional community, OAEC and Sowing Circle venture to model the kind of cooperation that offsets the high cost of healthy food. We are pooling our resources to make healthy food a financially affordable reality in the face of agricultural policies that subsidize industrialized junk food instead of locally grown fresh fruits and veggies. Sharing food costs and cooking responsibilities means that we can afford to buy high quality, whole, unprocessed ingredients in bulk because we ourselves are doing the processing. Pooling of resources makes sense in terms of equipment too. Each of us doesn't need our own personal Vitamix or set of cookbooks (or table saw, tractor, copy machine, etc. either). Common ownership allows us a level of infrastructure and a quality of life that most of us couldn't afford on our own.

Of course, all of those reading this magazine realize that sharing comes with a level of compromise that most people have not been raised to accept in a culture that emphasizes individualism over cooperation. We all have different food preferences, likes and dislikes, diets and food philosophies, but have come to accept that living in community and committing to consensus-based self-governance means that when we do what is best for us as a whole, in the long run, we do what is best for us as individuals. Consensus decisions are often made at a snail's pace and take longer than a quick vote, but are completely in line with our move away from a culture of instant gratification. In our commitment to self-governance through practicing the democratic arts, everyone can have a seat at the table.

Many of us in the eco-ag movement champion the "food theory of everything" with a belief that fixing the food system can be a solutions generator for a host of our nation's ecological, economic, health, and psycho-spiritual problems. Yet sustainability is a misnomer—we don't want to sustain mainstream America's current system, which is obviously deeply flawed, but rather are working on the ground to move towards food systems and models of community that heal environmental and cultural degradation.

As Brock Dolman, Sowing Circle member and OAEC Senior Biologist, has said: "This is a thrivalist movement, not a survivalist movement. Participating in activities that are regenerative to the cycles of life—watershed cycles, soil cycles, food cycles—can also be simultaneously regenerative to the human spirit and to human connectivity. Contributing to the health and vitality and betterment of the planet can and should also be invigorating for us. As David Orr would say, 'Hope is a verb with its sleeves rolled up.' And so let's do

Spring Salad Mix
excerpted from The OAEC Cookbook, p. 19

- Baby heirloom lettuces: Akcel, Forellenschluss, Merlot, Red Speckle, Pablo, Little Gem
- Baby beet leaves: Chioggia and Golden
- Cress: Wrinkly Crinkly Curly and Upland
- Green mustard leaves: Golden Streaks, Golden Frills, and Old-Fashioned Ragged Edge
- Kale leaves and flowers: Redbor, Winterbor, Dinosaur, Russian Red, Russian White
- Sprouting broccoli leaves: Purple, Spiagariello
- Baby Swiss chard leaves: Rainbow, Golden, Rhubarb, Flamingo Pink, Oriole Orange
- Arugula leaves
- Sylvetta arugula leaves
- Japanese red mustards: Osaka Purple, Giant Red, Garnet, Red Feather, Ruby Streaks
- Mache rosettes and flowers: Verte de Cambrai, Coquille des Louviers
- Baby amaranth leaves
- Baby spinach leaves
- Fava bean leaves and flowers
- Pea shoots, tendrils, and flowers
- French sorrel leaves
- Sheep sorrel leaves
- Plantain leaves: Buckhorn, Wild
- Dandelion leaves
- Mallow leaves
- Miner's lettuce leaves and flowers
- Chickweed leaves and flowers
- Red-veined dock leaves
- Salad Burnet leaves
- Shungiku leaves and flower petals
- Nasturtium leaves, buds, and flowers
- Chive leaves and flowers
- Wild radish flowers and young pods
- Yellow mustard and tatsoi flowers
- Society garlic leaves and flowers: Variegated and Green
- Chervil flowers
- Bronze fennel fronds
- Fenugreek leaves
- Dill leaves
- Garlic chive leaves
- Parsley leaflets
- Mint tips: Spearmint, Peppermint, Lemon Balm
- Sweet violet leaves and flowers
- Runner bean flowers
- Forget-me-not flowers
- Johnny jump-up flowers
- Cecil Bruner rose petals
- Abutilon flowers
- Calendula petals
- Anchusa flowers
- Tulip petals

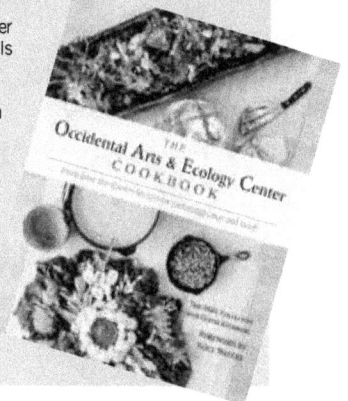

The Occidental Arts & Ecology Center COOKBOOK

this, but let's have fun while we're doing it. Let's find pleasure in the pursuit."

Most of the staff and resident cooks in the OAEC kitchen came to cooking through a combination of farming and communal living and have little to no formal culinary training. We take for granted our instinctual relationship to growing and cooking food, knowing from experience that **what grows together, goes together.** You could say we've acquired a high level of "vegetable literacy," as chef and author Deborah Madison calls it. Recipes are rarely used in the OAEC kitchen—not only is it extremely hard to find accurate recipes that are scaled up to feed a crowd, but we have mostly cooked by feel, improvising and teaching one another our tips and tricks, and collectively developing a style of treating vegetables rather than an actual body of hard and fast recipes.

We hire cooks from our team to prepare food for large workshops, but most nights of the year, especially during the winter slow season, the residential community of around 20 people shares dinner together by taking turns with the cooking. Like most American households with full-time jobs and busy schedules, each of us individually does not have time to make a healthy dinner from scratch every night. But with rotating kitchen duties, we each have to cook dinner only once every two or three weeks, if that. So when your night rolls around, it's like throwing a dinner party! We have time to plan ahead and take great pride in preparing something delicious and wholesome for everyone, each one trying to outdo the other with an over-the-top creation that we could never otherwise pull off on a daily basis.

Preparing a community dinner at OAEC usually starts with the question "What do I feel like eating?" Chances are, that's what everyone else wants, too. Is it time for an outdoor BBQ or a cozy dinner by the woodstove? Then comes a stroll through the garden to harvest the requisite salad plus whatever else is abundant and looking vibrant. What's in the "up for grabs" section of the walk-in cooler that needs using up? Check the chalkboard for a head count—who has signed out for dinner or is anyone expecting extra guests? Once all the variables are accounted for and a plan is made, it's time to dig in. Start to finish, most people take around three hours to pull it together, from harvest to dinner bell, plus another couple of hours for the cleanup—sounds like a lot, but the payoff is that for the rest of the month, it's simply a matter of showing up to the feast!

In the regular practice of breaking bread together, we cultivate a deep sense of commitment to the land and to one another. Because so many food cultures and traditions have been gobbled up by colonization and capitalism only to be regurgitated and sold back to

us in a processed, packaged form, Americans are ravenous for authentic food and authentic food culture.

So, in the spirit of Carlo Petrini's slow food "protest of pleasure," we resist the industrialized food system not only through voicing our resistance to pesticide use, factory farming, and other unsustainable food practices, but by living out the solution pathway and co-creating the kind of

> ## We resist the industrialized food system by co-creating restorative, celebratory, land-based culture.

restorative, celebratory, land-based culture we want to see thrive.

As Sowing Circle member and OAEC Executive Director Dave Henson puts it: "Without art and celebration, the revolution is no fun!"

Olivia Rathbone, lead author and project manager of The Occidental Arts and Ecology Center Cookbook: Fresh-from-the-Garden Recipes for Gatherings Large and Small *(Chelsea Green, 2015), currently manages the dynamic kitchen at OAEC and has tended the vibrant hearth of the community from the garden to the table for more than a decade. A lifelong farmer and cook, she orchestrates the inventive meals inspired by seasonal produce from the Mother Garden. See oaec.org.*

Fours Ways to Grow at Heartwood

By Sandy Thomson

Beth Walker's garden.

Here at Heartwood Cohousing, growing food is an important part of our community mix. We live in southwest Colorado, in the high desert. Growing food is a little harder here than in other places. We have to maintain faith that things will work out. The rains will come, the grasshoppers won't eat everything, and we need to help each other out—you never know when an early freeze will hit. We own a lot of land, 365 acres. Seventy of those acres are irrigated pasture or farm land and another five are irrigated around the housing cluster.

We have four different ways to participate in growing food on our land. The first and simplest is choosing to grow your own garden in your own yard. In permaculture speak, this is a zone one endeavor.

Beth Walker is one of our home gardeners. She loves her garden. It brings her joy and connects her to the land. It is a private thing to her—personal. It is only a step from her back door and she is fond of telling people that she just throws her leftover food scraps out her door into her garden. She enjoys watching them decompose and turn back into dirt. She feels satisfied when she is able to harvest food for her family and sometimes even enough to share with her neighbors. It is her sanctuary, a meditative space, a place of beauty and wonder. It is important to her and to her place in the community.

I remember the joy in her voice when she was telling me of the day she spent with Niema (a little neighbor girl) planting seeds. I know the sense of calm that comes to her face when she steps outside to enjoy her little garden. I am glad Beth has her garden and believe it is an important part of her experience of living in Heart-

wood. When I interviewed her, another important aspect that she shared with me is that it is a place where she can just do whatever she wants when she wants to. Oftentimes living in community can involve thinking of others a lot and asking permission and running projects by teams for approval, but in Beth's garden, she's the boss!

• • •

A zone two gardening opportunity is to be a member of the garden and greenhouse team. This team manages our 33-foot-diameter Growing Spaces growing dome and the raised beds surrounding it. I asked Rob Quinlin, one of our newer members, why he chose to be part of the garden and greenhouse team and this is what he shared with me:

"There's a feeling I get when I am eating a meal that was 100 percent produced from the land on which I live that allows me to feel a connection that I don't get from even eating in local restaurants where most of the food is locally sourced. I support the local food movement and applaud those businesses which strive to source ingredients locally. I vote with my dollar to keep those practices a possibility for the owners and encourage their dedication to further support local farms and have a connection with the surrounding land. There is something about eating food that is grown near to where you live that helps you feel like you are connected because you and the food are respiring the same air and growing with the same nutrients.

"When it's possible, cultivating the food yourself is a magical endeavor that puts yet another factor into the equation: sweat equity.

When I am eating a salad that was 100 percent grown in our community growing dome, I can taste the powerful Colorado sunshine. Each bite brings up memories of the beginnings of each ingredient. I remember preparing the soil, planting the seeds, thinning the plants, transplanting, tending, and watering them on my assigned days. I share the responsibility of tending to the needs and tasks of our community.

"One day a week, I get to spend anywhere between an hour to three hours in the sunny warmth of the dome tending to the plants and fish. Our dome is an oasis in the winter months where I get to give my time to the plants that give themselves to sustain me. It's a beautiful cycle that brings much more meaning to each meal. I value the fruits and vegetables of my labor, as someone who spent his childhood growing up in the kitchen and eventually working in kitchens. Having grown the ingredients I mix together is a very special opportunity to see a meal from start to finish. Sharing the responsibility of the growing dome with others is a convenient way to be involved in growing without feeling overwhelmed with the daily needs.

In the Harmony Garden, you can see and feel the beauty of Nature.

"I believe that the cooperative approach makes the experience even more meaningful, as it also builds the relationships amongst the members of my community. We get to learn from the wisdom each brings to the process, and thus cultivate our relationships alongside our plants. Aside from the joy of spending time with the plants and fish that live in our dome's water tank, and having the variety of food to harvest daily for a meal, we as the Greenhouse team also get thanks from our community members, who also get to harvest food for use in their meals at home. Knowing we are also sustaining our neighbors outside our family brings us all closer together, and hearing praise from our community at having such a bounty to harvest is another part of the reward for our work.

"I have learned so much about the care of plants during my time on the Greenhouse team, from both the plants and my team mates. The connection to what I eat, the relationships that our collective work has fostered, and the meditative time spent watering and caring for the plants has provided so much for me physically and mentally. There is no better way to find connection with both the land and the people than growing food.

"This work has brought me into sync with the things I used to see but didn't feel any connection to, like the seasonal movements of the sun, rainfall amounts, the temperature and humidity, and the slow but steady growth of the world of plants around me. It has also brought me into sync with the people around me as we collectively work toward producing healthy food to grow our bodies and spirits. Knowing that others also value the process of investing time and energy into the cultivating of both food and relationships provides a link that connects us above even the common value of healthy food for our families.

"To readers of your article, I would say: I encourage you to plant a garden, invite neighbors to help and grow food there, and offer what you harvest to friends. Even when animals eat your vegetables, and some unseen blight or frost damages the plants, or when you just get unlucky with the season, it will still be worthwhile when you stand back and look at what you have planted, the love and energy you have invested, and the harvest you get to enjoy. Get your hands dirty and spend some time tending to the soil that is underfoot all around you. It makes our time on this planet, spinning around the sun, more meaningful, and each meal a reward."

• • •

A little further away, but a bigger endeavor, is the Harmony Garden. This is roughly a two-acre deer-fenced area that contains fruit trees and bushes, a spiral garden full of perennial herbs and flowers and medicinal plants, and an old goat shed that has housed goats, turkeys, and now chickens and also has a place for tools and an area to relax out of the sun. It even has a small swing set and play structure for kids to enjoy. And bees. This is my favorite place to garden alone and with community members. It is always evolving, ever changing depending on who wants to participate and how much energy they have. Next year the upper half with the fruit trees in it will have about 50 chickens rotated around it to control weeds and grasshoppers and fertilize around the fruit trees. The lower half will be gardened by whichever families, couples, or singles want to have a bed or two to care for there.

We have work days to get everything ready, we share in the cost of manure, straw, tiller rentals, and even share seeds. Heartwood has an extensive seed bank that we are all welcome to take advantage of and contribute to. I see the Harmony Garden as a place for ceremony, for children to explore growing food, for anyone who wants to see how everything is connected, how beautiful nature can be. This garden is down in our irrigated pasture land. From there you can see the sun rise and set. You can hear the birds sing and see the eagle or hawk circle overhead hunting for mice or rabbits. I have seen coyotes

Enough to share.

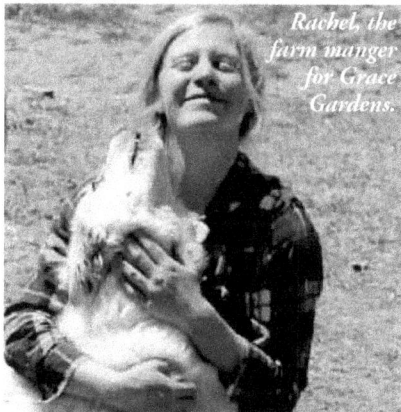
Rachel, the farm manager for Grace Gardens.

Beth Walker and Niema.

The Harmony Garden: Cole helping to harvest pumpkins.

growing food for Heartwood members—the fourth way to participate in food growing here. This is what she has to say:

"The mission statement of my little business is 'caring for the land, nourishing the neighbors.' I really enjoy working with the land that is stewarded and loved by our community. Equally so, I really enjoy nourishing my friends and neighbors at Heartwood. I am a strong believer in the importance of building local economies, and the little food system we have going here feels great to be a part of. I love that I can sell a lot of my products right here through our store. I can stock the store any time of day, and likewise, members of Heartwood can shop here whenever they want. It's the most convenient and socially responsible shopping I've ever heard of! We have had challenges with the store... mostly involving clear communication, expectations, and trust. But I think that we are getting better and better at making it work smoothly and sustainably.

"One of my favorite things about the design of Heartwood is the ease of helping each other out with little things. I have received farm tools, business information, chore favors, advice, and emotional and physical support...all for the benefit of my small farm business and personal well-being. Members of Heartwood hold a wide variety of talents and skills. I am so grateful to be able to lean on and bounce off of the members of my community in order for my business to thrive.

"I can't imagine trying to start out all alone as a farmer."

To sum it up, I would say that growing food plays such an important role at Heartwood that I could not imagine what life here would be without it. We have celebrations around the seasons as a result, we have amazing common meals that feature many things grown here on our land, and we have a deep appreciation for each other through the sharing of tasks and knowledge. ❧

from that garden. Rattlesnakes live there, along with skunks, squirrels, wild turkeys, and red-winged blackbirds. The sight of a mountain bluebird sitting on one of the fence posts silhouetted against a clear blue sky is an image I carry in my heart. To me the Harmony Garden is the heart of Heartwood. It is the heart of our land and it provides an almost spiritual connection to the land we are committed to stewarding. Not only does it provide food but it creates community. It provides a place away from the cluster of homes where you can see and feel the beauty of Nature. You can take a short walk and be alone with the plants and animals or you can go down with a group and experience the camaraderie of doing something enjoyable together.

• • •

Rachel, one of our members. was an intern here when we had a thriving farm and intern program. She learned to love the land and the community. She left but is now back running her own business

Sandy Thomson is one of the founding members of Heartwood Cohousing in Bayfield, Colorado (www.heartwoodcohousing.com). She and her husband Mac have raised three children at Heartwood. Sandy created and ran a homeschool co-op when her kids were little, helped create an organic farm on Heartwood's property, and is passionate about food and education. You can reach her at sandykthomsonrisk@gmail.com.

Belfast Ecovillage Produces Farm

By Sarah Lozanova

Sunday mornings at Belfast Cohousing and Ecovillage begin with Swiss chard, green onions, and piles of kale. Once a week, neighbors harvest veggies from Little River Community Farm, the three-acre on-site community supported agriculture (CSA) farm at the ecovillage. It is a worker-share arrangement, so neighbors dig in the dirt, snip, wash, and bundle the farm bounty together, while discussing recipe ideas.

Belfast Cohousing and Ecovillage is 36-unit multigenerational community in Midcoast Maine that has attracted members from all walks of life, including musicians, gardeners, educators, and naturalists. The 42-acre property was formerly a dairy farm, but is slowly turning into an ecovillage, with gardens, walking paths, bird watching, and many more ideas for the future.

Despite being a rural property, the homes are clustered to preserve open space and the built area is limited to six acres. Many of the super-energy-efficient homes are near net zero, with solar panels powering and heating the homes. The construction phase of the project is nearly complete, and only two units remain unsold.

"To me, a really important part of being a member of Belfast Ecovillage is the farm, where we raise food and work together," says Jeffrey Mabee, an avid gardener. "The CSA has really answered my prayers about that. Having young farmers using the land in such a responsible way feels right. The farm feels like the heart of any intentional community. It has a much greater significance than merely producing food."

The farm cofounders, Brian Hughes, Jenny Siebenhaar, and Amy Anderson, are all members of the ecovillage, and founded the farm last year. Hughes and Siebenhaar were farm apprentices in Europe in the early '90s, where they learned about permaculture and organic methods. They have managed three other CSA farms in recent years.

The farm at Belfast Ecovillage is unique because the current 22 farm members collectively own the land as members of the ecovillage, reside at the community, and contribute to maintaining the farm. An additional share purchased by community members is donated to the Belfast Soup Kitchen weekly.

"Little River Community Farm is the coolest CSA out there," explains Hughes. "Because the members also own the land and will have a long-term relationship to it, we can plant perennial crops like asparagus."

In the fall months, Belfast Ecovillagers start to notice the scarcity of cool storage space for fall crops. With slab-on-grade construction, the homes do not have basements. The common house, however, will have a root cellar, helping to alleviate this limitation. For now, many members can or freeze surplus vegetables.

It is common to see children at the farm workdays and harvests, where they develop a deeper relationship with their food and find an opportunity to learn. "I didn't learn where food comes from growing up," says Hughes. "I grew up in the suburbs and I was in my 20s before I knew what potato, beet, or carrot plants looked like."

Because Belfast Ecovillage is just completing the construction phase, farm projects have given members the unique opportunity to connect with the land and do physical labor together. Until this point, much of the community work has occurred in meetings—in planning and setting policies.

Some community members really appreciate how Belfast Ecovillage helps promote a healthy lifestyle. The weekly harvests help keep members active as they pick and haul the veggies. The community farm promotes culinary exploration and a high content of vegetables in the diet. Of course there is also a challenge associated with using a new vegetable such as kohlrabi or consuming all the kale that might arrive with a share.

"It is as fresh as you can get, like getting it from your own garden," says Hughes. "That impacts nutrition and taste. We're avoiding most of the carbon footprint of the food and we don't use packaging except for recycled bags."

In addition to the farm, there are several other multi-family farming initiatives in the community. There are two multi-household egg clubs, where members raise hens, while sharing the eggs, labor, and expenses. There have also been three multi-family flocks of meat birds during warmer months. Many Belfast Ecovillagers dream of having an orchard and then canning the harvest in the common house that is currently under construction. There is also interest in having livestock in the community, but the visions for the land are limited to the 36 acres available.

There is a widespread passion at the ecovillage for homegrown food. "Somehow when you are part of growing food, it feeds you more than just physically," explains Siebenhaar. "It feeds your soul and spirit and there is a beauty to this. It goes beyond calories, vitamins, and minerals." ~

Sarah Lozanova is an environmental journalist with an M.B.A. in sustainable management from the Presidio Graduate School. She has lived in several intentional communities and now resides in Belfast Cohousing and Ecovillage (mainecohousing.org) in Midcoast Maine with her husband and two children.

Photos courtesy of Sarah Lozanova

The Balancing Act of Farming in Community

By Coleen O'Connell

Cedar Mountain Farm's hay barn at Cobb Hill Cohousing.

Today started with sun but the sky has clouded as a major February northeaster blows into New England, promising a much-needed snowfall to deliver us from paths coated with treacherous ice. The children of Cobb Hill are anticipating a snow day and the best sledding conditions they have had yet this winter of 2014/15. A foot of new snow on our steep hillsides will delight not just the young, but a few of us old ones as well.

Meanwhile the cows, horses, sheep, and llama are nestled warmly in the barn. Calves are due so we'll see if any of them make their way into the world during the storm. The chickens probably won't venture out of their hut on wheels, but they will lay their eggs as usual. The car ballet (moving cars from lot to lot) will begin when the plow guy arrives to clear us out. We'll be in trouble if the electricity goes down and we can't chatter back and forth on our listserv advising where to move cars and when. The hustle and bustle of life on "the Hill," as we call it, will not be stopped by a mere snowstorm.

In 1991, Donella Meadows, coauthor of *The Limits to Growth* (1972), wrote in her nationally syndicated Global Citizen column, "Though I didn't grow up on a farm, I've been attracted to them all my life. When in 1972 I finally came to buy my own home, it was a farm. My psychological roots grew instantly into its cold, rocky soil. I have tried several times to leave it, reasoning that I could write more if I didn't spend so much time shoveling manure, that I need to be where the political action is, that I'm not a very good farmer anyway, that New Hampshire is a terrible place to farm. But I've always come back. Something deep in me needs to be attached to a farm."

She would eventually leave that farm in New Hampshire and move across the Connecticut River to the rural Upper Valley of Vermont, buying two adjacent dairy farms. With friends, she set out to found a "farm-based" community that would integrate principals of sustainability into all aspects of design and practice. The cohousing movement provided a useful model to help self-organize rather than re-invent the wheel. One of the original farmhouses became the headquarters of The Sustainability Institute, now the Donella Meadows Institute in Norwich, Vermont, and the process of planning and developing a cohousing community on the side of Cobb Hill went into full motion.

Moving with her to Vermont were her farming partners, Stephen Leslie and Kerry Gawalt. Choosing the rocky hillside to plant the homes left the prime agricultural fields available for farming. Kerry and Stephen and Donella would arrive on the property in the fall of 1999 with seven Jersey heifers, two Norwegian Fjord workhorses, and a draft pony named Bill. More people joined the development, moving closer to the community as the homes were being built. Stephen and Kerry began milking in 2000, and a group of Cobb Hill members began making cheese shortly after.

Farming Enterprises at Cobb Hill

Cobb Hill residents are co-owners of 270 acres of forest and farmland. Early in the development of the community, an enterprise system was started, allowing members to use common resources of land and buildings to bring sustainable agriculture and forestry products not only to the Cobb Hill community but also to the surrounding community and beyond. It is a free lease system with the idea that best practices will result in continued productive farmland and forest, with sustainability at the forefront of everyone's products. Money from sale of the development rights to the Upper Valley Land Trust and funds from the Vermont Housing and Conservation board were contributed to help make one of the homes qualify as an

rooms, and Frozen Yogurt (six flavors). Pigs and broiler chicken enterprises are in hibernation and might emerge again in the future. There are dreams of adding a few more enterprises. Local food is booming in Vermont and Cobb Hill is proud to be part of this movement.

Of the 23 families (40 adults, 16 children) living at Cobb Hill, few make their living through the enterprises at Cobb Hill. Most are hobby enterprises that might net participants a small profit in any given year. Most enterprises are co-operated by various members of Cobb Hill, which can change membership from year to year. Some have investment capital that can be put in or taken out; others are standing operations that need labor only. At last count, there were 18 adults involved in the enterprises of Cobb Hill, and one high school student who oversees the Community Chicken enterprise.

At Cobb Hill, you quickly discover that you are not on a typical working farm.

Your first impression upon turning into the drive of Cobb Hill is that you have entered a working farm. The large red barn with a Farmstand sign greets you, the silo stands tall against the sky, and the machine shed yawns at you showing off its riot of tools, farm equipment, pails, fencing, and countless miscellaneous gadgets. Once past the barn you have only to look up the hill to see the passive solar homes perched solidly on the shale bedrock hillside. You know you are not on a typical working farm.

"affordable" housing unit. It was written into the Land Trust Agreement that an affordable unit should always be available for a farm family.

Gathering momentum, the enterprise system has operated at Cobb Hill for the past 15 years now boasting many enterprises—CSA Market Garden, Jersey Dairy Milk, Cobb Hill Cheese with two Artisan cheeses, The Farmstand, Hay, Maple Syrup, Icelandic Sheep, Chickens, Honey, Shiitake Mush-

Cedar Mountain Farm is the enterprise started by Stephen and Kerry when they first moved to Cobb Hill with Donella. They produce sustainably grown vegetables, fruit, hay, flowers, milk, beef, and Jersey heifers. They use the Community Supported Agriculture system to market their vegetables, along with direct sales of their products through the Cobb Hill Farmstand (open every day for the passerby or local Cobb Hill or Hartland residents), private sales, mail order, and local farmers' markets. Wholesale accounts are set up with Cobb Hill Cheese and Cobb Hill Frozen Yogurt, Dairy Farmers of America Coop, area restaurants and farms, and 12 gallons a week of direct raw milk sales go to residents of Cobb Hill and the surrounding community. The Jersey heifers are sold through Jersey Marketing Services to supply the national milk market.

Making artisan cheese at Cobb Hill.

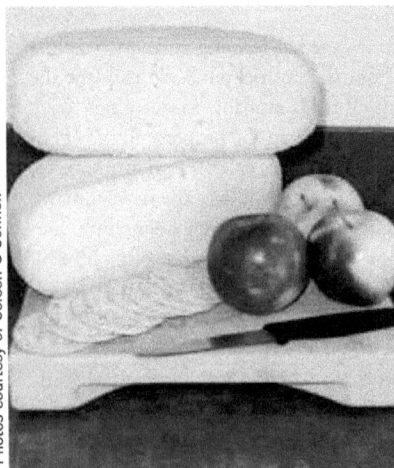

Photos courtesy of Coleen O'Connell

Plowing with Fjords at Cobb Hill.

Halloween harvest at Cedar Mountain Farm.

Cows grazing at Cedar Mountain Farm.

A fall day on the farm.

The farm business demonstrates the viability of using horses for traction power on the farm and to educate the public about the value of local-sustainable agriculture. The farmers have 17 acres in hay, 35 in pasture, and the balance in garden and greenhouses...altogether about 60 acres of Cobb Hill land. They feed an average herd of 50 young stock, steers, bred heifers, and milking cows, plus four working horses. (Cobb Hill Enterprise report, 2013.) Stephen is also an author, having published *The New Horse-Powered Farm* through Chelsea Green Publishers (2013); another book specifically on market gardening with horses is due to the publisher in a few days. He's not your typical farmer either.

Value-added products have enhanced the opportunities for this small-scale farm to gain recognition. Award-winning Cobb Hill Cheese and Cobb Hill Frozen Yogurt are products of the raw milk, rich in butterfat, of the Jersey cows. Owned and managed separately by other Cobb Hill residents, the cows are fed specifically to elicit the kind of milk needed to make the artisan cheese. A symbiosis is in play—without the quality Jersey milk, the award-winning alpine cheese would not be possible. Without the cheese, and the frozen market, the farmers would have to sell their milk on the larger volatile milk market.

Dairy farms in America have been on the decline for the past century. Vermont continues to support a small cadre of small-scale farms, but in the agribusiness world that has taken over, doing agriculture is a rare thing these days. Less than two percent of the US population now makes any of their income from farming and less than one percent makes all their household income from farming. Stephen and Kerry are committed farmers, loving what they do, doing it the best they can with what they have, yet struggle to support themselves and their daughter.

Struggles, Tensions, and Conflicts

So from all that you have read so far, you might conclude that the experiment at Cobb Hill is not only successful, but is a model for how one can do community and farming cooperatively. To some degree that is true, but taking off the rose-colored glasses, there have been struggles, tensions, and conflicts that have plagued this farm/community system over the years and continue to do so.

In the larger economic world of agriculture, as mentioned above, there is little support for the small-scale farmer. When Cobb Hill set out to do farming and community together, they devised what seemed like a wise and cutting-edge system to support a small farming enterprise. Fifteen years later, we are learning and growing from the conflicts and tensions that have surfaced time and again over the course of the community. The community support has come in the form of lease-free land, use of existing farm buildings, maintenance of those buildings over the years, and help with major tasks of hay and some field work.

As a newcomer to this community, I experience a lack of physical participation of the community in the farm for various com-

(without the investment expenses that keep many young farmers from fulfilling their dreams), they also have to contend with market prices for grains, hay, supplement, as well as the unstable prices for milk. They are too small to qualify for the subsidies that larger corporate dairy farmers might enjoy, but in truth most of the subsidies these days are going to mega farms growing soy and corn. So they must make their way through the small Vermont-focused agriculture grants that come through the state, and scale back any investments in infrastructure or stock to just those that they can afford from year to year.

Even though the Cobb Hill cheese and yogurt enterprises pay above-commodity prices for their milk, when you add vet bills, machinery, vehicles, gas, pasture upkeep costs, and other items to the list, you shortly begin to see that a 24-head milking herd and several acres of vegetables do not net you much in the end. A seven-day-a-week regimen of milking twice a day means the farmers must hire farmworkers in order to not exhaust themselves completely. By the time they are finished paying all the bills, there is little money left for Stephen and Kerry's salary.

Income variations among those who live at Cobb Hill can make farming among a cohousing community socially challenging. While Kerry rises at 5:00 each morning to milk, I personally work only half-time, and online, so I can pretty much do my work whenever I want during the day and week. I hear her crunch through the snow outside my window each morning as I turn over and thank my lucky stars I am not needing to milk in the dark at -21 degrees F, as was the case for Kerry this morning. I make a very modest salary but it is still more than what Kerry and Stephen make working 16-hour days on the farm. How

Income variations among cohousers can make farming socially challenging.

plicated and complex reasons. Some have to do with people's busy schedules and commitment potential for tasks, some have to do with insurance and what the farmers can invite people to do, some have to do with personalities and how communication happens. Ultimately this lack of participation remains a source of stress in the community that needs tending to on a regular basis.

From my interviews with residents it seems that most were attracted to Cobb Hill because of the farming aspect of the community. What a great place to raise kids and have fresh homegrown food! Most people at Cobb Hill know little about farming, however, and less about dairy farming, and have little knowledge of the market forces that drive agribusiness in this country. It is difficult to escape the larger economic systems that control agriculture in our country and world.

Though Kerry and Stephen can feel grateful and blessed to have lease-free land to farm

does a community manage and deal with income inequality? How do we talk about this without being whiney or eliciting guilt or shame? It is a conversation we are due to have.

Managing 270 acres, 125 of which are forest and a maple sugar bush, plus trails, and the infrastructure of maintaining 20 households plus a common house with three apartments, takes the time and energy of the larger Cobb Hill community. Tensions in the community can arise because there is much work other than farming to be done in a land-based cohousing community, and Stephen and Kerry have little time for anything beyond keeping the farm going and raising their young daughter.

How does a community that prides itself in the working farm balance its desire for broader community engagement, while accepting that farm life may not make community involvement possible? How do we accept that Kerry and Stephen are adding a great contribution to the community even without showing up? This stress is one we spend a good deal of time talking about and grappling with. Kerry and Stephen are beginning to see that though they are stretched for time, showing up makes a huge difference. Life at Cobb Hill

A waffle morning.

and in any intentional community is a balancing act.

Many could argue that the community could be more engaged in the farm, allowing for shared workloads, thus relieving Kerry and Stephen of some of their duties. Many would love to do this, actually. But it's nice in theory, harder in practice. As is often the case, it is more complicated to have volunteers than just do the work yourself. Certainly large actions such as putting up hay bales or weeding the corn patch can benefit from volunteers. But when raising animals, you want only those trained well or those in training to be the ones who deal directly with your most valuable resource. These cows are not just taken care of, they are nurtured here at Cobb Hill. Kerry is proud of her Jersey cows and she runs a tight ship in the barn. She holds to high standards and will not compromise on many things. You want a farmer in your community farm to have this work ethic and commitment. Running a farm by consensus or volunteerism is a recipe for disaster...and not just for the humans. Yet people like myself can continue to romanticize how wonderful it is to be living in a community with a farm, while I plan my two-week upcoming vacation to Hawaii.

An Evolving Vision

Almost 14 years since her death, Dana Meadows' spirit resides here at Cobb Hill, as do her ashes. Her dying at the beginning of this experiment left a community of people, overtaken by their grief, struggling with the task of figuring this all out without her extraordinary vision and collaborative spirit. Her words continue to guide us as we begin to take stock of the system we have created here for farmers and community to be in collaboration with each other.

We still hold out a sustainable vision for our world...hopefully using the definition that she spoke of in a speech in Spain in the fall of 1993: "I call the transformed world toward which we can move 'sustainable,' by which I mean a great deal more than a world that merely sustains itself unchanged. I mean a world that evolves, as life on earth has evolved for three billion years, toward ever greater diversity, elegance, beauty, self-awareness, inter-relationship, and spiritual realization."

Life at Cobb Hill continues. The car ballet went off without a hitch. We didn't lose power. We begin in 2015 to take stock of what has been created here. It is time to re-examine our assumptions, expose what isn't working, create some new dynamics, always looking for ways to intervene in the system. Dana would be proud to know that we are evolving this farm/community she loved. ❧

Coleen O'Connell recently moved to the Cobb Hill community from Belfast Cohousing and Ecovillage in Maine, where she served on the leadership team in developing the project. Coleen is the Director/Faculty of the Ecological Teaching and Learning M.S. Program for educators at Lesley University in Cambridge, Massachusetts. Her professional and personal passion has been to explore ecological literacy and sustainability in the context of our personal lifestyle choices. She has traveled internationally with students living in and studying the ecovillage movement. She can be reached at oconnell@lesley.edu and welcomes your comments or questions.

Summer at Cobb Hill

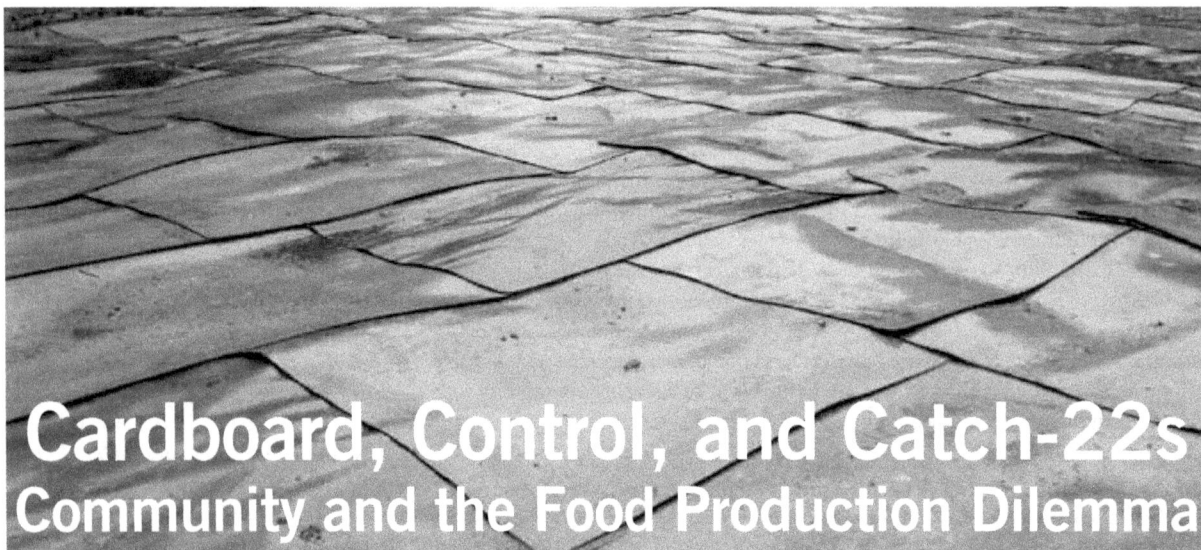

Moss Mulligan, 2015

Cardboard, Control, and Catch-22s
Community and the Food Production Dilemma

By Moss Mulligan

Editor's Note: *The author has requested pseudonymity, explaining: "This piece is intended primarily not as a critique of my community's gardening practices (gardening can be hard, often thankless work, even without random criticism in some magazine), but rather as an exercise in emotional release, self-reflection, and big-picture-assessment." We have honored this request.*

Cardboard. Not just a little cardboard—seemingly acres of cardboard. Cardboard topped by several inches of wood chips. A perfect formula for: suppressing annual weeds, yes, but encouraging perennial weeds. Tying up nitrogen in the breakdown of all that heavy-carbon material, so it is unavailable to growing plants. Creating a chunky and slivery woody-debris layer that, even when eventually mixed into the soil underneath, makes hands-in-the-soil gardening unpleasant if not impossible. Thwarting attempts to remove rhizomes of plants like quackgrass and bindweed. Voiding the garden of green living things, like cover-crop in the "off"-season, and introducing a barren, imported landscape dependent on (and reflecting the energy of) large-scale paper-product production, petroleum-fueled wood processing plants and/or wood-chippers, fossil-fuel-powered trucks and the roads those travel on, and the idea that we can just cover over what we don't like in life (such as those troublesome perennial weeds) and not have them come back stronger every time in reaction (which they do). We don't want to do the spadework, the forkwork, the hands-on work to address the problem in a more conscious, more effective, but more time-consuming way; we can cover over all those weeds in just a matter of hours, until all we see is: cardboard. And not just a little cardboard—seemingly acres of cardboard.

I myself have used cardboard to sheet-mulch many garden beds. Each time, I used the methods that I'd been taught, and that had proven effective. Cut down the vegetation underneath first. Remove all tape and staples from the cardboard. Be sure to overlap edges. Cover cardboard with a layered mixture of carbonaceous and nitrogenous materials (straw, grass cuttings, compost scraps, weeds, spoilt hay, manure), in effect creating a compost layer on top of the soil. Make this mulch *deep*—ideally at least six inches. And use this method only on an area that you are bringing into vegetable production for the first time or after at least several years of being fallow. This is a one-time conversion (of, for example, a lawn or a weedy disused area), to create or expand your usable

garden space. After this first sheet-mulching, it's fine to keep adding mulch every year, but cardboard should never again be necessary. Methodical attention to removing remaining perennial weeds that resprout through the mulch should obviate the need for any further choking of everything underneath. And, most important: leave wood chips out of the picture, or you'll have a very different, much less human-friendly animal for your vegetable garden soil.

Watching the transformation of garden areas that I once tended in my intentional community has been a lesson in letting go. Gardens that I used to spend hours in every day, filtering out perennial weed rhizomes from the soil in preparation for planting each bed, keeping the soil covered with green things throughout the year (the natural pattern in our mild mediterranean climate), giving plants individual attention, delighting in the beautiful, ever-changing artwork created by the diverse interplantings that I and those who joined me cycled through those beds—these have been turned into what look to me like cardboard-and-wood-chip-covered wastelands (and the parts that aren't cardboard-covered have no cover crop either—instead, they're being compacted and denuded by chickens and ducks that are allowed to free-range there). I would be very discouraged if I gave this situation energy—if I allowed it to matter to me still.

• • •

But I need to be honest with myself. Other things became more important to me than the task of keeping those gardens going in ways that would help my soul sing rather than cringe. Life itself shifted my focus elsewhere, by giving me a debilitating physical condition that made gardening painful and/or impossible for several years. I had to let go of the gardens I'd cared for so ceaselessly for so long. And in the way of community, other people, with other methods, temperaments, and preferences, stepped in to tend those gardens. Not only cardboard and wood chips, but rototillers (which I never used—I and my co-managers, interns, and apprentices gardened only with hand tools) now make at least annual appearances within every garden fence. Most of these gardens are empty of people most of the time, typically visited by work parties to accomplish big tasks. I no longer feel like going in there either—the wood-chip-laced soil, the clash with my aesthetic sensibilities, the foreign-to-me methods that I see creating only short-term (if any) advantages while contributing to longer-term problems, give me a desire to be almost anywhere else but in these places. The gardens used to be sanctuaries for me, but now I pass through them only quickly, if at all, usually accompanying children, who provide sufficient distraction that the distress I might otherwise feel isn't stimulated.

There's also more to this picture. Being free of the never-ending responsibilities of gardening has allowed me to open to so many previously neglected dimensions of life: in my own personal path and fulfillment, in my health and well-being, in interpersonal relationships, in community involvement, even in my sense of possibility, inner and outer evolution, and spiritual connection. Instead of constantly carrying an agenda, I feel more consistently able to be fully present in the "now." Time is now spacious enough to embrace the little and big miracles of life all around me (not just in the garden), and I find I enter easily into the wonder, curiosity, spontaneity, and joy of the community children that I now have time to give attention to. This ability to play a significant role in the lives of the young—and to make space for them to play a significant role in mine—feels easily worth the trade-off of no longer having any gardening responsibilities or even inclinations within my home community. Ideally, I'd combine these two elements—but given the choice, I'm happy to shift my focus to growing children rather than vegetables.

I'm obviously not a fan of my community's current food-production methods, but I don't think the practices that I used were actually sustainable or consistent with my deepest impulses either. I found a lot of joy in gardening—and still do, when I help friends in their gardens, away from the community—but in retrospect, my gardening efforts here were also fraught with contradictions. Whether in maintaining soil fertility (having chicken manure trucked in), in irrigating crops (using lots of grid electricity), in processing and storing food (ditto), in establishing work patterns that nourished rather than depleted those participating (I overworked and encouraged others to do the same), or in any of a slew of

In retrospect, my gardening efforts here were also fraught with contradictions.

other areas, my set of strategies often fell far short of something that, deep down, I could truly feel good about. Much of my continuing motivation depended upon a narrative of doing the best I could within an ethically and spiritually impossible situation, where every available choice was flawed, a Catch-22, when examined honestly. And in fact, almost every single modern approach I know to food production is fraught with similar, or worse, contradictions and problems—deleterious impacts on the natural world, on the people who participate and consume the fruits of the process, on future generations confronting an increasingly depleted world, and on our own souls as gardeners and farmers.

• • •

I would sum up these problems and impacts in a single word: control.

Most of our species' food procurement in modern times seems to be the result of our efforts to control the natural world—not to work with it. We decide what we will grow, and where we will grow it. We impose our

Moss Mulligan, 2009

Moss Mulligan, 2015

crops on the landscape. In order to make this happen, we also have to organize and in some sense control the people who will do the work. Virtually every cooperative gardening or farming situation that I have known of or been part of over the last 30 years—whether educational or production-oriented in focus—has encountered "control" issues among the people involved. I believe they're directly related to the fact that our food production is an attempt to control the plant and animal worlds too. Almost every cell of our bodies is built from the products of this control-dominated food production system, and we've been steeped in its paradigm our entire lives. It's no wonder then that we act it out in our relationships with each other, whether within or outside of the garden—but especially within, where the damage, the cultural wrong turn, may have originated.

Humans have always tended the land. But for most of our evolutionary history we were subtle gardeners, encouraging some plants and discouraging others within the palette of what grew naturally in the ecosystems we inhabited. We ate plants and animals but for the most part they were free, wild beings until we harvested and consumed them—and their relatives and offspring continued to live free and wild afterwards. And even after domestication started (as Michael Pollan has pointed out, this was a two-way process—we were domesticated by particular animal and plant species just as much as we domesticated them), our interactions with our "familiars" within those realms were for a long time much more nuanced, respectful, and equal than they are today. Only with the agricultural revolution was this order upended—something captured perfectly in one Native American's comment when the plow first arrived on the North American continent: "Wrong side up!" Most of us (except those gardeners careful not to invert soil layers, and those covering the soil with, ahem, cardboard instead) have been turning over the soil ever since, damaging not only the soil but ourselves in the process.

So it doesn't surprise me that whenever people get together to grow food, one person (usually he or she who takes most responsi-

> ## The plants and animals who fed us were free, wild beings until we harvested them.

bility) becomes the "problem" person, the one whose tendency to control (or sometimes, whose lack of the control needed to have any success in a control-based enterprise) rubs others the wrong way. I can likely count on the fingers of one hand the head farmers and gardeners I know, in communities and on farms, who have managed to avoid being labeled difficult or impossible to work with by some who tried to help—either for being a control freak or for not being in control enough. Even a hand that's had a run-in with the wrong piece of agricultural machinery would likely suffice for this count.

Another way must be possible—but the first step is recognizing that we have a problem. No matter what reassuring stories we may tell ourselves, simply growing "organic" food (whether using tractors, massive stacks of cardboard, or any other product of a control-based society)—and even doing that in community—will not save us from the fundamental contradictions the control paradigm has brought us. The words of Bob Dylan's "Idiot Wind" come to mind: "We're all idiots, babe; it's a wonder we can even feed ourselves."

Fortunately, it *is* a wonder. in a non-ironic way as well, that we can feed ourselves—that this whole world of life-nourishing-life exists, and that we're part of it. And as long as that's true, and as long as we're still managing to feed ourselves somehow, it's still possible to find *better* ways to feed ourselves. I predict this will be be one of the greatest challenges—and perhaps also greatest contributions—of communities and cooperative ventures in the next century, a century in which humanity will need to adapt rapidly rather than wallow in denial and delay. In the face of water shortages, soil depletion, climate weirding, peak everything, and massive social changes—and specifically, in transforming our relationships to food and most other areas of life—we will have to "shit or get off the pot." I look forward to it, as we definitely *won't* be in control, though the paths we choose will make a difference. ❧

Moss Mulligan is a communitarian, naturalist, and former garden coordinator who still occasionally finds ways to scratch the gardening itch.

From "Sketches of a life's last moments" by Claire Kerwin.

Glimpsing the Wild Within: The Sacred Violence of Eating

By Lindsay Hagamen

Editor's Note: *Vegetarian readers please be advised: this article contains graphic imagery involving animal slaughter and butchering.*

"People say that what we're seeking is a meaning for life...I think that what we're seeking is an experience of being alive, so that our life experience on the purely physical plane will have resonances within our innermost being and reality, so that we actually feel the rapture of being alive."
—Joseph Campbell, *The Power of Myth*

My hands, red with blood, are immersed in the still-warm flesh of the sow. With a knife sharp enough to take life swiftly, I cut through fat and muscle, trying to separate her head from the rest of her lifeless body. I'm struggling. With so much fat around her jowls, I cannot feel where to cut between the vertebrae. In my impatience, I resort to a saw, and with full-bodied strokes, push and pull the blade over the bone. It's neither elegant nor effective. But I need a way to ground myself—I'm in a state of exalted reverence.

We have just killed Willamena, a four-year-old sow we affectionately called "Willy." I helped raise Willy from a piglet, fed her nearly every day, and helped midwife her through three pregnancies. I learned from Willy new meanings of persistence, service, and love. I learned from her how far mothers will go to ensure the healthy survival of their strongest offspring. Willy inspired in me love, respect, and appreciation that created a powerful bond between us.

In the days following Willy's most recent pregnancy, I visited her pen regularly. On many of the visits, I found a limp piglet, so very peaceful, yet no longer alive. Willy's vision and hearing had been de-

teriorating and it had begun to impact her mothering. Currently, our land can only support one sow and her litter. So, with Willy's diminishing capacity to successfully raise healthy piglets, it was becoming clear that it was time to let one of her daughters succeed her. It was time to harvest Willy.

As the weeks passed, I resolved myself for Willy's coming death. On this day when we planned to harvest her, I spent a few hours with her, resting my head on her back, rubbing her belly, and scratching behind her ears. As she grunted contentedly, tears rolled steadily down my cheeks, wetting her skin. I would soon be taking her life, as she had taken the life of her own piglets.

There's a foreboding symmetry to it all: life feeding on life. The years of living in a forest, on a farm, one hour from the nearest grocery store, have instilled in me this humbling awareness about the web of life in which I am immersed. I sow seeds and harvest trees. I midwife the birth of pigs and then take their lives as dictated by the needs of the land and the demands of the seasons. This land is my grocery, my doctor, and my security.

My own existence is a collaboration of sun and soil, muscle and bone. Every day is an ecstatic celebration and a stoic fight. I too am vulnerable to the biting cold and the pangs of hunger. Coming face-to-face with my own place in the web of life has increased the frequency of my tears, the potency of my anger, and the quickness of my response. It has also enhanced the power of my love, the authenticity of my joy, and my desire to seek pleasure. It has ushered me into a life that is human, animal, and wild.

• • •

Humans have created stories since time immemorial. Mythological stories go far beyond a form of entertainment as they help us find purpose and peace in this remarkably complex, beautiful, and tragic world. Down through the generations, myths help pass the wisdoms that orient us to the world in which we were born, and guide us through the phases and stages of life. Myths have the power to shape lives and guide cultures.

One of the common themes in myth is a cosmology that reflects the subsistence practices dictated by the local ecology, helping place human culture in accord with nature. Joseph Campbell, a professor of comparative mythology at Sarah Lawrence College for nearly 40 years, shares a myth that establishes a covenant between the buffalo and the Plains Indians. The covenant affirms that the buffalo will come every year and give their lives to feed the people and the people in turn will bring them back to life through the sacred rites of the buffalo dance.

> ## Humans, squirrels, deer, coyotes, owls, and hawks—we are made from the same living Earth.

In the telling of this myth, Campbell offers that "the essence of life is that it lives by killing and eating. And that is the great mystery the myths have to deal with." These people, like most people the world over, were "living on death all the time, in a sea of blood." [*The Hero's Journey: The World of Joseph Campbell.* Documentary. 1987.] So this myth served to reconcile the human psyche with the harsh reality that life survives by eating life.

Campbell goes on to suggest that if we are to celebrate life for the miracle that it is, we must celebrate it as it truly is. But as a modern culture we are losing the capacity to distinguish between the "sea of blood" that flows from living a life in accordance with life itself and the "sea of blood" that flows from acting out of ignorance, greed, and aggression. Regaining the capacity to discern between these two dynamic forces may well save us from ourselves.

Today we live in a world that is full of needless atrocities. We live in a nation without guiding myths. We live in a culture where comfort, convenience, and progress disconnect so many from the places, processes, and creatures that are the sources of sustenance. What remains is a cultural crisis that is profound and widespread, a crisis of the conscious and our core identity.

What should we eat? Organic? Local? Vegetarian? Vegan? Raw? What if the animals are free-range? Or if the food will be otherwise thrown away? Maybe the answer lies in the Paleo diet? Or in the practices of Sally Fallon's *Nourishing Traditions*? We appear to be losing our bearings on how to relate to the very thing that gives us life and nourishment.

Emphasizing the importance of understanding local ecology in understanding ourselves, Wendell Berry observed that "You don't know who you are, if you don't know where you are." [Berry, Wendell. *Sex, Economy, Freedom and Community.* Pantheon, 1994.] I'd add that if you don't know the food you're eating, then you don't know who you really are.

• • •

Food is the most intimate connection I have with the Earth. When I eat, I am taking in the body of another being and making it part of my own. I am literally *incorporating* their cells into mine, their life into mine. I don't know of anything more intimate.

I can trace my life through the lens of trying to find right relationship with food. At the age of 10, I became vegetarian and pretended I was a calf at the dinner table. At 16, I became vegan, attended animal rights conferences, and recoiled at the horrors of factory farms, monoculture, and industrial agriculture. At 18, I started working on small-scale farms, helping to grow vegetables and fruit for local farmers' markets. At 23, I moved to Windward, a small land-based intentional community in southern Washington State, and started the process of integrating with this land—of consuming what this land provides at the nurturing hands of those who call it home. Seven years later, I am now of this plateau. Squash and greens and eggs and bone. Potatoes, lard, cheese, and plums. My body is made of the Earth I walk every day. I am bonded with those who too eat from this land—fellow humans, squirrels, deer, coyotes, owls, and hawks. We are made from the same living Earth.

I know that this process of healing, of unlearning and becoming human, is one in which I continually have to confront my deepest conditioning. I am no longer surprised when I find myself thinking something that a few years ago I would have considered heresy. The journey I am on is one that asks me to shed the things I carry that are not mine, and to integrate the part of me that had been lost. Through this process, I am slowly revealed to myself. Some parts are beautiful, some are unsettling. Some parts I can leave behind. Others, I learn, I cannot.

• • •

After I sufficiently tire myself with the saw and have made no meaningful progress separating Willy's head from the rest of her body, I humble myself and ask for help. Andrew takes the knife as I move around to take hold of her head. I sink my hands into the flesh and pull, creating more space between the vertebrae for Andrew to place the knife and sever the remaining connective tissue.

Sinking my hands into Willy's warm, bloody tissue ignites a series of conflicting feelings inside me. I feel horrified and content. I feel powerful and vulnerable, sickened and satiated. I mourn the loss of Willy's life—her contended grunts, her smile, the way her ears flopped when she ran towards food—and I simultaneously fill with a primal sense of comfort in knowing we have nourishing food for the coming winter. With Willy's body laying limp and dismembered in front of me, I have a heightened awareness of my own mortality—I can feel my muscles as they move and my lungs expanding with each breath—I know exactly what it would take for the life to flow out of my body as it has Willy's. Arising from the same primal place, I feel a heightened desire for my own flesh to engorge with blood, with life, and to surrender beneath the weight of a tender and impassioned lover.

Andrew looks up from where his attention has been focused on Willy's spine and our eyes meet. "Are you ready?" I nod. He swiftly separates the last of the connective tissue attaching Willy's head, and the full weight of her head falls into my hands.

At that moment, something shifts inside me: I stop fighting the part of myself that knows that these acts—killing, eating, living—are inherently violent. Holding her head dripping with blood, I feel like a monster. And I know I am. We just cut off Willy's head—an act that requires force, precision, and a desire to irrevocably damage something that was so meticulously (and miraculously) held together. I also feel intensely human. I feel alive and awake, captivated by my own physicality. I feel viscerally connected to Willy, to Andrew, to the grass underfoot, the trees at my side—to every creature who calls this land home. The weight of her head in my hands broke through another layer of the denial that had been keeping me from accepting the part of my humanity that is wild— the part of my humanity that is fighting for survival just like every other creature with whom we share this Earthly home.

We live in a violent world. I don't mean the needless atrocities that humans commit against fellow humans, against other animals, and ultimately against the land itself. I mean the violence of life feeding on life as a means of perpetuating itself. Of the lioness killing the zebra, of the brown bear catching the salmon, of the gardener pulling up carrots, of the deer eating the newly sprouted fir tree right down to the ground. A violence that I no longer want to deny and will perform with as much reverence as my body can muster.

For just as my body revolts against the experience of killing, so too does it find it deeply grounding. When my hands are immersed in another's flesh, every cell in my body knows I am alive. When my eyes catch sight of the beauty of the muscles or the intricate patterns of fascia and veins, I am mesmerized. When I am scraping the hide, a deep calm settles in. Even the first time felt familiar, like staring into the flames of a fire or feeling the beating heart of a beloved.

For me, harvesting another life for food—animals and plants alike— has become a sacred violence. I consider it part of the eternal dance of Life transforming itself from one form to another, and in the process infusing the transcendent into every mortal life form. It's a dance too complex for me to understand fully, but it's a dance that endlessly captivates me, and it compels me to engage wholeheartedly. And I do.

• • •

At Windward, we have, over time, developed rituals for killing animals. It's not the kind of ritual a modern pagan might imag-

ine. We do not declare intentions or call in elements. We do not sing organized song or stand in a circle.

The purpose, however, is clear. Blood, flesh, bone, and earth are present in their rawness and potency. If we are lucky, the wind and rain will spare us. Song is spontaneous, arising out of personal relationship with the animal. The connection between the humans is intensely palpable. The energy starts out solemn, grows reverent, sometimes becomes jovial, and ends in fatigue and cold fingers.

Earlier in the day the primary caretaker of the selected animal will prepare the space. By then, many will have already said their good-byes—feeding a special treat or scratching in the favorite places. Some draw pictures, others sing songs. Each person chooses what is most meaningful for them. Those who want to bear witness to the death arrive before the designated time. When that time comes, a sharp knife slits the jugular, or a bullet penetrates the brain. It's startling how quickly life can fade. My heart always sinks and my stomach tightens. And the beauty of the crimson blood as it flows over snow, around stone, or under leaves, takes my breath away. A bond forever connects those who are present for the taking of life.

On harvest days, everyone lends a hand. With repetition, individuals grow into specific roles: the one who wields the knife, the one who operates the crane, the one who ferries meat to the kitchen. We endeavor to use as much of the animal as possible, from tanning the hide to rendering the fat, from preparing the organ meats to fertilizing the garden with blood and bone. The parts we cannot use, we feed to other omnivores on the farm. Then there is processing the meat itself. For the larger animals, we gather in the kitchen to cut, sort, and package for freezing, sausage making, or dry curing. For a few hours we tell stories, make plans, or work in silence. It's a classic example of many hands making light work. And even then, making full use of all the animal can take weeks or even months.

Having many skillful hands becomes a necessity when we live with the raw elements of the land. When we rely on each other for our daily bread, community quickly becomes a viscerally felt network of security. Nurturing community is as much a necessity of living with the land as knowing east from west. Each of us here at Windward carries a deep understanding that we cannot do this—live with a forest, on a farm— on our own. We rely on each other to create that felt sense of integration that comes when we know our food, the life it lived, the ground it walked, its last moments. We live through partnership, with the forest, with the animals, and with one another. It is through these partnerships that we come to know ourselves and that we become fully human. It is in this violent harmony that I have come to find peace. ☙

Walt Patrick
Welcoming new life.

Lindsay Hagamen lives, works, loves, and plays on the high plateau that descends off of Mt. Adams in Wahkiacus, Washington. She is a Steward of the Windward Community (www.windward.org), lover of the Wild, and co-editor of the recently released collection Ecosexuality: When Nature Inspires the Arts of Love *(www.ecosexbook.com).*

Cool Pickles

By Albert Bates

Photos courtesy of Albert Bates

A recent post to one of The Farm's many Facebook groups included a page from an August 1981 internal newspaper, *The Weekly Beat*, that gave a tally of our canning progress that month—12,634 quarts of various fruits, veggies, sauces, and pickles. As I described in the Fall 2013 COMMUNITIES (#153), the Farm (Summertown, Tennessee) has now become carbon-minus, net sequestering more than five times the annual greenhouse gas footprint of ourselves and our visitors. We accomplish this primarily with our forests, but to a growing degree we do it with good soil management, including keyline, compost teas, and biochar.

So how do these two things, pickles and biochar, relate? Biochar is both a miraculous store of organic carbon and a nutrient densifier in organic and biodynamic gardening. It has the potential to restore our climate to pre-Anthropocene. It has the potential to end hunger. And lately we've learned something else—the power of biochar as a nonalcoholic digestif.

Frances D. Burton, in *Fire: The Spark That Ignited Human Evolution*, dates hominid use of fire to 1.6 to 2 million years before present, and charcoal cooking to the beginning of that period. We don't know when the discovery of the gastric benefits of charcoal first arrived, but it may have come from the observation of the habits of animals, such as red colobus monkeys in Africa, who improve their diet by seeking out char from the forest floor after wildfires, enabling them to relieve indigestion caused by toxins in some leafy greens. Mother monkeys teach their young to do this, as indeed our own ancestors may have taught their young, even before we had speech and flint tools.

It may have been our ancient taste for charcoal that coded a segment of our taste receptors to favor foods cooked over glowing embers. Consider the popularity of the Hawaiian *luau*, Indian *tandoor*, Brazilian *rodizio*, Colombian *lomo al trapo*, Argentinian *parallada*, Japanese *yakitori*, and Indonesian *satay*. In Thailand and Korea, they use a small tabletop charcoal hibachi for thinly sliced meat and vegetables. While you cook, the meat and juices drip down into the second chamber, making the meat low in fat and giving you a rich broth to use as a soup or a savory sauce. Both meat and broth contain traces of biochar.

Biochar works in your digestive tract the same way it works in the soil—by providing habitat for the microbiome. By partnering with our own unique gastrointestinal fauna we can stimulate phage immunogenicity, fight off infection antigens, and reverse toxin-loading. Biochar gives us an immune boost.

At the Farm Ecovillage Training Center, mentors and apprentices gather to make biochar pickles, a year-round way to get tasty trace amounts into our diet.

When making food-grade biochar, we generally select for our substrate a woody-stemmed plant such as bamboo. We fine grind the char, using a coffee grinder at the last stage, reducing it to a feathery powder.

See our recipe for Biochar Shiitake Pickles *(sidebar)*, and enjoy!

Albert Bates is author of The Biochar Solution, Pour Evian on Your Radishes, Climate in Crisis, *and three cookbooks, among other titles. He was part of the founding of the Global Ecovillage Network and shared the Right Livelihood Award in 1980 for The Farm's work in preserving indigenous culture. See www.thefarm.org and www.thefarm.org/etc.*

Biochar Shiitake Pickles
Makes 4 pints

We started experimenting with this right after we had harvested the last of our summer eggplant and hard rains brought us a bounty of shiitake. We finished making the eggplant pickles as planned, following my mother's recipe from *The Farm Vegetarian Cookbook*, and then we made shiitake pickles the same way, adding a sprinkling of biochar.

Ingredients
2 lbs shiitake mushrooms
1 qt cider or white wine vinegar
2 Tbsp pickling salt
2 Tbsp biochar
2 c extra-virgin olive oil
5 cloves garlic, peeled and sliced
8 jalapeño peppers, deseeded and quartered lengthwise
1 fresh chili habañero, deseeded and chopped finely
Onion powder
Garlic powder
Sprigs of fresh thyme, rosemary, and sage

Preparation
Wash and stem the mushrooms and slice them across the cap in strips. Place the mushrooms and jalapeño slices and garlic cloves in a mixing bowl, layering in 2 Tbsp of pickling salt and 2 Tbsp of biochar and a few sprigs of fresh thyme, rosemary, and sage as you go. Compress under weight overnight. This will bring a salty brine to the surface that submerges the mushrooms.

The next day, prepare sterilized pickling jars and have them at the ready.

Drain off the brine. If you prefer reduced sodium in your diet, briefly rinse the mushrooms in a colander but try not to rinse away the herbs and biochar. Sauté the mushrooms in a wok of preheated olive oil, adding dashes of onion powder and garlic powder and the diced habenero, about 5 minutes or until the mushrooms and garlic begin to brown. Using a slotted spoon, remove the pickled veggies and immerse in a bowl filled with vinegar. Immediately place the hot veggies and pickling marinade into the sterilized jars, filling them to the very top. Put the lids on tightly to heat seal, then set aside until cool. Clean the jars, attach sticky labels, and write the date and the contents on them. Store somewhere cool and dark—it's best to leave them for about 2 weeks before opening so the pickles really get to marinate well, but if you absolutely cannot wait, you can eat them sooner. They'll keep about 3 months.

—A.B.

Small and Large Miracles:
Food, Land, and Community at Kibbutz Lotan

By Alex Cicelsky

"Welcome to this circle. I'm impressed by all the small and large miracles that had to happen in order for us to be here, at this time, in order to share this meal together. You've come from around the globe—Nigeria and Ghana; Taiwan and Thailand; Switzerland, Germany, and the UK; Brazil and Colombia; the US and Canada—to join us here in Israel because you want to learn together with us to build and grow food while caring for our earth and communities. On the table, made with earth plasters and recycled materials, is food that we've harvested from the garden.

"Look around. This food forest was only a few years ago a desert—one of the driest in the world; only sand. We've built soil from our composted food scraps, watered it with salty water that we cannot drink, and welcomed ever-increasing varieties of insects, bees, and butterflies that together nurture and protect most of the fruits. There are no industrial fertilizers, no herbicides or pesticides in this garden. The dates are organic—grown and harvested by our children. The marula beer comes from the fruits of these trees that shade us. What we haven't produced ourselves is all local. We made the bread together and cooked it on rocket ovens, which we'll learn more about—these energy-efficient ovens are fueled with the trimmings of our trees without deforestation.

"Some of you bless a meal by standing in silence together. Others express appreciation to the land and the cooks. It is normal at Jewish tables to say a blessing over bread. This is an unusual blessing which literally says Blessed in G-d who brings forth bread from the earth. All the other ancient Hebrew blessings over fruits are direct—fruit of the vine, fruits from the earth. I've never seen bread grow out of the earth. The intention here is for us to be a part of the miracle of food—harvesting the grains, preparing them, and cooking the bread. In this simple blessing we learn that in order to feed ourselves we are an integral part of the holy process of caring for nature and adding our creative input into supplying our most basic needs.

"So for this celebration meal let's be intentional in our permaculture view as we be begin our course by gleaning a blessing from the culture of this land, the local culture, and our community's vision: *Blessed are we from the Source of Creation, as stewards of the earth from which we bring forth our bread and sustenance. Let's all share in this bread as a symbol of how, when we share our wealth, we all benefit and there is enough for all.*"

Food production has been at the heart and economic center of Kibbutz Lotan since before we moved onto our site. We started as an agricultural cooperative. We were pioneers in our 20s in an unpopulated desert, growing melons, tomatoes, onions, and corn in sand using drip irrigation, spending 12 hours a day harvesting, sorting, and packing. We planted date trees and nurtured

Photo courtesy of Alex Cicelsky

them for years until they produced fruits. We welded the sheds for cows and opened a modern dairy. For us—city folk, Israeli and from the four corners of the earth—the ideal of the kibbutz was to return to the land, to be the workers, owners, and managers of our egalitarian and socialistic cooperative. Our life cycles were dictated by the climate and crops: seeding, harvesting, and land preparation. We were delighted to learn the ancient, agricultural roots of the Jewish holidays as the fruits and grains—the symbols of each of the festivals—ripened at the appropriate season from our trees or were harvested in our or neighboring fields. We paid our bills by turning salty water and modern agro-technologies into high quality fruits for the winter markets in Europe.

The date plantations now produce 460 tons of dates—half on brackish water and the other from processed waste water from the city of Eilat. Last year our dates were recognized as the best quality dates in the country. Our cows produce 3.6 million liters of milk a year. Those branches make up half our community's income. It is very hard to make a profit from field crops like garlic, potatoes, and watermelon, as we compete with Iberia, North Africa, and the Jordanian farmers we trained to meet European food production standards. The sandy fields receive tons of composted cow manure, solar powered computers measure every drop of water at the plant's roots, and open fields of crops are now covered with screen houses into which specific insects are introduced to manage the pests threatening the monoculture of peppers promised to the winter markets of Tel Aviv, Moscow, and London.

Our communal dining hall serves three meals a day from fresh produce, almost all locally produced (Israel is a very small country). Meat or fish appear on the menu only five times a week. Shabbat (the Sabbath) and holidays are welcomed with community banquets or potluck meals beginning with song and blessings over bread and wine led by community members with birthdays or celebrating a special life cycle event. On Pesach (Passover) and Tu B'shvat (birthday of the trees) we have Seders (literally "order") where food items representing fortitude, fortune, empowerment, rejuvenation, pain, slavery, and freedom are presented in poems, story, and song. The fall harvest festival of Sukkot is celebrated in a huge shed of our date palm branches, erected each year, under which we eat for eight days and nights. The spring harvest festival of Shavuot is a dairy products feast.

Our educational branch, the Center for Creative Ecology, is rooted in organic food production, nature conservation, and environmental activism. In 1996 we decided to begin separating our community's waste streams and composting food waste. This was revolutionary because there were no recycling industries in the country. Tourists and regional authorities were fascinated by our ability to take food waste and turn it into soil, and our use of non-biodegradable waste as construction materials. We remembered Rachel Carson's cry in *Silent Spring* and dedicated research into reinvented desert agriculture. The result was the Gan Bayit—Home Garden.

Having learned about the permaculture techniques of companion planting and forest gardens, we tried growing vegetables and herbs without pesticides, herbicides, or industrial fertilizers which are necessary in the commercial agriculture around us. Where there was once sand and a single Acacia tree, there is now a food jungle of lettuces, herbs (including mint from Mt. Sinai), sweet potatoes, tomatoes, broccoli and cauliflower, beans and eggplants, edible flowers and amaranth, onions and garlic, guava and olives and figs. Butterflies and many varieties of bees help us tell the story to visitors that diversity in nature nurtures stability, which is a message too for our communities and societies.

The Gan Bayit was the first CSA in Israel and served as the training center for many of the urban gardens and permaculture training centers across the country. Students of ours developed therapeutic vegetable gardening projects for handicapped inner-city children, mentally challenged adults, and women in prison. Our Solar Tea House, the second solar-powered grid-connected public building in Israel (the first was a school up the road from us), is a gourmet vegan and vegetarian restaurant at the edge of the Gan Bayit, serving produce from the garden and eggs from our free-range chickens. Waste water from the restaurant is treated and returned to the trees in the garden (and of course the guests love the classy no-water composting toilets).

Butterflies and many varieties of bees help us tell the story to visitors that diversity in nature nurtures stability.

While upwards of 8,000 human visitors walk through the garden every year, uncounted thousands of birds, wintering on Lotan or passing through to Africa, stop in for rest, food, and water. For them we let all the plants go to seed during the short spring migration, as the rows fill with bird watchers and researchers who know that the Gan Bayit (and all of Kibbutz Lotan) is a world-class birding hot spot (check out the movie *Bluethroats before Breakfast* filmed in the garden: wildlifevideos.net/israel1_new.html).

Our permaculture course is unique as it is seven weeks long. We need that time to give students practical, hands-on experience and full-cycle observation in food production from soil building and composting to seed, seedling, pollination, weeding, irrigation, harvest, seed collection, and food processing and storage. They harvest what they grow, cook in solar ovens, grind the food waste to feed the biogas system, and cook with its methane.

While most meals are with the community, the students living in solar-powered, strawbale (renewable agricultural waste) domes in the EcoCampus make their own food twice a week in mass ovens and rocket stoves fired from the limbs of trees in the neighborhood. Meals begin with "tuning in," as they have learned that food is a miracle, best prepared and eaten together, in celebration outside under a canopy of stars.

Alex Cicelsky is a founding member of Kibbutz Lotan, where his work at the Center for Creative Ecology includes research, teaching, planning new ecological infrastructure and development projects, outreach, and resource development. For more about Kibbutz Lotan, see www.kibbutzlotan.com and www.tinyurl.com/lotanvid3.

Celebrating the Local, Shared Bounty at Groundswell Cohousing

By Julia Jongkind

Author's daughter picking kale to eat. She now picks dandelions and asks her mom to make them into cookies.

Welcome to Groundswell Cohousing at Yarrow Ecovillage (British Columbia). We are a group of folks who love food: growing it, eating it, sharing and preserving it too. It has been what holds us together through thick and thin. At a fundamental level, sharing food is what sets the tone for our community.

Our cohousing group started out on the Yarrow Ecovillage with two new homes and two old farmhouses. One mom suggested a simple and low-work but high-benefits meal sharing plan. One day a week we would all eat together—a vegetarian meal. Each week a different family would cook for the others, showing their generosity, and the others would receive gratefully. We have a few vegetarians and we wanted to keep the cost low for all cooks. We also were not interested on calculating who owed what, as it seemed to divide the focus of eating together away from enjoyment into penny-splitting. This idea was enacted and a few changes made. Five years and 30 households later, we still do not have our common house finished, but we do have five meals a week and still cook for each other in turns. (Members of each household can attend as many as they wish; two to three meals per week is probably average.)

Without a common house, we have dined together in a variety of strange locales. We did start by eating in each others' homes, but we grew too large for that to continue. We then moved our meals to the bunker silo—which was great in the summer. In the winter we built a greenhouse-like structure inside the bunker silo and strung it with fairy lights. It was a bit cool and dim, but we all fit and ate many meals in that rustic setting. As we continued to build more homes, the bunker silo was dismantled and we moved into the Garage Cafe—better lighting and heat! Alas, we grew too large for even this grand space, and another locale was set up. Part of the old machine shed had been cleared out and set up for office space for a number of folks who worked from home. In the evening, it became our cosy dining hall. Notice that not one of these locations had a kitchen—we are all experts on one-pot meals.

Just recently we have changed again. With five meals a week available, each meal group got small enough to eat at each others' houses again, with some creative seating. For example, on Thurs-days there are eight adults and 11 kids signed up for the meal. When we hosted that meal, we placed the coffee table in the kitchen and, sitting on cushions, ate around it next to the kitchen table.

What makes these meals so connective to the wider community are the stories of where the food comes from and how it is prepared. The chefs who describe their offerings when local—like from our organic commercial farmers on our land, or from this amazing farmer they know from our nearby farmers' market—have the most joy-filled tales to tell us about what we are about to eat. We all get a matching twinkle in our eyes as we look at the kale and potato soup, knowing it was harvested locally with love.

One typical summer meal was described as follows:

Today for your dining pleasure we have my nasturtiums stuffed with local goat cheese from across the river. In the salad we have fresh spring mix from Osprey Organics (standing right there) with roasted beets and fresh grilled zucchini. Here are a number of infused oils and vinegars to drizzle on your meal and of course rice and red quinoa. For dessert there are melt-in-your mouth brownies and fresh berries with cream.

By the end of this delightful and detailed description, we are all drooling and ready to rave about the amazing food as well. It also sets a happy and positive tone for our dining conversations.

In cooking for each other and having regular meals together with local and fresh ingredients, we all feel blessed to live with each other, surrounded by such flavourful bounty. This positive outlook seeps into our work in our community, making us all aware of how good we have it here and how fortunate we are to have generous neighbors who cook well.

I wish you the joys of great company and great food regularly. ❧

Julia Jongkind is a mom of four kids aged 10 and under. She has lived in cohousing communities for the last nine years and currently is on the facilitation team at Yarrow Ecovillage (groundswellcohousing. ca). She chooses to homeschool her children and finds that living in an intentional community makes that a far richer experience. She also works from home as a Learning Consultant with a distance learning program and is just finishing her Masters.

II

SHELTER AND ECO-BUILDING

Beyond Sustainability: Building for Health

accommodating people with environmental intolerances in intentional community living

By Julie Genser

I cried when I read in COMMUNITIES' Health and Well-Being issue (Winter 2009) about Fred Lanphear,[1] an elder of the Songaia community who was diagnosed with Amyotrophic Lateral Sclerosis (ALS) and appealed to his community to help him face this last stage of his life with grace. His community embraced him, tucking him in to bed every night, helping him stretch and do yoga, and celebrating his life with a ceremony while he was still alive and able to participate. His story stood in stark contrast to that of artist and poet Bene Barrymore, a senior disabled by a toxic brain injury.[2] Instead of enjoying her retirement years in comfort, surrounded by family, Bene struggles for survival each year during pesticide spraying season. The 77-year-old has severe environmental sensitivities and the neurotoxic fumes from bug killers cause her to flee the comfort and safety of her home to live in her car for months every year to avoid becoming even more debilitated. Not exactly the ideal vision of how to spend one's retirement years.

Bene did not get a celebration from her community honoring her as an elder when she got sick; instead she gets to face difficult symptoms and a life on the run completely alone. There is little compassion in our world today for people whose very existence questions the sanity of a global dependence on chemicals, pharmaceuticals, petroleum, and other substances that make our culture of capitalism go 'round. Unfortunately, there is a hidden population of thousands of others like Bene, fleeing their homes and neighborhoods to escape the daily poisoning our chemically and electronically addicted society blindly and indiscriminately inflicts.

A New Conversation

As Joshua Canter wrote in his article "The True Need for Community,"[3] "the element of community is one of the greatest factors in healing." Who needs healing—and thus, community—more than those who are ill? And so I want to start a conversation. The conversation I'd like to start is this: What are intentional communities willing to do in order to accommodate those with chemical, electrical, and other environmental sensitivities? Are intentional communities willing to be educated about the difference between green/sustainable and non-toxic? Are intentional communities willing to expand their notion of disabled, and count non-toxic housing and common facilities as necessary as a handicapped-accessible bathroom? Are intentional communities willing to accept that sustainability issues may have to be relegated to the back burner in order for some people merely to survive?

Some of the basic facts:
+ **There are thousands, if not millions, of people in the world suffering** from

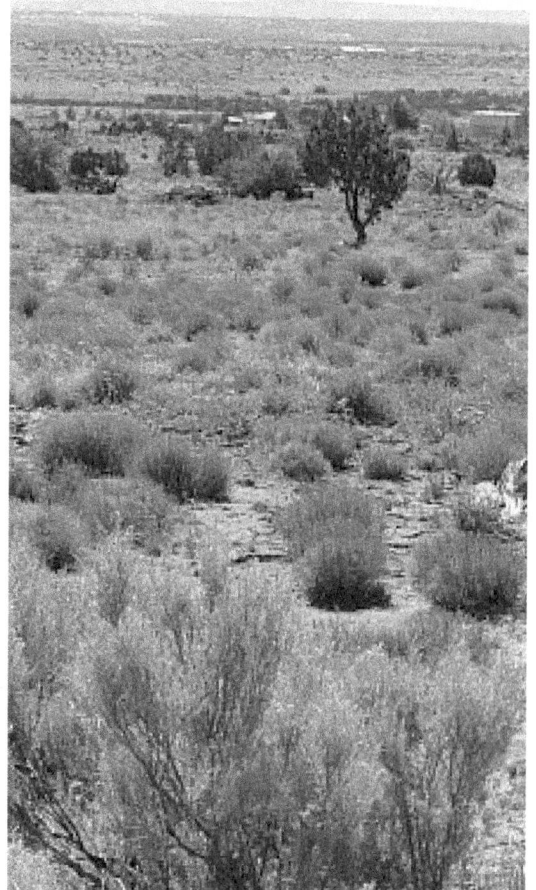

some form of environmental illness (EI) today, who experience mild to life-threatening physical reactions to extremely low levels of chemicals, mold, foods, electrical fields, and other environmental factors.

✦ **A large number of people with environmental sensitivities are homeless,** living in their cars, in a tent in the woods, in run-down trailers, or are prisoners in toxic apartments and homes across the country because they have no other housing options.

✦ Due to the nature of the illness, **many people with environmental illness experience rejection, blame, abandonment, ridicule, anger, and even assault** (from the intentional use of substances known to cause them bodily harm) from the people they know and love most. They often live in near isolation just to avoid exposure to the chemicals and other substances that cause them debilitating symptoms.

✦ Because of the loss and separation from most everything and everyone they

know and love, **many EIs experience post traumatic stress disorder (PTSD) as part and parcel of getting the illness,** and the daily trauma that comes from the social isolation imposed by the illness can sometimes feel worse than the physical symptoms themselves.

✦ **Many EIs lack access to medical care, food, and housing due to their environmental intolerance**—physician/health practitioner offices are inaccessible due to the use of air fresheners, cleaning chemicals, and perfumed patients and health care workers; food in supermarkets and even health food stores is contaminated by fragrant product displays located near open food displays; standard housing is usually rife with triggers: from formaldehyde in building materials and toxic glues used in construction, to mold, faulty electrical wiring, and air fresheners used by former tenants.

✦ **In order to survive and thrive, people with environmental illness must adopt non-toxic lifestyles that are very much aligned with intentional community values.**

✦ **There are approximately 2,200 intentional communities worldwide that might make ideal homes for those with environmental illness** due to their adherence to a chemical-free lifestyle, if not for a combination of any of the following factors:
• lack of tolerable non-toxic sleeping/housing accommodations;
• use of wood-burning stoves, gas, propane, and oil for heat and cooking;
• residents' past use of toxic laundry products (fragrance chemicals from fabric softeners and some detergents can stay in clothes forever, even if you have since switched brands to an ecological, scent-free product);
• residents' use of certain fragrant plant-based and other natural products such as essential oils;
• use of candles, incense, and other scented products in public, shared spaces;
• use of WiFi, cell phones, and other

Photos courtesy of Julie Genser

wireless technology;
• use/location of solar inverters;
• moldy conditions;
• tobacco/marijuana smoking policy;
• dietary restrictions (many with chronic illness may have dietary needs that are in conflict with vegetarian and/or raw dietary requirements that are common in many communities);
• ignorance about the condition.

The Ideal Solution

If one of the underlying intentions of "intentional" communities is to provide a healthy, community-based alternative to a more modern, technology-based life, then intentional communities could be an ideal living solution for those suffering from not only environmental illness but other chronic illnesses as well; for these are the people who are not thriving in conventional lifestyles and need to transform their reality the most.

But being sick can often mean not being able to function in nor contribute fully to a group situation—physically, financially, emotionally, or otherwise. It might even seem that someone recovering from a chronic illness could potentially drain the resources of a community. For this reason, many communities may hesitate to take on members with existing health conditions that render them unable to contribute as much as others to community life. Is it possible to shift this paradigm of illness-as-adversary so communities can actually look to their less able-bodied members as contributors to, rather than detractors from, their common goal? To see their cohabitation with differently-abled members not as a sacrifice but, as Sweigh Spilkin writes of her own journey with environmental illness, "a sacred part of a larger ceremony?"[4]

Illness as Opportunity

Monetarily speaking, those with EI do not have to drain the financial resources of a community; many are receiving Social Security Disability Insurance benefits and have a reliable monthly income. Those who are not able to contribute financially could barter services like food preparation or organic gardening.

Taking on members who are on a recovery path can provide a community with many opportunities for collective evolution, including the opportunity to: slow down and rethink priorities; appreciate different levels of health; deepen spiritually from members who have evolved in this way due to their physical limitations; be more deeply educated on the toxicity of everyday products; see how facing adversity together can serve as a powerful initiation to a new phase in communal growth; appreciate the preciousness of life in every single, beautiful moment. Community members can come to know that suffering/illness/disability is something sacred, a teacher to be valued—that from suffering, comes strength.

Needing to pay attention to certain details in order to accommodate those with finer tuned needs will only benefit the health of the community and the individuals that comprise it in the long run. For example, wood smoke—"one of the most harmful air pollutants we have on earth"[5]—is known to be a huge health hazard that contributes to asthma and other respiratory ailments in children and adults, yet wood is commonly used for heating at intentional communities. Wood smoke is also a big deterrent to living in community for those with EI. Likewise, the long-term health effects of WiFi systems and cell phones are suspect enough for whole countries to issue warnings to their citizens (Germany,[6] the European Union[7]) and yet are also frequently seen in intentional communities across America. Heeding the warnings that those with environmental illness call out through their immediate and more pronounced reactions to certain substances may help prevent your community members from developing cancer and other serious ailments in years to come. Any wise community will embrace these "canaries in the coalmine" and recognize their value in contributing to the long-term health and survival of the community.

Areas for Educating

Some of the issues that may potentially cause misunderstandings and difficulties between EIs and their communities, but may possibly be avoided through disability training, include:

• the inability to participate in community consistently;
• the need for some EIs to use water inefficiently in order to prepare clothing and bedding for use;
• communication difficulties due to physical reactions to toxins (confusion, memory loss, difficulty speaking);
• need for trauma processing;
• stress intolerance and mood changes due to neurological injury that may include damage to "fight or flight" center of brain.

What complicates the situation is that each case of environmental illness is completely unique, in terms of triggers, symptoms, and severity of reactions. Therefore, no standard rule will apply to all, as each person's specific needs will need to be understood and accepted on an individual basis.

Community-Minded

Interestingly, what I have noticed from running an online health community devoted to people with environmental intolerances for several years is the high percentage of creative and intuitive folks struck with this illness, two types that are typically drawn to a community-living mentality. Many artists, after years working with toxic art materials—paints, solvents, photographic chemicals, printing inks—become chemically sensitive. Musicians, dancers, actors, and other creative types typically take on low-paying toxic jobs to support themselves while trying to succeed in their art: housecleaning, house painting, construction, dry cleaning, warehouse work, flight attending; the list goes on. Once they have become more stable after the onset of debilitating symptoms, they often look for other avenues to express their creative spirit—possibly delving into meal preparation, energy work, leading group rituals—that could benefit community life. It also seems true that those who become living meters to the environment pick up on all sorts of energies, not just from chemicals and electricity. Many are highly empathic and attuned to the emotional states of others, some are clairvoyant, others are medically intuitive and able to "see" illness, and there are those, like myself, that find they can use physical touch to help transition others through crisis situations.

When I lived at the supportive Lost Valley community in Dexter, Oregon while attending their Ecovillage and Permaculture Design Certification Program several years ago, I quickly transformed from an impatient New York City girl into a barefoot

---

I know of many others who are environmentally sensitive looking for, but so far excluded from, community living.

being in touch with her natural world, and started to connect deeply to my intuitive self in a way I never had before. Community living can do this. I was gifted with three opportunities during my relatively short time there to listen to my deeper self and use hands-on healing to help others transition out of epileptic seizure, a sleep apnea choking episode, and past trauma. It was immediately after leaving Lost Valley that I developed severe environmental intolerance. I would love to find a pedestrian-centered community like Lost Valley that offers such healing safety from our toxic world—emotionally, physically, and chemically/electrically speaking—so that I can continue to develop this primal urge to facilitate healing during crisis situations that present themselves in a community setting.

I know of many others who are environmentally sensitive looking for, but so far excluded from, community living. There is Jamie Isman, a 34-year-old community organizer, activist, and facilitator of rituals that integrate earth and goddess spirituality with Jewish practice. Jamie is also a singer/songwriter, astrologer, clairvoyant, and all around mystic who loves to share her ethereal vision. An avid cook, she loves to nourish people with healthy meals including lacto-fermented and dehydrated foods. Disabled by environmental illness as well as a physical assault, Jamie recently fled the toxic urban landscape of Oakland, California to find refuge in the desolate mountains of northeast Arizona. Although she appreciates the beauty, peace, and clean air there, she is craving human connection that comes from community. Jamie seeks community free from all chemicals, wood smoke and barbecues, gas/propane, fragranced products, mold contamination, and cigarette smoke. You can contact her at jamieisman.com.

Mary and Keith, who both have mild chemical sensitivities, recently left their beloved home, careers, heath care providers, and dear friends in western Massachussetts in search of a safe ecovillage they could call home (read about their cross-country roadtrip here: maryandkeith.blogspot.com). Some of the gifts they have to offer a community include laughter, yoga, nonprofit program development, event coordination, nursing and hospice care, earth stewardship, elder/child/pet care, and cooking. They are looking for an ecovillage that is free of chemically fragranced products and essential oils, car exhaust, lighter fluid, wood smoke, fresh tar, and other pollutants. Speaking about their current adventure visiting intentional communities across America in search of a safe haven, Mary and Keith share their experience:

"Imagine yourself excitedly arriving to an intentional community that prides itself on living a sustainable life close to the land. To your dismay, you quickly discover that the members of the community use toxic mainstream products like Tide and Bounce, which adversely affect your health and pollute the earth. These products, incompatible with sustainable living practices, preclude you not only from membership in the community, but also from a healthy visit due to the deleterious impact on your health. As members of the chemically sensitive community, we strongly encourage and invite intentional communities to use all natural and fragrance-free products!"

Moving Forward

Community living is so badly needed for those with chronic environmental illness that I have decided to create a 501(c)3 nonprofit called re|shelter (reshelter.org) with my dear friend and fellow EI survivor Julie Laffin in order to address the housing needs of those with environmental intolerances. As part of our goal, we hope to explore solutions that facilitate the inclusion of those with EI in intentional community living.

Ideas we have on how to further this conversation:

• IC.org to provide a public listing of communities that are EI friendly/aware, including a contact person;
• Reshelter.org to maintain a private listing of EIs wishing to be placed in community;
• Intentional communities to incorporate specific language about acceptable personal care and laundry products, building materials, etc. into community rules, and—most importantly—to enforce these rules;

• Reshelter.org to provide a template for such language;
• Educational workshops to be given in participating intentional communities about accommodating disability from environmental illness;
• Reshelter.org to explore funding solutions for the creation of non-toxic housing in existing intentional communities as well as the formation of new communities

If there are any communities out there that are already accommodating those with environmental sensitivities and want to share their solutions, I would love to hear from you. To those communities interested in becoming a healthier, more inclusive home for those with environmental intolerances, please join this important conversation. You can contact me at planetthrive.com/contact-us or leave a comment under this article at planetthrive.com/2010/06/beyond-green.

To learn more about the housing needs of those with environmental intolerances, please see the resources at mcs-safehomes.com and read the *Safer Construction Tips for the Environmentally Sensitive* PDF brochure in the "tips" section. Also visit reshelter.org. Blessings to all those working to create a saner, more humane world.

Thank you to Jamie Isman and Mary Rives for editing assistance with this article. ❀

Julie Genser is a former photographer, writer, and certified holistic health counselor whose life was derailed by extensive food and chemical sensitivities. In 2004 she completed the Ecovillage and Permaculture Design Certification Program at Lost Valley Educational Center in Dexter, Oregon. A few weeks later she developed severe environmental illness and had to drop out of ECOSA Institute, where she had just begun an intensive semester in sustainable architecture. She now lives in the desolate beauty of rural Arizona, where she dreams of living in community like the one she discovered at Lost Valley. She provides online community to those with environmental illness through her website PlanetThrive.com.

1 Fred Lanphear, "Embracing a Terminal Illness," Communities: Life in Cooperative Culture, Issue #145, Winter 2009, http://communities.ic.org/articles/1327/Embracing_a_Terminal_Illness

2 "Bene's Battle", PlanetThrive.com http://planetthrive.com/2009/10/benes-battle/

3 Joshua Canter, "The True Need for Community," Communities: Life in Cooperative Culture, Issue #145, Winter 2009, http://planetthrive.com/2009/12/the-true-need-for-community/

4 Sweigh Spilkin, "Meaning as Medicine in Chronic Illness," PlanetThrive.com, http://planetthrive.com/2008/07/meaning-as-medicine-in-chronic-illness/

5 Gerd Oberfeld, M.D., "International Study of Asthma and Allergies in Childhood," http://burningissues.org/car-www/medical_effects/fact-sheet.htm

6 Geoffrey Lean, "Germany warns citizens to avoid using Wi-Fi," The Independent, September 09, 2007, http://www.independent.co.uk/environment/green-living/germany-warns-citizens-to-avoid-using-wifi-401845.html.

7 Geoffrey Lean, "EU watchdog calls for urgent action on Wi-Fi radiation," The Independent, September 16, 2007, http://www.independent.co.uk/environment/green-living/eu-watchdog-calls-for-urgent-action-on-wifi-radiation-402539.html.

Tiny Houses as Appropriate Technology

By Mary Murphy

The tiny house movement has been growing exponentially in recent years, both in communitarian circles and beyond. In an age of ballooning real estate prices, building a tiny home can seem like the only achievable path to home ownership for many people, especially for those who choose a livelihood outside the conventionally profitable professions.

In June of 2013 I moved into my own tiny house, which I had designed and built entirely myself using many recycled components. It cost me around $5,000 to build and the footprint of the house fits on a 72-square foot trailer that I can tow with a medium-sized pickup truck. The house has very simple systems (greywater, humanure, no electrical wiring) and I've lived in it in two different locations: one with electricity and one that is off the grid. In this article I intend to explore tiny houses as a form of appropriate technology, whether you live on or off the grid.

What Is a Tiny House?

First, let's define the term "tiny house." Usage varies throughout the movement, but in this article, let's say a tiny house is a house built on a wheeled trailer that conforms to the maximum trailer sizes that govern shipping containers and RVs. In the United States that means it must be no more than 8 feet wide, 13.5 feet tall, and typical lengths are 16, 18, and 20 feet. A classic tiny house would be 8x16 feet with a sleeping loft, giving it a footprint of 128 square feet.

My own tiny house is 5.5x13 feet, with a footprint of 72 square feet, with no loft. I built it so small for reasons of economy: the cheap (but small) trailer from Craigslist is what enabled me to afford the project. Many of the observations I make here will also apply to other forms of small housing, whether they are on wheels or not.

The reason so many tiny house dwellers build their houses on trailers is not just mobility, it is also a legal loophole: most towns have zoning that includes a "minimum dwelling size" which is much larger than some people need or want, and building codes requiring broad hallways, wide doorways, and a host of other details that make it difficult to design

that they are customized to the needs of their owners, sidestepping the waste of installing conventional systems just to meet building codes. Most tiny houses are owner-built, and even if the owner uses purchased blueprints, they inevitably customize the interior to meet their unique set of needs. Those needs can differ vastly depending on what other facilities are available at the tiny house site. Tiny houses are a perfect fit for communities that share bathing facilities, a laundry, and perhaps a kitchen: the smaller dwellings can

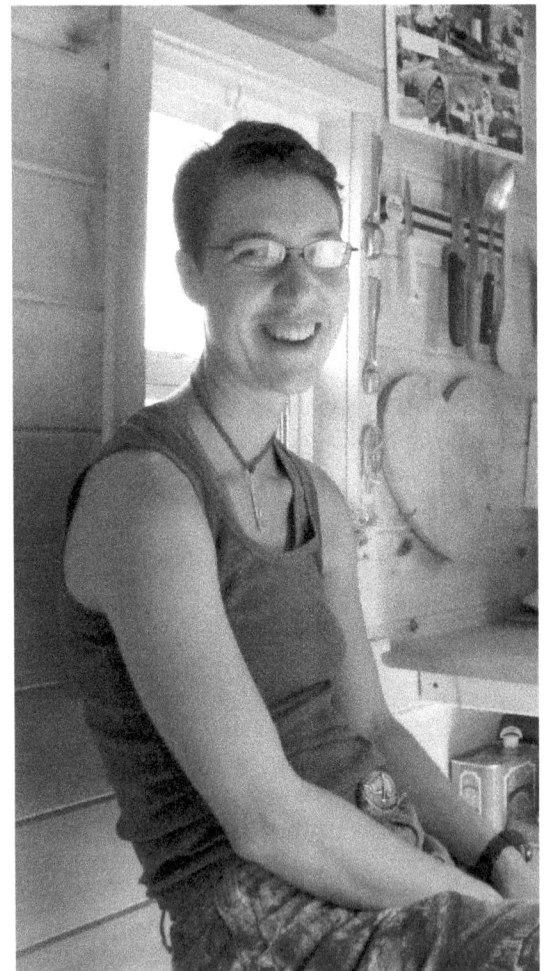

> Tiny houses are customized to the needs of their owners, sidestepping the waste of installing conventional systems just to meet building codes.

a small space that works well. By putting the house on a trailer, you are suddenly governed by RV laws instead, which stipulate a maximum trailer size rather than a minimum. Also, in many cases you will not have to pay property tax on the tiny house, since it is not attached to a foundation. The property tax loophole can be very appealing to intentional communities that want to add housing capacity without increasing their tax burden. Some municipalities have zoning that outlaws parking an RV or tiny house in your yard, so check with the authorities before you start building.

The primary reason that I consider tiny houses a form of appropriate technology is

be outfitted with fewer utilities and those needs can usually be met more efficiently by sharing the necessary systems with the community as a whole. For my own tiny house site, I rent a spot at a small organic farm. The other dwellings on the farm are two yurts.

Let's take a look at some of the systems tiny houses can have, and the range of choices available. Each person can customize their house with the systems that are important for their particular needs.

Tiny House Systems: Electricity

Some tiny houses are hooked up with full wiring for grid-tied AC power (or take the less technical option and run an extension cord in through a window). Others have a solar system for the whole house, while still others just charge a few batteries to run small lights and simple electronics. Needs will vary depending on whether the occupant(s) work at home or in another building, whether they like to stay up late or go to bed with the sun, whether they have medical needs that require reliable electricity, and a host of other factors. It is fairly easy to start with a simple system and upgrade over time, as funds become available or needs increase.

My own tiny house used to have extension-cord power, but in my fabulous new mountain-view site my house is off the grid. I light my little house with candles and super-efficient battery-powered LED lights. I charge my smart phone and computer in a nearby barn or in my car as I'm driving. This winter I'll need more indoor computer time to work on my business, so I'm researching small battery packs that can run a laptop (the Goal Zero Yeti 400 looks promising).

Telecommunications

Telecommunications are an important part of most of our lives these days. Since I'm running a small wilderness business from my home, these connections aren't optional for me. At a past site I ran both phone and ethernet wires from a nearby building into my tiny house, but at the current site cellular service was my only option. A smart phone gives me reliable phone and email access in my little home.

Heating and Cooling

I enjoy long cold winters in my home state of Vermont, and a serious consideration when building a house is "How much is it going to cost to heat all this space every year?" In hot climates, cooling costs can be just as significant. My house was built to be lightweight so it wouldn't exceed the weight limit of the single-axle trailer on which it sits. My R-10 foam-board insulation isn't made of sustainable materials and doesn't offer a top notch insulation factor, but the small 72-square-foot size makes the house extremely efficient to heat nonetheless. In its first winter I heated it with an electric space heater I got at a thrift store for $15, and even in an unusually frigid January my heating energy bill was only $80/month.

This year I am upgrading to a super-efficient, clean burning micro-woodstove (a technological improvement which is costing me over $3,000) that will allow me to use a local and renewable fuel source. I will sleep better knowing that my heating dollars are going to a local sustainable logger instead of fueling the perpetual conflicts in the Middle East. It's also great to know that, in a pinch, I could gather all the fuel I needed in my own backyard. Wood costs about $200 per cord around here, and the two cords I'm purchasing this fall should last me through this winter and much of the next. Also, I've built my house to be able to freeze when I go away for more than a day (it has no water pipes), so

I don't have to heat it when I'm traveling, which saves even more fuel.

Water

Water is a basic need, and we need to have enough for drinking, cooking, cleaning, and bathing. Some tiny houses are hooked up to a pressurized water supply and contain on-demand hot water heaters that provide hot showers and warm water for cleaning. However, insulating the

> On a grumpy day when living this efficiently can seem like a sacrifice, the beauty still speaks to my heart and makes the decision to live small feel worth it.

intake and outflow pipes well enough so that they don't freeze is a big challenge in cold climates when you don't have a foundation. Since it would require buried lines and a super-insulated (and possibly heated) water line between the buried pipe and the

house floor, it isn't a good option for tiny houses that may be moved frequently.

My own system is super-simple: a $30 five-gallon water container sits above my tiny bar sink. I fill it up at the pump in the farm's greenhouse and haul it up the hill about twice a week to use for washing dishes and general cleaning. The bar sink drains into a two-gallon bucket greywater container (free food service waste). Since I use only very small amounts of biodegradable soap in my sink, I can safely empty this bucket in the high grass near my home. In the summer I use a solar shower, and in the winter I'll shower occasionally at a friend's house or at the day-shelter in town. I do laundry at the laundromat. For drinking and cooking water, I keep several BPA-free water bottles filled up and at the ready.

Cooking and Food Storage

Heating and cooling food can take a lot of energy in a typical house. Some folks choose to install a small fridge, but then they must provide the electricity to run it. I avoid the electrical needs of a refrigerator by cooling my food in a large cooler (I re-freeze my ice packs in the farm's large meat freezer). I cook on a small burner that runs on denatured alcohol (theoretically a renewable fuel, although I'm told that current ethanol practices are agriculturally unsustainable). In the winter, my new micro-woodstove offers a second cooking burner.

Transportation

Transportation costs hinge on the location of one's home, and tiny house dwellers have the option to relocate their house as their transportation needs change. When used as an "urban infill" housing strategy, tiny houses can offer an affordable place to live in neighborhoods that are well served by public transportation systems. When tiny houses are sited in intentional communities, the option for car-sharing or even just occasional carpooling with fellow community members helps reduce the carbon footprint of rural living.

My tiny house is nine miles from Montpelier, Vermont, where I can do almost all of my errands in one compact town. Gas is one of my biggest housing-related expenses, but since

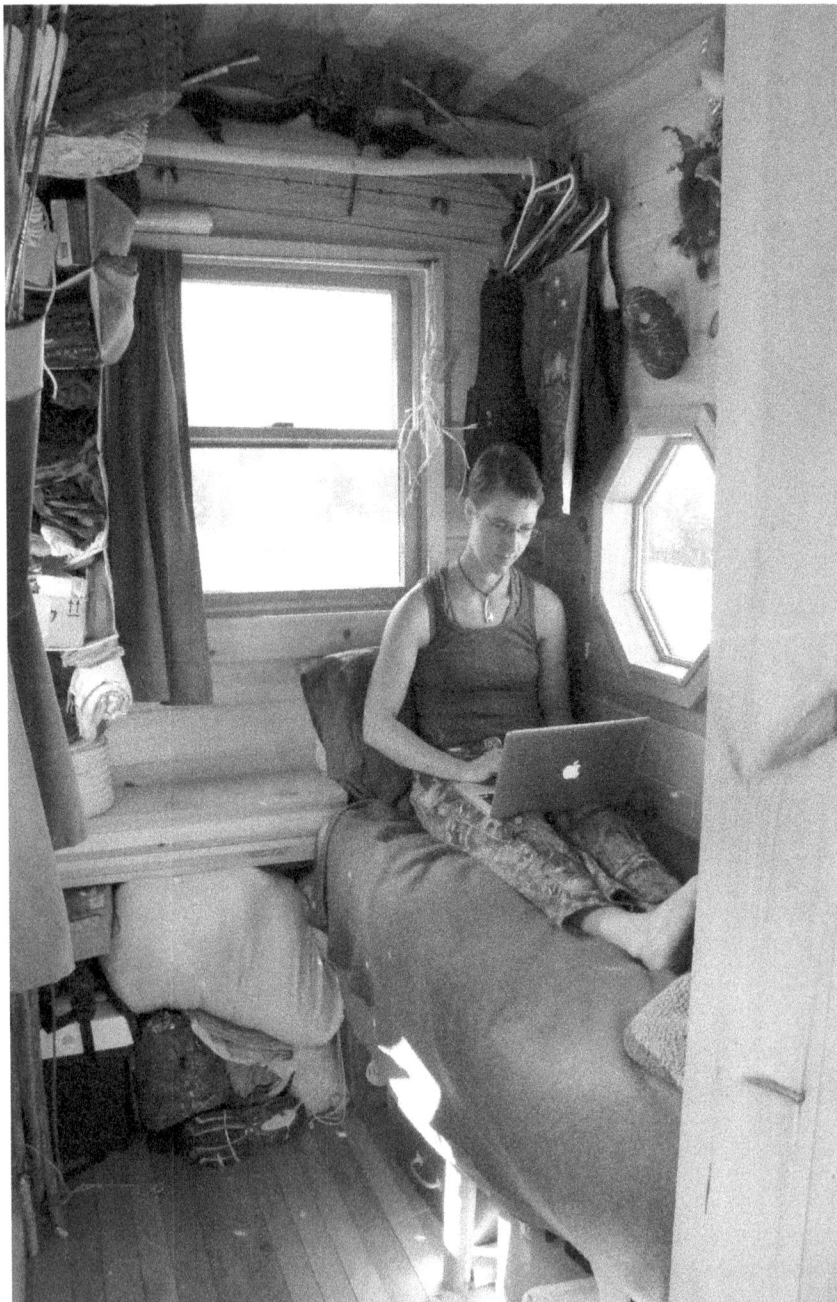

I primarily work from home running my on-site wilderness skills business, I don't have to commute every day. Once my business grows enough to support leaving my supplemental job, I will be able to reduce trips to town a lot more.

Limiting "Stuff"

Another impact we have on energy use involves how much "stuff" we consume. Manufacturing, shipping, and displaying commercial goods takes a huge amount of resources. Most tiny house dwellers find that living in a small space encourages them to consider carefully before making a purchase. After all, there's not much room, so buying another possession often means letting go of an older one. This helps prevent habitual engagement with the consumer economy, and limits purchases to things we truly need and want to have in our lives.

I'll admit that not all my possessions fit in 72 square feet, so I rent a room in a barn down the road to store most of the outdoor gear that I use in my wilderness business and a few of my personal possessions. Nonetheless, I pass by many potential purchases every month purely out of the knowledge that I don't have the space for them!

Inspiration and Beauty

Finally, I believe that truly sustainable forms of technology not only conserve resources, they also inspire us. Our dutiful awareness of the need for resource conservation fuels some of our lifestyle decisions, but the excitement of beauty and empowerment can prove to be a much more sustainable motivation for lifestyle change. In my experience people love tiny houses because they are beautiful expressions of their owner's aesthetic and values. Many people take the time to make their tiny houses beautiful, and the small size amplifies the effect of their efforts by drawing the eye to all the thoughtful touches.

Personally, my curved vardo-style roof was the biggest aesthetic choice I made about the exterior of my house, and that is what gives it such a fairy-tale appeal. The bold colors are also fun, and it's easier to make unique color choices when you can paint the whole house in one day with one can of paint! When the investment of time and money is low, people feel free to experiment.

When you're living in such a small space,

you want it to be beautiful and cozy—that's part of what makes it work. Inside my house, I spent a little extra money to get lovely honey-colored pine paneling from a local saw mill, and took the extra time to build windowsills and install nice trim. I've hung my three carefully chosen ceramic mugs from hooks by the kitchen window, and baskets made from natural wood and vines hang from hooks on my high ceiling, providing both extra storage and a simple charm. In a house with so few spaces and objects, it is worth it to make each one beautiful.

On a grumpy day when the resource-efficiency of my home no longer seems to outweigh the sacrifice of ample space and hot running water, the beauty still speaks to my heart and makes the decision to live small feel worth it.

Empowerment

Tiny houses are also incredibly empowering. When I tell people that I live in a tiny house that I built myself for $5,000 and with no building experience, their eyes light up. They start thinking, "Well, if she can do it, I could probably do it too..." I can certainly attest that waking up each morning in a house I built with my own hands has changed my perspective on the world. I start each day with a sense that anything is possible and dreams really can come true.

Sometimes we really can find simple, homemade solutions that solve a problem, increase our sustainability, and add a little more beauty and fun to the world. That's what makes tiny houses such an appropriate technology for solving housing problems both inside and outside of intentional communities. ❧

Mary Murphy lives in cheerful community with the other residents of Good Heart Farmstead in central Vermont. From her tiny house she runs Mountainsong Expeditions, a small wilderness company which offers spiritually-based wilderness trips and classes on The Sacred Hunt. You can view more photos of the tiny house on her website: www.mountainsongexpeditions.com/tiny-house.html. You can read more of Mary's writing in the book Stepping Into Ourselves: An Anthology on Priestesses *and in previous issues of* COMMUNITIES. *Feel free to drop her an email through the "Contact Us" page on her website.*

My Favorite Tiny House Resources

The Small House Book by Jay Schaffer. A philosophical and practical introduction to the tiny house movement, including many photographs and floorplans of the original Tumbleweed home designs.

Tiny Homes by Lloyd Kahn. A beautiful photo tour of hundreds of owner-built small homes.

The Very Efficient Carpenter by Larry Haun. Whlie not specifically about tiny houses, this book taught me all I needed to know to design and frame my house.

www.tumbleweedhouses.com. This company sells blueprints and kits for building your own house (if you don't want to design it yourself).

www.tinyhouseblog.com. Great articles from all corners of the tiny house movement, with many guest posts by owner-builders.

www.rowdykittens.com/our-tiny-house. Tammy Strobel's blog on simple living with her partner in their tiny house.

littleyellowdoor.wordpress.com. The cheerful and refreshingly honest blog of a young woman who built the tiny house of her dreams in California and transformed her life.

—M.M.

Who Can Live in a Tiny House?

Tiny houses do a fabulous job of solving the dilemma of the limited, excessively large, and overly expensive housing options for single people by creating an affordable and flexible housing option. If the owner's life outgrows the tiny house, it can be re-purposed as a home office, meditation room, guest house, or kids' playspace.

Many tiny houses are designed with a sleeping loft, which requires a decent amount of physical mobility to access, but others have floor plans that are all on one level and thus more accessible. I've yet to see a tiny house plan that is wheelchair accessible, and the wide clearance requirements of the wheelchair would be a big limiting factor in the design.

Are tiny houses a practical solution for a housing a couple? I know several happy couples living in tiny houses, others who tried it and the experiment failed (one relationship never recovered), and many more couples whose differing values about housing clash too much for them to ever try it. Both people must really WANT to live small for the idea to be worth trying. You should also consider each person's cleanliness standards, daily schedule (does one person go to bed early while the other is a night owl?), need for privacy, need for quiet time, and storage needs. The impact of all these differences will be more keenly felt in a shared space. Polyamorous relationships with more than two co-habitating partners would increase the complication and space-crunch significantly—I'd love to hear from people who are trying it!

What about tiny houses and kids? Single moms have been enthusiastically involved in the tiny house movement since the beginning, and I know one couple who was raising a toddler and an infant in their 18-foot tiny house (they moved to a bigger space after a few years). It all depends on the parenting style, personalities involved, and the family's ability to creatively solve the need for a balance of privacy and togetherness. I've heard of several older teenagers building their own tiny houses in the family's backyard. What an amazing gift to become a homeowner before you even turn 18!

Personally, I know I would not want to live in my 72-square-foot house with a partner. I love being king of my own castle and setting everything up just the way I like it. I built my house during the end of a relationship with a previous partner who thought tiny houses were a little crazy, and having sovereignty over my own tiny space felt very healing at that time, helping me affirm my own core values in a concrete way. When I moved into my tiny house I did worry a bit that the women I would want to date would think it was weird, but instead it has turned into an effective litmus test: if you don't like my tiny house, our values are probably too different anyway!

My current partner and I don't live together full time, but she often stays at my little house for long weekends and we love sharing the nest-like space: when I have company my single bunk folds out into a double bed that takes up an entire half the house, wall-to-wall. It is especially nice in the winter, since we don't feel guilty turning up the heat enough to be truly cozy in a state where many people are keeping their houses very chilly to save on heating bills. The small space also encourages us to take more walks outdoors in all seasons. If I ever get involved in raising children I won't want to do it in my ultra-tiny house, but I'm sure I'll love parking it in the backyard as a quiet personal retreat from the bustle of childrearing.

—M.M.

It Takes All Kinds
TO RAISE A VILLAGE

By Melanie Rios

Dome Village is home to a half-dozen people living at Maitreya Ecovillage in Eugene, Oregon who share a one-bedroom apartment while sleeping in their personal bedrooms made of cardboard and old political signs that the original residents of Dome Village built a decade ago. Their monthly expenses and ecological footprint are a small fraction of their neighbors', and they are happily living with their friends, yet their lifestyle is illegal. In 2009 the ecovillage received a notice from the city code enforcement department that we had one week to remove their bedrooms or face a $400 per day fine for illegal camping. Five years later elected officials were on hand for the ribbon cutting of "Opportunity Village," a city-approved collection of small bedrooms and shared common kitchen to provide temporary shelter to homeless people, and Dome Village was still thriving at Maitreya. What led to this happy outcome?

The short answer is that a healthy balance of strategies and a committed community were able to create a cultural shift that supported the emergence of creative responses to some of the challenges of our times, including climate change, social isolation, and a lack of affordable housing. Just as a healthy garden contains a variety of plants rather than a monoculture, a healthy activist community is populated by people playing a variety of roles. There were visionary leaders, early adopters, social organizers, advocates, inventive builders, resource contributors, government supporters, street occupiers, journalists, academics, and many others who played a role in this shift of culture.

Here I tell the part of this story that I personally witnessed, aware that this is just a small part of a much larger tale. There are many people not mentioned here who have contributed to the creation of these villages, and the emergence of Dome Village and Opportunity Village is part of an unfolding process that will likely eventually lead to legalizing and creating many more affordable, communal, and ecological places to live.

One thing that inspired me when I moved to Maitreya in 2002 was the nearby Dharmalaya Center, a beautiful strawbale building that was being built in the backyard of a family's house with the help of many community volunteers. Once built, the center hosted yoga classes, permaculture courses, and neighborhood gatherings. Frustratingly, a few years later the folks at Dharmalaya received a notice that this center operated in violation of city land use codes. A six hour public hearing took place in which almost 100 people spoke on behalf of Dharmalaya, with no one speaking against them. I noticed that the officials representing the government in this hearing seemed to be sinking into their chairs, not happy to be spoiling the fun of so many enthusiastic supporters. The outcome of this hearing was that Dharmalaya was allowed to continue operating their center with some restrictions. Possibly as a result of this legal encounter, Dome Village was later supported by city code enforcers, an unanticipated ripple I will describe in a moment.

Upon moving to Eugene I was also inspired by my new neighbor, Finn Po, who built the first dome at Maitreya. He voiced his dream of people living lives of voluntary simplicity close to the earth while sharing resources, and talked about the joy of living "house free" with low financial overhead and plenty of friends nearby. He slept in the dome he had built for $18, preferring this cozy nest to the indoor bedroom that he used for an office. Early adopters asked Finn to teach them how to build their own domes, and Finn invited them to share his kitchen and bathroom while they built and then lived in their dwellings. Within a few years there were a half-dozen tiny bedrooms clustered in a plum orchard near his rented apartment. I played the role of "social or-

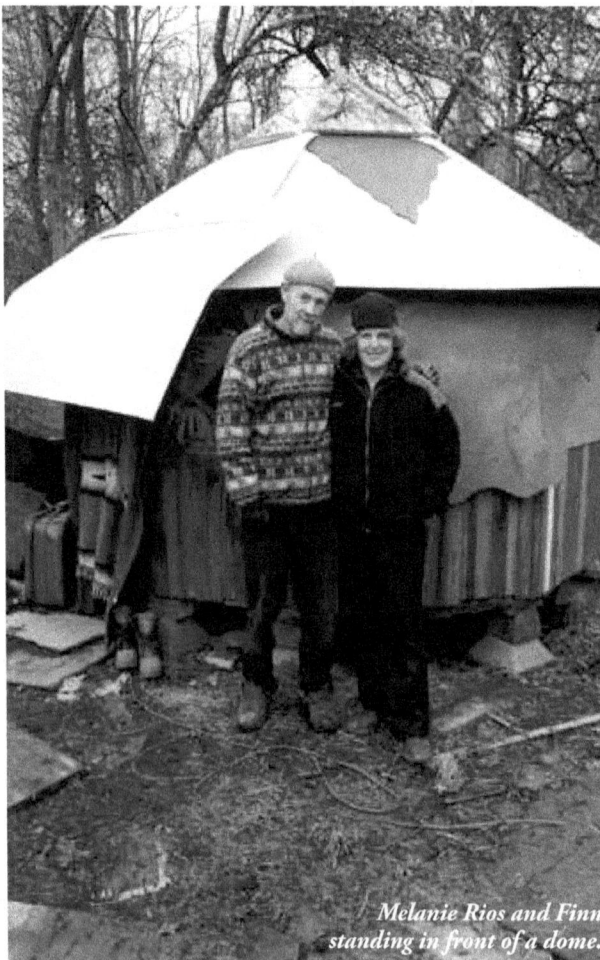

Melanie Rios and Finn standing in front of a dome.

ganizer" in this village creation by facilitating meetings amongst those sharing Finn's apartment and helping them integrate into the larger Maitreya community. Some of the "dome villagers" had been homeless prior to living there, some were students and activists appreciative of low-budget housing, and some were seeking a way to live authentic and simple lives in community. Challenges arose and were resolved through interpersonal conflict resolution as well as policy formation. Some policies were set by the landlord, such as banning candles and smoking in the domes and requiring drywall interior walls to improve fire prevention. Other policies were made by those living there, such as how long guests could stay. I wrote an article documenting why and what we were doing at Dome Village for *Permaculture Magazine* in preparation for addressing potential city concerns. (See sidebar for a description of a typical evening at Dome Village.)

At the same time, I worked with a Landscape Architecture class at the University of Oregon to design a model village for a three-acre property in Eugene, and these beautiful designs were displayed for a couple of months in the lobby of the city building department. I submitted a proposal for "ecovillage zoning" to the city that would make it legal to build this village. While the proposal was not approved and the village was not built, these ideas and images for creating a simple, ecological, and beautiful village percolated in the minds of those who passed through the building department and those who read the proposal.

Amidst all the hopeful developments, the moment arrived when

Robert Bolman, who owned the land where Dome Village was located, received a letter from the city requiring him to dismantle Dome Village within a week. A neighbor had become disgruntled by noise emanating from our chicken coop, and called the city to complain about that and our "illegal camping." Rob and I went downtown to talk with a code enforcer, where we reported that we had already moved the chickens to a location farther away from neighbors.

Regarding the citation of "illegal camping," we acknowledged the important role the code enforcer played in making sure people were not exploited and were safe in their housing, and described how we manifested these values at Dome Village. We said we were creating a demonstration model of how people could make the whole planet safer by decreasing our ecological footprint through shared simple living. We talked about the importance of pilot experiments for responding to a possible influx of climate refugees to the Pacific Northwest. We appreciated her for doing her part from within the government to protect people's lives, and said we were consciously operating outside the law with similar goals. We handed her a copy of the article I had written about Dome Village.

When we requested a hearing even though we knew that Dome Village was illegal, her eyes grew big. In this moment, I realized the lasting impression that the Dharmalaya hearing had likely made on the city code enforcers. Within 24 hours of our meeting they sent out an inspector who simply asked us to pick up the fallen plums on the ground around the domes. While the domes were not de-

> # The inspector simply asked us to pick up the fallen plums on the ground around the domes.

Brian Hurley at the Dome Village.

Melanie Rios

clared officially legal, it became clear that they could remain, which encouraged friends throughout the city to build dome bedrooms in their own yards. The neighbor's complaint turned out to be a blessing in disguise, an important step in this social movement to live collectively and lightly on our planet.

The impact of our work did not end here, thanks in part to the next player in our story, Erik DeBuhr, one of the folks who built a dome modeled on Finn's design. He experimented with new ways of creating small stand-alone bedrooms that were roomier and easier to build, founding a nonprofit called Community Supported Shelters to build these spaces he calls "conestoga huts."

In the meantime, the occupy movement arose, with hundreds of people in Eugene sleeping in a nomadic village that moved from street corners to parks and back. Many were homeless folks who came out of their cars and hiding spots in bushes to gather with activists taking a break from their homes, and through this process, consciousness rose in the city around the issue of homelessness. After the occupiers dispersed, the issue of homelessness remained alive, and city council meetings became packed with people expressing a desire to address the problem. The city council approved the creation of Opportunity Village and several other related initiatives.

People attended fundraising events with music and delicious meals and offered money and supplies for building conestoga huts. Churches allowed homeless people to stay in conestoga huts placed on their properties while folks were waiting for Opportunity Village to be approved and built. And this isn't the end of the story. There's a movement afoot to create more places like Opportunity Village in Eugene, as well as a village of tiny houses where people can live permanently. Other locales are citing the successful operation of Opportunity Village as they lobby for similar initiatives in their towns.

I've sometimes heard people arguing about what activist roles are most important, with some people declaring other people to be slackers, inflammatory, delusional, or enemies. Yet in the same way that our gardens rely on different plants to host beneficial insects, synthesize nitrogen, and prevent erosion, our movements rely on a wide assortment of contributors.

Our wisest social transformation guides are pointing to a different perspective that deemphasizes a sense of separation and judgment towards others. There is a need, they say, for those who take to the streets, for supportive public officials, for journalists, for artists and inventors, and for visionary edge-walkers and their followers. Musicians, cooks, facilitators, graphic artists, and conscious law-breakers also play their parts. There is room for those who oppose our ideas, for in responding to their concerns we become stronger, just as wind and drought can help plants grow deep roots.

Our power to transform the world multiplies when each of us collaboratively contributes that which is at the intersection of our gifts, our passions, and what the world needs. ❧

Melanie Rios is an urban gardener, musician, and intentional community consultant who lives in Portland, Oregon. One of her current passions is creating terra preta soil to sequester carbon, increase garden fertility, and establish a healthy sanitation system. She recently founded the Village Singers, a choir that leads work-party volunteers in singing harmony while they create gardens and cob structures. Melanie offers workshops and coaching in sociocracy, social permaculture, conflict resolution, culture shift, composting, and other resiliency-promoting topics.

Life in Dome Village

Dome Villagers say what they value most about their home is their relationships with their fellow villagers, and they seem to have created a culture where people contribute generously to each other. "Whenever someone needs help, I offer," says Jesse, "and folks help me when I have a need, whether it's to build a dome or bring in firewood." On one recent evening, a few people traded massages on top of sleeping bags rolled out in front of the stove. Coral said she was hungry for calzones, and Rafael offered to cook enough for everyone... A neighbor came by to ask if anyone wanted to help make a brochure informing our urban neighborhood about a "city repair" project he's organizing, and John volunteered. Later, a visiting traveler from Germany started playing some upbeat music, and some folks started dancing.

—Quoted from "Alternative America" by Melanie Rios, *Permaculture Magazine: Solutions for Sustainable Living*, Issue #56, Summer 2008.

How to Change a Law

A few ways to help change a law:

• Consider the law you wish to change. What is its intended purpose? What needs and values does the law support? What consequences of this law are a problem, and for whom?

• Consider solutions to these problematic consequences that still support the intended consequences of the law, assuming you support those intentions.

• Experiment with implementing these solutions, even if it means breaking the law. Keep refining your experiment to decrease what isn't yet working well.

• Document how and why you're conducting this experiment, and tell this story in person, in print, using social media, and through creative expression such as songs and theater.

• Support people who are creatively and productively breaking problematic laws by testifying at hearings and contributing resources.

• See the good in everyone, as this brings out the best in them.

• Nurture those who are on the front lines with food, friendship, and shelter.

• Take to the streets with signs and leaflets.

• Support change from within institutions.

• Listen deeply to those who disagree with you, and look for ways that their ideas can improve your work.

—M.R.

MY STRUGGLE TO
Legalize Sustainable Living

By Graham Ellis

"We shall require a substantially new manner of thinking if mankind is to survive."
—Albert Einstein

"This reminds me of how I grew up," said Hawaii County Mayor, Billy Kenoi, as he toured the rustic facilities of Bellyacres, an ecovillage in the Puna jungle of Hawaii. After hearing how just a few complainers had been able to cripple our community development model, he told me he learned at law school that the purpose of the law was to serve as a shield, not as a weapon. This has not been my experience.

Persistent complaints from a handful of people over the last five years have destroyed our chances of living the vision we shared when we created our community in 1987. We were a group of idealistic, anarchistic jugglers; not at all your typical demographic for community builders. We minimally cleared our land, planted tropical fruit orchards, built houses, jungalows, and community facilities, lived 100 percent from solar power, used catchment water, harvested our own lumber, raised chickens, and used horses for weed control and fertilizing. We built S.P.A.C.E. (www.hawaiispace.com), a 7,000 sq. ft. community arts center that became home to a charter school, a farmers' market, arts classes, community events, and performances. In 2008, I wrote that "we may be the most sustainable community development project in the US."

The problem is that the Special Permit I obtained in 2000 only allowed performance arts workshops and farm activities with building permits for S.P.A.C.E., four houses, and a workshop. Over nearly three decades, we had built a dozen jungalows, community kitchen, sauna, showers, and three extra houses, plus almost every service we provided our broader community was noncompliant. Being this far outside the law, we became severely vulnerable to attack from anyone with any kind of a grudge against our organization, our activities, or our personalities. In a world where it is impossible

Joe Hoffman, Isla Ellis, and Graham take a juggling break while building S.P.A.C.E.
Brad Lewis

The author at S.P.A.C.E. in 2008.

Isla Kral Ellis, daughter of the author, feeding chickens at 10 months old.
Photos courtesy of Graham Ellis

Allison Erickson Photography

to keep everyone happy all the time, especially irrational neighbors, we were an easy target and we have now literally broken apart under the weight of the laws that have been used as weapons against us.

It is my belief that the complaint-driven system of enforcement has been at the root of our collapse. This process, which exists almost everywhere in the US, enables alternative groups like ours the freedom to live in non-compliance with building and zoning codes and activities until someone files a complaint. The system gives amazing amounts of power to the complainer(s). The original complaint that brought our demise was instigated by a newcomer to our neighborhood who said applause at our shows "interrupted his TV viewing." He boasted he was "at war" with us and, since he hired a top local law firm, the Planning Department issued us a "cease and desist" order.

To this day, our ecovillage has never received a single warning or citation from the police for any noise ordinance violations or disturbances; ironically, the only person arrested by the police was this same neighbor for domestic violence. One month after launching his "bombs," our new neighbor moved away to work in the Pentagon (honestly). Within a year, he sold his house with a promise that the war was still on and he would file a contested case hearing. He left our whole community to deal with the fallout.

We were encouraged that 979 of our ecovillage supporters responded immediately by signing a petition; many also called the Mayor, and 423 supporters later submitted written testimony and spoke at hearings praising our ecovillage. We became a test case for the legalization of sustainable community living on our island, which caused us to be subjected to continual opposition and road blocks from County and State agencies. It has been five years and at least three feet of legal paperwork and we still have not had our Planning Commission hearing. We learned that once complaints have been filed (and if they continue to be filed, even from a very few vocal opponents) the authorities feel duty-bound to impose the law to its full extent to eliminate all non-compliant behaviors. They need to do this to protect themselves from being sued for not doing their legal duty. This applies even if they are aware that the complaints are frivolous, fraudulent, or purely vindictive, which dozens were. My six-year-old daughter's birthday party, which was attended by 30 of her kindergarten friends and finished at 5:30 pm on a Sunday, had a complaint filed, as did a memorial service for a 21-year-old resident killed by a hit-and-run that ended at 7:30 pm, also on a Sunday.

As the ecovillage founder and point person for all legal and financial issues, I have spent 18 busy years, and way too much of my energy, struggling to bring our organization into compliance, either by modifying our buildings and activities to fit into existing legal boxes or applying for Special Permits and State Land Leases or by attempting to get new laws adopted through the democratic process. I have now stopped this futile pursuit: I left my home of 28 years, moved with my family of seven, and found a good job as a development consultant for another nonprofit in an affluent community that has a legal structure and permits for its activities. I feel that I can now focus on building community instead of struggling with the law.

The sad fact is that grassroots sustainable community developments seldom conform to existing building codes or zoning codes. Even sympathetic and supportive members of the government bureaucracy have no boxes to put us in to rubber stamp our activities. Years of wishful searching online for models of legalized sustainable living that we could adopt produced just a few exciting prospects. I found examples of groups circumventing laws through the grace of

An unpermitted jungalow built in 1992, recently condemned.

Bellyacres interns Silver Luwick and Lyla Gibbons prepare sustainably home harvested native Ohia trees for building S.P.A.C.E.

This homebuilt yurt was the author's bedroom from 1987-1997.

A circus arts camp at S.P.A.C.E. taught by world champion and Cirque Du Soleil artist Annetta Lucero, but no performances permitted!

Photos courtesy of Graham Ellis

Seaview Performing Arts Center for Education under construction in 2007; volunteer labor and sustainable building materials helped us keep the cost to about $280,000 for 5,000 square feet.

Photo courtesy of Graham Ellis

supportive local government officials, I found councils that passed bills to allow a specific alternative development, and I found Earthship's Sustainable Development Testing Sites Bill (which has benefited only them). I found alternative building codes in Humboldt, Cochise, Nevada, Mendocino, and other counties for single family residences. I researched worldwide and all I found were communities like us struggling to find solutions to legalize truly sustainable lifestyles.

My research also unearthed endless government rhetoric spouting the benefits and challenges of sustainability. Hawaii State government adopted a grandiose "Sustainability 2050 Plan" in 2008, and has implemented very little, while Hawaii County adopted a resolution in 2009 that realistically warned "from a sustainability perspective, the problem is that we are creating ongoing structural barriers that actually prevent people from being able to meet their own needs. These barriers…include the abuse of political power and discriminatory government policies." Hopeful that local officials actually supported sustainability principles and would be excited about models practicing sustainability, I brought every elected official I could to visit our ecovillage and see what we were doing. It seemed like everyone was impressed.

We received recognition letters from our State Governor, Lt. Governor, two Federal Senators, and two Congressional Representatives. The Chairman of the County Council testified before a 2012 hearing, initiated to revoke our Special Permit, saying "This is exactly the kind of community development that should be duplicated around the island, not shut down." The Chairman of the Planning Commission had also visited our ecovillage and was another supporter. We had a partial victory: our existing permit was not revoked. We were front page news in our local newspaper two consecutive days and the struggle continued.

We had hired the best lawyer in town and together we worked hard on a creative application to amend our Special Permit to include all the activities our local community desired us to provide. We also proposed modifying the system for dealing with complaints. We engaged in numerous lengthy meetings and endless dialogues with our neighbors, County officials, and other local groups confronted with similar situations to ourselves. The Planning Department and the Department of Public Works were uncooperative: just when our lawyers thought our application was complete, they asked us for an unnecessary "Traffic Impact Analysis Report," then took forever to review it and request changes. It appeared they had every intention of stalling us until we died.

We recognized that the Special Permit process itself was flawed and so I founded and became President of the Hawaii Sustainable Community Alliance, an association of like-minded people (see www.hawaiisustainablecommunity.org) with a mission to change existing laws. We had powerful and productive board meetings every other week, and built a coalition of over 600 sustainable community advocates and 30 local organizations. Being

highly motivated, we successfully petitioned our County Council to pass a resolution in 2011 requesting our building department "to establish an alternative building code." We submitted a draft bill and even got a County Council member elected on the basis of his support for this reform; however, nothing ever happened. The administration just ignored it, claiming it was under review (apparently indefinitely).

In 2012, we succeeded in the passage of our second County Resolution, which requested the State legislature to support a Sustainable Living Research Site bill. We campaigned hard to get our local health food store owner elected as our State Senator. He's been a consistent supporter of all sustainability efforts, he plays Jerry Garcia in our community Grateful Dead cover band, and he introduced our Sustainable Living bill in the State Judiciary. That season, the bill passed through all four committees in the House, but was tragically killed by the chairwoman of the first Senate committee, who had a severe dislike for Grateful Dead-loving Senators.

In 2014, after a lengthy, tiring, and well fought campaign by our HSCA membership, the bill passed, almost unanimously, through all eight committees in the State House and the State Senate. We were jubilant and excited at the prospect, not only of having the first legislation of its kind in the country, but at the thought that it would enable all ecovillages and sustainable communities in Hawaii a chance of becoming legal without compromise. Sadly, it failed because the same Senator that killed the bill previously was chairman of the conference committee assigned to resolve minor amendment issues and she refused to give it a hearing, thereby killing it again. That event ended any faith I still had in the democratic process.

Concurrently with this process, we had an ongoing application with the Hawaii Department of Land and Natural Resources to lease a parcel of land adjacent to our community upon which we had illegally encroached with driveways, a horse corral, and a few jungalows in the early 1990s. The lease could have resolved these legal issues and given us a productive means to work within the system. I had successfully completed this application in 1998 and it went to the State Board for approval, but was tabled due to a review of nonprofit leases. It soon appeared to be forgotten so we let sleeping dogs lie and all was well for the next 14 years.

In 2010, a disgruntled ex-employee of our organization decided to use our encroachment on the State land as ammunition against us and, after he recruited the help of two loud and unsavory political wannabes, some complaints were filed and we reinstated the lease process. With the requirement for a detailed environmental impact assessment and opportunity for public input, the lease proved impossible due to the intensity of complaints by the same small faction lodged against us. It was irrelevant that the complaints were mostly frivolous, fraudulent, and vindictive, and we submitted great rebuttal letters. We initially had the cooperation of State officials who visited and

would take any action to comply with their judgment against us. The basis for this is the growing education taking place in Hawaii regarding the fact that under US law there never was a treaty of annexation with the Hawaiian Kingdom to make it a State of the Union and under international law there is a presumption that the sovereign State of Hawaii still exists under occupation by the US. This may be hard for anyone subjected to the official US version of history to accept; however, if you go to www.hawaiiankingdom.org/blog you can learn about the true legal status of Hawaii and current initiatives to rectify the illegalities. Our ecovillage membership was totally divided on this issue and we never reached a consensus-minus-two agreement in accordance with our bylaws. The fun that originally brought us together had been replaced by fear.

There is a fear amongst some that continuing complaints from the tireless few would cause the authorities to make us remove every single unpermitted structure on our land. Our own members have now demolished structures: perfectly good, sustainable cabins and community facilities in the face of fines and threats of further government action. The impact of our struggle for legalization has worn us down, stressed us out, destroyed our morale and, over time, created such a climate of fear amongst many of our ecovillage members that they have voted against us even having our own family birthday parties or celebrations on our own property—all totally legal activities. Without the fun community gatherings that originally brought us together and glued us together for nearly three decades, our intentional community experiment is dying.

The fun that originally brought us together has been replaced by fear.

admired our community project, but eventually, when they faced being exposed for bending the rules and risking their jobs to help us, they turned against us and we ended up being fined $53,000 and were given 90 days to remove all encroachments.

This, of course, was seen as absurd by everyone in our neighborhood, except a tiny minority, but it became the final blow in our community's effort to survive. Adding to the fear factor were erroneous Ethics Commission charges filed against our nonprofits, the HSCA, the Senator who introduced our bill, and the Planning Commission Chairman who had previously supported us. Needless to say, the charges were all dismissed; however, they caused us considerable stress and some feared that other threats made by complainers would even result in one of our members getting deported from the US.

Our ecovillage land trust has had a consensus-minus-two decision-making process since 1987 but we never had to deal with anything like the major issues that this State judgment brought upon us. About two-thirds of our 30 geographically-dispersed members who participated in the email dialogue chose to acquiesce to the demands of the State Land Use division. About a third of us believed that we should at least attempt to stall them by using the law as a defense. We proposed sending a letter asking the State of Hawaii to prove that they had legal jurisdiction and clear title to this parcel before we

Along with the three dozen members of my ecovillage and the hundreds of community neighbors, interns, and visitors who lived with us, I believe that we were pioneers in a movement that the world needs in order to thrive sustainably.

The struggle for legalizing sustainable living is happening in many sectors of society by many people, in many ways. My greatest hope is that others will continue with this work and find success, because ecovillages and intentional communities have huge contributions to make to society's search for better sustainable lifestyle practices. 🥄

Graham Ellis was an idealistic visionary when he founded Bellyacres ecovillage in 1987. He also founded Jugglers for Peace, Hawaii's Volcano Circus, the HICCUP circus, and the Hawaii Sustainable Community Alliance. He has been a champion for grassroots developments and has had great adventures pursuing a community-based sustainable lifestyle for 28 years. He now lives happily with his family of seven in a conventional home and works for a mainstream nonprofit organization that operates 100 percent legally.

S.P.A.C.E. Farmers' Market, voted the best on the island from 2008-14, now closed down.

ADVENTURES OF THE MINI MOON
Realities of building your own earthen house with reused materials and volunteer labor

By Jenny Leis

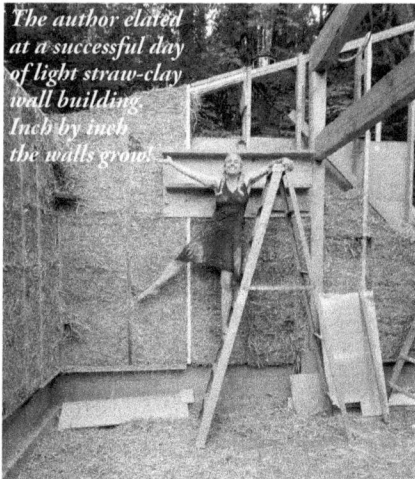
The author elated at a successful day of light straw-clay wall building. Inch by inch the walls grow!

Live music and horse manure plaster party! People offered all kinds of skills to make the workparties special!

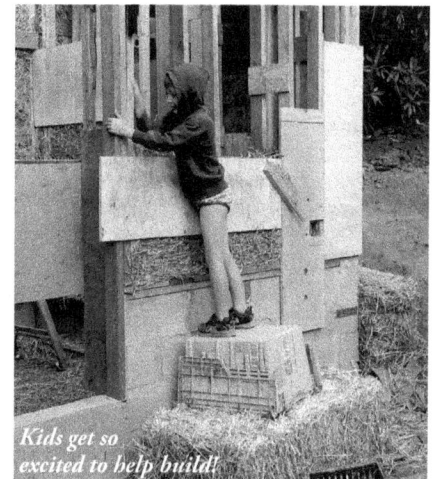
Kids get so excited to help build!

"*So when are you going to move in?*" Ummm, a year ago?

"*Horse manure? You built your house out of horse manure?*" Yup.

I didn't know what I was doing. I thought that after building a wood shed and a deck, it wouldn't be that much harder to take on an actual building—just a little 200 sq. ft. cozy home using volunteer labor and all local, natural, reused, creatively-sourced materials. Silly me! I'm writing this article now to share tidbits that I wish I knew before I started building the Mini Moon.

When I began this project, I suddenly became a general contractor for a project way beyond my abilities. The project I thought would take a summer is now two years long (and counting). Every time I meet a builder, I fall to the ground in respect: I had NO IDEA how complicated a building was. Every single inch taught me a new book of knowledge and complexity—how to space rebar in a concrete foundation (that you even need rebar!), how to estimate how much space 10 tons of small stones will fill (for the drain) and what kind of dump truck can be driven backwards down a long dirt driveway, what happens if you are a half-inch off in the length of some boards, what product will stick to windows and earthen plaster to be a flexible flashing (what flashing is!), what can be used to create a round gutter, what's the difference between nails and screws...and on and on.

And the labor! So far, I've had over 300 different people put their hands into this project. That's a lot of advertising and coordinating work parties. So while I was learning how to be a contractor and builder, I also put on my community organizer hat to recruit a nonstop flow of volunteers. Now I have 300 new or deepened friendships!

For years I've hung out with natural builders at my community and around Portland, Oregon (a hotspot of urban natural building) yet I'd never actually done much of the physical work. I was more of a talker, and even went on a national speaking tour about the community- and relationship-building power of natural building (many of you have heard about the Village Building Convergence). Now, I finally get it. It's awesome. Every inch of this building is woven with relationships, conversations, learning, sharing, loving touch.

The Basics

The Mini Moon is a 200 sq. ft. light straw-clay, cob, and recycled wood building with electricity but no plumbing. It's a satellite bedroom and mini-community center. I designed it specifically to have a dozen people in a circle for a meeting, good lighting and movable tables for art parties, the proper electrical lines to be a small music recording studio (foot-thick earth walls make the best sound quality!), and space for overnight guests and cuddle piles. I am community through

and through, and my deepest hope was that the Mini Moon became a hub for community activity. And it is working!

Context is key. I live at Tryon Life Community Farm (TLC Farm) in Portland, Oregon, a seven-acre public nonprofit community education center. About 18 of us live here within two residential collectives (The Bridgewalkers Alliance is specifically for people of color and trans folk; I am part of the other collective, Cedar Moon). On this land we host many events, workshops, and retreats. So when I called for workparties every weekend for two years, many people already had a relationship with this land and community, and for new folks TLC Farm was an attraction.

The Magic of Facebook; the Tenacity to Keep Asking

I hosted over 125 public workparties in 20 months. I rode the Facebook wave. I created a buzz and kept my public story consistent—for two years, my FB feed was a broken record. I posted a lot of photos, each time with a call to the next action: Come to the workparty on Saturday! Who has scrap plywood? Anyone know of a place to get reused windows?

It worked. Everywhere I go, people ask me about the project, comment on how hard I've been working, that it's taking so long (yeah, thanks, I know), and that they really want to help. It's created a buzz that people want to be part of.

And yes, it's hard to keep asking for help. I was embarrassed at times. But every time I asked, people showed up. And had a great time. And told me that my persistence was inspirational. So I kept asking.

I've learned that it's OK to ask because people will say yes when they choose to. I made sure to show my gratitude, explain how they made a meaningful impact on a big project, and tried to make it fun! It feels better to give than to receive, so when you find yourself asking for help, a lot, remember that you are also offering the opportunity for people to feel connected to something special.

Recipe for Successful Workparties

People who show up at workparties are cool. They are ready to work and I learned that I don't have to provide a lot of bells and whistles to make the experience meaningful. They came for a reason—to learn a skill or participate in a community activity or do something outside, not because I had great snacks or a live band (which I thought I'd have at every workparty—ha!).

People gave me a lot of great feedback about how I hosted workparties; here are some things I learned. My number one suggestion is to take time to share a warm welcome and a grateful good-bye for every person who shows up (details below). My number two suggestion is to be prepared! Know what you need to do that day and have the tools and materials at hand. No one likes to show up ready to work and then wait while you awkwardly fumble around.

Some more workparty secrets:

• **Honest advertising:**

Food. After the first couple workparties I got real about my ability to provide food so I always said to bring a lunch. I provided at least some snacks, but most people were perfectly happy to provide for themselves.

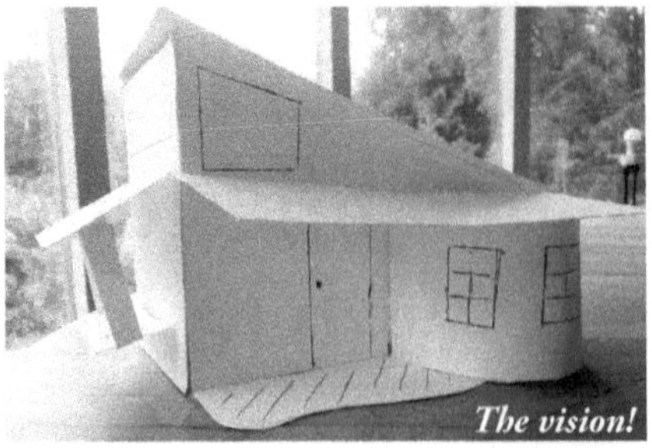
The vision!

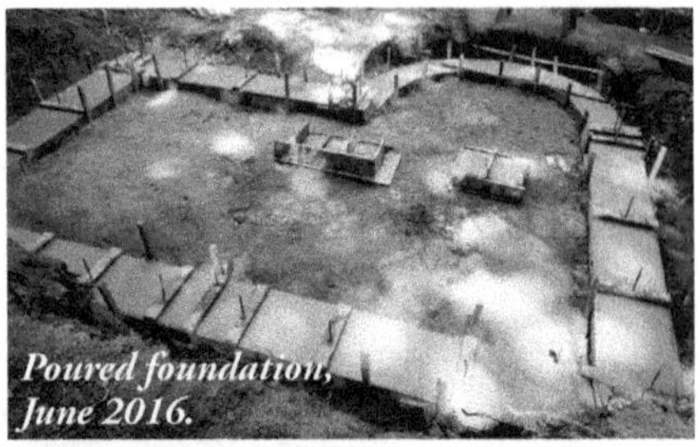
Poured foundation, June 2016.

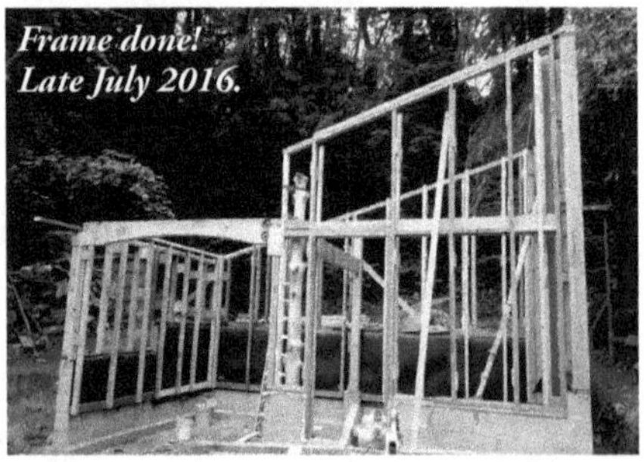
Frame done! Late July 2016.

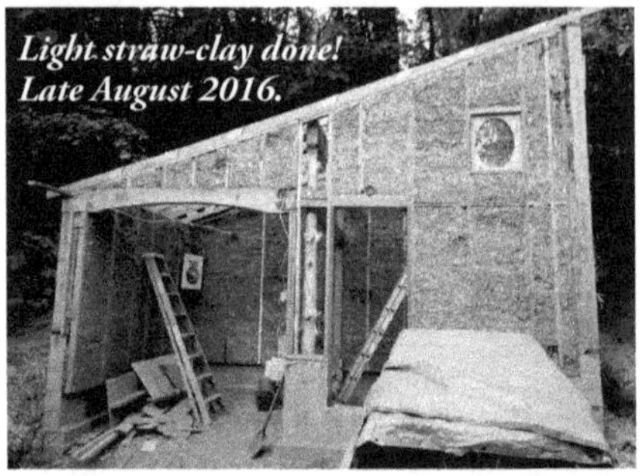
Light straw-clay done! Late August 2016.

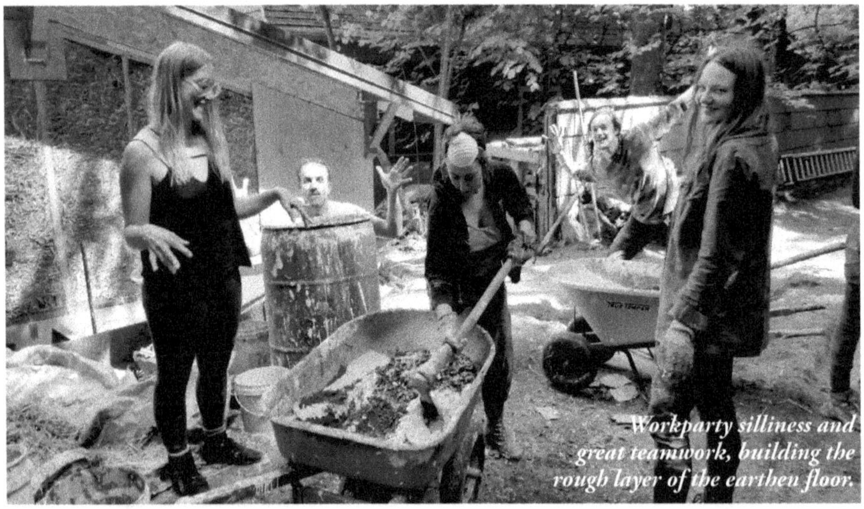
Workparty silliness and great teamwork, building the rough layer of the earthen floor.

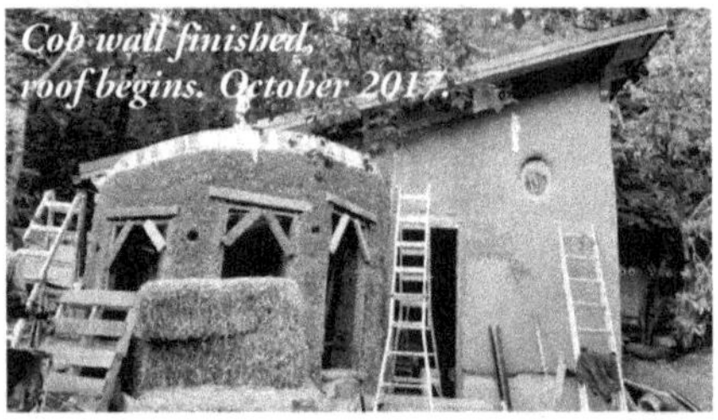
Cob wall finished, roof begins. October 2017.

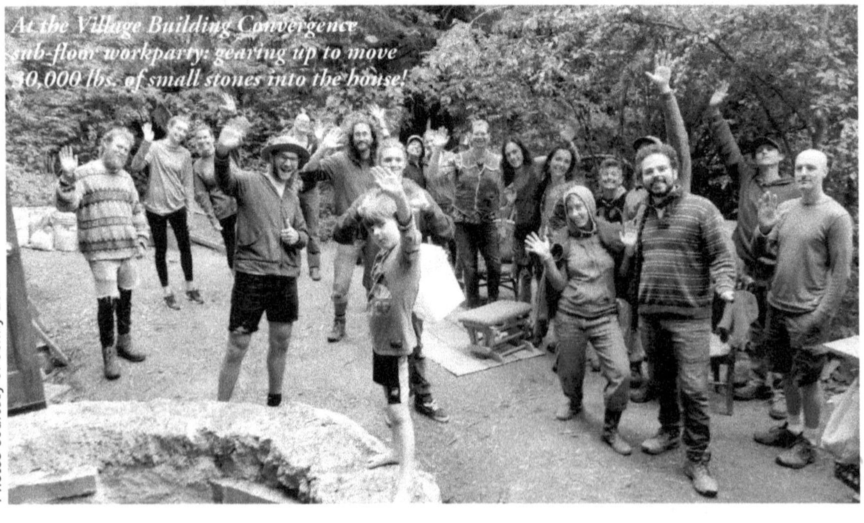
At the Village Building Convergence sub-floor workparty: gearing up to move 30,000 lbs. of small stones into the house!

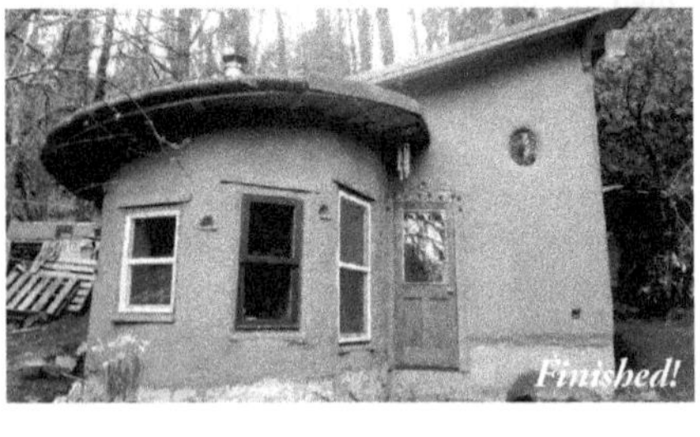
Finished!

Photos courtesy of Jenny Leis

Workplan/timing. Tell people exactly what they are in for, and if there will be options for folks of different ages/abilities. Have clear start and end times and stick with them.

Kid friendly? Make this explicit. Don't assume that kids will get in the way; in fact, they can be the most tenacious workers and creative visionaries, and I find that parents who bring kids to construction parties are damn cool and ready to work hard.

Dog friendly? I invited only dogs who could happily hang out on a leash.

• **A warm and connective welcome:** This is so important! Every time someone showed up, I stopped what I was doing and walked up to greet them. If someone has never been to your site before, they are likely feeling a little nervous or confused (remember they are walking into an active construction zone with tools and materials and partially built things everywhere!). I would always do the following:

Introduce myself with my gender pronoun (more on this below) and offer a warm welcome and gratitude for them showing up.

Find out what brought them here today.

Give a quick tour: big picture vision, what we're doing today, and how they can fit in.

Sparkles! At this point, they have received a lot of information, and I wanted to give them a quiet moment to take it all in and make a personal connection to the project. So, I gave them a pinch of sparkles (yes, I know, I know, microplastics...) to put anywhere they wanted in the project and I asked them to offer an intention for their work here today, or a blessing for the space, or TLC Farm, or the world: "Add your own bit of sparkle to the dirt!" Then I left them alone. I found that after people took a moment alone, they felt relaxed, happy, intrigued with my strange building site, and ready to go!

• **Meaningful work, something for everyone:** Some parts of the project lent themselves more easily to all-hands-on-deck-super-fun work, like building straw-clay or cob walls. Other days were more technical or heavy lifting. But no matter what, I always had a plan in my back pocket for someone with either less or more physical ability or knowledge. I tried to put everyone to use in appropriate ways. It felt good to have choices to offer.

• **Realistic and successful work:** Even on days where it felt like we trudged through only a small amount of work, I always made sure to celebrate what we accomplished. Everyone wants to feel their contribution was meaningful and that they helped out.

• **Community questions/conversations:** Inevitably people ask a lot of questions about the intentional community and education center. "So, how many people live here now?" is almost always the first question. I learned to anticipate the basics, share them up front in a condensed form, and politely say that I'm happy to answer more questions as we work or on a break. I also shared upcoming TLC Farm events and encouraged them to walk around and check the place out.

• **Photos:** Since Facebook advertising was so important to me, and I wanted to document the project, I took a lot of photos. It's very important to ask: Is it OK if I take your photo? And can I post it on FB?

• **A warm and connective goodbye, with gratitude:** Just as when folks arrived, when they left I always took a moment to stop, look them in the eye, and thank them for their contributions. These are very meaningful moments!

• **Sparkle in, Sparkle out!** Just as they took a quiet moment to "sparkle in" to the project, I asked people to "sparkle out" by signing my "Purple Sparkle Participation Book." In my little dirty sparkly notebook, I asked folks to sign their name and date, and whatever else they want-

ed—what they did that day, what it meant to them, etc. This helped people solidify the feeling that they were part of something special and to reflect on their own journey.

Gender

An unexpected aspect and extremely meaningful part of this project was learning how this building site became a safer space for people who identify as gender non-binary and/or trans. At least a dozen participants thanked me—and kept showing up—because they had been wanting to learn these skills and had not felt safe or comfortable at many other building sites. Building is a cis-male dominated world and not only was I a woman running this show, but I also made sure to include gender pronouns in introductions, and to do the work to teach folks who had never encountered concepts like gender non-binary. I used my gender privilege and workparty leader-power to intervene and gently teach cis-people if they seemed confused, used incorrect pronouns, or asked inappropriate questions.

Again, context is key: TLC Farm is known as a gender-variant-supportive place, due to the Bridgewalkers Alliance residential collective and monthly "Tranimal Nature" events on the land. Many folks from these communities came to my workparties. As a cis-woman, I was humbled to spend many hours over dozens of workparties hearing about their gender-related experiences in the world and at other building sites. I recommend for any workparty host to learn about the importance—and nuances—of including pronouns in introductions, at least as a start for creating safer spaces.

Ponderings for Intentional Communities

I'll be honest: this project was hard on my community. Not only did I disappear from other responsibilities on the land, but I also constantly asked for help and spilled stressful

Building with cob weaves so many stories and conversations into the wall!

Kids are builders, too!

Sparkles were added at the end of each major accomplishment. Here, the rough layer of the earthen floor.

energy to my community-mates.

When my community agreed to this project, they anticipated my physical and emotional stress and asked me to incorporate rest days and a daily practice into my schedule. I didn't. I let the stress consume me and obsessively kept working. I always felt like I was racing the rainy season. Every week, I needed to plan a workparty, learn the skills needed for that weekend, advertise, prepare snacks and materials, and then do the work. I was constantly exhausted, had trouble sleeping, and broke down crying a lot. My community-mates saw that I got myself into something way over my head and gently tried to slow me down, but I didn't listen.

Many workparty folks asked why my community-mates weren't joining in. I explained that they did a lot of late-night truck unloading and random heavy-object moving for me, and that they were there when I really needed it. If you live in a land-based intentional community, you know that there are endless projects and responsibilities. I didn't want to ask more of my land-mates; I was appreciative that they kept things going while I was focused on the Mini Moon.

But an element of resentment also grew, both directions. They were frustrated at my stress and non-involvement in things like weekly cooking chores, and I got sad when people didn't help at my workparties.

By the second year, I think my community arrived at some kind of balance. The majority of the work was done by me and off-site people. We realized that I was fulfilling TLC Farm's educational mission by having consistent natural building workparties and lively activities almost every weekend. I brought a lot of new energy and attention to the land project. And hopefully in just a couple more months, I will be done and can re-involve myself in the rest of the community work. Plus, the Mini Moon is already starting to function as a mini-community center, which my land-mates are now discovering as a lovely place for meetings, quiet work, and connective conversations.

Unexpected Magic

Even though I thought this would be a summer-long project and it turned into a ton of stress and work over two years, I am so happy with the Mini Moon. At this point, I just laugh at how long this is taking. As someone said to me, every workparty adds more love to my walls—more fun and great people. Now, I am a builder and this house is truly a community space—a beautiful, hand-crafted, relationship-full, cozy home for gatherings. I am humbled and honored to steward the Mini Moon! 🦋

Jenny Leis has always lived in community, most recently for 13 years in Cedar Moon, part of Tryon Life Community Farm in Portland, Oregon (www.tryonfarm.org). She loves bringing sparkle to the dirt!

The light-straw clay insulation is completed—a major success moment!

What I Learned about Local, Natural, Reused Materials

• Reused wood: It takes five times longer than new wood to source, pull out nails, avoid broken screws when cutting, deal with warped and mismatched boards...but it is so damn satisfying! There is so much scrap wood in cities! Neighbors have little piles left over from projects, new buildings have trash piles, dumpsters are gold outside of a remodel (old growth 2x4s!), and builder-friends often have extras. Friends would keep an eye out and text when they saw a fantastic free pile of wood—that's how I got my live-edge gorgeous trim!

• Clay, sand, straw: Every location is different so I will defer to all the natural building books to tell you how to do a soil test. Useful hint: find a pottery maker with clay scraps.

• Horse manure: Easy to get for free from farms, usually lovely places to visit. Fantastic plaster material, and quite fun to work with! (It doesn't smell when it dries, and has a lovely fibrous texture.)

• Hardware: You probably want to buy your nails and screws new and you will probably end up needing a ton more than you think. Invest in the giant boxes! Costs of hardware really add up!

• Styrofoam, gooey chemicals, Tyvek, tar paper, and other yucky stuff: Sometimes you just gotta use plastic/oil products, but the good thing is that I could reuse other people's leftovers. Best creative reuse story: my neighbor had Structural Insulated Panels sitting in his backyard for 10 years. Now, my "Cozy Cob Corner" ceiling is insulated with eight inches of styrofoam—a perfect example of using something un-enviro-friendly that would otherwise rot in a forest or landfill.

• Windows: More expensive than I anticipated, even used. Hard to get the same size so why not make them all different sizes? Tip: there are a lot of interesting-shaped large windows that get thrown out, so if you plan to have a big or odd window, find it early in your design process and design the wall around it!

• Sparkles: OK, so I know that microplastics are evil, but I really love sparkles. Every inch of this building has layers of sparkles built into it. I even took small handfuls and carefully blew them onto the wet plaster, inside and out. They are magical at night when they glint in light!

—JL

My Budget

I was told that you can have two of the magic three: good, fast, or cheap. I still wanted all three. "They" were right. I ended up letting go of the "fast," since I stuck with my value of finding used materials, which took a LOT of time on Craigslist and Facebook, and driving around town.

At the end of this project, I expect it to total about $18,000. This includes about $7,000 for consulting support and labor (at a few key moments, we hired some friends) and about $9,000 for materials. I also put in over $2,000 for gas/driving, snacks, and odds and ends. I didn't count my personal expenses—endless hours, many days of missed work, health care costs for hurt body parts—and the time of my superstar volunteers.

• Labor: $7,000 (consultant and some friend-labor)
• Foundation and drainage: $2,000
• Frame: $500
• Electrical: $400
• Light straw-clay insulation: $400
• Stove pipe: $500
• Windows and door: $500
• Cob wall, including foundation: $600
• Roof, ceiling, and insulation: $2,000
• Earthen subfloor and floor: $1,500
• Structural plywood and earthen plaster: $400
• Not counted: Snacks, gas-mileage, or the value of my time, volunteer time, and all of the free materials!

—JL

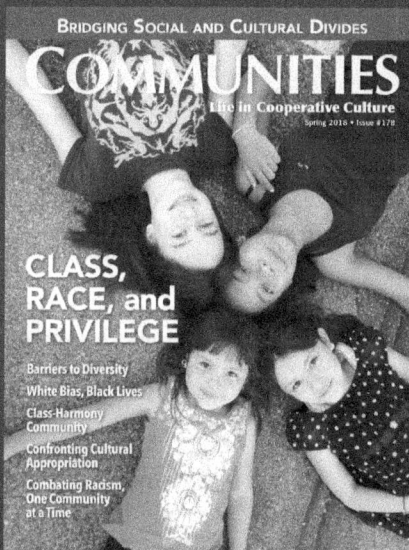

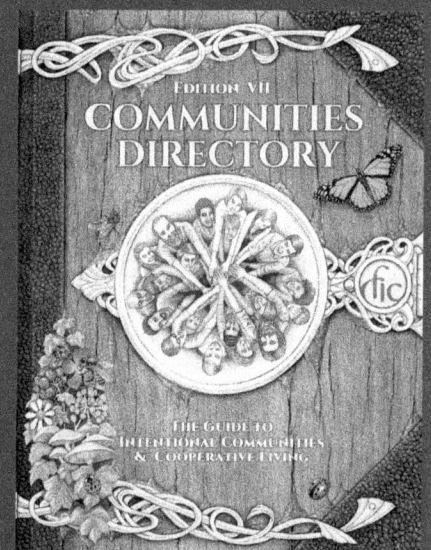

Lancaster Cohousing.

Panya Project.

BUILDING COLLECTIVELY
Is Greener, Easier, and Cheaper

By Jenny Pickerill

Building a house is hard work. A decade ago my mum and I built an eco-house together. We loved it—the freedom of designing what spaces we wanted, the excitement of choosing only materials we wanted to use, and most of all the pure joy of moving into the finished house. I have lived in many places but up until then I had never realised that a house could actually make me happy. Sitting on a reclaimed-wooden floor warmed by the sun streaming in through a draught-free window, knowing my water was being heated, and electricity generated, for free by the sun, I felt a surge of happiness.

I also suffered from a wave of exhaustion, a realisation that there was no money left, a worry about all the jobs still to do, and a fear about whether the house would stay standing, endure a storm, and if the systems (like the rainwater harvester) would carry on working. But it was at this moment, despite the work, stress, and worry, that I fell in love with eco-building and its possibilities. I also realised how terrible most of the other houses I had lived in had been. They were cold, damp, draughty, dark, and even mouldy. Since then I have been exploring how we can build better houses that are affordable, comfortable, and ecological.

Communities are sites of innovation and experimentation in eco-home design. I first encountered eco-building at the Centre for Alternative Technology in Wales, where they were experimenting with timber-frame and strawbale construction. The buildings of eco-communities shape many communities' functions. As Jan Martin Bang argues, "we are what we live in. When we plan our buildings, we are also planning what kind of society we want to create...we make the buildings and the buildings make us."[1]

Karen Liftin[2] calls this the "architectures of intimacy" where buildings in communities are purposefully designed to encourage social interaction. When designing and building using circles—as a house shape, as houses around a communal circular garden, as an arrangement for seating—the circle is used to avoid hierarchy and enables everyone to see each other. Building houses together is also a way to build community. Using materials such as strawbale which require little specialised training means anyone can get involved. Yet building collectively and in community is not always easy.

Eco-communities benefit from a shared work force, shared infrastructure costs, and economies of scale, and builders benefit from mutual support and a niche space in which to innovate and take risks. However, the costs of building in eco-communities tend to be the time required to make decisions and an experimentalism that can mean ignoring established building approaches or building physics. It is easier and cheaper to build eco-homes in communities, but the results are more variable.

Building in a community requires effort to be focused into communal systems of decision-making, living together, and processes of sharing. Numerous social and economic benefits result from this, but the houses themselves can suffer. In some cases eco-communities offer important space for periods of innovative and creative experimentation that go on to influence eco-home design elsewhere. But those who seek to focus on housing can be accused of specialisation or elitism, and be marginalised.

Opportunities

Building together is cheaper than building alone. Numerous strategies can reduce the costs of construction; building smaller houses, using cheap marginal land, using reclaimed materials, or reducing labour costs through self-build. Eco-communities use all these tactics and some have managed to build incredibly inexpensive homes. For example, Tony Wrench built his roundhouse at Birthdr Mawr (Wales) for a total cost of $4,000. However, eco-communities are also able to benefit from their size to reduce the costs of building by sharing infrastructure and devising cost-sharing schemes. LILAC (Leeds, England) developed a new home ownership model to ensure the houses remained affordable. Residents only pay a housing charge of 35 percent of their income. In effect the higher earners subsidise those on lower incomes.

Eco-communities also provide a ready pool of labour that significantly reduces costs. Labour costs in building are conventionally half of the total costs of construction. Communities also buy construction materials in bulk, further reducing costs. Clutching to the steep hillside of the Sangre de Cristo Mountains north of Taos, New Mexico, the Lama

Foundation has been building since 1968. Principally a spiritual centre, it has an eclectic mixture of eco-homes. Building here is a collective process and part of a spiritual practice for many; one resident said they "build with clay, mud, and love."

Building is a process of sharing—sharing tools, skills, and roles—as Chelsea Lord, a volunteer explains: "Building a building has to be a collective thing... In regular construction it's all portioned out...everybody is separate... It's just so un-cohesive and it ends up costing the homeowner so much for all these specialised people to come in with all these really expensive specialised tools. Whereas in natural building the same crew of people all build together start to finish, and you don't have to have a bunch of specialised tools and you don't have to have a bunch of specialised knowledge. If there is someone directing, you don't have to know how to use a nail gun or a [circular] saw. So it's just much more human, and then they're so beautiful when they're done, they just feel good."

Perhaps the most effective way to build more ecologically is by building smaller homes and by sharing large communal spaces and facilities. Eli Spevak (Peninsula Park Commons, Oregon) explains: "The most effective thing you can do is simply build smaller and attached housing. Most of the carbon impact of housing comes from heating it, so if you have a smaller space you do not need as much energy to heat it and if it is attached, side by side with your neighbours, then you also need less heat because the common walls share the heat across the buildings. One of the things we do is build smaller spaces and then have common spaces to provide a little extra space."

In Panya Project (Thailand), large communal spaces include the shared kitchen, gardens, sitting area, office space, laundry, workshops, greenhouses, guest space, and bathrooms. Panya Project is near Mae Taeng, Chiang Mai, northern Thailand. Established in 2004, the 10-acre site has become a place for experimentation and education in permaculture and natural building. Built using either sun-dried adobe bricks or wattle and cob, homes are purposely small—one house is just three metres by four and a half metres floor space, because it contains only space for sleeping and privacy. Most simply contain a bed and some storage space. All cooking, dining, and washing occur in communal spaces. This reduces both build time and material requirements.

Even in cities, eco-communities often offer small personal spaces compensated for by large communal areas. At Los Angeles Eco-Village, an eco-retrofit of an old brick apartment block in downtown L.A., residents rent private apartments with individual kitchens and bathrooms, but they share the gardens, bike storage room, bulk food storage, meeting space, and a large entrance seating area.

Despite the compact size, the physical and emotional sense of home extends far beyond the house. Peninsula Park Commons, initiated by Eli Spevak and Jim Labbe in 2003, is a cohousing development created by renovating six existing houses and building four new structures. Beyond the buildings lie the communal gardens and raised vegetable patches. Rather than stop the development at the edge of the plot, however, Peninsula Park Commons stretched out into the street and reclaimed the sidewalk with planters. Plant beds overflow and merge the communal garden with the public space. This is a very deliberate approach; in Eli Spevak's words, "we want to slip into existing communities." They hold

Lama Foundation.

Dance at Lama Foundation.

Open Day, Peninsula Park Commons.

Kailash Ecovillage.

Photos courtesy of Jenny Pickerill

community events like their annual community ice cream social and garden party to reach out and draw people in.

This sharing and communal spirit is a vital support mechanism for eco-building, especially when it involves risk-taking. Being surrounded by like-minded individuals and communal infrastructure provides invaluable mutual support. Kailash is an urban ecovillage situated in a 32-unit apartment building in Portland, Oregon. All the units are one-bedroom small apartments and the community is gradually eco-retrofitting the whole building. As Maitri, a cofounder of the ecovillage, argues, "you really have to be the model. You have to be what you want other people to be. So you really need to work on your own self first."

Encouraging change requires appropriate infrastructure, as Maitri explains: "We have individual [garden] plots so that people can put themselves into that and be creative. I think it's very important that people have that opportunity. Like the bike parking—we put those bike-parking racks and oh, we need two more already! You provide a community; people come and have a good time."

Challenges

If communities self-build they take time and energy away from other tasks. Even using external volunteer labour has costs—the time taken to train newcomers, the costs of repairing mistakes, or the inefficiency of unskilled labour. Lama Foundation struggled to maintain their buildings because they relied on volunteers to build, and yet natural materials were used which require regular attention and patching. The community didn't anticipate this need for maintenance. In Richard Gomes' words, "we are financially OK, but we do not have the staff to maintain the buildings. We need a bigger staff if we are to only have lime plasters;

that is why we have started to use some regular plaster—stucco—on external walls." (Stucco has a bigger environmental impact.)

The cost of labour—whether it is measured in time, efficiency, training requirements, or the consequences of using unskilled labour—needs to be understood. Diana Leafe Christian proposes that all eco-communities create a budget for labour needs: "if you don't create a labor budget, you'll be forever tempted to add new projects and ask the community to allocate labor credit for them, leaving you wondering why you have six half-done construction projects sitting around for years."[3]

Eco-building therefore requires significant negotiation, time, patience, and compromise, and careful attention to decision-making structures. The more democratic and shared the approach, the longer the process takes. At Kailash Ecovillage effort went into building community, as Ole explains: "We have a weekly community night...when we moved in the residents didn't know each other and now everybody knows almost everybody...so it's created a tremendous sense of community out of basically zero community before."

But they decided against the democratic approach in decision-making in order to save time and reduce conflict. According to Ole, a cofounder and owner of the land and apartments, "we're a hierarchy—we're basically a benevolent dictatorship here and we take the decisions and we invite a lot of community input but ultimately we are the decision-makers. I think for some people that actually is probably preferable because most people don't want to be involved in a lot of the decisions we do—they just want things to be done and maintenance to be done and there's no need for them to give any input in that."

Ole and Maitri adopted this approach because when they were part of a previous attempt to establish cohousing in Portland, they felt that

LILAC.

Tir y Gafel Ecovillage.

Peninsula Park Commons.

Panya Project.

Lama Foundation.

Los Angeles Eco-Village.

Panya Project.

the consensus decision-making approach paralysed the progress of the build. In Ole's view, "it just takes forever as there are so many voices... and they agonise over these silly things: the colour, the finishes, and stuff like that."

Lydia Doleman, a self-builder, argues that "buildings have the capacity to equalize people or segregate them."[4] Eco-communities need to design their buildings and shared spaces to accommodate diversity. While communities have developed new forms of interpersonal relationships, often rejecting the notion of a nuclear family, other forms of diversity have been paid less attention, especially race, disability, and class. Camphill communities seek to provide places for disabled people to live and work, and new cohousing communities are being designed for seniors, but in most eco-communities little provision is made for differently abled bodies.

Finally, Jonathan Dawson argues it is time for eco-communities to start to accept the need for professional support: "as planning regulations have tightened, it has become more difficult for groups to create substantial new settlements without professional assistance."[5] Eco-communities are generally quite poor at collaborating with professionals. While many examples of outstanding, high quality eco-building exist in eco-communities, in many other examples little reference was made to existing building knowledge, resulting in simple mistakes. Communities can fall prey to anti-professionalism, a rejection of the importance of experts, specialists, or building professionals such as architects and engineers.

The journey of Twin Oaks (Louisa, Virginia) exemplifies the tension between unskilled building and a professional approach. The community had the input of professional architects and builders who had given up their jobs and settled there. Over time some of these builders began to get frustrated with the need to work with volunteers and constantly teach others, and eventually a key builder departed. At Dancing Rabbit (Rutledge, Missouri), Alex Whitcroft, a trained architect, sought to overcome this tension by being a "brave specialist," someone who lived on site and worked with residents: "what is needed is not specialists but...brave specialists who can listen, ask the right questions, and design with communities while integrating their expertise."[6] This compromise approach is perhaps the most productive way forwards in terms of ensuring quality eco-buildings.

Ten things to consider when eco-building in community

1. Sharing space, objects, equipment, and skills reduces costs and environmental waste, but robust systems of sharing with clear agreements are needed.

2. Living in compact spaces works if there is communal space available to share, particularly access to green spaces.

3. There is a need to balance participation in eco-building and collective decision-making with the need to complete projects and take risks.

4. Without explicit effort to encourage diverse types of residents and self-builders, eco-building will likely remain the preserve of the white middle classes.

5. Although learning by doing is useful, the need to learn from the past, from experts and professionals, and to seek out existing knowledge is too often ignored, wasting time, effort, and resources.

6. That many eco-communities relied upon volunteers to build (and maintain) their houses has unintended costs. Sometimes this results in inefficient building practices, incomplete projects, failure to consider and plan for maintenance, and poor quality buildings.

7. Residents and self-builders rely upon mutual support in building their eco-homes, not just in sharing physical labour but also emotional support.

8. Eco-building does not necessarily require destroying existing structures. Such structures can be renovated and often there is still space in which to add new additional eco-homes.

9. Eco-communities' focus on social issues, on commitment, building community, and collective governance, has sometimes led to neglect of the need to learn and understand the physics of how buildings work.

10. Building by anticipating future change in occupiers, and thinking through how to, for example, maintain affordability, are essential to the success of eco-homes.

Jenny Pickerill is a Professor of Environmental Geography at the University of Sheffield, England. She has worked with many eco-communities worldwide and recently published a book, Eco-Homes: People, Place and Politics *(Zed Books). Information about her work and contact details are at www.jennypickerill.info.*

1. Bang, J M (2005) *Ecovillages: A Practical Guide to Sustainable Communities.* Floris Books, Edinburgh, pp. 124-125.
2. Litfin, K T (2014) *Ecovillages: Lessons for Sustainable Community.* Polity Press, Cambridge.
3. Christian, D L (2003) *Creating a Life Together: Practical Tools to Grow Ecovillages and Intentional Communities.* New Society Publishers, Gabriola Island, Canada, p. 165.
4. Flying Hammer Productions. theflyinghammer.com
5. Dawson, J (2006) *Ecovillages: New Frontiers for Sustainability.* Schumacher Briefings, Green Books, Totnes, Devon, p. 82.
6. Whitcroft, A (2012) Getting Ecovillages Noticed, COMMUNITIES #156, Fall 2012, pp. 29-33 (p. 30).

Harmonious Homemade Habitat

By Laura Harris

I had been dreaming of building a strawbale house for many years, despite having no experience with building. I was very idealistic, and using natural construction satisfied my goal to use nontoxic materials. I had lived in several urban intentional communities, but was ready to find a rural IC where I could build and farm. I had lived in Washington state for over a decade when I discovered Tolstoy Farm, and I was fortunate to be accepted by this decentralized community in eastern Washington. The climatic extremes of the Columbia basin are perfectly suited for strawbale buildings.

In 1997 I moved to Tolstoy Farm, which was formed in 1963 by hippies, back-to-the-landers, draft dodgers, and social visionaries. They had begun building structures out of whatever they could find. Builders who had started out as amateurs went on to work in the industry and became experts in their field. By the time I arrived some of the older homes were being remodeled and modernized; others had crumbled into ruins.

Between the knowledge of the people in the Tolstoy community, their willingness to teach and share tools, and the archive of success and failure that the existing buildings provide, I found a vast resource from which aspiring builders can learn. On the 180 acres owned by the community, much of which has been preserved as natural forest, there are raw materials that would not normally be available. There also exists a tradition of neighbors coming together and helping each other out when extra hands are needed. I discovered that this network of natural materials, experienced builders, and people willing to help out and share tools makes intentional community an excellent place for eco-design and natural building. The bylaws of Tolstoy Farm require residents to have as little environmental impact as possible, including that all homes be off the grid. This suited my ideals perfectly.

I wanted to design my house in order to utilize the natural forces to my benefit, while protecting my structure from destructive elements. I picked a spot near enough to a creek that I could hear the water flowing, but far enough away to avoid flooding and the inevitable migration of the creek bed. I observed the wind, the slope of the terrain, geology, drainage, availability of water, access, solar exposure (especially in the winter), privacy, rain and snow fall, fire safety, food and water storage, aging, proximity to other homes and tall trees that could fall on the house. I imagined my house in ruins, being able to compost back into the earth.

Observing these elements informed my eco-building design. I had hoped to use only natural construction materials such as straw, soil, clay, lime, rock, wood, metal, and water. But as I planned the structure, I had to also take into consideration how much money I had to build with and live on, which limited my time. I had

Laura pounding in corner brace. Experimental thatch structure can be seen in background.

D. Dolph

Concrete foundation with posts in place.

Completed log frame with roof before stacking bales.

Plastering workparty, southeast corner.

also to consider the wear on my body of doing such intense physical work, and the carbon footprint involved in moving materials around. So I ended up choosing to use concrete rather than fitted rock for my foundation, tar paper as a moisture barrier in the roof, man-made metal roofing, and a worn-out set of tires packed with rock to support internal posts.

Since recycled and repurposed materials are commonly used in eco-buildings, I felt good about reusing my old tires. Other Tolstoy residents have replaced fiberglass with insulation made from recycled jeans, reused old barn beams rather then buying lumber, and packed an unfinished house frame with light clay (straw wetted with clay slip and packed into forms). One house was made entirely of rocks and mortar, and several underground cellars and ice houses have lovely living roofs. A log cabin stands as a reminder of the beauty of wood in the round. Another resident used fibercrete (concrete mixed with shredded newspaper) to super insulate his walls and make beautiful stairs. I used cardboard, dogwood branches, and papier mâché for my ceiling rather than sheetrock. Repurposing and recycling can save money, energy, and reduce the need for resource extraction.

People who want to learn natural building and eco-design are drawn to intentional communities and become willing helpers in a fun and nontoxic work-play endeavor. Women and children become active participants, gaining skill and expertise not encouraged in conventional construction. Those with artistic inclinations will find fulfillment in the malleability of earthly materials. Natural and eco-building can be less expensive, yet more labor intensive, than conventional construction.

During my research and the two years I spent building my strawbale house, I learned some of the things that can go wrong:

• A wall coated with natural plaster needs a significant roof overhang, and the two-and-a-half-foot overhang I made is not quite enough. In the winter snow slides off the roof and heaps up against the plaster, degrading it.

• I tried using dry stone work for the floor and stairs of an attached porch, but it was very unstable. Later I used concrete mortar to stabilize the rock work.

• During a winter of very deep snow I had thick ice buildup on my metal roof. Once it started to melt, the whole sheet slid down and smashed my stovepipe. My partner then designed and welded a V-shaped ice splitter that we mounted above the stovepipe to prevent this.

• While it is soothing to have a river or creek flowing close enough to hear it, I have seen several

homes swamped during floods. I took care to place my house more than 100 feet away from the creek.

• My experimental papier mâché ceiling has held up pretty well on the inside, but not so well outside under the eaves. Moisture decayed the paper, allowing wasps, bats, and flying squirrels to move in. Last winter I removed the damaged areas and lined the eaves with hardware cloth and tar paper, which I secured to the top of the walls with a decorative arrange-

By utilizing the extra labor offered by community members, I created a super-insulated unique home with raw materials for under $5000.

ment of apple and pear cuttings.

• My adobe floor is soft and beautiful, but areas with heavy wear develop potholes and cracks. Chair legs bore holes as well. I have tried many different recipes for patching, and have found oat water mixed in with my usual mix of fine fiber, sifted sand, dirt, and clay to work wonders. Using a hole saw, I cut disks out of plywood, screwed them to the bottom of the chair legs, and glued a layer of homemade felt to the bottom. This solved the chair problem.

• I used scavenged one-and-a-half-inch pipe for my drain, and buried it under the adobe floor. I ignored the advice of a seasoned builder who said this was a mistake. The drain pipe got plugged up as predicted. I recently rerouted a new drain through the wall which feeds through proper drain pipes and into a buried hugelkultur greywater system.

• I visited a cob/strawbale hybrid cottage in Oregon where the builder had used curved saplings for window headers, creating an arch. The weight of the strawbales and cob stacked on top of this was too heavy and broke the window. Learning from this I made two-inch by 16-inch wood headers using a chainsaw mill and allowed two to three inches between the window and the header to accommodate settling of the walls. I filled this gap with long cigars of straw wrapped with string, and plastered over it. In some places I have successfully stacked 10 vertical feet of bale wall on top of these window headers without compromising the window.

Even when things go wrong and the natural builder has to undo and redo, this is a nontoxic job. Most materials can be reused, and there is little to no trash. Natural plaster and cob can be rewetted, remixed, and put back into action. While professional builders often use a modified cement mixer to blend plaster, I used the simpler method, mixing plaster on a tarp on the ground and squishing it with bare feet. This mix is safe for the skin; the clay in the mix can actually draw venom out of pesky bug bites. Once your feet are rinsed off from mixing cob or plaster, they feel super clean! This divergence from the caustic contents of concrete enables participation by young and old alike without protective gear.

Which of the many natural and eco-building options are best really depends on the climate and the locally available materials. Strawbale building has shown promise in climates with extremes of heat and cold, and where grains are grown. Light clay has been used to infill conventionally framed structures, replacing fiberglass. When plastered, the walls look similar to bale walls, but lack the extra insulating value. Old tires are filled with rammed earth in the earthship homes popular in the Southwest. Cob and adobe bricks are appropriate wherever there is enough soil; rock building, where there is an abundance of rock; log building, where there is an abundance of logs. Underground structures like cellars, ice houses, basements, and hillside hobbit holes are incredible temperature regulators but must be placed well away from flood waters and need good ventilation to prevent mold.

Retrofitting and remodeling with eco-materials is a good option for those wanting to replace toxic elements while saving the framework of a beloved home. When to retrofit or rebuild is a decision made after careful inspection of the structure. Is the design workable or inadequate for the conditions? Is the the frame rotten or infested with termites? If so you may regret the time spent trying to revive the dead.

As long as the frame and roof are sound and not infested with rodents or insects, it is likely rebuildable. If the foundation and location are still suitable, an eco-remodel is the best response to limits that a community may place on new construction. It may not save time nor headaches, as rebuilding involves tearing down and hauling off trash, then figuring out how to make what you want out of what is left. Retrofitting with strawbales requires extending the roof out and/or reducing the inside floor space, changing the window and door frames, and assuring the foundation is adequate.

I found natural building to be a fine way to live my ideals. By collecting downed trees I framed a house without the killing of live trees. By milling boards with a chainsaw mill I did not support the timber industry. By using local strawbales, dirt, sand, clay, and cardboard I avoided using sheetrock and fiberglass.

Two years after I started, I moved into an unfinished yet livable shell. By utilizing the extra labor offered by community members, I created a super-insulated unique home with raw materials for under $5000. It took several more years to finish the walls and floor. Now, in 2018, it has been 20 years since I started, and I also have a rock porch, a cob root cellar, a log-framed outbuilding, a greenhouse framed with curved saplings, and a cob bread oven. The most recent improvements include a well, a hugelkultur greywater drain, and upgraded solar power.

I hope my story inspires others to use natural building and eco-materials to construct durable, nontoxic, low-impact, energy-efficient, and creative structures. With determination, hard work, and the support of an intentional community, you too might be able to create the home of your dreams. ❧

Laura Harris is a 20-year member of the Tolstoy Farm community, where she enjoys communal living, organic farming, and fiber arts.

Laura's strawbale house in 2018.

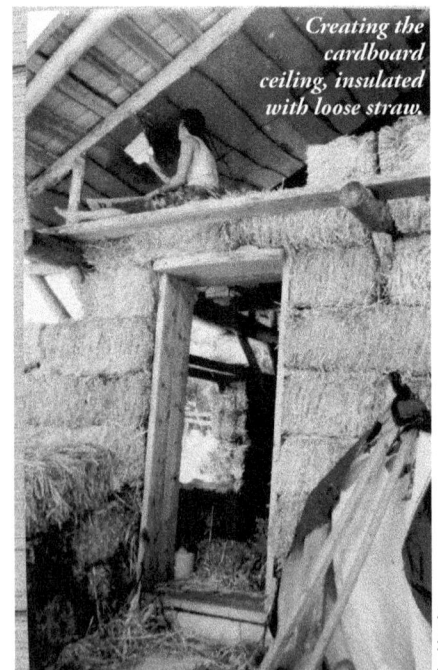

Creating the cardboard ceiling, insulated with loose straw.

Loft bedroom in Larkspur.

BUILDING IN AN ECOVILLAGE: LESSONS LEARNED

By Tony "Papa Bear" Barrett

When the founders of Dancing Rabbit Ecovillage were searching for our land, they had a short list of criteria to keep in mind. The freedom to explore alternative construction was on that list, so you could say that alternative construction is written into our DNA. It was certainly a large factor in my decision to join the community (located just outside Rutledge, Missouri) in 2006.

I first visited Dancing Rabbit in fall 2005, after abandoning a MFA program studying furniture making. The next spring, I came back as a work-exchanger/intern working on the Ironweed co-op kitchen, my first chance to really get my hands dirty. Before my work-exchange was over, I was designing and collecting materials for my first building project, a 400+ sq. ft. light clay-straw insulated cabin, named Larkspur. I have had the great fortune to earn my living doing what I love working in my community ever since.

Having studied furniture making, I was no stranger to design, tools, and joinery, but I had never designed or built anything bigger than a table before. What I now know about architecture, construction techniques, natural building, and building science has come from personal experience, research, lots of reading, asking others, and a healthy dose of making it up as I go along. Even after designing and building many structures over the course of 12 years, I often feel my knowledge is woefully lacking. Please keep this in mind when selecting the grain of salt with which to take these words.

Here are some of the lessons I have learned along the way:

Yes, you can build your own house. So long as you are reasonably handy and highly motivated, there is no reason you can not pull this off. Time, money, and skill are all you need, and to be honest, you could get away with any two of those three. Even a small building project is made up of hundreds of small, discrete tasks, but most of those a trained monkey could perform. A much more important part of the construction process than experience swinging a hammer is knowing how it all needs to come together, and in what order.

You don't have to do it alone. There is certainly something to be said about going out into the wilderness and carving out a shelter with nothing but your wits and bare hands, but there is nothing particularly heroic about solo building as a practice. In fact, it can be faster, safer, and more fun to work with other people—particularly when it comes to labor-intensive natural building techniques. If the people you enlist to help have more experience, all the better.

You don't have to do it all. Don't be afraid to bring in the experts. Don't know much about plumbing? Hire that part out. Really hate working with concrete? Ditto. This will (ideally) provide you with quality work, and save you from having to become your own expert in every trade.

Keep it simple. A building project of any size is complicated. Don't make it any more complicated than you have to, unless you really want to stretch your limits. In which case, why are you even reading this article?

Start small. If you are new to building, don't make your first project a 1000+ sq. ft. house. Maybe start with a chicken coop, a garden shed, or a garage. You will gain real-world experience understanding the building process with significantly lower stakes.

Gain experience any way you can. Volunteer for work parties, participate in workshops. Better yet, work on someone else's project first. You can earn money, gain experience, benefit from their experience, and ultimately not have to live with the inevitable mistakes you make.

You are going to make mistakes. There is no way around this. Your best bet is to learn from them, and not repeat them. Also, be open and honest about your failures—you may save someone else from a similar fate. May all your mistakes be small.

Prepare yourself. Building your own home will be an enormous undertaking. It will require more time, money, and materials than you think it will. I am still regularly shocked by how quickly even a small house will go through lumber.

Give careful consideration to your site. Understand the ways wind, water, sun, and shade move throughout the year on your property. Think about how your building will relate to both existing and future structures. Understand the local architectural vernacular—those design techniques have proven themselves a good match for your region. Familiarize yourself with Permaculture design, passive solar design, and consider incorporating them into your project.

Use more insulation. Code-minimum levels of insulation are simply not enough. Remember, a code-minimum construction project is the lowest quality project that can be legally built. Insulation is a great area to go above and beyond the minimums. Your building will perform better, and your energy requirements will be lower.

Reclaim materials. It is possible to save money while introducing character to your project by using reclaimed materials, whether that is lumber, flooring, lighting or plumbing fixtures. You can buy those materials from salvage companies, or salvage them yourself from dumpsters, demolition sites, or standing buildings. In my rural area, I have deconstructed many houses and outbuildings to salvage materials. Not only was I able to acquire materials at zero cost beyond my labor, but I also learned a wealth of information about how buildings are put together. As a bonus, reusing old materials in your project often adds instant charm and a sense of history.

Many ways to build. There are as many ways to build buildings as

The Bear Cave.

Alternating tread stairs in Larkspur.

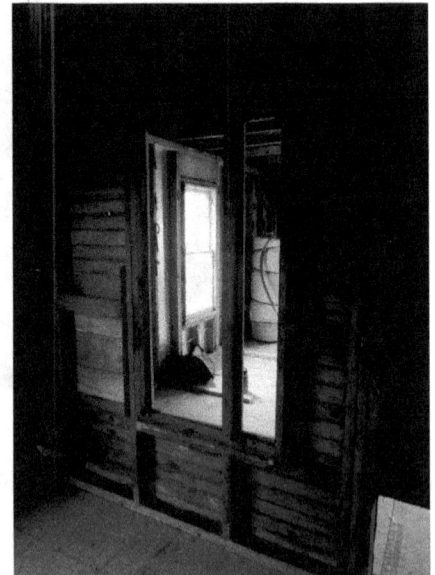

Building the porch on Larkspur.

Photos courtesy of Tony "Bear" Barrett

Lobelia.

The Tiny Trailer House.

Author with tiny book.

The Haven.

there are people building them. No two of the 100+-year-old buildings I have deconstructed were built the same way. I like to think that there is no one right way to build...unfortunately there are plenty of wrong ways.

Educate yourself. If you understand basic building science, and implement best practices in each aspect of your project, there is no reason your house won't be standing tall in 100+ years.

Know the code. Even if building permits and inspections are not necessary where you live, it is a good idea to know what the requirements are for such things as structural elements, electrical systems, plumbing, etc. You may choose to meet those requirements, or not, but you should be familiar.

Don't experiment for experimentation's sake. Find out what works well in your area, and why. Talk to and learn from area builders. Then you can sit down to design a building you know will succeed. Sure, you could try to insulate your walls with plastic bottles stuffed with chicken feathers, but maybe your neighbors have had a lot of luck insulating with local strawbales. You may want to repeat their successes rather than take a chance on your experiment.

Use the Critical Path. The Critical Path is the order in which a building project comes together. What are my next steps and what do I need in order to complete them? This will help prevent you from leaving something out, or doing things out of sequence. The longer and more detailed your Critical Path the better.

Water is the enemy. Apart from cataclysmic natural disasters, most buildings eventually crumble thanks to the presence of water. Water freezing under your foundation, or being blown into your wall or roof assemblies, can make short work of your building. If you want your house to last a long time, protect it from water with a good foundation, a good roof, and careful attention to flashing and drainage details.

Buy the best quality windows you can afford. Windows and doors are very high-ticket items and it is tempting to try to save money with lower quality, or reclaimed units. My choice to install reclaimed windows in our current strawbale-insulated home may have saved us thousands of dollars during construction, but it was the single biggest mistake I made in terms of efficiency and performance. Window and door technologies are advancing so quickly that it is now possible to buy windows with insulative values as high as R-10, roughly equal to that of a 2x4 wall with fiberglass batts.

Plan for the future. Remember that your life will be changing, and your building may want to change with it. Furthermore, you want this building to outlast you. It is important to think beyond your needs right now. Think about how your home will serve you as you and your family grow, and age. Due to design restrictions, the lofted sleeping area in my first cabin was accessed by an alternating-tread staircase. That worked great for me until my son was born—but then it seemed a bit too dangerous. The second house I designed for us is a single story with doorways wide enough to accommodate a wheelchair. Take the long view.

Know what is important to you. The more you know what you like and don't like, the more likely you are to love your new home. For instance, if you prefer to sleep in, maybe you don't want your bedroom on the East. If you are allergic, those strawbales may not be such a good idea after all. If you love cooking, go for a bigger kitchen. If you want to do a lot of food preservation, be sure to include a pantry. Even a small office area could make working from home a reality. If you have a fondness for wood heat, by all means include a wood stove. If you hate processing and handling firewood, maybe don't. A custom cabinet could display your extensive collection of widgits while also providing the perfect personal touch that says home.

Look for inspiration everywhere. I am constantly expanding my design vocabulary just by keeping my eyes open as I go about my day. I try to examine the buildings I interact with closely. How does this floorplan flow? What are the proportions of that window? That trim? How high is this ceiling? With the help of my ever-present sketchbook and tape measure, I can usually take note of the things that appeal to me, file them away in my brain, and pull them out the next time I am looking for a design solution. 🐾

Tony (Bear) Barrett, owner of Papa Bear's Tiny Homes, has been designing and building at Dancing Rabbit Ecovillage in northeast Missouri since 2006. When Bear is not building, he is often seen trying to keep up with his partner, Alyssa, and their son, Zane, around the village. Their strawbale home Lobelia can be seen featured in Small Homes, *by LLoyd Kahn.*

IONIA'S BARN PROJECT:
Where Community and Natural Building Meet

By Eliza Eller

It is a winter solstice dawn on the Kenai Peninsula in Alaska, and I stand almost 40 feet above the ground in our barn cupola, peering over the treetops at the first rays of the winter sun. I can see my breath in the frigid air, but the bright sun rays come streaming towards me like a river. This cupola is such an amazing space, I am frozen in time, dancing with the coming light, feeling like I am the first person in the world to see this day. The barn is magical, and this space will make a liberating special meeting area/meditation nook/reading loft when the barn is done. It's been a long nine years of building for our village, and we are more than ready for the barn to be finished. In fact, it's become a running joke: "When are we going to _____?" "When the barn is done!"

Ionia is a cooperative ecovillage located on 200 acres of spruce forest on the Kenai Peninsula in Alaska, created in 1986 by five disenfranchised families with members who experienced emotional traumas navigating modern times. The founding families met each other in the movement known as macrobiotics, and we had that love of simple plant-based foods in common. Coming from the large Boston-based macrobiotic community (our grandparent) we also all had a sense of human beings being part of natural forces, part of an infinite universe just like other natural phenomena; we were and are attracted to non-human-centric points of view. This is part of the foundational ethos of Ionia.

All of the original families received SSI disability benefits which barely paid the bills in the city. In our humble beginnings, we bought 10 acres of flat muskeg-covered land on the Kenai Peninsula, built a road, dug a well, and put up five tipis. For $500 down and $300 per month, we had a beginning. As one of the founding mamas, I felt happy and safe in our own little paradise in the making. It was a cold, snowy winter that year but we were cozy in those tipis: the kids ran around in the spruce forest and we cooked on wood stoves which we kept cranking 24 hours a day. We began to talk with each other daily in morning meetings, pool resources, and attempt to create a culture of trust, imagination, tolerance, and cooperation: we felt that "Shared sorrow is half sorrow and shared joy is double joy," a wise Swedish proverb.

Ionia has evolved over the past 30-plus years to become a bustling little village. Our kids have grown and gone off to explore who they are in the world, and many have returned to raise their own children as part of our endeavor, so now third-generation babies and toddlers are running around laughing and screaming. We have had 16 babies born in the last four years. Ionia is primarily a community of families, and our year-round population hovers between 40 and 50, of all ages and abilities, from newborns to elders. Many people join us in the summers to learn, help out, and sometimes to heal.

Spending time at Ionia is definitely a commitment of attention, reflection, and change. We are trying to create a way of life which embodies more social and environmental justice than modern times' usual alternatives. We mill spruce logs to build homes and furniture, and grow and cut firewood. Organic gardens, greenhouses, and a grain field help to feed us throughout the year. We share resources and pool strengths, providing an umbrella for all. We partner with local social service organizations, the State of Alaska Division of Behavioral Health, and the college to provide wellness and recovery training for people on the Central Kenai Peninsula who experience addiction, trauma, and emotional imbalance. Our activities usually always encompass macrobiotics, or whole foods for whole health, peer support and close family support, and simple, seasonal activities based in the natural world. Building with natural materials is a great fit for this community: we hope to live lightly on this pristine Alaskan land...plus natural buildings often need many hands.

In the first 10 years, the residents joined together to build 10 beautiful log cabins: first, five 1,400 square foot family homes, then five smaller cabins of various sizes as our kids grew up and more families moved in. In the beginning, we built the traditional Alaskan way with logs, and heated with wood stoves. We created our own design process, which is easy in rural Alaska where building permits are not an issue. All our cabins have open floor plans, on-demand propane hot water, and outhouses.

The long summers of daylight are our building season. Log building relies heavily on people with strong arms to lift logs. In our community, the women and children peeled logs every day for weeks and weeks all summer long. The guys mostly lifted purlins and wall logs into place, and everyone hammered the roof boards on. My young children learned to cook whole meals in that first summer, by necessity, as we built and built. When we moved into my family home, my kids dumped sand in the middle of the living room floor without a second thought because they were so used to living outside!

The cabins have housed numerous people over the years, and they continue to be a strong comforting presence, demonstrating the amazing beauty of nature, the financial and creative power of community, and a balanced mix of individual expression with community norms and neighborhood planning. However we needed more housing.

As the pressure to have a true common space finally boiled over, in 2001-2003 we gathered our strong young men and women, and all our experienced builders together to design and build a 12,000 square foot log community center, which was named the Longhouse. The Longhouse has a large and comfortable meeting room where we can gather in circle meetings, an administrative office with computer access, a music corner with many instruments, a sewing corner, plenty of space for private corners and storage, and a community-size kitchen, pantry, and root cellar. Ionia is known for its delicious, wholesome cooking; fermented foods such as miso, sauerkraut, kimchee, vinegars, and tempeh, plus sourdough breads, sugar-free desserts, and jams, are all made from scratch in the community kitchen.

The Longhouse is also where our morning meetings are held; it has a home-schooling circle for its youngest residents; we celebrate monthly full moon celebrations and holidays there; we let the youngsters run around together; and it is home to many, many conversations, therapies, planning meetings, sewing and art projects, classes, music jams, and other happenings in village life. It is also a way for the larger surrounding community to interface with Ionia, and has been the beginning of a more open era for us. For example, we began to have public cooking classes—and I learned to teach.

The Longhouse has huge log trusses which sweep across grand high peaked ceilings, wood floors, log post and beams, and log walls, as well as majestic soapstone masonry heaters which save us firewood and give us steady hours of cozy gentle warmth. The masonry heaters are of Northern European tradition, designed by Albe Bardon of Maine Wood Heat Company especially for this space, and built by a team of masons from all over the country. It was a sight to behold as they were built, and gave me so much respect for the all but lost art of masonry work. When they first agreed to build these massive stone heaters, they had some requests: a home to stay in on the property, and a build site that was roofed over, dry, and warm. Well, as they were arriving, we were rushing to hammer on the roof boards—literally as they set up to build, the roof was closing up. It was September and getting chilly, so it was dicey but we did it and the masons were quite gracious. They bunked all together in a log cabin, ate macrobiotic meals, and had never experienced such rustic and peaceful surroundings, full of wild children and wild eagles.

Photos courtesy of Eliza Eller

The Longhouse was another log building; there were miles of logs to peel and place, and every course of logs gave us new excitement and a feeling of accomplishment. We knew this method of building, yet as we have seen over the years, logs are lovely but not great insulators. The six inches of log is a poor keeper of heat, not to mention the many cracks between the logs. So when it came time to plan the next big project—the "Barn" as we have come to call it—we were perplexed as to what materials would be best suited.

The barn was conceived to be a series of shops: woodshop and wood beamery, mechanics shop, metalworking shop, pottery/clay shop, bicycle/cart shop, and a dojo/yoga studio. It has space for processing the harvest, drying beans, squash, seeds, grains, and sea vegetables, plus space for the spring starts. It has a hay loft (which hopefully some couples have rolled in!). Ionia, being a plant-based community, has very few animal residents, excepting a

matter how "green" (energy efficient) they may be. But then, one of our young men spent a winter volunteering in Mexico, where he helped to build with straw and mud. He called, super excited, and said that this was it—this is how we must build the barn.

Whoops, we might have a change of plan! We had to stop and think, frustrate the architect, spend more money we didn't have on his time, have mad planning meetings in the middle of the barn construction site, and finally—after much debate—decide that yes, this really did sound like a fitting alternative more in line with our values and more exciting to explore. This was a very backwards process and not recommended, but there you have community life, with all its complications and unknowns.

Luckily, homemade natural buildings are more suited for this kind of redesign-and-rebuild-as-you-go kind of organic process! The barn has been a learning curve from the beginning. Luckily, our architect is a patient, creative, flexible man with vision. He was able to dance with Ionia's group process and found a way to communicate our changing plans successfully with the fire marshal and permitting entities. This was a huge boon to us.

We researched, found some strawbale and straw/clay homes in Alaska, and traveled to talk with the builder-owners. It seemed to us that in our wet cold climate, strawbale has the best insulation value hands down, but it had other drawbacks: rodents enjoyed building their nests in straw in the long cold winters; and any rain or snow that found its way in created big mold issues. In our buildings, which are heated with firewood, and must withstand months of rain and snow, we started to look more seriously at the light straw-clay alternative.

Straw and clay creates a wall which is fireproof, thick and insulative, and hydroscopic—which means it can breathe, and wants to let in and let out moisture as it breathes. This means that no moisture barrier is wanted! This was a whole new concept, and quite welcome. It also means it needs a good hat (low overhanging roof) and good boots (dry and high foundation which keeps the walls off of the ground). The walls can be load-bearing or not, but it makes a gorgeous combination with load-bearing timber frames. There are many traditional and recently improved versions of building with straw and clay, from cob to adobe, but in our cold and wet climate, the method which makes the most

> Everyone, no matter age or ability, can get involved and get trained up in most of the tasks. It's been a great way to enjoy our collected energy.

few ducks, cats, and dogs so far, so it need not be a space for animals to stay. The barn has big dreams for becoming a folk school for learning traditional crafts, a house-building production line, and a model for alternative building methods and alternative energy technologies. It is yet another huge community-size building—3,000 square feet, with two stories plus a cupola. Ah yes, a cupola to better view solstice sunrise from...

But what to build it with? Our first idea was a basic post and beam skeleton, wrapped in Structural Insulated Panels (SIPs), billed to be super energy efficient and cost efficient. OK, so that was the plan...we hired an architect this time, to satisfy some of our grant funders, and created a modern design pleasing to all. It has a north overhanging roof for outside vehicle parking, huge southern roof for future solar panels, plenty of windows, and another open floor plan.

In 2008 construction commenced, with unique steel foundation posts, thick wood flooring, the first posts and beams. But wait, somewhere along the way, we had a series of discussions and decided we might need to switch to logs; maybe we couldn't live with the "ka ka" (made from oil) building materials no

sense is known as light straw-clay.

Our local Kenai Peninsula clay is perfectly suitable; dry baled Delta Junction straw is readily available. In the summer of that same year, our main building crew drove to Salt Spring Island in Canada for a three-week intensive natural building workshop called Econest. This exciting workshop connected us to the big wide world of the natural building movement and covered the basics of clay/straw and timber frame construction, combining lectures with practice. Returning as an inspired force, the building commenced in earnest.

We found a local natural builder to apprentice with, Lasse Holmes of Canyon Arts Natural Building in nearby Homer, who has helped us create a building system and style which supports all of us working together. Lasse has been an invaluable resource. With his help, we built from scratch a mechanized system for the production of straw/clay insulation and clay plasters. We found parts in junk yards and neighbor's back yards and fish packing plants to put together an efficient user-friendly production line which includes storage tanks and settling tanks, clay slip mixers, and a straw/clay mixer/tumbler. The Ionia sawmill is an integral part of this production line as well, and most of the posts, beams, and boards in the barn structure have come off our own mill. This has taken more time than expected but is enormously satisfying. In fact, all aspects of this way of building seem to take a long time, we are finding out.

Each summer's work has been accomplished by setting up a "train" of crews: each crew's daily tasks allow the next part of the train to move, and each crew's work depends on the last. The crews consist of saw millers, carpenters, clay processors, clay slip makers, straw fluffers, straw/clay insulation mixers, form builders, straw/clay stuffers, and plasterers. And this is Ionia, where we are all about the food, so don't forget the snack makers! Everyone, no matter age or ability, can get involved and get trained up in most of the tasks. It's been a great way to enjoy our collected energy, all summer long for many summers.

The barn now has been home to many natural building workshops, including rocket mass heater, timber framed bridge, and clay plasters. The staircase up to the cupola is the crown jewel, sweeping up in a square spiral of local wood. It was built as the last creation of one of our founding fathers, who died last spring. The barn is his legacy, along with countless other builders.

Master craftsmen have created doors that will last several lifetimes, and the clay walls breathe with you as you work, creating a nourishing fresh environment.

Within this process of building, we have confirmed and reconfirmed that simple hands-on collected natural activities are foundational to our way of life. Building the barn provides a tangible, accessible pathway for many residents to be involved in a community process; to learn new skills; to be drawn in by the teamwork approach and by the natural materials themselves.

The barn has connected Ionia to the larger natural building movement in Alaska, the lower 48, and all over the world. It has been an epic nine-year journey and has changed the pace and tone of our community quite a bit: it has brought in curious builders and volunteers from Taiwan, Japan, Europe, South America, other communes, and all over Alaska every year. A handful of our residents have been inspired to travel to other builds, and are planning homes here made from straw and clay. I feel we will always be building now—first to finish the barn, then to build homes here at Ionia, then onwards to homes around us in Alaska.

This summer is hoping to be the last major building season, with the final colorful lime and clay finish plasters. We welcome volunteers to come to Alaska to help with this amazing project. It is our vision that the barn can be a place to create, but also to retreat, to contemplate, and to reconnect with what is important to you. I have heard people give the barn credit for healing their traumas, and it's been a great meeting site for romances as well. I have become a budding natural builder, and much of my family has been involved with this building in ways that will forever imprint their lives. What will we do next? I guess we'll find out, "When the barn is done!" ❧

Eliza Eller lives on the Kenai Peninsula in Alaska at the village of Ionia (www.ionia.org). She spends her days growing food in the summers and carrying firewood in the winters, soaking in the arctic sun, organizing events and trainings, cooking, keeping in touch with her growing family, and scrambling to keep up with the ever moving generations of change at Ionia. She hangs out around guys who love building with clay and straw, and it is catching, so on a warm summer day, if she isn't weeding in one if the many greenhouses, one might find her, covered with clay, madly mixing a barrel of slip. For more information about volunteer opportunities this summer on the Ionia Barn Project, write eliza@ionia.org or call her at (907) 252-2314.

Cherry blossoms in front of the house. Having orchards and gardens on the south side of the house helps keep the solar clearing open, and makes good use of the space.

BUILDING WITH RESPECT

By Alexis Zeigler

Humans modify our environment more than any other animals. We want to, we have to, protect ourselves from the elements. Is it possible for us to do so while respecting the sacred creation? The answer to that question cannot be summarized in a simple list of commandments, but the complexity of the answers only underscores the importance of our mindfulness.

I have lived in community all of my life. I have built conventional buildings, super-insulated buildings, and a variety of renewable energy systems. I have also organized some successful environmental campaigns. Green building could be our salvation or hasten our destruction, depending on what we pursue and how.

When I teach green building workshops, I talk to the participants about three levels of planning to consider, each of more importance by an order of magnitude than the one below. The most important level is context—what are you building, where, who's using it, and for what purpose? The single family house on a mountaintop may have some appeal, but if you are driving an hour to work, another hour to pick up the kids and go shopping, and coming home to shovel firewood into the stove, you cannot add any "environmental" technology onto that situation to make it sustainable. Poor context means isolated. Good context means building the right thing in the right place. Though Americans have a near obsession with their own independence, by far the most important environmental "technology" ever developed is cooperative use—in a word, community. Community is THE technology that makes renewable energy viable.

The second order of magnitude is conservation and insulation. It is always cheaper to save energy with good insulation and conservationist design than to generate energy. Make no mistake, current incentives to put up grid-tie solar and other "renewable" energy sources on American homes instead of focusing on insulation and smart context have everything to do with politics and nothing to do with environmental protection.

Renewable energy sources are the third level of design consideration. Renewable energy when added onto conventional American buildings is a feeble supplement to fossil energy sources. Once one has considered appropriate context and developed wise conservationist design, then renewable energy becomes a powerful, liberating energy source that can allow us to live sustainably, and support communities that empower our democracy from the ground up.

Want to build green? Here's your checklist (and there is a resource section at the end with links to material sources):

1) Don't do it alone, or with just your spouse. Find a group to work with or live with. The more you can share, the lower your footprint will be. If you live in a tropical climate, the tiny houses are fine. If you live in a climate that gets cold, then free-standing housing will always have a devastating footprint compared to shared spaces.

2) What works great in one place would be foolish in another. A subterranean house that works great in New Mexico would be a hor-

rible mold pit in Virginia (absent significant mechanical ventilation). A strawbale house would work great in the Dakotas, and it would be silly in Florida. Environmental solutions are always local.

3) Spend your money on good roofing (enameled metal), good windows, insulation, and sub-grade insulation. The rest you can do as cheap as you want.

4) Don't get anything less than decent quality double-pane windows. Never, never, never rebuild and install old single-pane windows. A decent quality double-pane window will have the same thermal performance as a multi-thousand-dollar triple-pane if you put thermal curtains in front of the double-pane window. Beware there are numerous different kinds of "low-e" coatings, many of which are designed to keep heat out, not let it in (to minimize air conditioning bills rather than maximize winter solar gain). Do not buy cheap used windows.

5) Passive solar is a "no-brainer." There are lots of good design guides around. Don't sweat the details too much, just put a good amount of glass on the south side.

6) Don't think that adding a bit more insulation than most people use is a good level of insulation. I have made super-insulated walls with straw, crumpled newspaper, leaves, and bamboo. Super-insulated walls need to be 18 inches or so thick. Blowing lots of insulation in the attic is easy enough. If you live where it rains, you need to keep the moisture out of your thick walls. The "breathability" issue is bogus unless you are building a commercial greenhouse or bathhouse. You DO need good overhangs,

and some control over rainwater falling off the roof. While there are numerous variations of cob that work fine, beware that insulation and thermal mass are two different things. Walls of dirt and rock that conduct heat out of the building will burn a lot of energy in a cold climate.

7) Ask 10 different carpenters how to build a dog house and you get 10 different dog houses, nine of which keep the dog dry. There are lots of well-intentioned green builders without a lot of conventional building experience, and lots of conventional builders who get really nervous about changing anything. There is more than one right answer to any important question. Ask lots.

8) Avoid dead air spaces, especially in any climate with damp summers. Everything must cross ventilate.

9) Unless you are building a teepee, flat, straight building lines are cheaper, faster, and will yield a much tighter insulation shell. A flat ceiling is better. Clearstories and skylights are always heat leaks. Put your creativity into making an effective shell look and function better. The American norm is to sacrifice function to making buildings look like micro-mansions. Funk that leaks like heck is no better. Avoid hiring an architect. They draw pictures. Your kid can do that. An experienced carpenter is far more useful.

10) Plan your utilities as an integral part of the design, not something that simply has to conform around the edges of a pretty design. I always put the utility room in the middle of the bath and kitchen so pipe runs are short.

Cherry blossoms.

Sub-grade insulation: often overlooked, but very important. See resources list for cheap foam source.

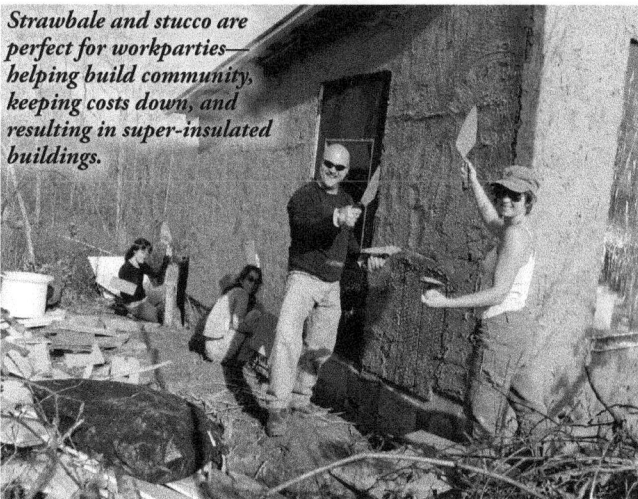

Strawbale and stucco are perfect for workparties— helping build community, keeping costs down, and resulting in super-insulated buildings.

Passive solar windows in strawbale walls make for deep window wells and great alcoves for plants and kids!

Photos courtesy of Alexis Zeigler

11) Do not not not even think about adding solar features until you have worked out the questions of context and insulation. I have seen some really expensive and ineffective solar heating and power systems added to badly insulated buildings. The results are not inspirational. Solar photovoltaic power is your last priority. Really.

12) Do not buy cheap or used appliances unless you have the ability to assess their energy use.

That's the nuts and bolts, and an opinion or two. We brought this all together at Living Energy Farm (Louisa, Virginia), and went a bit further. We built a community that is intended to run (and almost does) without fossil fuel. More critically, we designed it to be cheap so people all over the world can do what we do. We have found that people almost always confuse self-sufficiency and sustainability. At LEF, our definition of sustainability is focused on what seven billion people can do, not what we with privilege can do. Our focus on keeping things simple and widely accessible is unique, so far as we can tell.

Our design is intended to maximize the use of unskilled labor. Specifically, we use strawbales stacked inside a conventional (and cheap) stud frame design. In researching and working with strawbales, we realized that the rebar pins and cabling needed to build a load-bearing strawbale is more expensive than the 2x4s needed for a cheap stud wall, and that stud wall is also much cheaper than post and beam. Strawbales are simply leaned up against a wall by unskilled labor. Then stuccoed, again with unskilled labor. A good stuccoer can radically accelerate your unskilled stucco workers. Inexperienced people can move really, really slowly if not taught properly. Some strawbalers stick religiously to lime plaster on the outside. We use a bit of cement in the plaster and thus end up with a wall that can last for centuries without maintenance.

Building LEF has sharpened my focus on what works in green building. We run our entire economy on about 200 watts per person. But we did that AFTER we insulated well, AFTER we built a very integrated community with a high degree of shared use. The DC microgrid system we have built works really well, and is very different from anything else we have found. Our system is much cheaper than other power supply systems. It is also made of much more durable components. It is modular, so you can build it one piece at a time. It also has a multi-linear energy flow, so there is no such thing as a system-wide power outage.

There is a darker side to all of this as well. The hyper-productive American economy relies on consumerism, people buying gobs of junk they don't need. The pinnacle of consumerism is the American home, a micro-model of European royal mansions. That's one reason "green building" can be such a popular topic. At its worst, green building becomes greenwash for the greatest orgy of consumption in America. But we all have to have shelter. So where is the line between green and greenwash? The line is community.

Community is the "technology" that makes renewable energy work.

When solar photovoltaic is added to ordinary American homes, the ecological footprint probably increases because the energy demand is so high. In communities like LEF, we are using somewhere around two percent as much energy per capita as the average American, all of it renewable. Renewable energy applied to conventional houses and industrial economies is a weak, intermittent, expensive, and ineffective energy source. Once you have a good community design that needs two percent as much energy, then suddenly renewable energy becomes a powerful, enabling energy source that can make life comfortable and easy. It is no exaggeration to say that our future hinges on our ability to form effective community organizations.

Resources

- Overview of the DC microgrid system used at LEF (beware: this is a large PDF file): livingenergyfarm.org/raff20.pdf
- High quality DC brushless pumps: see Sun Pumps (some brushless and some brushed), Grundfos, Lorentz, and Robison.
- High quality, moderately priced wood-fired equipment: DS Machine in Pennsylvania. Great Amish company, they have water heaters, canners, furnaces, and other useful devices. They do not have a private website, but are listed on their county website, reallancastercounty.com/local-services/house/heating-cooling-hvac-coal-firewood-propane-fuel-oil-stoves/ds-stoves
- Good design for thermal curtains: kumeproject.com
- Good source for reclaimed foam insulation for sub-grade use, or for building homemade solar heating panels: insulationdepot.com
- Waterproofing admix we use in exterior stucco, cheap and nontoxic, much better than just adding a spray-on water seal. We have not used this product long enough to give it an unconditional endorsement, but so far so good: www.kryton.com/products/krystol-mortar-admixture-kma
- If you do use skylights, here is a design than can convert them from a thermal liability to a thermal asset. These can be homemade as well, with aluminum roofing metal: www.zomeworks.com/sunbender
- Solar hot water pumps, closed loop only: see El Sid pumps, numerous suppliers.
- Other solar hot water components, including very high quality stainless water tanks: www.aetsolar.com

Alexis Zeigler was raised on a self-sufficient farm in Georgia. He has lived all of his adult life in intentional community. He has worked as a green builder, environmental activist, and author. His book Integrated Activism *explores the connections between ecological change, politics, and cultural evolution.*

Reusing old tiles to make a rainbow mosaic in the shower.

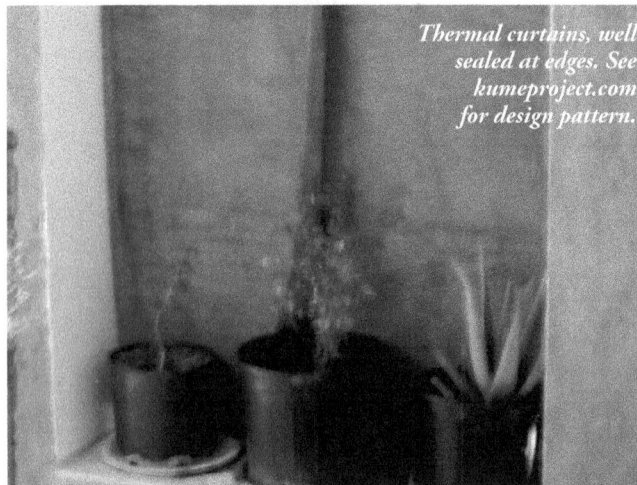

Thermal curtains, well sealed at edges. See kumeproject.com for design pattern.

ECO-BUILDING AT THE ECOVILLAGE
(I Have Built a Home)

By Arjuna da Silva

The author's home Leela, after completion.

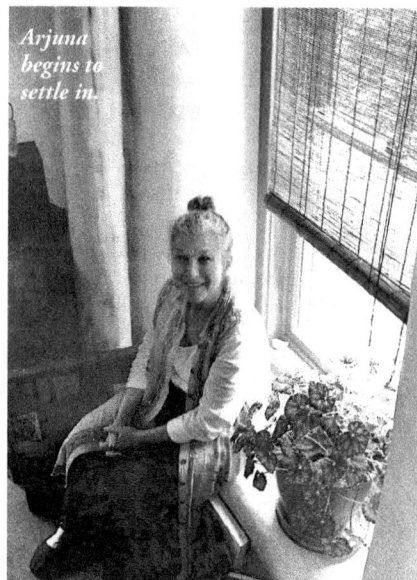
Arjuna begins to settle in.

There are several natural buildings at Earthaven (Black Mountain, North Carolina), designed and constructed with the Earth in mind—both to use as much of what we find right here on this patch of her, and to use materials with little to no negative impact on the planet. Some are timber-framed, some have simple rectangular designs, many have sheetrock interior walls, and most have earthen and lime plaster on the outside.

Those built primarily from earth and straw (and wood) are quite small—experiments to see how far folks wanted to venture into new and traditional modalities. They're all still standing and in good use today. One community-sized splendid result of our early forays into natural building is the 13-sided earth, wood, and straw Council Hall. If a room has ever been loved, it's this one!

I'm not sure why I latched onto the idea of natural building. The idea of building simple structures we could live well in, made out of easily available materials, thrilled me. I'd never owned a home, so I knew nothing about construction, but I was romantic about the aesthetics of spaces; the round, earth-toned warmth of a natural house promised me a luxury and comfort I felt I needed to feel.

When it came time for me to develop the homesite I'd leased at Earthaven, I got involved in what turned into a mystical journey that carried me from the most rudimentary sense to an ongoing experience of the dance of design and manifestation. "Leela," a sensual, earthy, womb-toned *being*, part temple, part hideaway, part evolving dreamscape, led the way.

In the eighth year of Earthaven, after several ideas for building within a pod design (shared facilities with radiating private spaces) disappeared into other folks' priorities, I got the idea of gathering my permie girlfriends for a design charrette on Site #7 in our Bellavia Gardens neighborhood, not far from the Village Center. We gathered outside my trailer on a lovely fall day, and I talked about my dreams of a home within the bigger home of Earthaven. Then we took measurements on the site, talked about water sources, wind tunnels, and solar angles, and dispersed to work on sketches focused on the key features I'd need to start with, including orientation, entrances and exits, facilities, connection to the commons, and so on.

When we compared all the sketches, some details were obviously similar and some unique, but I felt encouraged. I would have to mull over the designs, make some choices, and figure out the next step. But as the unfolding mystery would have it, one of the gals was an adventurous budding natural builder who suggested we walk back to the site and take a stab at designing the house. We stood where I thought the door was likely to be, and I followed her instructions about closing my eyes and imagining walking into the house. What would I see?

As I described where I imagined the walls would be, how far from each other, how they curved, she took notes. She jotted down where I said different things took place, adding questions to round out the sketch she was making. Where would the bathroom go? Would the toilet be in it? The resulting sketch could only be called an amoeba, but it didn't stop my friend from taking it seriously.

Another friend was learning the new AutoCAD program folks were talking about, and he agreed to mess with my amoeba. His result was a more symmetrical structure with more clearly defined areas. Then I made another deal: I said I'd have the foundation ready when my friend returned in the spring with a group of natural building interns.

Getting from sketch to foundation, however, became complex enough for its own chapter in this epic. Suffice to say, I was still figuring out how to dig the foundation when the group appeared. I had no foundation, no frame, no roof—and nothing much to offer a builder to get started on. There was an interlude for building accessory structures that helped the interns carry on learning about natural building, and we had some delightful plaster parties led by my friend (and Earthaven member) Mollie Curry of MudStrawLove.

Steveo is a local transplant, like lots of us, with considerable conventional building experience and a talent for sculpture. He'd worked with my natural builder friend on an adobe project and relished the idea of taking on a full-scale natural building project. His upbeat and confident personality got my attention, as he walked around the site, observing the little progress we'd made on the footprint, talking about rates for carpentry versus those for the mud and straw work. When, in a couple of hours, he'd already built a small shed out of scraps he found lying around, and set the tools and other materials inside it, I felt we were onto something with potential.

It took five years to build Leela (a Sanskrit word for "divine play"). During our first year, Steveo designed the timber-frame and we got several resident carpenters to put it together while he completed another job. We managed to pull a permit with the building department by explaining that the building was basically a timber-frame with masonry walls, and with

could be gently removed as the panel was pressed into place.

Following principles of passive solar design, most walls were made at least 24 inches thick. For the east, south, and west walls, we wanted plenty of thermal mass to radiate the sun's warmth into the house. (Remember, in summer the sun is high above and mostly beams its rays straight down, rather than at a penetrating angle to the walls and windows.) For the north wall, we wanted insulation instead of thermal mass, to shield the house from shady, windier zones, so we chose strawbale construction, learning to create specially shaped bales to fit angular spaces created by the roof line, managing—with Steve Kemble's expert guidance—to follow the curve in our foundation and meet the straighter side walls in unbroken connection. Steve brought many innovative techniques for "cutting" and "sewing" bales together, and we also used bamboo poles as studs to firm up parts of the strawbale "bricks."

On the inside, we designed an earthen wall with an arched opening above the hearth and an arched entryway into the kitchen and dining alcove. We were able to use compressed earth blocks (CEBs), made in a contraption that extruded big, dry blocks faster than we could pile them up. Although we didn't get our hands on that technology until all the exterior walls were in place, we got to use the blocks to create the arches.

To complete the design for the roof and upper-floor windows, Steveo built a clay model and we played with various cardboard roof panels and several cathedral-like rounded window shapes. Leela was built with wood, clay, and sand almost entirely from Earthaven. We bought pine floor joists wider than our trees could provide, and for some uses chose builder's sand rather than the cruder sand from our creeks. We made lime plaster for both interior and exterior walls to minimize mold, but were able to cover the interior arched walls with a reddish earthen plaster as they would be dried by the fire in the wood stove. Selecting pigment was an adventure, and Mollie was a patient provider of samples and test panels as we attempted to guess what a small patch of color would look like on an entire wall.

> My experience planning, building, working with others, and living in my house has been a dream come true on so many levels.

an engineer's signature assuring them that the ridge beam was broad enough. Neighbors at Earthaven built an Earthship (tire house), and they dealt with the county's lack of data by finding a local engineer who signed off on plans that had been approved in New Mexico.

Even with the roof up, though, it had to be slow going; one, because Steveo had other things to attend to and, two, because we could build only from May to mid-October since earthen and plastered walls that aren't completely dry will crack when they freeze.

In the beginning, we practiced techniques, embellishing our design as we went along. We hosted long weekends and weeklong workshops with dozens of pairs of hands plopping cob loaves onto foundation walls and smushing them into place, or pitchforking straw through clay slip for upper wall systems or (later on) mixing and spreading plaster on the interior (and even later on the exterior) walls. Though most folks were novices at this work, Steveo and good friends Mollie Curry and her partner Steve Kemble made sure that surfaces were well-shaped and smooth.

Leela is a 900 (somewhat) square foot, timber-frame construction with walls of cob, clay-straw, adobe brick, and a few other systems developed as we went along. On the second-story curved walls, for example, Steveo and several interns came up with the *chorizo*, a long, flexible sausage-like panel of clay-straw laid into wide strips of burlap, then rolled around a bamboo stake and carried up the scaffolding, where the bamboo

The other interior clay walls are plastered with a mixture of builder's sand and lime, which resulted in a beautiful shade of tan that complements the warm colors of all the poplar and pine posts, beams, and paneling. The deep rose-colored pigment we chose for the arched wall brings a rich and healing energy into the space. Each one of these decisions was treated with great care, some of them taking us weeks or longer to settle on.

Once Leela was all walled in, we could work through the winter, though often we had to quit when it was too cold. Perhaps the most challenging of all the aspects of the project were the earthen floors, which we only much later discovered are really *sand* floors, at least in this climate, with the lesser clay part essential for holding all the sand together. Our first few attempts, however, using a clay-heavy recipe, resulted in so much shrinkage and cracks that we had to do two out of three of them over. Luckily, our interns at the time were so determined that they worked tirelessly to fill, tamp, and repair the myriad cracking that made the living room floor look like a giant topographical map. Then Steveo did a hero's job of soaking and then pressing all the repaired surfaces into a smooth, flat, shining (after nine coats of linseed oil) floor. It took us two more floors before we got the recipe right, but Steveo always managed to come up with a way to make the best of things.

The last phase of construction was spent trimming, tiling, and delighting in opportunities to add lovely features and many spontaneously creative details. Meanwhile, the electric wiring, propane lines, wood heat, and water systems were finalized, the composting toilet was ordered, and a second-hand wood stove was refurbished and installed. Our final intern was with us the whole last year, and she was able to help us complete our work in time for me to move in at the beginning of winter in 2010, with wood heat, gas cookstove, bathtub, and on-demand propane-heated running hot water in place. The following year the photovoltaic system was designed and installed by neighbor friends learning the tricks of that trade.

Seven years later this past December, I can say I have logged more compliments and praises for the house than I ever could have imagined, not to mention the joy and comfort of living in it! There are still things to improve, such as adding insulated window and door shades downstairs on the south side, where we were a little excessive with the amount of glass we installed. (Classic passive solar design would have recommended at least one less window in the dining alcove and, possibly, one—not two—sets of French doors in the living room. I had to replace the initial solar panels and batteries by the time I learned how to manage the system, but now I'm getting additional amps twice a day from a shared micro-hydro station in the creek below, which has eliminated the use of a generator in our neighborhood for the past year.

While my experience planning, building, working with others, and living in my house has been a dream come true on so many levels, others in my community have not been so enthusiastic about working with earth and straw as their primary materials. Many folks who come to Earthaven now seem to be more excited about jumping into community life with both feet, meaning they prefer to move into something already built and available (though these are still in limited supply). And if they do have to build, they have mostly preferred to take the fastest route and use more common methods.

During the years we were building Leela, we started a nonprofit project called The Natural Building School and ran all our workshops and internships through it as a project of Culture's Edge. Within a few years after I moved into my house, though, the options for more natural building education became pretty limited, as no one had yet decided on building a natural house or other structure folks could learn on. There have been several natural building classes, introductions that let folks experiment with the basic techniques, but in general the Natural Building School is on hold here until someone comes up with a project we can sponsor.

In the meantime, there's plenty to do in an evolving ecovillage, both administratively and in developing our neighborhood, as new folks move in and the commons become a feature in our deliberations. I've started to pay long-needed attention to Leela's outside appearance, and a few features—stone knee walls, a stone patio, a swinging bench—have been added in the last few years that make a promising big difference. At the rate I'm going, there won't be a stage of completion, only the turning of a corner. But I can say, with a very happy heart, that I have managed to create a beautiful home that people will enjoy for generations to come. Praise be to the ancestors!

Arjuna da Silva was among the team of intrepid cultural revolutionaries who started Earthaven Ecovillage in 1994 and the educational nonprofit, Culture's Edge, in 1996. Her semi-professional life included many forms of psychotherapy and group counseling, but her passion for transformative community has used most of the last two decades in the unfolding Earthaven experience. Arjuna still focalizes the work of Culture's Edge at Earthaven. She was given the name "Shunyam Arjuna" (which means "emptiness of the morning sun") by the great spiritual master, Osho.

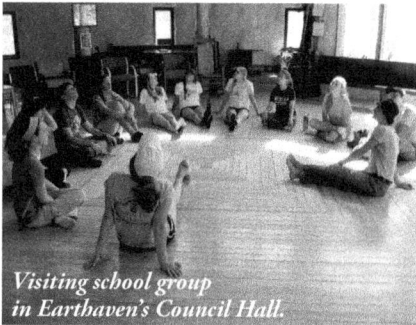
Visiting school group in Earthaven's Council Hall.

Adding a patio to the front of the house.

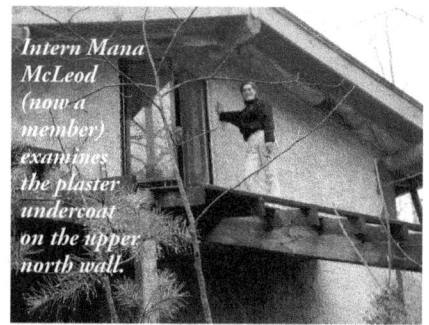
Intern Mana McLeod (now a member) examines the plaster undercoat on the upper north wall.

Interior arches today.

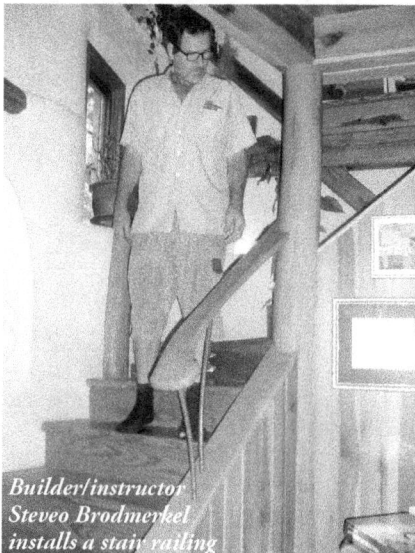
Builder/instructor Steveo Brodmerkel installs a stair railing

First workshop after the frame and roof were up.

Sue and Geoff Stone in front of their Earthship.

Earthaven Council Hall— Restorative Circles panorama.

139

GOOD NEIGHBOURS WITH EARTH:
Using natural building materials in community-scale construction

By Robin Allison

The annual Earthsong boat race on the pond.

"Mmmm, what's that beautiful smell?" asked the young visitor to Earthsong as she came into the common house, looking around with a small wondering smile. I ceased noticing the subtly fragrant, slightly spicy smell soon after moving into my new house in this cohousing community, but it is a typical first response of visitors. Earthsong houses smelt beautiful from the beginning, a combination of the resins of the solid timbers, and the natural tung tree oil and citrus thinners applied to the timber. Standard new construction often smells strongly of chemicals and can precipitate a headache within minutes. Our noses are highly sensitive organs that have evolved over millennia to give us information about our environment, and especially if something is healthy for us or not. Trust your nose!

Earthsong Eco-Neighbourhood is a 32-home cohousing community in Auckland, New Zealand. A fundamental part of our vision was to build to the "highest practical standards of sustainable human settlement." We chose materials that best fitted a range of sustainable criteria, including local and renewable where possible, low environmental impact and embodied energy, low toxicity, naturally durable, preferably reusable and recyclable.

But is it possible to use healthy and sustainable building materials in cohousing and still stay affordable? Does the group consensus process inevitably lead to compromises in green building decisions, or can it enable more courageous choices than a single household might consider? How much risk should a cohousing group take in trying less standard construction methods in order to build green? Earthsong faced these and other conundrums in our determination to be good neighbours to ourselves and the planet.

Appropriate sustainable building materials don't have to be expensive; many simple and effective solutions can be found using materials close to their natural state; cheap, beautiful, and sustainable. The rammed earth walls, solid timbers, natural oils and paints, and other sustainable materials at Earthsong have created a beautiful and healthy neighbourhood.

Innovative natural building materials are more typically used by owner-builders or passionate small-scale artisans building single homes. Owner-builders can respond to opportunities of material supply. They are willing to experiment, modify techniques on the job, and most importantly, they are willing to live with the (not always successful) consequences of experimentation.

Applying these same materials and systems to higher density multi-unit developments built by contractors in a profit-driven environment raises different issues and challenges. Commercial developers of multiple-unit developments look for design and materials acceptable to mainstream buyers. They value consistency of supply and reliable cost, and need a choice of contractors and tradespeople skilled in working with the materials for competitive tenders. They prefer no surprises in construction, and want predictable performance of materials so there are minimal "call-backs."

At Earthsong we operated in both of those worlds. We wanted to build a multi-home housing development, and we were a group of individuals with passion and drive and willing to innovate. We wanted to use natural and sustainable materials, and we needed a financially viable and cost-effective development. We set up a nonprofit company to be our own developer, and were willing to make braver choices than a commercial developer. And it was challenging!

If we want sustainable nontoxic materials to come into more mainstream use, it's essential that we talk about the challenges and learn from experience; even, or maybe especially, when it has been painful. Here are some of the challenges we found using natural building techniques for production housing. Some of these would apply also to one-off homes, but the logistics can get much more complicated with larger scale projects.

Craftsperson building techniques applied to production housing

In multi-unit housing, most would expect cost savings with repetition of design and processes and bulk buying of materials. This did not really eventuate in our case, because with rammed earth walls, timber structure, and lots of solid timber joinery and linings, they are crafted houses with a high skill and labour content.

One can argue, however, that using highly skilled labour is more sustainable and socially beneficial than using highly manufactured materials. Skilled labour usually makes possible the use of less processed materials with a lower embodied energy and shorter travel distances. Builders working with natural materials take pride in their work, and their skills are visible and valued. Skilled builders can respond to opportunities, working with the variable natural material to create something special.

Working with natural materials is usually healthier for the builders, and much more satisfying than the standard high-volume low-skill technology that relies on fossil energy use and highly manufactured products. Builders run on sandwiches, not fossil fuels!

Scale and density

With 32 houses on 1.2 hectares (three acres), Earthsong is considered a medium density development, and this affected both the design (two-story attached dwellings) and the means of construction (clusters of dwellings built by a single contractor). While it was not possible for individual owners to build their own houses, we did build in stages of two or more attached clusters.

Attached houses require good fire and acoustic separation between them. Rammed earth construction is brilliant for both; very little sound and no fire gets through solid earth construction. The upstairs timber-framed walls between houses, using standard detailing for party-walls, also presented no problems. What was more challenging was the external timber board-and-batten weatherboards on the upstairs walls. After much discussion with the local consenting authority to achieve sufficient fire separation between units, they accepted the external timber cladding with a small nib wall between houses to push any flame from one house away from the next.

Earth walls usually require a "good hat" to keep the high New Zealand rainfall off the walls. Two-story houses meant that the shelter of the roof was well above the ground-floor earth walls. Portland cement and agricultural lime aggregate was added to the rammed earth mix to improve durability and resistance to water penetration. In the later houses, small roofs or "hoods" were built above the earth walls to give local shelter.

Limited choice of building contractors

Any large building project requires contractors skilled in using the materials and systems involved. Because we were using non-standard eco-friendly materials and construction systems, there was only one company at the time skilled in rammed earth and of sufficient size to handle our project, so a competitive tender process was not feasible. Instead we worked early with the identified company to incorporate their cost-effective construction details into our design, and negotiated the contract

Earthsong houses surrounding the common house.

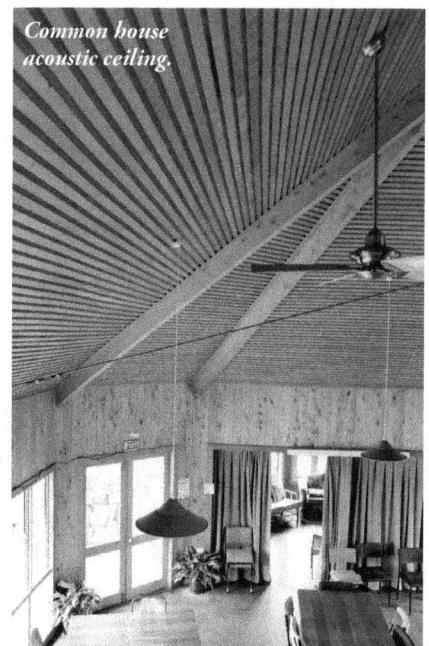

Common house acoustic ceiling.

Photos courtesy of Robin Allison

price and conditions. While they were well established in building single rammed earth and solid timber houses, they hadn't built more than one house at a time, so we hired professional project managers to work alongside and mentor them in the management systems required for such a large project as ours.

However, the unthinkable happened for us when three quarters of the way through building Stage I (the first 17 houses), the construc-

> We were committed to making buildings that foster the health and well-being of both the people who occupy them and the global ecosystems of which they are part.

tion company found themselves in financial difficulties largely caused by previous jobs and went into liquidation. This was a very serious setback to an already challenging project and we lost a substantial amount of money in delays, complications, and non-delivery of materials that we had paid for in advance.

Fortunately, almost all the rammed earth walls had been completed by then, and we managed to find mainstream builders willing to finish the houses, at great extra cost. We managed financially by deleting all non-essential items from the new contract and enlisting personal pledges from over 30 friends and relations to cover any shortfall at the end. Owners did their own painting, oiling, and sundry

other tasks, and paid more for their houses to cover the extra costs. It was very painful, but we managed to pull the project back from the brink.

Supply issues

Many natural building materials are not available "off-the-shelf." This entails finding a suitable supply well ahead of time, of appropriate quantity and quality, and often committing money up front to secure, and sometimes to process, that supply.

Timber was our biggest supply problem. Our houses have a lot of internal and external timber, all untreated and naturally durable species not readily available in bulk. In Stage I, the contractor proposed buying the living trees (mainly old farm shelterbelts) and getting them milled to ensure supply and save costs. They had to find and buy enough trees of the right species from several different sources, and get them harvested, milled, transported, and stored for seasoning. This required ongoing work for the contractors throughout construction, and upfront money from us to pay for it.

The winter that year was very wet. It was an ongoing problem getting enough of the right species and sizes of timber available and dry enough to use when needed. It created a major nightmare with the timeline, and no doubt contributed to the builders' troubles. The contractors' methodology may have worked for them on single house builds, but the logistics of processing the quantities required for 17 houses just proved too difficult. We didn't have the same supply issues in the later stages of building, however, as the Stage II contractor had a reliable supplier who sourced and supplied the appropriate timber when needed.

Variable materials

Most natural building materials are, by definition, less processed, less homogenized, and more variable. This is part of their charm, but can cause issues in construction, especially when building in bulk with added time and cost pressures. The ramming earth gave us problems late in construction.

Earth or subsoil suitable for ramming contains a range of particle sizes from fine (clay) to coarse (gravel). In some locations this occurs naturally and can be dug straight from the ground. If the local earth is not ideal, it needs additions of sand, lime, or other material to give an appropriate mix.

The earth walls in most of our houses are strong and beautiful. But problems appeared in the last stage of construction, with the walls having a crumbly surface and fine cracking. The strength of these walls was found to be acceptable, though lower than the earlier walls. The real

Attached terrace houses with nib wall in the timber cladding.

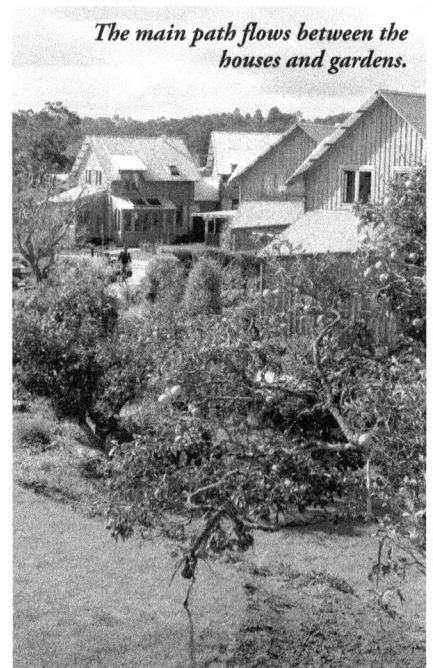

The main path flows between the houses and gardens.

problem was that they absorbed water, which we feared would weaken the walls and result in damp houses. Testing and soil analysis eventually showed that the clay content of the ramming earth had dropped significantly to almost zero. Some clay content is important because clay gives the initial cohesion to the material when the wall is rammed and being the smallest soil particle, helps the wall resist water penetration. In the few weeks between the soil being excavated for the pre-construction test wall and the actual wall ramming, the soil composition in the part of the bank being excavated at the time had changed.

By the time we realised there was a problem, the earth walls of three ground-floor units had already been rammed. Extra hoods were built around the building to protect the lower walls, and an earth wall sealer was used in some locations to minimize dusting and crumbling. Several mixes were trialed with test walls to develop a successful new recipe for the upper walls. It was very stressful and costly in time and money to both the contractor and us. But in this case the contractors worked hard with us to address the problem, and what we learnt has contributed to earth building knowledge in New Zealand.

Unusual design details

The other main area of difficulty and challenge has been in materials incompatibility. One consequence of pioneering new techniques to address environmental aspects of construction is that inevitably some mistakes were made, as other aspects of the materials were not understood or were overlooked. One example was the accelerated corrosion of unpainted zincalume (zinc/aluminium alloy coated steel) roofs through copper-laden runoff from the solar hot water panels. This was annoying but relatively simple to fix by applying protective paint.

Another example was more serious: corrosion of zinc flashings installed at ground level to protect the concrete floor slab insulation in the common house. These ground level flashings required substantial research, redesign, and expensive replacement. This was a painful process that delayed full completion of the common house by nearly two years, but we eventually found a solution that met our criteria of sustainability, durability, and ground-floor accessibility, and the repair was done.

All worth it in the end

This might sound like a litany of woes, but it wasn't all bad! While some problems were more complex than others, we found solutions for them all and carried on. It was a challenging journey, but we knew the journey was worth making, and we learnt a lot along the way that we can share with others. Few problems are insurmountable, and hopefully our experience will help others to anticipate where problems might occur and to plan ahead, so they don't trip you up in the heat of construction.

Do we wish we'd chosen more standard construction? No. We have beautiful, solid, timeless buildings, lovely to live in and with good thermal performance. The smell of well-being still infuses our lives 15 years later.

Is it possible to use sustainable materials and stay affordable? Yes. Many sustainable materials don't cost more than standard materials, although they might require more research and more effort to supply. There will often be a higher labour content, but also lower material and maintenance costs. It's a different aesthetic. Solid, natural timbers gain character with the knocks of age and use, unlike painted plasterboard which just starts to look shabby. Purchasers paid more money for the added costs of construction challenges, but our houses still ended up affordable relative to the standard housing market, and ongoing running costs for heating and cooling are very much less.

Does group consensus mean compromise, or more courageous choices? This depends on the strength of your vision and group commitment to sustainability. In our case I believe we held each other to account, pushed each other further to uphold our vision than we might have gone individually. The consequences of the difficulties were held by the group, not individuals, and together we stood stronger.

How much risk is reasonable for a group to take on? Again, it's up to the group to decide. Balance your vision and commitment with sensible, well researched decisions. We went out on a limb by choosing earth building, but it was backed up by solid research and professional support. We certainly had our issues, but those few challenging years have produced lovely buildings that will last generations into the future.

At Earthsong we were committed to making buildings that foster the health and well-being of both the people who occupy them and the global ecosystems of which they are part. We offer our mistakes, successes, and learnings in the hope of encouraging the wider use of natural building materials and systems in cohousing projects. ❧

Robin Allison was an eco-architect before founding and driving the development of Earthsong Eco-Neighbourhood. She now teaches and supports other community projects, and is writing a book of her cohousing experience to be published in 2018. See www.robinallison.co.nz.

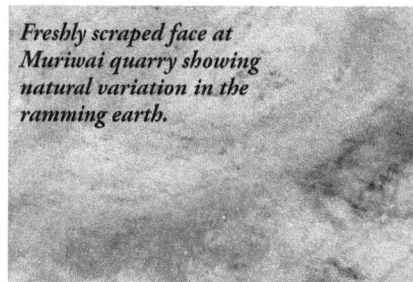

Muriwai quarry, the source of our ramming earth.

Freshly scraped face at Muriwai quarry showing natural variation in the ramming earth.

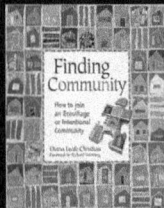

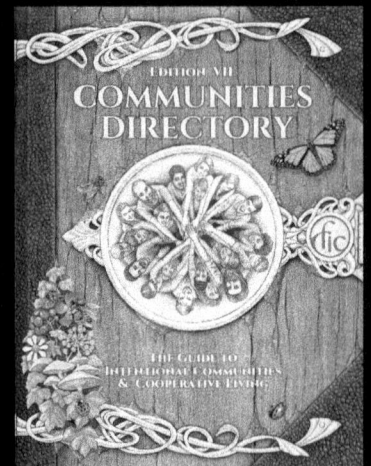

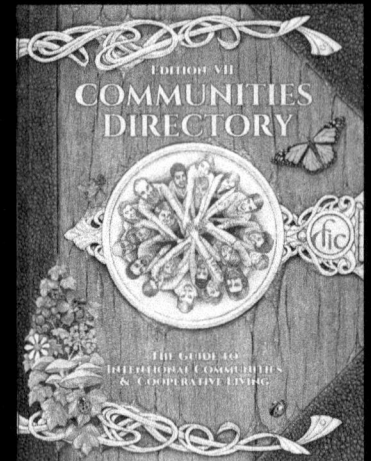

A High-Performance Building for Cohousing: From Vision to Move-In

By Michael Mariano

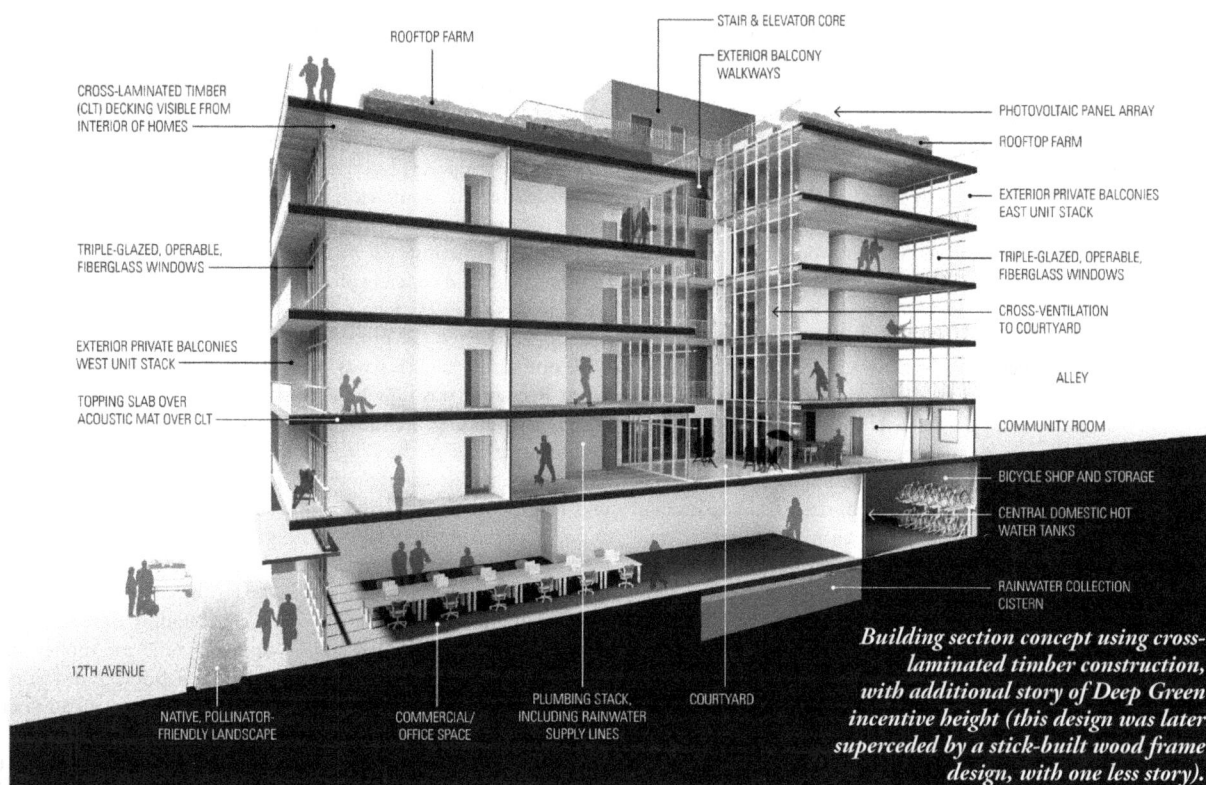

Building section concept using cross-laminated timber construction, with additional story of Deep Green incentive height (this design was later superceded by a stick-built wood frame design, with one less story).

So, you want to design, build, and live in community in the most ecologically positive building that can be built? This is the vision that my partner and I had as well, and here's the story and aspirations that took us on the decade-long course to move-in in July 2016, along with lessons learned along the way.

A Brief Personal History

The introduction to cohousing for my partner, Grace H. Kim, and me came in early 1992 with our Washington State University classmates at the Architectural Association in London during a study-abroad program. A Danish architecture professor and author of a book on the history of housing in Scandinavia, Jorn Orum-Nielsen, presented this concept of resident-developed housing, or *bofællesskab* in Danish. Back in the United States, architects Katie McCamant and Chuck Durrett had recently translated this into the English word "cohousing" in their seminal book, *Cohousing: A Contemporary Approach to Housing Ourselves*, published just four years prior.

During a subsequent month of travel in Europe, I visited a friend's father's friend who was a doctor in Milan, Italy. We were there for a week, staying in a five-story historic building that was owned by the doctor's extended family: he lived in the top-floor apartment with his family, his mother lived on the floor below, his brother below that with his family, a floor was rented out, and he had his doctor's office on the

ground floor. While a similar live/work configuration has occurred for millennia, it was entirely new to me. Fast-forwarding, our experience there was followed by completing our studies, architectural internship and licensure, six years living and working in the heart of Chicago, our return home to Seattle, a year-long certificate program in commercial real estate development for myself, and finally in 2004, the founding of our architecture practice, Schemata Workshop.

Site Acquisition

In 2006, Grace and I began a concerted effort to develop a cohousing project where we would live in community above our architecture studio. Our hope was to find a site in an urban village of Seattle, one that was within walking distance of public transportation, park space, arts and cultural amenities, healthcare, farmers' market, and grocery stores—criteria that has since been bundled into a concept called a high "walk score." We were fortunate to connect with a local real estate broker who intently listened to us, did the extensive legwork, and responded with potential sites to consider.

Around this time, we became familiar with and deeply appreciated the holistic approach presented by the International Living Futures Institute (ILFI) in their Living Building Challenge 1.0 (LBC). The LBC uses the premise that all buildings should have a positive, regenerative impact on the world, and not simply be "less-bad" than other buildings.

We used the LBC as a resource while designing Daybreak Cohousing, and later Dharma Rain Cohousing, both in Portland, Oregon. While Daybreak Cohousing is built and demonstrates the success of thoughtful passive design strategies, neither project achieves the high performance that each community professed as design began.

For our cohousing project in Seattle, we would attain as many LBC imperatives as possible: it was the right project, at the right time. Our intended location already met the LBC imperative of "Limits to growth" by considering only greyfield or brownfield sites, in an effort to make better use of land that has already been exploited. This opened up opportunities for previously developed sites—specifically, sites that are not on or adjacent to sensitive ecological habitats, erosion-prone or unstable slopes, nor poor soils, such as the peat or liquefaction areas common around Seattle.

The project would contribute to a walkable, pedestrian-oriented neighborhood, one that does not require building any onsite automobile parking. Some future residents were already living car-free and locally; some using public transit and local car-sharing; and others are avid walkers and cyclists. Bicycle use in the building would be encouraged by providing easily accessible, safe, and secure bicycle storage (including tandems, trailers, cargo bikes), and bicycle workspace. Showers and lockers would be provided for commuters in the commercial space.

After considering a number of different, scattered locations around Seattle, we focused our pursuits on a two-block-long stretch of geologically stable soil on the edge of the Capitol Hill Urban Village. For site acquisition, we would leverage the rent our architecture practice could pay for office space, as well as that of our personal residence. We found a site that was one-tenth of an acre, with 40 feet of street frontage on one side, and 40 feet of alley frontage opposite. A dilapidated, but still usable, single-story, unreinforced masonry building with 2,400 square feet of interior area had stood there since 1919, and a single-family home for the 20 years prior to that.

In mid-2007, we sent a letter of intent to purchase, and earnest money to the owner of the property, while we put our condo up for sale, hoping to use that profit as equity. Real estate sales took a downturn around the same time (eventually falling off completely), and we looked for investors that could make up our equity shortfall for purchasing the site.

To get a bank on board to finance the site acquisition, we proposed to keep the two tenants (a tattoo parlor, and an espresso cart) in the existing building and would hold their rents at their current rates. To increase revenue from the site in support of the purchase price, we designed and obtained a construction permit for a two-story, prefabricated component building to be erected on the unused and unbuilt portion of the site, to the east of the existing structure. The new building footprint of 20 feet by 50 feet would extend to the alley and partially cantilever over the existing building.

We collaborated with a local fabricator on a self-contained kitchen and bathroom module that would be delivered and simply plugged into the plumbing, electrical, and ventilation systems on each floor of the new building. The building structure would consist of prefabricated three-inch tubular steel frames that are bolted together in the field, with an exterior envelope of insulated metal panels and glass curtainwall outboard of the structure for energy efficiency. The fabricator and general contractor projected a four-month construction period. Within five to 10 years, the temporary building would be disassembled and moved to a new location. This would clear the site for a complete redevelopment of a multi-story, mixed-use building and cohousing community.

Course Correction: As we approached construction and mobilization for the drilled concrete pier foundation of the temporary structure, we were also finalizing loan terms for the construction project. Having recently completed the property acquisition with the same lender, we were optimistic, but this was early 2008, and the full impact of the Great Recession was now becoming apparent. Instead of erecting the temporary building, we moved our six-person architecture studio into the former garage of the existing building, with an entrance that took us past the espresso cart, and where a decade earlier "Hot Rod Pinstriping" had occurred, with hand-painted door signage that proclaimed the same. With the property now under our ownership, and a five-year loan term with our outside investors, we settled in to the quiet buzzing of tattoos from the other side of the wall, and the constant aroma of coffee. The unbuilt, prefabricated component building design, in which we invested a lot of research and development time and money—both personally and through the office—received a national award from the EPA for an unbuilt "Lifecycle Building," but the construction permit and shop drawings still lay in a flat file in the office.

Lesson Learned: Find a location for your future community that supports how you want to live, both now and in the future. An urban infill site takes advantage of the myriad of amenities, conveniences, and

Living Building Charrette with the Design Team, General Contractor, and City Deep Green Technical Assistance Group.

existing infrastructure to support livability. Be flexible, patient, take one deliberate step at a time, and accept that while some efforts may not come to fruition, they are not necessarily wasted. Everything described above led to acquiring a great site for our future cohousing community.

Building Community for Cohousing

In late 2009, Grace and I restarted offering monthly, local Cohousing 101 sessions (free and open to the public) that would raise awareness of the resident-developed model of an intentional community, and we discovered a variety of levels of interest among attendees. In early 2010, Grace and I announced that we had a site and if the location met expectations, they may be interested in an upcoming meeting to discuss moving forward. A number of families came and went during what we projected at the time would be a four-year development process. For some, there were too many meetings; it was going to take too long to complete; there was no off-site parking; homes were going to be too small and/or too expensive. The group adopted the placeholder name of Capitol Hill Urban Cohousing, or "CHUC" for short. With facilitation help, we wrote and coalesced around a vision and values statement, put up a website, and began design of the building in anticipation of the public meetings required to obtain City land use and building permits.

We hired a general contractor (GC) for pre-construction services that included members of the team that had just recently completed construction of the Bullitt Center about six blocks away from our site. They were in the midst of certification as a "Living Building" under the LBC, with required imperatives around net zero energy and water, nontoxic materials, and locally-sourced construction materials, among other criteria. With CHUC, we applied for permitting under the City's Deep Green Pilot Program, which was based on the LBC, and intended to encourage the construction of high-performance buildings. In exchange for our commitment to a 75 percent reduction in energy and water use over a comparable, code-compliant building, CHUC could receive a height exemption that could be used for an additional story of height.

We assembled a skilled design team, and held a kick-off/chartering meeting for the entire design and construction team at the Bullitt Center. With this momentum, we had our required LBC Charrette which brought together the entire team, led by a representative of the ILFI, along with a Technical Assistance Group (TAG) provided by the City that was comprised of local professionals with experience designing high-performance buildings. This day-long workshop and an integrated design process would help ensure the completed building would meet the goals for energy and water efficiency, along with our interest in achieving other "petals" of the LBC. The future cohousing residents were all committed to the highest performing, most environmentally positive building that we could possibly develop.

> It is difficult to reconcile aspirations for a great building (one that truly is good for the environment and its residents) and a building whose main goal is to provide for a thriving social network.

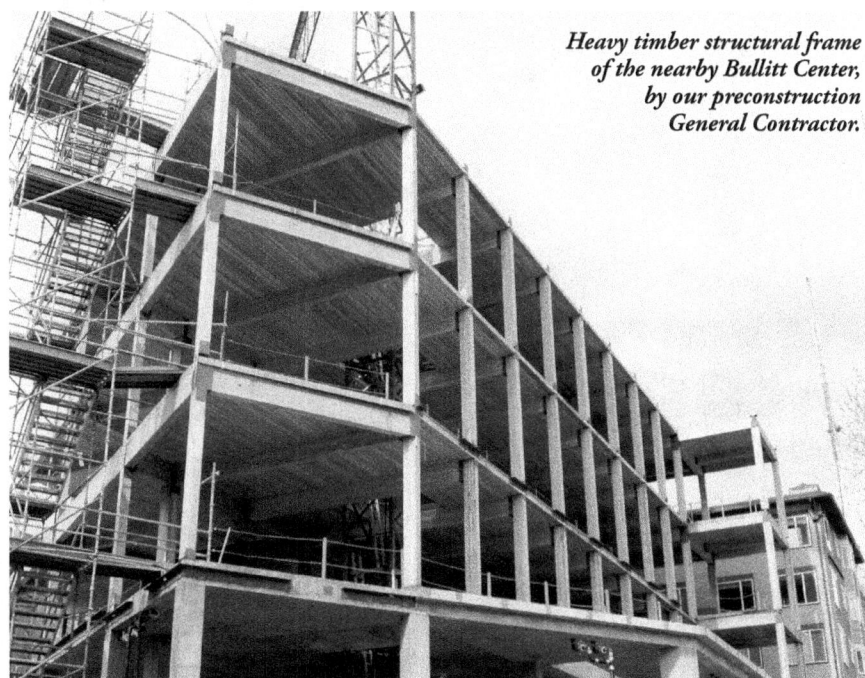

Heavy timber structural frame of the nearby Bullitt Center, by our preconstruction General Contractor.

Course Correction: None. The design team was united in pursuit of a building to fully comply with the City's Deep Green Pilot Program, or better.

Lesson Learned: This comprehensive approach to the design and project delivery effort, with the entire design and construction team closely collaborating, can help achieve a collective commitment and support for the vision, and ultimate success of the project. Unlike the speculative projects of this scale (and larger) that most members of the team work on regularly, here we could introduce them to the families that were going to live in the building. Be sure to reach out to the local building department to see what resources they may be able to offer in support of your project.

Structural System

At the outset of design, our priority was for resiliency—the early '70s British concept of a "long life, loose fit, low-energy" building, and what Stewart Brand in his book, *How Buildings Learn*, later articulated quite well as a systems approach to building. The primary structure would be clearly distinct and positioned in-board from the building envelope. Our design approach was informed by our Seattle experience living in a 1910 warehouse building in the Pike Place Market that had been later converted into housing, and the 1927 warehouse building that was later converted to office space and where we opened our architecture practice. To truly address flexibility for an unknown future, it is necessary to build a structure that would outlast all of the founding families and be a durable framework for future residents to live in community. Everything inside and outside this robust structural frame will eventually be replaced. The structure, however, will remain while exterior cladding deteriorates, window assemblies fail, electrical systems become obsolete, plumbing and mechanical systems are replaced, and interior walls are removed or relocated. In contrast to the temporal nature of all these systems, the primary structure and foundations are intentionally designed and built to remain fully functional for 250+ years.

In the interest of longevity, we investigated three different structural framing systems: 1) steel, 2) concrete, and 3) cross-laminated timber (CLT). Each of these could provide long-term flexibility related to interior partitions, and repair and eventual upgrade of building utilities and infrastructure. Due to our urban infill location and building out to the adjacent property lines, a steel frame would require expensive fire protection of all structural members, and we would still need the mass of a concrete deck for acceptable acoustic performance between homes. For a typical cast-in-place concrete building, current post-tensioned (P-T) engineering uses steel tendons to optimize the thickness of concrete and spans. Unfortunately a P-T system has an estimated 75-year lifespan, and we have a recent, local example of a high-rise that was entirely demolished due to early, pervasive failure of steel tendons. To avoid post-tensioning the concrete, we could use a dense web of mild-steel reinforcing, but this results in thicker floors than was our preference. Despite the nearly ideal acoustic and thermal performance of a high-mass concrete structure, we decided against this option due to the energy used in producing the cement, sourcing distance, and post-earthquake performance, assessment, and repair of concrete in our active seismic zone. Instead, we designed the building around a material that had already sequestered atmospheric carbon into trees that was then processed into CLT.

This CLT plank material is highly engineered and permitted under the Heavy Timber section of the building construction code. In addition to exceptional seismic performance, it also offered visible infrastructure and systems, such as surface-mounted electrical conduit, outlets, and light fixtures. Earthbound hold-downs at the exposed ends of CLT panel shear walls would also be visible and could be assessed after an earthquake. All plumbing would be consolidated to a limited number of vertical shafts through the building, with mechanical equipment, ductwork, and fire sprinklers visible and easily accessible within each home. While the Bullitt Center used an in-field, nail-laminated timber deck instead of CLT, our GC brought lessons learned related to fire-ratings and beam-to-column connec-

tions that we would also employ. With a CLT structural system, a lightweight-concrete topping slab is poured over a high-performance acoustic mat to provide acceptable sound isolation between homes, without having to suspend an insulated ceiling below the CLT deck and beams. CLT offered the attraction of visible wood ceiling and wall planes, in conjunction with the concrete floor that could be left exposed. Engineered flooring could be laid on top of the concrete for a more finished appearance, at the discretion and expense of the future resident.

Course Correction: Pre-construction services with the GC included two rounds of construction cost estimates. After reviewing and cutting everything that we reasonably could from the project, the cost estimate was still substantially higher than our budget could accommodate. The design team then redesigned the building from CLT to a more typical stick-built wood frame, over a first floor podium of mild-steel-reinforced concrete between the commercial space and residences above. A lot of the cost was also in how our selected GC delivered high-quality, well-crafted buildings. This simply required a lot more time and staff, as well as using reliable subcontractors that they could count on. We had to find a more economical GC, and chose one that had just completed an adjacent apartment building and provided a cost estimate that met our budget.

Lessons Learned: It is difficult to reconcile aspirations for a great building (one that truly is good for the environment and its residents) and a building whose main goal is to provide for a thriving social network, while connecting residents to light, air, food, nature, and community. Raising more investor equity would not work, due to the high interest we would pay for a loan subordinated to the bank. The future residents had already spent months running "sensitivity analyses" on a wide range of rent and equity scenarios and were using a reasonable principal and interest rate in our proforma. In order to increase the construction budget, we would need more low/no-interest "patient money" from the future resident families, but everyone had already contributed what they could. Time to get to work with what we could count on from the families that were committed to making this happen.

Net Zero Energy

LBC required that 100 percent of the project's energy needs be supplied by on-site renewable energy on a net annual basis, while the Deep Green Pilot Program required a 75 percent reduction of energy use over a conventional building. Our limited site and roof area had space for a 10kW photovoltaic system, which translated into needing to achieve an Energy Use Intensity (EUI) of 16. This low EUI is a challenge in a residential building, primarily due to daily hot water use by residents. To achieve the target EUI, we analyzed and optimized the building envelope using Passivhaus Institut energy strategies.

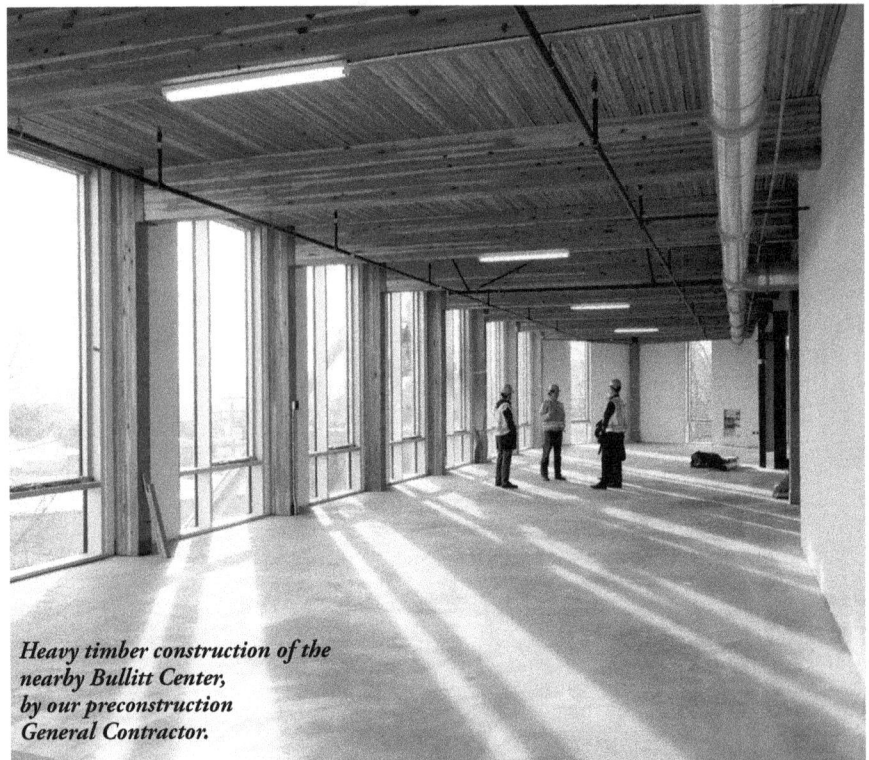

Heavy timber construction of the nearby Bullitt Center, by our preconstruction General Contractor.

148

To help ensure an airtight building with sufficient fresh air changes, the same fluid-applied Air and Water Barrier (AWB) refined specifically for and used on the Bullitt Center would be used on our building as well. Daylighting through individual unit configuration, shallow unit depth, window sizes and locations reduces the need for electric lighting. High-efficiency LED light fixtures with occupancy sensors, and efficient, Energy Star-rated appliances will be used throughout the building. Per LBC, no fossil fuels are permitted to serve the building, which also helps ensure indoor air quality by eliminating carbon monoxide output during cooking with natural gas. Cooktops are all electric induction for efficiency, and a central high-efficiency domestic hot water system serves all homes. A heat recovery ventilator (HRV) for each home was explored by the team, but we determined that energy use by the HRVs, and the noise generated, were both unnecessary and that a whole-house exhaust fan with fresh air supplied by window fresh air ports will be sufficient. Highly-insulated, full-height, operable tilt and turn, fiberglass-frame, triple-pane windows would provide for natural convection and night-flushing of the individual homes, taking advantage of the thermal mass of the building. A shallow balcony would extend the full length of the west façade, providing shading of the glass on hot summer days for interior comfort. All common area circulation space is unconditioned to reduce energy use of unoccupied space.

The commercial tenant (architect Schemata Workshop for a minimum five-year term) would commit to a maximum wattage allocation under the terms of their lease with the cohousing ownership entity, with a financial penalty if it is exceeded. The office space will use an electric hydronic baseboard at the exterior window wall, with CO_2 sensors operating windows for fresh air, which combine with bathroom exhaust fans to provide for necessary fresh air changes.

Course Correction: Due to construction costs, the rooftop PV array was not installed. As unit layouts were being refined, families moving into the west-facing homes stated a preference for interior space instead of exterior balconies. We omitted those balconies and designed an exterior sun-shading screen system that could slide out of view, but these screens were outside of the budget and omitted as well. Triple-pane fiberglass windows were too expensive to use throughout the building, and were installed only at the east façade of the sole residence with an exterior balcony overlooking the alley. Insulated, double-pane, vinyl windows are used elsewhere, while cost dictated a minimally code-compliant, fire-rated, insulated entry door and frame to each home.

Lesson Learned: A 10-year cost/benefit analysis of a variety of upgrades beyond energy code minimum provided guidance to the design team, with a final designed EUI of 31. We determined that an additional layer of insulation outboard of the wall sheathing that would substantially reduce thermal bridging, along with a continuous fluid-applied AWB, were low-cost options for a high-performance building envelope. Be sure, however, to find a qualified applicator that understands and can work with the specific AWB material selected. It's most practical to invest in cutting energy demand with a more efficient building, e.g., better windows and exterior doors, an efficient alternative to electric

Entry hall mosaic designed by a CHUC resident and assembled by the community.

resistance heating, and electric induction cooktops in all homes, before considering energy production.

Net Zero Water

LBC required 100 percent of the project's water needs be supplied with captured precipitation or other natural closed-loop water systems that account for downstream ecosystem impacts, in addition to onsite blackwater (sewage) treatment. The Deep Green Pilot Program required a vaguely defined 75 percent reduction in potable water usage and outflow compared to a conventional building, with no requirement for blackwater treatment. Due to our limited site area, high residential water demand, and the rooftop farm, we would need to also collect stormwater from the adjacent building to the north, which would supply a 20,000 gallon cistern under the street-level commercial space. Historically dry summers would be insufficient to refill the cistern, but rainwater would be used year-round for toilet flushing, clothes washing, and irrigation in order to minimize negative downstream ecosystem impacts. The lower roof with farm would discharge contaminated water, not available for use in the building, while the upper roof with PV array, along with water collection from the adjacent building rooftop would charge the cistern.

Course Correction: A secondary water supply system of "purple pipe," used solely for treated rainwater distribution to each home, along with the additional cost of excavation for the cistern, proved to be outside of the construction budget. At this point, it became apparent that we would not be able to achieve the City's minimum requirements under the Deep Green Pilot, and would need to back out of the program. This also translated into building only nine homes, versus the 12 anticipated with the height exemption allowed under the Deep Green Pilot program.

Lessons Learned: A multi-family apartment building is inherently challenging for water usage, in comparison to other buildings that have more commonly pursued the LBC. Residents shower, wash clothes, and have dishwashers. We would still have a central domestic hot water system that efficiently routes hot water to each home, along with high-efficiency plumbing fixtures.

Urban Agriculture

Our community made a commitment to integrating opportunities for and being stewards of urban agriculture, while making a positive contribution to a local food network. Toward that goal, we partnered with and received some minor financial support from both a local private university and a public college. A farm-to-table restaurant a half-mile south contracted with an urban farmer to oversee a majority of the farm that was dedicated to their food selection, production, and distribution. Staff from the restaurant can pick produce in the morning, and serve it in the restaurant that evening. At the same time, residents of the building will have access to designated areas for growing produce used in common meal preparation as well.

Course Correction: While we originally envisioned gardens on both roof levels, we omitted the elevator stop to the uppermost roof, which prohibited a farming use due to accessibility requirements of the building code. Construction costs were reduced by not reinforcing the upper roof for the heavy soil loading required by a garden. The upper roof is, however, designed to support a future PV array with conduit provided to the basement electrical room.

Lesson Learned: Be adaptable, while maintaining and finding a way to achieve the vision. Prospective residents who had expressed a commitment during early design to manage the farm instead moved to an actual farm, so the partnership with a restaurant was one way that allowed the farm to be used to its full potential. Installation of a PV array can still occur in the future, and after additional energy efficiency

upgrades, such as more efficient central hot water heaters, or cooktops, or wall heaters in homes.

Human Scale and Places

As described in the LBC, the project is designed to create human-scaled rather than automobile-scaled places, so that the experience brings out the best in humanity and promotes culture and interaction. Homes are organized such that there is a public-to-private gradient in the lives of residents, with kitchens immediately adjacent to common areas, and more privacy and seclusion offered further inside each home. The courtyard provides a human-scaled, intimate, vertical urban space that can be personalized, effectively serving as the central circulation path seen in other ground-related, suburban or rural cohousing communities. Salvaged brick from the original building paves a portion of the entry hall, and a prominent glass tile mosaic designed by a resident, with tiles set by all residents including the children, is a great reminder of the success of participation in building community.

The Common House, located on the second floor and directly adjacent to the outdoor patio, functions as a hearth/heart of the community and provides for communal meal preparation and dining three times a week, as well as informal gatherings, an impromptu "third place," celebrations, and fostering of community. Community spaces allow residents of the building to live larger than their compact and efficient homes would suggest.

In Closing

While aspirations were ambitious and paths toward a high-performance building were clear and exhaustively pursued during design, the single most significant goal was to live in community. With only 160 built cohousing communities in North America, adding one more to the list should be considered quite an accomplishment in itself. All nine families moved into the building over a three-day period in June 2016 to occupy six homes at 850 square feet each, two at 1,100 square feet, and one at 1,300 square feet. Common meals occur three times per week, and the building feels more lived-in every day. As with any construction project, we still have some challenges with warranty issues and maintenance to deal with, but staying focused made it all a reality. Be open to adapting the process in order to overcome the inevitable challenges along the way to be sure that future residents are all engaged in and committed to the project. Groups that are forming an intentional community need to accomplish the business of real estate development, while at the same time building community and social capital with each other. While participation by residents will fluctuate over the course of each of our lives, we will adapt, and living in community has proven to be well worth our collective effort. ✒

Michael Mariano is a principal and architect at Schemata Workshop, Inc. in Seattle, Washington, where his partner/spouse and their daughter live in the cohousing community above their office. Michael also co-chairs the Capitol Hill Ecodistrict, which anticipates certification in 2018 as one of the first-ever neighborhoods under the strict and holistic EcoDistricts protocol. CHUC is located at the geographic center of Capitol Hill and its population of 30,000 residents, and serves as the epicenter of their personal and professional efforts to improve livability while building community (schemataworkshop.com).

Recommended Reading:

Brand, Stewart. *How Buildings Learn: What Happens After They're Built*. Viking Press, 1994.

Leupen, Bernard. *Frame and Generic Space*. 010 Publishers, 2006.

EcoDistricts: www.ecodistricts.org

Capitol Hill Urban Cohousing: www.capitolhillurbancohousing.org

FROM BLIGHT TO BEAUTIFUL:
Renovating an Urban House By and For Community

By Lindsay Speer

Westcott Street house when first purchased in 2008.

Westcott Street house from the rear, 2017.

The start of it all: a compost bin

The first Bread and Roses Collective house is a large brick Victorian on a small lot on a residential street in the City of Syracuse, New York. In the early 2000s, when we first built our compost bin, the large lot behind our garage was an overgrown mess of broken box elders, Japanese knotweed, and piles of dumped trash, owned by an unresponsive slumlord. Our compost bin fit right in. As we spent time out there, we began to dream of urban gardens beyond our tiny Food Not Lawns front garden. When the land came up for sale in 2007, we knew we wanted it. What we weren't so sure about was the derelict, empty house that was attached to it.

The Westcott Street house had been neglected. A tarp covered the back third of the roof, which we had watched disintegrate over the course of five years. Water damage contributed to the whole place stinking of cheap chemical soap and mold, on top of decades of cigarette smoke. The old garage leaned precipitously. If we were to look for a second house to buy, this would not have been it, but to get the land we had to get the house.

The Bread and Roses Collective is a 501(c)3 nonprofit organized for providing affordable, sustainable, low-income housing. The first members of the collective moved into our first house as a rental property in 1997, and eventually organized themselves to form a nonprofit and purchase it from the landlord in 2004. We are a community of activists, often working for local nonprofits and engaged on our own time with various local campaigns, including fights for social and environmen-

tal justice. At the same time, we are building the world we want to live in at home, making decisions by consensus and working together to accomplish what none of us alone could do—

Such as buying and renovating a house.

When deciding whether or not to buy the Westcott Street house, the combined factors of already having a large mortgage on our first house and the state of disrepair of this new one gave many of us pause. As in many property transactions, time was of the essence. We came to an agreement that one of our members who could afford to would purchase the house, and at the very least we'd purchase the land from him. We'd take our time to consider the house's future. In the midst of this, the 2008 housing crisis hit and we ended up getting the property for only $57,000.

Should it stay or go?

Now that it was ours, we went to work pulling out the weeds, clearing out the junk, and expanding our compost operation to collect from a local vegan restaurant and a coffee shop to build the soil for the raised beds of our urban garden. We began to dream about what to do with the house. Despite its being legally owned by only one of us, the decision-making about its future was done collectively from the beginning. We came to the conclusion that the back third of the house was beyond saving. Should we only tear off that part, or should we demolish the whole house? Ultimately, the decision was made to save most of the house and design an addition to fit our needs and dreams. Bread and Roses committed to the project, and financed it through personal loans at interest rates below what the banks could offer.

"In retrospect, it would have been cheaper and easier to tear the whole thing down and build a new house from scratch," reflects Bread and Roses member Steve. Retrofitting the existing old house for energy efficiency and designing an addition to match its design was costly, in both time and money, but there were benefits too. "By keeping the existing house and carefully deconstructing the elements we wished to change, we saved a lot of material from ending up in the landfill. We also kept the character of the house, which is consistent with the neighborhood."

Hammering the nails out of every single piece of lath was an inefficient use of our time, although we now have a great supply of nail-free kindling for the highly efficient Avalon wood stove. On the other hand, removing the nails from larger old unpainted boards, installed before the days of pressurized lumber, was well worth it. They are now the sides of the raised beds in the garden.

Dreaming a future

The process in dreaming up what the future house would finally look like was extensive. The collective started by conducting interviews with each member about our hopes and dreams. We were lucky enough to have Simon, a longstanding guest at our weekly potluck who worked for an architectural firm, to guide us through the process of designing the addition of our dreams. He patiently worked with the collective and the architects through a consensus-based design—and

the redesign that took place as financial realities set in. A committee of four people led the extensive research and decision process, following the guidelines and broad decisions set by the collective (eight people at that time).

Key to the new addition was a large kitchen. The kitchen at the old house was small even by current single-family home standards. We wanted a kitchen in which we could host parties and workshops; a space that could serve as the hearth of the community. We also knew from experience that one bathroom was not quite enough for second-floor living quarters with five or more bedrooms. Finally, we wanted the first floor of the house to be accessible, both with an eye to accommodating anyone's eventual disability, and to currently provide accessible meeting space for the local activist community.

Eco-friendly design choices

We strove to build as eco-friendly as possible, but early on we realized that many compromises would have to be made in order to meet the City of Syracuse's building codes. We couldn't do strawbale walls, but we could use FSC-certified lumber. We had to hire a con-

Richard and Alison install ceiling drywall during the Spring 2012 Workweek with instruction from a friend.

Tearing down the back portion of the house, 2011.

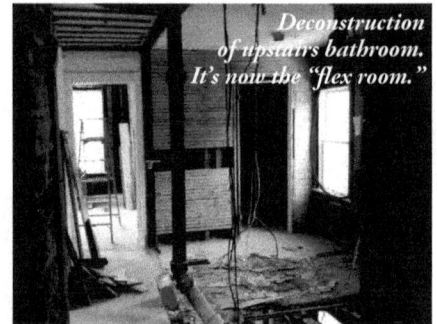
Deconstruction of upstairs bathroom. It's now the "flex room."

Original front stairs circa 2012.

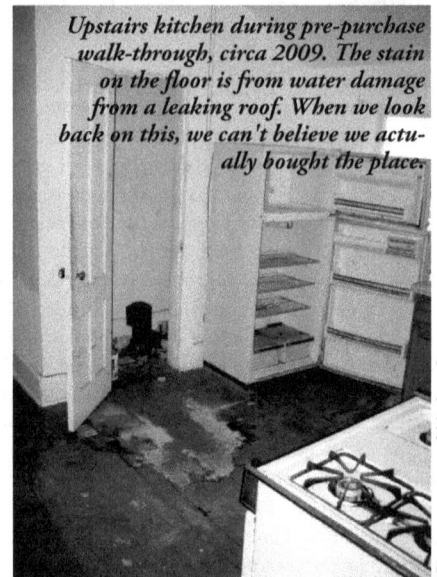
Upstairs kitchen during pre-purchase walk-through, circa 2009. The stain on the floor is from water damage from a leaking roof. When we look back on this, we can't believe we actually bought the place.

Photos courtesy of Lindsay Speer

2016 Native Plant Sale, organized as a joint fundraiser with the Alchemical Nursery Project, in front of the renovated Westcott Street house.

New kitchen as the tile is being installed.

A dining room built for a collective. We acquired the 17 ft.-long church pews from a Methodist church that closed down.

tractor to do the actual building envelope, as well as plumbing and electrical. Picking a good contractor is key, and it can be a challenge to find one who will work with a collective. Take the time to read reviews and listen to your gut. You want someone you can trust to build you a good house—this is not a place to cut costs or skimp. We may have saved ourselves many headaches if we'd had that advice.

We did most of the finish work inside ourselves, many of us learning along the way; it is amazing what you can learn from online videos. We taught each other the necessary skills and consulted often with friends and family. We hung drywall, painted, installed the tile and wood floors, cabinetry, countertops, internal doors, and trim. What materials we could, we bought secondhand, scouring Craigslist, the local Habitat for Humanity ReStore, and Freecycle. It was a continuous treasure hunt for the right items, with surprising finds like the granite countertops, or the wooden pews.

Our neighbors were another important source of materials. We carefully watched when

things went out on the curb as others remodeled their homes, acquiring a substantial number of doors coated with thick layers of old paint this way. We researched lead paint remediation and developed a process to strip the doors using a heat gun, citrus-based stripper, and careful disposal, always wearing N95 masks, gloves, and changing our clothes and shoes so as to prevent lead contamination elsewhere. When Jessica became pregnant she had her blood tested. Her blood lead levels came back as acceptable, a relief and validation for our process. To be extra safe she only worked on the later stages (staining, poly) of door refinishing through her pregnancy. Her daughter, now nearly three years old, is talkative and clever and has us all wrapped around her little finger.

After living for years in a large, drafty Victorian, we knew the importance of adequate insulation and double-pane, low emissivity (or low-E) windows to ward off the chill of Syracuse winters. We installed high-density foam panels for insulation, between the narrow four-inch studs framing the old portion of the house. If we had built new, this could have been a more eco-friendly material. We sprayed the attic with a thick layer of insulation, resulting in a roof with an R-value of 50.

The light-colored metal roof is an eco design choice. High reflectivity in the summertime means a cooler house, especially when combined with the used ceiling fans we installed in each room. By avoiding asphalt shingles we ensured we could use the rain water on our gardens. We installed homemade rain barrels at each of the downspouts, our contribution to the Save the Rain campaign to keep storm water out of our combined sewers and therefore out of Onondaga Creek and Onondaga Lake.

Most of our lighting fixtures were previously used, and we found some great deals on very pretty fixtures. When the electrician wanted light bulbs in every socket as he worked, Jessica diligently replaced every incandescent light he installed with LEDs. On-demand water heating not only saves energy, it also ensures that no one is upset someone else drained the hot water tank during the last shower!

We used a zero VOC stain with no petroleum distillates and Vermont Natural Coatings' Poly-Whey on all of our woodwork. The polywhey is a groundbreaking product developed in Vermont, made from dairy whey, a dairy industry waste product. It performs well and you can re-coat in a matter of a couple of hours as compared to traditional poly which requires at least 24 hours between coats, so it also makes the whole process much faster. All of the paint on the walls is also zero VOC. This was and is a great benefit, allowing us to work through the winters and while people are living in the house without headaches. By talking about the scale of our project and commitment to zero VOC with the owners of a local paint store, we were introduced to a zero VOC paint that was half the price of anything else we'd seen on shelves. Personal connection is everything.

Impact on membership

The building inspector awarded us a temporary Certificate of Occupancy (COO) in early 2014, allowing new people to move in and expand the number of hands working on the project, which has fluctuated between 10 and 13. We are working towards the permanent Certificate of Occupancy. We were surprised to learn that we had to install all the wood trim before a permanent COO would be granted, despite the rest of the house being fully functional. We had all the trim custom-milled but sent to us unfinished in order to save money. This has cost us in time as countless hours go into sanding and staining each piece. However the finished look, which matches the original trim of the house, is absolutely worth it.

In the 2000s, we would have work-weekends twice a year to maintain and improve the first house. With this project, we moved to work-weekends every month with people working on projects in-between as well. While some dedicated housemates stayed through it all, the amount of work involved did contribute to turnover. For a collective dedicated to providing housing to activists, it is a struggle to balance between building the house, working our day jobs, all while doing our best to contribute to local activist movements. Over the years, 40 members have all contributed to construction of the house. Some people have stayed only a short time; others gave significant years of their life to the project. Only four of us remain from those who made the decision to purchase the house, and I left for a few years. The biggest impact of turnover is the loss of acquired building skills, and the need to train and empower new members. Few people these days come to us with any practical building experience, but they leave with skills and confidence to tackle their own projects. Ultimately our project is not only benefiting our collective, but the community: five of our former members have now purchased and renovated houses nearby.

Even those who leave still appreciate the work they put in, and seeing the progress of the house. "I like coming back and seeing how I left my mark," observed Sienna when she visited recently, also noting how much she learned in the process. "The skills of building a house are transferable

to fighting for a cause: both need organization and people working together."

The secret to organizing people: good food

The once overgrown lot we originally coveted is now home to an urban permaculture oasis of 10 garden beds, three terraces, fruit trees, and rain gardens, providing the houses with abundant organic homegrown food. Our compost bin collection has grown from one to six with an impressive system of rotation. Many of the damaged trees we cleared were inoculated with oyster and shiitake mushroom spawn and have kept us happily eating mushrooms for years.

As the construction work winds down, Bread and Roses members find ourselves able to return more fully to the activism that brings us together in the first place. As the arena of national politics becomes increasingly chaotic, we find ourselves glad to be in a supportive community, with room to grow, personally and physically. For many members, it's the coming together in radical spaces with radical support that makes it all worth it. Here, we have bread, and we have roses too. ❧

Lindsay Speer is an organizer on indigenous rights, environmental justice, and energy policy. She is a graduate of Starhawk's Earth Activist Training Permaculture Design Course. Born and raised in Syracuse, she has lived at Bread and Roses from 2006-2010 and 2015-present. She is rooted deeply in this land and loves its crazy winters and glorious green summers. See @careoftheearth on Twitter.

Backyard with raised beds, circa 2014.

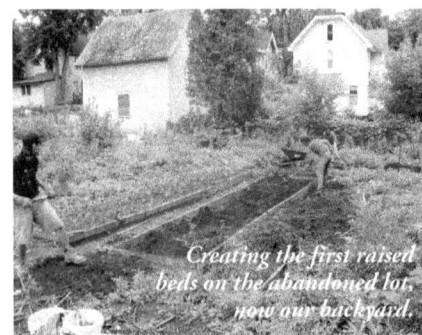

Creating the first raised beds on the abandoned lot, now our backyard.

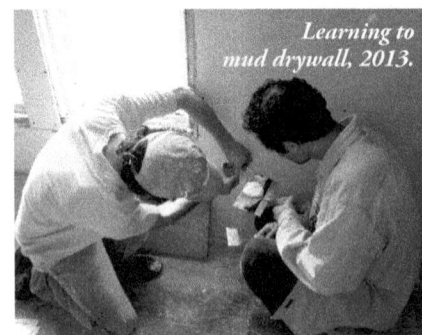

Learning to mud drywall, 2013.

III

ENERGY AND ECOLOGICAL FOOTPRINT

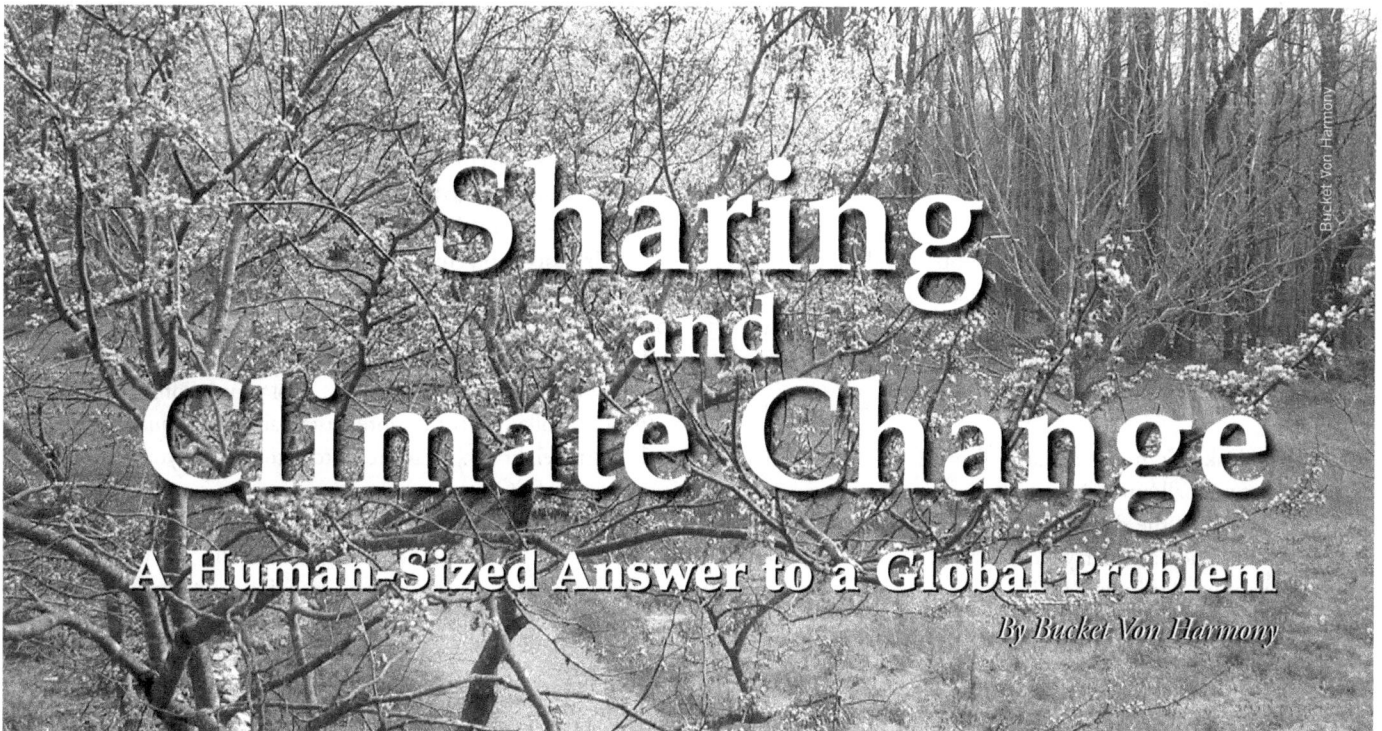

Sharing
and
Climate Change
A Human-Sized Answer to a Global Problem
By Bucket Von Harmony

The global community is facing a serious ecological problem. Unless we change our way of living we may be passing on to our children a world with rising sea levels, extreme weather conditions, and disrupted ecosystems. According to governmental studies done in the UK and EU, a global average temperature increase of over 3 degrees Celsius would cause irreversible changes to our environment, the effects of which may include a potential rise of the sea level of up to 7 meters and widespread water and food shortages.

Nathan Rive of the Center for International Climate and Environmental Research in Oslo says that if we are to have any chance of preventing the average temperature from increasing over 2 degrees, "we would have to cut global emissions by 80 percent by 2050."

How can we stop consuming resources and producing carbon at such high levels? Is it possible to do so and still maintain the level of comfort that we have in modern life? Are we willing to make the changes necessary, when the ultimate effects of our actions (or inaction) will not manifest until decades from now? We have the technology now that can help, but investment in these technologies on a massive scale is needed immediately if we hope to see the changes we need in place in time to make a difference. Government programs like carbon taxes might help motivate our industries to pollute less. However, in places like the European Union and the UK where such laws have been enacted, carbon reduction is still falling short of their goals. In addition, the US is the largest producer of carbon emissions per capita and is currently without comprehensive carbon emission regulations.

Don't give up hope yet! There exists today a solution that could drastically reduce the energy consumption and carbon emissions of the modern citizen, and it does not require new technology or a drastic reduction in quality of life. It is not anything new or complex; in fact it is something we all learned in Kindergarten. It is called sharing.

Case in Point: Twin Oaks Community

The bylaws of my home, Twin Oaks Community in Virginia, list ecological sustainability as just one of the many purposes of our community's existence. The primary intention of our community at its founding was to create a culture of cooperation, sharing, and equality. We certainly do care about ecological sustainability and hold many discussions on how we could do better. However, we have put most of our energy into finding ways to live cooperatively, communally, and comfortably.

Only 10 percent of our residents are grid-electricity-free, we have no buildings built with cob or strawbale, and we live with most of the comforts of modern life. Despite our lack of green technologies and our lifestyle of modern conveniences, members of our community consume far less resources than those in our neighborhood, in some cases by over 80 percent less!

Below is a breakdown of our resource consumption and how it compares to that of other people in our climate.

Gasoline:

The average Virginia resident uses about 530 gallons of gasoline per year.[1] Twin Oaks consumed about 15,267 gallons of gasoline in 2007. With an average adult and child population of 96, that would put our consumption at 159 gallons per person. That is *70 percent less gasoline consumed!*

Electricity:

The average Virginia resident uses 13,860 kWh of electricity per year.[2] Twin Oaks consumed 268,065 kWh in 2007. With an average adult and child population of 96, that would put our consumption at 2792 kWh per person. That is *80 percent less electricity consumed!*

Natural Gas:

The average Virginia natural gas consumer uses 302 therms of natural gas.[3] Twin Oaks consumed 16,221 therms of natural gas in 2007. With an average adult and child population of 96, that would put our consumption at 169 therms per person. That is *44 percent less natural gas consumed!*

Solid Waste:

The average American produces 1460 pounds of trash a year. Twin Oaks produced 18,780 pounds of solid waste in 2007. With an average adult and child population of 96, that would put our production at 196 pounds per person. That is *87 percent less solid waste produced!*

Twin Oaks Community has a fleet of 12 vehicles that we share between all our members. Each day one person runs into town to collect the day-to-day needs for us all. They also ferry people to their various destinations like doctor appointments or the library. By sharing our vehicles and carpooling, we are able to drastically reduce the amount of gasoline we use.

We all live in nine communal houses, each with different norms and culture. We use carbon-neutral wood to heat our houses. By sharing common space and having dormitory style housing, we consume much less energy to light and heat our homes than we would if we were to live in individual houses.

We serve lunch and dinner each day in a single building for our whole community. We are able to use much less energy to cook our food when we are using one kitchen to feed 90 people than we would if we each cooked our own meals.

What food and general necessities we do not produce ourselves, we buy in bulk. Because of this we greatly reduce the amount of packaging that comes onto our property. We send much less solid waste to the local landfill then we would if we were each to purchase our goods in individually wrapped packages.

By sharing so much we are able to live comfortably, but also greatly reduce our resource consumption and carbon output. Government programs and new technologies will be important in reducing our culture's output of carbon into the atmosphere, but there are things that we as individuals can do today to significantly reduce our contribution to global climate change.

Here are a few examples:

1. Join a food co-op! Use your collective buying power to save

> *By sharing so much we are able to live comfortably, but also greatly reduce our resource consumption and carbon output.*

money, while also reducing the packaging and energy used to deliver your food to your table. If there is not one in your area, start one! www.coopdirectory.org.

2. Carpool and ride-share when traveling! www.craigslist.org or www.rideshare-directory.com.

3. Join a housing co-op! Share a house with other like-minded souls, and share food costs and cook communal dinners together. You will save much more money and resources over living alone! directory.ic.org/records/coops.php.

4. Join an intentional community! There are thousands of communities out there with varying degrees of resource sharing and cooperation. ic.org.

5. Join an egalitarian community! Pool your income together with other folks to live a more sustainable and equitable life with your neighbors. Share resources to reduce your carbon footprint! theFEC.org.

6. Do you already live communally? Do an energy audit and see how your community is doing compared to others that live in your climate. Publish this information and let people know how effective cooperation and sharing is as a tool to battle climate change! Please send copies of your energy audits to bucket@twinoaks.org.

As times get harder, people will be looking for alternatives to our unsustainable economic model. We do need to look towards technology to help us and we do need our governments to regulate industry and lower emissions. These are issues of national and international politics and are beyond the reach of the average person.

However, by sharing more with members of our communities, we really can make significant and meaningful difference in our personal impact on the environment. We have the power to turn this crisis into an opportunity. By being examples for others to follow, perhaps we can make the necessary changes our world needs...one community at a time. ❀

Bucket Von Harmony is a member of Twin Oaks Community in Louisa, Virginia. Twin Oaks Community has served as an example of cooperative living for 41 years. Bucket serves as Co-Secretary of the Federation of Egalitarian Communities and is on the Twin Oaks Membership Team. Bucket also gardens, home schools a six-year-old, cooks dinner for 100 people, and makes tofu.

1. www.nationalpriorities.org/nppdatabase_tool (comparing 2005 numbers to our 2007 numbers)
2. www.eia.doe.gov/cneaf/electricity/esr/table5.html
3. tonto.eia.doe.gov/dnav/ng/ng_cons_num_dcu_SVA_a.htm
www.euractiv.com/en/sustainability/eu-climate-change-target-unfeasible/article-152154
www.metoffice.gov.uk/corporate/pressoffice/adcc/ExecSumFeb2005.pdf

www.stabilisation2005.com/outcomes.html
www.reuters.com/article/topNews/idUSL194440620070419
www.independent.co.uk/environment/3-degrees-chief-scientist-warns-bigger-rise-in-worlds-temperature-will-put-400-million-at-risk-474180.html
www.independent.co.uk/opinion/leading-articles/leading-article-the-dangers-of-pessimism-in-the-struggle-against-global-warming-474159.html
www.statemaster.com/graph/lif_ave_hou_siz-lifestyle-average-household-size

Revolutionary Communitarianism?

By Alexis Zeigler

We are facing combined energy, environmental, economic, and social justice problems of monumental proportions. We are also seeing a plethora of proposed solutions. Al Gore hosts an international concert to raise awareness of global warming, and Chevrolet is one of the primary sponsors. Chevron is running ads in major magazines encouraging people to conserve energy. Many developers and builders have jumped on the "green building" bandwagon, repackaging old plans in new green wrappers. These efforts range from well-intended to ineffectual, or just plain deceitful. We need a real conservation movement, and Intentional Communities are the sleeping giant of that movement.

I am an environmental activist and writer. As part of these efforts, I recently asked a number of my environmental activist friends to send me their energy bills. I looked at these bills, and conducted a comparison to the energy use at a few intentional communities. I expected the communities to have a smaller energy "footprint," but the degree of the difference was shocking.

Among my environmental activist friends in the central Virginia area, residential energy use varied considerably. The surprise was that the average energy use was *above* American average per capita use. How could that be? The American average includes many people who live in urban areas in apartments. For someone who lives in an old, uninsulated house, even if they keep the thermostat set at "painfully cold" in the winter, their energy use is still much higher than someone living in an apartment with other apartments on all sides.

There were other surprising discoveries in my rather non-scientific survey of energy use. The cooperative groups I examined had energy use levels from 75 percent below to more than 90 percent below American average per-capita residential use. Some co-ops probably don't do nearly as well, but that level of conservation is impressive. Put this in the context of the current debate over global warming. Various environmental groups have proposed radical carbon reductions goals in the range of 80 percent by 2050. This seems like an ambitious and noble goal. And yet some intentional communities are already conserving energy at a rate that is supposed to be our goal *40 years from now.*

The mainstream environmental movement has been trying to sell renewable energy by focusing primarily on production. We are supposed to believe that producing windmills, solar panels, and biofuels can create millions of jobs and eco-doodads that we can nail to the roof of every American suburban home. There's nothing wrong with alternative energy, but we have to understand that if we tried to power the beltways of America, to heat the homes of America, to turn the tumble driers and air conditioners of the modern industrial world with alternative energy, the results would be disastrous.

Fossil fuel is very concentrated—*extremely* concentrated—energy. We have grown accustomed to using small, cheap machines to use this concentrated energy to play with as we choose. Alternative energy—be it sun, wind, or biofuel—is widely dispersed, and in the case of biofuel, easily over-exploited. Renewable energy, compared to the plethora of fossil energy to which we are accustomed, is limited and very expensive energy. If we use it wisely, in a *very modest* fashion, it could serve us well. If we imagine we can solarize American suburbia to power our current lifestyle, then we are wrong. The ecological price of the machinery that would be required would not be sustainable by any measure.

Such issues are far more than academic. We live in a world that is already very polarized between rich and poor. This polarization has grown in an age of cheap energy. Now we are entering an age of expensive energy. What does that mean? It means the number of people suffering acute malnutrition has risen by 25 percent since the 1990s, from about 800 million to around a billion people. And that means a War on Terror, and Democrats that act like Republicans used to.

Does anyone have any illusions that President Obama is going to roll back the Patriot Act? Why not? Because our world is changing. The big pie of energy and resources is now shrinking on a per capita basis, and the only way we can continue to eat gluttonously is for others to eat less, or not at all. I wish I were just making metaphors. The hungry will fight back, and our politicians will continue, left, right, and center, to frame that battle in heroic and political terms, not in its real ecological context.

In the midst of these growing pressures, the Communities Movement is a sleeping giant. We can spend decades shaving small percentages of conservation off of the American consumer's wasteline, or we can point out that alternative energy—because of the physics of collecting and using diffuse energy—only really works if you use it cooperatively.

Let me sharpen the point. When the average American drives home from work, they want to eat, take a shower, maybe wash their clothes, and go to bed in their private apartment. They could drive a highly efficient hybrid car, but that costs tens of thousands of dollars. (There are some studies that suggest that the long-term toxic outputs from a hybrid car are higher than an SUV. See Trainer, Ted, *Renewable Energy Cannot Sustain a Consumer Society*, Dordrecht, Netherlands, 2007.) The machines required to provide alternative energy to a single individual in an apartment—solar collectors, batteries, and what not—would also be expensive. The payback, either financially or ecologically, on this equipment would fall somewhere between a long time and never *if it is used only by one or two people.*

Is the individual living in a apartment likely to do the research, and spend tens of thousands of dollars to buy a complex array of solar and energy storage equipment? Not likely. Are we going to seek and enforce the global economic inequality that allows the wealthy of the world to put eco-toys in their suburban palaces while everyone else goes hungry and cold? Can we provide these expensive alternative energy systems for each and every individual in the world, all 6.7 billion of us? Clearly not.

Could we provide alternative energy systems to every *community* in the world? Probably.

When alternative energy systems are used cooperatively, whether it be sharing between kinspeople in a village, residents in an intentional community, or even just people at a local laundromat, the cost of the machines is divided between the number of users, and the savings are multiplied. This dividing of the costs and compounding of the dividends is not trivial; it is the difference between the politicized greenhype of corporate environmentalism and the real thing. In intentional community, we have answers that are cheap, use existing mechanical and social technologies, and WORK!

The crucible in which community has historically been crushed is the challenge between sustainable, more egalitarian cultures and highly stratified states. The latter have great power to organize and motivate people. The former have a great power to be wise and sustainable. It is no wonder that modern social movements face the same challenge.

The dysfunctions of what we now call equality and consensus make for amusing stories about the endless "drama" of community living. I hope we have learned something from that drama, because the stakes are going to get much higher. History is calling upon us to awaken from our nap and act. We are going to face revolutionary change whether we like it or not. If we are wise, we will rise and lead it, instead of slumbering in the roadway until it runs us over. We have to find some means to bring people together, to generate commitment and cohesion, without creating an oppressive hierarchy. As far as I can tell, most in the communities movement are infected with the same disease that has so afflicted America at large. We respond to our immediate circumstance—relative comfort—rather than our knowledge that great changes are coming. We can talk about the coming changes, but a visceral, highly motivated response is lacking. Out of that motivation might be borne the highly coordinated, highly organized movement that is still at its heart as egalitarian and tolerant as it can be.

There are many efforts afoot these days to influence policy, to fix these our problems from the top down. I wish them luck, but we cannot wait. We need a bottom-up movement, one that does not wait on any policy changes. We need people who are willing to stick their necks out, to appear foolish and alarmist, to pursue the revolution that we know is approaching. That's you. ❁

Alternative energy— because of the physics of collecting and using diffuse energy— only really works if you use it cooperatively.

Alexis Zeigler is an activist, green builder, and orchardist living in central Virginia. He has lived in intentional community all of his adult life. More information, including articles, interviews, and downloadable books, can be found at his website, conev.org.

Cars and Rabbits

By Alline Anderson

Growing up in the San Francisco Bay Area, I was 26 years old before I went to Yosemite, 30 before I set foot on the island of Alcatraz; both trips happened because friends from out of town were visiting. Lesson learned: it often takes guests with fresh eyes to help us appreciate where and how we live.

I experienced this recently here at my home community, Dancing Rabbit Ecovillage (outside Rutledge, Missouri), with a visit from our friends Sharon and Dennis of Earthaven Ecovillage (Black Mountain, North Carolina). Seeing my own place through their eyes was a chance for me to revisit what has been accomplished, how some of our ideals have manifested into reality, and how by working together we can make a difference. Here's an example:

What separates the men from the boys, the wheat from the chaff, the truly eco-concerned from the cotton-headed ninnymuggins? Car use. While Dancing Rabbit receives a lot of attention for using biodiesel rather than petroleum, it seems to me that the way we utilize resources (in this case, cars) makes a much bigger impression, both socially and ecologically.

One of the stipulations when becoming a member of Dancing Rabbit is that we agree to—no, *choose* to—give up individual ownership of vehicles. For some this is not that much of a stretch; many Rabbits are avid cyclists, and have been getting around solely by bike for years. But for others, it is often a leap of faith; our American car culture is deep and wide, and for those accustomed to having a car available every second of every day it can initially be daunting.

It takes a bit of planning to divide car use for 35 people among three shared vehicles (two Jettas and a big ol' Ford truck). Each Sunday we gather in the Common House to do the "WIP," which stands for Week In Preview. Part of the WIP is scheduling the DRVC (Dancing Rabbit Vehicle Cooperative—yes, we are truly the land of acronyms!). Going through the week day by day, we figure out how best to utilize our vehicles. Who has a doctor's appointment, who needs to go to Kirksville for a conference, does the recycling need to go into Truman State?

Here's how this played out on a typical car trip: Cob and his son Duncan were taking the morning train from La Plata to Chicago, and Ma'ikwe was taking the evening train. They all needed to be dropped off at the La Plata station on Tuesday, albeit at vastly different times. Rather than make two trips, Kurt and I volunteered to drive, knowing that we both needed an eye exam in Kirksville. Sparky needed an eye exam too, so

she signed up to come along. And what the heck—since her train didn't leave until 8:00 p.m., Ma'ikwe called and got an appointment, too. Monday afternoon a group of Rabbits gathered to load the recycling into the back of the truck, and Tuesday morning the six of us piled into the front. We drove to the La Plata train station, dropped off Cob and a sleepy Duncan. We then drove 15 miles north to Kirksville and dropped off the recycling at Truman State's Recycling Center. Next, Kurt and I had our eyes examined while Sparky and Ma'ikwe did a little shopping on the square. We all met up for lunch, and then Kurt and I dropped Sparky and Ma'ikwe at the eye doc's while we did errands for a number of Rabbits: electrical supplies for Ted, custom cut glass for windows for Jeff's house, returning something to the Farm & Home for Rachel, picking up Sunflower Food Coop's order at HyVee, paintbrushes at the hardware store… At 4:00 Sparky and I reconvened at Washington Street Java Co. while Kurt and Ma'ikwe hightailed it to Bayview Supply to scope out supplies for the home she will be building next summer. With still a couple of hours before having to drop Ma'ikwe off at the station, we all had a delicious and relaxing dinner in town. After dinner, we stopped at the grocery store so that Ma'ikwe could get a few traveling treats. After dropping her at the train station, we had the truck back at Dancing Rabbit by 8:00 p.m. when Dan needed it to pick up another group of travelers at the Quincy train station, and were able to join the group celebrating Matt's birthday with games of charades and celebrity. (Whew!)

So what does all this running around prove? After living here for years, one tends to take it for granted; it's just how we do things. We do errands for one another, share rides, and cooperate the best we can. Yes, it sometimes is a pain in the, um, neck. But there is a certain comfort knowing that we can count on one another. We are all able to reduce our footprints just a bit— if each of us were to drive in our own cars on separate trips, we would use several times the petroleum used by the single trip.

Additionally, we not only save petroleum, we also save cold hard cash. By sharing the cost of car payment, maintenance, fuel, and insurance, our costs are startlingly less than when we each owned a car and each paid for our own. According to the Automobile Association of America, the national average cost for driving a car is $664 per month (AAA figured in average fuel, routine maintenance, tires, insurance, license and registration, loan finance charges, and depreciation costs; fuel prices

Photo courtesy of Alline Anderson

are based on late-2006 national averages). Just think how often your car just sits there in your driveway or garage. I don't know about you, but there are lots of things I'd rather do with my money than spend it on a car I'm not using.

So what if you are interested in car sharing and do not live at Dancing Rabbit or another intentional community? Why, what a GREAT question! Car Sharing businesses are popping up all over the country. Most of them offer vehicles by the hour or the day; many offer hybrids, and some even have pick-up trucks. One of the best resources around is Dave Brook's blog, carsharing.us. It is a wealth of information for those wanting to learn more, and for those who are not in big cities. Better yet, Dave

writes regularly, and is really tapped in to the Car Share world.

Change is in the air, and to make it work we all need to participate. What are you willing to do to help with the solution? I like how Frances Moore Lappé put it: "Hope is not what we find in evidence, it's what we become in action." ❃

Alline Anderson has lived at Dancing Rabbit Ecovillage in Rutledge, Missouri since 1999, where she shares her home with her husband Kurt Kessner, and her vehicles with 30 of her closest friends. Her latest adventure is launching The Milkweed Mercantile, an Eco Inn, Organic Café, and Green General Store. Learn more at milkweedmercantile.com.

Resources

- Zipcar (www.zipcar.com) in Atlanta, Boston, Chicago, London, New York, Philadelphia, Pittsburgh, Portland, San Francisco, Seattle, Toronto, Vancouver, and Washington D.C.
- UCarShare (www.ucarshare.com) in Berkeley, Madison, and Portland (both Maine and Oregon)
- www.citycarshare.org in the San Francisco Bay Area
- Philly Car Share (www.phillycarshare.org) in Philadelphia
- www.communitycarshare.org in Bellingham, Washingon
- www.igocars.org in Chicago
- Learn how to start your own Car Share: www.autoshare.com/beginners/guide.html

Ecovillages,
HOW ECOLOGICAL ARE YOU?

By Prudence-Elise Breton

I think of myself as a good "eco-citizen": I recycle, compost, and either bike or use transit in place of a car. I try to buy local or fair trade goods. During the winter, I insulate my windows to save energy. During the summer, I grow as many veggies as I can in my backyard. But when I look beyond my yard, I see overflowing garbage cans, cars left idling, and neighbours who have only ever grown a dandelion-free lawn. The situation is daunting. Are all my efforts the right things to do? What if we all were good "eco-citizens"? Would we really make a difference for the planet? I needed to see that another world was indeed possible, and when I discovered ecovillages, they seemed to be the perfect response. But how effective are their actions really? I decided to find out for myself by visiting a few.

My first visit was in 2004 to Ecohameau de La Baie[1] (Eco-hamlet of the Bay). Ecohameau de La Baie is a little settlement of one Community Supported Agriculture (CSA) farm and six houses, of which five are strawbale constructions. Ecohameau de La Baie is located in Saguenay, a city three hours' drive north of Quebec City, in the province of Quebec, Canada. The family that hosted me was very inspiring. They answered my questions regarding zoning, construction materials, and community rules. They also detailed their successes and disappointments. They gave me much to think about and pushed me to want to know more about ecovillages.

After this first experience, I wanted to visit some ecovillages in more organised and formal settings. I was looking for real models of an ecovillage, closer to an actual village and impressively ecological. After consulting Michel Desgagnés, who visited 40 intentional communities in Canada and the United States[2] in 2003, I chose two ecovillages located in the United States: Sirius Community in Massachusetts and Earthaven in North Carolina. While visiting these two ecovillages during the summer of 2005, I also stopped by Ganas (Staten Island, New York) for five days. Ganas does not claim to be an ecovillage. However, I thought it would be interesting to see the difference between ecovillages that are purposely working toward reducing their impact on the environment and another type of intentional community that is not specifically focusing on it.

I wanted to bring back from my trip an unambiguous image of their efforts toward sustainability. I did not know myself how to evaluate sustainability so I decided to use a sustainable development evaluation grid developed by a university instructor.[3] The grid has four dimensions: ecology, economy, social, and equity. Each of these dimensions includes various indicators to be weighted and scored. I thought the ecovillages would get amazing final scores, especially for the ecological dimension. However, my experience turned out to be a little different...

After my visit, I compiled the results for the four dimensions. To my surprise, the ecological dimension for all three communities had the weakest score. It seemed counter-intuitive that ecovillages should score so poorly in the ecological department. Why did ecovillages, which focus on sustainable development and ecology, not have better results? The reasons varied from one community to another: the use of cars associated with a remote location, being on the grid, low food self-sufficiency, absence of action plans, etc. The unanimous weakness that caused the relatively low scores for the ecology dimension, however, was the lack of data, monitoring, and evaluation.

Left: Ecohameau de La Baie (Eco-hamlet of the Bay) is a little settlement of six houses, of one Community Supported Agriculture (CSA) farm and six houses, of which five are strawbale constructions. This page: The picture shows the solar panels on the Second Neighbourhood Group (SoNG) houses at EcoVillage at Ithaca. Following an assessment of their energy consumption, solar panels will soon be installed on the First Resident Group (FRoG) houses.

I felt a sinking feeling about their poor scores for the ecology dimension but I was still buoyed up by the potential of ecovillages. Although ecovillages tend to neglect the evaluation of their activities, they are fully engaged in the process of working towards a sustainable future. All the communities I visited charmed me with their incredible capacity for *doing things*. Not only did they talk about sustainability, but they were also going out and trying to implement it on a day-to-day basis. Ecovillages provide a great place to live for their inhabitants. They take into account a respect for the natural environment and its ecosystems and educate the public about various aspects of sustainable living. Consequently, I decided to undertake a master's degree to study ecovillages. I wanted to know how, in detail, everything works—how they organize their ideas, people, and resources, to move towards sustainability. For my study, I decided to look at EcoVillage at Ithaca (EVI), in upstate New York.

I chose EVI because it seemed well structured, had two farms on site, had strong educational outreach, was accessible through the town transit system, and had a respectable population of about 160 inhabitants living in two dynamic cohousing neighbourhoods. Although my thesis research was about organization and not about evaluation, unlike my previous visits to ecovillages, I also looked at their monitoring and evaluation system in terms of ecological impact. Once again, the evaluation at EVI was mostly qualitative and irregular. During tours of the community, guides were using some statistics that came from more or less outdated research done by college or university students. Other statistics came from the energy task force committee regarding household energy consumption and transportation. However, no evaluation was done on the amount of compost, the amount of garbage and recycling, or their consumption of local food, and they only had a thin idea of the species and various plants growing on the land. No specific monitoring process was in place to make sure year after year that the community was progressing in reducing its ecological footprint.

My overall experience revealed the difficulty ecovillages have coordinating their mission and actions with measurable results. How can they affirm being ecovillages if they cannot certify, supported by concrete numbers, that their actions actually reduce their impact on the natural environment? How can they educate, influence, and convince a wider public that sustainable living is worth the effort if they do not present tangible results? How can they make the right choices to get closer to their ideal of a more sustainable way of life, if they have no data to rely on?

Evaluation of ecological activities is a real need for ecovillages. During my visits I heard comments regarding evaluation such as "we know it is important but can not do it—we don't know how" or "it's too much work." When asking for an estimation of how much waste was recycled, the person responsible for the recycling in that community told me: "I don't know, you'd have to empty the dumpster on the ground!" He seemed a little grossed out by this prospect. Evaluating is not easy; it takes imagination and time. I truly believe that ecovillages do not omit evaluation of their actions due to a lack of vision or carelessness. Thus, as an outside observer who believes in the potential of ecovillages, I would like to offer concrete and practical ideas on how to evaluate specific actions. The three simple examples of methods that I present could be used by all the communities I visited.

Compost

Compost is certainly an accessible way to reduce human impact on the environment. Among other benefits, composting reduces emissions of methane (CH_4), a greenhouse gas—300 times more harmful than CO_2—that is produced when organic matter decomposes in oxygen-starved landfills.[4] A nonprofit organization promoting compost to the downtown citizens of Quebec City, "Eco-Quartier CJC," in which I volunteered, is a good example. Eco-Quartier CJC set up communal compost bins in various public parks. They kept a digital hook scale and sheets in a waterproof bucket near each compost pile. Then, the willing participants were asked to weigh their deposit and note the amount on a sheet next to their name. At the end of the season, results were compiled to find how many tons were saved from going to the landfill. A big party was organized with the "composter-participants" and the numbers were revealed for each neighbourhood. It is amazing and fulfilling to realize how many tons are collected in only four months!

Energy Consumption

In 2005, EcoVillage at Ithaca devoted itself specifically to reducing its ecological footprint. It created the Energy Task Force

Committee that year to come up with long-term energy objectives for the community. The committee's mission included determining the current consumption of energy and resulting production of CO^2 emissions, then using this information to evaluate possible energy investments. The electricity usage was difficult to evaluate as the electricity provider refused to provide actual consumption data. Moreover, some residents in EVI were reluctant to share information on their energy consumption as they were afraid of being judged.

The Energy Task Force thus had to use a rough estimate based on a sample of households to assess electricity usage. They estimated fuel usage by sampling vehicle class (sedan, van, truck, etc) and estimating the miles driven per class, then measured carbon dioxide emissions by adding up results from electricity usage, natural gas burned, and vehicle usage over the next 10 years. They concluded that, on average, each household would spend $30,000 for gas, oil, and electricity bills over the next 10 years if nothing were to change. They brought these powerful numbers in front of the community decision-making meetings of both neighbourhoods of EVI. These groups gave the committee the mandate to look at energy options to reduce long-term costs, cut down pollution, and reduce dependence on fossil fuels. After a study made by a handful of willing burning souls, EVI will install solar panels on a number of houses, the common house, and the community pump house. The example of the Energy Task Force at EcoVillage at Ithaca shows that a better understanding of their actual situation allowed enlightened choices regarding their energy consumption.

The Energy Task Force concluded that, on average, each household would spend $30,000 for gas, oil, and electricity bills over the next 10 years if nothing were to change.

Local Foods

Our food choices have a tremendous impact on the planet. In the global economy, transportation requirements for food are high—such transportation ruins our air and sends tons of greenhouse gases into our atmosphere. According to the Natural Resources Defense Council[5], products grown in the United States travel an average of 1500 miles before getting sold. Ecovillages tend to diminish their *ecological foodprint* by growing food on-site and by purchasing as much as possible from local farmers. What is the proportion of local food used by the community? How much transportation was saved this year? I doubt that any community would have an answer. In most ecovillages, individual members control and buy their own food, making an exhaustive evaluation difficult. But communal meals could provide a good opportunity to make such measurements.

At the time of my visit to Sirius community, in summer 2005, vegetable production was managed by a Community Supported Agriculture (CSA) system. The rich soil of both their gardens produced an impressive amount of high-quality organic vegetables. In fact, at Sirius, I remember eating the best snap peas of my entire life! While helping the garden crew to separate the crops for the CSA members and the community meal, I thought that it would be easy to keep track of the quantity and types of vegetables consumed. These numbers could tell how productive long-term organic gardening can be. To go even further, the vegetable production could be compared with vegetables sold in the nearby markets to determine how much money and travelling was saved.

Conclusion

To go back to my original question, the one that first nourished my interest in ecovillages—"Is my drop in the ocean making a difference?"—I think the answer is yes. Because when I look at the accumulated efforts of ecovillages, I continue to be inspired. In an ecovillage, the power of living together—the support and motivation found in the immediate environment—helps inhabitants to continue working toward their convictions. If ecovillages would quantify these efforts, I think their demonstration would be even more powerful and would help them improve their own path to sustainable living. Ecovillages can use the measurable results of their own experiences in order to send a clear and universal message and inspire even more individuals to engage a way of life that preserves our natural resources and ecosystems for future generations. ✾

Prudence-Elise Breton is currently a Master's student at the University of Northern British Columbia (Canada) studying ecovillages. Her undergraduate studies in social work focused on community organization and local development. Interest in community living and passion for environmental protection led her to visit several ecovillages in order to experience their way of life and better understand their functioning.

1. Ecohameau de La Baie is one of the projects of the ecological research group called Le GREB. For further information, see website: www.greb.ca (French).
2. For further information, see website: www.cohabitat.ca/routedesecovillages/indexAmNord.html (French).
3. Villeneuve, C., (1999, reviewed 2004) Comment réaliser une analyse de développement durable?, Département des sciences fondamentales, Université du Québec à Chicoutimi (French).
4. US Composting Council, www.compostingcouncil.org.
5. Natural Resources Defense Council, www.nrdc.org/health/foodmiles/.

Photo courtesy of www.findhorn.org

Findhorn's Incredible Shrinking Footprint

By Jonathan Dawson

As with all truly living systems, Findhorn's strength lies in its ability to re-invent itself as the world around it changes. So it is that yesterday's ashram has become today's ecovillage. Not that the ashram has been abandoned. Rather, as we have climbed the dynamic spiral, so the aim—in some cases achieved, in others not—has been the integration of the best of each previous meme into a whole that is greater than the sum of its parts.

In the early 1960s, when the seeds of the community were sown, the word "ecology" was limited to the dusty corridors of natural sciences faculties. Transformation of consciousness was the core focus, meditation the practice.

And yet, among the founding members of the community, one—Dorothy MacLean—held strongly the vision of "co-creation with nature." Her ability to contact the intelligences in nature—devas specific to every plant and other natural being—underlay the community's ability to grow prodigiously-sized vegetables on the sandy soils of the Moray Firth in northern Scotland.

Dorothy's message that the nature devas were all too keen to cooperate with humans, not just in the growing of large cabbages but in the far larger work of healing the Earth, has provided the foundation and inspiration for much that has happened since in Findhorn on the ecological plane. It is the spark that has enabled the community's core spiritual impulse to manifest in ways that are increasingly relevant to a world facing converging ecological crises.

The achievements of the Findhorn ecovillage are documented in a 2006 study undertaken by the Stockholm Environment Institute. The community's ecological footprint proved to be the lowest ever measured for any settlement in the industrialized world—at 2.56 Global Hectares, less than half the UK national average, including the travel footprints of the 3000 annual course participants.

The following table and graphic from the report provides an overview of the study's key findings, including comparisons with Scotland, the UK, and the celebrated London green housing development, BedZED.

The community's home and energy footprint is 22 percent of the UK national average, for several reasons: Renewable energy

Table 22. Comparisons of the total Findhorn Foundation and Community ecological footprint and other ecological footprints.

Category	UK	Scotland	Findhorn	Bed Zed
Food	1.14	1.06	0.38	0.99
Home and Energy	1.35	1.33	0.30	0.36
Travel	0.85	0.99	0.51	0.26
Consumables	0.65	0.67	0.34	0.37
Services	0.41	0.33	0.29	0.24
Government and Other	0.47	0.47	0.35	0.47
Capital Investment	0.51	0.51	0.38	0.51
Total	5.40	5.37	2.56	3.20

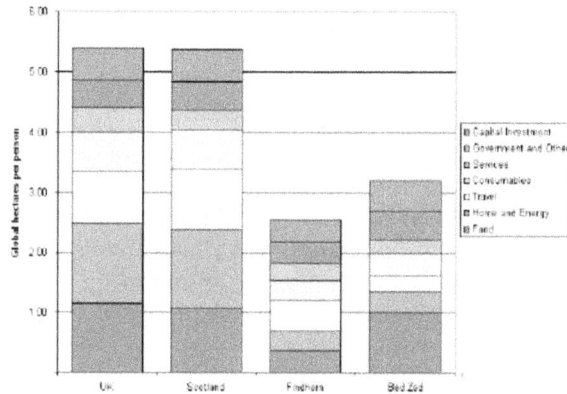

Figure 13. Comparison of ecological footprints for UK, Scotland, total Findhorn Foundation and Community and Bed Zed.

is generated on site through wind, solar, biomass, and geothermal technologies (Findhorn's four wind turbines, with a combined capacity of 750 kilowatts, generate 140 percent of the community's needs for electricity with the surplus being sold back to the grid). A growing number of highly insulated houses are replacing the old leaky caravans and bungalows that were home to early community members. And having almost 100 people—community members and course participants—sharing one large building, a former hotel in the neighbouring town of Forres, also produces large energy-saving dividends.

The community consumes a relatively large proportion of local, organic, seasonal, vegetarian food—no mean feat at more than 57 degrees north, the equivalent of northern Saskatchewan. A significant amount of this is grown at Britain's first organic CSA (community-supported agriculture) box-scheme, coordinated between three local farms. This enables it to record a food footprint just 33 percent of the national average.

Car usage was recorded as being a mere six percent of the national average; because there is so much employment generated onsite in a rich array of enterprises, few community members need to commute to work. (In the time since the study, the community has created its own carpool, dropping the car travel footprint even further.)

The community economy is distinctively vibrant at least in part due to the creation of a cooperative that has facilitated the investment of £600,000 of members' savings in community initiatives—including the wind park, affordable housing, and the community shop—and a complementary currency that keeps money circulating locally.

The footprint associated with "consumables," a general category covering consumer goods, is a little over half the national average, partly due to the sharing of equipment like washing machines and televisions, and partly because there is less need for luxury items in a community that provides so much of its own entertainment in home-grown choirs, dance classes, writing groups, and so on.

Finally, the community was awarded a zero score (the highest mark) for waste, since so much of this is recycled into productive use. This includes food scraps that are returned to the community gardens and the clean water returned to the local water table from the plant-based Living Machine sewage treatment system—once again, Britain's first.

In only one category did Findhorn's footprint exceed the national average; Findhorners travel two and half times further by air than the average Briton, the consequence of being a highly international community.

Now, things move on and it is time for us to re-invent ourselves again.

On the one hand, rising energy prices will necessarily drive us into a more bioregional world, with international travel becoming a progressively more expensive habit. This will be a challenge to an ecovillage that sometimes seems to defy the laws of physics: the further away from it, the higher its profile seems to be.

One task before us is therefore to become more enmeshed in our back yard, of greater service as an R&D and training centre to our own bioregion. This process is already underway, with myriad new locally-based initiatives recently launched, including strengthening ties with Scottish universities and the launch of CIFAL Findhorn, one of an international network of 12 United Nations training centres whose remit is the delivery of sustainability-related training courses to the staff and representatives of municipalities and other locally-based organizations (www.cifalfindhorn.org/). (The French acronym CIFAL stands for "Centre International de Formation des Autorités/Acteurs Locaux"—or "International Training Centre for Local Authorities/Actors.")

On the other hand, the most immediate threat we face as a species is runaway climate chaos, and not all of our efforts here at the local level will be effective in slowing that on the necessary scale and timeframe. The task is to provoke a mass public mobilization that will feed into the political process culminating in the UN Copenhagen conference in December 2009, which will decide on the international agreement to replace the Kyoto Protocol when it expires in 2012.

On this level, the Findhorn community is now engaged in a series of fun(d)-raising and public awareness campaigns linked to the 350 campaign (www.350.org) for an agreement at Copenhagen to stabilize CO_2 emissions to 350 parts per million. These include helping to set up a meeting between community representatives, scientific experts, and members of the Scottish Parliament, a series of pilgrimages that will converge on the Parliament on the same day, concerts, public educational events, and 350 logos planted far and wide, including in the

(continued on p. 71)

FINDHORN'S INCREDIBLE SHRINKING FOOTPRINT

(continued from p. 27)

local town's annual floral displays.

Tying together the threads of growing ecovillage activism in the face of the twin threats of peak oil and climate change, a new annual conference series launched at Findhorn in 2008—Positive Energy (PE). The first PE conference carried the strapline *Creative Community Responses to Peak Oil and Climate Change* and was the occasion for a great gathering of the ecovillage, transition, bioregional, and localization clans. The 2009 PE, scheduled for early October, focuses on the theme *Building Bioregional Resilience* and aims to further strengthen the links between intentional and more conventional sustainable community initiatives (www.findhorn.org/programmes/programme349.php).

These new challenges provide us with a rich and welcome opportunity to become a more truly Scottish community, one that is tied into the fabric of our own bioregion. As the links that tie us into relationship with our neighbours strengthen, so we can feel the gifts of solidarity and resilience deepen. ❋

Jonathan Dawson is a sustainability educator based at the Findhorn Foundation in Scotland (www.findhorn.org). He is recent President and still a serving member of the Board of the Global Ecovillage Network (gen.ecovillage.org).

Svanholm in Denmark Goes Carbon-Neutral

By Christina Adler Jensen,
translated by Pauline Kreiken and Nicholas Mickelsen

Svanholm, Denmark's largest intentional community and ecovillage, is a collective with a multi-functional agriculture operation, including dairy cows and sheep, and home to about 140 people. We began in 1978 when our founders bought 400 hectares (998 acres) on the island of Zealand, 55 kilometers (34 miles) from Copenhagen. Pioneers of organic farming in Denmark, we were instrumental in introducing organic dairy and other organic foods to Danish stores and supermarkets. About half of us work on site, in maintenance, administration, farming, cooking, teaching in our kindergarten, and the like, and half have jobs in the local area. As we are an income-sharing community, 80 percent of each person's income goes to Svanholm for taxes and common living expenses such as maintenance, food, electricity, and childcare; 20 percent is kept for personal use. We're also asset-sharing: new people contribute their assets to the community when they join, and get them back if they leave. We make decisions by consensus.

We have off-grid energy and other ecologically sustainable systems. We currently produce 68 percent of our own electrical and heating energy needs through two wind generators and a slightly archaic wood-chip furnace (fueled mainly by wood chips from our own trees). Unfortunately, because we're in a relatively isolated rural location, we're largely dependent on gasoline-fueled cars for work and leisure activities, which burdens our conscience. In fact, 14 percent of Svanholm's annual energy use is from driving cars! But this is about to change.

In the future, electric cars will be available in Denmark at a relatively decent price. Electrical recharging stations will be built along the entire Danish road system, ensuring a smooth transition from gasoline-powered vehicles to electric ones.

To power our electric cars in the winter, we installed a Stirling engine from the Stirling DK company in Denmark (www.sd.econtent.dk). This is a type of electric generator first developed by Scottish inventors Robert and James Stirling in 1816. The Stirling engine converts heat energy into mechanical power by alternately compressing and expanding a fixed quantity of air or other gas at different temperatures. (We use helium.) This pushes a flywheel around in a circle, which passes a copper coil back and forth through a magnetic field, which generates electricity. See animated graphics of different kinds of Stirling engines on Wikipedia (en.wikipedia.org/wiki/Stirling_Engine).

Unlike internal combustion engines, Stirling engines are quieter, more reliable, and have lower maintenance requirements. A Stirling engine costs more initially and is usually larger and heavier than a comparable internal combustion engine which produces the same amount of electricity, but a Stirling engine's lower maintenance costs make up for it.

We plan to burn woodchips from our forest to power the Stirling engine. Roughly 20 percent of the energy produced by the woodchips will be converted into electric power; the rest will be used for heating hot water. (We plan to install huge water tanks next to the engine.) The amount of woodchips required for this new project will be, on average, the same as that required by our current wood furnace. In the summer we'll get hot water from solar hot water panels, and electricity from our wind generators.

This way in the winter we'll provide our community with both hot water and electricity through a CO_2-neutral source, since trees yield only the amount of CO_2 which they absorb through their lifetime. (Trees would emit an equal amount of CO_2 through the process of breaking down if they were left to decompose on the forest floor.)

With a Stirling engine we'll burn 10 to 15 percent of our woodchips, and save an additional 15 to 20 percent on energy resources by replacing our hot water pipes with new, better-insulated pipes. The result should be a diminished use of woodchips and a more sustainable supply of electricity. In the near future we will also replace our out-of-date wind generators.

In December 2009 Denmark will be the site of the United Nations' Conference on Climate Change, hosted by the Danish government. The 1997 Kyoto conference on climate change attracted international notice; perhaps journalists from around the world will visit Svanholm during this one and finally put "ecovillages" on the map! ✳

Christina Adler Jensen is a journalist who has lived at Svanholm for three years. Pauline Kreiken and Nicholas Mickelsen also live at Svanholm. For more information about Svanholm: www.svanholm.dk, en.wikipedia.org/wiki/Svanholm.

A version of this article appeared in the July 2009 issue of Diane Leafe Christian's Ecovillages newsletter (www.EcovillageNews.org).

Car-Reduced and Car-Free Rural Communities

By Greg Ramsey

Kyle Gradinger

Kyle Gradinger

This page top: For approximately $2 per trip, a shuttle connects Torri Superiore Ecovillage (Italy) to the larger town of Ventimiglia in the valley, where village markets offer a variety of goods and services.
This page bottom: Twin Oaks Community (Virginia) collectively owns a fleet of about 18 motor vehicles (including cars, pickup trucks, cargo vans, and a mini-van) for approximately 85 adult members. Members do not have personal vehicles.
Opposite page top: A work bike in Vauban, Germany.
Opposite page middle: An Amsterdam commuter combines suit, briefcase, and bicycle.
Opposite page bottom: In another typical Amsterdam scene, a woman in a tight dress skirt and dress shoes rides a bicycle, carrying two additional passengers and an industrial work basket.

Many of us love the idea of living in a rural eco-community in order to reconnect to the land, to be close to rivers, forests, meadows, farmland, and wildlife—in a sense, to go back to our origins. It is certainly not a recent desire and is the impetus that has created the suburbs and the ex-urbs. So the three hundred dollar question is, should we continue on this path, and if so, are we doing it in a way that does not adversely impact those rural areas and the planet at large?

We know today that the most ecological practice is to locate community development close to existing infrastructure in towns and cities. This is done in order to reduce the impact of traffic into rural areas and to re-use existing structures. That being said, it is important to have small rural eco-communities or hamlets to encourage small-scale agriculture and to create rural stewardship. The general pattern has been to depopulate rural areas and for these lands to be assimilated by large national and international agro/forestry investment interests that promote monocultures with little regard for biodiversity. So placing eco-communities as stewards to sustain bioregions and polycultures instead of monocultures is a good thing if done appropriately.

Unfortunately, the automobile has a devastating impact on the development of these rural eco-communities. Roads are public enemy #1 to our waterways and wildlife habitats. Ever extending, widening, and adding roads and driveways further fragment our remaining wildlife habitats and farms, and create conduits for easy access to deplete our dwindling rural biodiversity. Some suggest that efficient cars running on renewable fuels will solve the problem—but nothing could be further from the truth. The impact of cars on our already fragmented natural communities and natural spaces would increase exponentially. So what can we do to reduce car mobility and its deleterious impacts on rural habitats and still re-populate rural eco-communities?

Minimize Car Intrusion

First, we can reduce how far and how many cars are allowed to intrude into rural areas. The less the car penetrates into the land, the more we will reduce impacts on the land. We can start by thinking of this regionally, and then seeing how it applies to single sites. At a regional scale, we can protect substantial areas and avoid the extension of roads into them in several ways:

1) Develop eco-communities closer to existing roads and services by shifting potential eco-communities from more remote

Kyle Gradinger

www.ski-epic.com

www.ski-epic.com

Automobile Impacts:

- The average car in the US emits 10,000 lbs. of carbon gas per year (three times its weight).

- The average American household generates eight car trips/day.

- 30 to 40 percent of the average American household energy consumption comes from automobile use.

to less remote areas that are more suitable for community development. Transfer of development rights is a common tool used for this purpose. More remote eco-communities should be preserved for very limited access.

2) Place conservation easements on the preserved areas to prevent future road intrusions into those areas.

3) Reduce the number of overall homes/cars allowed on particularly rural sites. Rural sites should rarely allow more than one unit per 20 acres (overall density) unless they are located within a couple miles (bike/cart access) of significant infrastructure/services/transportation center. If a particular property will not allow enough units at this density, then additional land should be preserved elsewhere to increase the number of units.

In this manner we can create a bioregional car-reducing transportation plan designed to reduce future wildlife habitat fragmentation and protect and maintain the integrity of the bioregion. This can be done at the scale of multiple counties, a county, or a portion of a county.

On an individual site basis, it is important to stop the car as close as is reasonably possible to the existing access road and collect the car there, restricting car access further into the site other than service access. Ecovillages and cohousing communities are good examples of how to collect the cars at the outskirts of the community and create an ideal walking-density community cluster. Any residents can then access further into the site on foot, by bicycle, or by electric cart.

Optimize Community-Based Transportation

Community-based transportation refers to cooperative local efforts to reduce car dependency. The intent is to create a walk and bike/cart zone (carbon-free transportation zone) connected to surrounding towns by an electric or biodiesel shuttle/bus.

The walk and bike/cart zone is designed for walking (1/8 to 1/4 mile) and for bikes/carts, including manual as well as electric bicycles and electric or biodiesel carts (20 mph or less), easily reaching one to two miles by persons of all ages. The Twin Oaks Community in rural Virginia provides bicycles for public use, as do some other budding ecovillages.

The heart of the eco-community should not exceed 1/8 to 1/4 mile (700 ft.-1300 ft. in length) to optimize walkability at a density ranging from four to 10 units per acre excluding agricultural areas. A minimum of 90 percent of the rural site should be preserved as farm land and wildlife habitats by locating the homes in a walkable compact cluster. Locating adjacent farming or market/crossroad communities within the one to two miles bike/cart area increases the overall transportation efficiency of the community, allowing multiple communities to connect by bicycle and electric carts and not be car-dependent.

Shuttles connect the walk and bike/cart zone several times per day to primary towns where lease-on-demand vehicles are available as well as links to buses and other forms of transit. In addition, shared vehicles may be available for commuting outside the walk and bike/cart zone.

(continued on p. 79)

CAR-REDUCED AND CAR-FREE RURAL COMMUNITIES

(continued from p. 59)

Every eco-community should have a community transportation management plan with funds set aside to insure the purchase and maintenance of community vehicles. Incentives can be formed to encourage planning for local micro-vehicle transportation and shuttles. Disincentives can be put into place to discourage single occupancy car trips and car ownership while funding community transportation with car impact fees. In Vauban, one of the first largely car-free communities in Freiburg, Germany, the majority of residents do not own cars. Those that do, purchase a parking space in a parking area outside the community for approximately $25,000.

Maintain a Local Micro Economy

Avoiding unnecessary commuter trips means having our daily life destinations within the local, walk and bike/cart zone area (two- to four-mile diameter). The most difficult of these destinations to maintain nearby is work! The Twin Oaks Community significantly reduces car commute requirements by providing a variety of cottage industries in the community and sharing a fleet of around 15 cars among 100 people.

So as we think of moving to a rural eco-community we should really ask ourselves what land-based workplaces can be incorporated into the community and how can their longevity best be protected. Examples of workplaces include farming, value-added agro-businesses, forest management, cottage industries, electronic cottages, artisanal shops, elder care, health services, education, and general services. The key is that these workplaces are supported by the residents of the eco-community in some form of enduring commitment. Once residents start going outside that area and commuting for goods and services, they undermine the local walk/bicycle/cart area market. Local resident member initiatives similar to Community Supported Agriculture can help maintain the local walk/bicycle/cart market.

In closing, if we can shift our car-centric culture to a walking and community transportation culture, we can look forward to preserving our rural areas while re-integrating eco-communities. I invite readers to respond to this article with examples in your community of how you have reduced car dependency, and we will incorporate those examples in a follow-up article. Also, feel free to contact us about the planning and design of car reduced/free communities. I can be reached at gramsey@villagehabitat.com. ❀

Greg Ramsey, M.Arch. and recipient of State AIA, National AIA, and United Nations Habitat awards, has committed a lifetime of study to pedestrian village and conservation planning. Greg is co-founder, principal, and chief designer of Village Habitat Design (www.villagehabitat.com) as well as co-author of Conservation Communities, *a village design primer. Greg works internationally as a workshop leader, conservation community planner, designer, and consultant (gramsey@usa.net).*

Community Makes Renewable Energy Work

By Alexis Zeigler

Renewable Energy is one of those terms that sound inherently virtuous, like peace or universal love. Once you start to look at how renewable energy is used in our time, the inherent virtue is washed away and a much more complex picture is left in its place.

That lesson was brought home to me recently when I was teaching a workshop about plant propagation. A fellow who had come to my workshop stayed afterward to chat. Turns out he works for the local power company, one not known for environmental thinking. He works in a generating facility that takes trees and burns them to make electricity. "The public doesn't understand," he was saying to me. He was upset to see the incredible volume of wood being consumed to produce only a tiny fraction of power demand. Indeed, if you study the issue, you realize that the United States burns far more energy than can be produced from bio-sources. (The estimates I have seen put our total current energy use at 25 percent higher than all the energy produced by all the green, photosynthesizing plants in our country in a single year, domestic and wild.) In spite of his concerns, he had to make a living, working in a facility that takes dozens of acres of forests every day and burns them to keep everyone's air conditioners and tumble dryers running. And the power company is getting tax credits to make "green energy."

The reality is that renewable energy cannot power the modern industrial economy—not even close. But there is another answer, and that answer is cooperative use. A few years ago I asked all of my environmentally minded friends to send me their domestic energy bills for three years. I added them up and compared them to American average residential energy use. I also collected energy bills for a number of cooperatives and communities. The results were staggering.

The average use of my conscientious friends, in spite of their efforts to insulate, moderate thermostat settings, etc., was *above* the American average usage. It turns out that if you own a house that stands by itself, even if you are saintly, you are likely to use more energy than a slob in an apartment that has other apartments around it. Lots of the apartment dwellers, slobs or not, are included in the American average. It was also surprising to look at the numbers from various communities. They dropped over a cliff from 60 percent of American average energy use all the way down to 9 percent. (That last number is for a group house that I built. That house is cooperative, strawbale, and solar heated.)

Fossil energy is concentrated stuff. Simple, cheap, small machines can convert fossil energy into heat or mechanical power. Renewable energy is, by comparison, slow and steady, dispersed, and intermittent. Every energy source has an

On a sunny day in a community setting, cooking using a solar parabolic cooker is no more difficult than using fossil energy.

Photos courtesy of Alexis Zeigler

A solar hot water batch collector becomes economical when shared.

Smokey the woodgas unit creates tractor fuel.

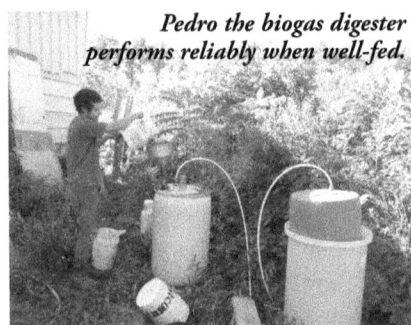

Pedro the biogas digester performs reliably when well-fed.

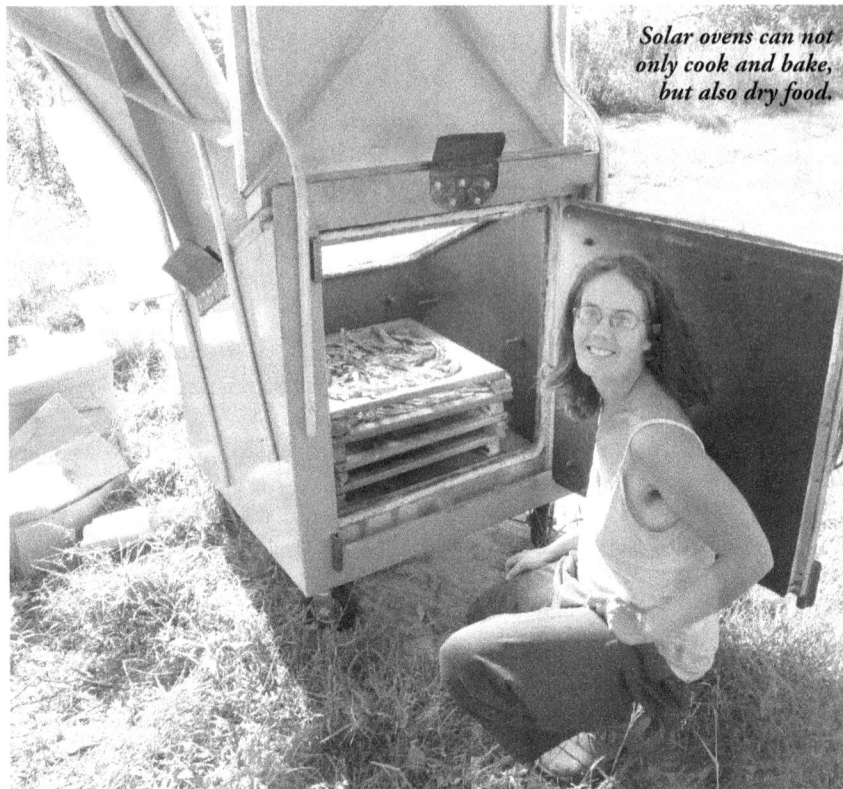

Solar ovens can not only cook and bake, but also dry food.

optimal economy of scale. The political reality of modern environmentalism is that it is easier for the environmental groups to sell supply-side solutions than to tell people to change their lifestyles. But physics don't care about politics, and the physics of renewable energy are that they don't work well on an individual scale. They work really well on a community scale.

Even a simple solar hot water system seems expensive and uneconomical for someone living alone, or even a small family. But at the community level, the costs are divided by the number of users while the overall efficiency skyrockets. I have built quite a few renewable energy systems. I would not have believed the numbers had I not seen them so many times now, but the mathematics of solar energy do magic when solar systems are developed for cooperative use. Shared housing makes solar energy work because it creates a modest economy of scale. If solar energy is cross-pollinated with good insulation and design, you can get extraordinary efficiencies at very modest cost.

These lessons have been sharpened even further as I have been working on a project called Living Energy Farm (LEF, livingenergyfarm.org). (I am one among many working on LEF, so my perspectives are my own.) At LEF, we have a solar parabolic cooker. We refer to it affectionately as the "death ray." That is because you can put a stick in front of it on a sunny day and the stick will burst into flames in about three seconds. No joke. The overall BTU (heat) output is similar to a gas burner on

---

At the community level, costs are divided by the number of users while the overall efficiency skyrockets.

---

medium. We use it a lot. We also have a solar oven that we use for baking as well as solar drying. Particularly on a parabolic cooker, solar cooking is no more difficult than using fossil energy. You just hang the pot up there and off it goes, just like you put it on a gas burner. Community makes it work. In the commuter culture, people don't have the time or space for solar cooking. In a community, a village, or a cooperative where one person can cook for others, solar cooking is simple, easy, and as sustainable as any technology could possibly be.

We also have a biogas system. We call that one Pedro, though I don't have a clue how that bubbly little beast got its name. It's like tending a woodstove. We have to feed Pedro and keep him warm. He makes gas pretty reliably at this point, though we will need a bigger system for the whole community. Fiddling with a gas digester is easy on a farm, in a community, or in a village. Community makes the technology

174

viable in a practical sense.

At LEF, we also have a woodgas system for our farm tractor. Woodgas was used heavily in World War II in Europe. It allows you to run a gasoline engine off of woodchips. But the important part is not the technology, but how and for what it is used. Even during the short duration of WWII, parts of Europe started to see deforestation problems as the trees were being cut to run the machines. Our bylaws allow us to use woodgas on the farm, in the community, but not over the road. We are on the second version of our system, and also heading toward a second generation of draft animals. These technologies work in community. They do not work in individualized society.

At LEF, we have a few solar electric systems, of different configurations for different purposes. (It seems like we can do what we need to do for the whole community with about 2300 watts.) In general, we try to use electricity when the sun shines instead of trying to store it. That means pumping water during the day and using drip irrigation. We are still building the main house. The irrigation water will run through the main house and suck heat out during the summer before the water goes out to the fields. Free air-conditioning, more or less.

The house is also solar heated with both passive and active (pumped) fea-

In summer, this 1400 watt array runs the main well pump. In winter, it powers blowers in the house that distribute solar radiant floor heat.

tures. Our commitment is to building reasonably cheaply so that our model can be replicated. Back in the 1970s, people built active solar houses. But they either used fluid systems, which require copper collection panels and are thus expensive, or they used air systems and tried to store the heat in rock beds for later use. Then they would have to store electricity to pump the heat back into the house later. They made complicated, expensive systems because they were working from a fossil-fuel paradigm. For us, we start with the assumption that we are designing our lifestyle to fit renewable energy, rather than trying to force renewable energy

systems to meet an individualized lifestyle.

At LEF, the solar panels that run our irrigation system don't do much in the winter as we don't need much water, so they run our solar blowers in the house. This close integration of systems works in community but breaks down across barriers of separate ownership of separate structures. The heat is stored in a high-tech material under the house called dirt, where it naturally conducts its way up into the living space. The living space is assumed to be in regular use with inhabitants who are capable of opening and closing windows, thus eliminating a bunch of batteries, computer controllers, and pumps. The sharing of expenses and space makes it financially feasible, desirable even, to invest more effort and money into features such as active solar heat.

Our lighting at LEF uses DC LEDs powered by nickel-iron (NiFe) batteries. NiFe batteries are an old technology. We have one with Thomas Edison's name stamped right onto the side of it, made by his company. The miraculous thing about that little battery is that it still works! Lead-acid batteries are much more popular, but they die after a few years and have to be replaced. (We ship them to the less-developed world where people are poisoned in the recycling industries.) The NiFe batteries are low-output. You can't start you car with them. That's why the lead-acid batteries are

This antique piston pump, good for solar energy supply fluctuations, pumps at low or high speeds.

175

This 500 watt PV array runs Living Energy Farm's construction tools.

so popular, because the presumption of power needs is so high. But for us, NiFes are perfectly suited to DC LED lighting systems that draw modest amounts of energy over extended periods of time.

We intend LEF to be financially self-supporting. We want to make sure our renewable energy systems are not just mechanically adequate, but financially feasible as well. We are earning our living with agriculture, growing open-pollinated seeds. My personal passion is for "perennial food," my term for fruit and nut trees. The individuation of the American lifestyle and the industrialization of agriculture to feed people disconnected from those farms has created many problems we need not recount here. Community-level agriculture creates opportunities for the integration of systems that supports renewable energy. Animal manure can feed a biogas digester. The chickens can eat bugs under the fruit trees, instead of using expensive and energy-intensive chemical sprays. Irrigation water becomes a heat-absorption medium. "Waste" biomass always finds a home. Machines parts, pipes, and various sundry mechanical widgets migrate from one project to another.

My experience with LEF has sharpened my understanding of the intrinsically supportive relationship between renewable energy and community. But even before LEF, the importance of using

renewable energy at a community scale instead of a private household scale was very clear. I have traveled the country giving slideshows and presentations about these issues, and about the relationship of energy supplies and the evolution of our civil society. I will not delve into that latter point here, except to say that ecological stress will be the death knell of democracy if we don't wise up.

Private ownership and control are deeply ingrained in the American psyche, and "the environment" is mostly an abstraction. If someone wants to invent a more efficient windmill or solar panel, that's fine, but we don't need it. If you want

to blame the powers that be, you can do that, but we are all sinners in the ecological catastrophe of our time. Good policies would help, but they are not what is most important. What is most important is for you to take the tools you already have, the information you already know, and get together with other people and act on it. Our entire political, academic, and religious tradition taken in total is a grand project to make powerful people look important. The reality is that we have always been in charge, and we always will be so. If you want to solve the environmental crises of our time, you need to work in cooperation with others to build a truly sustainable infrastructure based on renewable energy systems applied at the community level. That's where physics and politics meet. That is the path to a sane and sustainable future. ❧

Born on a largely self-sufficient farm in rural Georgia, Alexis Zeigler is a self-taught activist, builder, mechanic, writer, and orchardist. He has organized numerous successful campaigns focusing on political, environmental, and economic localization issues. He is currently working to build Living Energy Farm (livingenergyfarm.org), a zero-fossil-fuel farm that will be economically self-sufficient. He recently released a book entitled Integrated Activism *(North Atlantic Books).*

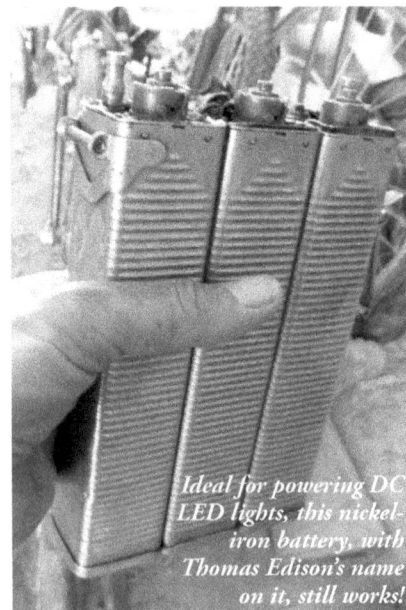
Ideal for powering DC LED lights, this nickel-iron battery, with Thomas Edison's name on it, still works!

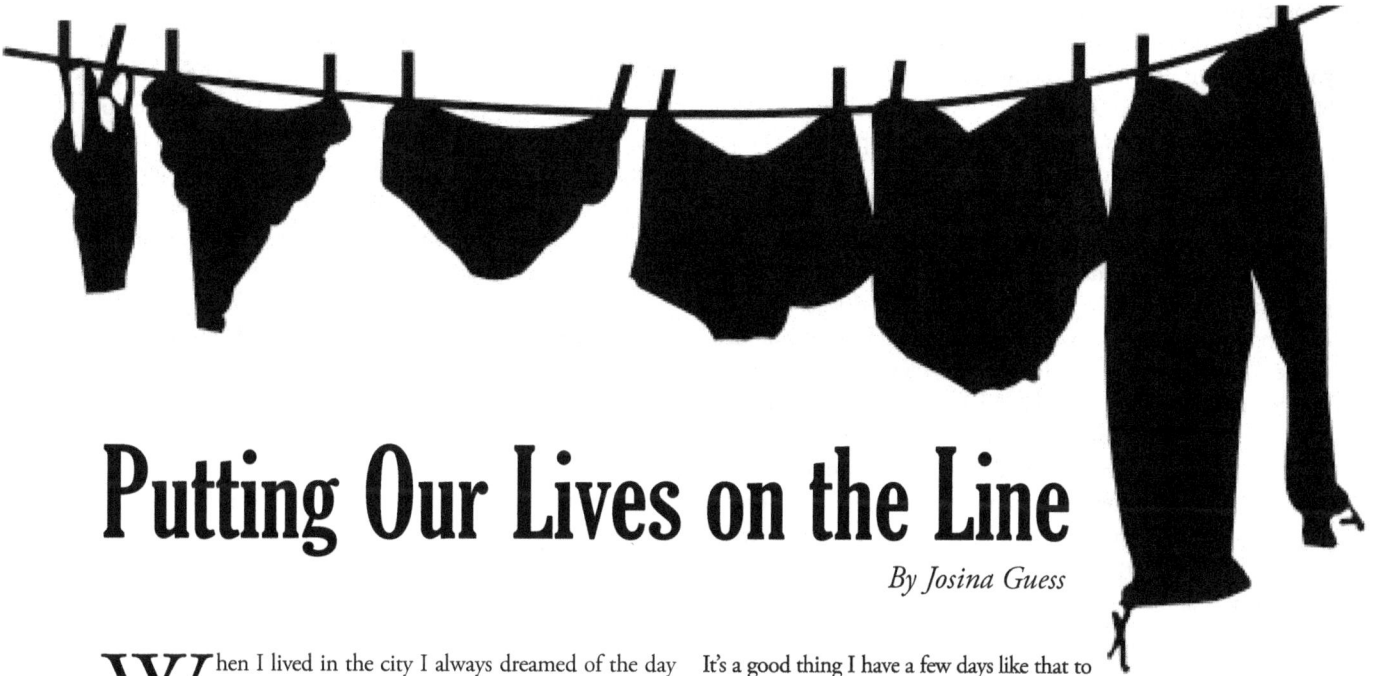

Putting Our Lives on the Line

By Josina Guess

When I lived in the city I always dreamed of the day that I might have a big clothesline. My fantasy began as a teenager in Washington, DC. My mom set up a small line in our big-for-the-city backyard and I fell in love with the smell and feel of sun-dried clothes. When I began a family of my own in Philadelphia I hung diapers and sheets on lines that criss-crossed over our cement postage-stamp of a yard. Sometimes I would chat across the chain-link fence with a neighbor who also hung her clothes. She lamented that fences now divided up the yards and alley in which children would play and community would form as clothes fluttered in the breeze.

Now that I live with my family at Jubilee Partners, a Christian service community in Comer, Georgia, my dream of a giant community clothesline has come true. And of course, as with most fantasies, the dream is tempered by reality.

As a small way to reduce our energy consumption, our community of about 40 staff and volunteers shares two (three, if they are all working) washing machines and one huge clothesline. The clothesline consists of 15 70-foot-long steel lines strung between three sets of very sturdy posts. When three families started this community in 1979 the clothesline was one of the first things they built. There is a laundry sign-up sheet in which each person or family has one or two two-hour slots a week in which to use the washing machines. We also have time set aside to wash guest linens, kitchen linens, and cleaning rags. The shared clothespins hang in sturdy gallon jugs that once held vinegar or maple syrup.

A community clothesline does much more than dry clothes with solar power; it can help to build community. It teaches the need for better cooperation and communication, requires deeper attention to the rhythms of nature, and provides a place for quiet contemplation and good conversation as well.

On a "perfect" day I will have our wash done very early and hang the clothes in the golden dewy morning to the serenade of birds flitting between blueberry bushes. After lunch I will check my laundry and find it nicely dried by the sun and breeze and I will have time to get it folded before the kids get home from school.

It's a good thing I have a few days like that to remember on the not-so-good days...like those when clean wash sours in a basket after a day of patiently waiting to be hung while my family and I flutter in six different directions; or when I bump my head as I try to hang or take in clothes in the dark because I can't find the headlamp or batteries for it. One evening my husband was taking in the clothes by moonlight when he saw three skunks digging in the grass beneath the clotheslines. Thankfully they did not spray. If they had I would be writing the story, "The day I gave up on the clothesline."

This summer we got so much rain that it really put my love for line drying to the test. Clothes would hang hopelessly sodden as the rain poured day and night without mercy. Some things would be so heavy with water that they would touch the ground below and need to be washed again. Sometimes towels would dry so slowly that they would begin to mildew and smell worse than before they were washed. The sun would shine and we would all rush to get laundry done and hung, but before the clothes had time to dry the storm clouds would form and we would then rush to bring in damp clothes before they became drenched. When the line is just not an option laundry hangs from makeshift lines in bedrooms, living rooms, and porches. On one particularly bad day, the rain seemed to finally break and the forecast called for only a 20 percent chance of rain but it poured three times. One community member shook his fist at the clouds in anger and drove his clothes to the local Laundromat to tumble dry. We do have our limits.

Though the heavy rains are bad, there are other forces of nature that can also hamper the romance of line drying. Here are some things I have learned: Hang clothes in mid-day and suffer the sun's heat, wait until evening and get bit by mosquitoes, oh and watch out for the fire ant hills. One can always hang clothes on the shady side of the line to avoid the heat of the sun, but during mulberry and blueberry season purple bird droppings will remind you that comfort comes at a price. It is important to pin things securely because heavy winds can tangle sheets and send clothes flying. One must take care to bring clothes in promptly and give them a good firm shaking lest wasps, bats, and bees take up residence. It is nice to let young children play in the sand while you are hanging laundry but be sure to grab those sandy hands before they grab your neighbor's clean sheets. Frozen fingers on crisp frosty clothes add an extra challenge to winter drying; be sure to dress warmly or just hang your wash to dry inside by the wood stove to get through the coldest days.

This practice of line drying also connects us with the majority of the people in the world who do not have dryers. As I was enjoying hanging laundry on a pleasant day my friend confided to me, "I hate hanging laundry." She grew up the youngest in a large family in rural Mexico and has put in countless hours hanging and taking down laundry. "It just takes too much time." Her honesty reminds me that my appreciation of line drying does not immediately impact the lives of my global neighbors and they aren't all enjoying it as much as I do. Yet I am still thankful that my kids are learning and working alongside her kids and sharing a common experience, even if they don't wax poetic about it the way I do. I do hope that even if we can't see it, our local choice to use less electricity is making a long-term difference for our neighbors around the world.

Through it all, we are certainly saving electricity, but there are times that I do still wonder, like my friend, about the overall efficiency of hanging out all our laundry to dry. Surely, we all could find other things to do with our time than brave the elements while we pin and unpin clothes from a line, day after day, week after week, month after month. Are those hours truly a good use of our corporate *human* energy?

The fact that we are all in it together makes a huge difference. Sometimes an unfinished conversation will carry over the next morning at the clothesline. Sometimes it is only at the clothesline where folks that don't normally make time to talk are standing still long enough to really check in with one another. There are times when my day has been so packed that

I've even suggested, "meet me at the clothesline" as a place for deeper conversation to happen. Even times of solitude at the line are valuable. Carefully pinning each item, I sing to myself and remember to pray for and give thanks for each member of my family. Glancing over at the sheets and embroidered pillowcases of a newlywed couple or the diapers of a new baby or the blouses of an elderly member or the bike clothes of an avid cyclist, I am reminded to pray for them too and be thankful for their presence in our community.

And yes, we see each other's underwear; this makes it hard to take yourself or other people too seriously. It can hardly be called

> # I've even suggested, "meet me at the clothesline" as a place for deeper conversation to happen.

heroic work to put our lives on the line in this way. In fact in this age of productivity and efficiency it could seem more foolish than valiant. But the daily task of hanging laundry forces us to slow down and it keeps us connected to the earth, to one another, and even—if we keep our hearts open—to God. Meet me at the clothesline if you want to talk more about it. ✒

Josina Guess lives and works at Jubilee Partners, a Christian community that offers hospitality and English lessons to refugees. Learn more at www.jubileepartners.org. She is a graduate of Earlham College and worked as a doula and children's minister in Philadelphia before moving to Georgia in 2011. She often thinks about what to write next while she is hanging laundry.

Author standing in front of the clothesline in the rain at Jubilee.

Clothesline in the snow.

Michael Guess

Generating Your Own Electricity: WHY AND HOW

By Mary Wildfire

Every community should have some kind of renewable power generation system. **Why?** Well, first, if yours is an ecovillage, having your own non-fossil-fueled power source enables your community to practice what you preach; it enables you to be a model of green living for the larger community surrounding you. It enables you to stop contributing to such crimes against posterity as the burning of coal, the drilling and fracking of shale gas, and the splitting of atoms.

Second, it gives you security. There's reason to believe that the grid will go down more and more often for longer periods, and/or get unaffordably expensive; setting up your own system now is a wise investment if you take the long-term savings into account. Depending how the converging crises of oil depletion, climate change, and corporate control of governments play out, some of those who keep waiting for solar, wind, or water power to get cheaper than grid power may find themselves making do with no electricity at all.

How? Making the conversion from grid power to producing your own involves research and choices. The first step is to determine what your current energy expenditures are, and look for ways to reduce them. A cheap and handy tool is the Kill-a-Watt (about $25), which plugs into a wall socket; you plug appliances into it, and it tells you how much power is being used. Your big energy hogs may not be the ones you think!

Also research what subsidies are available. There is a federal tax credit of 30 percent of costs, which may be rolled over into subsequent years if your tax liability is less than the credit. Many states also have tax credits or others subsidies; check www.dsireusa.org.

The third thing to research is which source of power your land best supports: Is there constant wind? Do you have a reliable stream with at least 10 feet of drop across your property? How about a good exposure to the south, without shading? Sometimes a hybrid system works best, if your stream or wind becomes weak in summer but that's when you get the most sun.

You also need to find the best spot for your panels, windmill, or water turbine. Often, solar panels are better mounted in the yard rather than on a roof: they work more efficiently in cooler, even cold, temperatures, and roofs build up heat. Also, it's easier to sweep snow off panels in a yard than to hang out a window in January to do it. But the roof may be a more secure location, especially in a city.

A key choice is whether to arrange an off-grid system or a grid-tied one. An off-grid system gives you independence—if the grid goes down, you are unaffected. But that's because you have batteries and a charge controller; with a grid-tied system you can save the cost of these things, using the grid itself as your battery. Given the arguments under "Why," you can see why my husband Don and I chose to go off-grid. But the other couple here, the Wilsons, are perhaps less paranoid, and more inclined to want to be part of a larger solution, so they chose a grid-tied system. As our community makes most decisions at the household level, we didn't need to agree on this. And it's worked out well making different choices because we have a line connecting the two houses—our own microgrid! Thus, when we go a week with no sun at all in winter, my household can take a kilowatt-hour or two from the grid, from the Wilsons' house. When the derecho came through in June 2012 and knocked out power, and the Wilsons' system went down as a result, we sent power the other way to keep their freezer going. Additional sharing may be possible when we find people for the other two leaseholds. Larger communities could also benefit from trading power in another way: between wind in the high places, water power in the lower places, and sun wherever the shade isn't. Some communities could use the money provided by high-earning members, while others with technical proficiency figure out the system, and anyone with time helps install it.

My husband figured out how to set up our system, then assisted the Wilsons with their grid-tied version, and then helped two other households in the larger community set up their own systems. He also created a website to share information about some of the technical tricks: find it at www.spectrumz.com, the Going Solar blog (there is also a link to "Hickory Ridge housing project," which is a slide-show of how we built our energy-efficient house).

We strive to live sustainably at Hickory Ridge in many ways. We have composting toilets, large gardens and orchards, rain barrels, and we're exploring permaculture ideas and grafting nut trees. But all those ways of recycling materials and energy are low-tech projects that can be added and worked with any time, as long as you have land and a few hand tools. Producing your own electricity is different. That's why I urge everyone to make it a priority, because the high-tech civilization that makes setting up such a system fairly easy now may not last. My household may use only a tenth of the electricity that the average US household does—but I'd sure miss it, if we didn't have that three kilowatt-hours or so a day! ᴥ

Mary Wildfire is a writer, activist, and gardener, living on a ridge in West Virginia. She is part of Hickory Ridge Land Trust. She admits to being a hippie and a tree smoocher, kind of a pinko, who believes subversion to be the highest calling.

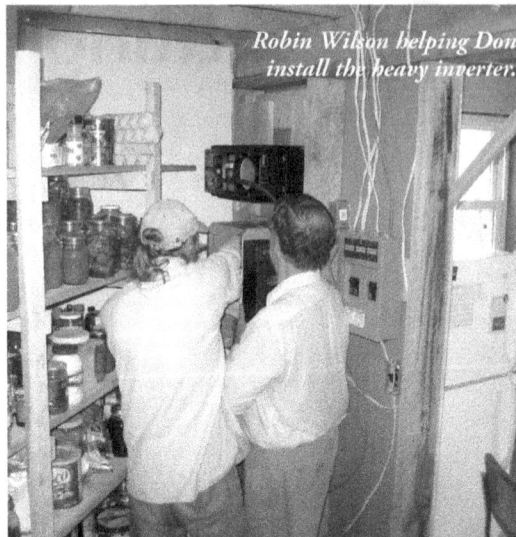

Robin Wilson helping Don install the heavy inverter.

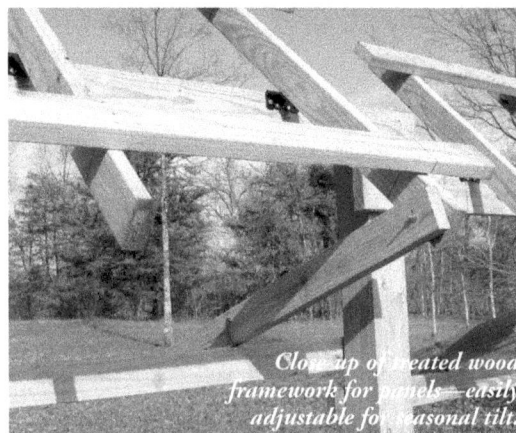

Close-up of treated wood framework for panels—easily adjustable for seasonal tilt.

The Wilsons' solar array, amid redbud in bloom with their home in background.

Mary Wildfire

GOING FOR THE GRID:
A Community Ditches Energy Independence to Get Greener

By Sarah Stoner

Five years ago, the community and I had just started our courtship. My family and I—husband and two young children—still lived among the bright lights of the city.

A few months into "dating"—which meant living on the 20-acre community land trust part-time each week during the membership process—the annual May Day Celebration rolled around. We had all just come off the typical long gray Washington winter. Our 10 adult members, gaggle of children, friends, neighbors gathered together in the sunshine. We danced barefoot in the cool grass, ate from the table spread with food and spring flowers. The band played under the cedar tree laced with tiny white lights—each powered by the solar panels just beyond the meadow. I turned my face up to the sun and let the lively beat wash over me. Sunshine converted to sound. It was like magic. I was in love.

Fast-forward to October—it's the start of our first full winter at Walker Creek living off-the-grid. The kids aren't asleep yet—our power keeps cutting out and they want their bedside Turtle Light to sleep. They are freaking out. I'm on a deadline. My laptop is sucking too much power from our back-up battery bank, but I need to finish the newsletter I am on contract to produce for a nonprofit in Florida, and it's too late to drive 25 minutes into town to the nearest coffee shop. Everything's closed. I am freaking out. My husband Ken is outside starting the backup generator—again. The lights turn on. The generator should be charging our eight deep-cycle batteries stored in the barn but it's not. The lights go out. The baby starts crying. Should I nurse Katey or stoke the fire? If I don't tend the fire right now I'll have to re-start it, the idea of which adds to my stress level, not to mention that Ken's out of earshot troubleshooting the generator and the kids won't be left alone in a dark house. I throw the little one on my hip and pull my rain jacket over her body and grimace as I hear my five-year-old wail to keep up through the slick mud. I grab two pieces of wood by the barn with my one free hand. I'm panting with anxiety.

So much for the simple life.

I'd visited friends in Colorado who power their house with the sun. They live against the backdrop of the Sangré de Cristo Mountains with a sun that beats down year-round. Other than that visit, I didn't have prior experience living with solar power. Even then, I noticed how often they stopped to look at the power meter panels. I didn't understand. Wasn't energy from the sun free? Unlimited? Abundant?

Isn't being able to generate your own energy, to be self-sufficient in terms of your power needs—as Walker Creek has been for more than 30 years—the ideal?

After a grand three-decade experiment in energy independence, Walker Creek Community has first-hand experience with two major misconceptions of off-grid living: that it's a romantic simpler choice involving homemade beeswax candles, self-sufficiency, life in the slow lane; and that it's a better environmental choice. We've learned as we've lived off-the-grid that in our case—it's not.

"I never encourage people to choose off-the-grid if they have utility power available," explains Alana Nelson, co-owner of Fire Mountain Solar, and part of the husband-wife team who led the joint effort to bring utility power up Periwinkle Lane—to the four households of our community, to the solar well-pump that provides water to our entire community, and to the two neighboring households who share an easement on our mile-plus dirt lane.

Tim and Alana Nelson have lived as neighbors to Walker Creek Community going on 15 years, ever since building their strawbale home up the hill from the community. The Nelsons' solar energy business grew out of living here on this land, off-the-grid. Alana explains that there are definitely appropriate situations for being off-the-grid. Among them: when it's so remote, like a cabin in the wilderness, that utility power is not an option; and when the cost to bring utilities to your home is so prohibitive—one of their clients was quoted $250,000 to run utilities a mile up their road—that an alternative-energy system is a smarter investment.

The houses that line the paved road to our lane have electricity, we live not 10 minutes from a vast hillside housing development, and beyond our fence we can see the 120-foot tall power lines rising above the cedar grove. The lines buzz like 1000 angry bees in deep winter when more humidity wets the air. Some days, we mock them with the smooth silver solar panels that sit on our roof. Other days, they mock us as we run outside to start our generator, bracing against the cold air.

In the late '70s and early '80s, just after the folks living at Walker Creek collectively donated the 20-acre property to the Evergreen Land Trust, a clear vision was already at hand. Walker Creek trust agreements articulate the commitment to be "an experimental ground for alternative technologies." Wind, water, and solar energy have all been a part of that experiment.

Today's members of Walker Creek are similarly committed. As established public school teachers, business owners, and tech freelancers who grow their own food and steward land cooperatively, members straddle the wide ground between back-to-the-landers and career professionals. Within this dichotomy Walker Creek also serves as an experimental ground for how the common US lifestyle—complete with computers, cars, and busy calendars—can co-exist with alternative energy choices.

Community member Aviathar Pemberton has made his home at Walker Creek Community for 28 years. He raised his three children here, off-the-grid, from babyhood to teenager-hood to young adulthood. Aviathar's evolution with alternative power ranges from candles to kerosene lanterns that smoked up the inside of his house to propane lights to electric automotive lights (like your tail lights) which he'd keep charged by run-

ning his car every few hours. Eventually he bought two solar panels to charge the set of deep-cycle batteries which charged the small 12 volt electric lights.

Around 1995, Aviathar, who also goes by V, began the process of adding more and more panels to his solar array, slowly converting his household to LED lights (which had just come out), building up a bank of back-up batteries, and investing in propane-run generators for our Northwest winters when there simply aren't enough daylight hours—or sunshine—to produce a reliable amount of power.

The Good, The Bad, and The Ugly

With simple doable new habits around energy use—not leaving appliances plugged in, using power strips, mastering the art of making toast on

Solar panels and tree branches blanketed with snow at Walker Creek Community.

the stovetop—our adjustment to living off-the-grid was surprising. Many days, our family hardly noticed the difference. Most days, I appreciate the forced consciousness around electricity, the small shifts in awareness, the ingenuity born from constraints. Who needs a document shredder when you have a fireplace for central heating? Who needs those kitchen appliances cluttering your counters when you can do it by hand? Can we figure out as a community how to build a root cellar in that hillside? There's something deeply satisfying about figuring out ways of doing things that you know have been done for hundreds of years before whirring, buzzing appliances with flashing digital displays came along.

And really, who wouldn't love the power of self-reliance—of learning how to meet your own energy needs? Winter storm power outages leave you utterly unaffected. Making your own electricity: it is magic.

The rewards of an off-grid system don't always come easy. We had warnings. As prospective members, we were told, "Some weeks, keeping the lights on and the water running and the house warm is a full-time job." But like when you're on the cusp of marriage and people tell you, "Marriage is hard work," sure, you hear them. But how hard can hard be? Only later, once you are in the daily, yearly unrelenting throes of your lights going out in the middle of cooking dinner, or as you walk at 6 a.m., again, through a pitch black winter morning shivering in pajamas and a coat across the creek to start the well pump generator for your shower before work—only then do you know.

I've tried to come up with a way to explain—more than "it's hard." And the best metaphor I can think of is this: visualize that energy-conscious person, like maybe you are, like the one I've always been, who turns off the lights when she leaves a room, even at the office; who turns off the tap when she brushes her teeth. Now picture a woman in Uganda, hauling a bucket of water. How does your relationship to that water change if you are her? How do your choices change when you only have one bucket? That finite amount is a far cry from water in the tap that you can treat with care—and that you can turn on at any time. That "bucket of water" is your electricity for the day when you live off-the-grid. It's an entirely different relationship.

Off-grid solar panels generate electricity, to use and to store to your bank of batteries. When there's no sunshine, you pull from the finite electricity stored in your batteries. So when it's cloudy or nearing nighttime, you have to consider what's left in your batteries, and how it fits with your plans—you might want to get some late night work done on your computer while your kids watch a movie. You can either make different energy choices, or turn on your generator to recharge your batteries enough to get through the night. Or you can choose to wait for enough sun to recharge your batteries, which may be tomorrow around 9 a.m., or...not. It could be cloudy.

"The batteries are the weakest part of an off-grid system," explains my husband Ken. Think of how your laptop or cell phone battery eventually holds less and less of a charge. Solar bank batteries do the same thing. And they have to be babied—bathed regularly in distilled not regular water. They can't get too cold. Even then, at $250 a pop, they need regular replacing. One bad battery can take your entire system down.

No doubt about it, living off-the-grid limits choices. Some you'd expect, others you might not. When your neighbor who raises grass-fed cattle offers up the chance to purchase a cow or half a cow from her, none of you have a freezer (electric) to store it. When you buy your Excalibur food dehydrator for the autumn abundance of apples and Asian pears and plums, you realize your house doesn't have the power to run it for the 24 hours it takes. So you store the dehydrator at your mother's house who lives an hour south in Seattle. It's an added bonus to work together on a big food project—and it also takes scheduling a drive down, kid logistics, hauling all the fruit to and fro, and getting to all this before the fruit rots. Each decision that affects off-grid power use adds up to a bigger picture layered with dubious environmental decisions and lots of logistics. So much for the simpler life!

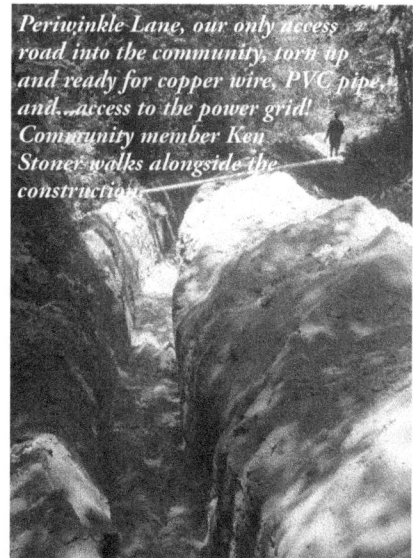
Periwinkle Lane, our only access road into the community, torn up and ready for copper wire, PVC pipe, and...access to the power grid! Community member Ken Stoner walks alongside the construction.

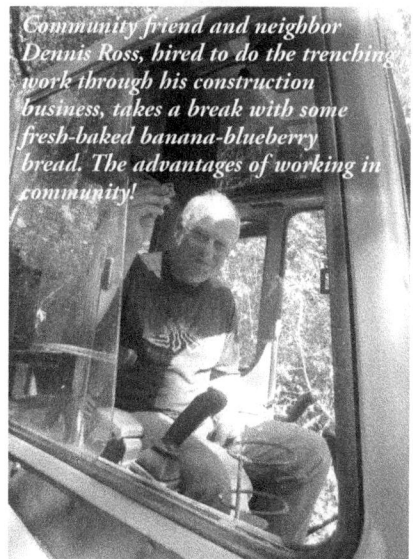
Community friend and neighbor Dennis Ross, hired to do the trenching work through his construction business, takes a break with some fresh-baked banana-blueberry bread. The advantages of working in community!

Photos courtesy of Sarah Stoner

183

Community member Aviathar Pemberton poses in the trench.

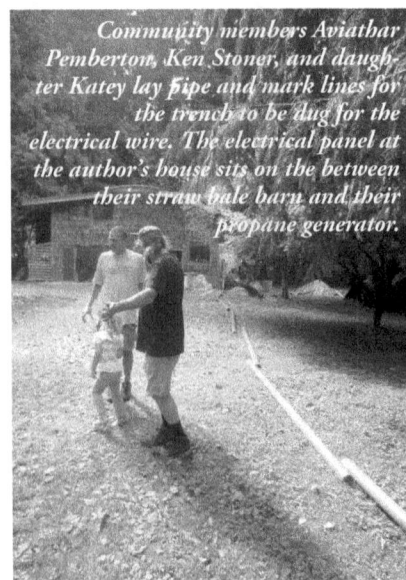

Community members Aviathar Pemberton, Ken Stoner, and daughter Katey lay pipe and mark lines for the trench to be dug for the electrical wire. The electrical panel at the author's house sits on the between their straw bale barn and their propane generator.

What's the big deal anyhow, to just run the generator whenever you need power? Walk with me for a moment, through this glorious forest of ours filled with native hemlocks and salmonberries, cougar and coyote, filled with shiny clean air that you breathe in as the forest breathes out. Walk through the cold winter air, clear as glass, under a sky held up by mossy trees. Now add in your polluting generator rumbling and roaring through the stillness. It really sucks.

Or maybe you sipped power today but your neighbor who makes and sells organic soap as a livelihood needs the extra power to finish up a batch. You get to hear her generator roar from across the creek. Polluting propane is a serious contradiction to living in nature.

Air pollution, noise pollution, and lifestyle constraints aside, the tipping point in our decision to join the grid was this: the opportunity to be a green-energy producer. "We spend all this money on a good off-grid power system and when the sun comes along and the system is at full capacity, there's this little switch that turns the panels off," explains V. "On summer days, our batteries are completely full by 11 a.m. After 11 a.m., that clean power goes to waste."

"Now we can capture all the excess energy that we weren't able to store in our battery banks in the summer time when the sun is shining in abundance and we can let someone else down the line use it," says Alana.

What Do We Stand For Now?

A few weeks ago, on one of our several "electricity work weekends," Ken and V along with another community member were discussing next steps. It was all sounding so serious. I wanted to add a little levity so, using my most syrupy New Age voice, I requested that we all hold hands in a circle and shout out the appliance we were most ready to invite into our lives.

"Toaster!"

"Hot tub!"

"Freezer!"

It's a brand new world in the woods of Walker Creek. How will we change, in terms of our energy consumption, now, with unlimited access to electricity?

Even with all the truths we've learned about the environmental costs, being able to declare that I live off-the-grid is a badge of honor hard to let go. What do we stand for, now that we can no longer declare as a community, "We are an example of off-the-grid living"—as we have for the last 30 years? "We are an example of a group of people with solar panels on our roofs" seems to lack the same punch.

What we *can* be is a net zero community. "With our solar panels we'll be able to bank enough credits in the spring and summer to get us through the winter," explains Alana.

But we won't be monitoring each other's household electricity bills, just like we've never monitored each other's propane bills when we were off-the-grid. At times, I was curious how we compared: households ranged from $40 to a whopping $250 a month in propane use.

Let's be clear that other folks might be able to pull it off better than we did—living off-the-grid, burning less propane—with fewer trees in the way, a larger solar array, a larger battery bank, and a larger budget. And here in the great Northwest, the bulk of our grid power is alternative energy: hydropower. For us, burning propane rather than using hydropower as a backup energy system for our solar array makes less sense. Take that same argument to the Midwest where the majority of grid power comes from burning fossil fuels—close to half of the US's electricity production comes from coal burning—and propane plus solar would be the better environmental choice.

Since our initial electricity meeting six months ago, we've not yet made time for

(continued on p. 75)

GOING FOR THE GRID: A COMMUNITY DITCHES
ENERGY INDEPENDENCE TO GET GREENER

(continued from p. 29)

collective discussions on how a grid-tie will alter our lifestyle and legacy. It's taken all we have to manage the pipe trenching work ourselves to lower costs. And to keep up with the vast and fast-changing information, deadlines, and decisions—loan payments, community dues increases, and a few crux moments requiring consensus from the four community households when members were spread all over the country on summer vacations. Many members admit they've been holding their breath, wondering if logistics would get in the way of seeing the project to the end.

They nearly did get in the way. Along the course of these fast-moving several months, balls were dropped, papers weren't read closely enough to catch important details, and neighbor relations nearly blew sky high—enough that several parties were ready to pull the plug on the project, no pun intended as it really wasn't all that funny how one oversight threatened to break a 15-year relationship between households.

And—we persevered. Walker Creek is committed not just to being an experimental ground for alternative technologies, but also to "principles of human cooperation and...the growth of a new culture and society." Community relationships remain intact. The email just arrived today: "PSE is coming Thursday to do the final hookups and then we'll have electricity!" writes Tim Nelson.

As for exactly how Walker Creek will evolve with electricity and with re-defining ourselves as a model for sustainable energy...stay tuned. A new courtship with power has just begun. Soon, we write our vows. ❧

This article was written using sunshine juice, with the occasional backup of a propane generator, a cursing husband, and the generous support of a Mount Vernon Library power outlet. Sarah J. Stoner is an American-born writer who was raised in Uganda, Morocco, Belgium, and Thailand. With nearly half her life spent spanning cultures, Sarah is now learning the language of staying put, growing her own food, running a household on solar power, and listening to the creek rush through her front yard. She explores identity and belonging at sarahhhwho.blogspot.com.

communities.ic.org

Burlington Cohousing's Excellent Solar Adventures

By Don Schramm

Cohousing in Burlington, Vermont had a long incubation period. We moved into Burlington Cohousing East Village in November 2007 after working towards it for 18 years. It felt like a Phoenix constantly arising from the ashes. Along the way we developed an in-depth mission statement that gave higher priority to affordable housing and engaged residents than to energy-efficiency and environmentally friendly power. While we tried to include passive solar, living roofs, tight and highly insulated structures, sustainable materials, and solar panels in our designs, our budget limited us to no living roofs and only conduits for future solar power. Since move-in, Burlington Electric Department and the State of Vermont have initiated a number of solar programs with incentives. As we have been weaving our way through our processes to get to a smaller environmental footprint, they have been stumbling their way through their processes as well.

East Village has enthusiastically embraced solar power after a number of skirmishes about private use of our common areas. Our physical community consists of a barn, two single family homes, 10 townhouses, a duplex, and 18 flats in the main building which also holds the common kitchen, dining room, living room, and guest bedrooms. All of these buildings have flat roofs except for the single family homes and our barn. We now have 175 solar panels providing 70 percent of our common use electricity and monthly credits on the electric bills of 11 of our 32 families. Of these panels, 83 are on the main building roof, 30 on the barn roof, 14 on one townhouse, and 16 each on three townhouse roofs. There are likely more solar panels to come and the issue of "private use of public areas" is still a hot one.

This issue grew gradually. When we moved into our newly built housing, we had exhausted our construction budget and there were many important features missing from our community. So the next two years we were busy repairing the 1940s barn that came with the land, building parking sheds, adding roof decks, creating guest rooms, furnishing the common kitchen, dining room, and living room, and many other smaller projects. We accomplished a great deal but at the same time glossed over some of the processes involved.

In the fall of 2009, two different families requested permission to install solar panels on the townhouse roofs above their heads. Both were approved by the Owners Association. The first family sailed through the process but ended up lacking the financing. The second family met some objections—first from several people unhappy overlooking their solar panels and second from owners concerned that eventually the community as a whole may want to use that roof for general solar power. That project went forward with the stipulation that in case the community wants our general solar system to be combined with those on this single townhouse, the owner would add her panels to the plan at no extra cost to her. Soon afterward 14 solar panels went

Burlington Cohousing Solar LLC members Charlotte, Barbara, Joan, and Don in front of some of the 113 panels that provide power to the community's common circuit.

Gail Holmes

up on her townhouse roof. This system used a single inverter and a set of storage batteries. Any power generated beyond what was used or could go into the batteries went out onto the electric grid.

At that stage our community began to confront conflicts that boiled down to individuals or families requesting some private use of public areas—in many cases roof space. A task force began brainstorming how to deal with such conflicts. There was unanimous agreement that the community as a whole owned all the buildings' "skins" and roofs. If we as a community agreed to use the space for everyone's benefit, there was no conflict. For example, we built a deck out over the third floor roof for community relaxation and gardens. That was a case of public use of public areas. When some families wanted to put air conditioner condensers on that deck then we had an issue. Those were eventually resolved by putting the condensers on the uppermost roof one story higher.

In August 2010 a consortium of three owners proposed installing 113 solar panels on the main roof and south barn roof. Other residents could have joined the consortium but chose not to. It would have been better if the Owners Association itself could have taken on this project but it did not qualify for the federal solar tax grants which was 30 percent of our total costs. So we formed the Burlington Cohousing Solar LLC which would finance and organize the project and sell the power to the Owners Association. Now the questions began to fly.

Would the panels damage the roof and if so who would pay for the repairs? Would they be insured and who would pay for that? How much would the fourth floor residents be disturbed by the installation? Were we truly being ecologically responsible in buying solar panels manufactured in other countries using resources and energy to ship them? The Solar LLC followed the new procedures for "private use of public areas," answered all the questions thrown at them, and started the installation that Fall.

Conflicts boiled down to individuals or families requesting private use of public areas—in many cases roof space.

While this was a "private use" in the sense that three solar LLC partners would get a return on their investment, it appeared to be for the overall good of the entire community. The majority of our common electric power would now come from solar. Our electricity rate would remain stable. In fact it ultimately went down $2,000 a year because our lower power purchases dropped us into a lower rate category. The Owners Association has the option of buying out the investors at a set cost anytime after the first five years. Through this process our Solar LLC had the assistance of Community Energy Exchange, an L3C organization which facilitates the development of community energy projects in Vermont. They helped design the system, choose the installer, set up the LLC, and do the general administration. In return they were given a small ownership stake.

The installer, Vermont Solar LLC, suggested that we use micro-inverters on each panel rather than a couple of inverters for the entire system. With micro-inverters, a problem with one panel will not impact the total electrical output of the entire array. Also micro-inverters are connected to the internet and the status of any panel

Burlington Cohousing Solstice Party Parade June 22, 2013 in front of townhouses with 48 solar panels.

Don Schramm

can be assessed online. There were some risks to this approach because micro-inverters did not have an established track record. Many of them actually failed on our main roof before the manufacturer decided that we had a gotten a batch of lemons and had the installer swap them out for newer versions. That was a year ago and we have had no failures since. Unlike the first solar installation with a battery backup, this one simply used the electric grid for "storage."

During the installation, we had a misunderstanding. A couple of residents lost their parking spaces when the crane arrived. They were upset enough that the crane had to be sent back while we resolved the dispute by providing more information and apologizing profusely. We had neglected to keep our neighbors fully informed of the details of what was going to happen. There was some peripheral "heat" around the issue that our conflict resolution committee helped ameliorate. The 113 solar panels have now been in operation for almost three years and have produced about 90 megawatt hours of power equivalent to offsetting 62.2 tons of carbon.

With this amazing success, one would expect clear sailing with the next solar project. That was not to be the case. In the spring of 2012 Burlington Electric Department opened a new solar program—Group Net Metering. This program enabled any resident of Burlington to install solar panels anywhere within the City and get credit on their electric bill based on how much electricity was produced by their panels. Ten families in East Village decided to give this idea a go. We estimated that after applying the Vermont Solar Incentive and the Federal Tax Credits, our per panel cost would be about $800 and each panel would provide $50 to $55 of credit each year. Various families would be purchasing different numbers of panels based generally on how much electricity they used. Together we would be installing 48 panels on two or three townhouse roofs.

"Which roofs?" seemed to be the major question. There are three blocks of townhouses that could handle solar panels. The duplex could take 40 altogether. One five-townhouse block could take 80. The other could take 64. We asked the townhouse owners how they felt about solar panels going on the roofs above their heads. One said she could not afford solar panels now but was planning to install them on the roof above her in the future and did not want to lose this opportunity. Another said they wanted to put a stairway up to their roof and sunbathe on it. Interestingly this family was one of those purchasing solar panels. A third owner said that she did not want solar panels on her roof. Four owners were supportive of having solar panels on the roofs above them. No one claimed that they owned their "roof" but there was a strong feeling that they should have some say about what happened up there.

Underneath the question of "Which roofs" were deeper questions. When is it appropriate to allow the "private use" of our "public areas"? For what purposes would we allow "private use" and how do we decide? Our task force had worked out a thoughtful procedure for residents to follow when requesting their "private use of public areas" and that was helpful when some residents wanted to build a stone wall and others to put in various types of sunshades. But the procedure did not go far enough. In retrospect we began to realize that we should never have agreed to the earliest proposals from residents to install their own solar panels without fully developing a policy for the "private use of public areas." The large solar project went through relatively easily because everyone seem to benefit from it. It too should have waited for policy development.

We were getting close to the deadline for the Vermont Solar

> ## No one claimed that they owned their "roof" but many felt strongly they should have a say about what happened up there.

Burlington Cohousing residents making pies using mostly solar power.

Joan Knight

Solar Powering Up Ceremony August 24, 2011 with Vermont Governor Peter Shumlin, Burlington Mayor Bob Kiss, Liz Miller of Vermont's Public Service Department, Solar installer Kirk Herander, and some East Village cohousers.

Governor Shumlin staff

Incentive, so we put off the full debate as to how we decide on what happens on our roofs. With three owners in one five-townhouse complex willing, we decided to put the panels there. We followed the "private use of public areas" procedures and got approval from the Owners Association to move forward with the installation with the stipulation that exactly which roofs the panels would be installed on would follow a community forum on the use of our roofs.

Nineteen people showed up for the forum and the discussion was lively. This was clearly a case of "private use of public areas" because the electrical credits generated by the new solar panels would only go to 10 of our 32 families. Nevertheless the project fit well our mission "to actively co-create and sustain a neighborhood that is nurturing to people and nature." Our hope too was that we would find the means in the future for the other 21 families to participate in group net metering and then the benefit would be community-wide. Some folks want energy independence similar to the first solar project that went in. That owner uses batteries to store power to use at night or when an outage occurs. Some suggested that a mix of energy independence for some households and group net metering for others might work best.

Questions were raised about conflicts of interest among the residents who would own the new panels. Should they be involved in the Owners Association's decision as to whether to go ahead? With our consensus-based decision process, conflicts of interest may possibly be less relevant because not just a majority but everyone needs to be on board. Is there a way residents can have some say in the decision as to what happens over their heads—at least if there will be serious disruption of their lives during installation or ongoing? The group net metering project sputtered its way through probably because "enough" of our residents seem to benefit. The 48 solar panels were installed in late Fall 2012 and started producing power in January of this year. Each month 10 families see a credit on their electric bills.

There is a move afoot to expand group net metering so that every family that wants to can participate and those who want to add more panels will be able to. Burlington Electric even has a program now of low-interest loans tied to property taxes

that will cost less each year than the savings on electric bills. This time though, the community seems to want a thorough thrashing out of the issues around "private use of public areas." This seems to be a debate about competing private uses of common areas. Although photovoltaics may be in keeping with our mission statement, we need not conflate "in the interest of the community" with "undertaken by the community." Essentially if it is not the Owners Association doing and owning a project, then we still only have one private use vs. another private use.

It is unlikely now that further solar panels will go up in our community unless we develop together a plan for a full build-out that all families will participate in. Perhaps we have to devise a method whereby individuals can invest and their financial interests will be protected but the community as a whole will own the panels. The discussion about how this might happen is planned for this Fall and it is likely to be a lively one.

General Project Details

Burlington Cohousing Common Circuit 25.4 kW Solar Project
Expected First Year Energy Production: 31.450 MWh
Developer: Burlington Cohousing Solar LLC with help from Community Energy Exchange L3C
Installer: Vermont Solar LLC www.vtsolar.com
113 Solon 225W Photovoltaic Modules with Enphase M215 Inverters
Total System Cost: $144,864.00
Less Federal Grant: $43,459.00
Less State Incentives: $24,069.00
Net Cost: $77,336.00
Cost per Solar Panel: $684.39
Cost per installed kW: $3,044.72
To view system go to: enlighten.enphaseenergy.com/public/systems/gyBG12559

Burlington Cohousing Group Net Metering 11.52 kW Solar Project
Expected First Year Energy Production: 13.868 MWh
Developer: Burlington Cohousing Net Metering Group with help from Community Energy Exchange L3C
Installer: Vermont Solar LLC, www.vtsolar.com
48 Solarworld SW240 W Photovoltaic Modules with Enphase M215 Inverters
Total System Cost: $57,610.00
Less State Incentives: $6,912.00
Less Federal Tax Credits: $15,210.00
Net Cost: $35,488.00
Cost per Solar Panel: $739.33
Cost per installed kW: $3080.56
To view system go to: enlighten.enphaseenergy.com/public/systems/3wpF144878 ❧

Don Schramm is one of the founding members of Burlington Cohousing East Village (bcoho.org).

Burlington Cohousing Energy Documents

Anyone wishing copies of the following documents—

A - Solar LLC Operating Agreement

B - Solar LLC Power Purchase Agreement with Burlington Cohousing

C - Net Metering Group Agreement

D - Solar Equipment Hosting Agreement

—may email noah@communityenergyexchange.com.

Establishing and Incorporating Renewable Energy Technologies in Camphill Communities
A Personal Journey

By Martin Sturm

Joining a small rural Camphill Community at the age of 22 in the west of Northern Ireland in 1988 felt for me like taking a leap back in a time machine.

After growing up on a well-mechanised farm at Camphill Community Brachenreuthe in the south of Germany and completing training as a biodynamic farmer on a modern community farm near Frankfurt (Dottenfelderhof), I found farming in the community in Northern Ireland a huge adjustment.

Neglected overgrown fields without infrastructure, the lack of any but the most basic farming tools, little money, and lots of rain were some of the farming challenges. On the other hand, a growing lifesharing intentional community was providing much-needed care, support, and day opportunities for adults with learning disabilities. In 1989 a complete changeover of responsibilities took place when the remaining pioneering family left. This meant taking on a substantial amount of additional responsibilities.

Building houses, workshops, and farm buildings formed a big part of daily life for my first 15 years in this community. Since I arrived we've also explored many ecologically-friendly technologies.

In 1989 the farm installed a barn hay drier using a dehumidifier heat pump and solar gain of the roof structure for drying. The hay drier has proven itself in an unpredictable climate. Drying costs are lower than the production of baled silage. And milk from hay-fed cows is healthful and can often be tolerated by people who may have milk-related allergies, making it particularly suitable for the needs of our community.

Clearing the land with its hedges and coppicing woodlands produced stacks of wood every year, most of which was formerly burned as waste. In 1996 I asked my peers in our community for permission to research the possibility of installing a wood chip gasification boiler for one or more buildings. I initially envisioned using only the waste wood of the estate.

I travelled from Scandinavia through Germany and Austria visiting wood boiler manufacturers, studied different technologies, and had discussions with the company owners seeking their personal support towards a possible installation in Northern Ireland. After significant technological learning, all relevant pieces for the choice of boiler fell together when Fröling, an Austrian based company, made an excellent offer and more importantly promised full technical support. We also agreed that I could install the boiler myself.

When I returned home with the good news, I presented a proposal to my community together with a detailed feasibility study showing considerable savings potential and environmental benefits. I was surprised to learn that the real challenge lay not in the realms of technology or funding, but in individual people's worries, feelings, and fear of change.

It took many meetings and conversations, and a fair degree of patience and determination. Finally, during 1998 I was allowed to proceed with the installation of a 320 kW Fröling Lambdamat wood chip boiler to initially supply four large buildings (expanded to include six buildings now) with heat and hot water through a district heating network using steel pre-insulated pipes.

We erected a purpose-built wood storage barn and purchased a Starchl screened wood chipper, together with wood chip handling equipment. We housed the boiler in a new multi-purpose farm building. In our negotiations with professionals over the installation of the district heating network, quotations returned exceeding the available budget three times. This situation necessitated quick learning. We purchased pipes from Denmark, hired a digger, and engaged a coded welder. With a team of coworkers we installed the district heating network ourselves below budget and on time.

At Easter 1999 the house where I live became one of the first buildings connected to the wood chip heating system; we took out the old LPG gas boilers and put a balancing vessel in its place. I will never forget how great the first hot bath felt, supplied with heat from our

CAMPHILL COMMUNITY CLANABOGAN
RENEWABLES FARM

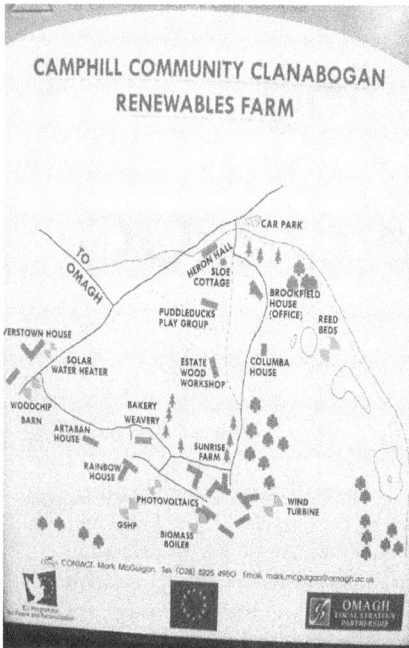

own virgin waste wood rather than from manufactured LPG gas.

In 2001, the Omagh Environmental Energy Consortium formed—a partnership of South West Colleges (Further and Higher Education colleges for the southwestern region of Northern Ireland), the local District Council, and two Farmers Unions.

Structural funding for the development of the local area became available and Camphill Community Clanabogan was used as a Renewable Energy Demonstration Project. As a result, we erected a 20 kW Jacobs windmill, supplying electricity for the community. Solar hot water panels fitted to one of our large buildings began supplying domestic hot water. A new 2 kW photovoltaic array fed electricity into the community. A ground source heat pump supplied the heat in an experimental root zone heating system in a large polytunnel in the garden. We also installed a further domestic wood chip boiler for a single dwelling.

The partnership with the college brought thousands of visitors to the community. Renewable Energy training courses and conferences were organised and partially held on site. The Northern Ireland government included the project in their white paper for the development of renewable energy technologies in Northern Ireland. The project won several awards including an all-UK Beacon Award.

Many other renewable energy installations were assisted throughout the country, in particular wood chip, pellet, and wood log boiler installations. Several Camphill Communities in Ireland and further afield received advice and sometimes hands-on help with installations.

In 2009 a successful funding application to the Low Carbon Communities Challenge awarded £450,000 and led to the planning and installation of a large district heating system for Camphill Community Glencraig near Belfast. A single URBAS medium temperature medium pressure biomass boiler, installed into a purpose-built boiler house with an output of 1000 kW, now supplied heat to 22 units through a network of district heating pipes with a total length of 3.2 km and a total project cost of £650,000.

The URBAS boiler is technology used in large wood district heating and power plants. This type of technology makes it possible to utilise very low grade wood biomass with up to 65 percent moisture content. A big advantage is that any waste wood from tree surgeons or sawmills can be used without the need for drying or screening of the wood chip. Cheap virgin wood waste material can be sourced and turned into valuable energy.

In its first year of operation the project has displaced 280,000 litres of oil and produced savings of around £100,000.

The Glencraig district heating project won the all-UK Renewable Energy Association Award 2011 for Best Community Project.

In my experience, engaging with communities about their own renewable energy possibilities is a journey which engages not only facts and figures but also many varied human factors and community dynamics. It is an excellent field for personal development and learning. ❧

Martin Sturm was born in 1965. His parents were then founder members of Camphill Dorfgemeinschaft Lehenhof. In 1967 the family moved to Camphill Brachenreuthe. After completing his training as a biodynamic farmer Martin moved in 1988 from Germany to Camphill Community Clanabogan in Northern Ireland, taking on the establishing and managing of what is now a 150 acre biodynamic social care farm. Besides many areas of hands-on practical involvement and in-depth experience in renewable energy systems with particular emphasis on biomass, Martin is part of the senior management team and registered provider of Camphill Community Clanabogan.

Energy Efficient Heating, Renewable Electricity, and Community Renaissance at ZEGG

By Achim Ecker

ZEGG's New Energy Plan

ZEGG has implemented a new energy plan after it decommissioned the former wood-chip burner which had served the community well for its first 20 years on the Bad Belzig site (about 80 km southwest of Berlin, Germany; see www.zegg.de/en/). The old boiler had an output of 850 kW and had been visited by some 1000 people from universities as well as politicians, since it was a pioneering example of its kind. The new system, serving ZEGG's 100 or so residents as well as its many guests, is based around a new solar-assisted biomass heating plant with the following components:

• 250 square meter thermal solar plant
• a new wood-chip fired boiler with 500 kW heat output
• a log fired boiler with 350 kW heat output
• three combined heat and power (co-generation) plants, delivering 45 kW heat and 15 kW electricity running on super-renewable wind-gas from Greenpeace wind generators
• heat recovery from a walk-in cooling and freezing unit of the central kitchen

This energy mix means that 100 percent of ZEGG's thermal energy requirements are met from regenerative sources.

In addition to the co-generation plants, in 2011 ZEGG installed a photovoltaic plant of 29 kWp (peak kilowatts). Together with the already existing PV plant it amounts to 52 kWp electricity produced. The co-generation plants produce electrical energy in a CO_2-friendly way because the excess thermal energy produced is used directly for heating water and buildings. This leads to CO_2 savings of more than 66,000 kg per year!

The electricity used by ZEGG is 100 percent regenerative. The combination of co-generation plants and PV panels meets about 90 percent of ZEGG's electricity demand. The rest is bought from Greenpeace-Energy.

ZEGG also completely renewed the underground site heating network. Deterioration of the pipes had led to heat losses of up to 15 percent (c. 150 kW), which will now be reduced to around four percent. Reducing energy losses through insulation is more important than producing (even renewable) energy. For this reason, we are also insulating the existing buildings on the ZEGG site using renewable materials. At the rate of one building every couple of years, we apply full thermal installation, including work on the facades, windows, roofs, and floors. This also needs to be combined with more energy efficiency like LED lighting, energy efficient household tools, etc. During the first 20 years of the heating grid's existence the heating energy demand dropped by more than 30 percent even though extra houses were connected to it—largely because of additional insulation and other improvements. These new investments ensure that ZEGG continues to be a model center when it comes to the use of renewable and regional energy sources.

New Energy from Holacracy

Restructuring the community and work areas to a holacratic system and organization two years ago helped us to take the necessary steps towards greater ecological sustainability. Decisions become faster and simpler to make and went very smoothly and easily here. Of course our long-famed training in working very intensively with ZEGG-FORUM and other methods has shaped our operational mode. We've learned to listen more to what moves others. It's helped us to decide to spend loads of money (around 800,000€)—which we essentially do not have—on being a very sustainable model; of course it will

Community tune-in exercise at the internal ZEGG community intensive conference, 2013.

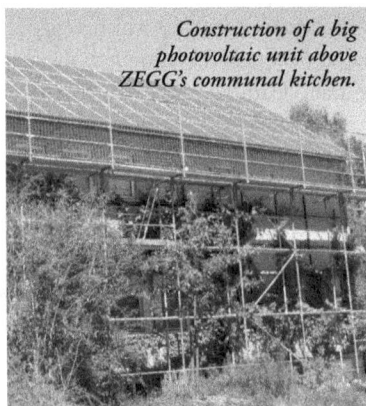

Construction of a big photovoltaic unit above ZEGG's communal kitchen.

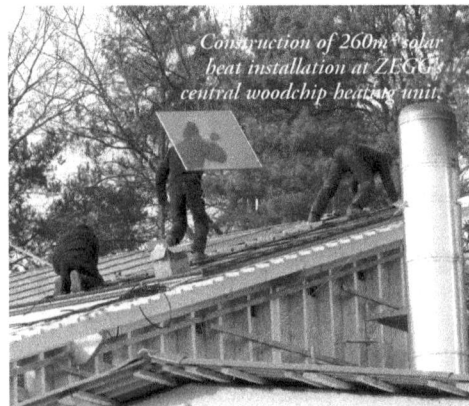

Construction of 260m² solar heat installation at ZEGG's central woodchip heating unit.

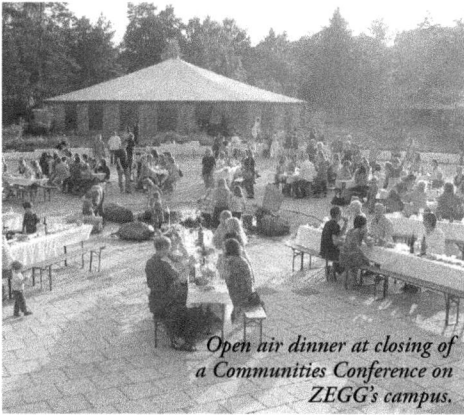

Open air dinner at closing of a Communities Conference on ZEGG's campus.

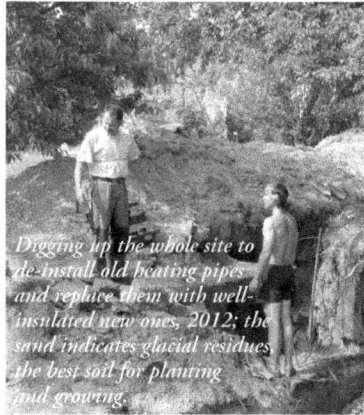

Digging up the whole site to de-install old heating pipes and replace them with well-insulated new ones, 2012; the sand indicates glacial residues, the best soil for planting and growing.

Closing ceremony of ZEGG's annual Summer Camp.

Photos courtesy of Achim Ecker

also save us money in the future from lower costs for fuel.

Our decision was well thought through, and acceptance was unanimous (we still use consensus decision making). As we are operating without inspired leaders or gurus, or a common ideology or creed, the fact that it worked easily reflects how much we've worked to develop good communication.

One topic where we do have arguments is whether to invest more in the seminar center for the guests that provide our main income, or to focus on better living conditions for ourselves, the people who run the seminar center. The first might generate more revenue or secure the income we have; the latter makes life better for us. But the focus on using renewables and being sustainable was never much of a debate.

Personal Choices and the Costs of Sustainability

Our ecological success as a community does not always extend to the "private sector" here. When it comes to the personal decisions we make individually—whether we use trains, buses, or bicycles in our travel plans, or airplanes and cars, like most of the rest of society—we aren't as consistent. Renewable things cost much more than non-renewables; taking a train is much more expensive than flying. We all feel constantly short of money, don't we?

While many are passionate about living sustainably, quite a few others in the community see steps toward a sustainable lifestyle as inconvenient. They believe they have sacrificed so much all their lives that now they want to focus more on their own comfort. Many still do choose to fly or to shop for "cheap and fast" rather than conscious and responsible.

Maybe this is a reaction against the dominance of community matters and values during the pioneering years? Then the private or personal came second or third, not first. First came service to the community and the world, as we were out to find a model of living that could counter all the atrocities we call daily life today. This did not feel like a sacrifice then, and even today I see it as being of service to something higher than just

my own needs. Of course, this is all easier given that my basic needs are met anyway.

One very important aspect of it all is that we are not dogmatic about our lifestyles. We do what we can and acknowledge the limits to this as well. It is a relaxed striving towards being as sustainable as we could be. This way seems better for our hearts—and healed hearts then will take more care of the earth by themselves, without dogmas.

Where We Are Now

We are proud to have grown out of being a very dogmatic community ("we know what the world needs and how we all need to live and we lead the way far beyond anyone else") during our first 15 years, to become a very welcoming and diverse place, open to all aspects of life, during our last 20 years. Sometimes I wonder if we are too diverse and in need of some more focus—but as it looks now, this focus could be coming as more and more of us are hearing this calling. A growing number of ZEGG people want to bring

> We are proud to have grown out of being a very dogmatic community during our first 15 years, to become a very welcoming and diverse place.

their actions into better alignment with their knowledge and thinking.

We also celebrate that we've continued to exist since 1978! To last this long, we must have learned something about social communication and cooperation. At ZEGG, I notice a high level of self-responsibility and self-reflection in most communication—very different from elsewhere in society.

As I see it, we are still far from ideal (keep in mind that I write and hold trainings about integral community building). We may rest on past successes and forgot that it takes constant effort to maintain what we've established. Past effort wears off. We don't have a common practice of ZEGG-FORUM any more. We have common Forum work in the community about four to five times a year, when we all meet to prepare plans or rebuild community.

Just starting is a renaissance of a striving for community

(continued on p. 77)

ENERGY EFFICIENT HEATING, RENEWABLE ELECTRICITY, AND COMMUNITY RENAISSANCE AT ZEGG

(continued from p. 37)

intimacy, after years when most here strove mainly for intimacy with a partner or with self. If it becomes strong, it will rekindle and reawaken our communication and transparency skills and practices, which have lain underused or dormant.

New Soil

One recent practical idea is kindling enthusiasm now—reawakening a longing to be of relevance for the world around us. We are working on a plan to replace all our flush toilets with dry separating toilets, using the urine and faeces in Terra Preta soils to restore fertility, save lots of water, and sequester carbon from the atmosphere (partly in biochar produced from organic waste materials). The grey water from showers and sinks would be cleaned and reused for irrigation and washing machines, turning us into a wastewater-free model settlement of the future.

I believe this would also bring us to more individual sustainability thinking and choices in our "private" lives. In many moments I can hear and feel the renewed change and the longing for yet a more coherent path together. So stay tuned! 🐦

Born in 1959, Achim Ecker is a trained social worker who values deep caring, compassion, and love for people and life. In the 1980s he was an intern at the Resource Center for Nonviolence in Santa Cruz. At ZEGG he is the chief Permaculturally-trained landscape designer and ecobuilder. For the last 20 years he has been teaching integral Forum and awareness training in German, English, and Spanish. Visit his website at www.zegg-forum.org.

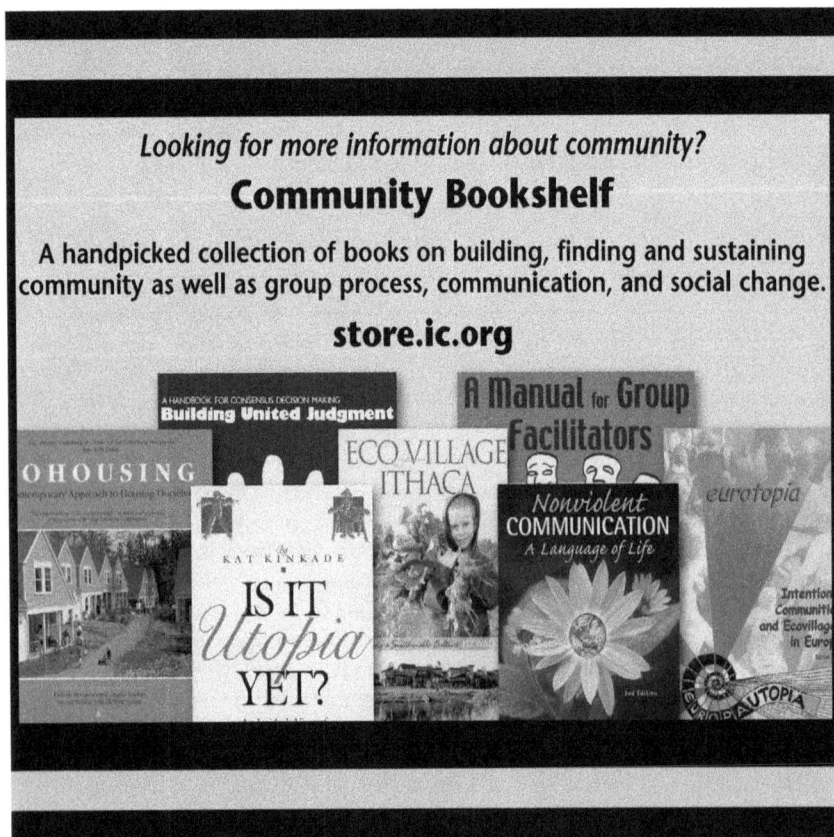

Energy Efficiency in Cohousing

By Charles Durrett

When it comes to energy use, *"show me the bills."* My electricity bill last year was minus $88, for the entire year. My highest monthly heating bill last winter was about $20, in the Lake Tahoe area.

A few years ago we designed a Unitarian Universalist Church in Fresno, California. Katie McCamant was the project architect. It was the first LEED (Leadership in Energy and Environmental Design) gold in all of central California. LEED today is the best we can do to institutionally and universally quantify "sustainability."

In the next year, we designed a 28-unit cohousing community right next door. Many of the folks in the Unitarian Universalist congregation were involved in planning and ultimately moved into the cohousing community. I was the architect for the cohousing community and when planning it I asked the group, "Do you want to do the cohousing as LEED certified?" They chimed in all at once: "No way! Chuck, if we have an extra $40,000 to $50,000 sitting around, we'll have them all converted to one-dollar-bills, grind them up and pour them into the walls as insulation; at least that way, we'll get something for it." It took somewhere between $40,000-$50,000 to get the 8" x 10" certificate for the church—and that was just the paperwork and buying the certificate. There was very little value added, and there was no way that the same client group wanted that rigmarole again.

I understand why the population wants a formula. To be honest, American architects have advertised conscientious, sustainable design for a long time, but have produced little more than rhetoric. In fact, a formula is necessary if not critical for 90 percent of the architects. They didn't start doing or trying to make efficient buildings until someone came along and started measuring things. The problem is that for people who see neighborhoods more holistically, they are measuring the wrong things. They are not measuring how low your energy bills were. Instead they are measuring how many bells and whistles you had. The bells and whistles

always cost more and break down more often, aren't simple elegant solutions, but depend on gizmos and money. The Energy Star refrigerator is not always the one that is the most energy efficient—you end up using the more energy wasteful appliance because it gets you a LEED point.

Similarly, the passive house is another good formula if you have excess money and want to spend it on currently popular ideas. Again it often appears that if we can just come up with the latest magic bullet (straw bale, a passive house, or similar) we will beat the game. The best game is to be a clever practitioner, perhaps making buildings that improve the most conventional building practices—just as the most efficient autos are "engineered" like the Prius and know the many details that really matter. Look to evolve and engineer aggressively rather than to find the magic bullet. Look to further the craft of good practices, even when they're conventional. We know that if we tweak conventional construction by 10 percent we can improve energy efficiency by 80-90 percent. Plan to employ carpenters and other artisans who can later modify buildings to new clients and uses.

Look at performance more than labels. People often say to us, "Oh yeah, that's like the passive house," or, "Yeah that will get you a couple of LEED points." That's not our concern. Our concern is: Do people love

> **Before moving into cohousing, one resident was buying five to six tanks of gas per month; now he buys less than one.**

living there? Is it a high-functioning community?—because that is *the* crux of sustainability. Above all else, if it doesn't work socially, why bother? Yes, we're looking to have the lowest possible energy bills, the best natural ventilation, natural light, low toxic material, sustainably grown lumber (if we used lumber), flooring that is completely biodegradable, and much much more. But all in the context of working socially, being beautiful and elegant (because people take care of what they love and love what is beautiful), and in the context of what is affordable—predictably affordable. We are wedded to serving everyone in the group.

When it comes to sustainability, show me the community. So much sustainability is embedded in community. Last night I had dinner in the not-quite-new cohousing community in Grass Valley, California. A resident said that previous to moving into cohousing he was buying five to six tanks of gas per month; now he buys less than one. That's because his all-important social life now happens *in* the neighborhood. Our 34-unit cohousing community in Nevada City, California shares one lawnmower, one table saw, one hot tub, one, one, one, lots of things. People there would think you were crazy if you proposed a second lawn mower. If I tried to co-purchase a lawn mower on the single-family house street I once lived, they would think I was crazy.

When people come to the table with intention of cooperation, anything is possible, including saving our species, and *that's sustainable.* ❧

Charles Durrett is an architect, author, and advocate of affordable, socially responsible and sustainable design who has made a major contribution in the last 20 years to a multi-disciplinary architecture and town planning—one that involves and empowers the inhabitants and enriches the sense of place and sense of community in both the urban and rural settings in which he works. Charles has designed over 50 cohousing communities in the United States, including Muir Commons, the first cohousing community in North America, and has consulted on many more around the world.

The Sun Touches Heartwood

By Richard Grossman

To create and live in a community which fosters harmony with each other, the larger community, and Nature.
—The Vision of Heartwood Cohousing

Perhaps my saddest day here at Heartwood was at a retreat a decade ago. One of my favorite neighbors said that he did not support using renewable energy because it didn't make financial sense. He pointed out that we were not an ecovillage. Fortunately, all our neighbors do not share that attitude. Since then the cost of the renewable energy infrastructure has dropped so that now it is competitive with conventional sources. Furthermore, we have devised a way to help our community afford what many of us feel is essential for our planet's future. Heartwood can feel the sun's power.

We take our community's Vision and Values statements almost as seriously as our Interpersonal Agreements. One of our Values is: "*Stewardship*: We live gently on the Earth. We are thankful for Nature's resources, being conscious to take good care of them and use them efficiently." We are living up to this Value more and more.

Heartwood Cohousing is located in one of the best areas in the US for solar energy. The sun shines here 300 days a year, but our climate is relatively cool because of the 7000 foot (2130 meter) altitude. This combination of brilliant sun and cool air makes photovoltaic generation of electricity very efficient.

Our community is medium sized with 24 homes and about 75 people, but we have as much land area as any cohousing in the US—we own over 250 acres (100 hectares) of wonderful land. Some is used for growing food on a large organic farm now with many animals. Much of our land is wild, with a few trails, for the enjoyment of wildlife and people. The sun keeps our crops growing and the woods healthy as well as warming and lighting the community. It would be a shame to not use the sun's energy to replace some of that otherwise generated by polluting fossil fuels.

Electricity and natural gas are amazingly inexpensive where we live in southwestern Colorado. We pay less than 12 cents per kilowatt-hour for "juice" from standard sources—largely from coal-fired power plants. Unfortunately, that cost does not reflect the true cost, because there are many hidden expenses or "externalities." Although these costs don't appear on monthly bills, they are real and often people elsewhere end up paying for them. Climate change from increased greenhouse gases is an example. Also, we all pay the government subsidies that support coal mining and power plants. What about the cost of black lung from coal miners? What about the health cost of particulates and mercury in the smoke? Good research suggests that our electric bills reflect only a half or a third of the true cost of electricity.

Some of us are more aware of the human impact on our planet and try to do what we can to minimize that impact. Unfortunately, many people are blissfully unaware. This continuum of understanding of environmental issues exists at Heartwood as well as in the rest of the country. Although I find this frustrating (as mentioned in the first paragraph), I am happy to say that we at Heartwood are better informed than most in our larger community.

Our attention to energy efficiency and harnessing the power of the sun started long before the first shovelful of earth was dug to build Heartwood. We create smaller individual footprints by living in a community and by clustering our homes. We chose energy-efficient building techniques and oriented our homes to maximize passive solar gain. About a dozen years ago, when compact fluorescents were becoming commercially available, one member gave CFLs as Christmas presents to every neighbor. Many of these are still shining and saving money.

After living here for several years we invited energy experts from our local electrical cooperative to talk to us about using less energy. We discovered that we could convert our community's electric meters from commercial to less expensive personal status. The money we saved went to buying "green" electricity—generated by wind or hydro. We have also encouraged members to pay the tiny increment in order to have "green" power in their homes.

Most of our vehicles are fuel-efficient. Many of us drive hybrids, but our rural lifestyle requires some heavy hauling. "Tritone" is a macho Dodge three-quarter ton turbodiesel truck available to members of the community. It is actually a combination of three vehicles (hence its name), and its prior use for forestry has given it its unique combination of dents. Its owners request only that users pay enough to cover the cost of fuel.

Heartwood now has five "solar systems"—three solar-thermal and two photovoltaic. Two of our straw clay homes were designed around their solar-thermal systems. The homes are well insulated and efficiently designed to be snug on even the coldest winter days. Much of their winter heat comes from the sun, and in the summer the domestic hot water is heated by solar.

The photovoltaic system on our home is seven years old. Although our roof is oriented perfectly, it is small enough that we could put only 10 panels on it. One of our criteria for the installer was we absolutely wanted the roof to be leak proof, since our bedroom is right underneath panels! Roofers tore off the old roof, installed a new waterproof membrane and replaced the metal. So far there have been no leaks and our bedroom is a little cooler in the summer because of the shade the panels provide.

Another criterion for our PV system was to provide about 85 to 90 percent of our electricity. This was an economic decision that was also forced by our roof area. The electrical co-op, with their net metering program, averages our production throughout the year. If the PV system produces more electricity than we use, they will buy the excess but at a lower rate than what they sell to customers. Well, last year I was surprised to learn we had actually made more than we had used, and so we received a small rebate. This increased efficiency was made possible by installing a new Energy Star refrigerator, some LED bulbs—and by turning off lights and phantom loads when they aren't needed.

What made my wife, Gail, and me decide to pay for this PV system? We have granddaughters. Now the girls are 10, six years old, and a newborn. We know that the world that they inherit from us will be very different from the world that we have enjoyed. In some ways it will be better, but we are concerned that it will be hotter and have scarcer resources. One of the actions that we have taken to try to make their world better is to employ renewable energy.

When we started thinking about having our own solar array there weren't many choices of installers in our area. Now there are more than a dozen, but back then I got only two estimates. One was appreciably lower than the other, but there was one major concern with that installer. Mick is a conservative Christian and I (a physician) am an abortion provider. I thought that sooner or later we might come to blows about abortion, so I brought up the subject early in our discussions. Mick had no problems working with an abortion provider and we ended up being good friends—and ended up with an excellent photovoltaic system.

Like most people and communities, we have limitations. Through the years we have dreamed of a photovoltaic system that could generate most of the "juice" for our community, but the figures just didn't add up for that dream to be economically possible. In addition, our electrical co-op has not yet made it possible to have "virtual net metering." Virtual net metering is necessary with a solar garden, where a large bank of panels provides power to multiple users. Metering of electrical usage becomes complicated since part of the electricity is from the utility and part is "homegrown." The Solar Garden Institute, based here in Colorado, has kept us informed of progress that is being made elsewhere in the US to make solar gardens feasible.

There are two pieces of good news. First is that the cost of photovoltaic systems is continuing to decrease. This, plus the rising cost of electricity, will make a solar garden more practical in the near future.

The other good news is political. One Heartwood member has used her political savvy to mobilize public sentiment. For years our electrical co-op had only one person on the board of directors who favored renewable power. Katie and a small group of people worked hard to get two more forward-looking directors elected last year. This year, 2013, all three "green" candidates won! Now our directors are split 50/50, with half definitely supporting renewable power. We expect that the board will approve a policy to support solar gardens soon.

Water to irrigate our community's private gardens and our "village green" has to be pumped to the housing cluster. We initially had a small capacity solar pump, but it wasn't long before our need exceeded its ability and it had to be supplemented by a gas pump. The gas pump was noisy, polluting, and a hassle to fill and run. We saved money for several years so we could replace these two pumps with a larger solar pump. Fortunately, the technology has improved in the past dozen years so versatile, high capacity pumps are now available. Also, solar panels have become affordable. Although this setup is relatively new at the time of writing, the new solar pump has been a great success!

What can Heartwood members do to compensate for their carbon emissions? Furthermore, what can Heartwood Cohousing do to be able to afford renewable energy systems? Fortunately we found a way to help with both. In the four years since it was started, our Renewable Energy Fund has collected over $2,000 of voluntary donations. Most donors give every month at the same time they pay their HOA dues. The Fund was set up to help people mitigate their unavoidable use of fossil fuels, and the money will be used to help the community switch to renewable energy.

We all depend on the sun for light and heat. Heartwood is making the transition from ancient sun power stored in fossil fuel to using the power of the day. We can feel good that, more and more, we have been touched by the sun. ❧

Richard Grossman and his wife Gail were some of the first inhabitants of Heartwood Cohousing, moving there in 2000. Dr. Grossman is an obstetrician-gynecologist who has helped families in the Four Corners region reach reproductive goals for over 35 years. His primary concern is the human impact on the natural world. His blog is available at www.population-matters.org.

The Personal and the Planetary:
Spiritual and Planetary Renewal at Lama Foundation

By Scott Shuker

I've always been an advocate of appropriate technologies and renewable energy. There is truly a guilt-free and burden-less feeling that comes with using them; turning on a light switch doesn't mean more tons of coal and uranium being mined, processed, and/or burned. A solar technician told me many years ago as we christened Lama Foundation's new solar array that "the only energy you waste is that which you don't use." This was a profound revelation for me. Since its beginning here in San Cristobal, New Mexico, Lama has embraced an off-the-grid lifestyle and was a pioneer in solar energy since its advent in the early to mid 1970s. We have never been connected to a public electrical grid system. Over the years, we have continued to use and innovate according to available solar technologies.

Lama is also a place for spiritual energy renewal. Through practices of meditation, chanting, hermitage, dancing, and daily service, people find serenity and fellowship as a means of healing and a much-needed "soul rest" from the frantic and often frightening pace of the modern world. I've always seen the personal in the practical at Lama, expressing our love of the planet through the choices we make on how to live on it. That is why we have invested so much in achieving sustainability these past 45 years.

Today, we are thriving. We combine active and passive solar design which meets almost all of the community's energy needs. Since the 1990s, we've centralized most of our 120 watt power in the Solar Shed which houses deep-cell batteries which store energy from the solar array, as well as equipment that then converts it for use to our many buildings—our own mini-grid. In addition to newer models, we continue to use solar panels which were being used in the 1970s. Large, south-facing windows allow the sun to keep the shed and batteries warm in the winter. The shed also houses a propane-powered generator as back-up when the power drain causes battery storage to get too low.

We've recently retrofitted our main Dome Complex with two glycol solar panels just outside the wash-house, which pre-heat cold water then send it to a standard propane water tank for holding. This cuts down significantly on the amount of propane used for water heating. The greenhouse nearby not only produces vegetables, it heats three rooms behind it (when the sun's out, of course). There is also a homemade outdoor shower system, a black-painted water tank inside a glass-enclosed unit, in which water is heated then gravity feeds to the shower head. Usually by mid-day in the summer, the water is so hot one must add cold water to make it comfortable.

The Community Center is also mostly powered by the sun. We once had propane-heated water baseboard heating for the entire building in its early days, but the system became so dysfunctional and high-maintenance we finally gave up. Instead, we decided to rely on other design features which are more sustainable anyway. Lighting power comes from the central array and we use compact fluorescent bulbs only. The kitchen is heated in the winter by convection, relying on a solar attic (often reaching well over 100 degrees Fahrenheit during the day) which heats then circulates hot air by fan to the kitchen as well as the mudroom. There is also a fan near the kitchen ceiling (which is 40 feet high) which circulates warmer air back down to the bottom. In the winter, we install translucent panels over rafters located halfway up, which retain more heat in the area that is actually used. The office nearby is now heated by a small solar collector which works on the same principle as the solar attic. A small 12 volt solar panel and fan push the warm air inside. A large greenhouse and skylight downstairs provide heat to the lower rooms, which are also heated by wood stoves. All residences are either connected to the central grid or have autonomous 12 volt systems employing one panel and two batteries. This is usually more than adequate for the needs of one or two people. The pump on the summer outdoor propane-heated shower system is powered this way as well.

A photovoltaic array feeds power to the Solar Shed, which houses deep-cell batteries and acts as the hub of Lama Foundation's mini-grid.

At the Lama Foundation in northern New Mexico, active and passive solar design and technologies meet almost all of the community's energy needs. Here, panels pre-heat water at the wash-house, while a nearby greenhouse produces vegetables and heats three rooms behind it.

Aspen A-frame 12V.

Our latest innovation and our proudest achievement in sustainable design resides in the Cottage Industries building. It is virtually self-sufficient. The electricity comes from the central community grid. Three glycol panels heat a radiant floor system along with large, south-facing windows. The indoor temperature, even on the coldest winter days, does not go below 60 degrees Fahrenheit. This allows our silk-screen ink to remain stable and not freeze, which has been a problem in the past. The CI building, which also houses a shower using heated water from the panels, is a very comfortable place to hang out or use a computer.

Using solar electricity does not mean total lack of waste or need for conservation. During extended periods of no sun (which are rare) and/or excessive demand, the batteries can get low enough to cause the propane generator to turn on in order to boost them to full charge. This uses more fossil fuel and shortens the life of the batteries. Panels, batteries, bulbs, cables, etc. all require intensive non-renewable industrial processes to produce, transport, maintain, and dispose of. We do recycle our batteries when they have worn out (though we've had our current store since the early 2000s). In the summer months and the shortest days of winter, residents must be extra conscious of power use so as not to require even more generator use.

For us, using this type of technology and design is a replicable model and has benefits for future generations. Many young people, from children to young adults, who may not have ever seen such systems, become more aware of how humans use and share energy, how that use impacts the system, the possibilities for a post-fossil fuel future, and its potential for low-or no-impact energy use. As a middle-school teacher, I've been able to actually develop a sustainable design curriculum based on the many concepts and applications I've learned at Lama. Doing so has created optimism and right livelihood for myself and a sense that younger generations are open to and even enthusiastic about renewable energy and appropriate technologies replacing the dinosaur of a fossil fuel energy system. I'm grateful to the Lama Foundation for this teaching and feel confident that the community will continue as a center for both the renewal of the spirit and renewal of the planet. ❧

Scott Shuker is has been associated with the Lama Foundation since 1995, joyfully remains a Continuing Member of the organization, and has been a prior contributor to COMMUNITIES *on Lama's behalf. He lives in Santa Fe, New Mexico.*

Loving Earth Sanctuary
Two Women's Quest for a Low-Tech Life

By Gloria Wilson

A newly forming community and innovative rural homestead in the hills of California's Central Coast, Loving Earth Sanctuary is based on the principle of "nourishing ourselves in a way that nourishes all life." Members will reside in their own simple dwellings and together work to pursue a life of land-based sustenance, inner growth, and service/sharing with the broader community.

A central tenet of this project is "radical simplicity," the effort to become more independent from fossil fuels, industrial mining, sweatshop labor, and other modern production systems that harm the Earth and people's health—while also cultivating a sense of abundance and contentment with life's simple joys. A rural life of material simplicity is also intended to free up more time for personal spiritual practice (of any faith or background), creative expression, and voluntary service to others in need. The project's two main founders, Gloria and Dori, are excited to build an egalitarian, consensus-based community on the land, and are open to new prospective members interested in this lifestyle.

In the following article, visionary and cofounder Gloria Wilson shares her own journey and reflects on the decision to live mostly free from modern technology.

My partner and I had a natural inclination toward Luddism from the start. We spent our childhoods dreaming about the "old days" of hand pumps, hen houses, and candlelight. While enamored with stories like *Little House on the Prairie* and *Caddy Woodlawn*, we also were motivated by our own sensitivities to modern life. We both recall how, as children, it was tragic for us to watch stars being consumed by street lights or to see a television replace jovial family dinners; we connected the dots early that technological advancements came with costs.

Nevertheless, culture has a way of ensnaring even the best-intentioned budding visionaries. In spite of our childhood fantasies, it didn't take long before we relied on computers and the internet for networking, information, creative outlet, and to some degree entertainment. Although we hadn't yet met each other, our ideas about technology were evolving on a parallel track. What had begun as hardcore "Amish" sensibility was now morphing into a more con-

ventional reliance on modern gadgets. Although still aware of the detriments posed by industrial life, we found momentary solace in the neo-environmentalists' solution for a greener future: solar panels.

At 15 I moved with my family onto 40 remote acres in the hills, where we put up a yurt and, after a year of mostly electricity-free living, set up a photovoltaic system. Living off-grid in a rural setting, I came into young adulthood optimistic about solar and other high-tech solutions to the myriad of current problems spiraling about my awareness. Convinced that solar provided the only realistic answer to climate change and peak oil, as well as a viable form of resistance to violence in the Middle East, I was able to reconcile my new-found love of internet chat forums and indie movies with my desire for world harmony.

It was, however, a tenuous relationship. On quiet nights in the crevices of time, when cricket sounds oozed through window screens, when I felt whole and complete simply being, I sometimes wondered if I really needed the modern world at all. I contemplated the losses: the mental fluster I felt from an overload of information, and the time spent in a virtual reality rather than the vibrant world around me.

• • •

While I spent balmy nights in the hills writing poetry by candlelight, my future lifemate was going on a journey. After graduating college with a degree in International Agriculture, she went in search of sustainable alternatives to the American Dream. Based on experiences at small farms across the continent, Dori was reaching the conclusion that small-scale local sustenance was one of the most effective means of resisting violence, whether in the form of sweatshop oppression, warfare, or environmental devastation.

But it wasn't until visiting Stillwaters Sanctuary (a project of the Possibility Alliance) in northeast Missouri that she began to question more deeply the role of technology in society and in her own future. Greatly influenced by Ethan and Sarah's commitment to a petroleum- and electricity-free sanctuary, she discovered that independence from computers, electric lights, power machinery, and all the modern appliances we take for granted was not only possible but also deeply gratifying.

At Stillwaters, Dori learned that even solar panels take a toll on the planet, from the mining of raw materials and routine dumping of toxic sludge, to the discarded batteries that store solar energy. She also learned about high cancer rates among computer factory workers, and how the mining of coltan (a component in nearly all electronics) is contributing to regional wars and environmental destruction in Central Africa.

This information was hard for Dori to confront. As a passionate writer, her relationship with computers was a strong one. Not only did the computer serve as an artistic medium, but she also relied on it as a tool for communicating important messages to a world in need of change. Like myself, she had come to believe that the benefits of using such technologies could outweigh the costs.

But after a seven-month internship at Stillwaters, Dori emerged

Illustrations by Dori Stone

with a different perspective. She'd witnessed a community of people living a beautiful, abundant, deeply meaningful life without using any electronics at all. Dori returned home to the Central Coast of California with a vision for founding a similar project in the region where she'd grown up. It was here, after over 20 years of living in the same circle of progressive local artists and activists, that our paths finally crossed.

By this point, I had started thinking seriously about living in a self-sufficient intentional community. Inspired by Gary Snyder's *The Four Changes*, I began to envision a self-sustaining village model for human life on planet Earth. I was already aligned with Dori in her effort to cease consumption of fossil fuels, but it wasn't until hearing about her experience at Stillwaters that I began to question my own views on "green technology." We discussed the impacts of solar panels and computers, from the depletion of rare earth metals to the hazardous e-waste resulting from planned obsolescence (products designed to break down and be replaced).

Ultimately, as much as we both appreciate the value of high technology for art and activism, we had to confront the fact that the "green tech revolution" is just another guise of the industrial revolution, a sly mask for the same oppressive system. Together we reached a shared conclusion that creating a life as free as reasonably possible from electricity is essential to our pursuit of a gentler life—one that not only enriches ourselves but nourishes the health of the planet and other people.

• • •

We know what our ideal looks like: using only materials we can acquire ourselves sustainably from the land where we live, harvested by our own hands. We feel that any system in which resources are extracted in far-off places or assembled by laborers obscured

behind factory walls is too vulnerable to corruption to be preferred over localized production, where we can truly know what we live on.

You may be wondering what I mean by "as free as *reasonably possible*." The truth is, we aren't sure yet ourselves. Having recently bought land (with the help of generous collaborators/supporters John Powell and Aron Heintz) in the Santa Lucia Mountains of coastal California and now on the verge of building community, we've been asking ourselves this very question: What exceptions to the low-tech ideal (if any) are reasonable, appropriate, or necessary for our lives?

Like our friends at Stillwaters, we face unique challenges posed by our land and local region. The criteria for affordable property, near our families and without strict building code enforcement, meant that any land we found would also have certain drawbacks. Our 40 acre parcel is beautiful, off-grid, and has usable wells, but unfortunately is located 35 miles from the nearest substantial town (Paso Robles) and 13 miles from the tiny community of Lockwood.

This presents a transportation conundrum. My parents and brother live up the road and carpool to Paso Robles five days a week for work. Although Dori and I use bicycles and public buses for getting around town, we've been hitching a ride there and back with my family about once per week. (With the exception of this trip between Paso Robles and our land, Dori is basically "car-free" and abstains from riding in personal vehicles, and I only accept rides when the driver is traveling to a particular destination already and has extra space in the car.) It burdens our hearts to be dependent on anybody's ongoing expenditure of fossil fuels, so we're actively considering alternatives. How can we engage with people in the nearest sizable population center, where many of our close family members and friends live, while also staying true to our deepest values?

Determined to try, we recently attempted a bike trip to Paso Robles from our land. The typical car route is 35 miles and takes an hour, but we've deemed that road too dangerous for cycling, so we took the longer but safer 52-mile route. After more than half a day pedaling over rugged terrain and country roads, we stopped 10 miles short of our destination due to a flat tire and intense summer heat. Although it was a fun adventure, we realized that bicycling as our sole form of transportation between the land and town (even just once per week) may not be realistic on an ongoing basis, especially when we consider long-term knee health and other factors in the equation.

This left us to contemplate more creative options. We've pondered the idea of riding to Paso Robles on motorized bicycles fueled by our own homebrew ethanol. We also could pedal from the land to Lockwood in just under two hours and catch a bus there. (Of course we're aware that public buses do run on fossil fuels, and this weighs on our consciences. However, we still consider public transit an acceptable "transition technology" during the shift to more sustainable and localized communities. In spite of its drawbacks, we believe that public transit could reduce modern society's ecological footprint substantially if utilized by more people.) We're also considering a team of mules to carry us to the rural community hall six miles away, and for picking up visitors in a mule-driven cart from the bus stop in Lockwood. One way or another, we're committed to be creative and adapt our lifestyle as necessary in order to live in a rural place with minimal reliance on gasoline or personal vehicles.

Another drawback of our region is the aridity. With no summer rainfall, the only way to establish fruit trees or grow warm season crops is by pumping groundwater for irrigation. Our property's main well already had an electric pump (to be powered by a generator), which we've reluctantly used a couple times for our initial work to restore and clean the well. This summer, we plan to build and install a simple hand-pump and windmill, in order to obtain water with no further use of fossil fuels. We're also eager to set up rain catchment barrels for the roofs of our house and barn.

An additional challenge of our location is that it's completely off-grid, which means no phone lines. (The folks at Stillwaters, although virtually electricity-free, still use a basic land line telephone.) Like our friends in Missouri, we feel that a telephone is a reasonable exception—in lieu of a computer—for coordinating logistics, connecting with others, and getting help in emergencies. Unfortunately, we don't have the option of a land line on our property, so we've resorted to a cell phone instead. We plan to build a cob phone booth with a small salvaged solar panel (and no batteries) to charge the community's phone during daylight hours.

Our phone calls are already kept in moderation by the steep hike to our call-spot, the only area on the land with phone reception, which helps keep the rest of Loving Earth a true sanctuary where people can remain present in their surroundings without the distraction of text messages or ringtones. While owning a high-tech, factory-made cell phone doesn't sit well with us, it's the best way we can think of at the moment to meet our needs for safety and for staying in touch with the broader world.

• • •

Despite the obstacles I've mentioned, the land is full of blessings. Every day I am joyfully reminded of the popular permaculture saying, "the problem is the solution." The fiery heat of the sun cooks our food in a homemade cardboard box solar oven. We've also been utilizing the waste of modern society by cooking on a fuel-efficient rocket stove made from salvaged aluminum cans, which can quickly boil a pot of water by using just a few sticks. Areas of dense brush on our land provide a source of rocket stove fuel, plant medicine, and good fodder for honeybees and native pollinators.

Our rural isolation has also allowed us to develop a more intimate relationship with the land. Recently somebody on the bus advised us to get a TV, unable to fathom how we could be content living "in the boonies" without one. We explained that our land is so rich in beauty it isn't necessary. At dusk we rush to the ridge to catch our favorite evening show—the sun flaming as it sets in a swirl of pinks and amber over the mountain tops. And every night we lie beneath the cinema of the night sky, fading into sleep amidst meteor showers and moonlight.

Yet even in this place of pristine natural beauty, the struggle to define our relationship with modern technology is an ever-present reality. It's a challenge each of us must face, exploring our values and setting our own boundaries. Throughout history the adoption of technology has happened without much thinking; new innovations merely get absorbed into a culture for the convenience they allow in daily life. I believe it's the responsibility of all thinking and compassionate human beings to question the ways we convenience ourselves, deeply considering the costs and benefits each new tool presents.

We live in a time when the benefits are far more discussed and championed than the costs, especially when it comes to "green technology" like electric cars or solar panels. A culture that forgets to watch its own progression is like an elephant with a bag tied over its head, bound to be a force of destruction, not by ill-will but by ignorance. This is what gives me courage to engage in the ongoing struggle for a better way. Like a salmon pushing against the weight of its stream, this struggle is one for life, a struggle we make for future generations. ☙

Gloria Wilson is a philosophy student, writer, naturalist, and cofounder of Loving Earth Sanctuary. To get in touch or request further information, please call 805-235-5547 or write to PO Box 2813, Paso Robles, California 93447.

Problem: In the face of rampant greed and short-sighted self-interest, it's so easy to lose connection to the extraordinary creativity displayed around this planet.

Response: Establish a centralized access point to sources of social and environmental inspiration — enabling activists and organizers, students and citizens to identify and amplify what might help our own acts of creation.

EXEMPLARS!

a free, searchable, living library of what is hopeful,

fascinating, and sustainable.

Visit www.exemplars.world

your portal to designing a sustainable future

Browse the 4 domains of **www.exemplars.world** For each Exemplar, the initial insight, the organizing strategy, tools, outcomes, and a link to websites.

View relevant essays and videos.

Submit Exemplars you have created or know of, as we expand the data base.

1. Cities, towns & communities

2. Businesses and organizations

3. Systemic interventions

4. Cultural sustainability

Curated by Paul Freundlich, pfreundlich@comcast.net

Founder, Green America

Technology in Service of Community

By Lindsay Hagamen and Walt Patrick

In the world of intentional communities, Windward has taken some paths that are different from the norm, and our relationship to technology serves as a good example. From the beginning, we've embraced technology as a way to fund the community through the creation of value.[1] But we've also been mindful of the principle "Technology in service of community, not community in service of technology" as a guide to how to use technology without letting technology use us.

When Windward was founded more than three decades ago, gasoline was 53 cents a gallon; today a gallon of gas costs about four dollars. We've come to see this trend in energy costs as an existential threat for communities like Windward that are located in deep country. We believe that developing technology capable of providing for our core physical needs is an essential part of ensuring Windward's capacity to survive and thrive in the future. As a result, the transformation of low-value materials into value-added products has become the central theme woven into the role that technology plays in the fabric of our community.

Windward's Relationship to Technology

We've come to see sustainable community as something that happens at the intersection of a set of carefully balanced systems. In order to keep that delicate equilibrium in play, we've learned how to weave a suite of technologies into our community's financial and life-support systems. Over the years, we've integrated key forms of social technology into Windward's culture, concepts such as representative consensus[2], freedom of conscience[3], and polyamory[4]. In a similar way, we embrace biological technology in our work growing gardens, raising animals, and stewarding the forest.

The Biomass-2-Methanol[5] process ("B2M" for short) lies at the heart of the community-scale energy technology we're developing. We believe that the on-site conversion of biomass into energy is a rural community's most credible route to achieving a high degree of energy sovereignty.

We've come to see energy sovereignty as a first level community priority for multiple reasons:

• Energy sovereignty protects us from rising energy costs as fossil fuels become more scarce and expensive;

• Access to energy ensures our ability to produce value-added products so that we have things to sell other than our labor;

• On-site fuel production gives us a competitive advantage in getting our products to market and something valuable to trade with our neighbors;

• A solar-based energy system will help shield us from corporate-driven fluctuations in the global economy;

• Developing a local, renewable energy technology manifests our commitment to being responsible stewards of Earth and tribe; and

• Producing our own energy will lessen our complicity in resource wars and economic imperialism.

To elaborate on that last point, we see energy independence as a matter of both ethics and economics. Windward grew out

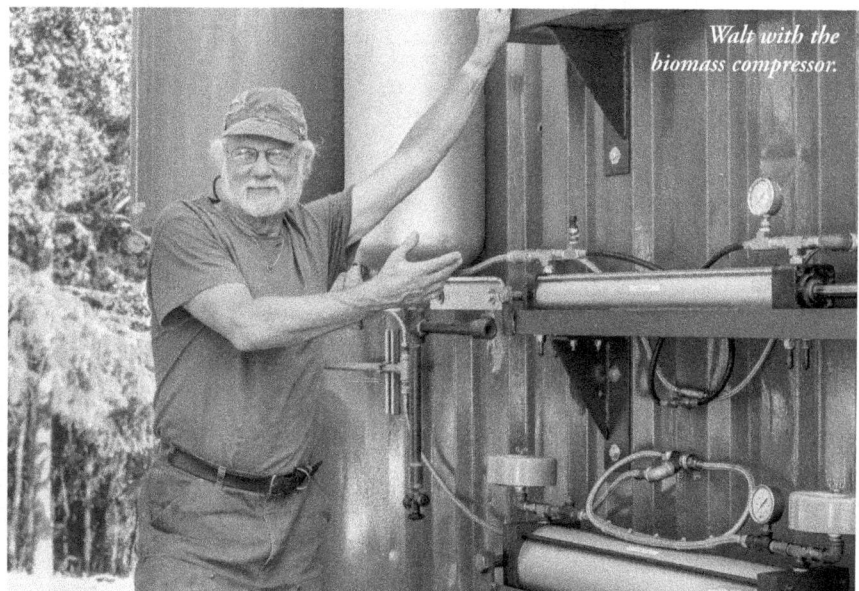

Walt with the biomass compressor.

of the anti-war protests of the 1970s and still embodies a deep desire to avoid being complicit in the resource wars that plague humanity today. For far too long, humanity has been digging coal from the bottom

goes way back. Our community drew its initial vision from Robert Heinlein's *The Moon is a Harsh Mistress.*[9] In turn, Heinlein drew from Upton Sinclair's EPIC Project and John Humphrey Noyes' Oneida Community[10]. Both Sinclair and Noyes were able to fuse cooperative association and technological enterprises in ways that have informed our effort to build on what worked for them. We proudly follow the path they blazed, paying close attention to what they did because it can be fairly argued that their successes created their greatest problems.

> **Too great a focus on technology—making it a priority over community—can lead to organizational collapse when political and economic conditions change.**

We're especially sensitive to the adverse impact that too great a focus on technology can have on a community. Pioneers such as Nancy and Jack Todd of The New Alchemy Institute[11] developed technologies that materially advanced the sustainable community tool set. Others such as Anna Edey of Solviva[12] demonstrated how sustainable food systems can open up profitable new markets in challenging climates. Yet perhaps the most important lesson their experiences drive home for us is how putting technology ahead of community can lead to organizational collapse when political and economic conditions change.

of its grave. We want to be part of creating a future in which energy comes from collecting the rays of the sun[6], not from mining down into the heart of the Earth.

We live in a rural county that produces large amounts of renewable energy[7], and our local power cooperative currently sells us the energy we need to power our washing machine for about a dime a load. Motivated by our long-term quest for energy independence, we take them up on the offer so that for now we can focus on developing the technology that will expand and strengthen our economic foundation.

Windward's Technological Lineage

Windward is no stranger to technology. In the 1980s we operated a foundry in southern Nevada where we transformed metal parts from junked cars into new products. In a sense, we were avid recyclers long before it became fashionable. We have a long-standing tradition of repurposing discarded resources, and it's a calling that we take great pride in. While our work here in south-central Washington State now-a-days revolves around technologies such as permaculture and sylviculture[8], we've learned how to operate our own sawmill, make bricks from our soil, use six different types of welders to maintain our heavy equipment, mix concrete for our buildings, and lots of other useful things. Essentially, we've learned how to use the technologies that best serve our vision and goals. In the process, we've found that most every project we get involved with brings with it an opportunity to expand our technological skill set, and each accomplishment builds our willingness to take on ever greater challenges.

For Windward, the concept of integrating appropriate technology into community life

Biomass to Methanol: Growing a Sustainable Future

The role that energy plays in community was summed up quite well by E. F. Schumacher: "It is impossible to overemphasize its centrality. It might be said that energy is for the mechani-

208

Claire preparing wool using a cyclocarder.

Ruben converts a dead tree into lumber.

Photos courtesy of Walt Patrick

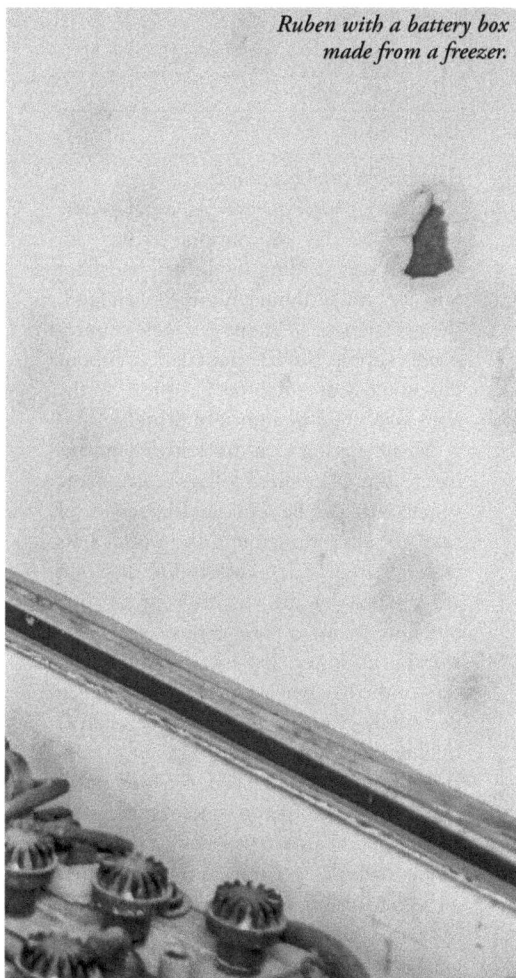

Ruben with a battery box made from a freezer.

cal world what consciousness is for the human world: If energy fails, everything fails."

The historical record shows that the crash of even one core system will threaten a community's survival, something which is especially true for its energy system. The landscape of the American West is littered with ghost towns that once prospered but then crashed when they exhausted some key non-renewable resource. As the age of cheap fossil fuels draws to a close, we believe that developing energy independence is a challenge that communities of all sorts must face.[13]

To ensure that Windward has the ability to meet its future energy needs, we are working through the challenges of converting the dilute energy stored in woody biomass into the concentrated fuels that a rural community like Windward uses and currently needs to buy. Throughout this research and development phase, we are committed to using open-source concepts to show others how to do the same. Each Earth Day, it's become a Windward community tradition to haul some biomass gasification equipment into Portland, Oregon, to show that there really is a homegrown alternative to relying on fossil fuels for energy, and to describe why our research is important to those who live in the city too.[14]

The first step of the B2M process takes advantage of the natural alchemy of photosynthesis: we use self-replicating solar collectors (a.k.a. trees) to capture sunshine, rain, and carbon dioxide in the form of woody biomass. We then process that biomass into wood chips which are versatile, compact, and easy to store.

The next steps are more involved. Gasification of woody biomass produces a fuel called wood gas[15] which can function as a replacement for natural gas and can be used to power our homes and tools. It's fairly straightforward to use wood gas to generate electricity and hot water that are used in the community. However, the subsequent transformation of wood gas into liquid fuels capable of operating cars, trucks, and tractors is more technologically challenging. So we're busy researching and building a prototype for the next step: converting wood gas into fuels that are more concentrated, portable, and biologically safe. Each type of liquid fuel has its pros and cons, but our studies indicate that the production of methanol as a replacement for gasoline[16] is the safest way to fuel community vehicles.

Describing the physical chemistry involved in the B2M process is beyond the scope of this essay.[17] However, this technology will enable Windward, and other communities like it, to produce its own vehicular fuel for community use and barter. The technology is also capable of generating other fuels such as dimethyl ether which can replace the propane and diesel that rural communities currently have to buy.

The B2M process is closely tied to forest stewardship. A forest is a living entity, and living closely with nature drives home the point that living things die. Each spring some trees die when they lose their grip on the saturated soil and blow over. Each winter some trees are killed when freezing rain snaps even full grown trees in half. Some trees die because of insect damage or from disease, and some of that material needs to be selectively cleared out in order to protect the forest's health. Responsible stewardship for our dry-land forest, or for forests that have fire as a natural part of the ecological cycle, also generates a substantial amount of woody biomass as low hanging branches are removed to minimize fire danger, and young trees are thinned out to encourage healthy tree density.

Removing the surplus biomass minimizes the fuel load and reduces the likelihood of a catastrophic forest fire. Instead of just piling it up and burning it, as many do, we're choosing to convert this forest fire hazard into wood gas and other more concentrated fuels that can be used to serve the visions and goals of the community.

Scale and Scope of B2M Technology

The sustainable production of methanol is an ambitious project, but fortunately, we're able to build on time-tested technology.[18] Indeed, little of the work we're doing involves inventing new technology, since gasification of coal was understood and widely used more than a century ago. Back then, most cities used gasification to convert coal into the gas that lit their street lights and cooked their food. Gasification was abandoned when a tsunami of petroleum swamped the world's energy systems, but with the rising cost of oil, gasification is poised to make a comeback. Much of the work that needs to be done now involves figuring out how to use woody biomass instead of coal, and then how to scale down and automate the production of methanol.

Still, it's a matter of scale. The gasification of woody biomass is limited[19] in ways that prevent it from being expanded into some desperate mega-system in order to replace oil in hopes of keeping the industrial-consumer complex going a bit longer. We're happy that B2M is a local-scale technology that's inherently limited to keeping an intentional community's lights on, its homes warm, and its goods moving to market.

Another benefit is that good stewardship results in a healthy forest that produces lots of biomass. That enables increased methanol production as a reward for good stewardship. Modern logging practices involve cutting down and hauling away whole trees including the vital micronutrients bound up in the wood.[20] That practice effectively strip mines

> Gasification was abandoned when a tsunami of petroleum swamped the world's energy systems, but with the rising cost of oil, gasification is poised to make a comeback.

the forest of the minerals trees need to live. On-site gasification retains those minerals on-site in the form of wood ash, a potent fertilizer[21] that is then returned to the forest to support new growth.

People who live in the city are impacted by the state of rural economies too. For example, rural people who abandon their land and move to the city because they can no longer afford the costs of rural life end up competing for jobs, housing, and all the other resources that support city life. Urban life is further impacted because life in the city depends on the resources produced by people living out on the front lines of land stewardship. B2M allows rural people to be the start of the fuel supply chain, instead of being stuck at the tail end—transforming the state of rural economies.

For city people to prosper, rural people need to be able to continue living with the land and sending food, fuel, and fiber into the city. Without country-grown food, the city starves. Without the fuels country people supply, the city goes dark. Without the watersheds rural people protect, the city's water becomes unfit to drink.

We are aiming to address these concerns by creating a localized village-scale energy system that can be replicated in service of rural communities around the world. Lots of people want to go back to the land, but are stymied by the challenge of figuring out how to meet their core needs. We're working to lower that barrier in anticipation of the day when solitary consumerism necessarily gives way to a new generation of intentional communities.

B2M is being developed as a well documented, open-source technology that can be copied wherever people have biomass to utilize—whether it's in the form of rice hulls or beetle-killed trees, logging waste or water hyacinths. Gasification is a process that separates the nutrients derived from the atmosphere[22] from the nutrients derived from the

Andrew with his home-built seed ball maker.

land[23] so that the former can be converted into fuel and the latter can be returned to support the next cycle of growth.

An Invitation to Support the Research

It's fine with us that this technology is not suitable for commercial exploitation.[24] We're not in this for the money—what we want is a reliable way to be able to meet our energy needs without doing harm. So rather than pursue government grants or bring in venture capitalists, we've embraced open-source funding. This path enables Windward's True Fans to accelerate our open-source research by providing recurring donations of as little as $10/month. We liken this funding approach to drip irrigation in that the money comes in at a steady rate, funds that we can use to purchase the parts needed to build the prototype. If you find the work we're doing to be worthwhile and you would enjoy having a front-row seat as it unfolds, we invite you to become a True Fan.[25]

In closing, we want to emphasize that technology is not a substitute for sound communitarian principles and sustainable ecological practices. Indeed, we see love, affection, and commitment as the qualities most essential to building a working model of what we think of as Love Based Living. But we also understand that it's much easier to manifest those qualities in a community that's well-lit and comfortable. We know

Claire getting firewood ready for winter.

that the future will not be simple; serious challenges lie ahead. But we also know that a hot bath, clean clothes, and a warm bed will help us face that future with deeper compassion, greater persistence—and more joy. ❧

Lindsay Hagamen is the President of the Windward Foundation and spends her time caring for the land and the people who tend to the land. Lindsay teaches permaculture and social permaculture in the Pacific Northwest and is a co-editor of an upcoming book on Ecosexuality. She is also the co-creator of the the EcoSex Convergence, an annual event that builds community around loving the Earth and one another (www.ecosexconvergence.org).

Walt Patrick is a founder of the Windward community with more than 30 years of full-time involvement in studying and creating intentional community. Since stepping down as Windward's lead director in 2011, Walt has focused on ensuring the community's long-term energy security through the conversion of woody biomass into the heat, power, and fuel a sustainable community needs in order to thrive (www.biomass2methanol.org).

1. Instead of striving to make money, our experience is that our long-term security is better served by focusing on ways to create value.
2. Representative consensus is a system of governance in which the members choose a committee that then develops a working consensus. For more details, see Windward's By-Laws at www.windward.org/windward/bylaws.htm.
3. The spiritual path which each member follows is a personal matter; nature is the only "higher authority" the community recognizes.
4. Many, but not all of our members practice polyamory, the practice of loving more than one person.
5. For detailed information, see www.biomass2methanol.org.
6. Using natural collectors such as trees instead of industrial products such as photovoltaic panels.
7. Deeply rural Klickitat County, home to 20,000 people, draws hydroelectric power from the Columbia River, has a string of wind turbines 26 miles long, and generates 27 Megawatts of power from its state-of-the-art landfill. Currently one third of the county's tax base is comprised of giant wind turbines.
8. "The cultivation of forest trees for timber or other purposes." (www.thefreedictionary.com/sylviculture)
9. End Poverty In California; see en.wikipedia.org/wiki/End_Poverty_in_California_movement.
10. See en.wikipedia.org/wiki/Oneida_Community.
11. See en.wikipedia.org/wiki/New_Alchemy_Institute.
12. See www.solviva.com.
13. White's Law, one of the core concepts of human ecology, tells us that, other factors remaining constant, culture evolves as the amount of energy harnessed per capita per year is increased.
14. See www.biomass2methanol.org/earthday2014.htm.
15. Wood gas contains carbon monoxide and hydrogen; natural gas contains methane.
16. Methanol contains 60 percent as much energy as gasoline, so more is required to go the same distance.
17 For loads of technical details, see www.biomass2methanol.org.
18. During World War II, more than a million vehicles ran on wood gas.
19 The energy density of woody biomass is so low that the energy required to transport it any notable distance exceeds the net energy in the biomass.
20. The mineral content of wood runs around four percent by dry weight.
21. Prior to the development of fossil-fuel based fertilizers, wood ash was the primary fertilizer available.
22. Carbon, Oxygen, and Hydrogen.
23. Magnesium, Calcium, Potassium, Phosphorus, Sulfur, Nitrogen, Boron, Copper, Iron, Manganese, Molybdenum, and Zinc.
24. Woody biomass lacks the energy density needed to justify the cost of long distance transport.
25. See www.biomass2methanol.org/support01.htm.

Life with the Solar Kitchen

By Frederick Weihe

A few years ago, we prepared ourselves for a radical experiment in energy sovereignty here in the Tamera Solar Village (Portugal). We had everything we needed to take our Solar Kitchen off-grid. With a group of people committed to live from food prepared only by a combination of solar thermal, biogas, and human labor, we entered into a period of discussion and communitarian decision-making—and all the nerves and excitement that accompany such a revolutionary step.

When there was nothing left but to go for it, we took a deep breath and...it was easy. In fact, it's hard now to remember what the fuss was all about, and the "experiment" never stopped. The Solar Kitchen is open to the elements and doesn't operate during the rainy winter season, but otherwise it is now simply one of our community kitchens, preparing food for up to 50 people every day. When people think of the Solar Kitchen today, they think of the tasty vegan food; the quirky, charming chef; the airy and comfortable seating areas for meals and gatherings. Guests in Tamera love to join the cooking team, not for a chance at the noble suffering of low-tech food-prep, but because the Solar Village is a nice place to be. The Scheffler mirror and biogas systems are beautiful, easy-to-use technologies with personalities.

These technologies are a success in our decentralized energy research. They *work*, and not only in the technical sense. As I'll describe, they support human beings living in cooperation with one another and with the cycles and rhythms of nature. These tools are firmly established in the life of the community, and they bring joy.

One of my jobs every day is to collect organic material to feed the biogas system....and already this puts me into contact with the logic of nature, in which nothing is wasted. What might otherwise be "trash"—kitchen scraps, leftovers, garden cuttings—have become valuable resources, wanted for the animals, for compost piles, and for our biogas system. I see, first hand, how this challenges the *buying, using, then throwing away* system of consumerism, and turns it into a flowing, regenerative cycle that supports the garden, the community, and the environment.

This job also brings me in contact with the other kitchens in Tamera, from which we get a lot of the raw materials for "Hulda" (the name of our biogas digester). I visit the large Campus Kitchen a few times a week, with its changing team of community members

Jessica the cook, at work in Tamera's Solar Kitchen.

and guests. The biogas-food containers are well-labeled but look a lot like trash-cans; I am constantly reminded—when I find cigarette butts and plastic wrappers in with the precious, energy-rich organic material—how deeply entrenched are the unconscious behaviors of disposable consumerism. The biogas system and I are educators, inviting people to participate in building a culture in which we take responsibility for everything we produce and consume...a world of closed natural cycles; a world without bottomless, throw-it-away-and-forget-it dumpsters; a society without hidden landfills on the edge of town full of toxic waste.

The Solar Kitchen interacts in a deep and dynamic way with the cooks and their helpers, too. New cooks typically think of the menu first, and then try to figure out how to make it. Often this is possible: thanks to the big mirror and Hulda, hot stoves are available almost all the time. But the Scheffler and the biogas do encourage some adjustment of styles; what ends up on the tables depends on the weather, the time of day, and Hulda's feeding schedule and changing gas levels. Some cooks experience this as a limitation; for others—for example our main "kitchen chief" Jessica—it is a part of the natural rhythm of life, like the seasons that bring different fruits and vegetables from the garden.

These are some of the reasons why the Scheffler mirror and the biogas system are such success stories in our research: not merely because they work well on the technological level, but because they fit into a more holistic picture, of sustainable community life in cooperation with nature. In fact, they don't only fit this new picture; they encourage and create it. They don't just let people feel ecologically righteous; they help people feel happy. They represent, for me, a step towards a kind of spiritual ergonomics, of which engineering and efficiency are only a part.

Our work includes the engineering and efficiency too, but that work can be done anywhere. Here we have a functioning community with a commitment to peace and sustainability: we can experience how the technology fits into our daily lives, in a meaningful human, ecological, and political context. We see and experience how people use the tools, and then we can go back to the lab and workshop to make refinements. The result is relevant for communities throughout the world. What we learn about these relationships between people, community, and technology can further inform our active research in other technologies, such as Stirling motors, heat-energy storage, innovative solar collectors, and resilient systems combining these different elements. Other groups are doing

wells and fireplaces, hearths and spring houses, gardens and stone circles, would not have acknowledged the distinction between technology and art, between doctors and shamans. I don't know if I believe in nature-spirits literally; what's important to me is the idea that objects made by clever human hands remain part of the natural world, fully in the flow of the cosmos. The fashioning of tools would not have been labeled or compartmentalized as "technology," but was rather a natural community activity. The ancient Celtic builders of Stonehenge—with all its marvels of stone-moving and astronomical precision—would not have been called astronomers or masons, but *druids*. Or probably just *people*.

This spiritual question is often with me, but I have to confess that the answers are still a long way away. I cannot claim to sense an invisible presence in the Scheffler mirror, the way I feel such a presence in a grandfather oak, or at our Oracle Spring pool. With its living, gurgling bio-mimicry, Hulda comes closer for some people; they sense it as alive. For my part, I can say that the question remains as a compass point, a question to walk with: How can we overcome the separation between human beings and the things they make? Sometimes I think we need to create rituals of inauguration, as our ancestors would have done, but I have a hard time really picturing what these would be. We are so deeply conditioned by industrial culture—in which people make tools to exploit nature—that it's hard to imagine how anything else would feel. Technology has become so fundamentally violent that sometimes I have real doubts about my profession.

But there are positive role-models: gardeners for example, and more specifically the Permaculturists, who do not exploit living systems but instead cooperate with them, in a way that makes those systems more alive and abundant while better serving human needs. My goal as a tech-

> My goal as a technologist is not to extract energy or exploit resources, but rather to intelligently and gently participate in the natural flows of energies, to serve life and my community.

good and important work, but few are doing *this* work, of developing community technology in community.

By the way, I don't use the word *spiritual* lightly. For our aboriginal ancestors, it would have been natural for human-built objects to be inhabited by unseen beings, in the same way spirits lived in trees, stones, and streams. But the ancient creators of

nologist is therefore not to extract energy or exploit resources, but rather to intelligently and gently participate in the natural flows of energies, to serve life and my community. We can and do talk about the kilowatts per square meter of sunshine, the UV resistance of fluoropolymers, how to get the hydrogen sulfide out of the biogas, and so on, but these discussions can lead to real, sustainable solutions only if we get the human and spiritual basics right.

To put it another way: technology carries information. All technologies, and the ways we use them, emerge from specific beliefs and narratives. Unless the tools and techniques are

(continued on p. 75)

Collaborators and Resources

Much of the technology used in Tamera has been developed in collaboration with cooperation partners. For more information about the Tamera Solar Village, please visit www.tamera.org/project-groups/autonomy-technology. For details about the Scheffler Mirror, see www.tamera.org/project-groups/autonomy-technology/scheffler-reflector, and visit the innovators behind it at Solar Bruecke: www.solare-bruecke.org. For more about our biogas system, see www.tamera.org/project-groups/autonomy-technology/biogas. For even more information about biogas as an energy solution for communities around the world, visit T. H. Culhane at www.solarcities.blogspot.com.

Author feeding the biogas system, with the Scheffler mirror in the background.

Photos courtesy of Frederick Weihe

LIFE WITH THE SOLAR KITCHEN

(continued from p. 53)

chosen carefully, they will tend to reinforce those unconscious beliefs and narratives. An individual family kitchen with plug-in appliances and a fridge full of grocery-store food is like a guide to a particular lifestyle, and a library of information about Western culture. Whether we are aware of it or not, technology contains a culture's answers to specific questions: What are the basic social units of civilization? What is energy and where does energy come from? What is the role of food in human relationships? What is the relationship between the human being and the living earth, from which all water, food, and energy come? Improving a technology that supports a lifestyle of alienated consumerism, to make it more energy-efficient for example, may be better than the alternative...at least in the short term. But it is not truly sustainable, because the lifestyle it serves is not sustainable.

The Solar Kitchen carries different information. It is a community kitchen, and this already is a revolutionary choice: we work together, cook together, share meals together. Our cooked food is prepared with the sun; we feel the immediate connection between our lives and the sky. Through the biogas system, we are in contact with the flowing rhythms of growth and decay. The tools can all be made with local materials and skills anywhere in the world, without relying on a globalized system of money and control. And simply by having our energy sources in our own hands, we are automatically more conscious of how we use energy.

My goal as part of the Technology Group is to support the emergence of a sustainable way of living which is not only more ethical, but truly more joyful and attractive than consumerism, with pleasures and luxuries that everyone on earth can have. And beyond this, we want to create awareness...through outreach and education of course, but also simply by sharing the technology itself. This automatically carries information: a community can build a kitchen for sure, but the right kitchen can also help build a community.

When I make morning coffee on the biogas, and watch Jessica elegantly swing the big gleaming mirror into place at the beginning of her cooking shift, ready to prepare lunch for gardeners, guests, students, craftspeople, technologists, and other community members, I know that this kind of kitchen can protect resources and nourish community anywhere. There's still a lot to be learned, more work to be done. But we have already created something that we love, and something we can share; we are on a good path. ❧

Frederick Weihe lives in Tamera, a community in southern Portugal. Born and raised in the United States, he has been living and working in Europe since 2000. He blogs occasionally at www.physicsforpeaceworkers.org.

A major new book series from the Fellowship for Intentional Community...

Wisdom of Communities

Each 8½"x11" book features between 300 and 400 pages of topical articles drawn mostly from COMMUNITIES magazine, intended to aid community founders, seekers, current communitarians, and students of intentional community in their explorations.

Volume 1, *Starting a Community: Resources and Stories about Creating and Exploring Intentional Community* includes both general articles and on-the-ground stories from intentional community founders and other catalysts of cooperative efforts.

Volume 2, *Finding a Community: Resources and Stories about Seeking and Joining Intentional Community* shares authors' experiences, tools, advice, and perspectives relevant to anyone searching for an intentional community to visit or to live in.

Volume 3, *Communication in Community: Resources and Stories about the Human Dimension of Cooperative Culture* includes articles about decision-making, governance, power, gender, class, race, relationships, intimacy, politics, and neighbor relations in cooperative group culture.

Volume 4, *Sustainability in Community: Resources and Stories about Creating Eco-Resilience in Intentional Community* focuses on food, water, permaculture, shelter, energy, ecological footprint, ecovillage design, eco-education, and resilience in cooperative culture.

Volumes 1 and 2 meet the need for one-stop collections of stories to help founders and seekers. Volumes 3 and 4 are primers on the variety of "soft" and "hard" skills and approaches that allow intentional communities and their members to endure, evolve, and thrive.

These books should broaden anyone's outlook on what is possible, how to pursue their dreams of community, and how to make their own lives and their communities models for a more cooperative, resilient culture—one that draws from the past while working toward a better future.

To order, please visit
**www.ic.org/community-bookstore/product/
wisdom-of-communities-volumes-1-2-3-4-complete-set**
(or search for individual volume pages as they are published in March, May, August, and October)

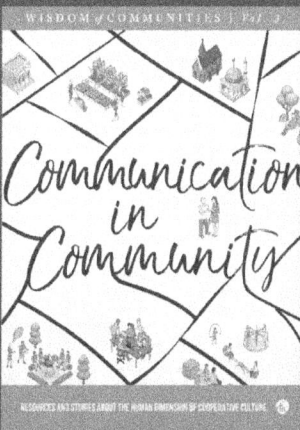

Living Energy Farm:
An Answer for Climate Change

By Alexis Zeigler

Living Energy Farm (Louisa, Virginia) is a community of people who support themselves without the use of fossil fuel. Our project has been built at modest cost so it can be replicated around the world. Living Energy Farm is a fully operational farm and community, not just an idea. LEF empowers us to dramatically reduce our dependence on the corporate economy, and it represents a viable solution to climate change.

There is a great departure between the physics of renewable energy and the politics of renewable energy. For the most part, renewable energy does not work on the individual level, nor does it work on the industrial level. Village-level use of renewable energy allows for a level of centralization and integration that makes renewable energy work fantastically well.

We have cooperative housing at LEF, not free-standing, single family houses, not "tiny houses." Cooperative use of resources is by far our most important "technology." Shared use allows us to acquire and build and integrate much, much better housing, water, and agricultural systems, and the various tools we need to support ourselves.

We build with straw bales by simply stacking them inside of a stud-frame wall. This is a fast and cheap way to build super-insulated buildings. This style of building is also well suited to large crews of unskilled workers who show up at community building parties. We can afford good insulation because we have pooled the labor and money of the people who share the use of the house. Our solar heating and cooling systems are both highly effective for us, and impractical for small houses.

At LEF, our main solar rack is six 30 volt photovoltaic solar electric (PV) panels. They are stacked in series. When you stack PV panels in series, just as when you stack batteries in a flashlight, the voltage adds up. So 6 X 30 V = 180 volts. Industrial motors are easily found for 90 V and 180 V DC. High voltage allows us to use small wires, and high voltage motors are cheaper and more durable than low voltage.

Storing electricity is expensive. The national electrical grid is powered mostly by massive coal plants that run all day and night. Constantly generating electrical power means they don't have to store it. But that comes at enormous environmental costs. Off-grid houses, on the other hand, usually rely on PV and use large sets of lead-acid batteries which are toxic, explosive, and short-lived. That is a poor solution.

At LEF, we do not have lead-acid batteries to support our houses or agricultural buildings. At LEF, we do not have any AC outlets or inverters because we don't need them and because such outlets are too easily treated as free energy, and thus encourage excessive use of electronic gadgetry. A lot of off-grid designs fail when the users plug in too many gadgets.

At LEF, we use electricity in two ways. The 180 volt PV rack supports "direct drive" equipment. That means a wire runs from the PV panels to the motors directly. That means no batteries necessary, no fancy electronics, no computerized controllers or thermostats, nothing but DC motors tied directly to the PV panel. The design of the DC motors has not changed since the 1800s. With direct

Solar cookers at LEF.

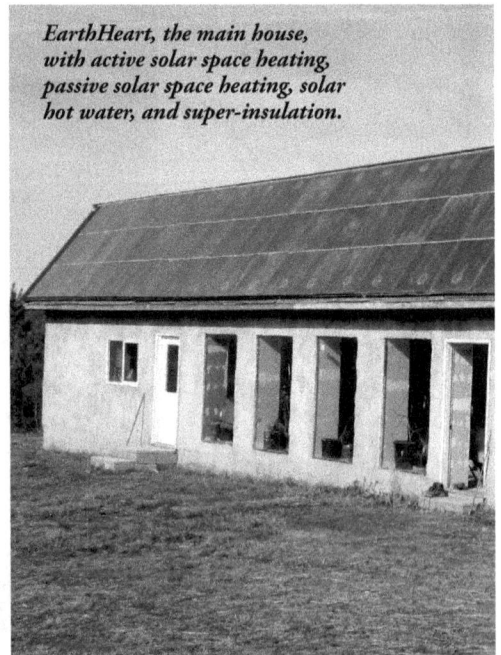

EarthHeart, the main house, with active solar space heating, passive solar space heating, solar hot water, and super-insulation.

Photos courtesy of Alexis Zeigler

drive, sun comes up, motors run. Sun goes down, motors stop. It's that simple. (We also use some smaller, modern DC "brushless" motors. Brushless motors are durable, but they are not available in larger sizes. They are also black boxes. If they stop working, there is nothing you can do about it. Brush motors are a simpler technology, though they do require some maintenance.)

An interesting difference between AC and DC equipment is that DC equipment tolerates overloading while AC does not. Imagine you wanted to accomplish a particular task, say grinding grain for instance. If you use an AC motor, then the instant there is any weakness—if the batteries fade or the inverter gets overloaded—the system shuts down. At LEF, our main 180 volt PV rack has a nominal output of about 1.5 horsepower. But with DC motors, they tolerate a huge range of power and voltage input. We can run motors when the sky is cloudy. The motors slow down, but they keep working. We can severely overload the system, turning on numerous motors adding up to two or three horsepower. Each motor slows a bit, but they still keep doing their job. Nothing shuts down until the sun goes down.

Our goal with our direct drive economy is to build machines that are cheap and effective, and to store energy in forms other than electricity. At LEF, we have slightly larger than normal water storage tanks. We have a DC well pump, not an AC pump, wired to our 180 volt PV rack. (Sun Pumps, Robison, and Grundfos are the companies with high-quality DC pumps.) Once or twice a day, we turn a small timer and charge the storage tanks. The

Food dried in the solar drier, a staple at LEF.

Lighting in the living room: 24 watts lights up a large space.

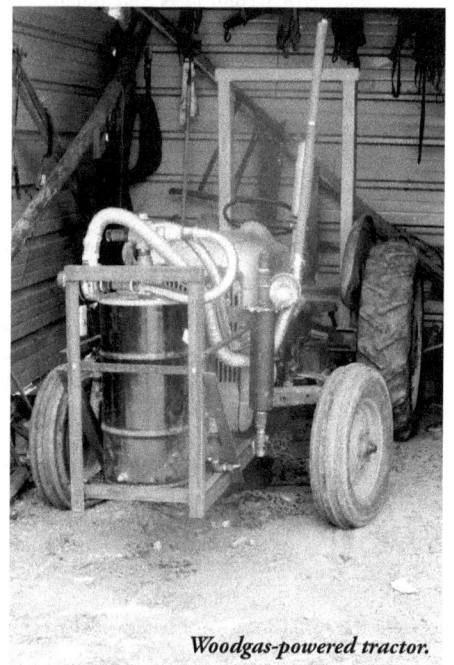
Woodgas-powered tractor.

217

pressure does fluctuate, and we have pay attention to what we are doing relative to the weather. That being said, we have all the water we need for domestic use and agricultural irrigation needs. There is certainly some embedded energy cost in making the equipment we use, but once installed we can use that equipment as much as we want without creating any pollution whatsoever. We have a high-output, reliable water system at about 10 percent of the cost of the "normal" off-grid model. The "integration" part comes in with all the other uses we get out of that 180 volt rack.

We have homemade, cheap, solar hot air collectors on the roofs of our kitchen and the main house. (The kitchen is separate from the main house in southern dog-trot tradition, thus keeping the heat out of the house when we are cooking and canning in summer). We have 180 volt direct-drive blowers that pull heat off of these hot air collectors and pass through coarse rock under the house and the kitchen. Again, the blowers simply come on and go off

teries, no fancy electronics.

At LEF, we use 12 V DC LEDs for lighting at night. Candles and lanterns would in theory be another option, but for daily use they are neither cheap nor effective. Also, burning your house down is not particulaly sustainable. DC LEDs are tremendously efficient. It takes two three-watt bulbs (six watts!) to light a room well enough to read the fine print in a book in the evening. The DC LEDs we use are, like the DC motors, tolerant of voltage variation. The LEDs we have are mostly rated for nine to 30 volts. A larger community would benefit from a 24 volt system for lighitng.

To power our LEDs, we use nickel-iron (NiFe) batteries. NiFes have an interesting history. We have a battery from an old miner's lamp that is decades old. It was made by Thomas Edison's company and has his signature right on the side of it. The amazing thing about this ancient relic is that it still works! NiFe batteries last a long, long time. To our knowledge, they are the only battery technology ever developed that does not degrade with each charge cycle. That, in theory, gives them an infinite lifespan, but in practice that's not quite true. Lead-acid batteries are delicate compared to NiFes. Lead-acid batteries are damaged by too much discharge of current. With NiFes, you can discharge them all you want and not hurt them.

NiFes were in heavy use in industry 50 years ago. If they are so good, why are they not used more? There are a couple of answers to that question. NiFes are large, heavy, and expensive relative to their power output. They are the opposite of a cell phone battery in every way. The modern power-hungry world has opted for short-lived, high-output, compact batteries instead.

In moving toward taking the LEF model to villages around the world, we realized that people living in non-industrial societies are often reliant on cell phones. If we in Virginia separate ourselves from commercial media, it is no big deal as we have numerous other means of access to information and resources. We cannot demand the same of villagers around the world. To test our low-voltage NiFe system, we have tied an automotive cell phone charger (as would plug into a cigarette lighter in a car) into out 12 V NiFe lighting system. We have found that we can charge as many cell phones and personal devices as we want, for ourselves, interns, and visitors, and the system has held up well. Charging directly from DC to DC (without going through an inverter) is much more efficient.

> ## We have been led to believe that living sustainably is difficult, expensive, reliant on new technologies, and involves personal discomfort. None of that is true.

with the sun. "Normal" solar heat storage has historically involved bizarrely complex systems using storage tanks, rock beds, and all manner of computerized controllers and pumps. We skip all that. The high-tech storage medium under the floor at LEF is dirt.

In the summer, the irrigation water headed to the fields passes through the house first, sucking the heat out of the house on its way. Presto: free air conditioning. This, again, is something that only works on a village level.

Our 180 volt solar rack also powers any mechanical devices we need. These include a grinder that grinds our grains into flour, as well as all manner of woodworking and metalworking machines. We can run any of the woodworking or metalworking equipment you would find in a woodshop or machine shop with our 180 volt DC motors.

Our bottom-line fuel is firewood. We use very little firewood compared to other "homesteaders," but we do use some. We collect dead wood, and cut it with manual cross-cut saws in the forest to get it small enough to haul home. (That's quick and easy.) Then we have a 180 volt DC buzz saw (buck saw) that efficiently cuts the wood into stove lengths. The saw is faster, and less dangerous, than a chainsaw. And it runs on sunshine, direct-drive, no bat-

We earn our living growing open-pollinated seeds that we sell in bulk to seed companies. To plow our fields, we use a woodgas tractor. Woodgas was the technology that kept Europe from starving during World War II. When Europe was cut off from fossil fuel in the war, much of the agricultural equipment was switched to woodgas. It is a complex and fussy process compared to other biofuels, but the feedstock (woodchips) does not compete with poor people's food as is the case of biodiesel and ethanol. Woodgas is made easier by the fact that thousands of people are using it, there are email lists for information, and several companies are making equipment. Our bylaws say that we use woodgas on the farm only. There is no biofuel that can power the American fleet of cars sustainably, and anyone who tells you otherwise is lying.

We have had draft animals on the property, and may again in order to assess their sustainability. Draft animals are much better from a self-sufficiency standpoint, as they can eat grass and regenerate themselves. But from a global sustainability standpoint, small tractors (in addition to hand work) are probably more sustainable than draft animals. Humans and our domestic animals now comprise a stunning 96 percent of the terrestrial zoomass (total weight of animals) on the planet Earth. Of everything we do, keeping so many ruminants makes them the largest single contributor to both species extinction and greenhouse gases. Draft animals are often integrated into the food production system of traditional farms. We favor a diet that contains as much home-grown food as possible. Given the financial and environmental costs of animal-based foods, both on our farm and the world at large, our diet is primarily focused around plant foods. Even though draft animals are clearly much less industrial than a small tractor, the tractor is probably more sustainable in a world of 7.5 billion people.

Finding sustainable and pleasant ways to cook food has been our biggest challenge. Currently we use both solar ovens and solar parabolic cookers. The parabolic cookers are less well-known, but more effective. They cook better in sub-optimal conditions. Numerous companies make models for sale, and they are not hard to build. Solar ovens can be purchased or homemade, but they need to be well designed to work well.

When there is not enough sunshine, we use a number of different wood cookers. Rocket stoves are the most efficient, though as with solar ovens, good design matters. (Stovetecs are great.) We have a little oven called a Butterfly that sits on top of any woodstove. It works okay. We have an Amish-made wood-fired canner that works great. It allows us to can a lot of food very quickly and efficiently in late summer. (Made by D.S. Machine in Pennsylvania; no website.)

We grow a lot of our own food. Some of our seed crops (like peppers) supply both food and seeds at the same time. We grow a lot of vegetables, and we are expanding our production of staple foods. We also grow naturally disease-resistant fruit and nut trees. Trees are one of the most resilient forms of agriculture because they have such enormous root systems. Tree foods also represent a zero soil erosion form of agriculture. We have done a lot of work to figure out which tree foods work well.

Growing all that food means we need to preserve some of it. The solar heating system for the kitchen doubles as industrial-scale food dryer (more systems integration that is only possible in a village). We simply divert the air that would normally be forced under the floor through a closet around the blower. The air is heated with sunshine and blown about with 180 V DC power. We can stack many layers of food-drying screens in the closet around the blower. We can dry large volumes of food quickly and efficiently, and with zero emissions.

We have been led to believe that living sustainably or reducing our "carbon footprint" is difficult, expensive, reliant on new technologies, and involves personal discomfort. None of that is true. Living a comfortable and happy life supported by renewable energy is easy if we are willing to adjust our lifestyles to the rhythms of nature. That's not what we are doing currently. The reality is that most of the people in the world today live a low-impact lifestyle because they cannot afford otherwise. Poorer people all over the world share resources and support each other. But consumption is power, and in order to hold onto that power, we hide behind grid-tied solar electricity, windmills, grass-fed beef, and a host of other layers of pale green paint slathered over consumer society. Real sustainability means that we have to share resources and live with some degree of modesty. And we have to call the Earth sacred. It is clear that mountains of facts will not convince us to change. We are destroying the sacred living Earth even as we sit and jabber about the ecological holocaust. The answers are not difficult. It is time we embrace them.

Born on a largely self-sufficient farm in rural Georgia, Alexis Zeigler is a self-taught activist, builder, mechanic, writer, and orchardist. He has organized numerous successful campaigns focusing on political, environmental, and economic localization issues. He is currently helping to build Living Energy Farm (livingenergyfarm.org), a zero-fossil-fuel farm aiming to be economically self-sufficient. He released the book Integrated Activism *(North Atlantic Books) in 2013.*

Direct-drive solar tools, grain grinder (in use), compressor, and bench grinder.

NiFe batteries: robust, nontoxic, and long-lasting, they power LED lighting at LEF.

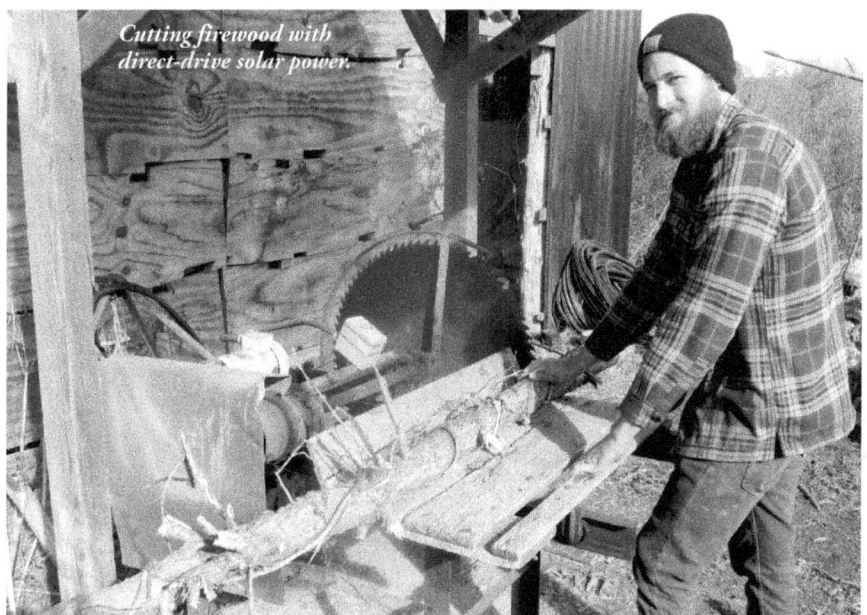

Cutting firewood with direct-drive solar power.

Limiting the Damage of Climate Change:
LESSONS FROM DANCING RABBIT

By Ma'ikwe Ludwig

Note: this article is adapted from the forthcoming book, Together Resilient: Building Community in the Age of Climate Disruption, *available from the ic.org website, May 2017.*

Communities—whether intentional, traditional, or formed in response to crisis—have a major advantage over individual efforts to address climate change: the ability to leverage sharing and cooperation as main tools for becoming more ecological. In my 2013 TEDx talk (www.youtube.com/watch?v=BS8YeDKKBcU), I dubbed cooperation the "Mother of All Sustainability Skills." Note that I frame it as a skill. Skills are learnable, and require regular practice to get (and stay) good at them. While cooperation is not a skill we are taught very much in our American education system, community living provides an immersive course in it. The members of almost any intentional community endeavor are going to have a lower ecological and carbon footprint than most of their go-it-alone neighbors are, because all communities share and cooperate to some extent.

Dancing Rabbit Ecovillage: A Case Study

The community that I know the best is Dancing Rabbit Ecovillage. I first visited DR in the spring of 1998 (the spring after the founders bought a piece of rough land in rural Missouri that had most recently been an abandoned pig farm). Thus commenced a very slow-motion courting process with the community: visiting, living there for short stints, going away again to try to form community somewhere else, visiting again, and then finally in 2008 moving back and staying for over eight years. I got to see a community go from the visionary stage, with Tony Sirna and Cecil Scheib saying to a group of us the first time I toured the community, "Someday a whole village will be here!," to being myself a central community member of that village and its nonprofit, living and breathing the reality of sustainability.

The founders did a lot of things right. Bucking conventional wisdom (or perhaps more fairly, stereotypes) these just-graduated-from-college smart young folks started from a place of relative humility and sought out a pre-existing community to be a mentor for them. That community, Sandhill Farm, had been started in 1974 by a group that included the Fellowship for Intentional Community's primary staffer for several decades, Laird Schaub. Laird is an expert in social dynamics, and

between the basic sensibility of our founders, Laird's wise counsel, and the lived experience of all the Sandhill members, Dancing Rabbit understood early on that the social dimension was incredibly important. (In fact, it is the most common place of failure in trying to have viable community. Most groups that fail do so because of a breakdown in conflict resolution skills, lack of facilitation skills to keep decision-making moving along in a solid way, or a general lack of understanding of the immense cultural shift they are taking on in moving from a competitive to a cooperative framework.)

The founders also set some very high bars on the ecological front for people joining. Six ecological covenants form the central agreements people make with each other and the community when they join. Here's the current iteration of those:

1. Dancing Rabbit members will not use personal motorized vehicles, or store them on Dancing Rabbit property.

2. At Dancing Rabbit, fossil fuels will not be applied to the following uses: powering vehicles, space-heating and -cooling, refrigeration, and heating domestic water.

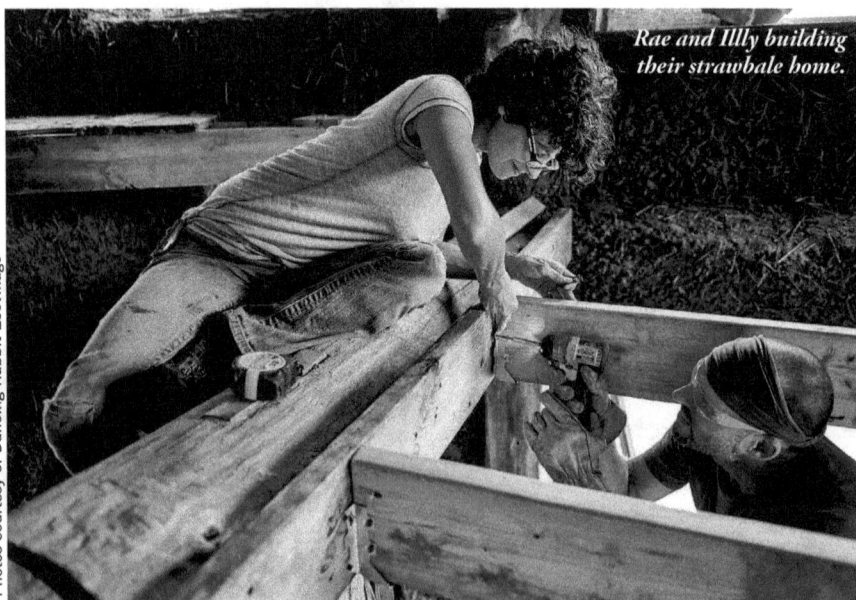
Rae and Illly building their strawbale home.

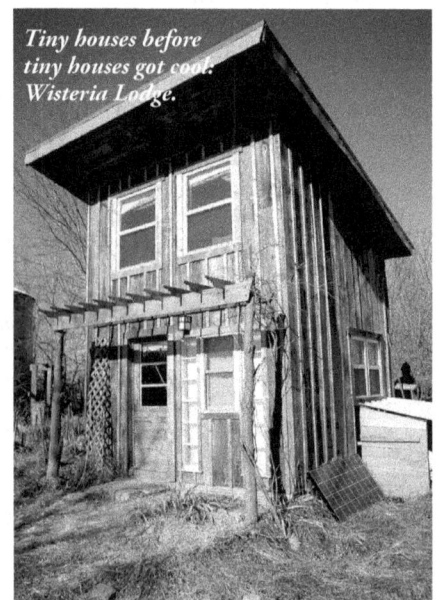
Tiny houses before tiny houses got cool. Wisteria Lodge.

Photos courtesy of Dancing Rabbit Ecovillage

3. All gardening, landscaping, horticulture, silviculture, and agriculture conducted on Dancing Rabbit property must conform to the standards as set by OCIA for organic procedures and processing. In addition, no petrochemical biocides may be used or stored on DR property for household or other purposes.

4. All electricity produced at Dancing Rabbit shall be from sustainable sources. Any electricity imported from off-site shall be balanced by Dancing Rabbit exporting enough on-site, sustainably generated electricity, to offset the imported electricity.

5. Lumber used for construction at Dancing Rabbit shall be either reused/reclaimed, locally harvested, or certified as sustainably harvested.

6. Waste disposal systems at Dancing Rabbit shall reclaim organic and recyclable materials.

That's a lot of things that the community regulates, but note as well how much they don't regulate. They say nothing about dietary choices, the square footage of homes, use of plastic or electronics...all of which are certainly ecologically impactful. The DR founders made a deliberate choice to regulate a handful of things that they believed were both very impactful on a person's (and therefore a community's) ecological footprint, and relatively easy to track, but that were less likely to lead to neighbors policing each other's behavior in an invasive way.

A policing environment is a common downfall of many well-intentioned sustainability projects: the holier-than-thou are, frankly, notoriously hard to be around for any length of time, let alone live with every day.

The founders had good discernment about what to regulate and not. For example, hiding the existence of a personal car on the property is hard enough that people don't try. Thus, from a "let's avoid policing" standpoint, banning personal car usage is relatively safe. On the other hand, smuggling a bag of Cheetos and a burger into the community would be sorely tempting (and a heck of a lot easier to get away with) if there were rules to be broken about meat or junk food consumption, and suspicions that someone is violating a rule can lead to all kinds of bad feelings.

I believe this particular filter of the DR founders has served the community well over the years. The danger is that people will conform with just this relatively limited list of restrictions and then have otherwise horrible practices, leading to very spotty gains in ecological progress. However, it turns out that happens only up to a point, and no further, because of the nature of consciousness.

DR members rely on people's ability to self-sort. They trust that people will apply to live in a place like DR only if they have a generally high level of consciousness around ecological practices. The high standards of the covenants help create a kind of litmus test for that. Frankly, if an American is willing to pry their hands off their personal car keys (one of the most amazing processes of consciousness shift you'll ever see) they are probably willing to do a lot of things, whether someone is standing over them demanding it or not. And to a large extent, that works at Dancing Rabbit.

So what has the impact been of Dancing Rabbit's set-up? Anthropologist Brooke Jones did her

Master's Thesis work on Dancing Rabbit's ecological practices, and later returned to continue collecting data. Here are the 2015 statistics she identified, expressed as the percent of average American consumption:

- 19 percent of water, over half from rainwater catchment (8.5 percent of municipal-source water)
- 13 percent of landfill waste, while doing higher than average recycling
- 14 percent of the US average of electricity used, including most of their business activities, and a net exporter of solar power onto the grid
- 5 percent propane/natural gas
- 6 percent of fuel for vehicles, owning 7 percent of the cars

Based on climate-related data I've studied and conversations with others even more up to

> ## If an American is willing to pry their hands off their personal car keys, they are probably willing to do a lot of things.

their eyeballs in data than I am, a 90 percent per capita reduction from current average American carbon emissions is the level I believe we need to achieve to live sustainably in the modern world. The numbers above put Dancing Rabbit right in the ballpark of that magic 10 percent mark in the areas measured. This very concrete example shows that sustainable is possible in these areas, and that community is a viable pathway to a low consumption future.

Two sets of data not included above are food and buildings. Jones learned in her early days of data collection that both of these categories are

Car sharing at Dancing Rabbit.

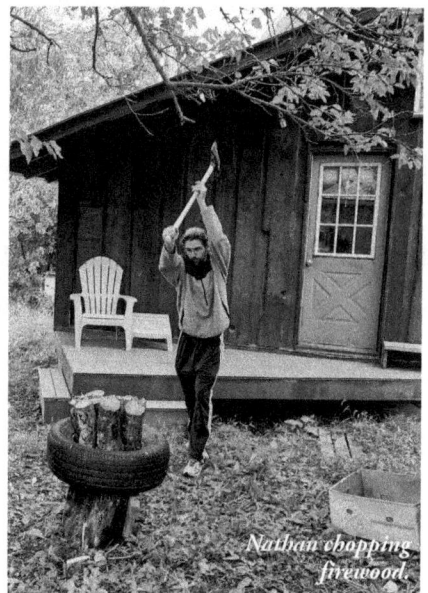

Nathan chopping firewood.

complicated to measure. Where the community car-sharing program makes it relatively easy to track miles driven in a year, the many sources of food community members rely on makes food footprints very hard to accurately measure. Same goes with buildings: a lot of factors go into determining the ecological and/or carbon footprint of a building (including the materials used, the distance they were shipped, the size of

the square footage is considered to be the best predictor of carbon footprint of a building (see www.opb.org/news/blog/ecotrope/graphics-reducing-energy-emissions-with-smaller-homes). Dancing Rabbit has one of the highest concentrations of natural buildings in the Midwest, including a number of strawbale and cob buildings, which are built using clay from their own property, straw from about 20 miles away, and sand from a local quarry. The ecological covenants also limit what wood can be used in construction to reclaimed lumber, locally sustainably harvested, and certified sustainable lumber. Most buildings also make use of passive solar and other green design techniques. Finally, none of them are heated with fossil fuels. (Technically, when someone is running an electric heater at night they may be pulling some coal-produced electricity from the grid, but it is more-than-replaced during the day by exported clean solar power).

> When we think about solutions to climate change, we need to look not only at reducing negative impacts, but also at increasing our positive ones.

In terms of food, meat eaters at Dancing Rabbit appear to consume less than the American average, with a portion of the meat being produced within walking distance of where it is consumed; similarly most people get a high percentage of their dairy products from an organic farm just a few miles away. And, predictably, there are people who eat little or no meat and dairy. Most people either grow their own gardens or try to get produce from farmers who live in the community, or from two of the

the building, and use of things like passive solar techniques...and then there is variation in how different renters or owners might occupy that building). It is hard to get really good numbers, especially on a low research budget.

Here's what we do know about Rabbit building and food practices, all of which bode pretty well for their having a noticeably lower than average footprint in both areas. Rabbits have, on average, about 30 percent of the personal space of most Americans and, since 80 percent of the carbon emissions in the life of a building come from occupying it (largely heating and cooling),

other nearby intentional communities (one less than a mile away and the other three miles away).

So we know Dancing Rabbit's food and housing practices differ from standard American practices, and are likely to produce lower carbon emissions, but we don't know the exact percentages the way we do from Jones' work in those other areas.

As the statistics above show, in terms of water usage, while the community does not choose to regulate it, it is still using a fraction of an average American's water per capita. Same with the number of miles driven—no rule prohibits being a gas hog, but the combination of community systems discouraging commuter lifestyles and casual car usage and the high degree of consciousness among people who join the community adds up to a very strong showing in the fuel conservation category. Witness also that the farmers growing organic food on the property have a lot of local buyers for their products, even though the community doesn't say you have to eat locally and organically. Thus, the idea that people who are willing to live with a strong batch of regulations are also likely to have consciousness beyond those particular regulated areas seems to be true at Dancing Rabbit.

Khaki Campbell ducks romping through the yards.

Many hands make light work.

Canning.

The author's former home, Moon Lodge (on right), at Dancing Rabbit.

FOOT PATH

Obviously resource use reduction and carbon footprint reduction are not identical, but they are very closely related. Dancing Rabbit also engages in a number of activities that positively impact their carbon footprint (such as having planted about 15,000 trees over the years). Thus, when we think about solutions to climate change, we need to look not only at reducing negative impacts, but also at increasing our positive ones, and DR deserves credit for working both ends of that equation.

Dancing Rabbit is an excellent example of what a group can do with a very strong focus on the social and ecological dimensions, and with strong enough worldview articulation early on. (In addition to the ecological covenants, Dancing Rabbit has sustainability guidelines that are more philosophical in nature and provide significant food for thought for members: www.dancingrabbit.org/about-dancing-rabbit-eco-village/vision/sustainability-guidelines.) They also made some very good decisions that set up their members to be able to operate with only one foot in the wider, unsustainable economy (though my sense is that the economic-dimension strengths of DR have evolved over time, not as carefully crafted by the founders as the social and ecological dimensions were). The choices to locate in a place with a low cost of living, to de-emphasize car culture and materialism, and to strongly emphasize resource sharing and casual labor swaps have led to the community being relatively economically accessible (especially for people who are either able-bodied or have strong skills that can be sold on the internet).

Another economic feature of Dancing Rabbit took longer to catch on but now colors the life of the community very strongly: the ELM system. ELM stands for "exchange local money" and is one of the most used local (or complementary or alternative, depending on what language you prefer) currency systems in the world. As far as we know, DR is the only place in the world where someone can pay for their food, housing, transportation, and utilities using entirely a local currency. Most local currency programs have found that the biggest barrier to being viable is people not being able to pay for some basic service with it. At DR, you can pay for nearly all of your basics with it. Thus, the ELM system has a very high annual per capita use rate: 10,840 ELMs are exchanged per year per person on average.

A couple other important features of Dancing Rabbit relate both to its carbon footprint and to its viability as a community socially: the option of subgroups (or subcommunities) forming for various purposes, and a particular form of subgroups, the eating co-ops. So far, the longest running of the subcommunities was Skyhouse, an income-sharing group within Dancing Rabbit that lasted for 16 years, and that also spawned Sky Kitchen, one of DR's numerous eating co-ops. These options are important because they give people in the village different economic, spiritual, and social options without the whole community having to get on board with deeper values alignment.

I characterize Dancing Rabbit as a village whose main structure is a series of overlapping cooperatives. These cooperatives give people the option of being part of deeper resource, income, and labor sharing, or choosing to be more independent. So you can be part, for instance, of the shower co-op at the Common House, or you can construct your own shower facilities elsewhere. Same with landline phone service, internet access, grid-tied electrical service, and the humanure system, all of which are formal co-ops anyone in the community can join or pass on. Co-ops have also formed around agriculture (e.g., the goat and chicken co-op) as well as any number of eating scenes, hosted in structures (including both standard-looking kitchens and seasonal outdoor kitchens) that are large enough to accommodate daily cooking for eight to 30 people.

This makes Dancing Rabbit pretty unique: you can live in this community and live your life as communally as you want, or you can live there and share only a few resources with others (the Common House and land are required to share, and if you are going to drive a car, you need to be in the Dancing Rabbit Vehicle Co-op). One of the best things about that is that as your needs change, as they tend to do when people are in different life phases, you can stay within your same community and just change the amount of communal versus independent aspects of your life.

Most intentional communities are designed with more of a one-size-fits-all model—you either income share, or you don't; you cook and eat all your meals together, or you don't; you have a shared electrical grid, or you don't. At Dancing Rabbit, all of those are options, and you can try out different things over time...without losing your social support network by having to leave the community to do it.

Finally, Dancing Rabbit is a fascinating mix of how to relate to technology use. While the community relies heavily on email communication and other electronic systems (the car-sharing system, bulk food ordering, local currency, and aspects of decision-making all require people to get on a computer with some regularity to be able to fully participate) there is a wide range of other relationships to technology.

Some people's homes look very similar to a standard middle-class American existence: running water, kitchen gadgets galore, electricity backed up by grid power so you have just as few days without power as anyone else in the wider neighborhood. And these homes were often built using power tools, sometimes even with heavy equipment to dig foundations and place beams.

Other homes are basically a glorified bedroom, with no electricity or running water—these residents rely on the Common House or other cooperative infrastructure to get those needs met. Some were built with hand tools only (or very rare use of limited power tools) and lots of work-party muscle to get things done.

Most houses fall between these two extremes. And that's OK. One of the cool things about Dancing Rabbit is that those variations are all OK. While occasional tensions arise around these issues, for the most part I experience Dancing Rabbit as being both a relatively judgment-free zone about those choices, and a place that deliberately celebrates the diversity of choices as legitimate expressions of sustainability.

Among other things, this can make it easier for people of various levels of financial means to make it work. It also helps with more diversity in able-bodiedness: if you need your water to come out of the tap (as opposed to hauling it), have some gadget for medical reasons, drive places instead of biking, or have a brick walkway leading up to your door, that's all fine. On the other hand, if you want to get by on $3,000 a year of income and do a lot of stuff yourself without investing in modern conveniences, that works, too.

When I think of what the future might look like for all of us, living more sustainably, Dancing Rabbit features very large in my vision. This community has pulled off some remarkable achievements, without governmental approval or support (aside from a Department of Natural Resources grant to build a pond for erosion control, and some Conservation Reserve Program funding); without the use of any fancy technology (beyond what is widely available, currently on the market); and with using learnable social skills such as deliberation, compassion, and cooperation as their main go-to's to figure things out. While this took strong intentionality, and this group was fortunate to be able to put together initial funding from members, friends, and families, there is nothing magical or non-replicable about what this community has done. In many ways, this was regular people with clear vision banding together for the benefit of us all. ❧

Ma'ikwe Ludwig has lived in community for two decades and is now part of a forming income-sharing ecovillage in Laramie, Wyoming. She serves on the FIC's Board of Directors, and is currently the Executive Director of Commonomics USA, an organization that works to bring together economic and ecological justice in the form of tangible legal, economic, and community systems. She is the author of one previous book, Passion as Big as a Planet. *Ma'ikwe does regular training and consulting with communities and nonprofits on group dynamics, functional consensus, and integrated sustainability models, with cooperative culture development being a main theme of all of her work.*

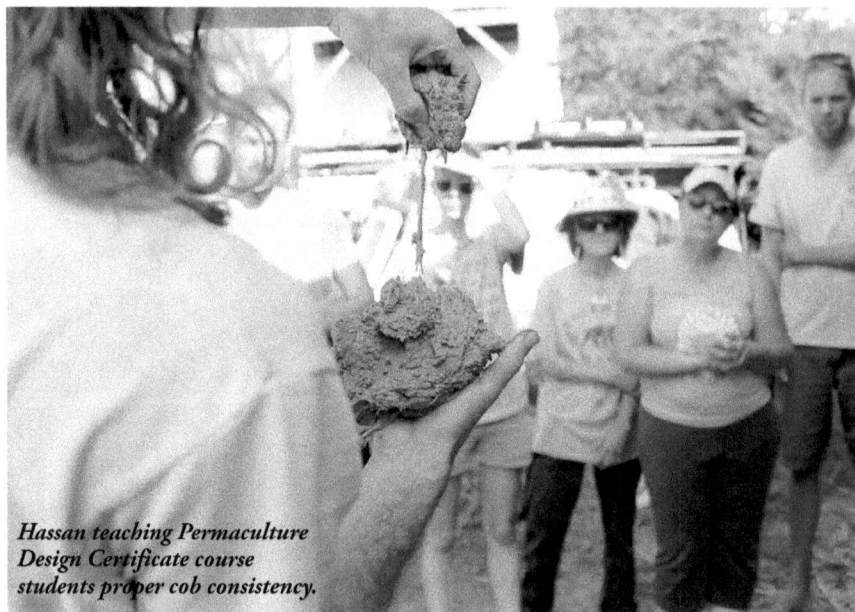

Hassan teaching Permaculture Design Certificate course students proper cob consistency.

A Four-Dimension Analysis of Dancing Rabbit

Dancing Rabbit is a prime example of a "Four-Dimension Community," one whose strengths derive in part from having engagement in all four areas the Global Ecovillage Network's curriculum says are necessary for deep sustainability. Here's a quick glance at ways I see the community doing well in these areas.

Worldview
• The community started with a clear vision, and took the time to articulate not only the covenants but also the more philosophical and challenging questions of how to re-think our relationship to the planet, each other, and global ethics.
• The recognition of the need for personal growth work has grown steadily over the years at Dancing Rabbit, and the visitor program (designed to introduce people to what they would need to know and work with if they joined the community) has a workshop on inner sustainability.
• The community has rituals that help reinforce the culture change that is happening, corresponding to both the annual calendar and the weekly rhythm of the community. And while these rituals are not religious, the community derives a sense of bonding, stability, and connection from these that is absolutely worldview-changing.
• The community has used consensus all along, which directly undermines the "in it for myself" worldview of wider American culture.
• Similarly, having a strong commitment to not being a commuter culture is a big worldview shift for Americans. Cars represent so much of Americanism: independence and freedom, casual consumerism—and even have become a symbol of adulthood. To let go of our primary relationship with the car is a big deal.
• Direct contact with nature is a large feature of most people's lives. Much of the community's food is grown right on the land; no roads are paved within the community and most people get around on foot through woodsy walking paths; and people frequently take longer walks on the 280 acres of land (most of which is designated as nature preserve). The natural world is a significant player in the community.
• DR practiced humility and a willingness to learn from other communities who had gone before them, a key element in their success. This humility continues in having an EcoProgress Committee, and regularly bringing in new trainers of new techniques.

Social
• Nonviolent conflict resolution is important at DR, and the community has put in place expectations, processes, support structures, and regular trainings to reinforce this.
• As noted above, consensus brings people into relationship with each other in a way that voting systems don't. The community also does regular training to build their skills in decision-making.
• There's a lot of collective fun created in the community—parties, float trips on nearby rivers, movie nights, telling of life stories, regular meal sharing, both planned and chance encounters at the swimming pond, and daily happy hour at the cooperatively run restaurant and B&B.
• Work parties get things done. Work is also a shared sphere, rather than an isolating one for many Rabbits.
• Systems support sharing: for instance, the online car sign-up is paired with time at the community's weekly coordination meeting to make for smooth sharing. Systems are also in place for the cleaning and maintenance of community assets (cars, the Common House, and the land) which helps with responsible management of the Commons.
• Dancing Rabbit's commitment to be a model and teach others means that thousands of people each year benefit from learning new skills and techniques, and being inspired to see that sustainability is indeed possible.

Economic
• The ELM system has a large impact—the money created in the community is used to provide interest-free financing for community entities, helping members put some distance between themselves and the predatory banking system. It also encourages people to think in terms of spending locally and keeping their money circulating within the local economy.
• Extensive barter and casual labor-sharing mean reduced expenses and a more human-engaged way of getting needs met.
• The choice to locate in an inexpensive part of the country, while challenging in terms of lack of job opportunities, served to both reinforce the "not a commuter culture" ethic of the community and make it more financially accessible for many people to join.
• No join fee means there is not an economic barrier to getting into the community.
• Collective buying power is put to work in many ways, including paying for the land, having access to equipment such as a big truck and a tractor, and even starting their own electric company to invest in a much bigger solar array than anyone could have done individually.
• The community has a very tight wage ratio (2:1), meaning that no one working for an official community entity can be making more than twice what the lowest paid person makes. This embodies economic justice and equity values.
• One of the best known businesses at Dancing Rabbit, the Milkweed Mercantile, recently went from being privately owned to being a cooperative.

Ecological
• Talking ecological issues is normalized in the community, allowing the problems in our world to be on the table, and therefore solvable with collective creativity.
• Meeting the ballpark 10 percent mark in resource consumption is a remarkable achievement; stay tuned for data on more categories.
• The most radical aspect of DR's ecological practices is the car co-op: four cars are shared by the full community, which has been as large as 65 adults in the last decade.
• Land stewardship is a big deal: the community has planted about 15,000 trees during its tenure, and there are several committees that work on the community's relationship with the property (from long-term planning, to insuring buildings are placed and constructed in as nurturing a way as possible, to planting those trees and other land management tasks).
• The net export commitment with green electricity insures that the benefits of DR's cooperative lifestyle extend beyond the borders of the property.
• Not resting on its past achievements, many people at DR embody a lifelong learning ethic. One of the current manifestations of this is a partnership with Midwest Permaculture, where many DR residents are able to get holistic design training in permaculture to help improve the overall community practices as well as design better individual projects.

—ML

ADDRESSING CLIMATE CHANGE:
Two Generations at Heart-Culture Farm Community

By Kara Huntermoon

" I want to *do* something about climate change," my 12-year-old daughter insisted. The immediacy of her feelings, and her earnest belief that she, personally, could do something momentous left me momentarily speechless. I remember that same urgency in myself as a teenager, before I realized the complexity of the problems facing us. Nevertheless, I have not stopped doing my part to solve those problems.

"We are doing something," I responded. "We're planting trees, growing food, and living in community."

My daughter shrugged me off. This is just her life, nothing unusual. She wants to do something *more* to address climate change.

But for many people, our life *is* unusual. Here's how those three actions specifically help mitigate climate change.

Planting Trees

Many people realize that planting trees sequesters atmospheric carbon. Trees inhale carbon dioxide, break it apart, use the carbon to build their body tissues, and exhale the oxygen (dioxide means two oxygen atoms). Besides reducing atmospheric carbon dioxide, trees and forests have several other beneficial effects on local climate, including the water cycle. Trees can prevent and mitigate drought, improve water quality, provide habitat for wildlife, and increase soil health. These are all important factors in mitigating catastrophic global climate trends. Here are some ways Heart-Culture (my community outside Eugene, Oregon) manages trees in response to climate change.

1. Plant more trees. At Heart-Culture, we are planting hundreds of trees as hedgerows and in food forests.

2. Heat with wood. This might seem counterintuitive, but wood can be a carbon-neutral way to heat a home, because the amount of carbon released into the atmosphere is equal to the amount the tree removed from the atmosphere during its lifetime. Fossil fuels (the source of electrical heating in most areas) can never be carbon-neutral. To make wood heat sustainable, use coppice systems, plant trees at the same rate that you are harvesting them, and/or don't harvest more than the annual growth increment from your woods. Use the most fuel-efficient stove you can afford in order to burn less wood.

3. Manage trees with coppice systems. Coppicing is a traditional form of silviculture in temperate regions with adequate rainfall. Basically it involves cutting a tree down, with the intention that it will grow back from the stump (called a stool). Coppiced trees grow much faster than a new tree seedling, because the mature root system remains underground. Coppiced trees can be used to produce firewood, fencing, tool handles, trellises, construction poles, and pretty much anything else you want to make out of wood. Several oak and ash trees volunteered on the edge of my garden, where they would eventually shade out my vegetable patch. Instead of removing them, I started an annual coppice rotation. Now I have a source for garden stakes and kindling that sequesters carbon and will never grow more than eight feet tall.

4. Brush Piles: Like most of our rural neighbors, we gather brush from landscape maintenance into a pile which we periodically burned. As our thinking about climate change evolved, it dawned on us that we were adding carbon to the atmosphere unnecessarily. Not only that, but we always saw insects, snakes, and birds fleeing for their lives when we burned the pile. Countless beneficial creatures must have died in those flames. We no longer burn the pile; we maintain it as beneficial insect and snake habitat. This means we have a large pile of brush and blackberry canes slowly rotting down near the garden. We keep adding to it, and it keeps rotting down. Instead of escaping into the atmosphere, the carbon is incorporated into the bodies of life forms and into the soil itself.

Growing Food

Growing food in your own yard means that no fossil fuels are used to transport it to you. This is especially true if you save seed, grow

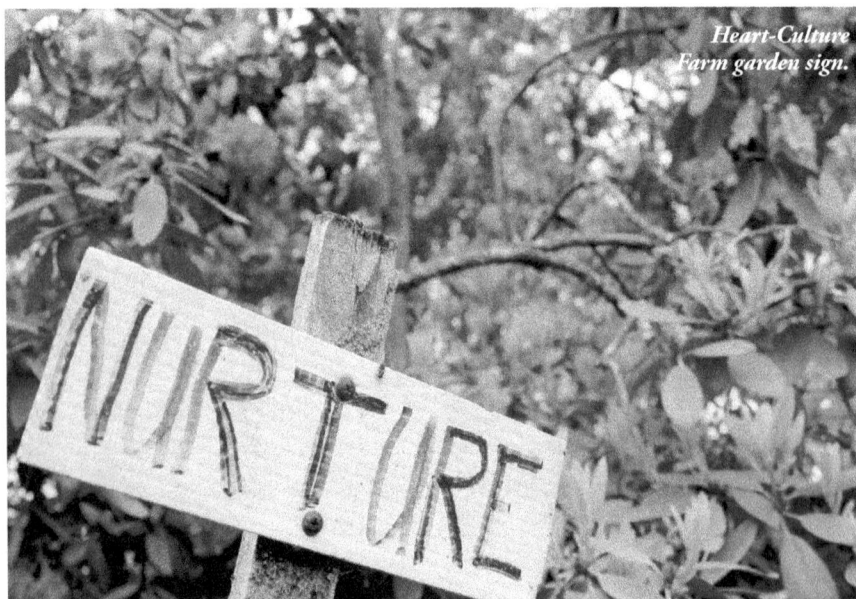

Heart-Culture Farm garden sign.

fertility on-site with animals and fertility crops, and preserve the harvest for year-'round use. My daughter sees me in the garden every day, feeding livestock, planting and harvesting, and preserving the harvest.

Hundreds of pounds of apples and squash arrived in our kitchen in a wheelbarrow this week. There are no stickers or rubber bands on this food. No plastic bags. No waxed cardboard boxes. The only gasoline required was to transport the trees to the farm 20 years ago, and the seed packet arrived in the mail. Next year my squash seed will be saved

that support several hundred species of butterfly and moth larvae. Songbirds build nests in the hedges, and feed those caterpillars to their babies.

When we grow gardens that provide yields for other species, not just ourselves, we increase the value of our gardens' ecological services. As environmentalist author Gene Logsdon pointed out, saving an endangered species like the blue whale requires international cooperation; saving an endangered insect species can be accomplished in a single backyard by the attentions of a single gardener. This is even more important in the face of climate-change related ecological collapse. Our gardens could reasonably become islands of safety for wildlife as well as essential food-production areas for ourselves.

Living in Community: Infrastructure

At Heart-Culture, we have old appliances. My cookstove is an ancient 1950s electric Frigidaire. Two burners no longer work, but we will keep using it for as long as possible, at which point we will replace it with the most efficient stove we can find. Since half of any appliance's fossil fuel use is embodied in its creation, any time a group of people share an appliance, they effectively avoid the large fossil fuel use of creating more. This is especially true when appliances are maintained and repaired for use beyond their expected lifespans.

Two other families at Heart-Culture use my stove for large baking projects, because they have only kitchenettes in their tiny homes. We have four stoves, three clothes washers, and three showers on the land; these are currently shared among six families and five single adults. In a culture that expects each family and each single person to have their own one (or more) of everything, we are forgoing the use of seven stoves, nine washers, and nine showers.

> In a culture that expects each family to have their own, we are forgoing the use of seven stoves, nine washers, and nine showers.

from this year's harvest, so I can honestly claim a 100 percent fossil-fuel-free squash harvest.

Permaculture gardening methods have a special place in carbon sequestration, not only because perennial plants act as carbon sinks, but also because the gardeners' management activities are less likely to rely on fossil fuel inputs. Permaculture orchards don't need to be tilled, sprayed, or mowed. We use geese and sheep to mow in the orchards. Chickens and ducks eat harmful insect pests. All these animals fertilize the trees with their manure. We attract beneficial insects and pollinators with guild plantings of flowers and herbs, as well as hedgerow trees

Our infrastructure is set up to support this choice by incorporating the use of tiny homes. Very small houses, these structures are less than 200 square feet each; some are only 80 square feet. A tiny home often acts as a detached bedroom, with one of the larger buildings as a support house for bathroom, kitchen, and living areas. The distance from their support house encourages residents to create outdoor living spaces with gardens, trellises, fire-pits, and solar showers. This increased connection with outdoor spaces definitely leads to greater awareness of the weather, and plants the seed for a different view of our own place in nature.

Embodied energy is a factor in building construction as well as appliances: how much fossil fuel use is needed to create the new structure and its components? Tiny homes use fewer resources during construction, which makes it easier to incorporate used and foraged materials available locally. They require less energy to heat and cool, especially if they are well insulated. It's easier to spend the extra money on better insulation when you need so little of it.

Edible daylily in Heart-Culture's garden.

The author's children care for a newborn lamb.

227

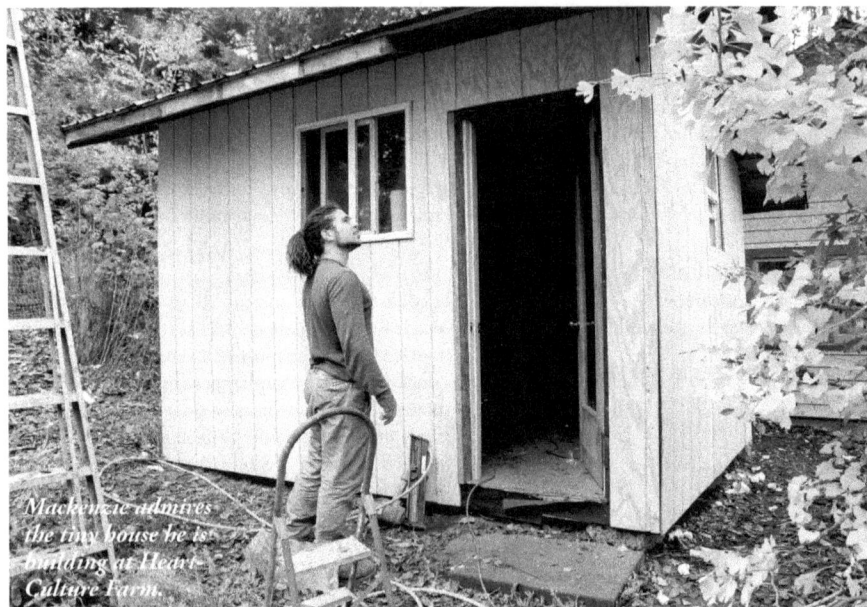
Mackenzie admires the tiny house he is building at Heart-Culture Farm.

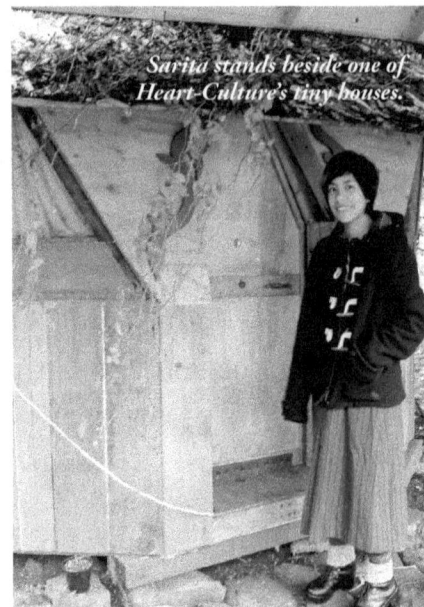
Sarita stands beside one of Heart-Culture's tiny houses.

In most cases a tiny home seems too small for a wood stove, but even with electric heat they can be very efficient. I lived with my toddler for nearly two years in an eight-foot dome with six-inch foam insulation. We used a tiny electric heater for 10 minutes on winter evenings, and snuggled under thick blankets to sleep. In the morning the entire home felt warm from our body heat. This was in Eugene, which is USDA Zone 8b, but even for our climate it was a very small amount of heating. Our support house was heated with a wood stove.

Living in Community: Economics and Social Justice

Climate justice is social justice. People of color, women, children, indigenous communities, and the poor are more severely affected by climate change because of lack of access to resources (including privilege) that would allow them to avoid personally suffering. Impoverished people cannot afford to rebuild lives devastated by drought, severe storms, and other climate disasters. They often live in areas more likely to be adversely affected by climate change, like flood plains. Federal funds intended to help homeowners rebuild after disasters don't help those who are too poor to own homes.

Tiny houses in intentional community can have another impact on climate change: addressing economic injustice by providing stable low-income housing. Many intentional communities are most accessible to educated white middle-class people, who have the knowledge and resources to seek out sustainable lifestyles. Like most other communities, Heart-Culture was founded by college-educated white affluent people. Over time, however, social justice has become a large part of our mission.

We set up our social and economic structures to reflect the goal of ending all forms of oppression. As a result, 90 percent of our current residents have incomes under the poverty line (compared to 16 percent of Oregon's population); 70 percent of our current residents are families with children (compared to 30 percent of Oregon's population); and 27 percent of our current residents are people of color (compared to 12 percent of Oregon's population). Half of our current owners group lives under the poverty line. Our buy-in system for new owners is designed to be accessible to even our most impoverished residents.

All our residents have access to 33 acres of community land, with barns, pasture, garden space, and woodworking shop. We live in a social environment which supports and encourages projects like sustainable gardening and resource cycling. For some residents, this is their first experience with interpersonal skills like mediation, consensus, and radical parenting. Others are well-versed in the "liberal" arts, but are learning for the first time about social justice, food-quality inequity, and white privilege.

Reaching Further

In terms of being a climate revolutionary, my child is right that we have far to go. We drive cars, depend on the nearby city of Eugene for our residents' incomes, and draw from the grid to power lights and appliances. However, we continually seek ways to bring our lifestyle into alignment with our values and with the survival needs of all life on this planet. My next project is to transition our entire community away from its aging septic systems and into constructed wetlands greywater treatment. I'm sure my daughter will help dig the ponds, and maybe I can articulate for her some of the reasons our new greywater system addresses climate change.

I'm actually glad my daughter shrugs off our revolutionary lifestyle as "just normal." It means

> It may turn out that raising children in community is my most effective form of climate justice activism.

she has a more empowered base to work from, and can reach further towards the goal of truly sustainable human settlements. It may turn out that raising children in community is my most effective form of climate justice activism. These kids will be able to see horizons that I cannot even imagine. I'm looking forward to following their lead.

All statistics for Oregon come from the US Census Bureau.

Kara Huntermoon is an owner-member at Heart-Culture Farm Community in Eugene, Oregon, where she raises kids and grows food. Her family of four earns $20,000 per year and eats half their diet year-'round from their own garden. She can be contacted through the Intentional Communities website, ic.org.

ECO-ENERGY
at Heartwood Cohousing

By Richard Grossman and the Common Facilities Team of Heartwood Cohousing

Heartwood Cohousing is fortunate to be situated on 361 acres of beautiful land. We have good irrigation rights—essential in southwest Colorado where there is little precipitation. Unfortunately, the irrigation water isn't always where we want it. Shortly after we moved in we installed a photovoltaic system that ran a pump, but that system couldn't keep up with the need.

So we got a gas pump which was effective—except for being noisy, requiring us to buy gasoline once or twice a week, and to walk a quarter mile to start it. We thought about a better solar pump and had a reserve fund to save up for it, but the money was accumulating too slowly.

Heartwood was first occupied in 2000, when renewable energy systems were very expensive and somewhat fragile. The cost of renewable energy has dropped amazingly and reliability has improved. We are also aware of the need to decrease our use of fossil fuels to combat climate change. To take advantage of these changes we started a Renewable Energy Fund (REF).

Contributions to the Renewable Energy Fund are voluntary, and are added to our monthly homeowner association bills. Fourteen households contribute regularly for a total of $152 each month. That adds up to almost $2000 in a year! The Common Facilities Team administers the fund—although that has been easy. The only decision that we have had to make so far was to use the money for the new, much improved solar pumping system.

We were fortunate to learn about amazing electric pumps that are made in Sweden that can run off of either AC or DC current, and are very efficient through a wide range of voltages. This is ideal for our situation where the amount of electricity generated by the sun varies so much. We decided to more than double the size of the solar array with a second set of panels and to buy one of those amazing pumps. Fortunately the cost was covered by a combination of the reserve and the REF, with just a bit left in REF. That was three years ago and the new pump is almost meeting our irrigation needs. This past summer we had to run the gas pump just a few times during a dry spell.

Why would someone want to increase their cost of living at Heartwood by contributing to the REF? While there are many generous souls here at Heartwood, there is an additional motivation. We all cause carbon dioxide to be emitted by our daily activities. Driving, heating our homes, the electricity to run our computers are some of the examples of activities that emit CO_2 from burning fossil fuels. Some people plant trees to absorb the CO_2 they emit. In addition to planting trees there are other ways to offset one's carbon emissions. One of my favorites is to pay for family planning; the fewer people, the fewer emissions. Another way, which is closer to home, is to invest in solar power generation, which will decrease the use of carbon-based fuels at a generating plant.

At the time of writing the balance of the REF is almost $5000, and I think that I know where that money will go, after the balance has grown a bit. This past year each team set its goals. Both the Common House Team and the Common Facilities Team want to decrease our

Finn Brunner

reliance on distant power sources and increase our use of renewable energy. The Common House Team put it best: one of their goals is to "bring a solar power system online to provide at least 80 percent of Common House power consumption within the next five years."

Even the most green-built structure wouldn't really be ecological if it is powered by a coal-burning power plant. Energy efficiency is of utmost importance in eco-building. Once efficiency is maximized one can consider the source of the power. Fortunately, for projects that don't have the cash to generate their own renewable power, "green" power is available in most parts of the US for a small additional cost.

One of our members once said that you have to plan and budget for renewable energy when you are building. The cost of solar photovoltaic systems was very high when our house was built. My wife and I added a rooftop PV system to our home when we could afford it, then we added another PV system to our carport to charge our plug-in Prius. There are now seven privately owned solar arrays (including four solar-thermal) at Heartwood. Furthermore, most people are careful to be efficient in their use of electricity and fossil fuels, and buy renewable energy for a small increase in price.

When we were planning our community two decades ago we planned our buildings so that they would be energy efficient and have as much passive solar gain as possible. Furthermore, most of our homes were also designed so that solar panels would be easy to add. Most of the 24 homes are highly efficient "stick-built," but we also have some alternative, extra-efficient building techniques. These include straw-clay, strawbale, and pumicecrete. And our workshop is strawbale construction.

Eco-building is important. It benefits not only the people who will live in and use the buildings, but also people of the future. It is important to be as energy independent as possible. If a person or community cannot afford the infrastructure to provide renewable energy at the time of building, they can be certain to build in such a way that it is easy to add later. Also consider setting up a fund to eventually pay for a renewable every system. It is an excellent way to offset inevitable carbon emissions! 🐋

Richard Grossman is a member of the Common Facilities Team of Heartwood Cohousing, Bayfield, Colorado (www.heartwoodcohousing. com). In 2000 Richard and his wife, Gail, moved from Durango, Colorado to Heartwood Cohousing—just a few miles to the east. Gail is a retired teacher and Richard a retired obstetrician-gynecologist. His major concern is overpopulation, and he feels that communities help us to live with smaller footprints. You can find his blog at www. population-matters.org.

IV
ECOVILLAGE DESIGN AND IMPLEMENTATION

Triumphs and Struggles
at Los Angeles Eco-Village

I (Ali) am currently sitting in the kitchen of my studio apartment in the Koreatown/Wilshire Center area of Los Angeles. As I write, I can hear helicopters overhead and cars speeding along Vermont Avenue—not the typical image that comes to mind when picturing life in an ecovillage.

Before I began living and working at Los Angeles Eco-Village (LAEV) in early 2008, my firsthand exposure to ecovillages was limited to rural communities. Yet I'm hardly a novice to the ecovillage movement, having spent the last three years visiting ecovillages worldwide and the last two working with NextGEN, the Next Generation of the Global Ecovillage Network.

Obviously, life in an urban setting is drastically different from life in a rural setting. In most rural ecovillages I've stayed at, my neighbors were my fellow community members, coworkers, and friends. The urban environment adds more layers of personal interaction.

As an urban ecovillager I interact with more people on a daily basis, simply by virtue of living in a city. I might see more people walking down a few crowded city streets on my way to buy groceries than I could in a week or even a month of living in a more isolated rural environment. But what stands out most to me is the increased interaction with city officials and local government.

ECOVILLAGE LIVING

BY ALISON ROSENBLATT & LOIS ARKIN

All ecovillages and communities striving to live with less of an impact on the earth have to deal with bureaucracy. What community hasn't had to prove to some government official that composting toilets and earthen houses are not only environmentally friendly, but safe as well? At some point in their existence, most communities face issues related to zoning regulations. But, as I've been learning at LAEV, the struggles over zoning and land use don't always have to do with land that they own.

LAEV has an inspiring record of working with local government to make the neighborhood more environmentally sustainable. Among its most visible accomplishments in this respect are the Bimini Slough Ecology Park and the Shared Street Project.

The Bimini Slough Ecology Park runs the length of one city block along LAEV's south border. Eco-Villagers helped the Bresee Foundation—a neighborhood nonprofit serving low-income youth and families—to get the 20,000 square foot street closed to traffic. In its place, the Bresee Foundation developed a park. The park features a day-lit streambed with native plants and trees that clean and absorb storm water, as well as a thick recycled tire floor on a children's play space and a teenage hang-out area made of local recycled concrete. Considering

City Councilperson Eric Garcetti makes a public statement. L.A. Eco-Village is in the background.

this was all done with public money, it's pretty impressive.

The Shared Street Project began in 1999 when, on behalf of the City of Los Angeles, Eco-Villager Joe Linton wrote a funding proposal to L.A.'s Metropolitan Transportation Authority for the creation of a demonstration shared street. The project aimed to make the street friendlier to pedestrians and encourage more neighbors to use the nearby subway and buses—to reduce auto use and auto dependency by widening the sidewalk and narrowing the street.

While the MTA approved the project for $250,000 in 2000, it did not schedule

LAEV founder Lois Arkin at the podium flanked by City Councilperson Eric Garcetti at the Shared Street Project dedication of macadamia trees. LAEV community members advocated for food-bearing trees in the public medians.

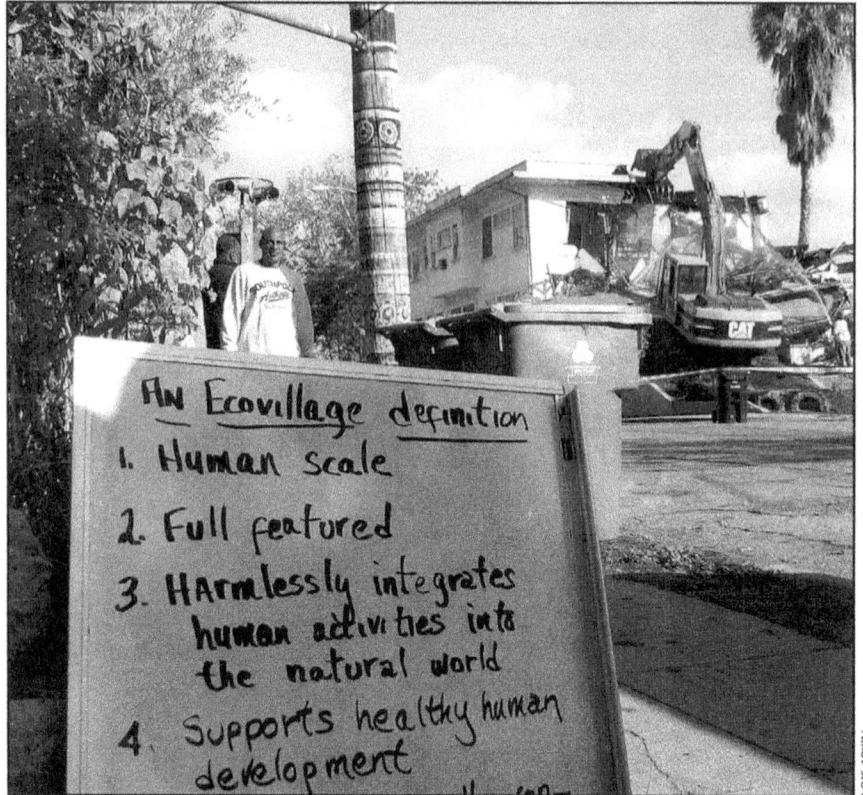

Bittersweet victories: The Los Angeles Unified School Disctrict earmarked the property across the street from LAEV (and by chance, the founding location of the L.A. Eco-Village) as a future school parking lot. Although the land is already bulldozed, LAEV is still hoping to save it, to be used as a horticultural project for children.

the money to become available until 2007. When 2007 rolled around, many of the neighbors had changed, along with the projected costs. Several LAEV members worked with the City's Bureau of Street Services, neighbors, and our City Councilperson, Eric Garcetti, to plan a series of community workshops to re-plan the project to get everyone on the same page once again. Eco-Villagers advocated for permeable sidewalks and food bearing trees in the public median, which would be still more costly to the City. Eco-Villager Lara Morrison researched potential new sources of public funding to make up for the projected shortfall. She did extensive research to help the city get comfortable with planting maca-

Other public officials are beginning to tour regularly to see how they can use our example in their own jurisdictions.

damia trees in the public median We all knew that, although in violation of established policy, this was the direction the City needed to move for our future food security. Now, as a result of all this public advocacy work, rainwater permeates the sidewalks, replenishing our groundwater, and macadamia trees are starting to fruit and will soon provide nourishment for our community and our neighbors. Other public officials are beginning to tour regularly to see how they can use our example in their own jurisdictions.

Unfortunately, engagement with city officials does not always involve such visually and ecologically exciting projects. In recent years LAEV has also struggled to save a major portion of the neighborhood from threatened condemnation by the Los Angeles Unified School District for a large new school, the need for which was questionable. When I first learned about the opportunity to move to LAEV, I also learned of this struggle, which could have devastated the neighborhood with the elimination of almost 40 units of affordable housing.

The work Eco-Villagers and their neighbors engaged in during this struggle was complex, effective, and best described by Eco-Villager Lois Arkin, one of the key organizers during the struggle:

Lois Arkin:

It was hard for me (Lois) to gear up for this struggle. I had done it a few other times during my past 25-plus years in this neighborhood. But since arriving at old age—I'm nearly 72—this kind of a struggle takes a bit more psychological gearing up. The 35-member L.A. Eco-Village Intentional Community (LAEV-IC) makes decisions by consensus. And since the IC neighbors didn't have a clear consensus on moving full force forward, just a few of us, acting as individuals, did all the initial organizing. It meant putting most of our other priorities on hold. We continued to report on our progress and needs at our weekly community meetings, not only to provide transparency to our activities but because we wanted the LAEV-IC to come to a consensus to both support and engage in the struggle. That consensus would represent political power, as well as fresh energy and moral support for what was ultimately a David and Goliath battle.

Nonetheless, not having the Community's initial consensus actually worked in our favor. Time was of the essence, so the few of us acting as individuals were able to move quickly in a variety of ways without needing to check back with the Community for consensus. We were working on behalf of the whole neighborhood rather than just the Intentional Community. This enhanced our rela-

Skills and processes that many Eco-Villagers had learned in community played an important role in our success. Looking carefully at the issues of the different stakeholders, and working at dealing with the issues, rather than just attaching ourselves to a position, were key.

tionships enormously with neighbors on the threatened adjacent block, many of whom we had not even met before, but who had lived in the neighborhood for decades. Through the creation of these new relationships and working to save their housing, we were building trust, learning about their needs, resources, and issues, and developing the potential to more effectively introduce ecovillage-type activities on their block in the future.

Much to their credit, the LAEV-IC did eventually mobilize—and boldly—as the risk of losing much of the neighborhood's housing and the threat of quadrupling traffic on our already congested street

became increasingly obvious to them. Most importantly, they began to see that there was a viable alternative site for the school close by, one that would not take any housing and would improve a degraded area which was also a brownfield, significantly contaminated from prior industrial uses.

So, ultimately, even though there was never a formal LAEV-IC consensus, dozens rose to the occasion. Or I should say "occasions," since there were many. We searched for alternative sites. There was an endless need to get neighbors to sign hard copy petitions to the School Board members. Eco-Villager Michelle Wong

Perseverance pays: On the Shared Street Project, L.A. Eco-Villagers advocated for eco-savvy ideas like permeable sidewalks to help allow rainwater to replenish groundwater. Here, LAEV friend George Patton gives a demonstration.

An LAEV-generated proposal to L.A's Metropolitan Transportation Authority rallied for the creation of a demonstration shared street. The goal: to make the street friendlier to pedestrians by widening the sidewalks and narrowing the streets, and encouraging more neighbors to use the nearby subway and buses, thereby reducing auto use and auto dependency in the neighborhood. Above: Tea Party as traffic-calming device!

created an electronic petition that garnered nearly a thousand signatures from LAEV friends throughout the world (www.gopetition.com/petitions/la-eco-village).

Other neighbors attended meetings with high-ranking public officials whose support we needed. There was video-taping to do at the large District-sponsored public meetings, where we were able to get hundreds of people to show up. A prominent eminent domain attorney was retained on behalf of all the building owners who were at risk of having their properties condemned. Some of us did outreach to the media. Although these activities took a lot of energy, it is unlikely our success would have happened without this multi-dimensional approach.

Skills and processes that many Eco-Villagers had learned in community played an important role in our success as well. Looking carefully at the issues of the different stakeholders, and working at dealing with the issues, rather than just attaching ourselves to a position, were key in this regard. Most Eco-Villagers practiced non-

violent communication in their letters and public comments, in contrast to many others who used language that was adversarial and contentious. Eco-Villagers were clearly working toward win-win solutions for identifying a new school site, using language that was strong but not aggressive, and using the power of their collective presence as a political tool.

Ultimately, the success of our struggle was capped with our close and long-term working relationship with the city's Community Redevelopment Agency and our City Councilman. Because these folks also feel passionate about not destroying affordable housing, they were able to use the power of their offices and informal relationships to convince the School Board authorities to make an alternative site selection. Nonetheless, in local politics, the squeaky wheel with a good cause does get the grease. Without the public support that we were able to generate, our elected official would have found it difficult to justify the time and effort it took to save the housing.

The "victory" was, nonetheless, bittersweet, and at the time of this writing may not be totally secure. Two issues came up: The School District's Facilities Department is planning to plunk down a parking lot for 137 cars on the property they already own in the LAEV two-block neighborhood. What to do? Start the next chapter of our struggle or simply be grateful that it is not a school for 1000 kids? Well, some of us had another idea for how to use the nearly two-acre site within our immediate LAEV boundaries: a car-free mixed use development, featuring a year-round indoor swimming pool using the hot mineral springs 2000 feet below our street, creating an educational biological living machine, using the hot waters for geothermal heating in the neighborhood, and creating an edible landscape around a cohousing development that would be marketed as affordable housing for school staff from all the schools in the area. Various School District officials have expressed real interest in doing innovative joint use projects, so this one is not out of the realm of possibilities. See the concept proposal at www.laecovillage.org/conceptproposal lausdcra.html. Stay tuned for more outcomes on that one.

The second piece of the bittersweet victory has to do with the alternative site selected by the School Board. That site, located primarily on District-owned property of an existing middle school adjacent to the LAEV neighborhood, will need significant remediation of soil contaminants. The school principal and several of the teachers, students, and parents are very upset at the disruption that will be caused by the construction and, more seriously, at the contaminated nature of the site. Others of us see this as an important opportunity to clean up the contamination and bring a currently blighted area back to life: an opportunity for another struggle that has enormous implications for the future of education in our intensely urban and toxic neighborhoods.

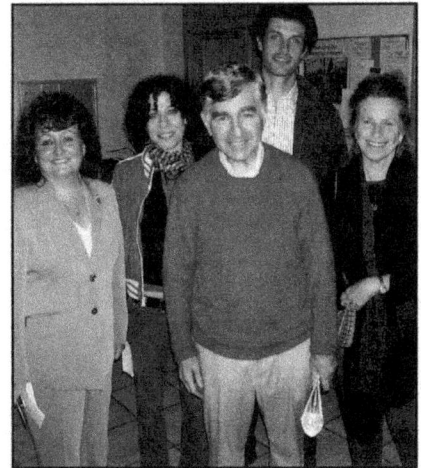

Former 1988 presidential candidate Michael Dukakis visits with L.A. Eco-Villagers.

I and many other Eco-Villagers continue to see ourselves as helping our neighborhood and the city at large reinvent how we live in the city. And perhaps with a little breathing space here and there, it has finally sunk in for me that the struggles never really end. The challenge is to keep seeing the opportunities in the struggles—that's what makes it really fun! ✻

Alison Rosenblatt lives at Los Angeles Eco-Village, where she is coordinating activities for the CRSP Institute for Urban Ecovillages. A former intern at Lost Valley Educational Center, she is also a founding member of NextGEN, the Next Generation of the Global Ecovillage Network. She represents NextGEN on the GEN board and is co-secretary of the Ecovillage Network of the Americas. She will enter the University of British Columbia's Cross-Faculty Inquiry in Education Masters program. She can be reached at alirosenblatt@gmail.com.

Lois Arkin is the Executive Director of the Cooperative Resources and Service Project (CRSP) Institute for Urban Ecovillages at Los Angeles Eco-Village, and is the Western US Ecovillage Network of the Americas Council Representative. She can be reached at crsp@igc.org. More information on L.A. Eco-Village is at www.laecovillage.org and www.urbansoil.net/wiki.cgi. Lois and Ali are the current editorial team for this Ecovillage Living Column.

Ecologically Speaking Communities

Enright Ridge Urban Eco-Village

By Kate Reidel

We can no longer deny the environmental crisis. While issues such as global warming and rapid species extinction are being accepted as real by science and state, they are but symptoms of the created disease that lies within the web of our culture. In a time when humans have depleted many of the Earth's resources and changed the nature of nature herself, the only thing we can do to begin healing from our mistakes is to begin thinking ecologically. The main question leading our human lives will have to cease being: How much money does it cost; can I make; will I need? Instead, people all over the world are going to have to ask questions like: Where do my major resources like food and water really come from and how are they being poisoned? How can I save resources and look for renewable ways to function in my life? And ultimately, How does this action enhance Earth?

It has been a misconception that humans were created for an economic system of production and consumption. The reality of our existence is that we are simply a part of the larger system of Earth, and economics is just one of the things that we humans do. In addition to the economic part of our lives, we also practice spiritual, cultural, educational, and political lives, all of which make up the larger dynamics of being human. The anthropocentric world view claims that we are the top of the chain of life, there is nothing that is above

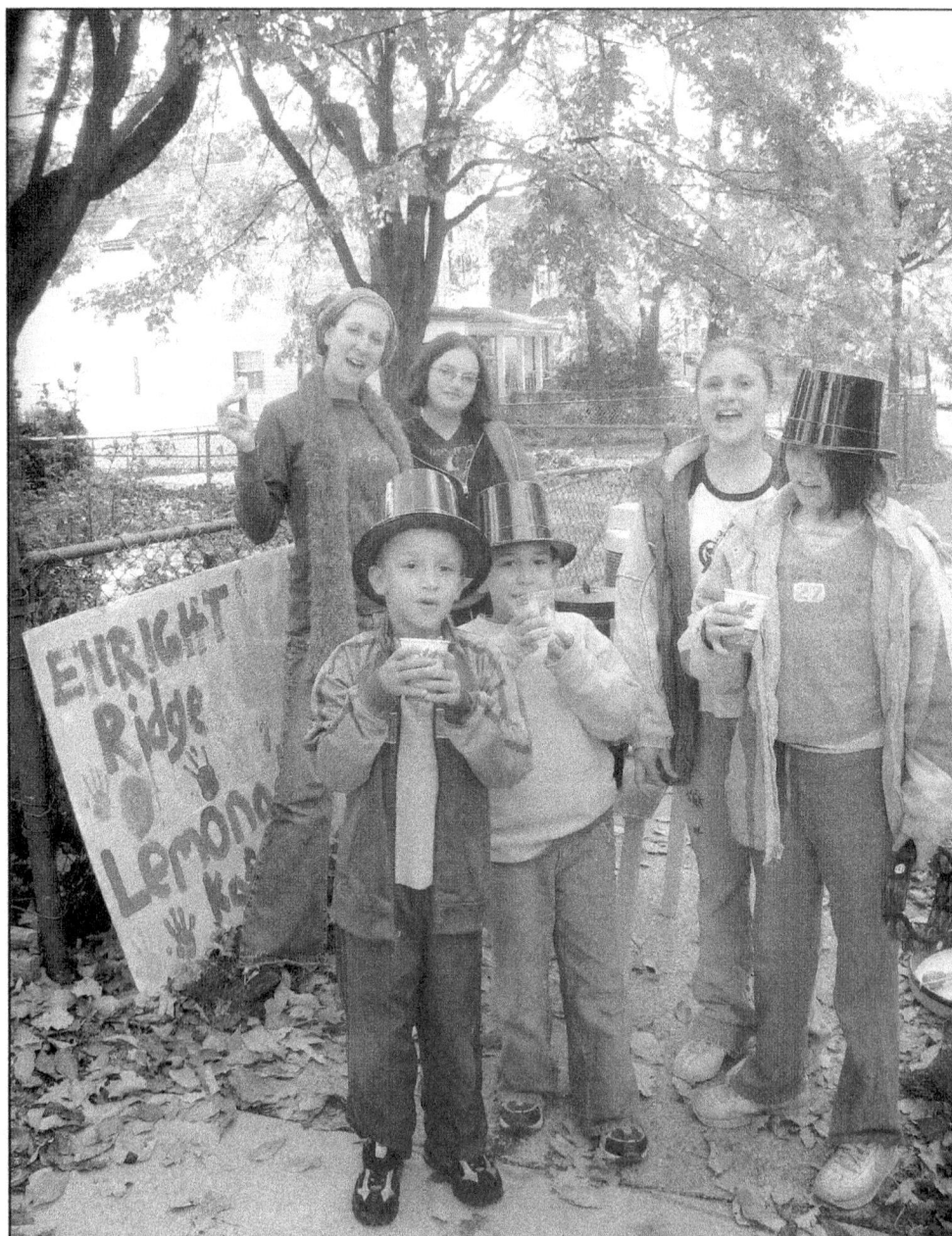

Lemonade stand community style! Residents and friends of Enright make some pocket change.

In an ecovillage, residents take responsibility for their own energy sources, food, and general well-being. Most ecovillages are small-scale, self-sustaining communities aimed at developing alternative ecological, environmental, and cultural standards.

our dominance. By asking how our action enhances Earth, we are shifting to an ecological paradigm that views the Earth as the larger, dominant system that holds our lives, just as it holds all other life on this planet.

When we ask ourselves the big question when it comes to our communities, what is our answer? Do our neighborhoods do more good for the Earth than harm? Do our cities clean more air than they pollute? The answer is that most do not yet, but they should and they will have to if we hope to live in a decent world. Where we live and where we work should be places that contribute to the quality of life on this planet, and they should provide us with a natural ecosystem in which we actively participate as humans. Ecologically-conscious communities are important for stepping into a new cultural paradigm and living as if the Earth mattered.

Ecovillages are one way to design communities with the Earth in mind. In an ecovillage, residents take responsibility for their own energy sources, food, and general well-being. Most ecovillages are small-scale, self-sustaining communities aimed at developing alternative ecological, environmental, and cultural standards. While rural ecovillages have sprung up across the world with success, urban ecovillages are a new

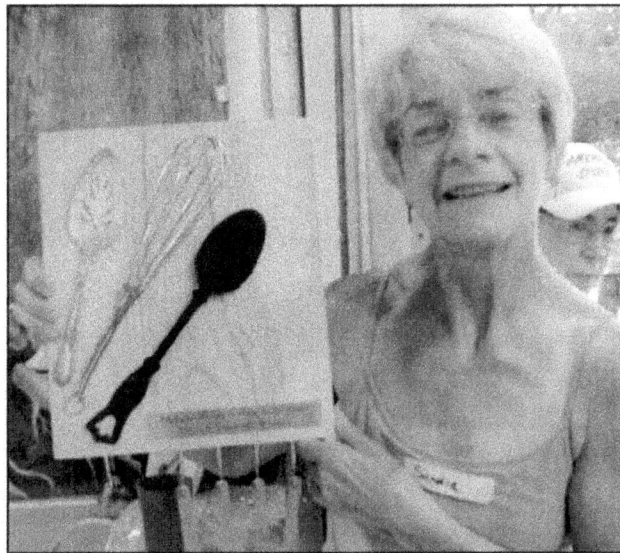

Dessert Champion of the annual Neighborhood Chili Cook-off Sandie Lett. To start a tradition, these custom-designed trophies are to be passed down each year from the old winners to the new winners.

concept that we must consider, especially because the human population threatens to destroy many of our natural areas already.

Here in Cincinnati, a community in Price Hill has organized itself to form an urban ecovillage with much success. Enright Ridge Urban Eco-village is a community fostering a sustainable urban neighborhood, which promotes preserving the

planet through social, economic, and healthy lifestyles and which demonstrates urban revitalization utilizing these principles. Our resources are abundant at this location. We are comprised of 90 households located atop a south-facing ridge only seven minutes from downtown Cincinnati. Accessible public transportation enables residents to stay connected to outside communities and resources, and the ridge we live on is surrounded by nearly 200 acres of woods, including a 16-acre nature preserve.

When we began to organize this existing community to raise questions of sustainability and preservation in 2004, residents spoke up about their desire to create a supportive community that actively advocates for their own safety as well as the safety of the Earth. The Enright Ridge Urban Eco-village was born from a deep concern for the well-being of the entire life community here in Price Hill.

Through many community events, discussions, and interactions, the residents of Enright have formed six committees that are the conduits for decision-making in the village. We have housing, promotions, communications, long-range planning, and green living committees that allow everyone who wishes to participate a fair voice in creating the neighborhood they desire based on what interests them. We currently have about a third of the residents who participate wholeheartedly, one third who appreciate what we are doing but do not attend many events, and one third of the people do not care either way. As we continue our efforts, more and more residents have become interested and we hope that more people will include themselves in our activities.

Work party at Enright.

Enright Hootenanny.

In the last two years, residents have accomplished many things together which have made Enright Ridge a safer, more beautiful place to live, where residents lead more fulfilling lives. Taking care of the land by picking up trash, growing our own food, and eradicating invasive species has added to our quality of life. A quarterly street-wide newsletter keeps everyone up-to-date with what is going on and also allows neighbors to get to know each other. The promotions committee organized a Home & Garden tour in 2006 that attracted people to visit our community, and is planning another one this year to showcase our progress. The housing committee has saved four houses in foreclosure from being bought by investors, then rehabilitated them using ecological principles and sold them to homeowners interested in learning to live more sustainably. This committee also purchased the apartment building and storefront at the top of the street, rehabilitated it, and rented the space to people interested in the ecovillage. It is now the new home of the Cincinnati Zen Center.

Residents of Enright Ridge Urban Eco-village have done this and much more to reach our goals of shifting our consciousness from an anthropocentric view to an Earth-centered view of life. There have been challenges along the way, including difficulties retrofitting old houses to save energy, pollution of the land from years of abuse, and little control over who moves into the neighborhood. But we have also had many encouragements along the way as well, including support from a financial foundation which lends us money for

The residents of Enright Ridge Urban Eco-village have done much to reach our goals of shifting our consciousness from an anthropocentric view to an Earth-centered view of life.

the ecovillage at low or no interest, allowing us to accomplish some of the loftier goals like purchasing property. We also received a grant to install rain gardens on the street.

Looking into the future, it is not easy to see how we will be able to continue living as consumers of the Earth, especially when resources are drying up and we are affecting the natural cycles of renewal. For Enright Ridge residents, the future is what we look forward to because we see the ability to change within ourselves. People of Enright were all once blind to the destructive behaviors of our society and have made strides in changing our lifestyles to honor the Earth. These actions are what give us hope for the future, because if we can live as if the Earth is primary, if we can create ecologically speaking communities, humans might just have a shot at saving the world. ✸

A resident of Enright Ridge Urban Eco-village, Kate Reidel is Volunteer Coordinator for the ecovillage and for Imago. Kate has lived in Price Hill for much of her life and is now completing her bachelor's degree in Human Ecology and Education as well as pursuing a Permaculture degree. Her hope is to use this practical knowledge of agriculture, energy, and natural systems theory to live sustainably within the ecovillage while teaching and learning alongside others who have similar interests. Kate is energized by being in the woods, hiking, reading, gardening, music, poetry, and deep conversation.

NOTES FROM THE EDITOR BY CHRIS ROTH

Chris Roth

An Ecovillage Future

What is an ecovillage? Robert Gilman defined it as "a human-scale, full-featured settlement, with multiple centers of initiative, in which human activities are harmlessly integrated into the natural world in a way that is supportive of healthy human development and can be successfully continued into the indefinite future."[1] That's a mouthful, and for some people, "ecovillage" has come to mean simply an ecologically-oriented community, even an informally organized one.

In reality, few if any current ecovillage projects may entirely meet the more restrictive definition, requiring a "full-featured settlement, with multiple centers of initiative." Most contemporary ecovillage dwellers still need to go to a larger village, town, or city, or into cyberspace, to meet some of their significant needs. Furthermore, we don't know if *any* of our current ways of living, even in ecovillages, can be "successfully continued into the indefinite future." (Not only are many eco-living techniques and technologies experimental, but the future itself is uncertain.) So by nature, all "ecovillages" in the modern world are *aspiring* ecovillages, hoping that both they and the rest of the world can grow into indefinitely-sustainable ways of being.

In this issue of COMMUNITIES, we've allowed a broad definition, letting groups self-identify as ecovillages, recognizing that in every case this is more a statement of intention than of full reality. Like Permaculture, "Ecovillage" is a concept-art-craft-science that can develop only through experimentation, exploration, and beginning attempts. It will take many smaller-scale efforts to develop more mature and robust ecovillages. These pages contain first-hand stories of some of these efforts. If the human species is to have a future, it will *need* to be sustainable in all the ways ecovillages strive for, and we or our descendants will likely recognize some of these stories as having been the seeds of that future.

• • •

As Laird points out in his Publisher's Note, ecovillages aren't only

about the future. Many or most of our ancestors lived in settlements that would have met ecovillage criteria—otherwise our species would have fallen off an ecological and/or social cliff long before the modern age. And it's also true that modern civilization has veered almost unimaginably far off the path of sustainability that allowed indigenous cultures to survive for thousands of years. At risk are not only healthy human development and community but the habitability of our planet.

I'm beginning to believe that ecovillages are necessary not just for a functional social order and a livable planet—but, on some deep level within each of us, for the fulfillment of our evolutionary natures, even the health of our own souls. Over the past year-plus, with an aspiring ecovillage as a home base, I've been exploring different settings, different ways of living, different forms of community. And what I recognize, again and again, is that I feel most alive when I am in consciously cultivated, directly experienced community with both people and the earth.

The separation from both of those that much of modern living imposes is devastating to who we are as people, and to each of us as individuals. "Business as usual" in the modern world—each individual or family in its own set of boxes, designed to separate them from the rest of the world—is neither usual nor natural. Living close to the earth in community with others is not a wild experiment or aberration, a flight of fancy or a pipe dream of the impractical. It is what sustained our species since the dawn of time. To return to that way of being, we need each other; going it alone will neither get us there nor leave us a viable planet or civilization in which to practice it.

For the Earth, for our communities, and for our souls, we need ecovillages—in all the diverse manifestations we can imagine for that term. ❧

Chris Roth edits COMMUNITIES *and lives at Lost Valley Educational Center/Meadowsong Ecovillage outside Dexter, Oregon.*

[1] Robert Gilman, "The Eco-village Challenge," www.context.org/iclib/ic29/gilman1; and quoted by Diana Leafe Christian, "Robert Gilman on 'Multiple Centers of Initiative,'" www.ecovillagenews.org/wiki/index.php/Robert_Gilman_on_"Multiple_Centers_of_Initiative"

Off the Grid and Out of the Trash Can

By Arjuna da Silva

At Earthaven in western North Carolina, and in a few of our neighboring communities, people are learning how to set up and live with modest photovoltaic systems, run gravity-fed water systems, reuse a majority of materials that pass through their lives, and reap the benefits of simpler living. In the center of Earthaven's property right before two creeks converge, there is enough flow volume and vertical drop of creek water to turn two small turbines in a micro-hydro station that powers infrastructure all of us and some of our neighbors enjoy. Assisted by a bank of solar panels, the batteries in this system can store enough energy to run our Village Center and several households and, even more amazingly, the woodshop and construction of its adjacent Village Arts Building.

Earthaven Ecovillage, where I've lived full time for the last 12 years, was founded on the broad principle of contributing to cultural transformation: reconnection to Earth, each other and, in some clear yet undocumented way, the Cosmos. Nothing in the earliest community documents, written before the site was ever chosen, said anything like "We shall create our own electricity!" or "We shall not deal with banks." While we were excited to take on alternative technology experimentation, we didn't intend to keep the banks out of it; it just turned out that way.

Founding Day, September 11, 1994: We agree to set up an organization that takes advantage of the lack of electrical poles on our property and to learn everything about living off the grid in ways we can afford. We also begin to draft bylaws describing a membership/ownership policy that will make it impossible for banks to finance members' investments. To own anything not portable at Earthaven is to be a "Full Member," a real person. We know we don't ever want to deal with a bank as part of our consensus Council.

In the coffee table book *Off The Grid*, Lori Ryker lists five natural categories of technologies that support off-the-grid living: Earth, with its thermal mass, geothermal, and composting potentials; Wind; Sun, for its photovoltaic power and hot water applications (not to mention its heat); Water, as micro-hydropower and also in rainwater collection and grey water reclamation; and Fire. She also lists a sixth technological category—the gas generators, batteries, inverters, and other gadgets that make it possible to use the other five. Above all, it is personally a thrill and an honor to relate to the power of natural resources as gods, these presences much of the modern world calls "weather." When Earth, Wind, Sun, Water, and Fire help us use their power, they grant us much wealth.

Electric Power

There is one micro-hydropower station at Earthaven, centrally located and serving the Village Center (office, internet lounge, kitchen, and Council Hall) and the Village Arts Building, plus several neighborhoods in a small grid that includes solar panels. The station provides up to 24 kilowatt hours of electricity a day. Though cloudy weather and poor maintenance can challenge a photovoltaic system, hydropower doesn't depend on the Sun, and generally needs

Tribal Condo.

Photos courtesy of Arjuna da Silva

less fussing. Water in our creeks flows night and day, all seasons. It can be disrupted if a flood washes out the intake or there's a break in the line, or if a crawdad decides to climb into it and gets stuck—in which case the upstream treks to repair a catchment become sought-for tales of local heroism. We envision a second micro-hydro station further on down the creek, below the confluence; it will eventually help provide electricity to several additional neighborhoods currently using only solar power. We already have the turbines we'll use, and I guess when the need and available funds and labor match up, we'll build a new weir and set it up!

Six trash cans.

Beyond the reach of our elegant micro-hydro "stream engines," everyone uses photovoltaics to power their homes and businesses. Many folks share power systems, either in multi-family buildings or between several small neighboring ones. Some folks manage with low battery capacity and small inverters (to power a light and a laptop), but most have upgraded to quality systems that allow modest to moderate use of power tools, audiovisual equipment, and appliances.

Success within Limits

Most Earthaveners started out with candlelight. My first utility upgrade was for hot water, not electricity. A neighbor installed a small on-demand propane heater in the trailer I owned and re-plumbed it with Pex pipe, which froze but never broke. It provided many, many showers through the years for friends and neighbors, and lots of hot dishwater—and still does via the current owner.

As we built houses, we learned to factor in larger systems, along with plans for earning, borrowing, or using savings to cover those costs. No matter how we paid (or are still paying), the hefty price tags make it essential to understand, maintain, and preserve our systems. We have to learn how to maximize battery life and to fathom meters and other component readouts. We may wind up grieving wasted money—and toxic materials going to landfills—as we discover our mistakes. Still, as we learn, we do get to celebrate arriving at the long-term system reliability we've been working for.

Wind, an excellent way to generate electric power, has not turned out to be dependable enough here, even on our ridge tops, to merit building towers and generating stations there. Sometimes the gods are busy elsewhere, or Wind and Water stay around fighting and we have a mess to clean up and a power shortage. Thus it turns out every now and then that bigger usages—particularly extended uses of power tools—may need to be postponed until the weather has been sunny, or augmented with a generator. Since oil products are still important to us as backup (not to mention for getting off of and back onto the land), we look forward to the day when some creative folks set up a methane generation system to offset propane and other gas uses.

Living off the grid doesn't require becoming an alternative energy expert, but I can't imagine doing it in isolation. Neighbors, and especially knowledgeable neighbors, help keep systems running. Meanwhile, we learn from them (and our conversations with each other) how to refine our systems and our use of them. Knowing how many amps per hour your system should provide becomes essential. Tuning in to system upgrade options through group purchases and even component trading becomes possible as the generations of various systems evolve.

On the subject of waste cycling, Earthaven members for the most part embrace the practice of making pee and poop available as fertilizer. Several neighborhoods have chickens, there is cow, goat, and sheep manure, and, of course, kitchen and other vegetable matter for compost. (Herein lies much of the fuel for methane digestion!)

SHRI house panels.

It took more than a decade for the first private flush toilet to be installed at Earthaven, and our public flush toilet went in two years ago at the insistence of the Health Department. Otherwise, folks poop in composting toilet buildings with rotating humanure chambers, in little buildings with 55-gallon drums, or in buckets they dump in drums or chambers. Several homes installed factory-built composting toilets, although I'd say the jury is out on whether these work well for us.

Besides ardent recycling, reusing, and refurbishing, we turn paper into mulch or compile it in "carbon dumps" along with stumps and roots and other non-reusable natural materials where it slowly turns back into soil.

Though we may have to work harder around home than we were used to "out there," we generally receive enough satisfaction from this "good" and "real" work to make it worth our while. I especially like telling people that our 70-person-plus-many-visitors population uses only seven or eight of the garbage company's giant canisters a week to contain all we create for the landfill and all our plastic, glass, and metal recycling too.

Design

In addition to active use of the Sun's power through photovoltaics, passive solar design is a soft Sun technology of its own. Once you've gotten the point—and particularly once you've spent time in a passive solar building—you will always wonder how anyone could have built any other way. I love how the walls (and the space within them) of my sweet, sweet house of earth, wood, and straw are heated by the Sun. In winter, the Sun's angled rays shine through my windows, warming floors and the ambient air. In a way, the Sun cools the house, as well, by the way it changes its angle in summer and doesn't shine in, so floor and walls stay cool. Simply by opening windows to the cool air of the mountains at dusk and shutting them again not long after sunrise, we can keep the house feeling cool and dry all day.

The Sun also heats a lot of the hot water people at Earthaven use. It is an awesome, marvelous generator! But despite the Sun's hot power, Fire for domestic use in heating and cooking is still significant to most of us. A wood fire in an efficient stove in a well-built structure warms the heart, dries a damp atmosphere, and supports the Sun's Big Fire warmth in winter, not to mention keeping the kettle on and letting the stew simmer effortlessly. Fire has also come back into popular use for creating fertilizer through biochar production.

Someone once asked me how we knew to build my house this way. I realized that it was just "in the air" when the time came to build. Permaculture having been central to the design conversation among members early on, the passive solar design message spread and was absorbed. By the time we were playing with sketches, orienting a building 14 degrees to the Southeast was an easy tenet to follow. Understanding why thick, thermally massive walls belong in the South, with thick, well-insulated walls in the North, was part of the local culture. Thinking about it, I see other evidence that we have already been transformed by the habits and practices we've adopted in our off-the-grid, out-of-the-trash-can lifestyle. "Occupy Earth!" could be our motto, not in protest but in literal intent.

Living off the grid doesn't require becoming an alternative energy expert, but I can't imagine doing it in isolation.

All of these efforts toward a modicum of individual and collective self-sufficiency are ways of insuring that our lives can remain productive and comfortable under a variety of future economic strains. The culture we are transforming and the lifestyle that is transforming us will have to turn away in so many ways from the cash economy as a dependable social organization. As Charles Eisenstein suggests in his book *Sacred Economics*, we are following the trajectory that leads to a culture where relationships are the currency of sustainability—never money. Relationships with neighbors near and even further away, those trying similar things and some who help solve and fix problems, build networks of support and knowledge—there's our ultimate wealth. ✥

Arjuna da Silva is an inveterate optimist, certified alchemical hypnotherapist, group facilitator, and visionary. She is currently settling into her gorgeous new home and landscape at Earthaven Ecovillage (www. earthaven.org), while beginning several book-length projects about life in the 21st century. Arjuna can be reached at arjuna@earthaven.org.

Aspiring to the Working Class

By Lee Walker Warren

One-hundred-fifty years ago, 90 percent of people on earth were farmers. This meant that every person in every family knew how to survive. Men and women knew how to work a field, fix tools, build a house, feed themselves. They knew how to raise animals, tend a winter garden, preserve food, grind grain, bake bread, and sew.

And then there's the invisible stuff that is second nature to land-based people. How to make allies of neighbors, trade skills, watch for signs in nature, learn about the cycles of water, wind, cold, and heat in their bioregion, take care of each other, and—most of all—give thanks.

Children knew how to survive as well. It is said of the Amish community, even today, that children "break even" by age seven and "turn a profit" by 12. I know one Amish family in Pennsylvania whose two boys, ages eight and 10, run the entire dairy herd by themselves—50 head of cows.

We now live in a world where folks don't quite know what to do when a light bulb burns out. Or where taking out the trash may be the only significant physical labor they do all day long. When we're that disconnected from creating our built environment and our food sources, I believe it leaves us feeling helpless and full of anxiety. Our culture has come to value the intellect over physical work. Yet our animal selves know how far we are from the body knowledge that has kept us alive since time out of mind.

For 10 years now I've managed work-exchange and internship programs at Earthaven Ecovillage, an intentional community in the southern Appalachian Mountains of western North Carolina. Young folks love to be here. They sense there is wisdom in this life. They come here to trade their time for food, housing, and an opportunity to live at an eco-village. When I put out a listing on our website or on idealist.org asking for help, I can get up to 10 responses a week from people wanting to experience this life. When they get here they are surprised to find that they are required to work in the

Photos courtesy of Lee Walker Warren

garden for hours, schlep building materials, and dig holes—things they'd never done in their urban or suburban lives. After a three- or six-month stint, I've had many of them tell me that the most valuable thing they learned was to work.

All of us at Earthaven come from the middle class. Some from the lower-middle and some from the upper-middle, but "wage-earners" all. We've all been educated and had significant choice about our lives. And we've been part of the generations-long move away from physical skill into knowledge-based work.

In order to live that way, we've had to rely on low-paid workers from across the globe who produce our cheap goods, and on "energy slaves." An energy slave refers to the human labor we'd need to support our modern lifestyle if we weren't relying on oil-based technologies (i.e. energy). I've heard it said that the average American uses 150 energy slaves. And because our energy slaves do so much of our work for us, nearly all of us grew up knowing nothing about simple physical skills.

I was raised as the grandchild and great-grandchild of European immigrants. They worked hard to make sure that I had a better life—a life that included education and opportunity. Even though my parents and grandparents had a garden, I did little work with my hands. I never knew how to use power tools, change my oil, or fix a simple garden hose.

Now I'm a farmer. I built my farm and my house and my neighborhood by hand, with other hard-working and collective-minded folks. I continue to maintain all those things through ongoing physical labor. Every day there is physical work. There is firewood to cut, projects to finish, all manner of things to repair, animals to care for, and constant plant growth to tend and tame. There is a learning of a new skill or a deeper understanding of a plumbing, electrical, or natural system.

I came to this life through my political, social, and spiritual awareness, and from my endless curiosity about the economic discrepancies in the world. My family sometimes shakes their heads in dismay. They want me to be happy, and think that I am, but they don't quite understand why I moved down a class level rather than up. They had given me every opportunity to do "better" than they had. Why hadn't I taken it?

Capitalism has long offered the possibility (or the illusion) to transcend the working class. Yet the more we move up on the economic ladder, the more we deal with "information" and the less we deal with the real stuff of life. Over the years we've so entirely moved away from physical work that

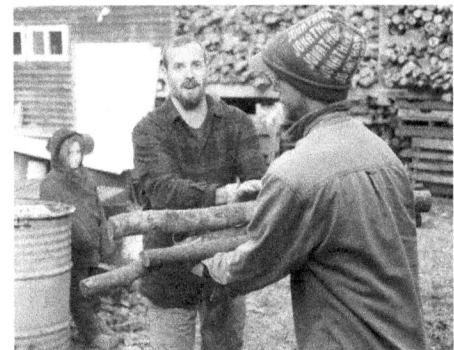

> ## Over the years we've so entirely moved away from physical work that people don't know where the stuff that sustains their lives comes from.

we now have a national obesity epidemic on our hands and a population of people who don't know where the stuff that sustains their lives (food, water, and energy) comes from. It took only a few generations to get here. The road back may be longer as we recollect the wisdom that was put aside by our ancestors. The process of remembering always seems to be more arduous than does forgetting.

Susan Patrice

Susan Patrice

Some of us, living in ecovillages and other land-based situations, are on the long, steep road to figuring out how to live responsibly again—to reclaim some basic knowledge that used to be just "good, common, sense." At Earthaven, we don't have low-paid workers running around putting our water and waste systems in, maintaining overhead electric lines (we're entirely off grid), or taking care of our lawns.

Last week I was shoulder deep in a pipe, cleaning out the gunk. Our rainwater

Working helps us remember our evolutionary potential—what these physical bodies were made for.

system had a take-away pipe underground that was leaking. In the city, I would have called someone to come and fix that. Out here, we need to figure it out ourselves. So I stuck my hand down into the pipe to pull away all the debris, and then kept digging. This project has taken weeks of investigation, fixing problems, fitting pipes, and digging. We finally discovered a crushed pipe and were able to fix the system. Sometimes, when working on a complex physical project, the ignorance and paralysis are hard to overcome. "Can't someone else do this?," "I'm not strong enough," "I don't know enough," "It's too hard," we think.

At Earthaven, we have a few choices:

1. We can pay someone to do all that stuff for us.

2. We can live with a lot lower standard of living than we grew up with in mainstream culture.

3. We can learn to be working class.

What you realize after being forced to do all these core-to-life tasks is that working feels good. The paralysis of a life of leisure and body-ignorance begins to fall away. Numb spots in the brain and in the muscles of the body start to activate and remember how to work together. The body responds to integration. Empowerment starts to creep in. Working helps us remember our evolutionary potential—what these physical bodies were made for. And getting it right gives us the courage and confidence to keep trying. When using a scythe or digging a trench, we often joke that we should set up an expensive "gym" on our farm so the city people can come get a good workout and actually help us accomplish something important at the same time. We imagine that everyone will benefit.

Part of the hope of ecovillages is to learn the skills that we've all lost through cultural amnesia—to regain strength in our muscles, brains, hands, and hearts to do what it takes to be responsible for our lives. And responsibility for our lives means not shipping out our waste for someone else to deal with, or importing food that someone else has grown, or being ignorant about where our water, heat, and power come from.

The work is hard. The doing of it is crucial. And the reward is indescribably satisfying. ❧

Lee Walker Warren a writer, herbalist, and the manager of Imani Farm, a cooperative homestead farm at Earthaven Ecovillage. She is a cofounder of the Village Terraces Cohousing Neighborhood (within Earthaven) and the Program Director of the Southeast Women's Herbal Conference (sewisewomen.com). She has lived in community for 15 years.

HEADWATERS - site plan

Ecovillage Infrastructure: The Skeleton of Community

By Gwendolyn Hallsmith

When you think of an ecovillage, the images that come to mind are generally pastoral—small pretty homes amidst gardens overflowing with organic vegetables, flowers blooming, children playing on swings suspended from graceful old maple trees. We focus on the visual and social amenities of living in community, and yet the physical and legal infrastructure are the less visible (but no less critical) components of an ecovillage community's success.

All too often, people try to form ecovillages without a solid understanding of the legal and technical issues associated with large numbers of people living on the same piece of land together. They find a large lot for sale out in the middle of the countryside, buy it, and start to make plans for communal living without first making sure that what they have in mind is even possible. This is not baseless speculation on my part—as a city planning and development director, I have been contacted by many groups over time that have needed help when they found themselves in a difficult situation.

Before you buy that beautiful property with the spectacular view, there are a number of questions you need to ask. First and foremost are questions about two critical life support systems that no community can be without—potable water and adequate human waste treatment capacity. Beyond that, you want to know what the zoning regulations are in the community where you plan to live, building codes, and any other regulatory issues that might apply to a large development project.

Water Supply

Just because there is a small brook flowing down the hill on the dream property you found does not mean it will be easy to create a community water supply. The EPA water supply regulations require that any system serving more than 15 connections or 25 people for at least 60 days a year be treated as a public water supply. Surface water, in these circumstances, requires treatment systems that eradicate critters like giardia and cryptosporidium, two parasites that make people very sick. These slow filtration treatment systems can be very expensive—it is often much more cost-effective to drill a well. But wells that can serve an ecovillage are also very difficult to permit. They require fairly expensive pump tests to demonstrate that the aquifer has the capacity to withdraw the water needed without robbing nearby properties of their water supply. The easiest way around all of these problems is to find land that has access to an existing public water supply. With a public water supply, the municipality or district takes care of all the regulatory requirements for you.

Human Waste

Second only to water supply are the systems you need to treat human waste. While many ecovillages want to reduce the impact on water by installing composting toilets, this does not eliminate your need to have either permitted septic systems or access to a municipal wastewater treatment facility. In Vermont and other cold climates, greywater is regulated, and composting toilets are not permitted in places where a conventional system or public sewer system is not available. Septic systems require good soils, and there are rules about how far from septic systems wells need to be. As with the water supply, the simplest way to manage human waste is to find land that has access to public sewer pipes and wastewater treatment systems. This way, even if you use composting toilets, there is a backup system.

Composting toilets and greywater management take careful planning and require ongoing attention. It is not advisable to simply throw the contents of a composting toilet into your compost bin. There is not sufficient evidence that even in an ideal composting situation where adequate heat is generated, this is enough to kill all of the viral and bacterial contamination that might be living in the compost. In Vermont, where we live, you are required to bury the composted material for two years before using it anywhere near plants for human consumption.

Greywater from sinks, showers, and laundry has many of the same issues. While it can often contain nutrients that help plants grow, it is advisable to use it on non-edible plants. Simply running a hose from greywater to the garden works in the summertime, but in climates where freezing occurs, this doesn't work. In Vermont a septic system or sewer treatment of greywater is required.

Zoning and Subdivision Regulations

These are laws passed by the local community about how land is used in town. The zoning typically tells you how many homes can be on an acre of land and what kinds of homes are allowed—usually a single or two family home is allowed without special permits, but as soon as you want to build more than that you need to provide more information. Zoning will also talk about uses allowed, design standards, and application procedures. Subdivision regulations typically deal with road standards for new roads going in to serve more homes and the other amenities needed when new developments are being proposed—sidewalks, curbs, signage, parks, bike paths, etc. Some states, like Vermont, have additional regional or state review of large projects. In Vermont, any intentional community with more than 10 homes would trigger review by the regional Act 250 Commission.

These review and approval processes, while important to maintaining the integrity of the environment and the community where the development is being proposed, can add a lot of time and expense to a project. They also add a layer of uncertainty, because with most land use review the answer at the end of the process can be a simple "no, you can't do this." Even if the answer is yes, there are sometimes conditions set on the permission that make it too expensive to complete. Never purchase land before you understand all the permitting requirements—it is not uncommon to condition the purchase on obtaining the permits prior to closing.

Legal Structure

Let me start by saying that I am not a lawyer, and this does not constitute legal advice. You need to get a good lawyer before contemplating any land purchase, subdivision, or other large development project. That said, there are several legal forms your community can take, and the form it takes will have an enormous impact on the life and decision making in the community. There are two forms you need to consider—the legal entity that owns the community and the form of ownership for the housing in the community.

Legal Entity/Owner Choices

Corporation: For the purpose of this article, this includes LLCs, S-Corps, and other similar entities. As I said, I am not a lawyer, and I'm also not a tax attorney. The advantage of a corporation is that it gives you protection from liability. LLCs and S-Corps behave a bit more like partnerships insofar as the income you derive from the corporate activities (and the loss) passes through to your personal income taxes, so you don't have to pay taxes twice. Since corporations are a legitimate legal entity, it also gives you a way to pass ownership on

in an orderly fashion; it is not dependent on the individuals who establish the community in the first place. The Headwaters Garden and Learning Center (the project I'm involved with) was established as a close corporation under Vermont law, which means that the current owners always need to approve new owners—hostile takeovers are not an option.

Nonprofit Organization: Given people's overall goodwill when they are setting up an intentional community, this often seems like the logical form to adopt. It allows for grants to be written to help cover the costs, and allows all sorts of good, tax-exempt activities—education, poverty alleviation, community service, health activities, affordable housing, etc. The problem with establishing your community as a nonprofit is that if you want to build and sell homes, or start community businesses, all the proceeds from that activity need to go to the benefit of the nonprofit. While having a nonprofit for the charitable work of the community is a good idea, it's not necessarily a good idea for the overall structure. Nonprofits will also tend to be corporations, which in turn will offer the liability shield of that structure.

Cooperative: Cooperatives will be structured by state law, but in general they will allocate benefits based on patronage rather than equity. A cooperative is owned and controlled by the people who use its services. For ecovillages, they may be a preferable choice, given their more egalitarian form. In Vermont, a cooperative also must be a corporation, either a for-profit or a nonprofit. So in this case, it also offers the liability shield for the individuals involved.

Options for Homeownership

Fee Simple Lots/Subdivision: Once the community identifies a large piece of land to use for several homes, one of the simplest ways to make home sites available for different people and families is to subdivide the land and sell lots. A homeowners association can be established to discuss and decide on community issues, but each homeowner would own their lot outright. While simple, this does not always offer the same degree of community control

(continued on p. 74)

ECOVILLAGE INFRASTRUCTURE: THE SKELETON OF COMMUNITY

(continued from p. 23)

over the long run, since fee simple ownership gives the landowners a lot of independence.

Condominium: If you think condominiums are only the large, multifamily developments you tend to find at ski areas and resorts, think again. A condominium is just a form of homeownership—it can include single family dwellings as well. The Headwaters Garden and Learning Center adopted the condominium form of ownership, because we wanted to have a higher level of community control over the different homes, and we also wanted a form of homeownership that was familiar to area banks and insurance companies. With our condominium, individual homeowners own a home site, but all the land is shared in common.

Cooperative: Like its counterpart in the owner entity category, a housing cooperative has a shared benefit for the people who are involved. It also tends to be established when the ownership entity is a nonprofit corporation. In Vermont, housing cooperatives need to be dedicated to the perpetual affordability of all the housing units, although in other places this is not necessarily the case. One of the advantages of an affordable housing cooperative is that the cooperative tends to own the property and its debts and obligations. This means that when units are transferred, the new cooperative member does not necessarily have to go through the mortgage process, but needs instead to come up with the funds for shares in the co-op.

Community Land Trust: Like the cooperative, this homeownership model is dedicated to perpetually affordable housing, and tends to be established as a nonprofit corporation. The difference between a cooperative and a community land trust is that with a cooperative, the members would be the decision-makers and own shares, whereas with a community land trust, the land is leased to the people who live there, while they are allowed to own their homes. Land trusts tend to have a board of directors, like most nonprofits, although there are models out there where communities combine the cooperative and land trust ideas.

Other Ecovillage Bones

Other important structural components of an ecovillage can include farming agreements, business structures, design rules, decision-making rules, conflict resolution processes, membership definitions, joining processes, financial responsibilities, insurance...the list goes on and on. It is better to think through a lot of these issues before you start living there—it's a lot harder to build an airplane in flight than it is to make sure all the landing gear works while it's still on the ground.

Go and visit other communities, ask them questions about what has worked and what hasn't worked. Get them to recommend good lawyers, engineers, and design professionals. It is always easier to work with someone who understands ecovillages than someone who has never heard of the idea before.

But beyond all the advice and assistance you can gather, ultimately what matters is what works for you and your fellow travelers, in your context, on the land you have found. Take it one step at a time, doing the best you can with what you have. Even if the structure feels more conventional than you would like, it is often easier to make change in small steps, rather than to be struggling with unknown forms while building a community at the same time. ❧

Currently Director of Planning and Community Development for the City of Montpelier, Vermont, Gwendolyn Hallsmith has over 25 years of experience working with municipal, regional, and state government in the United States and internationally, and is also Executive Director of Global Community Initiatives (www.global-community.org). Recently she has founded and developed the infrastructure at The Headwaters Garden and Learning Center, a new ecovillage in Cabot, Vermont. There are seven home sites, five of which are still available. Contact Gwendolyn at gwenhs@gmail.com.

From Camp to Village

By Andrew Heben

There is tremendous opportunity for sustainable practices within the tent cities organized by our unhoused populations here in the US. Instead of considering ways to improve living conditions within these marginalized communities, attention is typically directed towards rescuing people from their situation. This approach leaves people in an expected state of urgency and desperation to find conventional shelter, yet our stock of affordable and transitional housing continues to dwindle, and what does remain is often socially isolating and environmentally unsustainable. Rather than being rescued, members of tent cities are more often left to carry out a nomadic existence, forced by city officials to move from one space of underutilized land to the next.

A better approach may be to consider ecovillages as a model for reframing these informal settlements as a viable alternative. Let's address homelessness and sustainability together.

Ecovillages typically have personal, social, and ecological dimensions. Many tent cities already demonstrate strong personal and social elements—especially organized ones in which a self-governing community begins to emerge. They often ban theft, alcohol, and illegal substances in order to improve living conditions within the community and lessen the likelihood of eviction by the city.

Organized tent cities practice horizontal organization where people facing similar issues work together in order to help themselves. This opportunity for participation results in what Caleb Poirier describes as "a returned sense of agency," where people who became accustomed to being unheard all of a sudden make decisions that directly shape the community in which they live.

Mutual Support at Camp Take Notice

Caleb is the founder of Camp Take Notice in Ann Arbor, Michigan. What started over three years ago as a single tent in the woods evolved into a highly organized community of around 60 otherwise homeless individuals. After a series of relocations, the camp settled in its sixth location, where it developed organically for over two years in leftover space created by highways. In late June, residents found state workers constructing an eight-foot fence that would prevent them from returning to their long-time home. "It's not against Camp Take

Notice specifically," said Mark Sweeney, a regional manager for the Michigan Department of Transportation, "but more to prevent a homeless encampment of any kind in this location." While some received subsidies for one year's rent, over half did not. This insufficient, short-term solution could cost the state over half a million dollars.

During the summer of 2010, I stayed at Camp Take Notice to collect some first-hand research for my urban planning thesis project on tent cities. Instead of acting as an outside observer I decided I would much rather be a participant in this alternative community. Among other things, I found a prevalent gift, barter, and sharing economy in which goods and services were regularly traded without monetary exchange.

A fine example of this came during my lowest moment while staying at the camp. As usual, I started the day by winding my bike up the forested trail, over the guardrail, and began to ride on the bridge over the highway. A large truck approaching from behind caused me to swerve and scrape the curb. Looking down, I saw the piece that holds the chain in place had cracked in half. With only a few dollars I realized I would probably not be able to get it fixed during the rest of my time there.

For most this would not be a huge deal, but a bike is an extremely valuable possession in this situation. Being able to get downtown each day is imperative for campers to get food, showers, and other services. I chained my bike to the nearest

DIGNITY VILLAGE Aerial View from Southwest

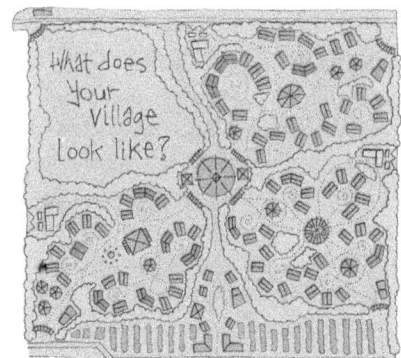

What does your village look like?

road sign and got on a bus since I had a meeting with the camp's nonprofit organization that afternoon.

After the meeting I walked the three miles back to camp to save bus fare, picking up my dejected bike along the way. As I entered camp, someone asked how my day was. I explained what had happened. As we examined the bike near the community's gathering area, others joined us, including Dave, who identified the broken piece as a rear derailleur. He said he had worked fixing bikes for years.

Usually reserved around me, Dave became quite engaged with the chance to help with a problem he was knowledgeable about. A number of old bikes were lying around so he suggested we replace my derailleur with one from an unused bike—a task for which we needed a special tool. We sought out Ethan, a military veteran with a wide selection of tools. Ethan sifted through a large case to find the right fit. I was able to remove the broken piece easily, and then start to replace it with a derailleur from an unused bike. But none of them fit my bike properly. I was still out of luck.

The next day I met with Caleb who, upon hearing my problem, helped me get a "Fare Deal" card which reduced my bus fare to $0.75. Panhandling a few quarters from time to time or recycling a few bottles was not a problem. Although my bike was still busted, I felt better about the situation knowing there was a network of friends to help when needed.

The experience also reaffirmed my belief in the personal and social dynamics of organized tent cities. Individuals facing similar issues work together in community, while simultaneously creating opportunities for personal healing and growth. The person with the problem becomes part of the solution.

Where Ecovillages Fit In

A key difference in this comparison is that ecovillages are villages of choice, while organized tent cities, though autonomous in nature, are camps of necessity. Also, outside of an often unintentionally small footprint, tent cities lack the ecological dimension fundamental to ecovillages. It takes a highly motivated community to take on such responsibility, and many people

Photos courtesy of Andrew Heben

Opposite page bottom left: Rendering by Mark Lakeman of existing conditions at Dignity Village in Portland, Oregon. Here, 60 otherwise homeless individuals have had the opportunity to move out of tents and into structures made largely from recycled materials.
Opposite page bottom right: Conceptual illustration by author for Opportunity Village Eugene. Currently, we are envisioning four self-governing neighborhoods of around 30 residents each along with a central village commons, a social campus with independent micro-businesses, and a village garden.
This page top: Two residents at "Nickelsville," an unsanctioned tent city in Seattle, work together to stay dry while another resident makes her rounds during a security shift. The community has a vision for transitioning to an ecovillage and has already begun to construct more durable structures with a defined path network.
This page lower photos: Self-constructed homes at Dignity Village along with a shared garden in raised beds.

believe homeless folks could never do it.

Portland's Dignity Village disproves this. Formerly known as Camp Dignity, the group was relocated dozens of times throughout the city, but continued to demand a "third alternative" to the street or shelter. Their relentless determination earned them a stable piece of city-owned land on which the settlement has existed for over a decade, slowly evolving from a camp to a village. Mark Lakeman, an architect who helped facilitate the vision for the village, describes the transition:

"[Camp Dignity] started off as tents but immediately they were self-organized into clusters. It was a nomadic form of a village at the start. As the camp was about to transition into more permanent settlement patterns, we realized the last 10,000 years were going to play out in a decade. They were going to be able to go from nomadic hunters and gatherers in a way—since they were subsisting off of what they could find—to settling and then establishing a system of pathways, nodes, and places; creating an urban fabric that actually reflected the people who lived there."

This vibrantly painted village of self-constructed homes and gardens sets a precedent for how organized tent cities can transform spaces into places. However, Dignity Village had a

(continued on p. 75)

FROM CAMP TO VILLAGE

(continued from p. 25)

few special individuals committed to building an ecologically-minded community, which is not always the case for tent cities. I believe this lack of motivation is not due to disinterest or incapability, but rather pressure to move on to more conventional shelter.

So, rather than focus on rescuing people from tent cities, an intentional community, such as an ecovillage, could adopt these unintentional communities, thereby broadening the reach of the current ecovillage movement. We can expand sustainable communities by including those residing in tents, the most basic of shelters!

At the simplest level, ecovillages could provide political support to a local tent city as a viable alternative to conventional housing. A network of support in the larger community is a key first step. Next, campers could become involved at the ecovillage, learning practical skills to apply in their own community. Ecovillagers could hold workshops at tent camps, providing hands-on education and catalyzing the transition from camp to village. While ecovillages expand their cause, organized tent cities could learn how to build and heat small, eco-minded dwellings.

Eugene, Oregon may soon break ground on such a model. Following the dismantling of the Occupy Eugene encampment late in 2011, the city formed a task force to find "new and innovative" solutions to the city's homeless problem. Their recommendation: "a place to be." At an Open Space conference at the end of March, supporters of this initiative connected with members of Maitreya Ecovillage, sparking the idea of a partnership between the two. One member is excited about building tiny houses for the village, while another is interested in presenting a model for more primitive structures that would be useful in the early phase. Yet another has offered to lend his knowledge of simple food production methods. We are working now to convince the City Council. ∿

An urban planner with a strong interest in self-governing tent cities in the United States, Andrew Heben currently resides at Walnut Street Co-op in Eugene, Oregon.

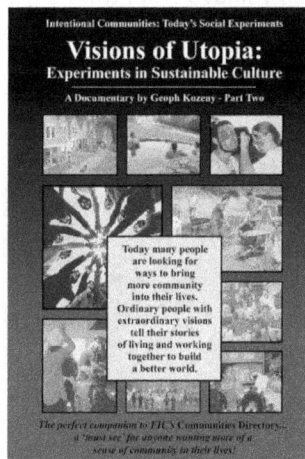

Good Neighbors
Top 10 Reasons to Live Next to an Ecovillage

By Alyson Ewald

There are local charms and delights in all the places I've lived—small New England towns, European cities of millions, Russian provincial centers. But I believe I've finally found the best place to live on Earth: right next to a thriving, growing ecovillage.

Sure, the ecovillagers themselves will usually tell you heaven is to be found inside their gates. And ecovillages, no doubt, are a crucial inspiration and model for all of us to learn how to survive on this changing planet. But they are not for everyone. Lots of folks have good reasons for living elsewhere, despite strong allegiance with the values of the village community. The great thing about this is that many of us are choosing to live very close by, generating a positively awesome neighborhood.

If living in an ecovillage suits you fine, then please by all means join one. As for me, here are the top 10 reasons I place my own personal paradise on the other side of the valley—but no farther.

10. Parties and peace. Virtually any evening of the week I can find something fun to do at the village. Many daytimes, too, can be filled with frisbee games, seed swaps, timber-frame bent raisings, dance classes, meditation, yoga, you name it. But personally, I'm beyond the age when I can keep up with all that. I like to have so many options in case I have the energy and spare time, but these days I appreciate being able to chill in the hammock or just sit at the pond watching my daughter play. And as a recovering workaholic I need to feel free of others' judgment whenever I do manage to hit that hammock even when it's a nice day and there are carrots to plant. Social joys or quiet solitude: it's my choice.

9. A safe remove from the soap operas. When I lived at the ecovillage I was always in the thick of things. If there was a tough decision for the group to make

Scenes from author's neighboring ecovillage, Dancing Rabbit.

Ryan Mlynarczyk

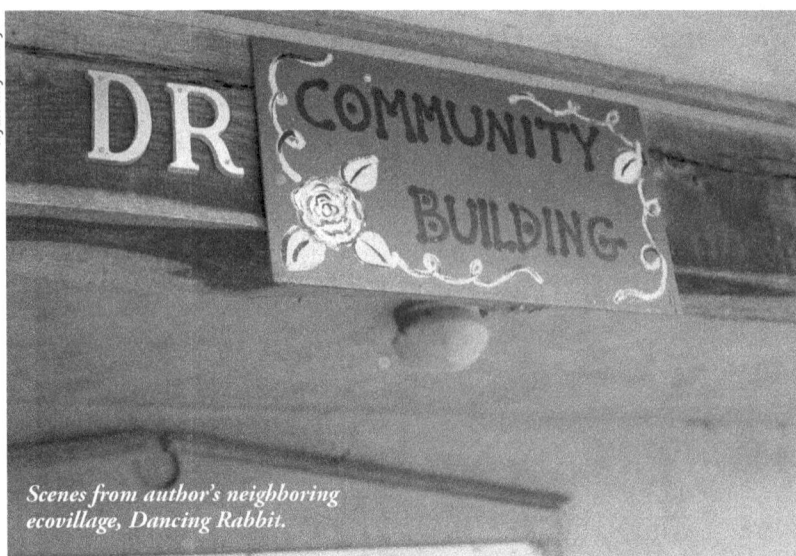

or a tricky social dynamic to navigate, I jumped right in, hungry to learn and eager to pull my weight. It was fascinating, but also pretty exhausting. Now that I live a stone's throw away, it's easier for me to pick and choose how much of the drama to get involved in. And I'm still close enough that folks can call on me for facilitation or mediation when they need someone like-minded who understands how the community works.

8. A home away from home (for me and for my friends). It's not infrequent for ecovillagers to seek a respite from all that drama and hubbub. Paradise, after all, can be a little overwhelming for us mere mortals. Then we go looking for someone else's little piece of heaven. It's not exactly that the grass is greener; it's that the grass is someone else's, so we don't have to scythe it (or feel guilty for not scything it, or annoyed at whoever scythed it improperly) before walking down the path to their pond. We can just go swimming.

7. Edge. Permaculture teaches us that the edge or boundary between two elements is a place of high diversity, opportunity, and growth. The edge is where the action is, a place of special creativity and productivity. Think shoreline, atmosphere, cell wall, forest edge. The social interface among the four eco-communities in our area (and between us and other local folks) is often the place where we get the best perspective on our conflicts and gain new insights on how to survive and thrive. Not to mention that it's good exercise crossing that boundary; I have a built-in mile-and-a-half round-trip walk any time I want to visit my friends.

6. Diversity and redundancy. Bear with me for a few more permaculture principles. Nature builds in lots of different strategies to ensure that essential needs get met. There is not just one kind of tree purifying the air, not just one type of plankton or mammal or insect or fungus or bird. Likewise, we need an abundance of ways to handle the converging crises that face us. No one ecovillage or community has all the answers, and some of our experiments are not going to work. It's going to take lots of us working those edges and tapping our widely varying creative juices to meet this challenge. Different strokes for different folks.

5. Stacking functions. The idea here is that each member of a landscape, homestead, or community performs a variety of needed tasks. We are all multi-purpose

Top Three Challenges of Living Next to an Ecovillage (But Not in It)

OK, so life here is not always a bowl full of (organic homegrown) cherries. Here are three reasons I sometimes find myself in the pits.

3. National exposure. I've just cooled off in our private pond and am hanging laundry in the buff while I push my young child (also nude) on our swing at the edge of the woods. Suddenly I hear voices. Walking along the path toward us come 15 strangers. Oh no! I forgot—is it the ecovillage visitor tour? A college class? Or maybe that's the TV reality-show film crew! In any case they are getting a full frontal of both me and my daughter. Is this illegal? And do I turn and run, or smile and wave? I could do without having to make this choice.

2. Isolation. It might seem odd to complain of both too much visibility and too much isolation. But despite all the tours and cameras, I do frequently feel lonesome and out of place. It's as if we don't quite fit in anywhere. We're not really ecovillagers, but not "locals" either. We're farming, but both camps seem to think we're doing it wrong. And most of us left our family and old friends far away to move here.

1. Out of the loop. This is the downside of getting to avoid the soap operas: I often have no idea what's going on in my neighbors' lives. I can no longer count on running into my friends casually, but instead must schedule dates if I want to catch up with them. I am (naturally) uninvited to ecovillage-only events or support groups. Ecovillagers frequently forget to forward us emails offering free scrap lumber or announcing a change in an event's time or venue. Also, a 15-minute walk can seem pretty long sometimes. So I generally miss out on things like early-morning yoga. I understand that I am choosing this distance, but the separation can be painful.

—A.E.

organisms, constantly absorbing new information and adapting our activities to suit our surroundings. An ecovillage is no different. It does not exist solely in order to promote a singular approach to living on Earth; instead it plays different roles for the different people and other beings who interact with it, such as protecting habitat, fostering cooperation, enhancing biodiversity, and planting the seeds for similar ventures to sprout up around it. My community and I are one of those sprouts. When we interact with the ecovillage, such as by setting up a child care collective or a mutual health insurance fund, I feel we're helping to multiply the roles the village plays in creating a cooperative culture.

4. Sharing the surplus. There are so many extra goodies generated when we live nearby. I have ready eaters for my sourdough bread at the ecovillage—and a great kitchen there to bake it in. At our homesteading community we have plenty of room for hundreds of fruit trees, livestock, poultry, and eco-farmed crops, which will someday serve the village well. The villagers likewise can provide cheese, yogurt, greens, veggies, candles, and pizza. And there's another commodity in good local supply: experience. The local brain trust on sustainable living is immense, making homesteading here a lot easier than going it alone.

3. Hope. I moved out here a decade ago because swimming upstream tired me out. I needed to feel like I wasn't alone, to see others making similar choices to mine, for similar reasons. Somehow it brings me even more hope and energy when I see a multitude of ways that communities around me are living in these times. From the commune that arrived here in the '70s to the Mennonites raising organic milk down the road, this place is full of folks who care about each other and about Earth. The more I cross the boundaries among these kindred groups, the less isolated I feel and the more optimistic I am about our chances of survival.

2. Resilience. Lately I've been hearing this word a lot. To me it combines diversity, flexibility, and strength, and without it we will perish. Our species must change course drastically and quickly in order to cope with a changing climate, and to avert as much suffering as possible. For example, we need to bring our food sources closer to home, and diversify the offerings each farmer provides. Three years ago, toward that end, we started a farmers' market in our town. The founders were a local business owner, a commune member, and me, with strong support from ecovillagers and Mennonite growers. We don't have time left to argue about tactics or dogma. Resilience requires that we set aside small differences and play to our diverse strengths as a flexible society of local communities.

And the Number One reason I live next to an ecovillage is...

1. Love. The person I've partnered with to raise a family doesn't want to live in a dense village. And I don't want to live more than a short walk away from my friends. Our four-year-old daughter tells us she loves where our compromise has landed her: close enough to walk to her play-dates, and far enough away that most evenings it's just us three enjoying a peaceful meal at home together. My unattached neighbors enjoy the proximity of a broad, deep, and growing dating pool, along with the opportunity to invite sweethearts over to our side of the valley for a quiet romantic getaway. I'm telling you, it's the best of all worlds. What's not to love? ᴥ

Alyson Ewald lives at Red Earth Farms, a homesteading community land trust she cofounded in Rutledge, Missouri. Previously she lived for several years at Dancing Rabbit Ecovillage, where she still serves on the board of directors.

Getting Ecovillages Noticed

By Alex Whitcroft

The Context

I am an architectural designer, originally from London, who's currently living at Dancing Rabbit Ecovillage (DR). How I ended up in the middle of rural Missouri is, as they say, another story. However, the long and the short of it is that in the summer of 2009 I stepped off a near empty Amtrak train at the Quincy, Illinois station into the humidity of a midwest summer and boarded a dusty white biodiesel-fuelled truck bound for DR to do a natural building work-exchange. I have stayed in contact ever since, and am now here designing the community's new common house—an ambitious new building to serve as the heart of the community as it grows from its current 60-ish people towards its 500-1000 goal.

I'm also on LUPP—Dancing Rabbit's Land Use Planning and Policy committee, which is responsible for crafting policy on village design, leasing of personal land, communal infrastructure, etc.

From Innovation to Influence

Intentional communities, including ecovillages like DR, often self-select locations with limited building codes or zoning laws, which restrict more mainstream developments; they often create small-scale solutions to problems which the wider culture deals with at the large/municipal level; they have been refining the consensus process for decades, while only recently the most progressive in the mainstream are starting to talk about crowd sourcing and decision making from the ground up. The list goes on. As a result, they can explore, relatively easily, radical sustainable ideas.

However, quietly going about fixing the world's problems is one thing; getting the world to pay attention is another.

My question is: can ecovillages not only be effective incubators for innovation and beneficial social and ecological change, but also make a notable difference in the wider culture?

The term "ecovillage" is a pretty broad term, covering all manner of communities, and trying to talk about them all together is rather difficult. So for the purposes of this article I want to narrow the focus. I would like to explore, using DR and the common house project, how this, and other similar radical ecovillages and intentional communities, might grow and take more centre stage in the wider conversation about sustainable society and development.

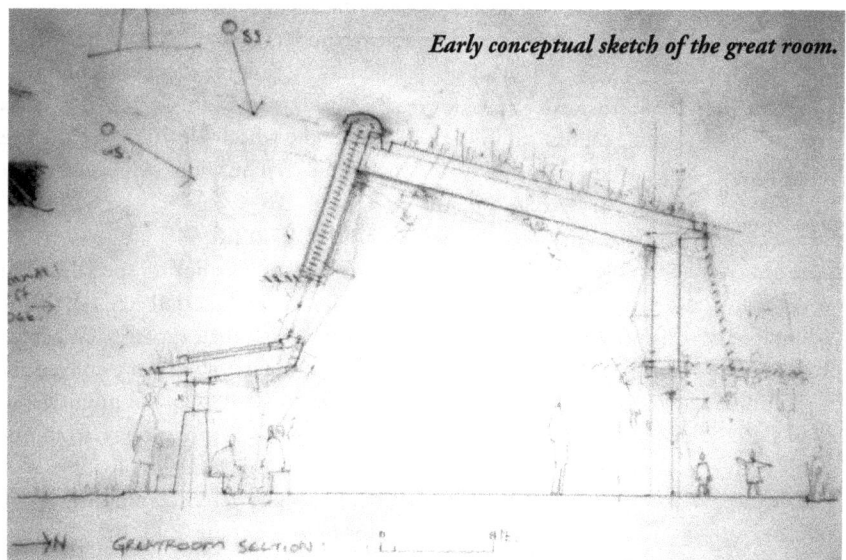

Early conceptual sketch of the great room.

The Reputation Problem

Only recently has the wider culture started to use the rhetoric of "green," "eco," "sustainable," "ecological," "lateral power," "ground-up decision making," "grassroots initiatives," and so on. The communities movement has been talking about and doing these things for decades. You would have thought that being that ahead of the curve would have been a clear and acceptable indicator that the communities movement had something the wider culture could learn from. However, even if you widen the net to encompass cohousing and urban communities, the communities movement is still largely a fringe phenomenon. It still struggles to shake off the "hippie" label that it has been landed with and be considered for what it is—a global community of well educated, intelligent people developing systems and social models the mainstream would greatly benefit from paying attention to. So what's the problem?

Arrival of the Specialist

In late 2010 I had a Q&A session with the whole DR community whilst they were considering me as the designer for their new common house. There were the usual questions like my previous experience, why I thought I was a good fit for the project, what my aspirations for the building were, how might I be compensated, and so on. But there were some unusual questions too, such as

1. Specialists are often arrogant "know-it-alls"—they come from a culture of hierarchies where they, as an "expert," are high up the pyramid—and therefore won't be able to operate in a less hierarchical, more mutually respectful culture.

2. Specialists are prescriptive "arse-coverers" and will hold back sustainable innovation and freedom in order to protect themselves or do things the way they normally do them.

3. Specialists have qualifications, bestowed on them by the mainstream, that are not necessarily valued by communitarians.

4. The knowledge and skills specialists have may not apply in a community setting.

The concerns are understandable.

1. Architects have a reputation for enjoying being in charge and doing a terrible job at listening to clients.

2. The mainstream world, including the building industry, can be a minefield of litigation, and as a result part of being a "professional" is that you cover your arse.

3. In part coming from the arse-covering routine, specialists often carry a lot of mainstream values, assumptions, and safeguards with them.

4. And finally, yes, community is a world unto its own and there will be a learning curve for even the most veteran specialist.

DR, like many communities, works by consensus and this model specifically teaches people that everyone is holding a piece of the truth—an idea that I am inclined to believe. No one comes to the table with nothing to contribute. However, the mainstream dogma of qualifications, specialisation, and "expertise," more often than not, tries to claim only a few people have the authority or know-how to speak.

However, in the spirit of consensus, there is a piece of truth the wider culture is holding, which is that many subjects are complex and great benefit is gained from experience. This applies to everything from agriculture to teaching, construction to facilitation.

Ecovillages tend to be overly cautious of specialists, while the wider culture is overly reliant on them.

Ecovillages tend to be overly cautious of specialists, while the wider culture is overly reliant on them. Neither situation is ideal.

There are also financial implications of hiring lots of specialists which communities like DR tend not to be willing or able to support—especially when, by hiring specialists from further away, they would cause money to leave the local economy.

By pushing specialists away, DR can create a situation where 1.) They have to re-invent the wheel—learning for themselves what the right specialist might already know, and 2.) The wider culture can disregard them due to their lack of credentials.

"How do you think you will handle having 50 very opinionated people as a client?" "Well, I hope," I said. When asked if they had any concerns, a few people voiced that they were sceptical of hiring "an architect"—an outside specialist.

Part of the problem, as I see it, is that the radical end of the alternative culture spectrum (I include ecovillages here) often tends to distrust specialists.

Opinions on this vary, and every community's relation to specialists is going to be slightly different, so I'm going to talk about DR and my experiences.

There seem to be a number of main concerns:

A Middle Ground

What is needed is not no specialists but, as Stefano Serafini of P2P Urbanism said, brave specialists who can listen, ask the right questions, and design with communities while integrating their expertise. What Serafini is calling for is a merger of the knowledge base and reputability of a conventional specialist with skills related to consensus and crowd sourcing that communities already have.

Another piece of a solution is for communities like DR to attract specialists into the community. With specialists living and working within the community a number of things happen: 1.) The community is able to pay for specialists without money leaving the local economy; 2.) If the community is economically depressed, the specialists can adjust to and charge a local living wage when working within the community and therefore be more affordable; and, last but by no means least, 3.) By living in the physical and social context of the community, rather than working remotely, the specialist can both gain and offer valuable trust and knowledge.

And so here I am, testing the theory—an outside specialist living and working at DR and designing in partnership with the community.

Why Be Normal?

Another part of the issue is that ecovillages often seem to actively encourage the outsiders' view of them as woo-woo and disconnected from, or unsympathetic to, the wider culture. There is an air of pride around being weird. I can entirely relate to this—I hate to be labelled "normal." And anyway, all radicals get called weird. However, to change the wider world, you need to move gradually from being called weird to being called visionary. That process happens by gaining respect.

So the question is, how can radicals do that? The answer is, interestingly, the same as in consensus and NVC (Nonviolent Communication): by giving others a means of assessing your position in a way they can relate to. If you are in a consensus meeting and two people each can't hear what the other is bringing to the discussion, you try to use their language; compare the issue to examples they already understand or agree to; match their energy; reflect back to them what they said so they feel heard; etc.

The wider culture won't listen if it thinks ecovillages are out of touch, not understanding the wider culture's reality/values. Ecovillages should use the same skills they are already honing for their internal politics to relate to the wider culture.

Making the Common House Relevant

Let's use the new DR common house as an example. As a community, DR decided that it wanted this building to be a flagship for the community, an example of cutting edge sustainable architecture, and a tool for the community's outreach and education efforts—in themselves important pieces of being noticed.

There were a number of things to demonstrate: that DR is building a viable economy; that the alternative construction materials and techniques employed at DR are compatible with modern building standards; that this project was as sustainable as the cutting edge in the wider culture. It's not unusual for *really* eco projects to get a large chunk of their funding from donations or wealthy institutions. As a nonprofit, DR could have opted for this route. However, we agreed to pay for the majority of the project ourselves. We also decided to pay people a local living wage to do the construction—a move away from the volunteer and work-exchange culture often found here. This would help strengthen our internal economy, give a sense of ownership, and also show that we were creating here an alternative, but viable, economy. That's an important piece for the wider culture to understand.

We also wanted to use natural, local materials such as clay, strawbale, and natural plasters, as these have a considerably lower embodied energy than more processed/manufactured products, and are great in terms of biodegradability, toxicity, etc. However, we were aware of the need for energy efficiency, airtight-

"Artist's impressions" of the building design, produced to help communicate the project.

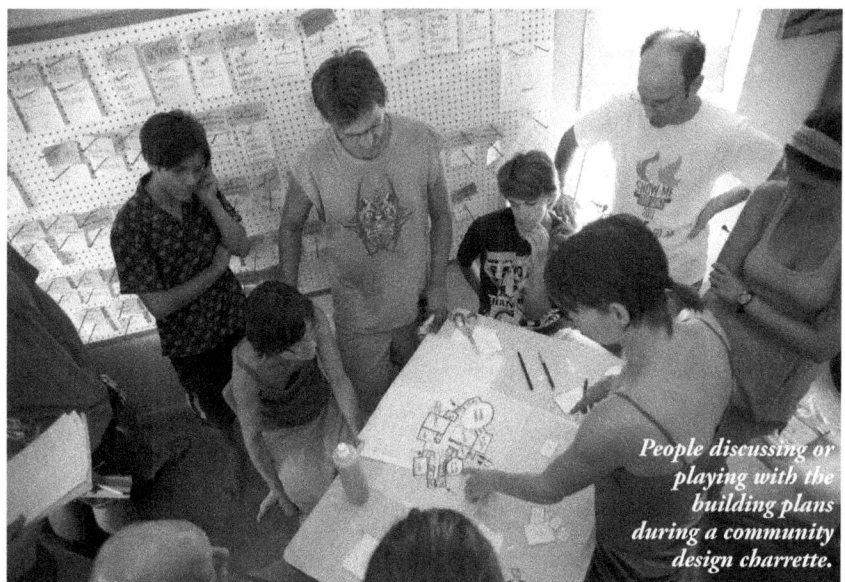

People discussing or playing with the building plans during a community design charrette.

ness, damp-proofing, integration of modern services/equipment (like a commercial kitchen), managing labour costs (which can be very high with natural materials), etc. All of these are also currently valued at the progressive end of the wider culture. As a result we chose to use a hybrid of natural building and green building, using the best features of each. If the wider culture could dismiss the project as a "quaint little building at a commune" they probably would, but a building that meets every sustainable benchmark the wider culture currently thinks about, integrates the most advanced building systems, does it in a way that challenges the current thinking, but is still understandable to someone holding that wider culture's viewpoint...that is a powerful tool.

Similarly, as a means of translating the unorthodox nature of the project into language understandable by the wider culture, we decided to pursue LEED and LBC (Living Building Challenge) certifications. Both are green building certification systems that assess and try to quantify how eco a building is. LEED is widely known throughout the construction industry and is rapidly becoming the de facto standard for green building certification in the USA. Certifications are graded from Bronze through to Platinum. We have our sights set on Platinum. LBC is newer and much more stringent. As I write this only three buildings in the world are currently certified as "Living Buildings." However, LBC is already gaining a reputation as the most thorough certification system around.

When first discussed, the idea of spending time and energy fulfilling mainstream certifications was seen by some people in the community as a waste of time, or selling out. It is true that LEED Platinum at least will make little to no difference in the ecological performance of the building. However, that's just the point—ecovillages are already nonchalantly exceeding the wider culture's standards and not shouting about it. By achieving LEED Platinum DR is showing, without any room for argument, that they can match the wider culture blow for blow. By achieving LBC DR is going further—showing it can match even the most cutting edge aspirations of the wider culture. There's not much room for ignoring that.

Replicability

Communities are, to use the currently trending term, "evolutionary" or "emergent" rather than top-down designed—that is, they emerge and evolve as a result of a set of inputs much like organisms, not like a toaster, which comes into being when someone says "behold the toaster" in all its pre-defined top-down-designed glory. As a result, they are difficult to transplant. It's not like buying a more energy efficient appliance (such as a toaster) or fitting your house with solar panels. You can't do community on your own, and you can't just buy it. You can't manufacture community, you have to grow it. The question is, how do you make it easier?

As I see it, if the vision of ecovillages is going to spread, then two things need to be in place: 1.) available and affordable teaching and education opportunities so that people who want to can learn about them, and 2.) replicable systems as a foundation/toolkit for founding communities.

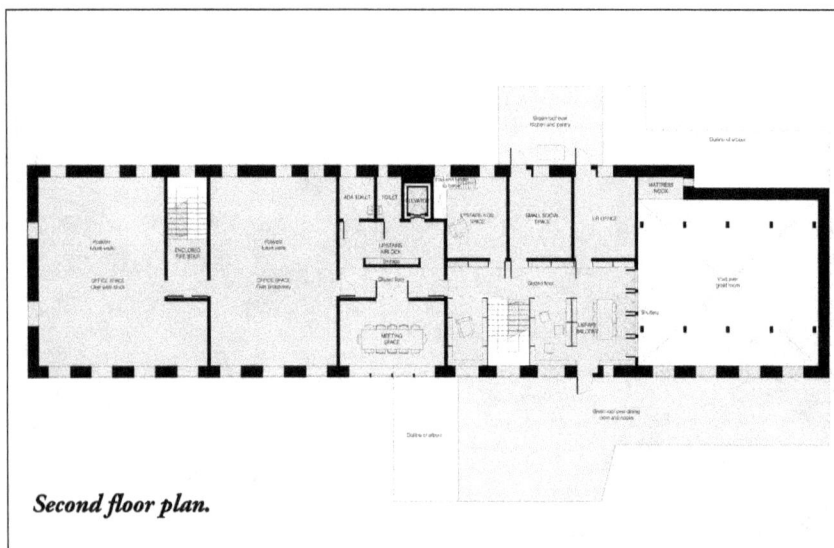

Second floor plan.

Educational Reach

At DR the first part is already under way. DR runs a range of educational programs and workshops including tours, short-term visitor programs, and seasonal work-exchanges. The community is also working to expand its educational options with paid courses including natural building and Gaia Education's Ecovillage Design Education program.

At most of these kinds of events the audience is made up of people already involved or in touch with the communities movement.

The next step then is to get people who are not already tuned in to the alternative culture scene attending events, and through that reach further into the wider culture. Interestingly, events like Off Grid Blues—a blues dancing weekend held at DR, which was attended by a wide range of people, many of whom had no previous exposure to an ecovillage but went away touched and impressed—show that the right courses/events at an ecovillage can bring in people from outside the normal crowd. This happened because people were attending something not specifically alternative culture based—blues dancing.

The same model could be applied to other areas, such as alternative construction workshops aimed at teaching mainstream contractors how they could use natural building techniques, or consensus training courses aimed at teaching mainstream professionals how to facilitate, work more openly with clients, etc.

Eco-Rules and Regulations

DR will be 15 years old this autumn. Over the last decade and a half it has put together a wide range of policies, guidelines, and committees to administer and guide the community.

To date DR has been regulated largely by socially enforced "guidelines" and a set of seven ecological covenants. Although these have been pretty successful so far in maintaining the integrity of the village's principles, there have increasingly been difficulties where individual needs/choices—such as commuting by car to work, or material choices in construction projects which the covenants don't specifically prohibit but seem to stretch the bounds of what is socially accepted, etc.—have begun to show the limits of the current systems. Without a more robust system there is a risk of increasing dilution of DR's mission and ecological performance. However, there is resistance to further "rules and regulations" that some people see as limiting their ability to explore, innovate, or simply do things their own way—their freedom.

It's a difficult balance to strike, as over-regulation and prescription in the mainstream world are part of the reasons to move to community. On the other hand, community already imposes some remarkably restrictive lifestyle rules. For example, at DR you can't own a private motor vehicle—that's a big ask for the average Westerner, let alone the average American. So why are a few more regulations such a scary proposition? Part of it may be that it's very easy to talk abstractly about vision-level wishes and even construct systems to get there. It's different living day-to-day where time, emotional energy, health, and money are all bottom-line pressures whose limits we have to deal with.

So the million Whuffie question is: could more structured and enforceable rules protect the vision of communities like DR, or are they more likely to choke innovation and risk restricting accessibility due to increased financial or energetic demands? I think that, if they are designed well, regulations, with room for exceptions, would benefit communities like DR.

Another of our hopes in pursuing LBC certification on the new common house is that, by sharing the research and methods, DR could adopt LBC, or their own version of it, as a kind of sustainable building code—in the manner mentioned above. This might then be a transferable tool that others could use.

In the LUPP committee, we are working on expanding DR's current guidelines around buildings and neighbourhoods into a set of more fully fledged appropriate holistic planning and zoning regulations, covering things like density, water management, passive solar, designing to encourage community, and so on.

If we can create clearly articulated systems that benefit the communities themselves, and are transferable to settings in the wider culture, maybe these can provide the DNA by which to propagate ecovillages.

> ## Could more structured and enforceable rules protect the vision of communities like DR, or are they more likely to choke innovation and restrict accessibility?

Minor Shifts, Major Effects

I don't want to see ecovillages watering down or sugar coating the radical ways of living that they are exploring in order to win favour in the mainstream. On the other hand I am excited about those same radical ideas and lifestyles and would love to see them spread as far and wide as they can be.

I think that by making some relatively minor shifts in the way ecovillages like DR operate and relate to elements of the wider culture—such as specialists, standards, and course participants—ecovillages can gain leverage and affect real, notable change. ❧

Alex Whitcroft is a multi-disciplinary architectural designer whose work focuses on holistic sustainable design, craft and close collaboration with craftspeople, exploration of materials, and blending innovative and traditional materials and technologies to create beautiful, robust, ecologically sound, culturally specific architecture. His website is alexwhitcroft.co.uk.

Creating eCohousing

By Vivian Vaillant

"Vivian! You are just in time for check in. Two sentences that say where you are right now." Michael, one of the longest-term members to live onsite at The Yarrow Ecovillage, is facilitating our monthly community meeting. As I turn the corner I let out a sudden gasp of delight.

"I'm just..." My voice catches in my throat. I'm working on not being so darned emotional. I try to gather my thoughts. "I'm just so taken aback by the image of you all! And I'm so grateful!"

My neighbours and neighbours-in-waiting are gathered in the old bunker silo that doubles as a sun shade, rain shade, community kitchen, and bike shed. There are about four old couches filled with smiling faces. Chairs and benches make up a second ring of smiling faces. We have become an enormous group. The oldest members and the very newest all gather together to go through the business of the day. I run back for my camera. Some memories are worth taking pictures of.

The meeting is full of important details about the filing of legal documents, community contribution hours, and the startling realization that in 20 days our bunker silo needs to be emptied for demolition. Demolition!? How can that be? I joined this project two short (and very long) years ago and every meeting, BBQ, and other important community moment has happened in this barn. When I came here last summer the barn was my kitchen and comfort. I've had long talks by candlelight in this barn! I've played men-against-women pictionary in this barn (and the women won, by the way!). And now it is coming down to make room for the final stage of construction. In two and a half short years we've gone from no buildings to 16, and now we count down the months to our final construction.

Did we make mistakes? Certainly. We could write a whole book about things we'd recommend no other group do. I think I can safely say we have done one thing very well. We consensed that cohousing be the mechanism to do the housing portion of the ecovillage.

At The Yarrow Ecovillage we strive for a more sustainable life by relying on a deep sense of community. Years ago the community (then very small) asked themselves a defining question: "If you can only choose one, which is the higher value? Community? or Sustainability?" The answer came back a resounding "Community." Not what you'd expect from an ecovillage. May I defend? The reason was that by prioritizing strong community connections, sustainability would naturally follow.

We are surrounded by like-minded people who teach us, push us, and offer us helping hands in a way that lets every family strive for a higher level of sustainability. Some families are more committed, or farther down the path of learning than others. We allow for imperfection as we all learn and grow. We'll all do better next time. By placing community as our highest priority we have also become attainable to a broader group of neighbours. We actually have homes to sell people! We have a site plan, and a common house. People know what they are getting into. People also don't have to feel like the perfect vegan yogi to come here. All we ask is that they respect our prior agreements, and that they are personally striving to be a little bit better every day.

Bunker silo meeting.

I really think the cohousing model helps us achieve that. While our homes are not the cob, strawbale, or yurts we once sort of wished we could build, the more conventional cohousing homes that Charles Durrett has designed for us hold human connection as the highest priority. Everything, from the distance of front doors and the set-up of the mail room in the common house to the locations of our gathering nodes, is designed with the highest level of human contact in public spaces balanced with high levels of privacy in private spaces. This allows for us to live in close proximity without being stuck in each other's faces all the time. We like it very much.

Cohousing—or in our case "eCohousing"—has been in North America for over 30 years since Charles Durrett and Kathrine McCammant brought it from Denmark. In 30 years over 150 cohousing communities have been built across the US, and another 25 in Canada. More begin development every year. The major hurdle for cohousing projects tends to be the acquisition of land. In our case land was not a problem. We had 28 acres of land and not enough people to get all the work done. By bringing Charles on board we were able to attract more people quickly. Every family that comes brings new talents and new ways to have fun. We are on a roll.

If I could send a few words of caution with this great recommendation of the cohousing model they would be these:

1. If possible, hire a cohousing architect before you build any of your buildings. A good place to start looking is the cohousing.org site, or in Canada, cohousing.ca. We had some existing buildings from before Charles came into the picture—our "phase one" of development. It was difficult, but not impossible to work around them. They are pretty, but they impacted the flexibility of the overall site plane.

2. We did have one shortfall within the process: front closets were a priority that was not met. Because we are a farming community, an entire mud room in each house would have been very nice. In the end we've found ways to adapt and meet our needs; however, I think this miscom-

The village from the farm.

munication could have been avoided by holding a community meeting to discuss the plans before Charles arrived to garner our feedback. When he comes, his time is spent very quickly between city officials and community meetings. His time for feedback is limited. Community efficiency would have helped us immensely.

3. Stay away from any custom homes. They will surely cause your community more strife than they are worth. Consider that in cohousing your highest value becomes your community connections. Our experience has been that custom homes have cost both the custom home owners and the community at large more stress than they are worth. I think a good rule to adopt would be to allow only floor plans that are used at least twice in the site plan. If someone wants to design something custom, it should be fine as long as it is salable to more than one family. This will go a long way to fairness in the sales you have to do to newcomers. As the head of marketing I can tell you that it is difficult to explain to newcomers why some of our units are so specialized when the other 18 are exactly the same as each other.

4. As much as possible build all of your units at the same time. Phases of development are tiring and costly. You stand to save a large amount of money by building out simultaneously. It is also nice to do one big move-in month rather than having some people afar and others on-site.

5. When cohousing architects speak, please listen to them. They do know what they are talking about.

While we've almost completed our multigenerational cohousing project, we've also begun a seniors cohousing group. In the final picture our ecovillage will be a 20 acre organic farm, a multigenerational cohousing, seniors cohousing, and commercial development. We are on the main street of a small town with all of our basic needs within walking distance. The journey has been long. Thousands and thousands of hours have been put into our project to date. Love, frustration, and overwhelming commitment will get us to completion. (Is there such a thing?) As we celebrate 10 years since we bought the land, I can tell you that adopting cohousing has allowed us to move at a much faster rate. I believe the key to our long-term success will be the human-centred architecture cohousing has brought. And what luck for me that this is my sweet home!

• • •

For more information on cohousing you can read *Creating Cohousing* by Charles Durrett and Kathryn McCamant (we're a chapter in the latest edition). See also the websites www.cohousing.org and www.cohousing.ca. ❧

_____

Vivian Vaillant is one of the many people who have worked hard to make The Yarrow Ecovillage a successful reality in Yarrow, British Columbia (see www.yarrowecovillage.ca).

Coming of Age: 21 Years of EcoVillage Planning and Living

By Liz Walker

"To promote experiential learning about ways of meeting human needs for shelter, food, energy, livelihood, and social connectedness that are aligned with the long-term health and viability of Earth and all its inhabitants."
—Mission statement for EcoVillage at Ithaca—Center for Sustainability Education

Last night a group of four dozen people gathered in the Common House for a simple vegetarian dinner of curried lentil soup, hearty cornbread, and a salad made from three kinds of greens from our onsite farm. After the dishes were cleared, a third of the group stayed on for an in-depth presentation by Jesse Sherry, a PhD student from Rutgers who is studying the ecological footprint of several ecovillages and comparing their impact to that of the average US citizen. Using data generated from about half of the 60 households who live at EcoVillage at Ithaca (EVI), Jesse found that the EVI average was about 2.4 global hectares (gha) per person, compared with 8 gha per person for the national average. This means that people who live in our community use only about 30 percent of the resources (for travel, heat, food, water, and waste) of typical Americans. Lest we get too self-congratulatory, the two other ecovillages studied—Earthhaven in North Carolina and Sirius in Massachusetts, were at 1.8 and 2.1 respectively. We were doing well, and with more collective effort we could do even better.

Looking around the room, I remembered our "Envisioning Retreat," 21 years ago. In June of 1991, 100 of us camped out in a field during the week of the summer solstice and dreamed of creating an ecovillage together. While fireflies flickered around our tents, we talked of our vision: to create a community of up to 500 people, with thriving organic farms and a vibrant education center just outside of Ithaca.

As with the presentation we had just heard, I was struck at how far we have come, and at the same time how far we have to go. At age 21, how have we matured, and how are we still struggling to live out our values? What have we learned that may be useful to the broader society?

Forming an Identity

Early in the development of EVI, we chose to appeal to middle class Americans. We wanted to create an alternative lifestyle that would demonstrate a far more ecological approach than mainstream culture, yet that would be

seen this type of community. However, cohousing brings some key principles into play that have been highly successful. Our two (soon to be three) densely clustered neighborhoods are centered on winding pedestrian streets that offer a congenial place for kids to play, neighbors to chat, and conversations to unfold around picnic tables and sand boxes. There is a delightful sense of wandering through a park as one follows the path past unique front-yard gardens blossoming with a profusion of flowering plants.

The Common Houses offer a common space for several community dinners each week, kids' indoor play space, home offices, common laundry facilities, and a place for ongoing classes, celebrations, dances, and special gatherings. There is a nice balance between people's private lives and the ongoing life of the community.

Another key choice was to actively farm the land. We chose land with abandoned agricultural fields that we have gradually been bringing back into production. Right now we have two working farms: West Haven Farm has 10 acres under production and grows certified organic vegetables and fruit for 1000 people a week during the growing season. Kestrel's Perch Berry Farm is five acres and has a U-Pick operation with seven kinds of berries. Both farms are operated as CSAs, with member families from all over the county. In addition, we have several thriving community gardens for the residents, and a growing agricultural education program, Groundswell Center for Local Food and Farming, which will soon reclaim 10 acres at EVI for small-scale incubator farms for low income beginning farmers.

EcoVillage at Ithaca was started by a

attractive to a wide variety of people. We wanted to influence development patterns, and make a difference through our example.

This influenced many of our subsequent choices. We wanted to be accessible to visitors and students, so we decided to develop on land that was just two miles from downtown Ithaca, New York, a progressive college town that is home to Cornell University, Ithaca College, and TC3, our local community college. We have a steady stream of visitors who come to EVI on tours, to do research, to visit, or to buy produce from our farms. A common comment from visitors is, "You know, I could actually see myself living here."

Another early decision was to use the cohousing model. In 1991, cohousing was so new to the US that none of us had ever

nonprofit organization (now called EVI–Center for Sustainability Education), and a big part of our initial work has been to grow the ecovillage itself from a vision to a real, living laboratory. At times it has been hard to separate out the identities of the living community and the educational work. Once in a while there is a clash between our nonprofit mission (which seeks to bring in visitors, support research, and "grow the vision") and some of the residents who want to enjoy quiet lives without the disruption of more visitors or more neighborhoods.

Gaining Skills

As our ecovillage has developed over time, we have grown in our capabilities. Our initial cohousing neighborhood was the first in New York State, and we had all the challenges of convincing our local planning board, bankers, insurance agents, and the NYS Attorney General's office that we were legitimate developers. Now we are actually the ones writing new zoning regulations; not only do we anticipate they will be adopted by our county, but also hope they will be of use around the country.

In 1997, when our first resident group, "FROG," was built, no incentive programs were in place to help fund renewable energy. Now, in 2012, we have just installed a brand new 50 KW ground-mounted solar array which is producing 60 percent of the electricity needed by all 30 homes in FROG. Smart meters tell us how much current we are using in our homes or as a whole neighborhood. Our second cohousing neighborhood, "SONG," built in 2002-2004, was able to take advantage of incentive and rebate programs that returned approximately 50 percent of the value of the investment. Out of 30 homes, almost half sport photovoltaic panels (solar electric) and four use solar thermal (hot water). Our third neighborhood, "TREE," currently under construction, plans to make extensive use of photovoltaics and solar thermal. Incentive and rebate programs now return about three quarters of the original investment, making it crazy not to use them.

In addition to expanding our renewable energy capacity, our green building efforts have also become more sophisticated over time. From simple passive solar duplexes in FROG, to examples of strawbale, structurally insulated panels (SIPs), and timber-frame buildings in SONG, we are now aiming for Passive House (PH) certification in TREE. The Passive House standard is "arguably the most stringent energy-efficient building spec in the world," says Chris Corson in the May 2012 issue of *The Journal of Light Construction*. "The big picture goal of the Passive House movement is to nearly eliminate housing's share of climate change by slashing energy consumption to about six percent of that used in conventional homes." In the TREE neighborhood, we are aiming not only to greatly reduce energy consumption, but also to show that it can be done affordably.

With 15 years of community living under our belts, we've also grown tremendously in our collective ability to solve conflicts. And we've had some doozies! One community-wide conflict that took over a year to resolve was figuring out a policy on outdoor cats. Our group seemed pretty evenly split between those who wanted to restrict cats from hunting (cats kill millions of birds a year), to those who felt that their beloved pets should have the freedom to roam. After a dozen or more tense meetings in "salons" (non-decision-making discussion groups), neighborhood groups, and whole village meetings, we finally reached consensus on a long-term policy that would restrict each of the three neighborhoods to no more than two outdoor cats apiece. The

short-term policy allowed existing neighborhood cats (including four owned by one person) to be "grandfathered" in. While it was a compromise that thrilled no one, it allowed us to finally drop the issue, and move towards a more ecological long-term policy, while not penalizing those who already owned outdoor cats.

Facing Challenges

While we have a good track record on many fronts, there continue to be challenges in others. I'll pick two for now: achieving more racial and income diversity, and long-term community burnout.

While our goal has always been to be an inclusive community, we have had only mixed success. In some respects, the village population is quite diverse, with ages from two to 82, people with varied types of jobs, and spiritual backgrounds ranging from observant Jews to Bahai, Christian, and Earth-based spirituality. There are a few people with major physical disabilities, and several children with major developmental delays. There is a fairly small lesbian, gay, and bisexual population currently, at just five percent of the adult residents.

When it comes to income level, most people are middle class, although there are some residents (often renters) who are low income, and others who are quite wealthy. Over the years we have tried many different strategies for keeping housing as affordable as possible. We have used standardized design and construction in FROG and TREE, with options for self-building in SONG. We also received a grant from the Federal Home Loan Bank for SONG that enabled us to pay the down payments for six affordable homes in SONG. In TREE, we are aiming for very affordable pricing based on building 15 apartments in addition to 25 houses, standardizing design

and construction, and using a nonprofit development model in which the group itself acts as general contractor, while hiring a very experienced builder. But I think the most successful strategy may be that TREE will also offer 15 percent of its homes as rentals, allowing people to live here who would otherwise not have the capital needed to buy a home.

We probably have least diversity in race. Currently we have 15 percent people of color (compared to 20 percent non-white population in Tompkins County, and 33 percent in the City of Ithaca). There are very few African Americans at EVI, a situation we would love to change. There are currently several efforts aimed at bridging this gap. Quite a few of our residents have taken a five week course called "Talking Circles on Race and Racism." Several of our residents have been trained to lead these sessions, which aim to create a dialogue between whites and people of color. There is also an onsite, ongoing weekly study group on bridging the gap between environmentalism and social justice.

Another challenge we are facing is how to keep the energy going for the long term. After 15 years of living in community, we are currently facing a problem of burnout. It is often hard to make the quorum for our monthly village meetings, our work teams sometimes don't have enough participation, and many community meals (there are four dinners a week) have low attendance. What is wrong? We've been trying to figure it out.

Our cook team has been especially hard hit, and we've noticed a few trends. Many more people have specialized diets than even five years ago. The cooks are now responsible for making meals for a wide variety of dietary needs: vegans, vegetarians, gluten-free, nightshade-free, kid-friendly, and various combinations of these. There are whole families who are on meat-oriented diets to correct severe allergies. What's a cook to do?

Part of the solution seems to be to simplify the meals, aiming for one-food-fits-most (e.g. a vegan, gluten-free main dish can feed most people). We are also trying to find ways to appreciate the cooks, who may put in between two to six hours to prepare a meal, then have it scarfed up quickly, with people rushing off for another evening activity. It's sometimes hard to keep the culture of community going when the societal trend is chronic busyness and isolation. The good news is that we are consciously addressing this, and experimenting with different ideas, including monthly coffee houses and special celebrations. In addition, with the influx of new TREE residents moving in over the coming year, there will be lots more people to partake in both cooking and eating community meals.

Stepping Out into the World

While we have always been engaged in educational work, in the last several years our efforts have grown dramatically. Part of this is through establishing partnerships with other groups. Our nonprofit arm currently has formal partnerships with Ithaca College Environmental Studies Department, Tompkins County Planning Department, Center for Transformative Action, Cornell Cooperative Extension, Tompkins County Climate Protection Initiative, New Roots Charter School, and many other groups who share our values of sustainability and social justice.

Partly because of these partnerships, EcoVillage at Ithaca–Center for Sustainability Education has landed two major federal grants. One, a three year USDA grant, funds Groundswell Center (already mentioned) to work with beginning farmers. This program has taken off like wildfire, and is bringing together local food justice groups with farmers, and like its name, creating a groundswell of interest in local food and farming. Every week from spring through fall, a couple dozen aspiring farmers meet for hands-on classes that teach everything from business planning to nutrition to organic weed control. The excitement is palpable.

Last April we also received an EPA Climate Showcase Communities Grant in partnership with the Tompkins County Planning Department. The three year grant (one of a total of 50 around the country) allows us to study the lessons we've learned from building EVI, and apply those lessons to three new pilot projects (the TREE neighborhood, an urban infill "pocket neighborhood," and a new residential eco-development of 70 homes planned on county land). We'll study energy usage of future residents a year before move-in as well as a year after move-in to find out the most successful strategies for cutting greenhouse gas emissions. It is thrilling to think that one of our very earliest dreams—to

> **One of our very earliest dreams— to actually influence mainstream development to become bright green and community oriented—is underway.**

actually influence mainstream development to become bright green and community oriented—is underway.

Looking Towards the Future

In the very near future, our population will increase by a third, to about 250 people. Our per capita ecological footprint should also shrink substantially, with the construction of Passive House buildings in TREE, and new solar arrays. As our ecovillage continues to grow and mature, we also plan more onsite businesses, a dynamic EcoVillage Education Center, more farming, a more racially and economically diverse group, and we hope, ever-deepening community ties, both to each other and to this gorgeous Finger Lakes regional community of land and people. ❧

Liz Walker is cofounder of EcoVillage at Ithaca, and serves as Executive Director of the EVI–Center for Sustainability Education. She has authored two books, EcoVillage at Ithaca: Pioneering a Sustainable Culture, *and* Choosing a Sustainable Future: Ideas and Inspiration from Ithaca, NY, *both published by New Society Publishers.*

Growing Up in EcoVillage at Ithaca

By Allegra Willett

The wind is rustling through my hair and I can feel the rough texture of the straw beneath me. "WE MUST RIDE ON!" comes a call from my left. Emma is our chieftain and we are riding our faithful wolf mounts onward to save a tribesman. Of course we aren't; our imagination is so full bodied that the hay barrels beneath us are magically wolves. The weaponry we so proudly carry across our backs is simply grapevines twisted with twine. We had journeyed into the forest that surrounds our village alone with small saws earlier that day, scavenging for vines with curvatures perfect for our new bows. After our bows were strung with twine we headed into the goldenrod fields to select arrows that would fill the makeshift quivers that rested behind our non-dominant shoulders. For weeks on end we would run freely through the woods, climbing trees and making forts with sticks and moss. We stalked through the high grass behind the village pond, making grass houses and pretending to hunt. The freedom our land allowed, and that with which our parents gifted us, made us grow with the opportunity to explore our surroundings and learn from what we saw around us.

In the evenings after our community meals we would gather all of the children in our cohousing village and don our darkest clothes so we could slip into the shadows while we played "dark tag," our version of cops and robbers. I can still remember running to the veggie-oil-powered bus that housed our French Canadian visitors and asking them to play with us in the darkness. One of those times we were running beside the pond in the pitch blackness with one of the men from the bus. I was yelling, "RORY, RUN FASTER!" to a girl who lived a few houses down from me. Tim, a fast boy from the other team, was hot on our heels and I knew that Rory wasn't a fast runner. Suddenly the Canadian scooped her up in his arms and ran her into the safety of our village, with her screaming and laughing for him to put her down.

Dark tag was the time for all of us to get together to play, no matter what our age differences were. The village would ring with laughter and shrill screams from boys and girls jumping out of the blackness. You could tell a really good game was going when the village was silent with all of us stalking each other from our hiding places. My generation of EcoVillage kids created dark tag 15 years ago; we are legends here and the game is still played today.

Growing up in a cohousing community was full of freedom for me as a child and I had very little awareness of the housing experiment EcoVillage was known for worldwide. To me EcoVillage was a home with endless space and time for exploration. I have always imagined life to be a series of adventures that should never be taken for granted. When I was returning home from interning at Disney World this past January, I remember sitting in the observation car on the Amtrak Auto Train that runs from Sanford, Florida to Lorton, Virginia. We had just passed through the Georgia border, and I was looking out the window as the sun was setting, wondering what adventures the world had in store for me next. I could almost feel the future, yet it was more like smoke than an actual texture. It is hard to grasp the exact shape my future will take but the smoke tells me that the future adventures are as sure as my dark tag teammates waiting to be discovered in the shadows. ❧

Home-schooled at EcoVillage at Ithaca, Allegra Willett is now in her late teens. She wrote this essay for her college entrance application.

Fifty Years On:
Living Now in the
Findhorn Foundation Community

By Lisa Sutherland

I first heard about Findhorn whilst kneeling in a mountain of mulch, trellising beans through the brown stalks of sunflowers. I was taking a stranger for a ramble through the diverse abundance of the garden I was tending using permaculture principles, common sense, creative need, and long conversations with the plants and landscape. My guest was delighted by the story of how the lawn of this small suburban plot in a semi-industrial area in Durban, South Africa had become a community project that shared the healing power of nature with all who were willing to learn and care for the garden. "Have you heard about Findhorn?" she said, and that was it, I felt something deep within me hum and from that moment on, a journey of discovery began.

Three years later, I found myself on the threshold of a communal ecohouse in the housing cluster called Bagend, all my worldly goods packed into a suitcase and a backpack. I had come to Findhorn to answer the call of love, a call that led me to participate in the first Findhorn Ecovillage Design and Education Training.

I had great dreams of creating an ecovillage in South Africa, with the intention of housing the many children families orphaned through AIDS. Most people settle for a house—I wanted an entire village! Now, six years later, these ambitious dreams have waned and the anxiety to change the world single-handedly has softened into the valuable wisdom that I am not alone on this journey. Indeed, there is a global wave of people dedicated to being the change they want to see in the world, committed to the inspired action of social and environmental justice, investigating new ways of living and growing together, honouring all life on this planet.

Here, living within the Findhorn community, I am reminded every day of the call to hold the faith and vision of a better world. I only need to look outside my office window to see the demonstration of building this future. The grass roof on the guest lodge is the playground for insects, its structure designed to harness renewable energy and its walls welcoming in the guests who, like me, are drawn to experience this demonstration of a community aspiring to harmonious and sustainable lifestyles.

This year, the Findhorn community is celebrating its 50th birthday. From its humble beginnings in 1962, this constantly evolving community is now home to more than 400 people creatively exploring how to live more consciously and sustainably on this planet. It is difficult to define the Findhorn Foundation Community in relation to place. Although The Park, located on the beautiful Findhorn Bay, is a demonstration of ecological buildings, the social and spiritual impulse of the community reaches far beyond, indeed to all four corners of the globe. This global community includes the many people who have been inspired by their experiences here and have taken them out into the world, seeding many projects in their hometowns, from meditation circles to sustainability projects. The Findhorn ecovillage is unique because it addresses sustainability not only in environmental terms, but also in spiritual, social, and economic terms and this moves the concept of community beyond the site and into the realms of the heart and mind and spirit.

The focal point of everyday life in the community is the practice of the founding spiritual principles of inner listening, co-creation with the intelligence of nature, and

Photos courtesy of Lisa Sutherland

270

taking inspired action.

The community encourages everyone to engage in their own form of spiritual practice and offers numerous opportunities to explore various ways of connecting with the intelligence that is at the heart of all life. In the gardens, the Celtic festivals are celebrated to mark the seasons; every year we hold a festival of Sacred Dance, Music, and Song; and people hold and share various faiths. I can start my day by lifting my voice in chorus, harmonising with others as we sing the songs brought to us via the Taizé community in France. I can also attend daily group meditations in the Main Sanctuary deepening the practice of inner listening and being still.

This diverse community includes holistic businesses, artists, builders, healing professionals, a community shop, a café, an eco-friendly printing company, a Steiner school, a theatre complex, and associated retreat and workshop centres—all linked by a shared positive vision for humanity and the earth. I consider myself blessed to have all these resources at my fingertips. I can buy local, organic, fair-trade food, hold my meetings in the warmth and welcome of the café, read our information on eco-friendly paper that considers the impact on the planet and not just profit, benefit from the renew-

we share with our guests. I begin my working day with a check-in—an open space in which to hear where everyone is at, to assess what might be needed to support one another, and to identify the work tasks that have priority. Once a week we have time to meditate and share together, valuing the need to nurture the relationships we have with one another. Periodically the team comes together for supervision, to examine the conflicts, the edges, and the issues that are at play in our field. The business of the Findhorn Foundation is not just task, it involves a dedication to being aware of the way in which we go about our daily work and how we are in relationship with ourselves, one another, and our world.

Sound like heaven on earth? It is, and this Eden also has its share of snakes. Accommodation is one of those. For five years I lived in communal housing, eventually choosing to move into a flat of my own in the village because I realised I needed space away from the hustle, bustle, and intensity of community life. As well as providing for individual needs, the community faces the challenge of providing affordable housing for a ballooning aging population and the numerous young families who settle here in this child-friendly environment.

The question of minimum wage is a

The community walks the fine line of being innovative and having to adhere to government policy.

able energy that powers my office, dance in the spacious beauty of the Universal Hall, attend courses that ignite my spirit, and find the support and nurturing I need as I continue to discover the depth of my personal journey.

The experiential programmes and workshops offered through the Findhorn Foundation share practical steps for personal and global transformation. Working for the Findhorn Foundation I am supported by the daily practices

hot issue at present and the Findhorn Foundation has realised that it is no longer possible for all co-workers to receive this basic remuneration as it does not meet the needs of several people. With regards many issues, the community walks the fine line of being innovative and pushing boundaries and having to adhere to government policy and law. There is a raw edge where different

(continued on p. 76)

271

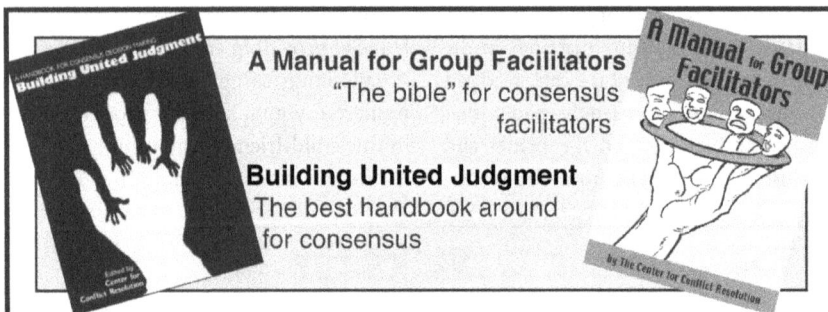

FIFTY YEARS ON: LIVING NOW IN THE FINDHORN FOUNDATION COMMUNITY

(continued from p. 43)

beliefs clash concerning lifestyle choices; for example, car and property ownership, where to shop, what to invest in…rich debates that keep us connected and sometimes divided.

Recently, with new property developments, we are faced with the issue of how big can the local community get without losing sight of its original impulse. It has also generated ideas about how to hold this growing community together so that we may continue to thrive into the next 50 years.

Almost everyone I have met in this community is a gardener of some kind—whether actively putting their hands in the earth to bring forth the bounty and beauty of nature, or cultivating the full radiance of their life's purpose. Here I live amongst people who recognise humanity's interdependence with all of life and affirm the values of love, service, integrity, responsibility, and personal leadership.

The ecovillage at Findhorn reflects the community's commitment to work consciously and harmoniously with nature. The ecovillage includes caring and cooperative relationships, healthy ecological practices and building techniques, responsible energy generation and use, recycling, organic food production, and sustainable social and economic structures, and serves as an inspiring demonstration of new directions for humanity and the planet. Here I have everything I need and it is a blessing to live with a sense of integrity, knowing that all that I source comes from a place that values life in all its forms, and strives to demonstrate sustainable, harmonious living practice. ❧

Lisa Sutherland was born in South Africa and made the biggest leap of faith and longest journey of her life six years ago, when she came to Findhorn to experience the reality of communal living. She now lives in Findhorn village, works part-time for the Findhorn Foundation, runs a complementary therapies practice, and is studying further in Complementary Medicine.

Earthsong Eco-Neighbourhood— Rebuilding Community within the City

By Robin Allison

Turn off busy Swanson Road in the western suburbs of Auckland, leave your car in the carpark to walk between clusters of houses into the heart of this urban community, and you find yourself in an oasis of calm, beauty, and abundance. Neighbours stop for a chat on the path, children race past on their tricycles, and the loudest sound you hear is the birdsong. This is Earthsong, home to 69 adults and children in 32 homes nestled amongst gardens, paths, and a village green on only three acres of land.

Earthsong is an eco-neighbourhood based on the twin principles of cohousing and permaculture. The founding vision, still strongly held by residents today, has three equal components: sustainable design and construction, respectful and cooperative community, and education by demonstration. At Earthsong we are relearning the skills and benefits of belonging to a community, and rebuilding a healthy interdependence with each other and with earth.

Launched at a public meeting in 1995, the project grew as people joined and worked together over several years developing the foundation agreements of effective group procedures, legal and financial structures, and site and design criteria. In 1999 they purchased the land (a former organic orchard), then worked with consultants to design the whole development, and contracted with builders to build the project in stages. While the first residents moved into their homes in 2002, the last homes and siteworks weren't completed until 2008.

Communities such as Earthsong add another layer of belonging into the standard suburban model—a layer of community relationships and governance, that doesn't reduce our personal autonomy in our own homes but adds the enormous richness of a cohesive neighbourhood within the more impersonal wider suburb and city.

Design for Sustainability

What makes Earthsong an eco-neighbourhood? Earthsong itself doesn't have the shops, businesses, school, or other facilities suggested by the term "village," so we are happy to be known as a housing neighbourhood. However we are a short walk to the shops, library and community facilities, bus stop, and train station of our local suburban centre.

Within our neighbourhood the site layout, buildings, and services are designed to work with the natural landform and climate. Rammed earth and natural timber give the houses a solid and timeless feel, with plenty of windows to let the sun warm the coloured concrete floors for passive solar design. Solar water heaters, nontoxic materials, natural oils and paints all add up to low-energy and healthy houses.

Clusters of two-storey attached dwellings are arranged along the common pathways and shared courtyards, surrounded by old fruit trees and lush new plantings. Homes range from one-bed-

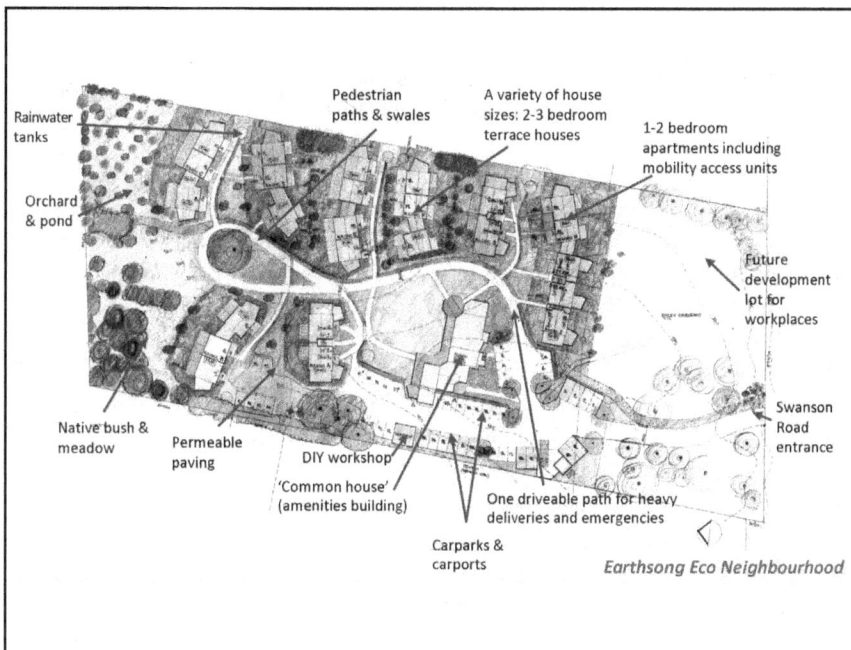

Rainwater tanks

Orchard & pond

Native bush & meadow

Permeable paving

DIY workshop

'Common house' (amenities building)

Carparks & carports

Pedestrian paths & swales

A variety of house sizes: 2-3 bedroom terrace houses

1-2 bedroom apartments including mobility access units

Future development lot for workplaces

Swanson Road entrance

One driveable path for heavy deliveries and emergencies

Earthsong Eco Neighbourhood

Earthsong common house.

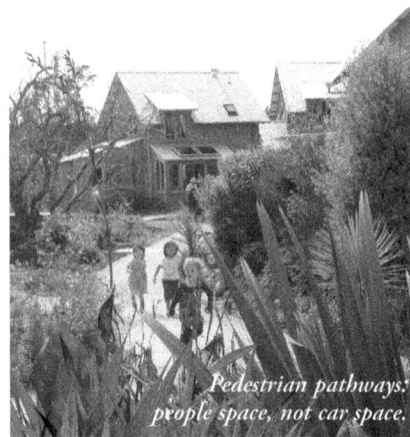
Pedestrian pathways: people space, not car space.

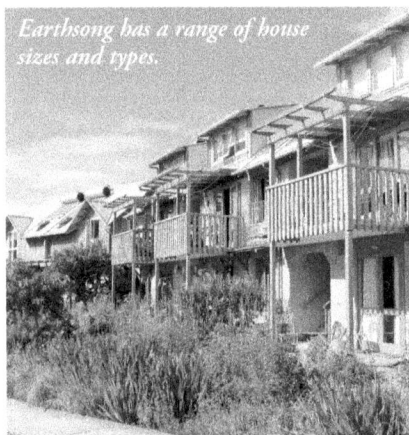
Earthsong has a range of house sizes and types.

Neighbours gather on the path.

Photos courtesy of Robin Allison

room studios to four-bedroom houses to suit all ages and different household types. Easy gradients on all paths allow full accessibility, and seven single-level houses are designed for those older or less mobile.

Roof water is collected for reuse in the homes. Surface rain water flows into densely planted swales (shallow dish drains) beside the paths, and down to the large pond, home to frogs and ducks, reducing water runoff from the site. A comprehensive permaculture site design includes gathering nodes and children's play areas, vegetable gardens, native bush and orchard areas, water management, and composting.

We couldn't include everything we wanted at the time of building due to cost or regulatory obstacles, so we built in the ability to upgrade later. There are cables inside the walls of each house to assist later installation of photovoltaic panels, land area is set aside for more water tanks, and networks of spare conduits in the ground allow for future internet upgrades. Sustainability includes affordability, and our approach has been to achieve as much as we could across the full spectrum of environmental and social sustainability and to be willing to let go of perfection in any one area.

Community Aspects of Sustainability

What we have learnt at Earthsong is that social and environmental sustainability are complementary and mutually reinforcing. Many of the sustainable design aspects of our neighbourhood were made possible not only in *addition* to a social and cooperative structure, but *because* of our social cooperative structure; the two have always gone hand-in-hand.

One example is our car-free neighbourhood: we place a higher importance on our relationships with one another than with our cars, so we designed the carparks at the edge of the site. This has both social and environmental benefits—land area that would otherwise be driveways or road is freed up for productive gardens and community living space, for children to play safely and neighbours to interact as they come and go from their houses.

By sharing resources, we have access to increased facilities and "common wealth" while we use less overall. At the heart of the neighbourhood is the common house, our much-loved community building owned jointly by all the house-holders and providing shared spaces including the large dining/meeting hall, sitting room, large kitchen, childrens' room, guest room, and shared laundry. The individual houses are well-designed but compact (100 square meters for a three-bedroom home) because they don't need a spare bedroom for occasional guests, or a living room large enough for large parties or meetings. Even eco-friendly construction uses significant energy and materials so building smaller houses and having shared facilities makes good environmental sense.

Living within a diverse and supportive neighbourhood makes it easier for individuals to make low-energy, sustainable choices. With good systems of management, equipment such as lawnmowers, garden tools, and workshop tools can be shared. Carpooling and car sharing are much easier to organize and manage when we already know and trust one another.

Working alongside my neighbours on a cooking team for a common dinner or a working bee in the garden is a great way to build the social glue of relationships that maintains community. Cooperation also happens on a daily informal basis, from child-care arrangements to moving furniture or watering the garden when a neighbour goes away. It's all about building connections between people and valuing the sense of belonging.

Another powerful way that being part of a cohesive community can facilitate environmental responsibility is that we learn from each other. Designing eco-friendly buildings and neighbourhoods is an important first step, but the behaviour of the occupants is at least as significant when it comes to the overall impact. It takes extra effort to live a more sustainable life, to resist the gravitational pull back to doing things the "normal" and therefore easier way, but in community we can help each other with information, support, and accountability.

One example is electricity use, which can vary widely even between identical houses with similar numbers and ages of inhabitants, because of the habits and behaviour of the residents. As a cooperative neighbourhood we can facilitate

behaviour change in a number of ways, through information exchange and education, sharing ideas and tips about how to manage the systems more efficiently, internal pricing plans that reward low users and discourage high use, built-in feedback mechanisms, and accountability by making individual house use transparent to all. All of these mechanisms are in place in some form at Earthsong, with the result that 32 homes and the common house are functioning with an electricity supply of the size that usually supplies six houses in New Zealand.

"Through living at Earthsong," one resident told me, "I have become aware of permaculture and have seen it work in practice. With the support of neighbours I am now implementing permaculture principles in my garden."

"My education focused strongly on decision making and producing 'optimal' results," another said. "Our consensus decision-making process here at Earthsong makes me realise how much learning we lose by reducing decisions to numbers. In the beginning I just wanted to get done with the rounds and the meetings; now I value them for providing insight in the thought processes and mindsets of my neighbours."

And another: "I buy much more organic food for myself because it seems strange to live in a healthy house on a certified organic property and fill the fridge up with non-organic food."

Eco-Neighbourhoods within Eco-Cities

Earthsong has become a catalyst in the rejuvenation of the wider suburb. The

front portion of our site will be developed as eco-friendly shops and offices, to link the housing with the wider neighbourhood, enhance the adjacent commercial centre, and provide work opportunities for both Earthsong residents and the wider community. Several residents have been deeply involved in local community development projects, working towards a more socially, culturally, and environmentally sustainable suburb or "ecovillage."

Like a healthy organism with healthy organs made up of healthy cells, sustainability needs to operate at all levels: the individual, the household, the neighbourhood, the village, and the city. A flourishing, sustainable "eco-city," by definition, would include many flourishing, connected ecovillages and neighbourhoods, of an appropriate scale to encourage cooperation and healthy relationships. It is increasingly apparent that we are all part of one vast, complex planetary system or organism, and eco-neighbourhoods and villages offer fertile environments to re-learn the skills of interdependence and cooperation that will contribute to the health of our beautiful earth home. ❧

An architect, Robin was the initiator and development coordinator and is now a contented resident of Earthsong Eco-Neighbourhood (www.earthsong.org.nz). She is a fellow of the New Zealand Social Entrepreneur Fellowship, and is profiled in the recent book How Communities Heal. *Her chapter is available at tinyurl. com/hchallison. Contact robin.allison@ earthsong.org.nz.*

The pond: home of ducks, frogs, and herons.

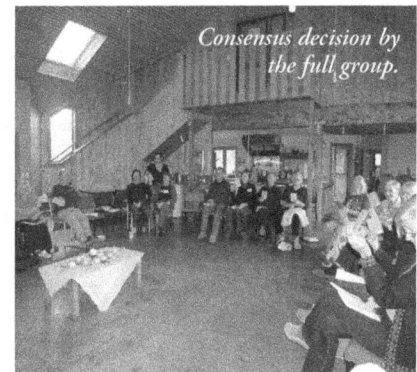

Consensus decision by the full group.

Dandelion Village: Building an Ecovillage in Town

By Maggie Sullivan

It may seem impossible to create an intentional community inside an existing city with all the difficulties in zoning restrictions, red tape, and political jockeying. However, Dandelion Village successfully navigated the legal hoops to form an ecovillage within the city of Bloomington, Indiana and their success can be replicated elsewhere. Their keys to success were understanding the process, identifying allies in positions of power, and communicating with complete transparency about their goals and plans.

While rural ecovillages can provide better opportunities for farming and connecting with nature, urban locations have their own benefits, like car-free living, sewer systems, public libraries, better school options, a market for goods produced by the ecovillage, and a more vibrant social scene. Danny Weddle, one of the founders of Dandelion Village, dreamed of creating an ecovillage in his college town and gathered a group of five people who were ready to make it happen. "We looked for a property that was 15 minutes from downtown on a bike," said Danny. Their original vision was of a 50-member community on a permaculture-designed urban farm with members living in small, minimalist cabins and sharing a communal building with the kitchen and bathrooms. This design would allow higher density than typical single family home developments while maintaining much more greenspace and focusing on "hyperlocal food production."

By scouring the property listings and keeping an eye out for "for sale" signs, they located a potential property just south of town. They held a series of work sessions to produce a 14-page ecovillage development plan. At the same time, Danny, Zach Dwiel, and Carolyn Blank set up casual meetings with a few sympathetic city council members, such as the chair for Bloomington's Peak Oil Task Force. These city council members were very supportive and had many suggestions on how to navigate the planning process. Their chief advice was to start talking with the city planning department immediately to determine their options and the best approach for obtaining approval.

Like many fast-growing communities, Bloomington has extensive development guidelines geared towards preserving the exceptional quality of life valued by its citizens. Simultaneously ranked as one of the best college towns, one of the best places to retire, and one of the best gay/lesbian communities, its local culture is artsy, diverse, environmentally conscious, and progressive. Happily, the staff at the planning department was intrigued by Dandelion Village. "Many of the goals of this project...are things the city has been dictating and encouraging through the Growth Policies Plan," said development review manager Pat Shay, commenting on its compact urban form and its use of an otherwise hard-to-develop lot. However, the project was a challenge because it did not meet traditional zoning requirements. "This was a new issue for Bloomington," said planning director Tom Micuda. "We did not have a code for cohousing and that meant we had to go for rezoning for the land. Essentially we did a PUD." PUD (Planned Unit Development) was

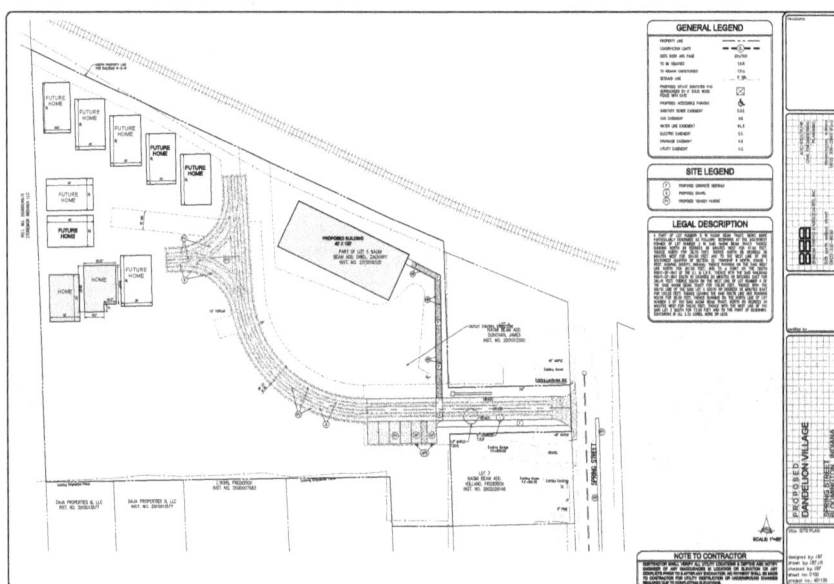

276

Dandelion Village bees.

Photos courtesy of Maggie Sullivan

Dandelion Village greenhouse.

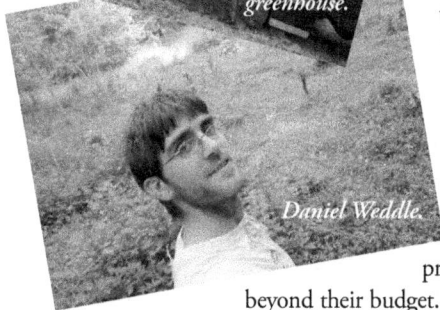

Daniel Weddle.

a large chicken flock of 50 hens, a small herd of goats, barns, and only two parking spaces for the entire development with the understanding that the members would live largely car-free.

Several plan commission members were skeptical of the idea and many were concerned about having farm animals near a residential neighborhood. However, they were impressed by the group's dedication and preparedness and intrigued by the idea of a project countering the "McMansion trend" seen elsewhere in the city. They did advise the Dandelion group that their PUD request would not be approved without plans developed by a licensed engineer. They also listened attentively to the neighborhood residents who came to the meeting and voiced deep concerns. In response, the Dandelion Village group began canvassing door-to-door to talk with their future neighbors and understand their fears.

Most of the concerns revolved around the idea that a hippie commune would bring in drugs and undesirables, not to mention crowing roosters and loose goats eating their peonies. "It was the issue of 'we're not familiar with this—what will it do to us?'" said Tom Micuda. Many neighbors were also concerned about the impact on existing problems like lack of neighborhood parking and flooding issues. The neighborhood streets routinely flooded during large storm events and there were concerns that any sort of development in the area would make it worse.

The Dandelion group continued to talk with neighbors and even helped relaunch the Waterman Neighborhood Association. They also incorporated water retention structures into their site design. Instead of causing additional flooding problems, their development was designed to improve the situation by holding back runoff from the adjacent neighborhood to the north. "We approached from a permaculture prespective," said Danny, describing how they elected to turn waste into a resource. "Water is one of the most critical flows you can possibly have. There has been a drought for the last three years so we said

designed mainly for developers looking to do large neighborhood developments and allows developers to propose a layout different from the standard pattern. Generally, the idea is that the city gives some sort of concession to the developer (for example, higher density) that is mitigated by the developer offering some benefit to the city, often in terms of subsidizing additional infrastructure costs or helping the city meet one of its development goals like preserved greenspace.

While things were advancing with the planning department, the Dandelion Village group had less success purchasing a piece of land. The owner of the first property raised his price 20 percent, pushing it beyond their budget. Danny, Zach, and Carolyn continued their search via Google Earth and by bicycle. Another promising property fell through before they stumbled on an unusual location that became their ultimate site. It was an odd piece of land sandwiched between a train track, a trailer park, a cemetery, and the blue collar Waterman neighborhood. After conducting environmental studies to determine that there was no contamination from a nearby salvage yard, they purchased the 2.25 acre property for $57,000 and resumed work on the PUD approval process.

Although the Dandelion group had quietly rallied support for months, their first official presentation was to the Bloomington Plan Commission in March 2011. This 11-member board reviews all proposed site developments within city limits and makes a recommendation to the City Council to grant or deny project approval. As part of the process, neighbors were notified of the project and invited to attend the Plan Commission meeting. "In all my years as planning director, Dandelion Village is the most unique project I've ever worked on," said Tom Micuda. "We also had to work through what I would call the fear of the unknown and the fact that ecovillages and cooperative housing are not within the lexicon of standard plan commission members so we had to educate about what that meant."

For the first meeting, Danny and the ecovillage group developed site sketches and proposed development layouts. Their initial strategy was to ask for far more than they thought would be approved, which would allow some room for negotiation. They asked for a density of 15 houses and 75 people as well as site exemptions to allow composting toilets,

(continued on p. 77)

DANDELION VILLAGE: BUILDING AN ECOVILLAGE IN TOWN
(continued from p. 48)

'Let's be selfish and hold that water as much as we possibly can.'"

Hiring a watershed engineer was not cheap but allowed them to present a much more professional set of plans to the Plan Commission at their second hearing. Through the negotiation process, they ended up reducing their density to 30 adults and 10 children with 10 small houses and one large communal building that could contain up to 15 bedrooms as well as a large kitchen and dining hall. They had originally hoped that the small houses could be built without kitchens and bathrooms but that would have classified them as a commercial development (e.g. residence camp) and required the installation of sprinkler systems in all buildings—nearly as expensive as putting in kitchens and bathrooms! They did get permission to have both chickens and goats on the site as well as barns for their agricultural equipment. Composting toilets were abandoned in favor of city sewer connections.

The Plan Commission officially approved their request for a PUD in August 2011. By then, public sentiment was generally in favor of the project and the neighbors who had voiced the strongest opposition began admitting some respect for these crazy young people and their vision. Curiosity replaced concern and the project was unanimously approved by the Bloomington City Council in October as an excellent example of walking the sustainability talk.

By this point, Danny and the other ecovillage founders were worn out but happy. They knew there were still three more permitting steps required and they now had the engineering support needed to develop their final plat for the site. In April 2012, they submitted the final plans for review to get their grading permit, which essentially approves their watershed engineering. Simultaneously, they applied for building permits so that the first two homes could be constructed in the summer. As part of their PUD agreement, they must complete all site grading and basic infrastructure (e.g. storm water retention ponds and main roads) before applying for an occupancy permit, which they hope to acquire in the fall. Once the first founders move in, they will start work on two small community houses and the large community building that will provide a gathering space as well as bedrooms that can be rented out to generate income for the ecovillage and house other members as they build their own permanent homes.

The Dandelion group is thrilled by the location and are excited that they have already formed a bond with their new neighbors. "After a year and a half of politics, it feels great to be through the political process and almost ready to break ground," says founder Zach Dwiel. "I'm super excited to start building and stop politicking." While their community has continued to form over potlucks and planning sessions, the members look forward to working side by side building their new home.

Danny acknowledges that this is still the beginning, for both Dandelion Village and for encouraging ecovillage development everywhere. He will be busy for the next couple of years helping the community develop and take ownership of their property. After that, he plans to return to the planning department to propose that their development be used as the model for a new zoning category specifically for ecovillages. "I feel the greatest effect we can have on the ecovillage movement is to set the precedent of a cooperative housing zoning category for the city of Bloomington," says Danny. He hopes this will pave the way for similar developments in Bloomington and even be adopted in other communities. Perhaps someday his ecovillage zoning category will even become the new normal. ❧

Maggie Sullivan is a Bloomington, Indiana native with a passion for sustainability and a deep love of the Midwest. She co-writes the green living blog www.greencouple.com with her husband Will and serves as president of the nonprofit Center for Sustainable Living. Her favorite ecovillage is Lost Valley Educational Center where she studied permaculture in 2005, and she looks forward to having an ecovillage in her own hometown.

Living the Questions

By Coleen O'Connell

Joanne Moesswilde

Jeffrey Mabee

Jeffrey Mabee

I n the small coastal village of Belfast, Maine, an ecovillage is brewing. The ingredients have been steeped, following the recipe of a cohousing project and the dream of becoming an ecovillage. Years in the planning, with designs percolating and group processes filtered through, we broke ground in fall 2011. The first homes are being built as I type this. Move-in for the first residents is slated for May 2012.

Forty-two acres at the edge of town, two miles walking and biking distance to downtown, 36 households will stand. Sandwiched between horse farms, the land is open with hay fields while the Little River defines its southern border. Beautiful views of the coastal Maine hills will greet us each morning as we wake in our south-facing sun-dependent homes.

What are our dreams for becoming an ecovillage? The mission for Belfast Cohousing & Ecovillage is "to be a model environmentally sustainable, affordable, multi-generational cohousing community that is easily accessible to Belfast, includes land reserved for agricultural use and open space, and is an innovative housing option for rural Maine." (www.mainecohousing.org)

Our mission opens many small but significant questions to be decided as we grapple with giving definition to that irascible word *sustainable*. What, exactly, are we trying to sustain? A way of life? The planet? An ecosystem? What will truly make us an ecovillage? So far we answer this with plans for farming, growing our own food, putting food by, shared resources, a neighborhood of the old-fashioned type where the village raises the child, living in harmony with the land, allowing there to be

space for the more-than-human world... an ecological vision for sure, but one that is still only a vision and not yet real.

In the design process, we started with houses, of course. How to arrange them became clear when our decision was to go with a solar design; next came the decision for duplex/shared wall houses. (Now this pushed the psychological boundaries of middle to upper-middle class folks!) Then came a significant pivotal decision to get off petroleum (at least for our homes—we'll deal with cars later...a much stickier issue), and thus the hiring of the local Design/Build team of GO Logic who build to German Passiv Haus design standards. (See sidebar for more information.) Given the climate in Maine, where 90 percent of the winter home-heating fuel is petroleum based, this was a radical decision. Not even gas cook stoves with those telltale propane tanks outside will exist for our homes. Nor will we have wood stoves as back up—we didn't want to breathe each other's smoke. For some of us, imagining a winter without a wood stove as, at the least, back-up heat for a snowstorm that takes the grid down, is akin to heresy. Thank goodness the prototype house that GO Logic built a few miles away is performing to Passiv Haus standards and we have seen the data and are assured that we will be warmed by the sun as we are cocooned within the super-insulated walls of our homes.

With a mission in place to become sustainable, affordable, and multi-generational, we have mostly failed on one account: affordability. By making the decisions we did, we have left out most of the young Maine families that reside in our area. Affordable, we came to understand, is relative. Our prices work for out of state or urban-dwelling prospective members, but are not affordable for most of the young families

279

that already live here. High-paying jobs are not plentiful in these parts, known mostly for its beautiful scenery, recreational summer boating, and organic and conventional farming. The affordability issue also squeezes on the mission to be multi-generational. Because of the costs, we have easily attracted older, close to retirement-aged people who are trading larger homes for a small, energy-efficient home, while we have struggled to retain young families with children under the age of 12. When you look at the demographics for cohousing communities around the country you will find highly educated, progressive folks, with plenty of discretionary time on their hands, and income levels that rank in the middle to upper-middle class range—hardly the demographics for Waldo County, Maine, which is one of the poorer counties in our state. But we do have families with children and for that we are grateful.

These issues have been compounded by the timing of our project. The land was bought in July 2008, with our spirits soaring as months of planning were turning real when people plunked down money to buy the land. August, one month later, the economy collapsed, caused, in part, by a burst of the housing bubble. This project is a testament to the sustained vision held by its members in that we were able to break ground three years from that land purchase with 21 houses sold. Since ground-breaking we have sold three more. We continue to market the remaining 12 units with the goal that the project will be complete with Common House by the end of 2014. Given the bad financial climate, we were also counseled by a former cohousing developer, John Ryan, to do our own self-financing, saving all the paperwork and oversight that shaken bankers would hold us to. Though risky, it has proven to be a way forward in this devastated housing market. As each house is built, the risk becomes less and less. Our final goal is to sell the last remaining houses so that work on the Common House can commence. When the Common House is complete, the main characteristic for a

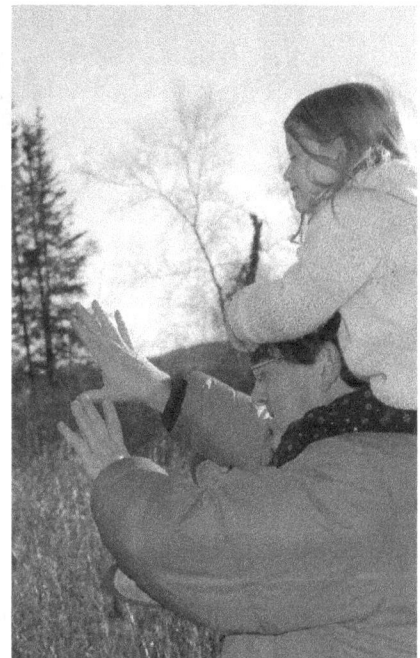

Photos by Steve Chiasson

Passiv Haus

A Passive House (Passiv Haus in German where it originated) is a very well-insulated, virtually airtight building that is primarily heated by passive solar gain and by internal gains from people, electrical equipment, etc. Energy losses are minimized. Any remaining heat demand is provided by an extremely small source. Avoidance of heat gain through shading and window orientation also helps to limit any cooling load, which is similarly minimized. An energy recovery ventilator provides a constant, balanced fresh air supply. The result is an impressive system that not only saves up to 90 percent of space heating costs, but also provides a uniquely terrific indoor air quality.

A Passive House is a comprehensive system. "Passive" describes well this system's underlying receptivity and retention capacity. Working with natural resources, free solar energy is captured and applied efficiently, instead of relying predominantly on "active" systems to bring a building to "zero" energy. High performance triple-glazed windows, super-insulation, an airtight building shell, limitation of thermal bridging, and balanced energy recovery ventilation make possible extraordinary reductions in energy use and carbon emission.

(See www.passivehouse.us/passiveHouse/PassiveHouseInfo.html.)

cohousing community will be in place, but then the challenging task of turning all of this into an ecovillage will remain.

As you read this, the first gardens will be producing the first crop of food. The Land Use Committee is deep into its design for the use of the common land: where to put the community gardens; how much acreage to set aside for the CSA farm; how to run that farm; where will the chickens, sheep, pigs go, the soccer field and playground for the children, the campfire ring for nightly sing-a-longs? This part is not a dream; it is hard work and the task of getting 24 households (and eventually 36 households) to agree to the design is a process in and of itself. The growing skill level of managing the decision-making process of a large group of people has brought us from a traditional consensus model of decision making to moving toward the practice of sociocracy, or dynamic governance. This is both exciting and riddled with obstacles—time being one of them. Distance between members is another. Difference of opinion is always an issue, and issues of power ever present. We have finally scheduled a weekend workshop and are bringing in a renowned facilitator, John Buck, to get us started on dynamic governance.

Sociocracy comes to us from The Netherlands. A Dutch businessman proposed this method back in the '90s as new way of running his business so every person would be respected and included and the interests of the minority as well as the majority would be heard (O'Rear and Buck, 2000). The format and ground rules offer a built-in efficiency such that a large group of people can make decisions together without getting bogged down in trying to come to a full agreement within all its membership. It is a process of consent, where the decision can be made if no one raises a reasoned or paramount objection to going forward with a proposal that has been put on the table.

We learn to trust the committees that come up with the proposals and the outcome is that we are all able to live with the decisions. The efficiency factor is most attractive to us, after four years of mostly successful but often slow and stressful consensus processes. We are excited to finally have a clear sense of at least the first 24 household members. Previous facilitation and decision-making trainings have been lost on many people who have come and gone from the project. We have spent money to train people, only to see them leave the project, including most of the founding members. With purchase-and-sales agreements in hand, we can safely move ahead with the new sociocracy training in hopes that the groundwork we are laying now, before we move in, will see us through many years of successful decision making as we collaboratively build the community we have envisioned.

We are slogging through the muck but the vision remains clear. The larger Belfast community is watching us. This is a small town after all, where the networks weave and wind themselves across every sector of the culture. We are under scrutiny. Will we truly accomplish all that we set out to do? Will we be the gold standard for what the word sustainability really means? Will we become yet another example of the growing ecovillage movement? Will we be the hippie village that most folks think we are? Or will we be a group of middle to upper-middle class people living comfortably on a nice piece of land in nice energy-efficient houses?

As Rilke so brilliantly advised, "Be patient toward all that is unsolved in your heart and try to love the questions themselves like locked rooms and like books that are written in a very foreign tongue. Do not now seek the answers, which cannot be given you because you would not be able to live them and the point is, to live everything. Live the questions now. Perhaps you will then gradually without noticing it, live along some distant day into the answer."

Here at Belfast Cohousing & Ecovillage, we are living the questions. ❧

Coleen O'Connell, a member of the Belfast Cohousing & Ecovillage community, has served on the leadership team for the project. Coleen is the Director/Faculty of the Ecological Teaching and Learning MS Program for educators at Lesley University in Cambridge, Massachusetts. Her professional and personal passion has been to explore ecological literacy and sustainability in the context of our personal lifestyle choices. She has traveled internationally with students living in and studying the ecovillage movement. She cofounded a small ecovillage, Ravenwood, in the midcoast region of Maine which has been a teaching laboratory for Lesley University and the Audubon Expedition Institute (now the Expedition Education Institute). She can be reached at oconnell@lesley.edu and welcomes your comments or questions.

References:
O'Rear, Tena Meadow and Buck, John. "Going Dutch," COMMUNITIES, Winter 2000, #109, pp. 38-43.
Rilke, Rainer Maria. (1903.) *Letters to a Young Poet.*
www.passivehouse.us/passiveHouse/PassiveHouseInfo.html
www.mainecohousing.org

Nashira:
An Ecovillage from the Grassroots

By Giovanni Ciarlo

Attending the Llamado De La Montaña (Call of the Mountain) Bioregional Gathering in Atlantida Ecovillage in Colombia this last January, and witnessing the emergence of the new Latin American organization, C.A.S.A. (Consejo de Asentamientos Sustentables de las Americas), was one of the most enriching and energizing experiences I've had in recent times. And although I really wanted to visit other Colombian ecovillage projects while I was there, I had time to see only one, Nashira, an urban ecovillage near the Colombian city of Cali.

Nashira, which means "Love Song" in the ancient local language, was one of the most amazing ecovillages I have ever visited. It is run by low-income women heads of households. This reflects a widespread social problem in the outskirts of cities in Colombia, where decades of civil conflict has left many women to manage and sustain the household. A Nashira pamphlet states *"The Nashira project goes beyond offering just housing solutions, it seeks to provide a better quality of life, offering a secure and nutritious supply of food within the compound, an environmentally friendly atmosphere, and a source of income through the development of workshops where women can manufacture their own products."*

I arrived in Nashira just before sunset. I was introduced to some of the residents and shown to a unit where I had a reservation to spend the night. I was met by Osiris, the 30-year-old son of Marta, the head of the house. As a sign of the changes undergone by ecovillage members, Osiris is a social sciences faculty member at one of Colombia's rural Universities, and was visiting his mom for the holidays, something I thought was itself out-of-the-ordinary for people in the lower-income social class. He showed me to my room, a spacious, well-lit single bedroom on the second floor of the 700-900 square foot home that Marta had helped to build during one of the training sessions offered by national and international ecovillage consultants.

I hurried to meet Osiris outside for the last bit of daylight to give me a flash tour of the ecovillage. Nashira was founded by a donor who gave the municipal authorities 30 hectares of land to build an 88-home ecological development for women heads of households with matching donations from government housing development funds. To date 48 units are already built, mostly with the sweat equity of their owners, who formed cooperative groups to learn and help each other to build small, attached, efficient, and durable housing units with the assistance of some additional materials, donations, and capacity training. Both national and international organizations spent time teaching ecovillage design and hands-on skills, from village economics (including small businesses that can operate from inside the village) to food production, decision making for self-governance, natural building, bed-and-breakfast ecotourism, a local solidarity economy, alternative renewable energy technologies, and waste management for recycling and recovering of industrial byproducts. One of the organizations doing the trainings is Change the World, where several ecovillage activists in both GEN and ENA work to bring low tech solutions to indigenous and marginalized people and natural reserves in Latin America. Among them is Beatriz Arjona, one of the organizers of the Llamado de la Montaña event and a member of Aldea Feliz, another ecovillage active

Head of household and daughter at Nashira Ecovillage outside Cali, Colombia.

Giovanni Ciarlo

in RENACE Colombia—the Colombian ecovillage network, now C.A.S.A. Colombia.

Osiris showed me the common house, a remodeled pre-existing farmhouse where now there is a computer lab and community center. Across from the common house is the solar restaurant, where one can find pastries and coffee during the weekends, and during special events there are cookouts using solar reflectors to grill, boil, fry, or bake many different local dishes with food grown on site. A dirt drive path passes the communal dry toilet built with bottles, mud, and bales of hay. It is beautiful, with the air of a temple or a pagoda where one would go meditate. Art is everywhere, complemented by well designed landscaping that takes advantage of the location to create gardens and paths around the site.

The shallow pool that children play in during the hot sunny days of the tropics is equipped with a converted bicycle pumping mechanism that is instructive as well as functional—pumping water from the well below to fill the pool and to create a waterfall from about eight feet up a wooden tower. The sound is soothing and children use it as a play station while they shower and enjoy the water and the sun.

We were able to see a number of housing units, and greeted people as they came outdoors to wave at us in the last minutes of dusk before dark. Osiris explained how there are several window-stores in some of the houses that sell snacks and beverages as well as some fresh and canned goods and cooking supplies. He told me that people form cooperatives to have more buying and selling choices. He showed me the partridge egg co-op, the chicken co-op, the cassava processing co-op, the recycling and restoring center, the children's daycare, and the rest of the land.

I was blown away at the achievements of this adventurous group of women. They all came from very disadvantaged sectors of the urban population. Most of them lived in shantytowns and cardboard shacks before getting the opportunity to apply and be selected for the project, creating an ecological community of similar women from the grassroots and poorest families in the Cali region.

Nashira impressed me because it is the first example I have seen of an ecological community, aligned with values promoted by GEN, which has emerged from the bottom up. It is a response and a solution to the housing and poverty issues of the oppressed, in a country that has seen decades of civil strife and violence affecting the majority of people, especially those living in the lower economic rungs. It was created not by a population from the privileged sector of society but by the poor, uneducated, economically distraught women leaders with families and dependents of all ages. Added to this mix was the right combination of aide and guidance of national and international agents, alongside committed activists and individuals empowered to help people from the oppressed sector improve their livelihood, because they believe it is possible and it should be done.

Before going to bed I spent time chatting with Marta, Osiris, and Natalia, his younger sister, about growing up in this village, and the opportunities ahead for them. They were upbeat and positive all the way. Natalia is also about to start college, where she hopes to study architecture so she can help others build affordable sustainable housing. The next day I took a refreshing cold shower, and as part of the cost for staying overnight, received a hefty breakfast of partridge eggs and toast followed by fresh brewed coffee. They even arranged calling a taxi to take me to the airport in the early hours of the morning. That's what I call *"Hospitalidad Latina."*

Seeing Nashira was like taking a breath of fresh air in the middle of the wilderness. It has given me renewed hope for a new society, that I like to refer to as *the reinvention of everything*, from our worldviews to the way we govern ourselves, the way we relate to Mother Earth, and the way we create local cooperative businesses that aim to provide right livelihoods to community members.

Giovanni Ciarlo cofounded Huehuecoyotl Ecovillage in Tepoztlán, Mexico in 1982. He is a Board member of Global Ecovillage Network (GEN) and is active in Gaia Education as developer of ecovillage design and education materials. He traveled to Colombia as council representative of ENA (The Ecovillage Network of the Americas). He also performs Latin music in the United States and Mexico with his group Sirius Coyote. Contact him at giovanni@ecovillage.org.

Owner built houses and food garden (casava, bananas, and other local foods) at Nashira ecovillage built after training in Permaculture and self build workshops.

The ENA and CASA group in ecovillage Atlantida, Colombia.

Publisher's Note BY SKY BLUE

ECOVILLAGES and the FIC

Intentional communities have evolved considerably over the last 200 years, but the sharing of common values has always been a core feature. Historically, religion has provided these values to most groups who want to carve out a space where those values can be practiced intensively. Religion still plays an important role for many communities, but increasingly the drive to create a different way of life has come from a different kind of analysis.

Ecovillages embody one of the most contemporary and nuanced approaches to collective living. The philosophy behind the concept comes the closest to replicating a religious foundation, but in a secular form. I say secular, though many in ecovillages would say that there is a deeply spiritual element. Many within the ecovillage movement see all life as connected and sacred, and believe that some form of greater force or consciousness is at play. Whether this is couched in more scientific or esoteric terminology, it's also commonly associated with an analysis of social justice, and, perhaps most importantly, an analysis of global ecological destruction and the need to create sustainable lifestyles and communities.

The term "ecovillage" came into use with Robert and Diane Gilman's study, *Ecovillages and Sustainable Communities*, for Gaia Trust in 1991. This document led to the conference in 1995 that birthed the Global Ecovillage Network (GEN), which has acted as the centralizing force for the ecovillage movement ever since. As with other types of intentional community, no one has a monopoly on the term ecovillage, there's no certification program, and any group that chooses to identify as an ecovillage may do so.

GEN currently defines an ecovillage as "an intentional or traditional community using local participatory processes to holistically integrate ecological, economic, social, and cultural dimensions of sustainability in order to regenerate social and natural environments."

Gilmans' study offers the definition, "a human-scale, full-featured settlement in which human activities are harmlessly integrated into the natural world in a way that is supportive of healthy human development, and can be successfully continued into the indefinite future."

"Human-scale" and "full-featured" capture a lot of what's important about intentional communities. These terms tie in with what GEN describes as the four dimensions of sustainability: social, economic, ecological, and cultural. They acknowledge the multifaceted nature of our lives as human beings on this planet. This connects to a fact I love to share, which is that the root word of "eco" is the Greek word *oikos*, meaning home. "Eco" isn't just part of "ecological" and "ecovillage," it's part of "economy" as well. Economy is not just about money; it's about how we as a society provide for our basic needs.

A central idea behind ecovillages is that how we provide for our basic needs should not be divorced from the social and cultural aspects of our lives, nor from the ecological impacts of how those needs are met. Ecovillages remind us that it's all connected: where we lay our heads, where we make a living, all the goods and services, the relationships and culture, the natural world, the technology, the governance, the caring and loving and growing and cooking and building, it's all part of it, and we're all in it together.

The sickness and unsustainability of our society are reflected in the radical disintegration, segregation, compartmentalization, and isolation not only of people but of the various aspects of people's lives. This scenario not only allows, but encourages us to make choices from a narrow, self-serving, fear-based perspective. If we can re-integrate our own lives, and our lives with each other's lives; if we can bring each other into our homes, and make decisions about our home together, on a micro scale; then we can begin to cultivate the caring and compassion and intelligence necessary to make decisions that consider people on the other side of the planet. GEN has been a crucial advocate for this worldview in the recent evolution of the intentional communities movement.

The FIC was already an established organization when GEN formed and when its local ambassadors, the Ecovillage Network of the Americas (ENA), started organizing. It was unique that there was an existing organization like the FIC in the regional networks GEN was developing. ENA focused its work on Latin America, in part because the FIC was already active in the US and Canada, and because they didn't want ENA to be dominated by white English-speakers from North America. For the last 20 years, the FIC and ENA have had important connections and overlaps, but have maintained separate activities. In 2012, the Latin America contingent spun off from ENA to form El Consejo de Asentamientos Sustentables de las América Latina (CASA), and the Ecovillage Network of Canada (ENC) formed. Around 2014, ENC and US-based ENA, along with the newly invigorated youth arm of GEN, NextGEN North America (NextGENNA), started a dialog with the FIC about establishing a partnership.

Inter-organizational politics are never simple, and the dialog had its challenges. Then last year GEN held a 20th anniversary celebration at Findhorn Community in Scotland, its headquarters. Players from each group attended, sharing in this important milestone and plotting a path forward. I was honored to participate in this, along with people from communities from dozens of countries on every continent. It was amazing to experience an affinity born from a radical experience of community between people from such a diversity of cultures. GEN has truly managed to create a global movement, and FIC clearly needs to be a participant.

It's with great pleasure that the FIC presents this issue of COMMUNITIES on Ecovillages around the World in partnership with GEN and Gaia Trust. The FIC is also pleased to have signed on to a partnership agreement last Fall to re-establish the Global Ecovillage Network of North America (GENNA). Additionally, GEN recently hired our beloved Business Manager, Christopher Kindig, as its Operations Director (and also IT Director), putting him in a key position to foster collaboration (see his comments in the sidebar).

While the FIC does offer its services globally, its focus is on North America, particularly the US and Canada, and this isn't likely to change. Partly it's an issue of capacity, but it's also an issue of what's appropriate. A US-based organization should not be the direct service provider to communities in India or West Africa. This is what GEN is about, fostering regional networks by and for the communities in those regions, that can provide the support those communities need.

GEN's vision is of a world of empowered citizens and communities, designing and implementing their own pathways to a sustainable future, and building bridges of hope and international solidarity. The FIC is proud to be part of this movement and, in this issue, give you a glimpse of what global transformation looks like. ❧

Sky Blue (sky@ic.org) is Executive Director of the Fellowship for Intentional Community.

More on the FIC-GEN Collaboration

It is an amazing privilege to work with both FIC and GEN! Long before I had ever heard the term, I knew somewhere in my heart what an ecovillage was, and yearned for it. Now I am excited to come to work every day because it means helping brilliant and passionate people in both organizations to grow this movement towards ecological communities, and spreading ecovillage technologies and lessons to the larger society.

In addition to this special issue of COMMUNITIES, we are also partnering to offer more Community Bookstore titles through a new store on ecovillage.org. Most exciting of all is that FIC and GEN agreed to collaborate on their databases, which will add thousands of community listings to each directory, and further enhance the detail and usefulness of the information. Connecting the sites together is a tall order, but the stakes are much higher. Humanity has to unite around a more sustainable, resilient, and satisfying model of society, and ecovillages around the world can play a vital role.

—Christopher Kindig

Anna Jackson of Meadowsong Ecovillage uses an artist's conk (Ganoderma applanatum) as a canvas to celebrate interspecies community.

Photo by Kyle Shepherd, Artwork by Anna Jackson

Around the World in 80 Pages

Among all the issues of COMMUNITIES I've edited, this one has by far the largest proportion of non-North American content. That is no accident, given the theme. Compared with North America, especially the United States, most of the rest of the world has an undeniable head start in creating replicable ecovillage models. In an era when even US citizens are waking up to the myth of "American exceptionalism"—when documentaries like Michael Moore's *Where to Invade Next* and political campaigns like Bernie Sanders' are reminding people that other countries have much to teach us about creating healthy societies—American communitarians too may be ripe for embracing the simultaneously humbling and empowering truth that people on other continents are, in general, significantly more advanced in ecovillage development than we are, with a few notable exceptions.

This wasn't always the case. Turtle Island was home to many long-lived indigenous ecovillages (before that word existed, and before those ecovillages were decimated by the effects of white settlement and conquest of the "New World"). Remnants of those ecovillage cultures survive, but they are understandably reluctant to invite more conquest or cooption by outsiders, and are also at a considerable economic, social, and political disadvantage in the modern world. Some of the white settlers' more traditional ways of life, in small towns and in farming or spiritual communities, contained significant ecovillage elements, but they too have largely faded out or been substantially diluted. People who have *not* been part of those generations-old traditions together, who are not united by blood, tribe, and history, do not have an easy avenue to join into or replicate the surviving North American models.

And although the continent is also replete with examples of non-

human "ecovillages" in the natural world—from ant hills to prairie dog colonies to heron rookeries to aspen groves to oak savannas to redwood forests—those tight-knit, interdependent, regenerative communities too are not necessarily looking for new members, especially of the modernized bipedal variety.

Fortunately for the ecovillage movement, the world is larger than North America, and ecovillagers around the world have created networks to help spread the word even to "late adopters." Foremost among those networks are the Global Ecovillage Network (GEN) and its various branches, and a primary catalyst of these groups' work has been Gaia Trust, established by Ross and Hildur Jackson in 1987. Gaia Trust's latest of countless essential contributions to the ecovillage movement is sponsorship of this issue of COMMUNITIES. Sponsorships like this embody the spirit of visionary cooperation that, in these challenging times, is so essential to the continued evolution of our species and of its social strategies. While helping keep us out of the red, they also enable the collaborations—like that between our staff and GEN staff and activists—that make this magazine a joy to work on. We'd especially like to thank Ross Jackson, Maya Norton, and this issue's many authors for their unique, substantial, practical, and inspiring contributions to the creation of this volume.

Please consider subscribing (if you don't already), giving gift subscriptions, ordering back issues or "Best of COMMUNITIES" collections, and/or supporting COMMUNITIES and the FIC in other ways, so that we too can continue to be catalysts in the movement for a more cooperative, regenerative world.

We hope you enjoy this issue!

Chris Roth lives at an "aspiring" ecovillage in Oregon (see lostvalley.org).

OVERCOMING APARTHEID
—the Global Ecovillage Network

By Kosha Anja Joubert

Two roads diverged in a wood, and I—
I took the one less traveled by,
And that has made all the difference.
——Robert Frost

I was born into apartheid. The word itself comes from my first language, Afrikaans. It means "to set apart" or "to be in a state of separation." In the South Africa of my childhood, people were set apart by the colors of their skin. And even though it was a country that was abundant with diverse cultures, I grew up in the incongruent monotony of an all-white neighborhood and an all-white school. It simply did not feel right. Even as a child, I started asking uncomfortable questions of my parents and teachers. As I came to realize the depth of injustice and pain the system inflicted, I became a very angry youth, and as a young adult, after moving to Amsterdam, I became an anti-apartheid activist.

I studied cultural anthropology and linguistics in hope of learning how to bridge gaps through intercultural communication and help heal what was broken apart. Unfortunately, that is not what was taught at universities in the late 1980s. What I started to understand, though, and fully realized later, is that apartheid did not die in the early 1990s in South Africa. It was alive and kicking then and is alive and kicking today, being reinforced with every fence and every wall that is going up. On a global level, people's access to healthcare and wealth, their level of education and their freedom of movement are all decisively influenced by the passport they carry. And, on a more fundamental level, as humans we have set ourselves apart from the natural world and other species that share the planet with us. The abolition of apartheid is still waiting for its fulfillment, even in South Africa.

In order to acknowledge our oneness with all living systems and live accordingly, we need to have courage. We need to leave the highways that lull us into a false sense of security and start exploring some of the roads less traveled, both within and beyond ourselves. As Einstein said: "We can't solve problems by using the same kind of thinking we used to create them." We need to start thinking and seeing things afresh, experiencing and being in our bodies anew.

Scientists posit that we are aware of only around five percent of the total information that flows through our nervous systems. We could know so much more. We could practice broadening our awareness. We could shift the habitual pathways we travel within our own nervous systems. If we take a moment now to focus on our breath, on the in- and out-flow of air, on the stillness that lies within this movement, and how it connects us to all living things around us, we can sense our awareness shifting into a more connected and spacious mode. In a similar way, we can change the well-trod avenues we follow in our everyday realities. This is a time to have courage and go to places we haven't been to before, make connections we haven't made before, and create new synapses, insights, and solutions.

When I was 23 years old, in 1991, I walked a path less traveled. Nelson Mandela had just been released from prison. The transition was finally coming, but tension and violence were at an all time high in South Africa. I returned to my country on a pilgrimage, wanting to walk its land and finally visit all the places where I had not been allowed, or had not dared, to go before. I was told I would be raped, if not killed.

Setting off on foot, on a journey of about 1,000 km, from Stilbaai, the site of all my childhood summer holidays, up the east coast to Port St Johns in the Transkei, I felt a mixture of fear and determination. For the sake of my own integrity and healing, I felt I had no choice but to do this. People were shocked and sometimes amused to meet a young, white, Afrikaans woman walking through townships and deserted stretches of wild nature, sleeping in the dunes, swimming through rivers. I lived off the food and water that was offered to me and encountered nature, animals, humans, and even God in a way that healed something deep inside of me.

Finally, close to Port St Johns, I ran into a community where people of all skin colors were living, building huts, and tilling the land together, learning about each oth-

What Are Ecovillages?

Ecovillages are intentional or traditional communities, consciously designed through participatory processes to regenerate their social and natural environments. The social, ecological, economic, and cultural aspects are integrated into a holistic sustainable development model that is adapted to local contexts. Ecovillages are rural or urban settlements with vibrant social structures, vastly diverse, yet united in their actions towards low-impact, high quality lifestyles.

—KAJ

er's cultures. They had found a niche, in one of the so-called "homelands," to live their dream of the future. They were living their dream in the now; without fighting existing structures.

Seeing this shifted something deep inside of me. I realized I could invest my energy in more effective ways than through protest. Since then, I have sought to be part of building the new instead of fighting the old. This small community around Port St Johns became my entrance point into the Global Ecovillage Network (GEN)—a worldwide web of seeded dreams and roads less traveled. I started visiting communities around the globe, following an inner red thread of nomadic movement signposted by word of mouth recommendations that led me from one ecovillage to the next. I became witness to an emergence of a new culture rising slowly through communities around the planet where people came together to manifest their vision for the future.

Each of these communities is, in their own way, bridging the gaps created by apartheid, healing relationships with the living systems of which they are a part. People are understanding that if we don't wake up and consciously design our own future, past and present realities will surely shape it for us. And in that process we might lose so much that is precious. In intentional and traditional, rural and urban ecovillage projects, people choose to reconnect to nature, to each other, to the past and the future. They choose consciously to create solidarity and prepare the ground in respect for future generations.

After celebrating the 20th anniversary of the Global Ecovillage Network in 2015, today we reach out to around 10,000 such communities all over the globe. Each of them is a local expression of the same universal exploration: how can we become true to our potential as humans? How can we heal apartheid, the separation within us, between us, and connecting us to the natural world? How can we honor life as a whole, rebuilding the connections that have been broken in the social, cultural, economic, and ecological areas of life? And in this process, these communities learn and demonstrate that, not only is there no need for us to destroy life, not only can we *sustain* life, but we can actually *regenerate* life around us if only we set our minds and hearts to it. We can tap into our intelligence and wisdom and find the solutions needed.

We can regenerate the humus and the soils around us, composting and sequestering carbon through biochar, working hand in hand with microorganisms and the cycles of life. We can replenish the water tables that we have depleted in so many places. We can channel each precious drop of rainwater into catchment systems, swales, and water retention landscapes, supporting the much needed moisture to enter our soil instead of running over it, causing erosion. We can learn from nature and set up systems that produce no waste and use minimum effort for maximum effect, systems where each element fulfills multiple functions and is strengthened, through multiple connections, to become much more resilient.

We can learn how energy runs through sunlight, winds, water flows, geothermal heat, and biomass, and we can find abundant sources for our energy needs, transitioning to 100 percent renewables in the coming decades. We can replant the forests that are the very lungs of this planet. We can grow our food in ways that support life. While even one child still goes to bed hungry, alone, and afraid, our work will not be completed. We can reconnect to our love for place, and respect for heritage, as a source of inner power. We can solve our conflicts and integrate our traumas. We can combine the best of our traditions with the most innovative solutions and ingenious updates that technology has to offer. We can find ways to marry our love for the planet with our need to make a living and rebuild economies that serve life instead of profit.

We can do all that. Communities around the planet are playing their part on the frontlines of implementation right now. But we can only do this when we come together, letting go of our fears that there is not enough, and instead rebuilding cultures of sharing and solidarity. Generosity creates abundance. Ecovillages have been finding local solutions to global challenges. In ecovillages, we have developed lifestyles that are fulfilling and meaningful, while at the same time allowing us to tread softly on the earth.

When I started out on my journey in 1991, ecovillages were hidden right at the very end of all those roads less traveled. In the past 25 years, ecovillages and the ecovillage way of life have started rising to the surface of mainstream culture. In some countries, ecovillage strategies have actually broken through the surface into visibility—leading to top-down support for bottom-up community-led approaches to sustainability. In Senegal, the government has seen how such communities can bring about positive change and have established an ecovillage program with the goal of transitioning 14,000 villages to ecovillages. In the Gambia, a bioregion of 13 villages is following this example. In Tanzania, the government has started with three pilot ecovillages and is now expanding the approach. In Thailand, Myanmar, Bangladesh, and India, we see community-led networks of change emerging from a similar impulse.

The UN Sustainable Development Goals aim to make cities and human settlements inclusive, safe, resilient, and sustainable by 2030. Within GEN, we have been saying that,

Kosha Joubert with members of GEN's communities in Africa.

in effect, every village needs to become an ecovillage and every city a green city in order to support life to thrive around the world. The question of how the ecovillage approach can dramatically be scaled up, without losing its core value of locally owned, participatory processes, has become central.

In the past years, GEN has identified five closely related program areas, which, when combined with and galvanized by practical solutions, educational tools, consultancy expertise, and funding, may well provide an answer. GEN is developing consolidated support systems for the following impulses:

1. **Showcase Ecovillages:** celebrating the most inspiring existing examples and solutions
2. **Ecovillage Incubation:** developing tools and support systems for setting up new intentional ecovillages
3. **Ecovillage Transition:** developing tools and support systems for transitioning existing settlements to sustainable settlements/ecovillages
4. **Greening Schools for Sustainable Communities:** working with green schools as hubs for community-led sustainable development
5. **EmerGENcies:** a guide for rebuilding communities after disasters and building communities with, by, and for refugees

In order to support the above, GEN will:

• Further develop its own **educational strand**, while continuing to collaborate closely with Gaia Education, GEN's daughter organization
• Cultivate tools and skills for **social entrepreneurship** at all levels of the organization
• Work closely with academia in applying **participatory action research** to monitor, evaluate, and further evolve best practices
• Initiate a **GEN Consultancy**
• Engage in **political advocacy** in order to inspire the integration of ecovillage strategies in sustainable development plans

I believe that we can create a world that is at peace with itself. A world that lives within its own means. That we are able to come home to this planet, abolishing apartheid and stepping into right relationship with everything around, understanding that we can be caretakers, guardians, and lovers of life while we are here.

So let me ask you: what are the roads less traveled in your life? What are those dreams and visions that are calling you to change your habits? Where are you are invited to expand and what gaps will you close by traveling into unfamiliar territory? Who are the people you know that you need to have a conversation with, that you need to listen to, whom you have been avoiding? Maybe you feel interested in exploring your own cultural roots and coming into alignment with your higher purpose? Would you like to explore the ecology of your everyday life more deeply? Do you know where your food, your water, your energy comes from? Which ecosystems in your environment could you enrich through simple action? Maybe it's the windowsill in your kitchen or the space around a tree in front of your house? How do you aim to change the economy of your life in order to focus on sharing and not only your own personal profit? And who is part of the network of friends that you want to create the future with?

Another world is not only possible. She is on her way. On quiet days I can hear her breathing.

—Arundhati Roy

Kosha Joubert serves as Executive Director of GEN International, and sits on the Advisory Board of GEN Africa. She has many years of experience as an international facilitator, trainer, and consultant and has worked extensively in the fields of curriculum development, international collaboration, and sustainable development. Kosha grew up in South Africa under apartheid and has been dedicated to building bridges across all divides ever since. She has lived in ecovillages for the past 25 years and been a driving force in GEN for eight years. Kosha is also a cofounder of Gaia Education, which develops trainings at the cutting-edge of sustainability, and coauthor of the internationally applied Gaia Education curriculum, the Ecovillage Design Education. You can see her TEDx Talk on Ecovillages here: youtu.be/gGbuOBCGfmQ.

CREATING THE IDEAL INTENTIONAL COMMUNITY
(OR REVITALIZING AN EXISTING ONE)

I, Sahmat, grew up in intentional communities and have lived in 10 of them. I have been so dedicated to Community with both humans and Nature that I've been called "The Community Guy". The communities I grew up in shared a fairly strong "sense of community". I call this deep and sustained sense of community "Common-unity" because it's a state of unity we share in common, with the unique individuality of each human and each species still honored. It's this state of Common-unity that I've found most valuable in life and to me it's the main reason for living in an intentional community. When a group is deep in Common-unity together, there's a shared sense of love, joy, and peace that tops any other group experience.

However, I've found that in all the communities I've lived in, the sense of community is not nearly as deep and sustained as it could be. It's precisely this lack of Common-unity that is the root cause of the catastrophic global suffering of racism, wars, child abuse, abuse of women, environmental and species destruction, etc. So the ultimate goal is ending global suffering through "Global Common-unity": the spreading of Common-unity throughout the world by forming a global network of Common-unity-dedicated Communities.

So I've spent my life learning how to create Common-unity-dedicated communities that share true Common-unity: a deeper and more sustained sense of community. There are two keys to starting a Common-unity community (or moving an existing community into deeper Common-unity):

1. The first key to Common-unity is for everyone to be "Common-unity-dedicated" as their top common priority. This doesn't seem to be the case in any existing community, which results in focus and energies being bled off into other priorities. So maintenance of Common-unity doesn't get enough time and energy.

2. The second key to Common-unity is to learn "Common-unity Skills", skills that must be practiced to maintain Common-unity: Speaking from the Heart, Empathetic Listening, Emptying of Ego-attachments, Conflict Resolution, Consensus, Heart Wound Healing, Cooperative Housing, and Cooperative Economics. Modern culture does not teach us these skills.

We at the Alliance for Global Community have developed free workshops that train you in these Common-unity Skills. The workshops contain the Sharing Circle process developed by M. Scott Peck, a Nature connection exercise developed by John Seed and Joanna Macy, healing exercises developed by Byron Katie and Richard Moss, and exercises in creating Cooperative Housing and Cooperative Economics. We've tested various versions of these Common-unity Skill Building workshops over the past 25 years, and we've found them to be quite effective in teaching Common-unity skills that can help maintain Common-unity. If you'd like to start a Common-unity-dedicated community, or if you'd like to bring more Common-unity into an existing community (perhaps through a Common-unity sub-community or "pod"), you need to learn or improve these Common-unity skills as soon as possible.

To find out how to sign up for a free public Common-unity Skills workshop or schedule a free workshop for an existing group or community, please go to my website thecommunityguy.org There you can also find out how to get a free copy of the book "Skill Building for Global Common-unity". You can contact Sahmat directly at info@thecommunityguy.org or at 434-305-4770.

COMMON-UNITY WITH HUMANITY AND NATURE

ECOVILLAGES WORLDWIDE
—Local Solutions for Global Problems

By Leila Dregger

An ecovillage can be a traditional village, a city quarter, or an intentional community that improves the lives of its members and the environment in a conscious and participative process. Ecovillages in Europe and the United States mostly follow the desire of members to lead healthier and more communal lives. In the Global South it is different. There it is often directly about surviving: about food sovereignty, protection and survival in areas of crisis, or ways out of poverty. We invite you for a trip to ecovillages throughout regions of the world.

Did You Know?

...that the ecovillage Crystal Waters in Australia, with a population of 200, simultaneously acts as a wildlife reserve?

...that in Orissa, one of the poorest areas in India, over 200 villages of indigenous people are transforming their communities into ecovillages?

...that during 13 years in Latin America, the traveling community of La Caravana taught villagers, farmers, youth, and children sustainable living techniques?

...that the ecovillage Hurdal in Norway has developed the "Active House" and created a green business by building eco-friendly houses?

...that Eco-Valley in Hungary produces an abundance of grain and vegetables to feed its 200 residents several times over, and that it effectively offers social work to some of the poorest communities nationwide?

...that the Peace Community San José de Apartadó in Colombia has formed a neutral village in the middle of an armed conflict zone and its more than 1,000 peasants have been in nonviolent resistance against expulsion for 18 years?

...that the Healing Biotope Tamera in Portugal with 170 members and a Love School at its center has ecologically regenerated an area of 220 acres of land which had been in the process of desertification?

...that the Konohana Family community in Japan has 100 members that are engaged in new agricultural methods for healthy food production and cares for psychiatrically vulnerable people?

...that the fast growing ecovillage Schloss Tempelhof in Germany with its extended economic and legal know-how has established a foundation that supports many other ecovillages and emerging intentional communities?

...that the Republic of Damanhur in Italy with more than 1,000 members was building a secret underground Temple of Humanity for more than 10 years before it was discovered and turned into an officially recognized piece of art?

Future City Auroville, India

In 1968, on the Coromandel Coast in South India, the Tasmanian traveler Joss Brook heard for the first time of the idea to found a future city: Auroville. This vision attracted cultural refugees, hippies, and truth seekers from America, Germany, and France who started to build themselves a different life. Many of them left the project—the early life of poverty in the ecovillage was too harsh—but Brook stayed. "We spoke with old village dwellers who had a huge knowledge of herbs. They were singing while planting rice, and communing with plants and animals. Through them we made contact to the soul of the original forest which grew here once."

Sekem, Egypt.

Photos courtesy of Global Ecovillage Network

Favela da Paz Brazil.

Simon du Vinage

Today, there are about 2,000 people from 40 countries living in Auroville. On the formerly barren plateau we now find houses of wood, adobe, and natural stones in the shade of many trees. Big solar systems serve for cooking and producing electricity. A daily stream of tourists visits Matrimandir, the sacred center of Auroville.

Brook's team planted a 400 hectare wide green belt and built 1,000 miles of ditches and earth dams to conserve rainwater. For Brook, it is the growing forest, not Matrimandir, that is the most sacred place of Auroville.

Meanwhile, experts from Damanhur ecovillage of Italy help the government to develop sustainability concepts for the whole region, collaborating with the local population. In the nearby city of Pondicherry, they turned a public dump into a recreation area.

Brook: "This is Auroville: people from all over the world together with locals try to find the way of sustainability. The most important thing is to perceive the soul because in the soul we find the memory of the future garden."

Favela da Paz, Sao Paulo, Brazil

According to the United Nations, the Jardim Ângela neighborhood in Sao Paulo used to be one of the most violent slums in the world. Criminal activity, drug dealers, youth gangs, street children, and poverty dominated the streets.

When he was 13, two major events occurred in the life of Claudio Miranda: his best friend was killed and he was arrested. "The policeman pointed his gun at my head and demanded that I play my saxophone to prove that I was indeed a musician. It worked. Since then I have known that music is life energy."

Much has changed since then. Today he calls the police his friends. Claudio, his brother Fabio, his wife Hellem, and many of their friends run a samba school that offers street kids an alternative to drugs and violence. After visiting the Tamera ecovillage in Portugal he had a larger idea: "I will call it Favela da Paz—slum of peace."

They turned their family home into an ecological center with a biogas digester for cooking on the roof, a solar shower, and a permaculture garden along the walls. Hellem: "Of course the neighbors became curious. Today we run courses in vegetarian cuisine and urban permaculture."

Coming together and learning, instead of fighting and stealing—this launched a process of change. The parents of the neighborhood planted trees in the schoolyard. They fought successfully against the Brazilian government's plan to destroy their Favela

in preparation for the FIFA World Cup in 2014. And every month there is a big samba party on the streets.

Sekem, Egypt

Many years ago during his university studies in Austria, Dr. Ibrahim Abouleish from Cairo got to know anthroposophy. He returned home with a big vision: he saw wa-

> # Sekem engaged the children to pick chamomile in the morning— under the condition that they could go to school in the afternoon.

ter, trees, animals, and people thriving in the middle of the desert. "Trees gave shade, the land turned green, flowers exuded fragrance, and insects and birds showed their devotion to the creator as if they spoke the first Surah of the Quran."

Forty years ago, he purchased a property in the north of Cairo and drilled a well. This is how Sekem started—and today it is an ecovillage, a farm for medicinal herbs, organic cotton, and cattle, a hospital for locals, an alternative university, and a Waldorf school; it also supports several ecological industries and crafts workshops.

Sekem introduced the idea of organic agriculture to Egypt. Hundreds of farmers learned to cultivate and market cereals, herbs, and cotton without chemicals.

The idea of "the chamomile kids" was controversial but effective. As the local population could not afford to do without the salaries of their children, Sekem engaged the children to pick chamomile in the morning—under the condition that they could go to school in the afternoon.

Today the ecovillage combines Islamic and anthroposophic cultural elements. Every morning, all the thousands of coworkers—from farmers to managers—gather in a morning circle: a symbol for equality and wholeness of the vision.

Abouleish: "Sekem has become a model for sustainable development throughout the world. We want to prove that through our work and investment in education we can compete with the best companies of the world."

Kitzeh, Ukraine.

Photos courtesy of Global Ecovillage Network

The SICE Ecovillage Initiative for Syrian Refugees in Sweden

Fayez Karimeh from Syria, 43, father of three, maintained a reforestation project in Yabroud before the war. After neighbors chopped down his trees for firewood, he searched the internet for alternatives forms of energy and came across instructions for building a biogas digester. While constructing it, he came in contact with the European ecovillage movement. When his city was bombarded he decided to take his family to safety in Europe. Tamera in Portugal offered him temporary residency, enabling a legal means to escape his country.

"Tamera was a cultural shock for me," he remembers. "I had never heard of ecovillages before, and now, coming from a war zone, I met this community that tried to act peacefully in every element of life."

After three months he continued to his country of choice, Sweden, and decided to build an ecovillage for refugees. "Ecovillages for refugees have many advantages," he elaborated during a talk in the University of Uppsala. "The refugees help with the ecological revitalization of the host country, and at the same time learn techniques that will later help them to rebuild their country."

It is very important for Karimeh that those techniques include social skills: "The communities need knowledge about social communication, basic democracy, and conflict resolution."

On April 1st, 2015, Karimeh founded the association SICE: the Syrian Initiative Craftsmanship Ecovillage. Under SICE's auspices, he organizes seminars in Swedish ecovillages: about clay building, harvesting wild fruits, building natural sewage systems, and more. Many Swedes support the idea, and two communities have offered land to establish the first refugee ecovillage in their country.

To learn more, visit their website at www.ecovillage.nu.

Kitzeh, Russia

Kitezh is a community dedicated to the nurturing of foster children. The hamlet, around 360 kilometers south of Moscow, is surrounded by forests and consists of just 16 houses, a school, a workshop, and several outbuildings, including a cowshed. Though its "footprint" is naturally small, ecological sustainability is not its first priority.

In the latter days of the Soviet Union, radio correspondent Dmitry Morozov observed the plight of street children living without the support of parents in his country. In the chaotic post-Soviet years, he set out to create a community that would offer a different way of life, aspiring to the best of human values. The community, now led by Maxim Aneekiev, helps children adapt to everyday life, overcoming their trauma and pain. Children learn care and love, not by listening to adults, but by exploring a therapeutic environment of challenges.

Morozov: "Perhaps it would be best to develop the adults first before they work with the children, but in reality, they develop alongside the children. This is the natural way. Through the reflective awareness of the reality of everyday activity...adults understand the necessity to change and work with their own attitude towards life. By helping others they are helping themselves."

The community's weekly meetings help bind it together. Kitezh's work has become better known in the region and in Moscow through the Role Play Games run during the holidays. These events, lasting up to two weeks, are designed to help children confront their own issues with courage and with the support of their friends. Through these public events, Kitezh expands to take in children who come from "good families" but are not thriving in the region's normal schools.

The Green Kibbutz, Israel

Kibbutz Lotan in the southern Arava desert was founded in 1983, established as a pioneering community experiment in combining the ideals of egalitarian society with creative and liberal Jewish expression, and a political agenda of disengaging religion from government. The founders were a group of 60 young adults, aged 18 to 24, from Israel and around the world.

With its many ecological activities it is a catalyst for environmental consciousness in Israel—and for liberal Judaism. With all its environmental efforts—land preservation, bird watching, waste separation, recycling and composting, renewable energy, energy conservation—the kibbutz has made a direct impact on the region. Over 50 percent of the electricity used in Eilat, Israel's southernmost city, is produced today by solar panels, and the region practices significantly more waste separation and recycling than Israel's other regions. Cofounder Alex Cicelsky: "We're proud to be reminded that we were the catalyst for these developments."

The compact photovoltaic system that powers the EcoCampus, housing students from the Arava Institute for Environmental Studies, where students live in 10 highly efficient passive solar strawbale houses, produces five times more electricity than it needs—even when air conditioners are turned on high all summer. The EcoCampus kitchen runs on biogas. It has no-water toilets and a greywater system to showcase for the 10,000 people who come every year to visit and learn from their work.

Making community decisions and airing issues publicly is both the challenge and strength of the kibbutz. Cicelsky: "In the beginning, everything was discussed in our general assembly. Now, more is processed in committees and then resolutions are brought for approval."

Leila Dregger is a graduate agricultural engineer and longtime journalist. She traveled for many decades to all the world's continents, encountering various communities and peace projects to identify and write about diverse lifestyles. Her primary areas of focus are peace, ecology, community, and women. She has worked for 25 years in press and radio and is a screenwriter and director for theater and film. She was the editor of the magazine The Female Voice—Politics of the Heart. *She was press officer for the House of Democracy in Berlin, the ZEGG community in Belzig (both in Germany), and the Tamera ecovillage in Portugal, where she mainly lives today. From 2012-2015, she was the editor of the Global Ecovillage Network (GEN) International newsletter. She teaches constructive journalism for young professionals and students, as well as in crisis regions. She is the author of several books.*

Leila is also helping Tamera host this year's conference of the International Communal Studies (ICSA), July 1-3, 2016, entitled "Community approaches towards inner and outer peace." ICSA was formed in 1985 during the international conference held at Yad Tabenkin, the Research and Documentation Centre of the Kibbutz Movement, in Israel. The international conferences of ICSA enable scholars and members of kibbutzim and communes to meet and exchange views and research. The participation of scholars at the conferences has promoted many reciprocal visits of kibbutz and communal scholars to kibbutzim and communes around the world. As an international organization ICSA maintains contact with parallel associations like the Communal Studies Association in the US. For more information, please visit www.communa.org.il/icsa.

CREATING CARBON-NEGATIVE
COMMUNITIES:
Ecovillages and the UN's New Sustainable Development Goals
By Rob Wheeler

At ZEGG ecovillage in Germany, 400 people dine outside during a Whitsun festival.

Achim Ecker

The Global Ecovillage Network (GEN) and its many ecovillage communities have long striven to be good planetary citizens and to live in ways that are as sustainable, nurturing, and harmonious as possible. We are now working to help achieve the United Nations' new Sustainable Development Goals (SDGs) and to fulfill the Paris Climate Agreement; and you can help too. The SDGs were adopted by the UN last September. Many describe them as the most ambitious and inclusive set of goals to which the UN has ever agreed.

The SDGs include 17 primary goals and 169 more specific targets. They encompass such objectives as achieving full and productive employment and decent work for all; ensuring access to adequate, safe, and affordable housing and basic services; doubling agricultural productivity and the incomes of small-scale farmers; implementing resilient agricultural practices while strengthening capacity for adaptation to climate change; doubling the global rate of energy efficiency; ensuring access to affordable, reliable, sustainable, and modern energy for all; and sustainably managing and efficiently using natural resources—all by 2030.

These intentions are certainly challenging, but achievable if we set our hearts and minds to it. Ecovillages are already showing how these goals can be met.

GEN and the UN

I have represented GEN at the United Nations for the past 15 years. I have lived in an ecovillage community, and in my career as an educator and acivisit visited many more.

During that time I have come to recognize ecovillages as among the most sustainable communities on earth. I have also become familiar with the UN's new SDGs, having participated actively in the meetings at the UN that developed them and evaluated how they could be achieved.

GEN and our ecovillage communities are already well on our way towards helping the UN and the world's people to reach these targets and goals. For example, many ecovillages are leaders in developing and using organic farming, regenerative agriculture, biochar and carbon sequestration, biological waste treatment processes, natural building practices, and innovative means of producing renewable energy.

I joined a GEN delegation that participated in the UN's Climate Summit in Paris in December, and helped to put together a special website for it, looking at how ecovillages are helping to address and prevent climate change. I want to share with you some of the many ways that ecovillages around the world help create a more just, equitable, and sustainable world and ways in which you and your community can participate.

Transitioning to Clean and Renewable Energy

Goal 7 of the SDGs calls for ensuring access to and substantially increasing the share of renewable energy. The world community is finally taking notice and investing in the transition to a truly renewable energy future, but we still have a long way to go. According to REN21's 2014 report, renewables contributed 19 percent to our global energy consumption in 2012, but almost half of this still comes from burning fuel wood. More than a billion people still lack access to electricity. And an estimated seven million people die each year from indoor air pollution from cooking and heating fires—mostly women and children. It is thus a challenging goal but one that can definitely be met.

Dyssekilde Ecovillage in Denmark provides one example of what we can do. Almost all of the houses have a greenhouse built in on their south-facing wall. Passive solar heating is particularly efficient in houses with brick or other dense walls that absorb the heat, shortening the active heating season by a month both in autumn and spring.

When the ecovillage first started, wood was a popular fuel as it was relatively cheap, easily obtainable, and, when sustainably harvested, CO_2-neutral. Many of the older houses are therefore heated by wood-burning mass ovens—heavy brick or stone ovens in the middle of the houses. They are fired once a day to very high heat, which gives a cleaner combustion and less pollution. The brick or stone then absorbs the heat and slowly releases it during the day. These ovens typically utilize 95 percent of the biomass energy and are thus ideal for home heating in Scandinavian and other cold climates. Many also have built-in ovens for baking and cooking.

When the Dyssekilde community built their communal house they decided to heat it with geothermal energy. This system works by absorbing heat from the ground via long tubes dug approximately 1 meter into the earth. These are filled with water and an anti-freeze solution. Electricity provided by wind power runs a compressor that boosts this relatively low heat to 30-40 degrees C, which is then used to heat floors, radiators, and tap water. Many houses also have solar water heaters on the roof. Finally, in order to be self-sufficient they built the first windmill in the area in the mid-1990s. Communally owned, it produces two and a half times the electricity needed for houses in the village. (See www.dyssekilde.dk/uk/node/126.)

Increasing Productivity and Income with Solar Dryers

Hakoritna Farm in Palestine has had great success with solar dryers. In Palestine, farmers cannot export their products because of the checkpoints and separation wall. Given the nation's minute size, farmers' livelihoods are compromised as fruits and vegetables of the same variety ripen simultaneously, often flooding the market and driving down the price farmers can ask for their crops. Farmers therefore reap insufficient profits to cover their input and labor, especially when the produce is organic. But by installing solar dryers they are able to preserve vegetables and fruits for the winter, thus getting a much better price and increasing food sovereignty.

People used to put produce on rooftops to dry but would have to take it down at night; and if it rained all could be ruined. The solar dryer makes things easy. It is essentially a plastic sheet tunnel with solar-driven fans to maintain the right humidity. The fruits can dry in just a day.

(You can read more about Hakoritna Farm in Palestine, along with many other ecovillage success stories, in GEN's new book Ecovillage: 1001 Ways to Heal the Planet, available on the GEN website at www.ecovillage.org/node/5746 and on the FIC website at www.ic.org/community-bookstore/product/ecovillage-1001-ways-to-heal-the-planet; it is also reviewed on page 80 of this issue.)

The Tamera ecovillage in Portugal has also been using a solar dryer that has proved itself many times over. Similar solar dryers are also used by fishermen in Bangladesh to dry fish, farmers in Togo for bananas, and merchants in China for spices. One half of the floor

Ecovillage Design Education course, Palestine, 2015.

Biogas system for refugee camps and slums.

Photo courtesy of Global Ecovillage Network

of the tunnel-dryer is painted black and serves as the "collector." Here, solar radiation is transformed into heat. The air is heated and thus has a lower relative humidity. A fan then blows the air across the goods to be dried, where it absorbs moisture. The sunlight falling on this drying area helps to vaporize moisture in the food. Because the fan (in the far triangular end of the tunnel-dryer) is powered by a photovoltaic (PV) module, the interior temperature can be kept constant. (You can find a detailed guide on constructing a solar dryer at www.solare-bruecke.org/Bauanleitungen/Tunneltrockner_dt.pdf.)

Biogas Digesters Can Be Cheap and Easy to Build

At Tamera, they have also built several biogas digesters that run almost entirely on kitchen and garden scraps from the community. With biogas from the first two they are able to cook on one burner for 10-20 hours a day. They estimate that this type of a system is 400 times more effective than a system using cow manure. With biogas, the kitchen can remain in service through the rainy winter season, during which time direct solar power is not sufficient. They are now planning to power a refrigerator and a generator with biogas. (See www.tamera.org/project-groups/autonomy-technology/biogas.)

T.H. Culhane from SolarCITIES helped Tamera construct and install the digesters. He has worked for years with the local people in the poorest neighborhoods of Cairo, Egypt and in other African countries to develop decentralized solutions for energy supply. They use what is available—buckets, plastic canisters, hoses, old gas cookers—to assemble a whole system: the biogas digester, an attached gas reservoir nearly as large as the digester, the inlet for kitchen waste, the outlets for gas and liquid fertilizer, and the cooker and other devices that use the gas. (See solarcities.blogspot.com.)

Cleaning Up Charcoal and Creating a Mini Grid in the Developing World

The European Union provides funding for a number of highly successful ecovillage climate projects in Tanzania that utilize multi-sectoral interventions. Zanzibar Community Forests International has assisted villagers in using a new method to produce charcoal, replacing the traditional earth mound technique with a low-cost retort kiln, doubling production efficiency. It takes half as much wood to produce the same amount of charcoal—and in turn consumes only half as much forest. This process cuts production time in half and reduces emissions up to 75 percent. (See forestsinternational.org/innovation/post/can-we-answer-tanzanias-charcoal-question-one-small-answer-at-a-time.)

In Tanzania, only 14 percent of the people have access to electricity. So they set out to design an electricity system for the island of Kokota in Zanzibar, spanning the entire island and empowering every single inhabitant. This meant providing electricity to over 80 homes and three public buildings. With no previous access to electricity, Kokota's energy demands were simple: people wanted electric lighting so they wouldn't have to keep buying and burning kerosene, and to charge their mobile phones. They figured out that a week's worth of energy to meet basic demands for a single household could be stored in a small motorcycle battery. So the community generates renewable energy collectively at a central location and then distributes it via a fleet of small carry-home batteries—a "portable" microgrid. (See forestsinternational.org/innovation/post/how-do-you-build-your-own-portable-microgrid.)

Sequestering Carbon and Improving Soil Health with Biochar

A number of ecovillages have also been experimenting with and offering workshops on making and using biochar and on building biochar pits, kilns, or wood stoves. Not only can biochar dramatically cut down on carbon emissions, it can also help to sequester vast amounts of carbon in our soils, while restoring soil health and increasing productivity.

In regions as diverse as the high mountain valleys of Costa Rica and the agricultural fields of western Kenya, biochar cook-

> ## A rich loamy soil, up to a meter deep, can be restored in a matter of years.

stoves are now being used to both clear the air and enrich the soil. Biochar is a type of charcoal produced when biomass burns in an oxygen-free environment. It can boost water and nutrients in dry, depleted soil while serving as a vehicle for burying the carbon that contributes to global warming.

At The Farm ecovillage community in Tennessee (US), they have been regenerating and replenishing depleted topsoil by putting biochar and compost tea into the soil using a keyline plow, which cuts into the soil surface without turning the earth. A rich loamy soil, up to a meter deep, can be restored in a matter of years.

In Germany's ZEGG ecovillage, the soil is sandy so they decided to use biochar (terra preta) to improve the soil quality in their gardens. Terra preta (literally "black earth" in Portuguese) owes its name to its very high charcoal content, and is made by adding a mixture of charcoal, bone, and manure to the otherwise relatively infertile Amazonian soil over many years.

According to a *National Geographic* news article entitled "Biochar Cookstoves Boost Health for People and Crops," three billion people worldwide rely on highly polluting open-fire cookstoves. The article goes on to say that a Seattle, Washington-based company, SeaChar, is testing a new style of clean cookstove that produces biochar. It can be built using local materials: a five-gallon steel paint bucket, some corrugated steel roofing material, and half of a one-gallon tomato sauce can.

In addition to wood, the stove burns garden debris, dried animal dung, corncobs, and coconut husks. A family cooking a pot of beans will use 40 percent less wood with this Estufa Finca stove than with an open-fire stove, while showing a significant reduction in exposure to harmful smoke. These stoves reduce particulate matter emissions by some 92 percent and carbon monoxide emissions by 87 percent. SeaChar offers a biochar buyback program too, through which households can earn an extra $15-20 per month by selling the biochar produced by their cookstoves—a huge boon in the developing world. (See news.nationalgeographic.com/news/energy/2013/01/130129-biochar-clean-cookstoves.)

A family cooking a pot of beans will use 40 percent less wood with an Estufa Finca stove than with an open-fire stove.

They built and use a Kontiki steel kiln at ZEGG to make the biochar, and have figured out an ingenious way to charge it. Biochar is extremely porous. It absorbs water and nutrients and can thus deliver them to the plant root zone. But if it is not charged by soaking with either liquid nitrogen or a compost tea, or being mixed into a compost pile, biochar soaks up, holds, and thus depletes the land of available nutrients.

At ZEGG they wanted to lower the nitrogen and phosphate levels in their wastewater to improve the quality of their outflow water. They discovered that urine has the highest content of nitrogen and phosphorus, much more than human feces. In fact, 80 to 90 percent of the nitrogen we shed and 50 percent of phosphorus are in the urine. So they started soaking biochar with urine from their waterless toilets in barrels for approximately four weeks. They then use composted leaf earth, clay, bokashi, grass clippings, and charged biochar in layers to set up a compost stack and let it sit covered for a year before putting it into their gardens. (See Terra Preta Production, Part II: Waterless Urinals—Charging Terra Preta at ZEGG, sites.ecovillage.org/article/terra-preta-production-part-ii.)

You will find many articles, videos, and instructions on making and using biochar on the GEN climate website at www.ecovillage.org/COP21 or more directly at ecovillage.org/node/5998.) Numerous organizations and businesses are also listed on the Global Alliance for Clean Cookstoves website that sell biochar cookstoves or help communities make and install them. See cleancookstoves.org (enter biochar under search).

So by making biochar and investing in cleaner energy production we can achieve many of the UN's SDGs: improving soil health, increasing agricultural productivity, reducing hunger, reducing water pollutants, and improving human health; while reducing carbon emissions, sequestering carbon, and reducing deforestation.

These are just some of the best practices and success stories being carried out in ecovillages that can help us deal more responsibly with the climate crisis while also achieving the SDGs. You can find many more examples and details under Success Stories at www.ecovillage.org/cop21.

Rob Wheeler has represented the Global Ecovillage Network at the United Nations for the past 15 years. He has participated actively in the global Earth Summit Conferences in Rio de Janeiro, in Johannesburg, and the annual meetings of the UN's Commission and now High Level Political Forum on Sustainable Development in New York. Rob used to live at the Heathcote Ecovillage Community in the US, and has worked for more than 25 years as a teacher and environmental educator. He co-organized and led a Sustainable Community Campaign in Santa Cruz County in California for five years in the 1990s and has been a peace, environmental, and political activist and organizer for most of his life. Every year he joins millions of people around the planet in celebrating his birthday, or rather Earth Day, on April 22.

At Dyssekilde Ecovillage in Denmark, using distance-appropriate transport reduces carbon footprints.

Hildur Jackson

LEARNING IN ECOVILLAGES AND Getting a College Degree

By Karen Stupski and Giovanni Ciarlo

Ecovillages are fun places to live and put into practice sustainable life styles, but they are also powerful sites of learning where people can discover and practice new ways of knowing, being, and doing, and create a more sustainable, peaceful, and socially just world.

From ecological practices such as permaculture and natural building to social skills such as decision-making and facilitation, ecovillages provide an abundance of learning opportunities. A new partnership between Goddard College in Vermont, and Gaia Education, a charity organization based in Scotland, enables students to earn college credit for their ecovillage-based learning. This partnership also creates the possibility for students to design a college experience that includes learning in ecovillages and other organizations doing cutting-edge work in sustainability and social and ecological justice. This article explores some of the benefits and challenges facing these community-based programs.

The Power of Ecovillage-Based Learning

Why are ecovillages such powerful sites of learning? It is not just the immersion in the physical location and ecological technologies that make ecovillage-based learning so powerful, but rather the alternative learning methods that are used. The methods of mainstream education, where students sit in classrooms, listen to lectures, and take tests, result in learning that is disconnected from the world and from the students' whole self. If students come to ecovillages and these same methods are used, the learning experience will be nothing special. However, ecovillages use alternative methods such as democratic pedagogies, reflective immersion, action/experiential learning, and holistic education. And these make all the difference in the world.

From 2006 to 2010 students came to Huehuecoyotl, a 34-year-old intentional community in central Mexico for three weeks of immersion studies in community development and leadership for social change. After an initial understanding of community research and needs assessment methodologies, they presented various projects that they could implement in the community. These led to creating recycling stations, wheelchair access ramps, garden improvement plans, community house beautification, and much more—a benefit to the community and a rich learning experience for the students, who received college credit for their work.

Democratic Pedagogies

Democratic pedagogies use education as a vehicle for social transformation through inquiry into power relations and the creation of democratic communities. Democratic educators share power with students as co-creators of knowledge and implement more egalitarian social structures and processes within the learning community. These methods give students more control over their individual and collective learning and they also promote deeper relationships and support within the community of learners. In addition, they help students to see the unjust social structures that perpetuate oppression in society, understand their own roles within those structures, and gain practical tools to help dismantle oppression.

Immersion

Most people learn about community living and group dynamics by immersing themselves in a community and learning bits and pieces of organizational skills that they need to live together and carry out common chores. This was the case with Huehuecoyotl. Its founders didn't start out knowing much about natural building or food production, but they used their experience and skills in theatre to buy land and create a community from scratch by acting out what they envisioned their community to look like, in both the so-cial and the environmental aspects, and integrating spiritual and economic elements as the need and opportunities arise. Students who participate in ecovillage-based education programs have similar immersive learning experiences.

Action Learning

The students who came to learn at Huehuecoyotl were faced with problems on the ground from day one. They got to meet community members and talk about issues and aspirations of the community right there. The solutions they then offered were based on action they could take. Many ecovillages engage in an action learning process without even realizing it, as in the case of needing to start a school for their young children, or building a shelter using natural local materials. These activities bring participants in close contact with the aims of the group, and learning takes place as those involved create systems and processes for tackling common challenges. At ecovillages, students engage in action learning, helping to identify real problems and implement solutions.

Holistic Education and Systems Thinking

Holistic education is based on the premise that an underlying cause of our current environmental and social problems is our tendency to deal with elements of systems as though they were isolated parts. A holistic approach to education helps students develop their ability to deal with whole systems by taking elements that traditional education treats as separate and integrating them into a larger whole. Holistic education is interdisciplinary, making connections among the humanities, the social sciences, the natural sciences, math, and the arts. It addresses the whole person, valuing

and nurturing students' intellectual, emotional, spiritual, and physical development. Finally, it helps students understand the Earth as a whole system to which they are intimately connected. Ecovillages embrace a holistic worldview which permeates ecovillage-based educational experiences.

The Challenges of Ecovillage-Based Learning

If ecovillage-based learning is so powerful, why isn't it more popular? There are many challenges that limit the ability of both ecovillages and students to engage in ecovillage-based education. Many ecovillages are small and have limited time, energy, and resources. This is illustrated by Andres K. Cobos, one of Huehuecoyotl's members, who says that he often doesn't have the time to prepare the spirituality-based teachings that he offers, because he must focus on issues pertaining to the immediate survival and long-term viability of the ecovillage. While it is true that students can help with projects and bring much-needed energy and resources to an ecovillage, community members still must make a significant effort to organize the educational programs and support the learners so that they have a high-quality experience. Ecovillages may not have members who want to do

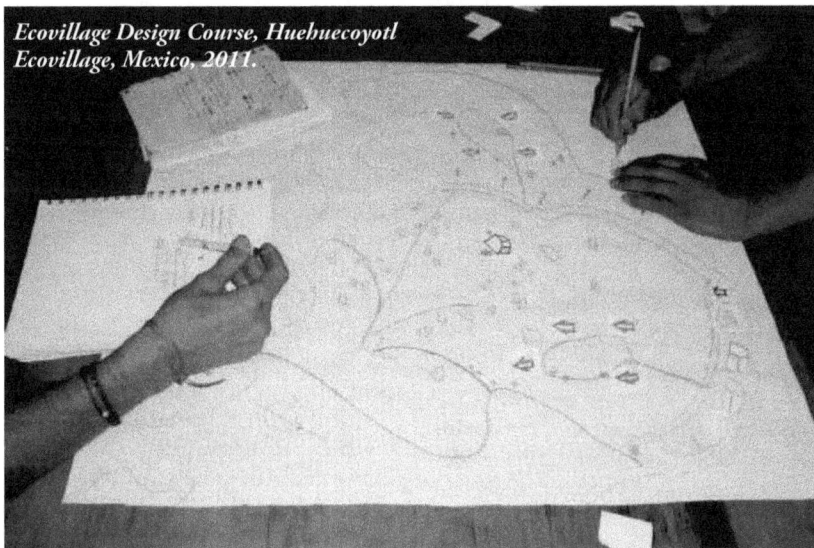

Ecovillage Design Course, Huehuecoyotl Ecovillage, Mexico, 2011.

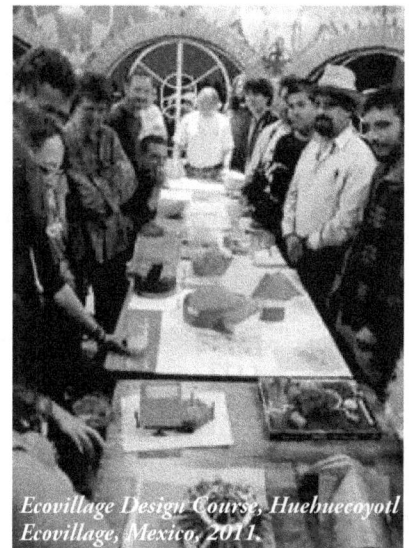

Ecovillage Design Course, Huehuecoyotl Ecovillage, Mexico, 2011.

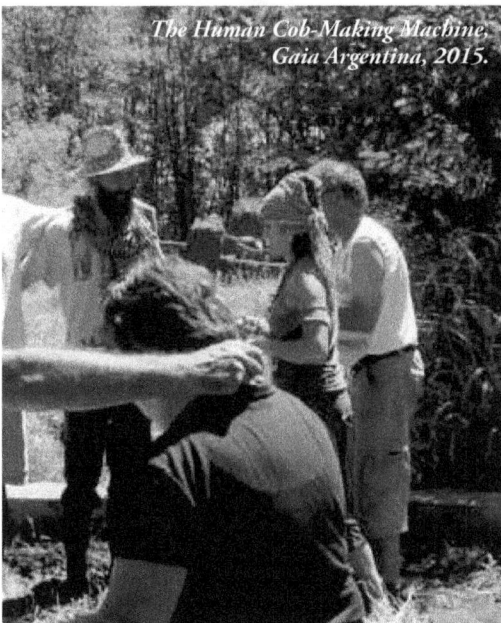

The Human Cob-Making Machine, Gaia Argentina, 2015.

Ecovillage Design Presentation, Gaia Argentina, 2015.

Photos by Giovanni Ciarlo

educational work or they may lack the expertise to develop curricula and organize high-quality educational programs. Most ecovillage-based programs that do exist cannot offer college credit unless they partner with an accredited academic institution.

The biggest challenge for students may be the lack of accessibility to ecovillage-based learning. The number of ecovillages offering educational programs, while growing, is relatively small and they are not widely known in mainstream culture. Sometimes, when students do participate in an ecovillage-based program, the experience may not be all that they had hoped for due to the challenges faced by the host ecovillage, as mentioned above. Students who want to earn college credit for their ecovillage-based learning have an even more difficult time, as there are few accredited ecovillage-based programs and those in existence face continuous enrollment challenges.

The Global Ecovillage Network (GEN) and Gaia Education

Fortunately, there are two organizations within the ecovillage movement that support the development of ecovillage-based education. The concept of "ecovillages" was born and made popular with the emergence in the 1990s of the Global Ecovillage Network (GEN). GEN's mission is to network ecovillages around the world in an effort to move human communities towards a more harmonious existence with each other and the Earth. Shortly after its creation GEN realized that the increasing number of self-identified ecovillages in its network had parts of the pieces for becoming a sustainable settlement, but education was a much-needed piece in helping them become more coherent and effective in developing their many systems, be it in the social, ecological, economic, or worldview aspects. To accomplish these new educational goals Gaia Education was created out of the ecovillage experience, and the curriculum that resulted from this effort became the basis for Ecovillage Design courses in over 40 countries in all continents, and online. The realization that ecovillages could become the immersion site for learning about community sustainability has revolutionized the way people learn to create community, or transition their community towards a more resilient path. Gaia Education provides valuable resources to strengthen ecovillage-based education around the world.

The Ecovillage Design Curriculum

The educators who developed Gaia Education's Ecovillage Design Curriculum, a group that playfully calls themselves the GEESE (Global Educators for Environmental Sustainability Education), includes ecovillage founders, sustainability practitioners, and educators from around the world, many of whom have academic training and research credentials in addition to personal experience creating ecovillages.

Each of the four dimensions (social, ecological, economic, and worldview) includes five modules and features learning goals, content, resources, and experiential learning activities. In addition, Gaia Education has published four books with reading materials that support each module. The curriculum is available for free on the Gaia Education website and it is an amazing resource for learners and ecovillages. Students can use it as a self-study guide and ecovillages can use it to supplement their own educational programs or partner with Gaia Education to offer a certified immersion course. It is also offered online in a learning community that includes an immersion experience in an ecovillage or sustainability center, often in partnership with ecovillages, universities, and training centers around the world.

Gaia Education offers a step-by-step guide on how to organize a course, and it offers a limited amount of small mentoring grants to help with the cost of organizing a course in economically challenged locations, thus addressing some of the biggest challenges facing ecovillages that want to organize education programs. For quality control, course organizers are required to have the students fill out an online evaluation form. The results of these evaluations over the past 10 years show that students around the world have had overwhelmingly positive and transformative experiences in these EDE courses.

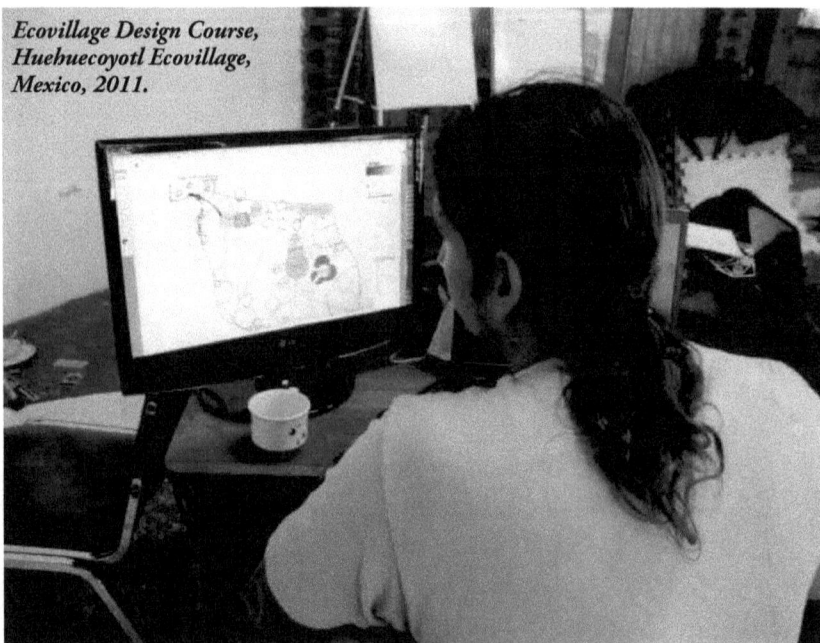

Ecovillage Design Course, Huehuecoyotl Ecovillage, Mexico, 2011.

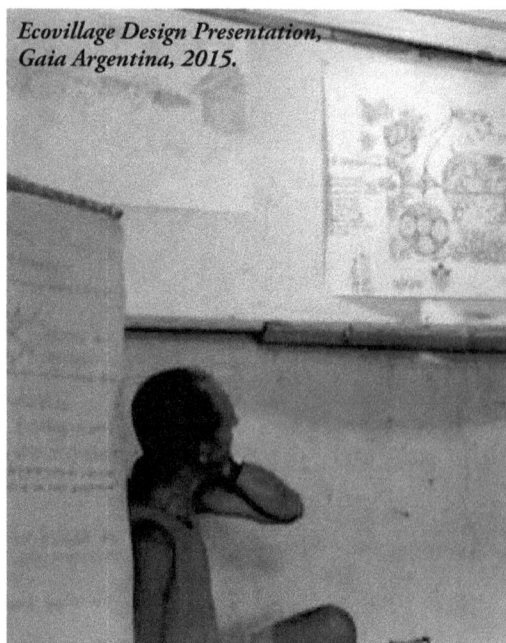

Ecovillage Design Presentation, Gaia Argentina, 2015.

In addition, the online course, called GEDS (Gaia Education Design for Sustainability), is a valuable resource for groups wanting to start an ecovillage, as it covers the basic information needed to develop

ecovillage-based learning through immersions and action learning projects. With Goddard's program, students can spend their college years living in ecovillages while earning a bachelors or masters degree. Many students at Goddard pursue degrees based on the ecovillage experience, including the current academic director of Gaia Education, Giovanni Ciarlo, who earned his M.A. at Goddard (SBC 2008) before taking a position with Gaia Education, and Cynthia Tina, who completed her B.A. degree with a focus on ecovillages and sustainable design (IBA 2014). Thus, it seemed only natural that Goddard College and Gaia Education would work together to provide degree credits to students.

> ## This institutional and grassroots partnership didn't come easy or fast. The key issues are academic rigor, instructors' credentials, and documentation of learning.

one, and can also supplement any onsite ecovillage-based training program.

Goddard's Sustainability Degrees and Ecovillages

While a number of mainstream colleges and universities have partnered with ecovillages over the years, Goddard College is a leader in alternative education and has many unique advantages that make it an excellent fit for ecovillage-based learning. Goddard is a small, progressive, liberal arts school in Vermont that offers low-residency programs leading to accredited bachelors and masters degrees. It has a radical pedagogy: there are no classes, no tests, and no grades. Students create their own study plans and are assessed on a portfolio of samples from their work. They can live anywhere and are free to engage in

A Partnership and its Obstacles and Challenges

In July 2015, Goddard College and Gaia Education created a partnership that enables students to earn up to 10 transfer credits if they complete the online GEDS course and enroll in a bachelors program at Goddard. In addition, students who enter the college through this partnership are eligible for a $1,000 scholarship. They can then go on to design their own individualized study program to earn an accredited bachelors degree focusing on the study of ecovillages or any other topics they wish to pursue.

This institutional and grassroots partnership didn't come easy or fast, as the promoters of this academic partnership have been talking and exploring options for nearly 10 years. The key issues are academic rigor, instructors' credentials, and documentation of learning. The accreditation body that accredits Goddard college's degrees is the same body that accredits other institutions in New England, including Ivy League schools like Harvard and Yale. Goddard could risk losing accreditation if the board found that its academic credits did not meet strict guidelines.

The criteria for this partnership illustrate important challenges that must be overcome when ecovillages partner with academic institutions to offer accredited programs. The issue of academic rigor was addressed by a thorough review of the GEDS curriculum to ensure that it offers college level learning and meets high academic standards. In this process, the content of the GEDS course was correlated to Goddard's degree requirements so that students could earn credit in specific wide knowledge areas, such as natural science, social science, and the humanities. The issue of instructors' credentials was resolved through Gaia Education's rigorous requirements for the instructors who are hired to teach the GEDS course. Finally, Gaia Education requires the students to document their learning through comprehension, critical thinking reflections, and a team design comprehensive case study portfolio, so that learning outcomes can be assessed and substantiated.

Another significant challenge is lack of resources and institutional capacity. Goddard College is a tiny school in comparison to many mainstream colleges and universities. While it has an abundance of innovative ideas and visions, Goddard does not have sufficient funding to pay for the labor required to bring all these ideas and visions to fruition. However, thanks to a grant from the Jeld Charitable Foundation, which supports the Fund for Experiments and New Initiatives at Goddard College, a team of faculty was empowered to work on developing the partnership with Gaia Education and other organizations doing cutting-edge work in sustainability and social and ecological justice.

Into the Future

In his article on "Ecovillages and Academia," published in the Summer 2010 issue (#147) of COMMUNITIES, Daniel Greenberg articulated a vision of the larger potential of ecovillage-based education: "While programs offered through Living Routes and individual ecovillages are a good start, we need to further collaborate with academia to create 'communiversities' where students can spend years in ecovillages and other related organizations and gain the background and skills needed to enter the workplace as professionals in fields as diverse as appropriate technologies, habitat restoration, sustainable agriculture, group facilitation, holistic health, ecological design, and green building." (p. 37)

(continued on p. 76)

LEARNING IN ECOVILLAGES AND GETTING A COLLEGE DEGREE

(continued from p. 35)

The Gaia-Goddard partnership is a step in that direction, making much of that vision possible for students.

Both Gaia Education and Goddard College also have other partnerships that can deepen and expand the learning opportunities available to students. For example, Gaia Education has partnered with the United Nations Sustainable Development Goals and uses the EDE course as a key component in grant-funded sustainable development projects. And Goddard College has partnerships with other organizations doing work in sustainability and social and ecological justice such as the Permaculture Institute of North America, Food First, and Yestermorrow. Students can engage in experiential learning with all of these partners.

Together, ecovillages, Gaia Education, Goddard College, and their partners give students the opportunity to have a global, transformative, and impactful experience where learning is integrated with work on meaningful projects that help to create a more sustainable and socially just world.

Giovanni Ciarlo (Gio) is an ecovillage activist and educator. He also performs and records with his musical group Sirius Coyote in both the US and Mexico, where he cofounded Ecoaldea Huehuecoyotl, an ecovillage based on the arts and ecology (www.huehuecoyotl. net). He is the Academic Director for Gaia Education, former advisor in the M.A. program at Goddard College, past president of GEN (2009-2011), and the recipient of the FIC's 2016 Kozeny Communitarian Award.

Karen Stupski is a sustainability educator, nonprofit administrator, and communitarian. She currently serves as a faculty member at Goddard College, Development Director for the Gunpowder Valley Conservancy (a watershed organization and land trust), and Executive Director of School of Living (a community land trust). Karen lives at Heathcote Community, where she coordinates the permaculture education program. She holds a Ph.D. in the history of science, medicine, and technology from Johns Hopkins University and a Post Masters Graduate Diploma in Organizing Learning for EcoSocial Regeneration from Gaia University.

In 2003, "La Cité Écologique" was founded, in Colebrook New Hampshire, on 315 acres of beautiful land surrounded by forest and mountains. Our ecovillage gives priority to education, optimal living to its members, a cooperative culture with resilience in its development and social entrepreneurship. So far, we have built one single family building, two large community residences, where people live in a kind of condo arrangement, and one community building (all powered by solar). We are expanding new building projects, to give a home to growing families and/or new members. We've created businesses, non-profits, a nonprofit school, and an organic farm, that helps better serve ours, and the local community. Visitors are welcome to our annual Open House in June, and Harvest Celebration in September. Guided tours, and internship programs are also available from May through October.

Contact: Leonie Brien (603) 331-1669
www.citeecologiquenh.org

La Cité Écologique
of New Hampshire
An Ecovillage since 2003

YARROW ECOVILLAGE:
Cohousing as a Building Block to the Ecovillage

By Charles Durrett and Katie McCamant

Following the first cohousing community in the United States, Muir Commons in Davis, California, cohousing has not only continued to expand throughout the US and Canada, it has also become a model for other housing types (senior housing, nonprofit affordable housing), and a building block for other larger communities, ecovillages in particular. Yarrow Ecovillage is one such project. True to the cohousing concept in general, it aims to re-establish many of the advantages of traditional villages within the context of 21st century life.

The site of this community is a former dairy farm, left inactive in the 1980s. Quite conveniently, the site is also on a main road that connects the small town of Yarrow (drained by decades of suburban sprawl, and now incorporated with its neighboring town of Chilliwack) with both urban Vancouver (to its west) and the natural beauty of the Fraser Valley. Yarrow Ecovillage offers the possibility of creating a new town center for Yarrow, a place for living combined with commerce. The 25 acre site on Yarrow Central Road in Chilliwack, British Columbia, includes a 33-unit intergenerational cohousing project, a 30,000-square-foot mixed-use area (commercial, rental units, learning, etc.), a 20 acre farm, and a 17-unit senior cohousing community.

Yarrow Ecovillage is designed to offer an exceptional combination of cohousing, sustainable living, farmland preservation, a live/work community, a learning center, and a mixed-use town center. Three main elements—living, working, and farming—along with many other activities and amenities such as learning, socializing, sharing, teaching, playing and visiting, are designed to come together to provide a model for environmentally, economically, and socially sustainable lifestyles. In order to accomplish the many objectives of the ecovillage, the city of Chilliwack worked with the resident group and its architects to establish an entirely new, custom zoning code. The result is an Ecovillage Zoning designation that includes residential, commercial, cottage industries, work space, public open space, recreational space, and farming.

The "town" of Yarrow has a population of about 3,000 people. It once had a concentration of commercial buildings and houses along its main street, and twice the population. It was a rural but functional small town surrounded by farms. Like too many rural towns, Yarrow's commercial viability is eclipsed by big box stores scattered between farmland, new residential developments, and previous downtown corridors. As a result, it is nearly impossible to shop, dine, be entertained, or go to school, the library, or the park in the area without getting into a car.

Although technically part of the city of Chilliwack, Yarrow is about nine miles away from Chilliwack. (For financial reasons, the town of Yarrow was incorporated in 1980 with its larger neighboring city, population 80,000, because it could not afford its own in-town infrastructure—sewer, water, schools, police, fire, administration). The community's disparate but numerous fruit and vegetable markets and smattering of small retail stores are too spread out to have any long-term commercial viability, much less culturally create any sense of place. Their dispersed locations do nothing to contribute to the kind of personal relationships that stitch a town together.

Ecovillage Zoning:
A New, Sustainable Land-Use Concept

In the winter of 2010, MDA and a few of the members of the Yarrow Ecovillage development team met with the city manager of

The ecovillage is filled with fun!

Photos courtesy of Lindy Sexton

Chilliwack, as well as the heads of planning and public works and other staff—nine city officials in all. To begin the discussions of the site, the officials opened the zoning map, the parcel map that designates the allowable land uses for all of Chilliwack and the surrounding incorporated areas. Parcels were designated for farming, residential and commercial, or a park, a school, and so on. Then we came to the 25 acre site on Yarrow Central Road, the address of Yarrow Ecovillage. Its zoning was (in capital letters) ECOVILLAGE—the first site in Canada that we know of, and perhaps in North America, that is a zoned ecovillage.

Cohousing as Essential Building Block to Ecovillage

The 33-unit intergenerational cohousing community completed in 2015 is the first building block of the ecovillage and plays a critical role in creating the culture of the place. In building it, the group learned cooperation and development skills, as well as how to brainstorm, discuss, and decide; it is the place where well-intentioned citizens learn to make consequential decisions together to accomplish their environmental and social aspirations. It is also where the relationships built during the design and development process carry over to everyday interactions and relationships now that the community is complete.

The Getting-It-Built workshop, an essential piece in starting cohousing communities, was a large catalyst in this process, taking the group from being $700,000 in debt for seven years with four houses, to finishing the 33-unit cohousing community in two years. Cohousing is the foundation upon which other players at Yarrow Ecovillage (such as merchants and farmers) model their legal structure to achieve a cooperative corporation. That is, they have learned how to invest together and, most importantly, how to get things done by working together.

The second and most public component of Yarrow Ecovillage is a 2.5 acre mixed-use area (commercial, learning, etc.)—effectively a town center. It includes 30,000 square feet of commercial space offering services, and places for work and creative opportunities, to the greater neighborhood. Yarrow Ecovillage and its new commercial area—including a yet-to-be-built 17-unit senior cohousing community, a refitted classic old dairy barn, and a completely

walkable environment—functions as a small town center. Its co-developer, the Yarrow Ecovillage Society (YES) Cooperative, continues to bring clarity of vision to the process. YES originally owned the site and works with new entities such as the Mixed-Use Development group (MUD) to best create the synergy on-site that will continue to set everyone up for success. Many of the original organizers of YES moved into the cohousing on-site.

The ability of the group to work together effectively yields the best strategy for accomplishing the sort of new town center that redevelopment agencies dream of. Yarrow Ecovillage is already a high-functioning hub and will grow to be a place where people can purchase locally grown organic produce (some grown on-site), park once and shop at four or five locations, meet a friend for coffee, work, get to know their neighbors, or take a class or two. It will be a place where families, seniors, and even teenagers will want to congregate. The goal is to not only enhance commercial viability and create a quality living environment, but to create a culturally viable and culturally vibrant place.

A 20 acre organic farm is located adjacent to the cohousing community. Some of the people who live in the cohousing community co-own and operate the farm, and like the commercial area, the farm is a separate partnership, managed by people with agricultural expertise (the business of farming), while remaining an important part of the larger whole—Yarrow Ecovillage.

Cohousing Site Design

In January 2010, we held a site design workshop with the group to plan and focus on the cohousing site. The outcome was a site plan that achieved the group's objectives. It added a diagonal pathway that links the cohousing site in the middle with the mixed-use site at one end, and the other end serves as a sight line, giving the residents a view of an existing silo that will continue to be preserved in the redevelopment, along with the heritage barn.

The cohousing site includes 33 private residences with a variety of housing types (duplexes, flats, townhouses, and shared houses), a common house, and ample programmed and unprogrammed open space. A new 3,900-square-foot common house is built at the intersection of the pedestrian pathways alongside the parking area on the east side of the site. This central area accommodates a terrace (connected to the common house) and a children's play area (across from, but separate from, the common house terrace). The location of the common house contributes to the overall functioning of the community as a gathering place. It is visible from private homes and the path that links them to the parking area. In this way, residents pass it on their way home and are likely to drop in.

Yarrow Ecovillage is designed to foster a sense of community along the pathways and

A view of
Yarrow Ecovillage.

The original barn still exists.

Gerry, one of the village sages, with a couple of young residents.

The group planned their ecovillage together.

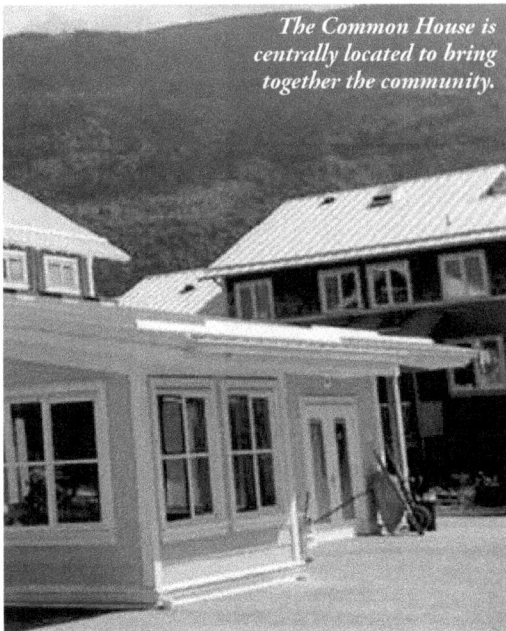
The Common House is centrally located to bring together the community.

YARROW CENTRAL ROAD

MIXED-USE AREA

COMMUNITY FARM

Yarrow Site Plan.

in the various outdoor spaces, balanced with adequate room for privacy in more secluded areas, such as private backyards. It is also well suited to passive and active heating and cooling possibilities, and overall sun control.

Reviving the Town Center

The town center is almost as old as human settlement. Members of Yarrow Ecovillage understand that the combination of positive, usable public space, combined with commercial activity and spaces for creativity and learning, activate the environment. Such public space doesn't just provide retail opportunities; it provides opportunities for meaningful human interaction. Over time, these spontaneous, informal interactions may grow into more formal friendships. You get to know the person who bakes your bread, grows your carrots, or relaxes in the public square on a sunny day, and he or she gets to know you and your children. The variety of relationships and diversity of people, skills, and interests will likely establish a vibrant culture of learning, doing, and being—as a functional, interrelated society.

Cohousing Design to Facilitate Community

Yarrow Ecovillage, while a model project in its own right, is part of a larger, growing trend in neighborhood design in which cohousing has played an important role.
(continued on p. 77)

YARROW ECOVILLAGE:
COHOUSING AS A BUILDING BLOCK TO THE ECOVILLAGE

(continued from p. 43)

We have seen many cohousing communities, like Yarrow Ecovillage, that begin as small infill projects and, over time, bring new life to an entire neighborhood. Yarrow Ecovillage is no different and has the potential to catalyze other developments nearby, helping to stem the tide of sprawl in this beautiful valley. As an infill project that reinvigorates a former, under-utilized site with a variety of uses, it is a model to be expanded upon in similar rural settings.

The Yarrow Ecovillage group has successfully completed a design and construction that captures a true *genius loci*, the spirit of a place that is memorable for both its architectural and its experiential qualities. This combination also allows for a wonderful balance of economics, ecology, and positive social space. This type of calculated diversity assures flexibility and longevity for Yarrow Ecovillage. The cohousing, first in the development process, is really the kingpin of the larger whole. It is the cornerstone or the incubator for thoughtful and efficient processes and investment models in the future. It not only catalyzes the Yarrow Ecovillage larger whole, it also helps to synthesize the three separate endeavors to accomplish the overall goals of the ecovillage.

In Conclusion

At one point, we were talking to the city about adding the 17-unit senior cohousing community. We asked, *can this work?* The city replied, *we don't know, it's zoned as an ecovillage—you tell us. We don't claim to know anything about ecovillages.*

And they were correct. It was up to the residents to come up with what made sense from an ecological, economical, and social point of view. Where is the synergy that will make it an ecovillage? What the group has designed couldn't be more sophisticated, more synergistic, likened to the organic villages of old that you find in southern France. Those villages were created before development became big box and big subdivision. Like when human environments were human scale—that's Yarrow Ecovillage.

McCamant & Durrett Architects | The Cohousing Company is an architecture and consulting firm with offices in Nevada City, California. Principal Architect Charles Durrett and his wife, Katie McCamant of Cohousing Solutions, have become well known nationally and internationally for the design of cohousing communities, sustainable design and development consulting. Since 1987 the firm has provided complete architectural services for a wide range of clients. Charles and Katie have published many essential cohousing books, including Cohousing: A Contemporary Approach to Housing Ourselves, Creating Cohousing: Building Sustainable Communities, *and* Senior Cohousing: A Community Approach to Independent Living. *MDA has adapted its cohousing design experience to affordable housing developments and senior neighborhoods. Other projects have included custom strawbale homes, mixed-use developments, town planning, commercial projects, and childcare centers. MDA's Lindy Sexton helped with the editing of this article.*

Want an Ecovillage? Stay Put!

By Abeja Hummel

Last spring, for the first time in my 43 years of life, I noticed when a bird returned from his winter migration and started singing to establish his territory. I was ecstatic! It was the Pacific-Slope Flycatcher, but it wasn't that I am in some way partial to the Pacific-Slope Flycatcher. It was that I NOTICED.

And here's where I get sad. How is that I, with my "eco-girl" persona, always outside doing something—playing, working, hiking, biking, climbing—never noticed what any young indigenous child would have found obvious? How is it that I just learned that there is information that humans can understand in the language of the birds—the pleasant "elevator music" that was rarely noticed in the background of my life? Why? Because no one around me noticed, either.

I've logged some time and miles on this big blue spinning ball, and I've got stories, let me tell you! Places I've lived. Trails I've hiked. Mountains I've climbed. Continents I've traversed. Communities I've visited. It's been fun and exciting.

Yet, in all that exploring, what I found was that the people I admired most were the ones who were connected and committed to their homes and their lands. Adivasi villagers in India fighting the government to protect their homes from being flooded by big dam projects. Quechua Indians of Peru maintaining their ancient system of trade, festivals, and work-exchange from the alpaca farmers on the top of the mountain, to the citrus farmers in the valleys, and all the villages in be-

A nest of Pacific Slope Flycatchers in the eaves of author's house.

Tom Shaver

tween. Dancers in Swaziland carrying the reeds they harvested for building in a celebration dance.

These people knew where they were from, and I was jealous. I always struggled to answer that question," Where are you from?" Growing up we moved about every four-five years to follow my dad's work. Am I from Utah? Kentucky? Michigan? Virginia? It was always new. Always interesting. And in our time off from school, we'd load in the car and drive far away for a family vacation, somewhere different and exciting every year.

You may recognize yourself in parts of this story. Cheap oil has made ours the most mobile human culture in history. Moving can be a very valuable step forward in your life. And it's important to travel and be exposed to different cultures, new ideas, other ways of doing things. But we've kinda over-done it, and it's destroying our ecosystems and our communities.

Probably around three-quarters of the inquiries we get from people interested in community are from folks in their 60s. A regular statement I get from folks in their 30s and 40s who come

through this land—many of whom consider themselves very eco-conscious—is "I would love to be a part of this community, but I *need* to travel and not feel tied down."

How can we care for a place if we're not there, day after day, month after month, year after year paying attention? Who will notice the changes—be it the early return of the Pacific-Slope Flycatcher or the slow creep of box stores and parking lots? "Wasn't that Walmart always on that corner? Doesn't anyone remember the forest? No, none of us are actually from around here."

Even setting aside nature, how can we develop deep human community connections if it's always so easy to move on to "greener pastures"? Our lack of commitment to place is mirrored in our lack of commitment to each other. I know, I've lived in and left three intentional communities now. I'm a great Facebook friend and all, but those pictures of your kids don't really amount to a relationship with them.

If you, like I was, are part of some "ecovillage" in a foreign country (for me it was Costa Rica), knowing that you'll need to come back to the States to visit family and make money every year, then I have some sad news for you. That's not "eco." And that's not a "village." Sorry.

One of the most radical forms of resistance we can perform right now is the act of being content in one place, despite its being mundane and inadequate. Staying put and paying attention. Being there for the land and each other. And what's really cool is, that it IS exciting, interesting, and fun. Each year that I witness the same cycles in the same place, I go deeper, notice changes and nuances, and get excited about what I know is coming, like an old friend.

I've lived here at Emerald Earth Sanctuary for nine short years now. Longer than anywhere I've ever lived in my life. What's to keep me here in this, my fourth intentional community, when the world is so full of options and this place is such a headache sometimes? Maybe it's my relationship to the Pacific-Slope Flycatcher. 🐦

For reasons still mysterious to her, Abeja Judy Hummel has spent 17 of the last 21 years living in intentional communities in Virginia, Costa Rica, and California. You'll now find her well-ensconced at Emerald Earth Sanctuary in Boonville, California with her husband Tom, 10-year-old son Garnet, a rotating band of community members, a herd of wily goats, some fat chickens, and a Pacific-Slope Flycatcher family in her eaves. Abeja has been fascinated with bird language since learning of its existence several years ago. See www.birdlanguage.com or www.8shields.org for more information.

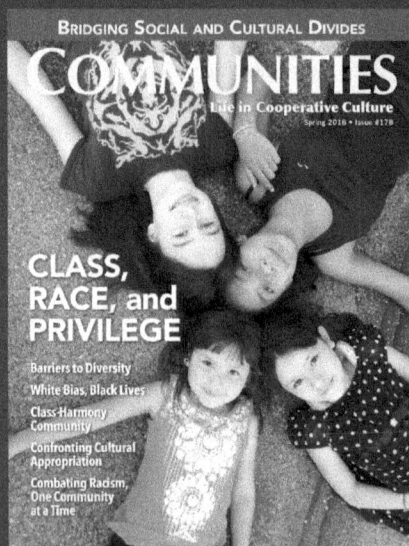

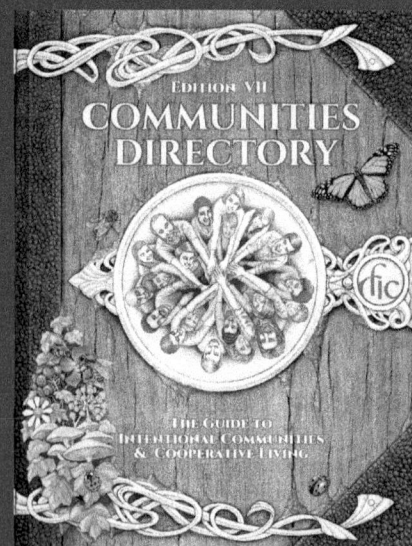

A ritual in progress at Emerald Earth's labyrinth with people writing on a sculpture the author created.

Land and Culture Collaboration

By Tom Shaver

At Emerald Earth Sanctuary outside Boonville, near-coastal northern California, we are called upon to "heal the relationship between humans and the earth." No small task... yet it's one I have taken on wholeheartedly over the past nine years. The land has shown me that a relationship of mutual support and reciprocity is available for us to choose—with the land and among ourselves.

As I read and network to seek others thinking similarly, I sense a growing movement aimed at building a nature-connected culture that supports ecosystem vitality. Since the basic component of this emerging culture is a small group of people intimately related to a specific area of land, I see how ecovillages could play a pivotal role in this movement.

I greatly appreciate that the founding members of Emerald Earth, in the early years following the purchase of the 189 acre property in the late '90s, devoted so much energy to building a deep spiritual relationship with the land. I sense that the spirits of the land are accustomed to people evoking their presence and that the spirits are adept at presenting themselves in ways that people can comprehend.

A second wave of residents thankfully created the physical and organizational infrastructure that allows me to feel largely disengaged from destructive mainstream culture. I get to live in a home built of materials from the land, eat food that was mostly grown or foraged here, use electricity and water from our own systems, and contribute my voice to our annual planning and long-term visioning.

As we delve more deeply into how to inhabit this land in an ecologically responsible manner we have come across the notion that the ecosystem of this area evolved with human participation (*1491*, Charles C. Mann). We began studying native land management practices in which the materials for life were derived from activities that supported the reproductive success and habitat quality of the species harvested (*Tending the Wild*, Kat Anderson). I began to realize, contrary to popular belief, that ecologically sustainable native cultures lived in balance with their environment, limiting their take to no more than the ecosystem could easily handle; that they actually provided ecosystem services that far outweighed the amount of materials they took for human use.

We did some experimental burning of grassland, building up to covering about an acre swath. We made a plan for revitalizing an oak woodland area. We took over a cow herd share operation and began practicing rotational grazing to build soil according to principles of Holistic Resource Management. I started taking on the notion that we, too, could have a relationship with our land such that we give to the ecosystem more than we receive from it.

This realization led me to notice how things I was already doing fell in line with this notion.

As I forage for mushrooms, I have gotten in the habit of throwing bits of past-mature or rotten caps up hill, far to the side or in an area far away that looks like it would be good habitat for, but is currently devoid of, that mushroom. I am called to help the organism to spread in space in ways that it wouldn't do normally. My intimate connection with mushrooms—through sometimes daily forays to find them, eating them, providing them for group meals, selling them to the public, and leading workshops in mushroom foraging—compels me naturally to serve the organisms that give me and my family life and livelihood.

A pivotal moment in our group happened during discussion of a plan for managing a three acre section of oak woodland. It was an area of crowded canopy with stunted underbrush and mossy soil. It is likely that this area was kept clear of underbrush by Indian burning, then overgrazed by settlers who left the landscape degraded. We discussed ideas for bringing vitality and diversity to this zone

browse height. These then sprouted new growth which is now a convenient source of fodder to coppice and bring to the goats. We also are reserving some branches to put into debris swales that increase water retention. The plan gets modified based on new information that was unforeseen at the beginning.

As one of the main people choosing which trees to cut or save, cutting fodder for the goats, and processing the woody material into wood chips, biochar, firewood, and lumber, I have a very deep connection to the process. When I see how the ecosystem benefits while we get materials for life, I experience a profound sense of belonging to the land. When I hunt, I know that the animals I cull were supported in life by my actions. When I eat, amend garden beds, or feed the woodstove, I know that those materials for life came from the gift of my creativity and facilitation to the land.

Having some experience with a few pilot projects, we are looking at taking on larger-scale efforts. We are working with a forester to plan a timber harvest to improve the health of the dense second and third growth forest. I am drafting a Land and Culture Collaboration Plan to provide a context for our activities in support of the ecosystem. I've come to realize that there is only a very

---

What was once a pocket of foreboding gloom is now an inviting, vibrant landscape where wildlife abounds.

---

through the introduction of domestic animals. I felt a wave of energy flow through us as the group mind came together in common purpose to boldly insert ourselves into the ecosystem to support its vitality.

The plan called for marking the trees to save, the ones to bring down in the first round of felling, and those to put in the "wait and see" category. We sought to preserve diversity of tree species while allowing more sun to reach the ground. Since we were feeding the leaves to the goats, the pace of felling was determined by the rate that the goats could consume the fodder. The bare branches were later either chipped or burned to produce biochar. The larger branches and trunks were bucked for firewood. We borrowed a portable saw mill to produce lumber from the larger fir, redwood, and oak trunks.

As each section opened up, we brought in the cows by distributing piles of hay. Each day a new area was trampled and left with a deposit of manure. Then we brought in the mobile chicken coop to distribute the manure and further stir up the ground surface. In some areas we spread a mix of pasture grass seed. Mostly we just let the native grasses and forbs reestablish. What was once a pocket of foreboding gloom is now an inviting, vibrant landscape. Wildlife—deer, pigs, turkeys, and quail—sweep over the area in greater numbers. A nearby colony of Acorn Woodpeckers became more raucous.

As we proceed, new opportunities present themselves. The approach on some oak trees, rather than felling them at the base, was to cut the major limbs, leaving a living trunk above

limited amount of impact I can have on the landscape in my lifetime. What occurs to me to do is to initiate a culture of human collaboration with the ecosystem that can be passed from generation to generation, building and morphing over time.

As I look at our forest, I see that it has been clearcut and used as sheep pasture for many decades, then selectively cut again about 40 years ago. I see that it is growing back very crowded. Many trees are deformed or stunted. I see how eventually things will get sorted out with mostly redwoods dominating the stand. I can also envision the next generation beyond the current one. My ability to see the forest as a living, changing entity is related to my experience of being

View of the land including labyrinth.

Photos courtesy of Tom Shaver

Goats eating brush at the barn.

Solar panels and power house.

Dense redwood forest.

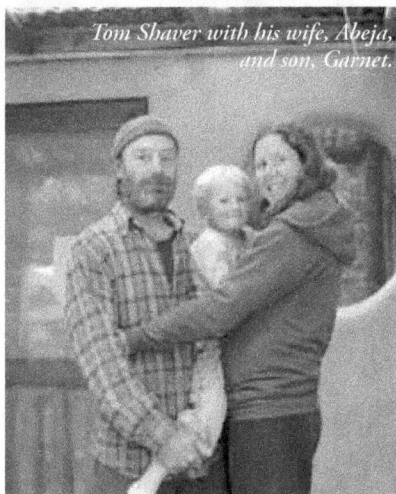

Tom Shaver with his wife, Abeja, and son, Garnet.

involved in the oak woodland area and roving over the forest repeatedly throughout several winters while mushroom foraging. I see what I could do to support the growth of the trees that are likely to emerge from the chaos, how I could encourage the buildup of duff to increase the depth of the soil, and that I could lay branches on contour to enhance the infiltration of water. It is out of empathy and knowing that I can do something helpful for a living being I am in relationship with that I am compelled to take action.

The ecosystem of my place calls me to participate in its growth and change. I see what I could do to support ecosystem processes such as biomass production, succession, and water cycling. I am inclined to facilitate greater diversity by discouraging elements that crowd out others, encouraging less well represented elements, and introducing elements that add functionality. I sense that I am engaging the land in a conversation in which I do something with the intention of helping and the land answers by exhibiting greater vitality. The materials for life that I get out of the process are the thanks I get that encourage me to continue and deepen my motivation to further the conversation. In this way, the ecosystem itself is in the lead. I am a follower with a clear role.

As we come to grips with our inability to stop global climate change, I'm wondering if I am experiencing the paradigm shift of consciousness that humankind needs to undergo. My inclination to participate in the growing, changing ecosystem leads me to see that, if I can be one with the ecosystem, then I will be one with the change.

As I look at what I might do to bring to others the experience of belonging to place, I have been attracted to the deep nature-connection practices of the Nature Awareness movement (8 Shields Institute). I realize that, even though I sense in myself a natural proclivity for perceiving the pattern language of nature, I have a long way to go and that I need mentoring and community support to take to higher levels my capacity to perceive what nature has to communicate.

I also recognize the need to shed the debilitating historical trauma that I hold from many generations of separation from the land. Indigenous cultures have rites of passage and vision quest practices that I have not gone through. I see that I need to build a culture around me to enable my deeper connection to nature. This is the same culture that is needed to carry further the work of engaging constructively in ecosystem processes into perpetuity

Fortunately, humans are programmed mentally and socially to operate optimally in the context of a culture that plays a supportive role in the ecosystem. All of us have ancestry who, for millions of years, lived in cultures that constructively participated in the vitality of their home place. It is only in the last few thousand years that a malignant civilization has arisen that has deliberately separated people from their home place and dismantled the cultural forms that held people in supportive relationship to their natural environment. A major task of our time, as I see it, is to reconnect people to the natural elements of a home place and rebuild the cultural forms that provide us with a constructive role in our local ecosystem and community.

Ecovillages, especially those in relationship with a large land base, are particularly strongly positioned to play a catalytic role in creating the eco-positive culture that will displace destructive civilization. Planning to play a long-term constructive role in ecosystem processes is more easily done for a specific area of land that is controlled in perpetuity by the group doing the planning.

Because it is hard to envision an eco-positive culture when one is dependent upon the current destructive one, the efforts to lower their ecological footprint make ecovillages more capable of being culturally creative. Ecovillages are well positioned to build in the archetypical forms of eco-positive culture—such as mentoring, rites of passage, and ceremony—that enable people to shed emotional baggage, connect more deeply to nature, and clarify their role in nature and society.

As ecovillages seek to derive more and more of their lives from place through regenerative land management practices, the creative process of designing systems to process goods for the ecovillage can be scaled up to the level of cottage industries that produce surplus for the public. I see, waiting to be developed, a whole new marketing realm—beyond Organic, Wildcrafted, or Local—which is something like "Buy Regenerative Culture."

As we learn how to engage constructively with the ecosystem, we learn to be more deeply aware of each other and what we can do to support others. At Emerald Earth Sanctuary, while just beginning to immerse ourselves functionally in the ecosystem, we sense that the land is directing us on the path of regenerative culture, and what we can offer people is a taste of the experience of having a constructive role in nature. We are in the midst of putting together a program of eco-positive cultural training oriented toward establishing these cultural forms within our core group while training others who will return to their own communities with eco-positive cultural mentoring skills. We are also looking at ways to infuse our local community with these cultural forms.

I can see how these principles of eco-positive culture building could be applied to neighborhoods and other social groupings. Groups could arrange to build relationships with private or public nature reserves. I see how roving bands could have a series of land areas that they rotate through in a year, doing constructive work in the ecosystem while building

eco-positive cultural forms.

That I have a vision of eco-positive, place-based culture is a product of my life experience and time spent living in emerging ecovillages. Lately, I've been harvesting seaweed and foraging mushrooms as a big part of my income. Together with my relationship to the land and my community, I see how my whole life has led me to this point of alignment such that I get to experience, even if for fleeting moments, the human culture that I envision. It's challenging for me to express in words what I feel in my gut. My sense is that I am receiving a message from nature. I hear her say "Come play!"

While I feel compelled to deliver that message to the world, what occurs to me to concentrate on at the moment is providing people with the experience of playing a constructive role in nature. Emerald Earth Sanctuary is an ideal palate to work with. The land already speaks to people, but the work of creating an intentional program of personal transformation is just beginning. I'd love to network with people who are interested in building eco-positive, place-based culture.

Tom Shaver lived at Loma Mona Ecovillage in Costa Rica before moving to Emerald Earth Sanctuary in 2007 with his wife, Abeja, and son, Garnet. Tom's professional life spans from possum trapping in New Zealand, to teaching English at an Islamic boarding school in Indonesia, to decades of carpentry and grassroots political organizing. Tom builds flammable symbolic forms that people add to in meaningful ways and then burns the resulting sculpture ceremonially.

Round pole building work.

Pool and waterfall in the creak that runs through the middle of the land.

Clearing in progress.

CLOUGHJORDAN ECOVILLAGE:
Modeling the Transition to a Low-Carbon Society

By Peadar Kirby

Photos (all taken at Cloughjordan Ecovillage, Ireland) by Davie Philip

While Ireland was living through the most severe economic collapse of its history since independence, a group of pioneering people were sowing the seeds of a new society through founding the ecovillage of Cloughjordan. Seeking to model sustainable living for the 21st century, the ecovillagers conceived their project during the boom years of Ireland's Celtic Tiger in the late 1990s and early 2000s, but by the time the infrastructure was being laid in 2008 and the first houses built in 2009, the Irish banking and construction sectors were in freefall and the ecovillage became the country's biggest building site.

Now with 55 houses built and a population of around 100 adults and 35 children, Cloughjordan has been recognised as one of Europe's most successful "anticipatory experiences" showing the way to a low-carbon society. As an educational charity, it draws thousands of people a year to learn the lessons of this pioneering community. Central to those lessons are the combination of some modern technologies that help lower emissions, embedded in a resilient community that seeks to foster a rich sense of interdependency, not without its tensions.

Among ecovillages, Cloughjordan is unusual in that its founders decided to integrate it into an existing urban settlement. They chose the small village of Cloughjordan (around 500 people) in county Tipperary. A site of 67 acres (27 hectares) was available on the south side of its main street, on a train line, and some leading people in the local community recognised it as an opportunity for regenerating a village that was in decline. Before buying the land, members of the ecovillage project worked with children in the local schools and with the residents of Cloughjordan to win support for developing the project.

Cloughjordan ecovillage therefore models not just ecological sustainability but also rural regeneration, drawing visitors to the existing village and fostering a new social, economic, and cultural dynamism. Readers of *The Irish Times* voted Cloughjordan one of the 10 best places to live in Ireland. The ecovillage embodies the important message that low-carbon living does not mean reverting to the privations of the past, but can be the catalyst for drawing together a diverse group of people who, through their wide range of talents, make it a lively and interesting place to live.

Integrating with the Natural Environment

The greenfield site that was bought behind Cloughjordan village was developed in a way unique for an Irish urban settlement. The village's planners confined the residential area to about one-third of the site closest to the main street, while devoting a further area beyond that to support services and amenities including a district heating system, an eco-enterprise centre, allotments for growing food, and a community farm. Ecovillagers have planted native varieties of apple trees in this area; throughout the village, various varieties of herbs and fruit bushes create an "edible landscape." An area of 12 acres (5 hectares) devoted to farming in a biodynamic way constitutes one of Ireland's few Community Support Agriculture (CSA) projects.

On the final third of the site, devoted to woodland, villagers planted 17,000 trees in 2011—mainly native species such as oak, ash, Scots pine, birch, rowan, cherry, hazel, and alder. This is regarded as an amenity area for visitors and a contribution to promoting biodiversity. A labrynth, built according to an ancient Celtic layout, provides a quiet space for reflection amid the woodland. According to the ecovillage website (www.thevillage.ie), "the community's land use plan is based on the principles of environmental and ecological diversity, productive landscape and permaculture." The design of common and private areas includes corridors for the movement of wildlife, and the composting of organic matter to regenerate the soil and avoiding toxic or other harmful substances is strongly recommended to all members. Since all are responsible for the upkeep of the common areas, the community organizes regular periods of communal work on the land (the Gaelic word "meitheal" is used for these, recalling the traditional practice of communal work among Irish farmers).

Central to the success of the project is the combination of low-energy technologies and robust community living. The Village Ecological Charter, drawn up by members, contains the guidelines for the development of the built and natural environments so as "to reduce the impact of the project on the natural environment and so promoting sustainable development." This includes detailed and specific targets for energy supply and use, plans for land management, water and solid waste, construction (including materials, light and air, and ventilation), and community issues such as transport, social and communal facilities, and noise and light pollution.

Towards Low-Carbon Living

Combining both cutting-edge technologies and some traditional technologies gives a rich and unique mix to the ecovillage. One of its most innovative features is its district heating system, the only one in Ireland powered by renewable sources of energy. This supplies all the heating and hot water for every house in the ecovillage, using no fossil fuels as primary energy sources and emitting no greenhouse gas emissions. (Electricity supply to drive the pumps and for other purposes is taken from the public mains at present, but there are plans for on-site generation in due course.) It saves an estimated 113.5 tonnes annually of carbon that would be emitted by conventional heating systems for the number of houses served. Though the ecovillage has the largest bank of solar panels in Ireland, these haven't yet been commissioned due to faults in their installation; the district heating system relies on waste wood from a sawmill about an hour away.

Members buy sites from the cooperative which owns the estate (of which all site owners must be members), building their own houses to their own designs, in keeping with the principles and specifications of the Ecological Charter. As a result, many different building types have been used, including passive timber frame with a variety of insulations and finishes, Durisol blocks (blocks of chipped wastewood bonded with ecocement), sheep's wool, cellulose (shredded newspaper), hemp-lime (lime is a tradi-

314

tional Irish form of finish but the addition of hemp, a fibrous plant material, gives it strength and insulation), cob (clay, sand, and straw), a Canadian stick-frame house with double stud walls (with no cold bridging), and kit houses, while natural slates or recycled plastic roof tiles and "green roofs" are widely used. These provide a colorful variety of different designs and finishes that gives the ecovillage a very distinctive look compared to other residential areas in Ireland. It also has some of the lowest Building Energy Ratings (BER) in Ireland.

The ecovillage includes Ireland's first member-owned and -operated CSA farm. Some two thirds of ecovillage households are members and the rest come from the wider Cloughjordan community. Currently it grows 4 acres (1.6 ha) of vegetables, 1 acre (0.4 ha) of cereals, 1 acre of green manure (humus building), and 6 acres (2.43 ha) in permanent pasture. Members pay a monthly fee (around €130 for a household of typically two adults and two children) and can take what food they want from a central distribution point that is supplied three times a week, all year around. Two part-time coordinators act as the main producers, are paid from the farm budget, and are answerable to the farm board which is elected by members. They rely on WWOOFers (Worldwide Opportunities on Organic Farms) and interns as well as on the voluntary labour of members when called upon.

Not only does the form of food production and distribution link the producer and consumer in a deeply interactive relationship, but it changes practices of consumption since members rely on whatever food is available according to the season, the weather, and the amounts planted. The farm also contributes to the resilience of the ecovillage itself, lessening reliance on commercial producers (often very distant), improving greatly the quality of food consumed, and enhancing skills and practices among members. It recently returned to the use of horses to plough the land to avoid the compacting that resulted from the use of tractors, and has hosted public demonstrations of horse-drawn ploughing.

The farm also links in with other projects through which ecovillagers earn a livelihood, such as the award-winning Riot Rye bakery and baking school, members who turn the food produced in the farm into tasty wholesome meals for ecovillagers and visitors, and the Green Enterprise centre with Ireland's only community-based Fab Lab (fabrication laboratory with 3-D printers). Ireland's largest cohousing project is being developed in the ecovillage to offer low-cost accommodation to those who want to come and sample life or live in the ecovillage. All these exemplify the "ecosystem of innovation" through which synergies grow, enhancing each of the elements of ecovillage life.

> # Horizontal rather than hierarchical management ensures that bottom-up initiatives flourish while preserving the coherence of the project as a whole.

Community Resilience

Beyond the technologies, both ancient and new, what is essential to the character of the ecovillage is that it is an intentional community. The dense web of interconnectedness that characterises relationships is strengthened and at times tested through a myriad of different kinds of activities, from the often tense discussions attempting to reach a community consensus on key issues to the enjoyment of community meals and parties where rich encounters take place. A special Process group exists to facilitate community interactions, and the monthly community meeting establishes a period in which any member can voice any issue that is troubling them, including issues of grievance and pain caused within the community. Successful community, then, depends not on avoiding or minimising pain and tensions but rather on facilitating their expression in an atmosphere of mutual respect. A diverse membership, which includes professional facilitators, counsellors, and psychotherapists, helps this process.

Finding a governance structure that reflects its values is a particular challenge for any intentional community, particularly one as complex and multifaceted as an ecovillage. By 2007, the existing organisational structure of Cloughjordan ecovillage based on multiple committees was under strain, unable to deal effectively with the many tasks and challenges facing the project. This led members to turn for support to consultants Angela Espinosa and Jon Walker, who promote the use of the Viable Systems Model (VSM) in cooperatives and large communities looking for alternatives to traditional hierarchies. This resulted in the restructuring of the ecovillage governance structures according to the principles of VSM, identifying the primary activities (PA) of the project and establishing groups to promote them. Two PAs exist in early 2016, one on education and the other on land use. A Development PA, looking after the development of the built environment, has recently been disbanded as it wasn't working well, and a replacement is being put in place. Each PA has a number of task groups within it responsible for different aspects of the primary activity.

The PAs are known as System One groups in VSM. Supporting these are what are called the meta-systemic management functions, Systems Two to Five, each of which fulfills essential functions in the organisation. These include a Process group to oversee the smooth functioning of the whole structure and to resolve problems as they arise, and a coordination team drawing together the activities of all the various groups and providing a monthly reporting mechanism to members. System Four involves keeping a close eye on what is happening in the wider society so as to strategically relate to developments. This led to the establishment of a Navigation group. Finally, System Five involves oversight and direction of the whole project, and includes the Board of Directors and the monthly members' meeting supplemented by an Identity group which deals with issues of membership and purpose. VSM allows a horizontal rather than a hierarchical management of the project, which ensures that bottom-up initiatives flourish while at the same time the coherence of the project as a whole holds together.

Ecological Footprint

Having put in place the means to transition to low-carbon living, the ecovillage needed evidence that it was succeeding. This required measuring its ecological footprint and comparing it to other similar communities in its locality as well as nationally and internationally. The concept of the ecological footprint (EF) is widely used internationally to quantify

the amount of carbon emitted by a household through measuring energy consumption, waste assimilation, food consumption, water consumption, built land area, and travel impacts. Aggregating household measures allows an estimate for a community to be produced. In mid-2014 all households in the ecovillage received a survey that gathered data to measure the EF of ecovillagers. The survey used a measure developed at the Centre for Environmental Research at the University of Limerick and implemented in communities in the region by Tipperary Energy Agency (TEA), which compiled and analysed the results. The survey covered the following areas:

• Household characteristics (number of dwellers; size and type of house)
• Household energy use and its sources
• Household waste (amounts and disposal)
• Food consumption and its origin
• Transport (modes and frequency)
• Water use, including water-saving measures and water harvesting

The questionnaire achieved a 94 percent response rate, indicating a high level of interest. Based on the survey, an EF of 2 global hectares (gHa) was estimated for the ecovillage, the lowest recorded for an Irish settlement. This compares to an EF of 2.9 gHa for the nearby town of Ballina after a four-year campaign to reduce its footprint, 3.9 gHa for a commuter community, and 4.3 gHa for 79 settlements throughout the country. Apart from measuring the ecovillage's EF, the results also allow the sources which constitute each of these EFs to be compared. The Global Footprint Network, an NGO which has developed and implemented the methodology for measuring EFs internationally, estimates an average EF of 4.6 gHa for Ireland (www.globalfootprintnetwork.org). It recognised the significance of Cloughjordan's EF by including an article on it in its newsletter. Globally, it is estimated that the maximum EF for each human being that allows them to live within the planet's biocapacity is 1.8 gHa. Based on this, ecovillage residents would currently need 1.1 planets to continue living the way they do. A plan for the systematic reduction of the ecovillage's EF with targets and periodic measurement to establish progress is being developed in early 2016.

International Recognition

Cloughjordan ecovillage faces many challenges. It is still only in its early phase of growth with more than 70 sites yet to sell, which will draw in new members and more than double its population. Yet already it is winning national and international recognition. Cloughjordan won the National Green Award for Ireland's greenest community three years in a row from 2012 to 2014 and won a gold medal award at the 2013 International Awards for Liveable Communities (LivCom), also known as the Green Oscars, hosted by Xiamen in the People's Republic of China and supported by the UN Environmental Programme (UNEP). The Milesecure consortium of 15 research centres throughout Europe was funded by the European Commission to learn the lessons for European policy of how to transition to a low-carbon future. As part of its research, it examined 1,500 projects all around Europe to identify the most successful "anticipatory experiences" to help guide EU policy. Among the 23 finally selected was Cloughjordan ecovillage and it was the only project to be highlighted in the "manifesto for human-based governance of secure and low-carbon energy transitions" that the consortium wrote as one outcome of its three-year project (see www.milesecure2050.eu). In these ways, the project is helping establish itself as a beacon for the challenging future that confronts humanity. ❧

Peadar Kirby is Professor Emeritus of International Politics and Public Policy at the University of Limerick. He is the author of many books on models of development in Ireland and Latin America. His recent books include Adapting to Climate Change: Governance Challenges, *co-edited with Deiric Ó Broin (Glasnevin, 2015) and* Transitioning to a Low-Carbon Society: Degrowth, austerity and wellbeing, *co-edited with Ernest Garcia and Mercedes Martinez-Iglesias (Palgrave Macmillan, forthcoming in 2016). He is writing a book on pathways to a low-carbon society to be published by Palgrave Macmillan in 2017. He was one of the first residents of Cloughjordan ecovillage in 2009 and is currently chair of the Board of Directors of the ecovillage.*

TRUE SUSTAINABILITY:
Indigenous Pathways

By Dan Schultz

Editor's Note: *We offered contributors to this issue this prompt (among many others): "Robert Gilman has defined an ecovillage as 'a human-scale, full-featured settlement, with multiple centers of initiative, in which human activities are harmlessly integrated into the natural world in a way that is supportive of healthy human development, and can be successfully continued into the indefinite future.' How does (or doesn't) this definition resonate with your understanding or vision of 'ecovillage'?" The founder of Maitreya Mountain Village chose to respond:*

Since 2008, Maitreya Mountain Village has defined itself as an ecovillage primarily using the yardstick of sustainability. Gilman's definition of ecovillage is fine, but I find the terms "human-scale" and "full-featured" too nebulous and "harmlessly integrating" innocuous. I like that concise, pithy word, "sustainable," overused, borrowed, and bludgeoned as it may be. It's brassier. It raises the bar for our responsibility as members of the human race. A sustainable culture speaks to the depths of generations all the way to genetics and back to Genesis.

If you're thinking I'm about to get up on my high horse and sing some kumbaya song or sermon, let's get that out of the way. Whether sustainability is a difficult tune to dance to or not (I'll get to that later), we've stumbled regularly since we began this project. We have not been, nor are we now, purists. But I have personally witnessed people move beautifully to the drumbeat of sustainability: the indigenous tribes.

Years ago, I had the good fortune of living amongst native Amazon tribes and also with the agrarian Nepalese. These pure of heart form the true sustainable communities on our planet. To me, their daily lives were a testimony and a template. In contrast to urban American life, the word that seemed most fit to describe their culture was "sane." It was a breath of fresh air. My experiences there (among others) were profoundly influential and led to the creation of Maitreya Mountain Village.

At the time Nepal was the so-called "poorest nation in the world" yet I witnessed no signs of squalor. They were a happy people. While they made their clothes or baskets, while they farmed and foraged for food, both the Huaorani and Nepali people smiled often in conversation with each other and when they sang, too. When they were still and silent, I felt the peace within them. In a moment of indulgent imagination I pictured the tribesmen in our world, handing over their credit cards at grocery stores, obsessing over their iPhones. It robbed them of something.

My friend, author, and eminent radical environmentalist Derrick Jensen believes that the only sustainable communities are the ones that resemble the indigenous ones, and

he's a vociferous opponent of civilization, inasmuch as it is defined as city life (civilization, from *civis*, meaning citizen, from Latin *civitatis*, meaning state or city). He posits that civilization and cities can never be an ethical or sustainable model for human society, largely because they denude landscapes (through mining, etc) to import resources to the high-density populations and inevitably lead to ecocentrism, human supremacy, slavery, and violence. It's hard to argue with that but, as Derrick says, no one is really talking about it much.

Here at MMV, while we haven't returned fully to the ancient ways, we're talking about it and transitioning toward it. Let me tell you a few of our successes and shortcomings, at least as I contrast them with the practices of my more pure and native friends.

We do not make our own clothes, but we do buy them at thrift stores. Not my underwear, though. Nope. Straight from the evil corporate behemoth Walmart (one of a few "big box" stores that are the only options in our remote area), and probably and unfortunately made with child slave labor, seven thousand miles away, or something like that. Darn it.

Our living systems combine livestock, forage, horticulture, and permaculture, producing much of our own food, but we still shop at Safeway twice a week through the winter (even though we *could* produce 100 percent of our own food). Non-organic and even GMOs work their way into our diets sometimes. It happens.

The mountainous landscape is advantageous in that it allows us gravity-fed water systems right from our springs. Still, the water runs into polypropylene storage tanks and PVC plumbing. Alternatively, we could make our own watertight containers and carry water up from the rivers.

Rainforests here love to grow mushrooms and we recently hosted an educational community mushroom foray/walk with over 30 people registering—it was marketed entirely on Facebook and email. It's not what the Huaorani do. Oh well.

I use concrete, a chainsaw, and a few weeks ago, we actually installed a satellite internet dish. We're still questioning whether this is really right (for us). But for now, e-commerce is part of how we participate in the cash economy, so we can pay our car insurance and property taxes. Those demands are real. But seeing someone staring motionless into a rectangle, absorbed by its flickering dots, seems out of place here. I imagine that WE may be robbed of something.

We're not the only ones who make compromises to integrate homesteading-permaculture protocols into (mainstream) market-monetary economy. Bill Mollison and Sepp Holzer, icons of the permaculture movement, made such compromises, fully acknowledging the virtues of heavy (fossil fuel) equipment, like excavators and bulldozers. At least we're in good company there. But I would be intensely interested as to what Henry David Thoreau (my mentor and hero) or the Huaorani chief would have to say about chainsaws, bulldozers, and a sustainable culture. What a conversation!

No matter how I look at it, we still don't measure up to the tribes. For now. I long for their purity of heart, their unwavering social responsibility and integrity. But I do not apologize for our compromises. I am OK with keeping one foot in the door of mainstream pragmatism and one in the door of a radical idealism. I am hoping to connect the two.

Our area here in the very north of California is rich in its own native history—home to the Tolowa, Yurok, and Takelma tribes, whose presence is felt even today. They collected and processed acorns as their staple food from the plentiful supply of tan oak trees. We follow in their footsteps, and participate in the community acorn festival in October.

MMV honors ritual as the native peoples do. I recall that the Huaorani woke every morning about 5 a.m. to share about the dreams they dreamed. Ritual keeps community together. MMV members practice Heart Club once a week, sharing feelings, hopes, fears, gratitude, whatever is alive in us.

There's so much to do, not only to "save the planet" but enjoy the fruits of community the old-fashioned way—by returning to a land-based culture where people think in terms of cultivating a relationship with their environment and caretaking it for generations, even centuries. I feel enlivened by the idea (and we're doing it with fig trees) of planting shade trees which we will never sit under.

I truly believe that sustainable culture and community is making a grassroots comeback. People from all walks of life are deeply drawn to it—I think they can feel the need for this change in their bones. So many of us feel disenchanted with the unsustainable precisely because we are all hardwired as humans to live in community, with real connection to other human beings and the living environment that surrounds us.

Transitioning both as individuals and

> We are all hardwired as humans to live in community, with real connection to others and to the living environment that surrounds us.

as communities, we can look to the indigenous tribes for guidance on how to get there. But these truly sustainable, traditional ecovillages are dwindling fast. There are only about 150 million tribal individuals left worldwide, less than two percent of the world population. But as their contemporaries, we neo-ecovillage peoples can carry the torch forward. As the unsustainable machinations fail and fall away (by definition, they have to), we can consciously transition into a sustainable, better world by building bridges from our modern knowledge to their ancient wisdom.

Dan Schultz is co-director of Maitreya Mountain Village (www.maitreyamountanvillage.com), which creates intentional, caring community and farming in an off-grid, wilderness setting. Dan hosts and produces a talk radio program called New Culture Radio focused on sustainability, and together with his partner Jane leads Transition Del Norte in Northwestern California.

Photos courtesy of Dan Schultz

V

ECO-EDUCATION

Seeking an Alternative Education

By Alison Cole

Ann Nguyen and Alison Cole of Boston, Massachusetts are setting sail to Auroville, India to learn effective solutions for human communities in a meaningful environment.

R. Buckminster Fuller once said "I live on Earth at present, and I don't know what I am. I know that I am not a category. I am not a thing—a noun. I seem to be a verb, an evolutionary process—an integral function of the universe." Fuller is not alone in this revelation. It is this discovery—that of being a verb, an integral function of the universe—that leads a person to realize their inherent worth and the interconnectedness of all things. This consciousness brings with it a lifestyle of intentional balance and harmony—a renewed sense of stewardship.

So what's a verb to do in a land of harsh nouns, industrial adjectives, and wasteful superlatives? This is the question my friend Ann and I are seeking to answer. Although our habitat of Boston, Massachusetts exudes an ephemeral layer of ecological consciousness, the physical and social landscape is trapped under its own urban weight. The excellent universities here promote changes of the mind, but hardly changes of the heart. Ann and I believe that the mind and heart are not mutually exclusive, and that both are essential to our human relationship with the environment. From this we decided to outsource our education to a place where both are held in equal regard.

In our search for an alternative education, we found ourselves magnetized to Auroville, a village located outside Puducherry in the Tamil Nadu state of India. Auroville (meaning "City of Dawn") was founded four decades ago on a plot of arid land by a multinational group of people as an experiment in spiritual and ecological community. Ann and I are fascinated by Auroville's newness, its diversity, its mission, but mostly its challenges. Is it possible to create a place for all walks of life to live in balance with merely dirt and willfulness? In Auroville, the answer seems to be *YES*. The "City of Dawn" presents itself as the ideal classroom for designing human solutions. It is my personal desire to build wastewater recycling systems using only biology and basic materials. Ann desires to design energy capture-transfer devices with simple materials. The multi-collaborative Auroville Centre for Scientific Research promotes simple technologies and provides opportunity for any interested person to learn the trade—to be a verb.

We also found ourselves drawn to a reforestation project outside Auroville in Sadhana Forest. It is a new endeavor run by Yorit and Aviram Rosin to rehabilitate the arid land and its waters by planting indigenous tree species. Their progress has been significant in the first few years and serves as a wonderful example of simple technology restoring balance to the earth. Ann and I will live and work there as we transcribe the methods of the Sadhana Forest Project into an open-source (free for all) online course for the internet-based Peer2Peer University.

When we speak to others of our desire to base our education in Auroville, few people fail to mention how far away it is from Boston. Some folks also mention to us the "noun-ness" of flying there. In response to this, we have decided the "verb" thing to do would be to sail to India, rather than fly. Sailing will be an excellent addition to our self-designed curriculum of skill-building and hopefully an example to our peers that, *YES*, two young women from the city can sail a boat across the seas to another life. In fact, classrooms of middle school students from disadvantaged neighborhoods in New York City will be corresponding with us throughout the entirety of our journey. The relationship is facilitated by a non-profit called Reach The World which enables classrooms to follow world travelers as a means to provide unique geographical and cultural curricula so often lacking in poor urban schools.

We feel that our generation has great potential to rid themselves of the noun and embrace the verb—to be conscious in-

dividuals who tend to the garden of life. We hope that our education in Auroville affords us the skills necessary to promote human growth, not stunt it. But most importantly we hope that we can transfer the skills and ideas of an evolved and whole human community to our peers here in the land of nouns.

Check out our project at www.alternativegradschool.com. ❁

Alison Cole and Song Anh "Ann" Nguyen are 24 and reside in Boston, Massachusetts. Alison grew up in the woods and received a degree in Marine and Freshwater Biology from Napier University in Edinburgh, Scotland. She currently works as an educator and lobbyist. Ann is a native Bostonian and holds a degree in Social Thought and Political Economy from the University of Massachusetts as well as a certificate in International Conflict Resolution from the Five Colleges Consortium. She currently works in global wealth management banking and instructs sailing.

Top: Dormitory for volunteers. It is made of natural local materials using traditional building methods. Above: Two children (of volunteers) pass the photovoltaic panels that supply electricity in Sadhana Forest. This site is not tied to the grid.

Chris Roth

Sarah Wilcox-Hughes and Keren Ram make beeswax candles at the electricity-free Possibility Alliance Sanctuary outside La Plata, Missouri.

Education for Sustainability

I'm listening to the rain fall on the roof of Karma, the passive solar residence at Sandhill Farm where I'm staying this spring. In these first few weeks of March, I've helped with and learned about peach tree pruning, maple syrup production, vegetable growing in northeast Missouri, food fermentation, and how best to navigate snowy, then muddy rutted farm roads by foot and by bicycle. I've seen and heard new birds nearly every day, deciphered some of the branching patterns on still-leafless deciduous trees, and (at the electricity-free Possibility Alliance Sanctuary, where I stopped for a few days before arriving here) learned some of the nuances of beeswax candle-making, bathing in a basin of woodstove-heated water, and accompanying a singing bilingual two-and-a-half-year-old on guitar.

In both of these communities, I've met and gotten to know people for whom education is not something they did in school, then were finished with. Life in these rural, land-based communities is an ongoing learning experience—and it's shared with others. It happens through direct experience and personal connection—a combination of conscious instruction, mentorship, osmosis, projects undertaken together, and the organic unfolding of daily life in these settings. It involves how we relate to one another and to ourselves—not simply physical living skills or knowledge about the world "out there." It involves multiple generations of people, most of whom are not blood-related but who consciously create a family feeling as a community—who eat together, meet together, share work, help and support each other through personal challenges, and learn from one another. Some are long-term members, some (like me) exploring, some intending to stay just for the growing season as interns, some simply visiting. Without exception, from what I've witnessed thus far, they are inspired by what they are doing, valuing and valued for their roles in these communities, and involved in an active quest to help a more community- and earth-focused world emerge. They not only embody it themselves, but they share their lives with others who are also sincerely interested in and called to this path.

No one here is stuck in a rut, resigned to the "grind" of a formulaic existence, counting the days to retirement (or too overwhelmed even to count). The only serious ruts in which people seem to get stuck are in the roads, but then they pull each other out or flag down a helpful neighbor.

For most of the past quarter-century, I've been fortunate to be part of such settings—places where I can hear the rain fall on the roof (not drowned out by traffic), get my hands in the soil, and learn about others and myself on much more profound levels than those allowed by merely superficial interactions. I have almost no memory of much of what I studied in my academic schooling, but what I've learned through direct, experiential engagement with rural life, ecological living, ecology, and community doesn't even need "recalling"—it's part of who I am. True, I have learned, then at least temporarily forgotten, many plant species names—but what's really important on this learning path doesn't fade away with time, but just gets richer. I feel more able to deeply appreciate community, life on the land, the natural and human worlds, and learning itself than I ever have.

Lately, I am particularly happy to be reminded of the power of small-scale educational programs—the internships, apprenticeships, and mentorships carried out by countless intentional communities, small organic family farms, and other groups trying to live more sustainably and create a better world. Personal connection, individual attention, a valuing of the whole individual—these are priceless gifts when they accompany an educational experience, and they are natural outgrowths of a healthy community setting. They lead not only to better learning of sustainable living skills, but to ongoing, sustainable and sustaining, human relationships. They lead to generations of people who feel more connected, and therefore who are more likely to care and act to assure that future generations have a livable world to inhabit as well.

While intentional-community-based sustainability education programs come with their share of challenges (many detailed in this issue), ultimately every one of them has a tremendous amount to teach its participants—all of whom, whether nominally facilitators or students, are in reality both teachers and learners. The increasing integration of more traditional academia with intentional community (also described herein) offers great promise as well. The alternative to a fragmented world is one which becomes more whole, and it will require an integration of community and a holistic approach to education.

As Pete Seeger points out, the world cannot be saved by impersonally large groups following a single formula, or by homogeneous, one-size-fits-all projects, no matter how nobly conceived. "I'm convinced that if there is a human race here in 100 years, it's not going to be big things that do it; it's going to be millions upon millions of small things."[1] Small projects which deeply touch the lives of those who participate in them inspire further connections, more teaching and learning, continued evolution in our individual and collective understanding of what constitute sustainable ways of living and social organization—and more direct experience of the hopeful reality that one person at a time, one step at a time, from the ground up, the world does change. ❀

Chris Roth (editor@ic.org) edits COMMUNITIES.

---

1. Inteview with Jeremy Smith, published November 9, 2007, www.chud.com/articles/articles/12479/1/EXCLUSIVE-INTERVIEW-PETE-SEEGER-PETE-SEEGER-THE-POWER-OF-SONG/Page1.html.

Live and Learn:
O.U.R. Ecovillage Builds Learning Community

By Elke Cole with Javan Kerby Bernakevitch

My name is Elke Cole and I am a communitarian...no, wait, strike that, that's a little vague...I'm a natural builder...ummm maybe not quite it, I'm not just a builder...I, I, well I live in community.

That's not a bad start to describe the way I live. I live and learn. Or is it that I learn and then I live? Maybe it's both. And I dance learning and living every day here at One United Resource (O.U.R., or OUR for short) Ecovillage on Vancouver Island, British Columbia.

Here on the island we can live outdoors from late April to mid October. This means that a large part of the on-site programs I'm involved in are conducted during this time, as off-site learners can come and camp in fine favourable weather.

Those of us who live here year-round occupy conventional and natural buildings, yurts and trailer spaces in winter, and some join the camp as soon as weather allows. I am fortunate to have my living and work space in what we affectionately call the Art Studio, destined to be an "artist in residence" accommodation complete with gallery space and studio. Here I am able to plan programs, complete all necessary computer work, and work on my personal design projects. Come sunshine and summer, I'm outside wearing the teacher and program leader hat. My living space then becomes the private refuge from being "on." Taking a break from the public hats of teacher and leader, I can step from the public realm into my own personal space, where I recharge, reload, and relax from work. Besides removing myself from others, I've found another way to let people know that I'm on time off: I put on a skirt!

There is a great appetite in the world for examples of sustainable land use, and in our "show me it in action" world, seeing really is believing. We share examples of natural homes, permaculture in action, composting toilets, greenhouses full of greens in April, ponds for irrigation, chickens, ducks, sheep, pigs and most importantly how all of us people live and work together!

I understand that tours and public inquiry form part of my agreement here: raising awareness and promoting our workshops support my work as designer and teacher. There is a business side in all of this: we intend to make a living right

Photos by Elke Cole

Opposite page top: Author's sleeping alcove. This page top left: Garden with cob lovenest and greenhouses from the art studio. Top middle: Setting up camp at O.U.R Ecovillage. Top right: Plaster fun in the village. Bottom left: It's all about food. Bottom right: Father and daughter relaxing.

here. Some of us have small individual businesses here, and the nonprofit organization operates accommodation and food services as well as the school.

Living in the middle of a demonstration site means living under observation. So when the public tours come through, I make my living space look good for the pictures and then... go for coffee.

There are about a dozen of us sharing the ebb and flood of seasonal activity. Living here means holding space for those who come to lend a hand to the site.

There's always more work than hands, and the core group of people struggles to find time for deeper connection. We have families and partners, meetings and work, and everybody needs some quiet time. As much as we respect personal space and time, it's often not easy to claim. What keeps us here is a sense that what we do is important on a larger scale. There's a greater calling that brings us into community to live and to educate ourselves and others.

For OUR school (TOPIA: The Sustainable Learning Institute) every season is another adventure: I personally don't want to get stale by teaching "on automatic," so I continually look for ways to do things differently. At the same time I understand that invisible structures carry us through our work. These structures consist of agreements that govern how we work and live together. We organize ourselves in teams: the kitchen team works closely with the garden team to feed us all. I start with this team because good food is at the heart of every successful workshop!

OUR kitchen also processes a lot of the produce for winter consumption by drying and canning. The ongoing challenge is to provide good food on a tight budget, and try to work with all the different politics that come up when we discuss sustainable food issues. One response to that is "OUR Food Manifesto," written in 2008. This document helps to educate visitors, interns, and potential residents

of OUR approach to food and its transformation through our kitchen. As our garden becomes bigger every season, so does the percentage of food harvested on site.

The garden team cares for the growing area that's protected by an eight-foot deer fence (with perimeter expanding!) and includes two large greenhouses. In 2009 the gardens were filled with song. The Sustainable Food Production team strongly believed what our ancestors knew instinctively—song is part of a strong work ethic. Their voices carried throughout the land, giving the other teams an opportunity to pause and question, "What does work entail?"

Questions our garden looks to answer are: how do we feed the number of people on site in a climate that has most output late in summer, while programs are heaviest in early to mid summer? How do we continue to keep and build soil while obtaining and improving yields?

(continued on p. 74)

LIVE AND LEARN:
O.U.R. ECOVILLAGE BUILDS LEARNING COMMUNITY
(continued from p. 17)

How do we find a way of managing our energy and how can we integrate new people?

On a developing site there's lots of work for builders. The building team is made up of residents, a few hired workers, instructors, interns, and students practicing a combination of conventional skills and natural building. The natural building program works on real building sites, of which there are always a few underway: you may learn foundation work on one, cob on another, and finish plaster on yet a third structure. This means that interns can see and work on buildings in all states of completion.

We call it "slow building": buildings take longer to complete when main components are part of our teaching and our season for programming is limited to favourable camp season, typically May to September.

None of our activities would function without the support of the office team. Like it or not, administration is a lot of work and requires fantastically capable and hard-working people. Here I've seen programs flourish or flounder with the work of the administrative staff. This is the place of first contact: the voice you hear when you call, the place where everyone is received, and where connection is made. This is where funding proposals are written, registration is handled, bookings made. It's where books are kept and websites are maintained. This is truly where the magic happens.

Lastly I want to acknowledge that most of us are having to wear many hats. On the same day I am asked to, accept, and choose to be a designer, builder, coordinator, mentor, blogger, communicator, team member, hearthkeeper, partner, and friend.

Whew...that's a lot of hats. Good thing I have a strong neck. Not to mention a strong sense of self.

And here's my motivation: How do I create a good life in this time of change?

My answer is building personal connections, doing things together, learning from each other, and sharing the work. That's what has me wake up in my cob sleeping alcove facing the sun and ready to face another day as a communitarian, I mean natural builder...ah heck with it...to face the day with my friends and family.

And that's good enough for me. ❀

Elke Cole is a Natural House Designer, builder, and educator. She lives at O.U.R. Ecovillage on Vancouver Island, British Columbia, where she coordinates the Natural Building Skillbuilder programs and has her consultation and design business, Houses That Love You Back. Please visit www.elkecole.com, read her blog "on building and being" (www.elkecole.com/weblog.html), or email naturalbuilding@ourecovillage.org.

Javan Kerby Bernakevitch has been a long-standing environmental educator, professional communicator, facilitator, and editor. An O.U.R. Ecovillage resident, Javan continues to expand his knowledge and passion for sustainability through permaculture as a teacher-in-training and designer, piloting top-bar honeybee hives, natural building with a special interest in finish plasters such as waterproof tadelakt, and engaging public talks and workshops on permaculture and sustainability. He continues to actively contribute to his community through his passion for sustainability and by collaborating on articles with community residents.

A brief history of education in sustainability at O.U.R:
Including the 2010 season we have
- 10 years of courses in community process (Way of Council), alternative energy, organic food production,
- and natural building
- nine years of sustainable food production internships
- eight years of Natural Building Internships
- seven years of Permaculture Design Certificate Courses
- and new in 2010 the first Canadian Permaculture Teacher Training

Teaching Hands-On Workshops in Community

By Michael G. Smith

As the sun sets on the last day of the workshop, some of the students pack up their campsites, offer heartfelt gratitude and goodbyes, and drive away. We can still hear two of them hammering away on the roof of the new building, installing rafters in the fading light. Several others cook up an impromptu evening meal; they've decided to stay an extra day to work with me tomorrow on the first layer of the earthen floor. My friend Margaret is exhausted but ecstatic. In the last five days, with the help of 20 former strangers, we have almost completed the walls of a new guest cottage in her backyard. One of the walls is made of strawbale, now plastered inside and out with a thick clay base coat; another of cob with a sculpted altar and inset stained glass windows; a third of slipstraw; and the last of wattle and daub. The students learned each of these techniques, as well as basic soil analysis, ecological clay harvesting, the fundamentals of passive solar design, and much more. We also found time to tour the other strawbale buildings in the community (Maxwelton Creek Cohousing in Washington), to harvest wild cherries and bake them into pies, to sing and play music around the campfire.

In these moments, so many things I love come together in one place: sharing good food, fire, and stories with

The author (center) supervises the construction of an earthen oven during a one-day workshop.

Anne Frobeen

Top: *A two-month apprenticeship gives students time to learn complex building skills. Above: At Emerald Earth's Natural Building Intensives, students get to experience a wide range of techniques; here, cordwood masonry with cob mortar.*

new friends, feeling sore in all my muscles but satisfied in my heart. This workshop achieved many goals at once. It provided training and knowledge in natural building to a diverse group of students; it created a beautiful example of low-cost construction using local materials; it went a long way toward getting my friend a place for her children and grandchildren to sleep when they visit; it gave me a good excuse to spend time with her and her family, and some income as well; it supported the development of another intentional community. Beyond those immediate effects, more subtle influences on the students, the community, and myself will emerge over time.

I've spent most of the last 11 years at Emerald Earth Sanctuary, a rural intentional community and learning center in northern California. During that period and the previous six years, I've been involved in planning, coordinating, and teaching well over 100 workshops, ranging from one day to two months in length. Most of these have been hands-on trainings for adults on natural building techniques, but other topics have included permaculture, local foods, and appropriate technology, and I've also worked occasionally with children. Besides Emerald Earth, I've taught at 10 other intentional communities in western North America. I realized recently that this experience teaching in so many different communities could allow me to make some general observations about workshops in community settings,

and perhaps to offer useful advice to communities wanting to start on-site educational programs.

Intentional communities and education are a natural fit. Many communities consider part of their mission to educate the public, at least about community structures and processes such as consensus decision-making. People who wind up at communities often have knowledge and experience related to health and sustainable living, making them potential in-house instructors for programs on these subjects. Workshops, camps, conferences, and other events can provide much-needed income in a way that harmonizes with community values and goals. Communities often have the infrastructure necessary to host groups; they also frequently have members with good skills in planning and coordinating events.

Educational events in communities also present unique challenges. Workshops, especially longer ones, can exert a big impact on long-term residents. Typically, some community members are more involved with a workshop than others. Those most involved shoulder the great majority of work but also reap the most benefits, including income, professional development, and the rewards of direct interaction with the students. Residents taking a less active role in the program will still feel the impacts, including the noise and mess created by a large group of visitors, possible rescheduling of mealtimes and meetings, and being bombarded by questions about what it's like to live in community, where to dump the compost, and so on.

It's critical that all community members be supportive of the educational mission. Usually this is not a problem in theory, as a desire to educate and share is common in community. However, resentments can build up if members feel saddled with tasks and impacts that they didn't agree to. Make sure that all responsibilities are clearly defined and assigned beforehand. These include publicity, registration, menu planning and shopping, cooking and cleaning,

Students and staff at the completion of a week-long Natural Building Intensive at Emerald Earth.

These weekend events (some have been up to a week long) are part open house, part free workshop, part networking opportunity for sustainability enthusiasts and community seekers. Each work party typically includes four three-hour work sessions, an extensive tour, a sauna and/or fire circle, and a talk about our community history, decision-making process, membership, and financial structure.

These events funnel many first-time visitors into pre-arranged times when we know we will be available to orient them and answer their questions. We usually host between a dozen and 30 people each time, which is much easier for us to manage than the same number of visits spread over a couple of months. Visitors appreciate the opportunity to visit a community and learn some skills practically for free (we ask only for a small donation to cover food costs) and we feel good about opening our doors to anyone who can get here, being a resource for people to learn about community and sustainable living, and at the same time getting some needed help with on-site projects.

During each work period, we like to have three different projects happening simultaneously to allow visitors a range of choices and to let us make efficient use of their help. We tend to save up projects that can benefit from a number of unskilled workers directed by one community member: things like turning garden beds, mixing cob, or digging swales. Almost every session becomes a mini-workshop, starting with a basic introduction to the task at hand and how it fits in with the bigger picture of living on our land. With tools distributed and the work underway, the explanation often continues in more depth, or else morphs into a more free-ranging discussion.

> *Work parties have a significant side benefit: they let community members develop teaching skills in a low-pressure setting.*

curriculum development, project planning and coordination, guest facilities, dealing with money, and site cleanup. Make clear agreements up front on the use of common facilities, how income will be distributed, and any other aspects of the workshop that will affect residents.

Workshops can be structured in many ways, each of which is more appropriate for certain topics than others. Even primarily hands-on learning programs can vary a lot in their length and formality. These variations obviously create different benefits and challenges for the community. What follows is a brief description of the formats I'm most familiar with, along with some observations about how each of them benefits and challenges the hosting community.

Work Parties

Between four and six times each year, we host public work parties at Emerald Earth.

Work parties have a significant side benefit: they let community members develop teaching skills in a low-pressure setting. We also host formal workshops in which students pay for instruction in natural building and other skills. To run high-quality workshops, the instructors must first have practice not only with the workshop topic but also with demonstrating and explaining it. Work parties help solve the dilemma that teaching skill comes largely from practice, but that it seems a bit unethical to charge people for inexperienced instruction.

One-Day Workshops

For communities looking to grow an educational program, a series of one-day workshops is a great way to start. Daylong workshops allow you to focus most of your energy on the educational mission, without so much investment in meals, facilities, and other responsibilities that come with longer events. A short workshop allows you to try new things and develop skills and experience with minimal stress.

One-day workshops are most appropriate for general introductions and for simple hands-on topics. Boiling down the essence of a complex topic (permaculture, for example, or intentional community itself) into a series of concise presentations and exercises can be a valuable challenge. I find one-day workshops best suited to teaching a single practical skill, such as making cordage or building an earthen oven.

Usually people are less willing to travel far for a one-day as opposed to a longer course. At Emerald Earth, we get a higher percentage of students from our local community in one-day workshops than in any other educational format (except for children's summer camps). Offering inexpensive learning opportunities to our neighbors feels good. However, I have also been surprised at how far people will drive for a daylong class. Last November, several students drove between three and six hours to attend our one-day Acorns for Food workshop. Because we're in a remote location an hour from the nearest budget accommodation, we decided to let workshop participants stay with us the night before the class, which in turn made us take on serving breakfast. This is an example of how hosting events becomes more complex when you attempt to accommodate diverse needs. Before another workshop last year, we put in about a day of extra work to make

Hands-on intensives are a dynamic way to learn new skills. Here, students at Emerald Earth build slipstraw and strawbale walls.

Brent Levin

our facilities accessible to one student in a wheelchair. In my opinion, this was well worth the effort, but it added to the predictable stress of last-minute preparations.

Two-Day to Two-Week Intensives

To teach a more complex skill or set of concepts requires longer than a day. I've led dozens of cob and natural building workshops lasting around a week. The length of the workshop should be tailored to the learning goals, and it's a good idea to make these goals clear beforehand, both to the organizer/teachers and to potential students. In a few days, you can teach someone how to mix and build a cob wall; learning to build a house take a lot longer. We've taught a couple of Introduction to Carpentry workshops lasting three or four days. Everyone gained a basic understanding of woodworking tools and methods, but I noticed that the level of confidence that people left with corresponded to the amount of experience they had when they came. To develop trust and comfort with a new set of technical skills takes most people a long time.

Project-based classes like natural building workshops require a huge amount of preparation up front. For our Natural Building Intensives at Emerald Earth, we usually spend between one and two days of prep time for every day of teaching. We spend this time working out designs and construction details, acquiring and preparing tools and materials (sharpening chisels, soaking clay, cleaning buckets), organizing the site so that a large group of students can work safely, and so on. This does not include the many hours devoted to course publicity, inquiries and registration, menu planning, shopping, cooking, campsites, and facilities. Running the same class year after year on the same site can eventually become a matter of routine, but successful classes are rarely if ever pulled together at the last minute.

So what's the payback for all this investment? Intensive workshops can be a reasonable source of income. Typical prices these days for residential workshops in sustainable skills run between $75 and $100 per day; sometimes much more. With 15 students in a weeklong workshop, you might bring in $8,000 to $10,000. Even if the workshop requires six weeks of paid work (let's say two full-time teacher/coordinators, one full-time cook, a week or two of preparation and organization, and a week or two of administration) plus expenses (food, materials, advertising, site use fee or community tithe), everyone should be able to make a living wage. You will have to decide how many paying students you need to make the accounts balance. We offer a discount for early payment to encourage people to sign up in advance, so that if we have to cancel due to low enrollment, we can do that with plenty of notice. Students may be buying airplane tickets, taking leaves from work, and lining up house-sitters; I prefer to give them a month's notice if the class is going to be canceled.

The building workshops that I teach are usually organized to contribute useful work to a project. I've seen many small buildings get started in short workshops; walls can go up quickly with a large group of excited students. But I've never seen a building completed in a workshop. It's easy to overestimate the amount of work that will be accomplished. When students are paying to learn, the primary emphasis needs to be on education rather than on production. I suspect that if I were to put all the hours I spend planning and organiz-

Students taste samples prepared from seven species of oak at Emerald Earth's Acorns for Food workshop.

ing courses into building instead, I would usually get just as much built. Obviously, getting work done is not the main goal of the workshop; my point here is that it should not be, or everyone is likely to end up disappointed.

An experienced teacher learns to accommodate different learning styles and to provide instruction appropriate for each student's level of experience. Having two or more instructors present is always helpful. Sometimes one of us will lead the majority of the group while the other works with stragglers who are not yet comfortable with previously introduced concepts or skills. Or one can direct the more advanced students on a special project so they don't get bored while the rest keep working on basic skills. Ideally the teaching staff will include a range in age, gender, and background; that way each student is more likely to find someone to relate to.

That point brings to mind the most painful experience of my teaching career so far. It was a weeklong cob workshop, the very first I taught as lead instructor. My co-teacher and I were both young men in our 20s, with more experience building than teaching. By chance we ended up with a group of students who were mostly women, many of them in their 40s and 50s. By halfway through the week, many of the women were skipping my lectures and gathering elsewhere on the property for their own discussions. They had decided they had more to learn from each other than

By halfway through the week, many of the women had decided they had more to learn from each other than from me, and they were probably right.

from me, and they were probably right. Unfortunately, I lacked the skills to bring the group back together, perhaps by creating an open forum for the students to share their experiences rather than sticking with my planned agenda of presentations.

Changes to the schedule or structure partway through a workshop should not be made lightly, but sometimes circumstance demands them. Last year in a building workshop, for example, my co-instructor noticed a disturbing gender dynamic. Most of the men were actively involved in raising a strawbale wall while many of the women stood back or moved on to a secondary task. We delayed the next building session for a discussion on the topic that I found fascinating. The students included about an equal number of women and men, as well as two transgender folks and a person in a wheelchair. They came from six different countries of origin and native languages, and ranged in age from early 20s to 60s; altogether an extremely diverse group. Were the two hours we spent discussing gender issues a valuable use of group time? At the very least, everyone got to hear a perspective very different from their own. In situations like that, I try ask myself: What is the most valuable thing to model and teach? Is it natural building skills (which is what the students signed up for), or is it a culture of awareness, respect, and honest communication, the core values of this community?

Perhaps the greatest value of longer residential courses like these is the break they provide from students' daily lives. I prefer to teach in a setting where students eat and sleep as well as learn and work together—ideally, all within walking distance. This strengthens the social bonding and support within the group and gives people the experience of being part of a community (albeit short-term) with shared interests. I've seen many life changes come out of residential workshops, including lasting friendships and partnerships (I won't get started on those stories) and the breaking of destructive old habits. Communities are ideal containers for this sort of transformation to occur. At Emerald Earth the experience of living in community for a week seems at least as valuable to most students as whatever practical skills or knowledge they take away with them.

We like to involve students in as many aspects of community life as possible during their stay. As a matter of course, they always help with after-meal cleanup and dishwashing, as well as building-site cleanup and preparing materials. Individuals may volunteer for more complex tasks like lighting the sauna, leading a morning circle, or helping to cook a meal. These kinds of activities enhance the experience of being part of an interdependent community. Occasionally, they can also create unexpected complications.

Some years ago I was doing support work at another community during a two-week Permaculture Design course. Part of the students' daily chore rotation included harvesting salad greens from the garden. They got to learn some garden botany and to exercise their creativity by selecting from dozens of varieties of edible greens. Late one morning the frantic lunch cook called me into the kitchen. The student harvesters had mistaken poison hemlock for fennel and the highly toxic leaves were peppered throughout several pounds of salad. It took three of us an hour to make sure we had gotten every leaf out and that the salad would be safe to serve!

Longer Educational Programs

Established Natural Building centers now commonly offer longer hands-on train-

ings, usually from six weeks to three months. I've been part of teaching four such programs here at Emerald Earth and three elsewhere (two at intentional communities). These programs are often called "Apprenticeships," although I prefer the term "Skillbuilder" used at O.U.R. Ecovillage. If you're trying to teach a complex set of skills like building, after a month is when you really begin to see the payoff. Most people seem to take that long to get so comfortable with a new set of activities and habits that they begin to incorporate the change into their self-identity. If we want to prepare people for professional work in natural building, teaching, and other skills, long programs like these are a good way to do it.

One of the gifts of a long class like this is the opportunity to develop deep relationships between instructors and students. I find that a month after a one- or two-day workshop I won't remember the names of most of the students; in a week-long class, students may or may not make a lasting impression; but the students I've spent two months with very often become long-term friends and colleagues.

If the workshop's influence on students is at all proportional to the students' impact on me, there seems to be a sort of a law of conservation at work. You can either have a little impact on many people, or a lot of impact on a few people. The shorter a workshop is (and the cheaper it is), the more accessible it is to people with busy lives, many interests, or limited resources. You can also usually accept more people into a short workshop, if for no other reason than that the logistics are easier. And obviously, you can pack more short workshops into your schedule than long ones. So the best formula for exposing a lot of people to your ideas is to offer many short inexpensive workshops.

On the other hand, if you want to make a really big impact on someone's life, you need time. Our two-month apprenticeships at Emerald Earth had two full-time instructors for a maximum of six students. This allowed us to give each student individual coaching nearly every day, and to introduce dangerous tools like power saws that just do not make sense in a large workshop.

In any program longer than two weeks, social dynamics within the group become a major contributor to its success or failure. Most people, stimulated by a learning experience in a new environment, can be "nice" and avoid conflict for a couple of weeks. If they find they aren't getting some of their needs met, they can usually suck it up until they get home. This is less likely when the program goes on for many weeks. Often during periods of discomfort and stress, the differences between personalities will rise to a head. I strongly prefer to include the skills needed for working and living together as an explicit part of the curriculum, spending time each week on things like conflict resolution, meeting facilitation, and understanding different learning and leadership styles. We called our apprenticeship "Natural Building in Community" to make this emphasis clear. It's also important to have open discussions periodically about what is working and what isn't, and for the staff to either work to resolve issues or to explain why they can't. I've seen the failure to directly address conflicts and expectations lead to persistent unresolved social tension among students or between students and staff.

Of course, the functioning of a group is not just the result of planning, structure, and the skills of the staff. Over the four years that we offered two-month building apprenticeships, the levels of social cohesion and support amongst the groups varied widely. One year in particular stands out in my mind as a model group of students. They were three women and three men, with a broad range of backgrounds and ages. They actually spent one of their spare evenings each week in a self-organized study group where they shared notes and discussed how they could support one another's learning goals. This was in welcome contrast to the previous year, which had sometimes felt like a summer school for reluctant teenagers. The orga-

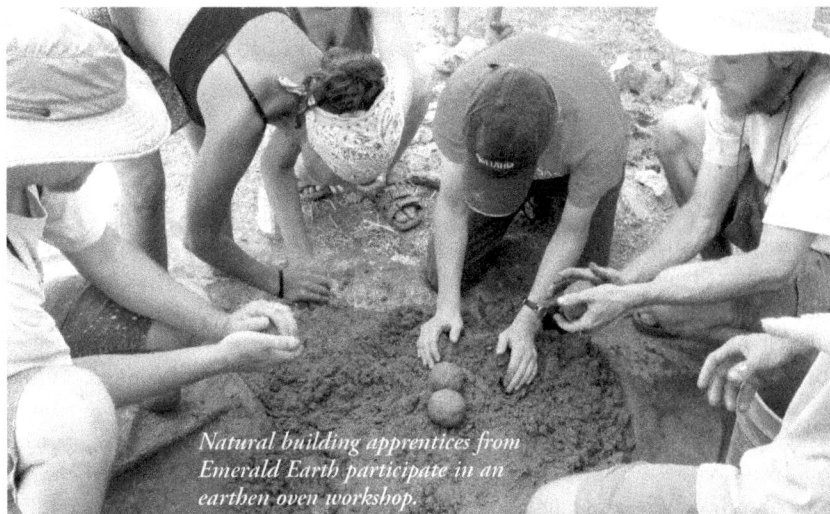

Natural building apprentices from Emerald Earth participate in an earthen oven workshop.

I've seen the failure to directly address conflicts and expectations lead to persistent unresolved social tension.

nization of both programs was similar; the main differences were the personalities of the students. Careful selection of self-motivated learners goes a long way toward the smooth functioning of an educational program.

Long programs like these require a major commitment on the part of the instructors, and may have significant effects on the hosting community. Community members who are not directly involved with the program may feel excluded from the social bonding taking place among students and teachers, or stretched thin taking care of business while the course leaders are occupied, or impatient for the program to end and life to get "back to normal." At Emerald Earth, we have felt these tensions, but the advantages to the community seemed to balance them out. With longer building trainings (over a month), the contribution from student work finally gets to be significant. We used our apprenticeship programs as a way to fund some of our builder/teachers to stay on-site working on community projects rather than seeking paid work elsewhere.

Internships or Work Exchange

Educational programs can vary in the formality of instruction as well as in length. Combine long duration with

low formality and you get an internship or work-exchange program. At Emerald Earth, we have offered work-trade positions for the last 10 years, ranging from two to seven months. We've found that these programs offer many of the advantages of long formal trainings, but with fewer negative impacts to the community as a whole.

The exchange in "work exchange" is mostly not financial. At most, we ask work traders to cover the costs of their food, but usually we split this expense with them 50/50. We offer them a place to live and learn and contribute and they offer us their labor and energy. Work traders come primarily for the experience of living in community and for general exposure to sustainable living skills. There may be some "classroom time," but most of the learning takes place on the job in the garden, kitchen, or building site. Any additional time we spend on instruction is compensated by increased productivity. Work-exchange therefore does not generate income for community members. It may or may not pass along knowledge as effectively as a paid apprenticeship. A formal training usually helps people pick up a specified set of skills in a relatively short time, whereas work exchange gives them broader exposure to everything happening in the community and the opportunity to develop a more personalized niche.

We find that, compared to apprentices and students, work traders reach a much higher level of social integration with the community. This is partly because their time is less scheduled with educational activities and they tend to spend time more evenly with all members. Work-traders, unlike apprentices, attend weekly coordination meetings where they see more of the inner workings of the community and have the opportunity to respond to emerging needs. The difference may also be in part because their primary focus is to be of service to the community rather than to learn specific skills.

Our 2009 work exchange program proved an exception to this rule. We offered two different focus areas: one on building our new common house and the other on gardening, animal husbandry, and food production. Each group worked about 30 hours per week in their focus area, directed by a non-overlapping subset of community members. This arrangement allowed us to get a lot of help in both areas from well-trained and dedicated teams. However, despite weekly sharing circles, shared mealtimes, and one afternoon per week spent working together in mixed groupings, we found that the split focus led to a surprising level of disconnection and even tension between the two teams. Partly because we were all so busy with our assigned tasks, some of the work traders (and members) were not finding time to develop friendships outside their focus groups or to resolve conflicts resulting from shared space.

This provided yet another lesson for us on how the structure of a program affects the social harmony of the community. As we design our programs for this coming season, we have tried to incorporate these learnings, as well as many others from the last decade of work parties, workshops, and work exchange. How to plan and implement educational programs that best serve us and our students is an evolutionary process for Emerald Earth and for communities in general. The stories of our successes and failures can be among the most important sparks of that evolution. ✱

Michael G. Smith is the author or co-author of four books, including The Hand-Sculpted House *and* The Art of Natural Building. *He is interested in the role intentional communities can play in the re-development of sustainable place-based cultures. Email him at michael@emeraldearth.org. Emerald Earth's course offerings and work-trade description can be found at www.emeraldearth.org.*

Some advice for communities wanting to start educational programs:

Start small. A series of one-day or weekend workshops on topics you know well can be a good way to start. Keep your costs low and try to run the workshop even if you don't get much enrollment. That will give you experience and start to establish your reputation as a learning center.

Develop programs based on your strengths. Ask yourself, "What does our community do best?" That is probably what you should be teaching.

Get help from outside instructors. If you don't have a reputation and experience running workshops, hiring a high-profile instructor from outside your community can help get the public's attention and provide a model for you to learn from.

Create programs that interest you. Bring in outside instructors to teach classes that you and other community members want to take. You may not make much money that way, but it will probably be cheaper than several of you traveling to study somewhere else.

Consistency and quality fill workshops. Word of mouth is a cheap and highly effective means of advertising. If you offer the same workshop repeatedly, students who enjoyed it will recommend it to their friends.

Make community structures visible. No matter what the topic of the workshop, visitors will be curious about the community. Being transparent about how your community works is good advertising for you and for the communities network as a whole.

Offer scholarships or work-trade. It's hard to balance covering your costs and paying your staff with making the workshop accessible to people with less money. Some effective solutions include scholarships, work-trade positions, and sliding scales. Differential payment scales can also help attract specific populations to your workshops. For example, our first two Natural Building Apprenticeships at Emerald Earth ended up with only a single woman student each. The third year, we offered scholarships specifically for women, and the ratio of women to men was equal. By the following year, we had one man and five women in the program, a complete reversal from two years previous.

Seeing the Good in the World:
Connecting Communities and Students for Sustainability Education and Transformation

By Joshua Lockyer

Photos courtesy of Joshua Lockyer

"I think a lot of people subscribe to the idea that intentional communities are cloistered away, and only focused on improving their own immediate societies. It was wonderful to see how each and every place we visited articulated how important it was to extend the benefits of cooperative living to everyone, not just those who actually live with them."

T his quote from one of my students indicates the impact that visits to intentional communities have on students in higher education. As an anthropologist and environmental studies teacher, I believe that providing students opportunities to experience intentional communities is an excellent way to explore the nuts and bolts of sustainability and participate in positive social transformation. This short article explores my experiences in this area and presents a call for communitarians and academic researchers to come together for a broad discussion about connecting communities, students, and academic institutions for sustainability education and transformation.

Intentional Communities in a Summer Field School

"This was one of the most educational and fun experiences of my life and I truly went home with a new perspective on our society and my life in general."

In the two years after finishing graduate school in 2007, I taught about intentional communities mostly in the abstract. I gave brief lectures on them in my introductory anthropology courses and even taught a one-credit freshman seminar on ecovillages. Throughout, most students did not show the greatest enthusiasm. A topic that held my attention for 10 years was not captivating for my students.

This began to change during summer 2009 when I co-taught a field school on the human ecology of the Southern Appalachian region during which we took students to visit a number of intentional communities. These visits came on the tail of several weeks spent learning about transformations in human-environmental relationships in the region over the last millennium. These transformations tended not to be positive in nature. From European colonialism and its effects on native cultures and landscapes to industrial-scale timber harvesting and mountaintop removal coal mining to the decline in agroecological diversity in the region, a series of negative scenarios confronted us. While it was exciting to immerse ourselves in the landscapes and communities in which these changes occurred, the experience was not particularly uplifting.

However, we also wanted to bring to light positive trends in the region: Cherokee cultural revitalization, an elk reintroduction program, renewable energy projects, local and organic food movements, and intentional communities. Moving roughly chronologically through the environmental history of the Southern Appalachians, toward the end of our itinerary we turned our attention to groups of people attempting to reinhabit this place. At this point, the tone of the course and the attitude of the students began to shift. Perhaps it was my own enthusiasm. My knowledge about the region was rooted in my long-term relationships with several intentional communities there. I think that seeing and talking with groups of people engaged in deliberate endeavors to change their relationships with each other and with the surrounding environment provided a sense of positive possibilities.

Learning about the communities was challenging as well. How could people choose to share ownership of land and other property with so many other people? How could people be willing to sit in meetings discussing minor details for so long? How could people put up with not having cell phone access 24 hours a day, seven days a week? These seemed contrary to what students expected from life. Students were also challenged by the practical, daily realities of community life. We spent 48 hours at an ecovillage and during that time, I was the only one to use the composting toilet. Students yearned for a "real" shower. Bathing in the creek didn't do the trick. Still, I could see that these experiences began to open up new possibilities for them. Simply seeing that other people could do something different was empowering.

Undergraduate Research on Intentional Communities

"I think intentional community building is one way, one step to creating a better world. It's great to see these communities in action instead of just having an abstract idea of what they are like."

Fast forward to spring semester 2010. A colleague and I received a small grant for research on intentional communities. The grant was part of a larger, campus-wide project that aims to determine how research, public policy, and citizen action can combine to contribute to more "livable lives" in the region surrounding our campus. Recognizing that intentional communities are inherently formed in

Opposite page: Students in the Human Ecology of the Southern Appalachians Summer School take a tour of an urban permaculture community in Asheville, North Carolina. This page top: Students in the Human Ecology of the Southern Appalachians Summer Field School take a tour of an ecovillage outside Asheville, North Carolina. Above: Students in the St. Louis Intentional Communities Research Group learn about cohousing at an emerging cohousing community in St. Louis, Missouri.

pursuit of lives more livable, we believed their endeavors should inform the larger project. Rather than simply writing a report or doing library research, we decided to get our students actively engaged with some of the intentional communities around campus. We wanted them to experience the transformative potential intentional communities hold and to use their fresh perspectives to help us bring this potential to light.

We chose to use appreciative inquiry to engage community members in discussions focused on the most positive aspects of their communities. Following on the idea that intentional communities are creating the change they wish to see in the world, we ask mostly about not the problems that local communitarians are responding to, but the solutions they're creating. Our research focuses on community members' experiences of the ways in which community living contributes to things like increased economic security and social support, a better sense of health and well-being, and reduced ecological footprints—all essential components of any transition to a more sustainable

(continued on p. 75)

SEEING THE GOOD IN THE WORLD: CONNECTING COMMUNITIES AND STUDENTS FOR SUSTAINABILITY EDUCATION AND TRANSFORMATION

(continued from p. 31)

society. While our goals could be achieved through reviews of the growing academic and community literatures on these topics, the quote above suggests that facilitating direct student experiences of intentional community holds much greater potential power.

Student Engagement:
Personal Inspiration and Social Transformation

"I really enjoyed the trip and how much it opened my eyes to the good in the world. You don't always get to see how much people care and appreciate everything they have, so much so that they extend themselves to others who are less fortunate in such a profound way."

"I was very humbled by the determination and passion with which each community pursued their goals, but also equally inspired by the grace they had in accepting where they were in that process."

"The common thread is an intense and deep love for those you are working and living with. I was truly envious of the kind of emotional relationships those people had with each other. It's an amazing thing."

A whirlwind tour of five local intentional communities at the beginning of the semester was the students' introduction to community living. Student responses to this tour reflect the power of this experience. Students were clearly inspired by the positive and moving examples presented by the communities we visited. In a world increasingly filled with bad news that can overwhelm one with a sense of powerlessness, intentional communities reverse this dynamic.

Intentional communities were seen as a manifestation of the potential good in the world. We visited communities dedicated to serving the homeless and others in need. We saw a variety of communities struggling to meet their goals and recognizing that the process of striving for something better is as important as actually getting there. Perhaps most powerfully, we encountered groups of people who care deeply about each other and about the places in which they live, people who were not afraid to speak openly and with emotion about these things even in the midst of a group of strangers.

Our all-day tour was long and tiring, but subsequent discussions indicate the students clearly took a lot from it, including a better understanding of what intentional communities are all about. Students are now excited about their research papers and projects and don't seem to need much prompting to get the work under way. Each student has selected a particular community to research in greater depth via frequent visits and interviews with community members throughout the semester. Perhaps more importantly, students are engaging these communities on an intensely personal level and contributing to the broader process of social and cultural transformation.

Sustainability is clearly not just about new technologies that enable us to use natural resources more efficiently. Nor can sustainability be achieved through research and public policy alone. Moving toward sustainability will require broad cultural transformations that can be brought about only as people reengage with each other

intentionally in local communities. My experiences over the last couple of years suggest that actively connecting students with intentional communities holds great potential for helping to initiate the kind of societal transformation that a quest for sustainability entails.

Connecting Communities and Students for Sustainability Education

I know there are many others out there who share my sentiments and who may have much greater experience with this topic. I would like to suggest that we create a forum where we can share our experiences and support each other in furthering the transformative potential inherent in engaging higher education students with community living. Perhaps we could come together at the Communal Studies Association annual conference for formal and informal discussions. Fellowship for Intentional Community events may provide appropriate venues as well. I am open to other suggestions. If you are an educator, communitarian, activist, or student who is interested in strengthening connections and increasing opportunities for interaction among communities, students, and academic institutions, please contact me at jlockyer@wustl.edu. ✺

Joshua Lockyer teaches anthropology and environmental studies at Washington University in St. Louis, including classes on intentional communities. He would like to thank the following students who provided quotations used in this article: LeeAnn Felder, Annie Rose Fondaw, Gabriella Torcise, and John Wargofchik. He would also like to thank all the communities and communitarians who have helped him and his students along this journey.

Sustainability:
Reflections from an Eco-Warrior

By Bruce Davidson

The thrill and the wonder of opening one's heart to the complexity and beauty of all life can be both terrifying and exhilarating. Letting go into this wonder is really what sustainability is about.

Joy and fulfillment come into your life when you consciously act to enhance your own and others' well-being. That joy far exceeds any satisfaction that might come from the accumulation of wealth or power.

Society has created a system of value not tied to the good of all beings. The dilemma is how to emerge from the delusions of what constitutes happiness or a good life, i.e., consumption and consumerism, and recognize that happiness and fulfillment occur through serving the well-being of all. Having worked on this for 36-plus years, I'm greatly encouraged to see the stranglehold of materialism on humanity's consciousness now loosening its grip and giving way to sincere interest and movement towards sustainability.

Our local town reflects this shift in consciousness. When Sirius Community first decided to put up a wind generator for electricity, in 1999, the town balked at the idea. After countless meetings with the board of health and a very long process, we received provisional permission to go ahead. Six years later, the town invited me to join their energy committee because they wanted to put up a wind generator behind the town hall.

People have come to Sirius with the idea of learning the nuts and bolts of green building, alternative energy, and permaculture. More often than not, they are confronted with the limitations in their attitudes toward life

Bruce Wilson

Opposite page: Bruce climbing the wind tower. This page left: Sirius Community Birthday Gathering. This page right: Elana and Llani Davidson repairing Kailasha.

that create their road blocks to living sustainably. What they learn—what helps them most—is to take responsibility for their experience and to open to what truly constitutes a joyful, satisfying life: simple living; positive, heartfelt human connections; and service.

In order to live sustainably, one must do more than teach or learn skills. One must embody the principles and values that lead to a sustainable life: love, compassion, and a commitment to the highest good for all beings. Without embodiment, skill learning becomes another theoretical or intellectual exercise. The most successful educational experiences are simultaneously intellectual, spiritual, and practical; they come through the combination of the head, the heart, and the hands, and through living the principles and values that create an environment where everyday life is a sustainable statement.

At Sirius, people have discovered themselves and the joys and possibilities of a new way of living, one where connection with others is important, living simply is valued, time spent working together is joyful and fun, and meditation brings peace. Significantly, they discover that they are not alone and there are others who share their values. The change in consciousness is deep and profound and influences their lives long after they leave.

Many people come to Sirius wanting to change their lives. Sometimes they are no longer satisfied with the "good" life they have created for themselves. Sometimes they have been through a life-changing trauma. They are open.

A man from an extremely wealthy background came to Sirius, bringing with him all the family pressures and expectations that accompany inherited wealth. He ended up in one of the smallest living spaces in the entire community. Through the process of living here, joining in the meditations, working with me three days a week, and participating in all aspects of

community life for roughly three years, he found the inner confidence to live simply. He felt at peace with his commitment to use his wealth to support projects promoting planetary peace and well-being.

One of our apprentices came from a gang in New York City. Roughly 18 years old, he had a chip on his shoulder and was enmeshed in the culture of violence and revenge. On his first day, he refused to participate in anything. He came to meals and wouldn't clean up, he wouldn't accept being told anything, and he was disruptive. Instead of getting angry, we worked to give him love. Instead of getting frustrated, we were determined to be accepting and to model right relationship. After two months in our apprenticeship program, he became willing to participate fully in the life of the community. When he left, he saw more possibilities and a wider horizon for himself. He now wanted to become a professional green builder. He returned to his previous environment, determined not to get caught up again in the negative downward spiral of gang violence.

We hosted an international program for youth from all over the world, mostly from affluent backgrounds. One indigenous aboriginal male teenager, coming from a reservation outside Los Angeles, California, felt alienated from the sustainable vision of his elders. Because of his background and because he had been hostile and mistrusting of the rest of the youth group, I invited him to help me run the sweat lodge ceremony. He called the reservation to get permission from his grandfather. After the ceremony was over, he was radiant, a changed young man. He told me that because young people from all over the world had participated in, accepted, and were deeply moved by the sacred ceremony of his people, he felt he and his traditions had value, and was now able to open up and connect with them.

(continued on p. 76)

Sirius Community

Sirius Community, 72 Baker Rd, Shutesbury MA 01072 USA, 413-259-1251, www.siriuscommunity.org, teaches spirituality and sustainability by demonstrating them as a way of life. For 31 years Sirius has taught courses on permaculture, organic gardening, natural building, simple living, and land stewardship ecology. We host our own programs for interns, apprentices, and guests, and facilitate tours of our site which include use of appropriate technology (wind- and solar-powered), vegetable-oil-powered vehicles, and composting toilets. Our conference center and facilities are also used by outside presenters. We interface with the larger community by doing presentations, have a strong educational presence on the internet via our website, and continue to develop social and spiritual connections with the local neighbors and community.

SUSTAINABILITY: REFLECTIONS FROM AN ECO-WARRIOR

(continued from p. 33)

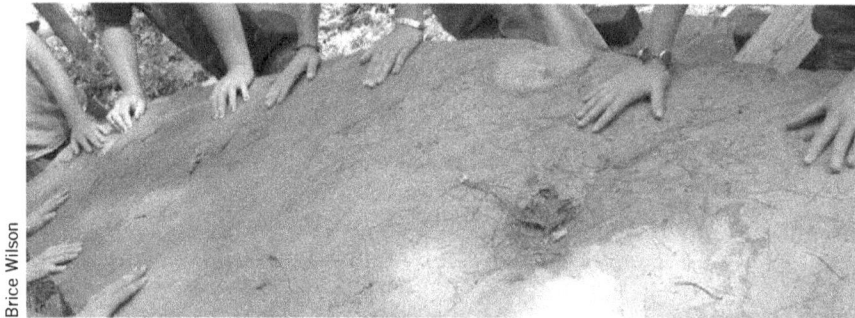

Brice Wilson

My own path towards a sustainable life also required a 180 degree change in attitude. I came from the mainstream baby boom values. At one time I had two sports cars, three motorcycles, and numerous girlfriends. In the 1960s, I joined the Marine Corps and did service during the Vietnam War.

After my tour of duty, when I was recovering from a broken leg received in an auto accident, an older woman whom I didn't know approached me and told me she was a healer. She said she could help me by doing hands-on healing on my leg. I thought the idea ridiculous, but when she put her hands on my leg and it immediately improved 50 percent, she got my attention.

She began talking about spiritual things, meditation, reincarnation, karma, eastern philosophies, and gave me some books to read. She emphasized that there was a spiritual component to life, that we are spiritual beings, that all life is sacred, and that if I really wanted to know truth, I would have to go within and find it myself.

I read all her books and more. I became a vegetarian and started meditating every day. My attitude changed from one that was concerned with sports cars, motorcycles, experimenting with different states of consciousness, and wanting stuff, to one more centered within.

After two years of deep reflection and personal transformation, I had a spiritual epiphany in the Sierra Nevada mountains in California. Through a meditative experience of oneness, I realized that all the things I was studying were true, that a spiritual reality weaves itself through all creation, and that I would spend the rest of my life serving it. I was 26 at that time. My view of eco-sustainability came to me with my epiphany in the mountains: all life is sacred and everything is interconnected. If you live from that understanding, you become a deep ecologist.

Six months later I went to Findhorn Community, where I discovered a group of like-minded souls. I stayed there for four years learning more about the spiritual components of sustainability and about living in community, before coming to Sirius to help ground a similar vision in this country.

That was 32 years ago. During that time I have learned many lessons. Some of the most important, I think, are: doing what you know in your heart is right; deep patience; and non-attachment to outcome, knowing that needed changes will come.

For many years, some of our visitors expressed the attitude that our sustainable practices seemed appealing, but not necessarily applicable to their lives. Now they say "please tell us how to do that" or "we need your help." I now notice that a lot of our practices and those of other sustainable communities, including conflict resolution, green building and technologies, permaculture, consensus decision making, even composting toilets, have found their way into the mainstream.

I have learned that to effectively catalyze change, an attitude of absolute non-judgment and acceptance is essential. The opening of hearts and minds to new ideas does not happen in an atmosphere of criticism. For example, a group of corporate CEOs interested in developing more sustainable practices within their companies visited us. By putting aside our preconceived ideas and judgments and embracing them wherever they were in their process, we were able to engage in meaningful dialogs about the best ways forward, and received an invitation for future collaboration.

My most important lesson from living in community all these years is this: change that will last, that is truly sustainable, comes from changing consciousness. A new paradigm for a sustainable future grows naturally from connection with our deeper nature—call it what you like, "the force," Buddha nature, Christ, Jehovah, Allah, it makes no difference. Once someone has experienced the sacred in themselves and in all life, a commitment to harmony and sustainability follows, and the entire earth and all beings become the community we choose to serve wherever we are. ✤

Dedicated to creating sacred space both indoors and outdoors, Bruce Davidson is a founding member and President of Sirius, an ecovillage and spiritual community located in western Massachusetts. He is a former member who served as coordinator of the Core Group of Findhorn Community, Scotland. A meditator for the past 38 years, green builder, gardener, and teacher, he also lived in a Zen Buddhist community. He continues to be a member of human kingdom, with all its frailties and vulnerabilities.

Ethan Hughes

Ecovillages and Academia

By Daniel Greenberg

We are living in a unique time, not just in human history, but in *planetary* history. From the war in Iraq to the war on rainforests; from global markets to global warming—it is clear we *must* learn to live in ways that honor all life. Yet, as a species, humans seem almost evolutionarily unprepared to address the global issues facing us. For the most part, business is going on as usual; governments—at best—are thinking ahead only to the next election; and, as Oberlin Professor David Orr has said, "We are still educating the young as if there were no planetary emergency."

We now need to move beyond the industrial era and begin to train leaders for the 21st century—leaders who know how to *heal* the Earth and build durable economies and sustainable communities. But how? Einstein once said, "We can't solve problems by using the same kind of thinking we used when we created them." So perhaps we also need to move beyond the ivory towers of traditional academia and create campuses and pedagogies that are better able to educate for a sustainable future.

Worldwide, ecovillages are striving to create high quality, healthy lifestyles *and* low ecological impacts. These ecovillages are developing and refining ecological and social tools such as community-scale renewable energy systems, ecological design, organic farming, holistic health and nutrition, consensus decision making, and mindfulness practices such as yoga and meditation.

Ecovillages are increasingly being used as "campuses" where students learn about sustainability while actually living it. Ecovillages such as Crystal Waters (Australia), Findhorn (Scotland), and Auroville (India), and, in North America, Sirius, EcoVillage at Ithaca, The Farm, and Earthaven, have already had considerable successes as educational centers and in creating ongoing partnerships with government agencies, research centers, and schools of higher learning. And organizations such as Living Routes are helping to build bridges between ecovillages and academia by creating college-level semester programs based in ecovillages around the world.

Why Academia Needs Ecovillages

To understand why ecovillages offer ideal campuses for sustainability education, we need to compare them with traditional universities. Regardless of what classes students take, the following list illustrates the hidden curriculum, or "metanarrative" as Chet Bowers would call it, that students learn simply through their day-to-day participation and involvement:

Conservative vs. Experimental

Universities tend to be burdened by cumbersome bureaucracies and are slow to change. In fact, the basic structure of universities has not significantly changed since the Middle Ages.

Ecovillages are physical and social "laboratories," experimenting with new technologies, social structures, and worldviews. They tend to have a trial and error mentality and are quick to adjust to changing conditions, challenges, and opportunities.

Hierarchical vs. Heterarchical

The power structure of universities is very top-down, with power emanating from the president down to the provosts, deans, faculty—and, at the bottom rung, students. The hidden agenda is one of "power over" and submission to authority, which is consistent with the conventional attitude that humans are meant to dominate and subdue nature.

In ecovillages, there is a wide diversity of relationships and members tend to interact on more or less an equal footing. Individuals might cook a meal together one day, sit in a budget meeting another day, and perhaps help harvest vegetables on yet another. These interdependent sets of relationships help members get to know each other on many levels and better understand the complexity of living systems.

Competitive vs. Cooperative

Universities are competitive on all levels—among students for the best grades; among faculty for grants, tenure, and recognition; and among schools for prestige and endowments.

While competition exists within ecovillages, the norm tends toward cooperation with members assuming as much responsibility as they are willing to handle. The success of individuals is typically viewed as inherently tied to the success of the community as a whole.

Fragmented Knowledge vs. Transdisciplinary Knowledge

Universities have responded to the exponentially increasing rate of knowledge generation with ever more sub-specializations within disciplines. Pat Murphy, director of Community Service in Yellow Springs, Ohio, refers to the "silo" mentality of higher education where institutions "stockpile" knowledge within discreet containers that are functionally isolated from each other.

Ecovillages recognize that real-life issues rarely exist within the boundaries of disciplines. For example, the decision to put up a windmill requires knowledge within the fields of appropriate technology, engineering, regional and community planning, governance, and even sociology and anthropology. The decision to create an organic farm crosses disciplines of agriculture, nutrition, philosophy and ethics, business, education, and communications, among others. While able to train specialists, ecovillages are uniquely positioned and equipped to train much-needed *generalists* who posses "lateral" rigor across disciplines to complement "vertical" rigor within disciplines.

Academic Community vs. Living Community

Many students claim that "gaining a sense of community" is a primary motivation to attend college. While this is certainly available, it is also true that most relationships in academia are mediated by specific, rather narrow roles—student/teacher, fellow researcher, classmate, etc.

If a sense of community is the goal, wouldn't it be more fulfilling to immerse oneself in a "living" community where members have a wide range of relationships, hold a common vision, and are committed to each other's long-term growth and development? Small class-size, the use of authentic assessment methods, and the creation of "learning communities" in which students have opportunities to deeply reflect on and share about their experiences further support their learning and growth.

I believe humans are "hard-wired" for community and tend to resonate with human-scale institutions in which they can both know and be known by others. Margaret Meade, the noted anthropologist, observed that for 99.9 per cent of our evolution, we lived in tribes. Many people in modern, "developed" countries have lost a sense of community so thoroughly that their closest acquaintances are characters on TV shows. The sense of belonging that students experience within ecovillages both awakens and fulfills a need that many did

not even know they had. And once nourished, this sense of belonging tends to expand to include ever broader communities—both human and non-human.

Theoretical vs. Applied

Academic types tend to stay in their heads—and their armchairs—and maintain a detached, theoretical perspective of the world. Researchers use the myth of "objectivity" as a rationale to stay removed from their subject matter and, consequently, often create knowledge, but rarely wisdom.

Ecovillages, in order to survive and prosper, must focus on practical knowledge and wisdom that can be applied in real-world settings. Theory is in the service of "what works" rather than the other way around. Ecovillages are inherently "experiential"—a word that many universities are loath to even use. Students often claim they learn more through internships and service learning opportunities than in even the best seminars.

Secular vs. Spiritual

Not only are most universities very hands-off, they also tend to separate our heads from our hearts—and typically only care about our heads. Consequently they tend to support a Cartesian view of the universe as a soulless machine to be manipulated and controlled by humans.

While some are explicitly religious, most ecovillages embrace a larger, more eclectic spiritual container in which members are supported to be "in process" and engaged with large questions of life and meaning. Yoga, meditation, and silence are common features of many ecovillages, and students on Living Routes programs have pursued vision quests as a way to deeply reflect on their relationship with themselves, each other, and the world.

Large Footprint vs. Small Footprint

Universities are beginning to incorporate more ecological design and building, but for the most part they are still incredibly resource-intensive institutions and not very attuned to their impact on their region or the world. Recycling and compact fluorescents are recent phenomena on many campuses and very few campuses even attempt to buy food locally, not to mention organically.

Ecovillages strive to live well, yet lightly. While many assume ecovillages aspire to self-sufficiency, this is rarely accurate. Most

look to their bioregion or watershed as the unit of land and culture that should become more self-reliant. Ecovillages often serve as regional catalysts for reducing ecological impacts by supporting local initiatives such as organic agriculture and local distribution networks so resources do not have to be shipped great distances.

Cross-Cultural vs. Cultural Immersion

Most campuses enroll students from a variety of cultural backgrounds. Yet typically these lifestyles and traditions are subsumed under the melting pot of the academic culture with few opportunities for cultural expression or exchange.

In ecovillages, perhaps because they are "living" rather than "academic" communities, there tend to be fuller expressions of members' cultural backgrounds through festivals, rituals, language, and food. Even further, in traditional, indigenous ecovillages, students have the opportunity to truly immerse themselves in vivid and full-featured cultures that both honor the past and are consciously reaching towards the future. For example, on Living Routes' programs in Senegal, US and Senegalese students join together to explore sustainable community development within indigenous ecovillages, which provide rich contexts for cross-cultural exchange and understanding. These programs are frequently life-changing experiences in which students experiment with and adopt wholly new ways of being and thinking.

Problem Oriented vs. Solution Oriented

Last, but perhaps most important, universities tend to be primarily focused on dissecting and understanding "problems." It is obviously critical that we continue to study and better understand the serious local and global issues facing us. But there comes a point when students "get it" and need to either do something about it or risk becoming overwhelmed with negativity and despair. Worse, some students even become emotionally numb in an unconscious effort to defend their hearts against the seemingly insurmountable social and environmental problems facing humanity and the Earth.

Ecovillages give students important opportunities to be a part of the solution and learn how they can make a positive difference in the world. They are not utopias, but after spending time living and learning in an ecovillage, students can never again say, "It can't be done," because they see people wholly devoted to right livelihood and creating a sustainable future. It then comes back to students to ask themselves, "What am I going to do? How can I make a difference in my own life and in my own community?"

Why Ecovillages Need Academia

The above comparisons may seem like an argument to run, not walk, away from traditional academia, but there are also important reasons to build bridges and work together.

First, academia is changing. With an increasing internationalization of the curriculum, interest in community partnerships, and recognition of the need for ecological design and interdisciplinary research, universities are beginning to see ecovillages as natural collaborators. Also, technological changes such as the internet and distance learning are making the large infrastructures of campus-based universities increasingly irrelevant and out-dated.

Second, universities are not going away anytime soon. In the US, higher education is approximately a $350 billion/year business. That's the GDP of Belgium! And this is not counting the *trillions* of dollars invested in facilities and resources. And universities are where the students are! Two out of every three high school graduates in the US go directly to college, and nationwide more than 16 million students are currently enrolled. Worldwide, by 2010 there were expected to be approximately 100 million college students (well more than the population of Germany!) and this number may reach 150 million by 2025.

Third, ecovillages need help in order to reach their highest potential. As advanced as ecovillages are in terms of providing campuses for sustainability education, I believe they are still in *kindergarten* in terms of what is truly needed to educate professionals capable of building the institutions and systems required for a sustainable world to be possible. While programs offered through Living Routes and individual ecovillages are a good start, we need to further collaborate with academia to create "communiversities" where students can spend *years* in ecovillages and other related organizations and gain the background and skills needed to enter the workplace as professionals in fields as diverse as appropriate technologies, habitat restoration, sustainable agriculture, group facilitation, holistic health, ecological design, and green building.

The fourth and most important reason for ecovillages to reach out to academia is that college-age students represent a powerful leverage point in the world's "Great Turning toward a more Ecological Age," as Joanna Macy refers to it. Many talk about members of the college population as "emerging adults" in that they are mature enough to ask the big questions yet also open to radical alternatives and new life directions. Emerging adults are key to the dissemination of emerging paradigms, and the world desperately needs leaders who are able to think—and act—outside of the box. The novelist Frederick Buechner once wrote that, "Vocation is the place where one's deep gladness and the world's deep hunger meet." Never before has this been more true—or necessary. Building bridges between ecovillages and academia is literally building bridges to a more sustainable future. What an amazing time to be alive! What an honor to be a part of this Great Turning! ✳

Daniel Greenberg has studied and directed community-based educational programs for over 15 years. He visited and corresponded with over 200 US intentional communities for his Ph.D. dissertation on children and education in community, and later spent a year at the Findhorn Foundation in Scotland working with children and families there. He is the founder and Executive Director of Living Routes, which develops accredited ecovillage-based education programs that promote sustainable community development. He lives at the Sirius Community in Shutesbury, Massachusetts with his wife Monique and their two daughters, Simone and Pema. This article is adapted from a chapter written for the book Beyond You and Me: Inspiration and Wisdom for Community Building *(Permanent Publications, Hampshire, UK, 2007).*

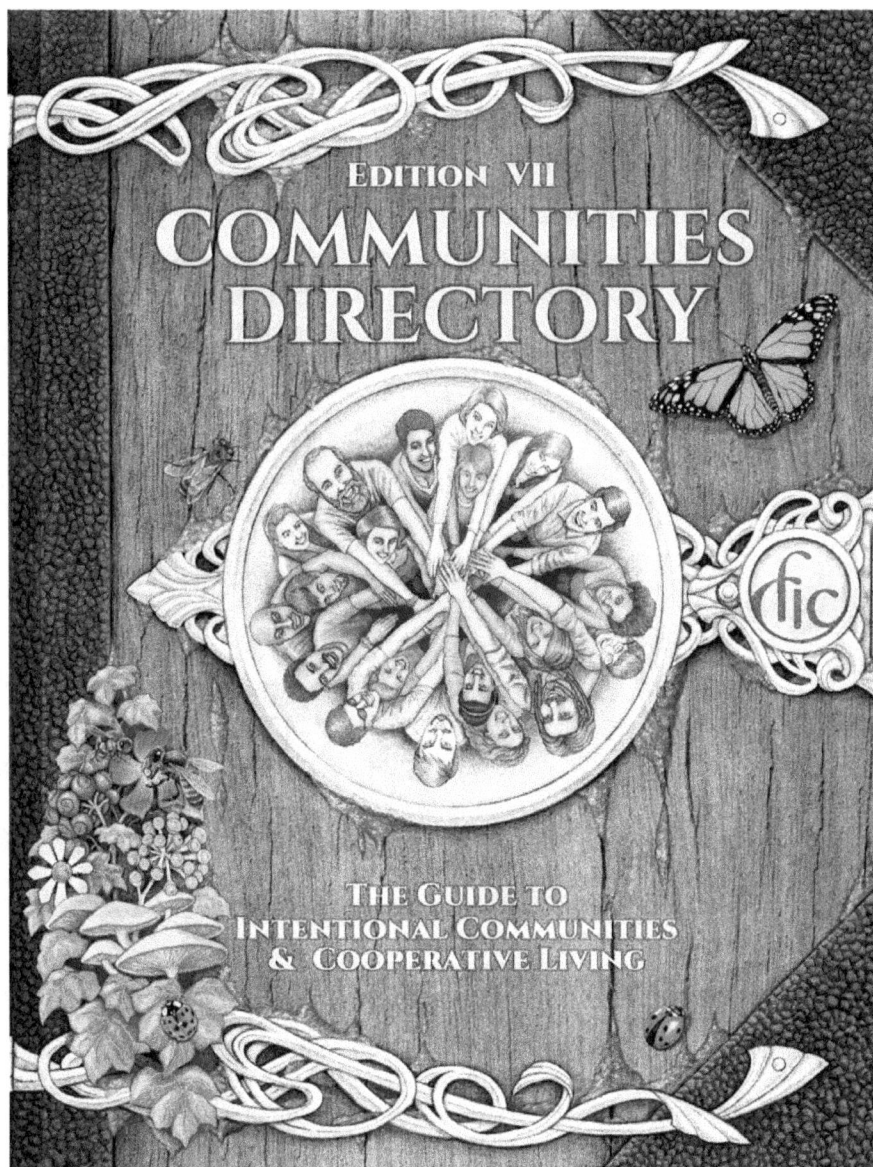

Communities Directory book!

In addition to profiling more than 1,000 communities, this new book includes full-page maps showing where communities are located, charts that compare communities by more than 30 qualities, and an easy index to find communities interested in specific pursuits. Also included are articles on how to start or join a community, the basics of group dynamics and decision-making, and countless additional resources and links to help your community thrive!

Order your book today: www.ic.org/New-Directory

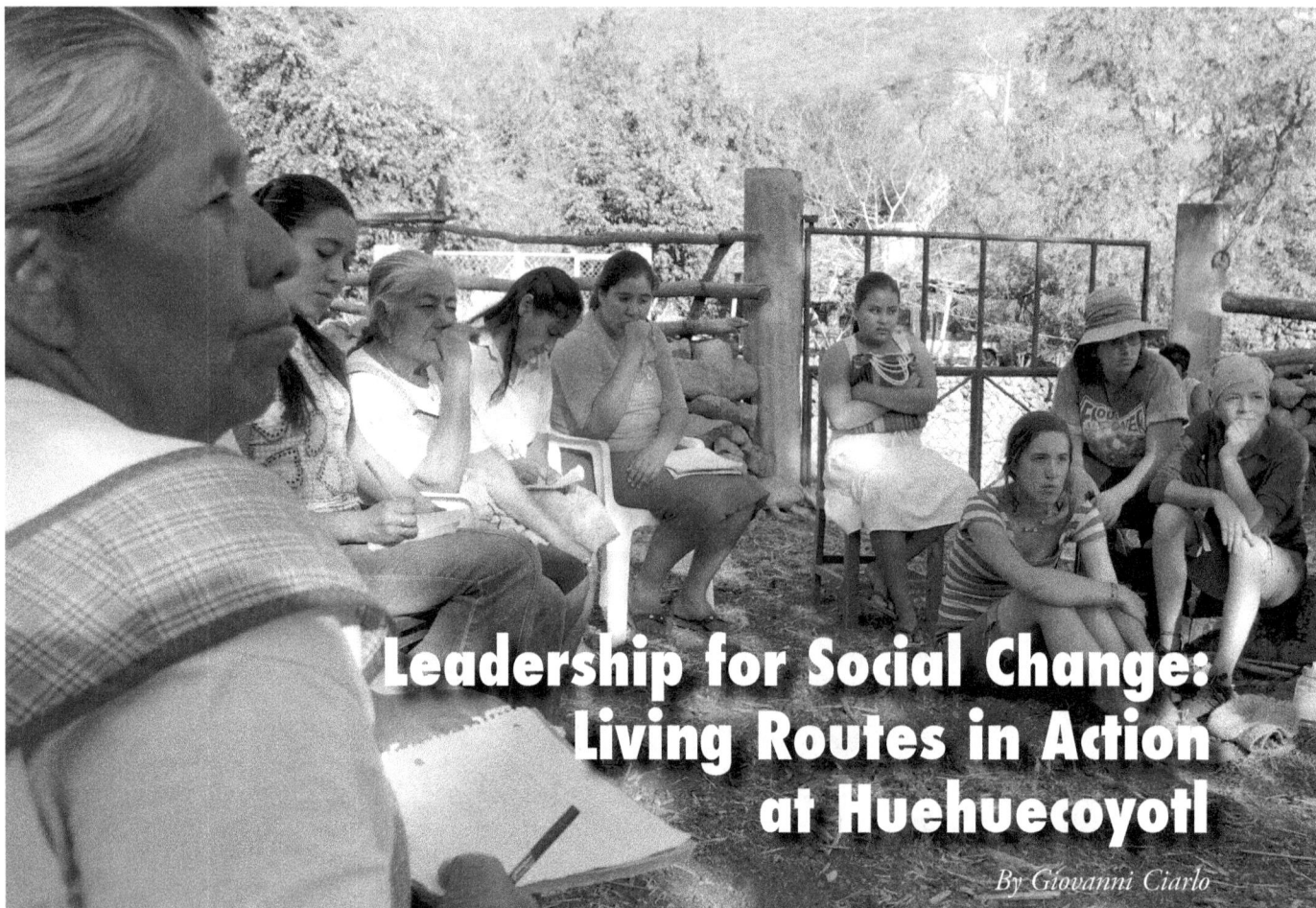

Leadership for Social Change: Living Routes in Action at Huehuecoyotl

By Giovanni Ciarlo

Huehuecoyotl Ecovillage was started in Tepoztlan, Mexico in 1982 by an international group of artists, environmentalists, and social activists with the vision of creating a demonstration model of sustainable community living, where we could engage in action-learning education, creativity, and fun-filled activism. After many years of living and learning about various aspects of sustainability (personal, social, and ecological), and exploring how to develop healthy and empowering leadership qualities in ourselves and others, in 2005 we partnered with Living Routes, a study-abroad organization based in Amherst, Massachusetts that offers college-level sustainability study programs rooted in ecovillages around the world. Through Living Routes, we offer a condensed version of the leadership style we have developed in a three-week January term course titled Leadership for Social Change. Students learn basic facilitation techniques, compassionate communication tools, and self-awareness skills that explore their social identity and their emerging values of social justice and inclusiveness.

Students are taken through an action-learning process of discovering their strengths and personal skills in a group setting, with the ultimate goal of researching, developing, presenting, and implementing a community service project that meets strict criteria of sustainability, group integration, and limited resources.

The first week of this program focuses on academic work related to facilitation and communications skills, with a good amount of

personal discovery and social identity exercises. Then the students go on field trips to get more acquainted with Mexican culture and heritage. One of these trips takes the students to meet a women's organization that works through local campesinos groups (subsistence farmers) to help the poorest families in the state meet basic needs of nutrition and economic security. The organization provides micro-credit funding to families and individuals to start small businesses in their villages. Students also visit small poultry operations, a shoe store, a nopal (cactus) farm, an ecotourism park run by locals, and other examples of leadership projects that make a direct difference to the communities in which they are located. Informed by this background, the students then research, interview, propose, and decide with ecovillage members what service project they will dedicate their last week to completing.

The first year we hosted this action learning program, the students decided to build a bus stop on the road where Huehuecoyotl's driveway starts. This was well received by the community and the local people who rely on bus service but have no defined place to wait for the bus or to take shelter from the rain when waiting. However, this admirable service project presented some unexpected challenges that the course organizer (I) had to deal with after the students left the ecovillage. As it turns out, the municipality of Tepoztlan, where our ecovillage is located, had been locked in a struggle with the local bus service company about where they would put three bus stops along the route that goes past Huehu-

the works. It took quite a bit of smooth talking with officials, and the support of a couple of local residents who attested to the benefit of the project to the local community, before we were dismissed with a light scolding and the project got approval. It has been one of the most used public spaces in the area, and a big success with the local community. But it also taught us an important lesson in local politics and conflict resolution.

Another year, students decided to build a new recycling center for the community. Since the old center was only a temporary shack that was untidy and falling down, this was a perfect opportunity to create a model recycling station to separate the various recyclable materials coming out of the community: paper, metal, glass, plastics, etc. This project was partly inspired by the installation in one of the houses of a new roof using recycled material made from plastic water bottles. We had been recycling all the plastic that entered our community for the past 25 years, and only now realized that we could get it back in the form of plastic roofing panels guaranteed to last for 100 years and not leak.

Our students designed and built a spacious recycling room, closed off from invading animals and organized with signage and containers for each material. It actually blends nicely into the landscape and looks stupendous with its bamboo walls, metal roof, and elegant round adobe back wall. It is centrally located with easy access for the pick-up service. This has been one of the most successful demonstration projects the community has to share with the outside world. People come from the surrounding villages and households to look at it and take back the idea

to recycle in their own places. It has also become a feature of our tour of the community whenever we have groups looking for the application of sustainable systems.

The projects implemented by Living Routes students have greatly benefited our ecovillage and the surrounding area. We are proud of the leadership our students have provided and the improvements they've made to our community while learning by doing, just as we did from the beginning of our own collective undertaking. The challenges have been to choose projects and activities that integrate well with the needs of the community and the local bioregion, while making the best use of the students' skills and criteria. Few students had ever mixed concrete before, or designed a building, or even dealt with local politics, but these experiences have made them more aware of the issues and dynamics of leadership for social change through personal and group action and engagement. ❋

Giovanni Ciarlo is a cofounder of Ecoaldea Huehuecoyotl (www.huehuecoyotl.net), and a consultant in sustainability and ecovillage design. He has an M.A. in Sustainable Communities and Socially Responsible Businesses from Goddard College, Vermont. Giovanni is the president of the board of both the Global Ecovillage Network (www.ecovillage.org) and Living Routes (www.livingroutes.org). He lives in his ecovillage in Mexico with his wife Kathleen Sartor part of the year, and leads arts in education programs in Connecticut with their musical group Sirius Coyote (www.siriuscoyote.org) the rest of the year.

ecoyotl—and about who would decide. By building the stop ourselves we had inadvertently bypassed their authority.

A few days after the students left, I got a visit from the planning department asking that I come in and explain why we did not take a permit for the bus stop. This was a big surprise, because for the last 23 years we had never needed to take out a permit before building our houses, or any other construction in our community. We always get the paperwork approved after the fact. I suspected a bribe request was in

Student Reflections

"I was really glad to have the opportunity to interview so many of the community members because I feel this was an integral step in choosing a worthwhile project. So often students on community service projects think they can change the world in one project—that they can just sweep into a place, build something, and have the residents be eternally grateful. I'm glad this certainly wasn't the sentiment among our group, and we took care to ask those most familiar with the local issues rather than assume our own knowledge to be superior."

—Rebecca Berube, Living Routes student, Huehuecoyotl, January 2010

"At first I thought that the classroom work was dull and pointless, but I realized quickly that I was learning a lot. By not only learning about leadership, consensus, and communication, but also getting to act on these lessons and use them to create a real, touchable, feasible goal, I feel like I really learned." —Emma Hutchens, Living Routes student, Huehuecoyotl, January 2010

Olympic-Sized Community

By Satyama Dawn Lasby

Two years ago I decided to take the plunge. That is, I decided to leave my corporate job in Vernon, British Columbia as the General Manager of the Chamber of Commerce and do exactly what I wanted to do. I wanted to live in community. I wanted to serve, experience unconditional love, and study meditation and yoga from authentic and traditional sources. I wanted to travel for a full year. At the end of all of that, I also wanted to live out a special dream: to live and work in Whistler, BC for the 2010 Olympics.

I have managed to do all of that, and coming out of the other side, I am now passionate about educating others about community and living sustainably.

To prepare myself for the time I was going to spend in India during my year of travel, I decided to live communally at a retreat centre in British Columbia. It was my first intentional community experience and a difficult one due to personality clashes with one of the owners and the mere fact that it was owned and not truly communal. The couple who owned it wanted to have several couples working the land in exchange for the living accommodation, but that vision wasn't in place at the time of my residence. It was still a retreat centre hosting wonderfully educational courses on self-development, but no one (other than the owners) lived there permanently.

I was one of about six volunteers who worked in exchange for food and accommodation. I learned a lot about communication through our daily meetings, based on the Findhorn Foundation model, in which we would plan out the day's work, food preparation, discuss how we were feeling, etc. I also learned about vegetarian cooking, composting, recycling, wind generation, and what it takes to run a retreat centre without a lot of resources. This experience prepared me for living at the Osho International Meditation Resort in India, and has helped make me the person I am today. That person, in this moment, is working for the 2010 Olympic Winter Games in Whistler, BC, and occasionally writing for magazines and teaching yoga classes.

My previous careers focused on event planning. As a person who lives their dreams, I wanted to work for the biggest event in the world. When I was done with my year of travel, I made my way to Whistler to make that dream a reality. Finding accommodation, let alone a like-minded community, is no easy task in Whistler. It is a tourist destination, so many people from all over the world live in shared houses, working for the winter season so they can enjoy skiing or snowboarding on a daily basis. After two forced short-term moves, I ended up in one of these shared houses due to its location near to the village, a "community" of sorts, but not a conscious one, with five Australians, two English, one Korean, one French, two Kiwis, and me, the only vegetarian, the only one who meditates, the only one who owns a home and a vehicle. It is a year like no other, where rents are at an all-time high at $1100/ month for a room, and landlords cash in on the number of people they put into a house that is shared.

One of the great things that happened in this house was the education of my housemates from all over the world. As a Canadian familiar with how Whistler functions as a resort community, I was able to see how the young people in this house learned about sorting and separating tin, plastic, glass, paper, cardboard, and compost. Whistler aspires to be a sustainable community, and because of its proximity to wildlife (bears, racoons, and other friendlies), the municipality puts the responsibility on the city's residents to bring their waste

352

to the depots, already sorted, instead of leaving it curbside. Until Whistler, none of the people in the house had ever sorted, or been responsible for the waste of 14 people and their guests. Reuseable shopping bags and more conscious buying choices happened organically as it quickly became apparent how much waste was produced in the house.

Synchronistically, I landed a job with the Resort Municipality of Whistler working for Whistler Live!, an arm of the RMOW designated to produce all of the entertainment for the Olympics and Paralympics. It was a dream job, with the added bonus of being the sustainability coordinator for the organization, aligning with the province's commitment to host the greenest games in history.

It was a seemingly odd work situation, as I, a communal, hippie yoga teacher, was now in the midst of the millions of dollars being spent to put on the games and entertain the masses. I went to work on my sustainability assignment in between trips to the recycling depot and Whistler's famous Re-Use-It Centre.

To eliminate bottled water in the village, Whistler Live! provided all staff, contractors, and our entertainers with stainless steel water bottles that they could keep and refill. As many as 50 artists and performers were in our green rooms at once. All catering was done with washable dishes so money would not be spent on disposables. Artists were educated about Whistler's sustainability procedures, and given a document the community is very proud of, Whistler2010, which

I, a communal, hippie yoga teacher, was now in the midst of the millions of dollars being spent to put on the games and entertain the masses.

was designed with Smart Growth principles and full input from the community. Whistler Live! was also instrumental in eliminating air pollutants from fireworks by removing the fireworks from the nightly "Fire and Ice" show.

My position with Whistler Live! was one with merit because of the educational aspect and ability to share Whistler's vision of a sustainable community with the world. The most educational element of living this dream, however, was learning how dreams change when they become reality—like fantasies lived-out, or like our feelings about things we want, once we get them. Dreams change, people change. I am living the dream, yet when interacting with thousands of people each day through the Olympics, I am also conscious of the work that needs to be done to really educate people on how to live with greater awareness of the impacts of lifestyle on the environment. One small group of people (the performers for Whistler Live! and our municipality staff) are being exposed to our good efforts to preserve the planet, but there are so many that could benefit from that same exposure, as I watch hundreds of people stroll down the village only to throw their Starbucks coffee cup in the garbage instead of taking the time to recycle it.

While I am fortunate to be paid to be living my dream, it also puts me in the position of knowing just how much is being spent on the games. The expenditures of the Olympics are not sustainable. There are so many ways that money could have been saved where it wasn't. In fact, it seemed like it was there to spend, and then spend more because government funding was easily presented. While working for the Olympics was an "old" dream lived out, I can't help thinking how much I have changed since taking the plunge. Where I may once have been fascinated by titles, money, and marketing, I am now happier, and much more conscious of excess. The excess use of any resource, especially money, is no longer acceptable to me, no matter what the cause. ❀

Satyama Dawn Lasby is a freelance writer and artist living in Whistler, British Columbia at the moment. Dedicated to discovering and teaching the way to the truth through meditation and yoga, she also likes to live in experimental situations. She can be reached at satyamadawn@gmail.com or found at www.meditationforathletes.com.

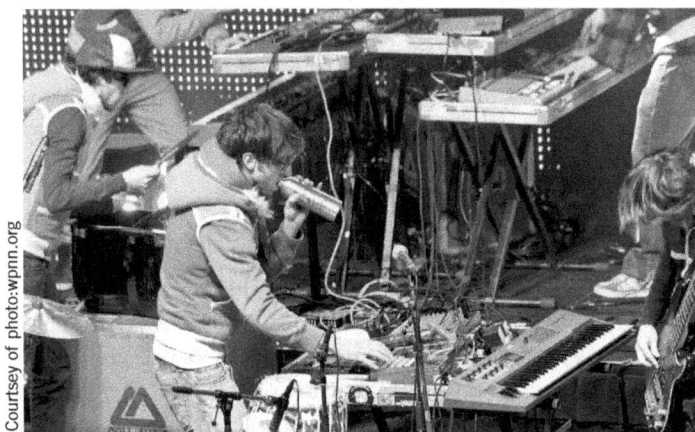

Misteur Valaire, one of the bands hired to entertain the masses during the 2010 Olympic Winter Games, drinks from stainless steel water bottles to prevent the purchase of plastic water bottles. Three bands per day were hired to perform, plus street performers, live artists, storytellers, and singer-songwriters.

Intentional "Colonies" and Tropical Sustainability

By Jon Kohl

Though Copenhagen negotiators wrangled and wrestled over cap-and-trade, technology transfer, mitigation funds, and other large-scale, multi-billion-dollar proposals to tackle climate change and move toward (energy) sustainability, they did not pay much heed to community transformation. Despite the lapse, many communities have transcended concern for merely their own environmental impact, and now reach regional and even international audiences with a sustainability message. Consider the ecovillage BedZED in England, Findhorn in Scotland, EcoVillage at Ithaca in New York, The Farm in Tennessee, Dancing Rabbit in Missouri, Lost Valley Educational Center in Oregon, or any of a host of others.

Despite the ascending role of intentional communities (ICs) in developed countries, intentional communities in developing countries require a different model for them to become both socially relevant and active promoters of sustainability.

In such countries, for ICs to be sustainability educators, they must offer more than educators, education centers, and a group of people dedicated to implementing sustainable technologies in their communities. In fact, the model often transplanted to developing countries makes such projects seem more like intentional colonies than intentional communities. And perhaps no country better demonstrates this phenomenon than Costa Rica.

By virtue of its high ecological attractiveness among foreign tourists and retirees alike, and its proximity to the United States, Costa Rica makes the perfect destination to study how development requires more than transplanting a successful northern model into southern waters where the concept of intentional community still strikes people as a foreign, perhaps even zany, idea.

The Intentional Colony

What then constitutes this transplanted model, the intentional colony, and why can it preclude sustainability education? The model exhibits the following characteristics, though any real IC may only exhibit some.

Strangers in a Strange Land

In Costa Rica we have several dozen ICs founded by foreigners and populated principally by foreigners, especially from the US.

Distant Shores

Foreigners often seek beaches, distant mountains, or secluded forest retreats, far from major population centers, to build their own "little paradises" as marketing materials often boast.

A Lot Different

As in the US, a common model to finance such communities is for one person or a group of partners to acquire a property and then subdivide it into heritable lots which they then sell to those who value the concept and can pay—most frequently foreigners. As site plans distribute lots along roads so that each landowner can enjoy a chunk of forest or beach frontage, lot layout inhibits resident interaction.

For the Rich and Mobile

Just as in the US, this model largely excludes those who cannot pay, and Costa Rica does not require low-income housing within IC projects. In fact, most municipalities have no master plan at all to influence their development.

Where Are the Locals?

Consequently, except for local caretakers or those who earned the beneficence of owners, Costa Ricans remain excluded from such projects.

Local Benefits for Foreign Members

Most well-intentioned ICs import quality sustainability and spiritual practices to Costa Rica. Communities here specialize in yoga, spirituality, biodynamic agriculture and permaculture, human potential, conservation, holistic healing, and other laudable perspectives. Some communities have innovated the use of biodigestors, tree houses, natural building technologies, and solar power. Yet many communities restrict these activities largely for their own members.

Furthermore, some communities cater almost exclusively to foreigners in marketing abovementioned services, partially because local populations do not yet appreciate the value of holistic cleanses, natural medicine, group meditation, or even nonconventional agriculture, and also because they could not afford such services in any event.

The English Way

The communities often operate mostly or exclusively in English (with some notable exceptions), and their websites are completely English-oriented to the United States or Europe. Last year I attended the first conference of intentional communities in Costa Rica. Everyone spoke English, while the only Costa

Rican participants were those who worked on the host farm.

Community educational materials are largely in English because, in general, most educational materials in environmental and sustainability matters are produced in the US with very few being adapted to the Latin American context. My wife is a professor at the University of Costa Rica in environmental education and interpretation, and her students regularly struggle to obtain educational material adapted to Costa Rican reality.

Hardware over Software

IC advertising often focuses on the more tangible and attractive tropical rainforests, solar panels, rows of organic tomatoes, and other aspects of community hardware. They much less advertise a community's capacity to resolve conflicts, cooperate in the management of community buildings, or make consensus-based decisions. My wife and I contemplated buying a lot in just such a community project where the developer (a great guy with great intentions) was selling an IC concept and the first time we potential buyers met each other was to settle lingering doubts before settling our down payments. We felt no sense of community, trust, or transparency. The developer's

lawyer even refused to meet with us. Consequently, and with the recession's dissuasions, the deal fell apart.

Intentional Colonies Make Sustainability Education Difficult

My assumption of sustainability in an IC context means that the IC nudges the region's place and people (not just its own property and its own people) toward sustainability. Otherwise the IC is little more than an intentional outpost, oasis, enclave, or colony. Some will argue that such well-intentioned communities assist foreigners in foreign lands to adopt more sustainable practices, and that the community itself, through wise land management and food production, is in fact sustainable with its concomitant educational value. Those definitions are fine and understandable, but to be generators of sustainability education, ICs must offer something more. Localization is key to sustainability and an IC can't promote localization if the locale doesn't benefit and integrate into the community's value chain.

Thus this environmentally sensitive model presents a hard sell for sustainability education, given its sociocultural, geographical, financial, and legal isolation, even though the colony serves its members and goals well. To be relevant to Costa Ricans or to locals anywhere in promoting sustainability, ICs need to take a different approach.

An Alternative Model Offers Solutions

Solutions are the better part of criticism. I am involved in an IC project, the Querencia Experimental Center for Carbon-Neutral Communities, that has studied the colony model and designed a new model that integrates an opposite approach to each point above, and hopefully when fully developed proves relevant to all Costa Rica and beyond.

Dion and Emilio represent an apt composition for Querencia's membership: the two hold one American and two Costa Rican passports.

355

Because intentional communities are still new to Costa Ricans, it has been challenging to convince Costa Ricans to join.

Composed Largely of Costa Ricans

Querencia starts out largely as a project of Costa Ricans with some foreign members who are committed to keep the project largely in Costa Rican middle-class hands. My criticism in this article is with community development models, not with individual foreigners.

Nearby Shores

For Querencia to be relevant to Costa Ricans, it must locate where most Costa Ricans live. Therefore we seek land within an hour and a half of the capital city. If our community locates beyond the distance a school bus would readily travel on a day visit, then we are too far.

A Lot Different from Lots

Our project must be accessible to middle-class professional Costa Ricans, a socioeconomic class, as in the US, that finds itself frequently left out of both assistance programs and commercial capital availability. Instead of a private corporation, the ecovillage portion of the Querencia Experimental Center may be managed by a cooperative owning the land and houses. Members own shares and build equity rather than own private lots.

Capitalization through Social Benefit

Private communities must capitalize through private means, thus raising costs and excluding Costa Ricans; a project that has high social benefit, our assumption goes, means that we can mix donor funding with private capital to finance our project. We also will provide social services, mainly educational, interpretive, touristic, training, and community outreach, as additional income streams.

Benefits for All Audiences

Our community will be the principal teaching tool for interpreting and educating about low-carbon and sustainable living. In a sense, the ecovillage is a living museum, and everyone who lives there necessarily contributes to the cooperative's business. Querencia has already formed an agreement with one Costa Rican-based school that offers sustainability courses for foreign university students and credit (www.earthedintl.org).

Spanish First

Spanish is the first language of Querencia. Our website is in English too because we are part of an international community to better leverage our social mission. We have also initiated discussions with a local university to develop a Costa Rican-centered curriculum for studying climate change and community.

Hardware and Software

Sustainability, just like a computer, requires both hardware and software to operate. Querencia thus focuses on building and energy technologies (inspired by Colombia's Las Gaviotas community) as much as the social and cultural techniques necessary to have a sustainable and functioning community (inspired by Mexico's Los Horcones community). In fact one of our founders is a Costa Rican psychologist who specializes in behaviorism and behavior change.

To summarize, the Querencia Experimental Center for Carbon-Neutral Communities is a nonprofit organization that researches and promotes sustainability techniques specifically adapted to developing country communities, both rich and poor, rural and urban, intentional and non-intentional. The ecovillage will be in effect the center's laboratory (in a similar way to B. F. Skinner's classic *Walden II* community), accompanied by a robust interpretive program (three of us founders are professionals in heritage interpretation and environmental education) that aims at a wide variety of audiences within Costa Rica.

Not without Its Challenges

Though the project has not yet capitalized, we already grapple with a number of challenges inherent in the model.

While the concept has attracted significant foreign interest, because ICs are still new to Costa Ricans, it has been challenging to convince Costa Ricans to join. This places us into the semi-vicious cycle of needing money and members to get land, and needing land to gain the credibility necessary to get money and members from within the country.

A corollary is that somehow we must maintain a balance between interested foreigners and Costa Ricans, to ensure the project remains largely Costa Rican.

Because spending capacity is lower for Costa Ricans than foreigners, we still have the challenge of financing houses. While we feel confident the concept and the NGO can garner exterior funding for land, for nonprofit projects, and even for the visitor center, no donor will likely contribute to our houses.

We strive to use transparent, participatory legal entities such as an association and a cooperative, but we also feel a strong pull to use a less transparent corporation that can much more rapidly get things done. Likely the secret is to forge the right mix of legal entities.

We hope in addition to work with many institutions throughout Costa Rica, especially its ICs, to better leverage and adapt their vast well of experience to Latin American society. Costa Rica has already committed itself to carbon neutrality by 2021, so if its ICs can help it reach that goal, then we can truly demonstrate the value of intentional communities, not colonies, in a post-carbon world. ❋

Jon Kohl (www.jonkohl.com) works as an international consultant in protected area management as well as a founding co-member of Querencia (www.querencia.co.cr).

Towards a Seventh Generation

By Understanding Israel, M.A. Education

There are many things to be shared with the Four Colors of humanity in our common destiny as one with our Mother the Earth.
—Resolution of the Fifth Annual Meetings of the Traditional Elders Circle, 1980[1]

The Six Nations Iroquois Confederacy mandated that its chiefs consider the influence of their actions and decisions on the seventh generation yet to be born.[2] What do our children retain from our dedication to sustainability as a community?

In my intentional community, we practiced organic gardening, recycling, seed preservation, water quality enhancement and conservation, and a variety of other earth-friendly habits. But what sustainable practices did our children retain and take to the next generation? I decided as part of my work towards a Doctorate in Educational Leadership to ask them.

They are grown now, with the youngest being 21 and the oldest 46. Via Facebook, email, and phone conversations, I queried 12 of the children who represented a cross-section of the youth I helped care for during my 26 years in our community. Ten replied.

I used this definition of sustainability graciously lent to me by Native Hawaiian elder, Puanani Rogers: "Aloha 'aina, malama' aina, ahupua'a style living... Aloha 'aina simply means to love and respect the land, make it yours and claim stewardship for it. Malama 'aina means to care for and nurture the land so it can give back all we need to sustain life for ourselves and our future generations, and, an ahupua'a is an ancient concept of resource uses and management based on families living in a division of land that connects the mountains to the reefs and the sea."[3]

Our children were raised in an educational environment based loosely on the principles of John Holt.[4] The schooling was classified as "experimental" status under the laws then in place affecting homeschooled children in Washington State.[5]

I discovered that all the mothers who responded (and one grandmother) were teaching the next generations about gardening, recycling, and careful selection of healthy foods. All the mothers felt they were not doing enough. However, I am sure they are also feeling overwhelmed with responsibilities of young children, husbands, and jobs. They are definitely doing their part as an integral link to the future of our planet.

In contrast, the men who responded recounted that it takes a lot of work to prepare the ground, plant the seeds, maintain organic practices, and finally harvest the bounty. In reflection, I wonder if perhaps we depended upon the men in our agrarian community for a heavier workload? However, the good news is that most of the men, along with most of the women, were taking responsibility to recycle, and were practicing resourcefulness by limiting their consumption of products that negatively alter our planet. The men also often mentioned a factor that cannot be easily measured: the inspiration to create a sustainable life based on the simplicity of childhood experiences in general. Tam Hunt, now an attorney with his own company Community Renewable Solutions LLC, which is focused on environmental practices, reflected: "Seeds are planted at all stages of life and they bloom

> *What sustainable practices did our children retain and take to the next generation? I decided to ask them.*

(continued on p. 77)

TOWARDS A SEVENTH GENERATION

(continued from p. 45)

at unpredictable times."

I want to encourage those who now are working on their first generation as a community. I hope my research, in some small way, can assure you that your dedication to sustainability will make a difference on this planet. The time spent teaching your children now to love and respect the earth will help us all move towards that seventh generation. ✿

Understanding Israel received her Masters in Education through the Antioch First People's Program at Muckleshoot Tribal College in 2008 at the age of 64. She is currently a second year student at Argosy University Seattle, working towards a Doctorate in Educational Leadership. She received the Southern California Motion Picture Council Humanitarian Award for her help in mentoring over 168 children in her home as an educator in a community in the Cascade Mountains of the Pacific Northwest. She received her B.A. in Education from Pacific Lutheran Univeristy and taught in the ghettos of Harlem, Washington DC, and Appalachia before joining and living in her alternative community for 26 years. Understanding Israel is currently active as a Native American storyteller in the Pacific Northwest and as Operations Manager for the National Association for American Indian Children and Elders. She can be reached at ravenspuppets@yahoo.com.

References:

1 Famous Quotes. (n.d.). *Indigenous People.* Retrieved January 21, 2009, from (www.indigenouspeople.net/quotes.htm)

2 Seventh Generation Fund for Indian Development—Indigenous non-profit organization. (n.d.). *Seventh Generation Fund for Indian Development—Indigenous non-profit organization.* Retrieved January 26, 2010, from www.7genfund.org.

3Puanani Rogers, Ho`okipa Network, Lihu`e, Kaua'i, Hawaii, www.sustainablemeasures.com/Sustainability/DefinitionsCommunity.html

4Prast, K. (n.d.). Homeschooling movement is growing, so is "unschooling"—Practically Speaking. *Blogs—MyCommunityNOW—Blogs.* Retrieved January 13, 2010, from blogs.brookfieldnow.com/practically_speaking/archive/2009/01/08/homeschooling-movement-is-growing-so-is-quot-unschooling-quot.aspx.

5Lowry, H.. M. 1991; Washington Homeschool Organization. (n.d.). *Washington Homeschool Organization.* Retrieved January 26, 2010, from www.washhomeschool.org.

Hippie Communes—Past Present and Future. (n.d.). *60s & Further: A Spiritual Garden that Rocks.* Retrieved January 25, 2010, from http://60sfurther.com/Communes.htm

Michelle R Davis. (2006, December). "Unschooling" Stresses Curiosity More Than Traditional Academics. Education Week, 26(16), 8. Retrieved January 24, 2010, from Education Module. (Document ID: 1184796981).

Ethan Hughes

Busted, Almost Bludgeoned, Possibly Broke
Hard Lessons from the Trenches of Sustainability Education

By Lee Icterus

To counterbalance some of the more upbeat stories shared in these pages, our pseudonymous author offers a few cautionary tales. According to Lee, "these are subjective snapshots, simplifications of multidimensional realities, and could be told in many different ways. In real life, even the 'villains' in these tales, from the decaffeinated code enforcement officer to the would-be-but-weren't homicidal maniacs to the doomsaying finance manager, have many redeeming qualities. They were simply parts of a bigger picture—the kind of picture that could happen to anyone."

Busted.

After 14 years of engaging in what we considered victimless crimes, we had to confront the plain fact: the gig was up. Ours had not been the usual victimless crimes—enjoyment of certain illicit substances, kinky sexual behavior among consenting adults, taking postage stamps to outer space, etc. We had transgressed not through overindulgence but through voluntary poverty and simplicity, planet care, and permaculture. We had been trying to educate for sustainability, but the law was not on our side.

We knew we'd been violating both building codes and zoning laws. We'd built multiple dwellings on a rural piece of land zoned for only one single-family residence. We'd obtained no building permits, and used construction methods and materials that conflicted with the codes and never would have gained official approval in the first place. We'd installed no flush toilets, no septic systems, no heavy-duty driveway with firetruck turnaround. We'd built among the trees, rather than cutting them down around dwellings as required in this forestry zone. We had been flying under the radar.

The founder had reassured us that the building code and zoning people would never visit, because they would never stray more than 30 minutes from their coffee pots. Because their office in town was a 45 minute drive away, we felt safe. Then several things happened that left us vulnerable: a key individual left the community on particularly bad terms; we adver-

tised locally for an open staff position; and the county planning department hired a new enforcement officer apparently less addicted to coffee and more attentive to the local newspaper classifieds. In a sequence of events that still remains mysterious, the unthinkable happened: both our infrastructure and our community received what amounted to "death sentences."

The motive behind our crimes had been simple: a commitment to educating the public about sustainability. Our research and education center aimed to train responsible "world citizens," especially those intending to work with local people in less-developed countries to help them meet basic needs for food, water, shelter, and fuel more self-reliantly. Instead of consuming the disproportionate amount of resources that average North Americans do, we wanted to take no more than our share based on equitable distribution throughout the world. And instead of plundering the planet and living at the expense of other creatures and ecosystems, we wanted to find balance with our environment. We tried to utilize primarily local renewable resources, at less than the rate of replacement, aided by appropriate "do-it-yourself" technologies and ecological gardening and forestry methods. We didn't believe in "out of sight, out of mind." In fact, to teach people to recognize and take responsibility for the results of their consumer choices, we forbade any trash or recycling from leaving our 40 acres: all materials brought onto our land were used, reused, or refashioned on site, or put into our own unauthorized dump at the corner of our property.

Limiting our population to a single family, as the zoning laws required, would have thwarted our strong educational mission, which depended on a community of unrelated adults and the ability to host additional interns and course participants. We needed places for all of these people to sleep, eat, and congregate, and we also wanted our approaches to creating infrastructure to be replicable in any "third world" situation. Plus, we had almost no money, and didn't believe in debt or even have access to loans. This meant using almost exclusively discarded and local resources. We built most dwellings for no more than a few hundred dollars (less than the amount building permits and inspections alone would have cost us, had we built legally). Little of our lumber was inspected or stamped, and few of our other building materials (wattle and daub, straw, wood shavings, cob, etc.) even had standards to measure up to—our county banned them entirely from use in construction. In the interests of nutrient recycling, we also broke the laws regarding human waste and greywater.

We believed in respecting the limits of our local and global ecosystems, with an approach to materials usage and economics that was replicable, indefinitely continuable, and socially equitable across cultures and across generations. Unfortunately, our attempts to model "third world conditions" and live sustainably within them—to make best use of what was around us, put permaculture ideas into practice, and live by "natural law"—were themselves not sustainable, due to the enforcement of human law.

How did it turn out? To oversimplify a bit: we hired a land use consultant and an attorney, found some fortunate legal loopholes to allow us to maintain our existing population levels on the land, tore down most of the old structures as we raised money for and built new ones, compromised in many areas, redefined some of our goals, and kept an educational focus while transitioning from an aspiring "third world sustainability site" to an aspiring "first world sustainability site."

The take-home lessons? Consider carefully before locating your activities in a part of the country in which they may be illegal—and be prepared to deal with, and challenge when necessary, the anti-permacultural rules, regulations, and laws that stifle efforts to embody and teach sustainability.

"I'll hit you over a head with a sledgehammer!"

This death threat was the final straw in one carpenter's troubled tenure at our community. He received an eviction notice later the same day. But if we'd been wise, we never would have taken him on.

We endured a similar trial with another individual, who threatened to blow a hole as big as a basketball in the middle of a fellow staff member.

The reasons for provocation (an attempt to hold an individual accountable to community agreements, and a rivalry between two dogs, respectively), while minor in themselves, seemed beside the point. In addition to their capacity for making violent threats when feeling insecure, the two individuals shared a common trait: we'd accepted them into our group because we felt we desperately needed certain work done, rather than because we felt comfortable with them as people. And why did we desperately need that work done? Because we had an already-advertised and enrolled sustainability education program to run.

If we didn't complete our new dormitory before the start of the summer, our summer students would have nowhere to stay, as the county had declared our previous student housing illegal.

Unless we could find some help, fast, we would need to cancel the program. To the overstressed, understaffed building crew, Josef seemed like a godsend (or Gaiasend). He had met a couple staff members at a party and asked if he could visit. When he arrived the next day, they drafted him into pounding some nails. It turned out he liked to pound nails, and had no pressing other commitments. While he displayed some disturbing tendencies (an inordinately loud voice; a fondness for telling anyone who would listen how to trick pay phones into letting you dial anywhere for free; a self-reported history as a spy for several different governments; a freely acknowledged status as an "illegal foreigner" with, nevertheless, what he described as a free pass from any police department in the country; a cigarette addiction that, increasingly, did not respect "no smoking" zones; and a strangely "wired" energy accompanied by a long-sleeves-only clothing policy, which became significant to us only in retrospect), he seemed to many group members like a relatively harmless eccentric who posed little risk. Besides, we really, really needed his help.

That was until, eventually, it was not his help that seemed indispensable, but his absence. Unfortunately, he then inflicted further damage by convincing a friend of our group to take him in, stealing from our friend's neighbors, and finally fleeing the area before his status as a drug addict and dealer came to light.

In the other case, we had welcomed Glen into our group as part of a "package deal." His wife worked quite effectively in an administrative department essential to our success as an educational center. In fact, we had waived our normal intake process, and a representative from our group had apparently "guaranteed" them spots in our community, if they would only move to our site and work with us. They arrived with a large moving van (itself a bit of a red flag in our simple-living community) and while Glen's wife caused no problems, Glen himself immediately showed his capacity for generating conflict. Knowing that none of us is without blemish or fault, we decided to try it out anyway. Some of us had misgivings, growing from minor to major, but Glen was a many-sided, often likeable person, despite a seemingly lackadaisical work attitude, an unpredictable (sometimes alcohol-fueled) temper, and, eventually, an obvious capacity for lying. The bottom line: our organization desperately needed the work that his wife was providing, in order to fill our educational mission. Or we thought we did, until, the death threat.

In both cases, we managed to survive the departure of the formerly indispensable individuals. In the latter case, Glen nearly sunk the organization on his way out—he'd planted a certain illegal weed on our land, which came within a few yards of being discovered by the authorities. As a parting gift, he also threatened us with a $25,000 lawsuit (for breach of a contract that existed, fortunately, only in his mind).

The take-home lessons? Among many others: *do* look a gift horse in the mouth, and know that desperate measures sometimes yield desperate results. Accepting individuals into a group in the interest of expedience to serve one's educational mission can provide unanticipated lessons of its own. If you are lucky, you will dodge the bullet.

Our finance "team"?

"Sparring partners" was more like it. One was a died in-the-wool optimist, another an intractable pessimist. When they described our financial situation, one of them didn't see the glass as half full and the other as half empty. One of them saw the glass as three-quarters full, and the other as (at least) three-quarters empty. Was it the same glass? We could never know.

Had our economic footing been inarguably sound, we would not have been confronting this dilemma of figuring out whom to believe and what to do. For years we had struggled to make ends meet financially. Our commitment to serving the public through educational programs had kept us going through thick and thin, but our chronically understaffed and underfunded organization alternated between minimum wage salaries and layoffs, and we never knew what the next financial cycle would bring. "Job security" was not in our vocabulary. Only people who could afford to commit themselves to our mission, knowing that it meant never earning much, would stay around for long. We relied heavily on intern and volunteer labor to keep our programs going—a system that seemed to work, for those involved in it, but which hardly matched the model of a thriving, growing business.

Unfortunately, our lack of adequate resources also left each employee overworked, and often too overwhelmed to learn much about other areas by spending time outside of a specific realm of responsibility. For example, the office staff almost never made it out to the vegetable gardens—and yet, because of our organizational structure, the office workers had most of the say over how we operated as a business, including funding and staffing levels for work on the land. At the same time, those involved in on-the-ground sustainability activities stayed so busy with their hands-on, land-based work, and with guiding and teaching interns, students, and visitors, that little of their energy or patience remained for engaging in the administrative or business side of things.

That the finance team itself couldn't come up with a clear assessment of our economic health only added to the disarray. As a result, we each heard what we were most predisposed to hear and believe. The pessimist's voice tended to be loudest, and when his own family's finances started looking grim, and his wife needed to get a job in town, he seemed to transfer that reality onto the rest of the group. When we created a list of the group's challenges during our annual retreat, he wrote "EXPECTING THE ORGANIZATION TO BE YOUR SUGAR DADDY" in large caps on the white board. He saw staff members as burdens on the group, and believed that the rest of us (like his wife), with the exception of himself and a bare-bones crew, should also get jobs in town.

How could our educational programs and service mission possibly function without anyone to implement them? To many of us, this did not appear to be a question that he asked or cared about. In fact, he believed that, with the world and economy "going down," we'd soon be confronting a far different reality anyway, one in which money played no role at all and in which small groups of people would need mainly to watch out for themselves.

For most employees, already working for minimal compensation and with too much responsibility, his message lowered morale. Meanwhile, his counterpart on the finance team asserted (less stridently) that we were actually outperforming our budget and needed to maintain our current staffing in order to bring in necessary income, fulfill our mission, and continue our activities, with all their positive local and non-local effects.

Those of us with a more optimistic, hopeful bent saw the pessimist's rants as reflecting his own worldview rather than our situation, and persisted in staying in our jobs and moving forward with our departments' plans. But the fault line in our finance depart-

The founder had reassured us that the building code and zoning people would never visit, because they would never stray more than 30 minutes from their coffee pots.

ment spread to the rest of the staff. We lost at least one highly qualified employee, who decided to get a secure job in town rather than deal with the apparent uncertainty of working for our group. With encouragement of several administrative staff who believed in privatizing different parts of our organization's work, another employee decided to become an entrepreneur instead, resulting in further splits in subsequent years as we tried to reconcile coexisting public and private systems of growing food and offering education. Staff and resident turnover soon reached unprecedented levels.

Lack of unity about how to approach work that was deeply satisfying to some, but not all of us; the economic demands of combining innovative sustainability education programs with attempts to "walk our talk"; the financial challenges, in the midst of an ailing consumeristic culture, of serving those on an alternative path, who often had few funds to spare; varying perceptions of the larger world, its direction, and what "sustainability" within that world meant; clashing personal psychological makeups; escalating staff turnover...all of these begged the question: Is it possible to educate others effectively about sustainability if your group itself has not found a way to live and work together sustainably?

In the end, despite the challenges, educational programs continued, thanks to valiant, self-sacrificing efforts by countless individuals over the course of many years, but key questions remained unresolved and future prospects uncertain.

The take-home lessons? Running homegrown eco-oriented educational programs is not for the faint of heart. Fear and a scarcity mentality can significantly hobble work that relies on hope for creating a better world. Unlikely things—some might call them miracles—do happen (otherwise, our group would never have come into being)—but only if given the opportunity. And healthy, well-functioning community may prove to be the most essential ingredient in learning and teaching about a sustainable world. ❋

Lee Icterus writes nonfiction (and, some would say, fiction) from the backwoods of America and the heart of community.

VI
FINDING RESILIENCE IN COOPERATIVE CULTURE

The Nature of Our Work

By Stacie Whitney

Community living, Non-Violent Communication (NVC), process work, and conflict resolution become buzzwords when you live at a place like Findhorn (an international holistic education center and spiritual community/ecovillage of more than 300 people located on the coast of northern Scotland). I've spent years living, studying, and working in groups on everything from consensus decision making to holistic health.

I recently spent two weeks visiting my family in the States, and all of it—all of my expertise and practice—flew right out the window when I revisited my old family dynamics. The temper I thought I'd left behind bubbled up from its place of deep rest. The wall I've been working so hard to chisel away day after day rebuilt itself within hours, and fortified itself with an extra layer of bricks. Years of self-growth and improvement were suddenly nothing but words and concepts as I reverted to my old patterns, dynamics, and lifestyle choices. I heard myself responding to questions that my parents asked me with mere grunts, and I even discovered one gorgeous sunny day that I'd locked myself in our room (my husband was witness to this experience), in an ever-so-teenage display of emotional shutdown.

On return to Findhorn, I've slowly been able to chisel the wall back down to a place where I can take responsibility and apologize for my actions. But with the perspective of distance comes the unavoidable question: How do we translate all of this work that we do in community out into the rest of the world? Because if we don't, then why are we doing the work in the first place? In other words, can we make the transition from "I" to the greater "We"?

This question has huge implications for the communities movement—not only in interpersonal relationships and group consciousness, but also in being demonstrations and training centers for the rest of the world. We can be as low-impact and carbon-neutral as we want, but if it doesn't translate into a formula that empowers visitors to make shifts in their own lives, then we are deluding ourselves into thinking that we are "being the change."

I run a semester study abroad program here at Findhorn, entitled "The Human Challenge of Sustainability." And indeed it is! Often students come here expecting us to have all the answers and be the vision of zero-carbon perfection. What they inevitably learn is that we are striving, and it is an ongoing journey. If we "reach" the goal, then perhaps we have not set our sights far enough ahead. Our aim is to empower young people to confront the challenges in the world today, and to work toward sustainable solutions, using different approaches, worldviews, and awareness than originally created the situation. So while we do show them our wind turbines and explain how they provide us with enough energy to sell some back to the grid, we also work with them to be creative about their own energy usage when they return home. We are not teaching the methods, we are teaching the thinking that brought us to discover this method for ourselves.

How we view the world, and our role in it, is the keystone to positive global change. I've recently been contemplating the world situation in light of changing worldviews. While there is a pungent whiff of hope in the air on the tail of the Obama Inauguration, it is important to keep in mind what it is that invites us to hope in the first place. Obama represents change, a divergence from old patterns of thinking, and yes, even a bit of idealism. This combination of attributes adds up to empowerment.

The times I am closest to, and most in-tune with my family,

are when I refuse to believe the stories I learned in all those years about who got more attention and who played what roles in our dynamics. The reason I fell back into old patterns on my recent trip was that I forgot that I am allowed to think in a different way. One of my greatest strengths is seeing one situation with unlimited viewpoints. And this is where I can meet an old stagnant dynamic head-on. We can all do this, if we can accept that change is not only inevitable, but it is also *good*.

We will not prevent global climate change by converting all electricity sources to wind turbines. We will, however, halt it, if we can use our deep, intuitive, creative selves to continually evolve, adapt, and create according to what is needed and what is available. With each month that passes here at Findhorn, I become clearer that this is the work we do so well here.

I will not have lasting peace and contentment in my personal and family life if I stick to old patterns and habits. It is this "out-of-the-box" thinking, which so many of us have been accused of, that is so desperately needed at this stage. If we limit ourselves to using only a few established methods, then we are allowing ourselves to be stuck in a process of repetitive, limited thinking. And now, more than ever, is a time for the new. What we are hoping to spread is a fire for rapid, creative, urgent, and beautiful change. ❀

Stacie Whitney, M.S., is an environmental educator and writer with an ardor for positive perceptual shift as a change agent in today's world. She has traveled, worked, adventured, and lived on both sides of the Atlantic, on both land and sea, and now lives in Findhorn with her husband. For more information on the Findhorn Foundation and community, please visit www.findhorn.org; for more on the Human Challenge of Sustainability, see www.findhorncollege.com.

Left page: The Nature at Findhorn Beach. This page top: Findhorn Community Semester (FCS) students in the field discussing their worldviews. Middle: Labrynth at Findhorn Beach. Bottom: FCS students enjoying Findhorn dunes with wind turbines in the background.

All photos courtesy of Stacie Whitney

How Ecology Led Me to Community

By Chris Roth

In Communities, *we like to feature personal stories about real experiences, rather than abstract theories or dry analyses. In this article, our editor plunges into the fun. He asks that you imagine listening to the following story around a crackling campfire, and remember that "I" is just a figure of speech, and might just as easily be "you"...*

I'd never been one who tried too hard to conform, but my marching to a different drummer became decidedly more pronounced in high school. There are various ways to describe what happened: you could say that trees started to speak to me, or that long-distance running connected me with the natural world in new ways, or that an earth-centered spiritual awakening led me to find that that "God," increasingly elusive in church, resided in the outdoors instead. Whatever the explanation, I started to take my guidance from ecologically-oriented voices that seemed at times audible only to me, but which spoke clear as crystal and left little doubt about what I needed to do.

One might think that "marching to one's own drummer" would lead one away from community, into isolation and even hermithood. But in fact this particular drummer led me invariably toward community, which I discovered to be inextricably intertwined with ecology. Although I was marching without a map, with little idea where I'd end up, the outcomes seem inevitable in retrospect.

Here are just a few of the off-beat marching orders I received and the mysterious places they took me:

"Avoid Cars!"

I had never liked cars. As a young child, I had to be coaxed to get into them, and I never experienced that automotive fascination that many boys develop. I disliked the noise, the fumes, the confinement, the danger, and, as I learned more about them, their other impacts (ecological, social, economic, political). In the wake of the mid-'70s oil crisis, I wrote an editorial in my high school newspaper inveighing against excessive car use. Most of my classmates, meanwhile, eagerly anticipated and then celebrated the day when they were allowed to drive and own a car. I walked, biked, ran, and tried to stay out of mo-

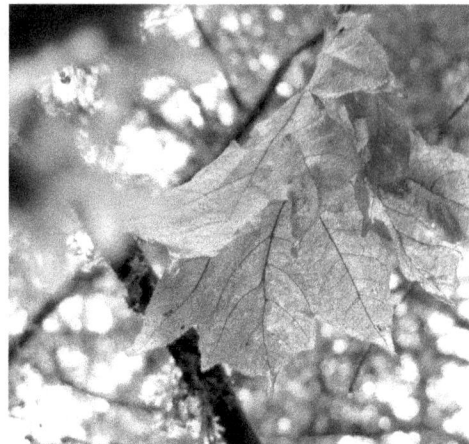

tor vehicles. The drummer I was marching to told me that the world could not sustain them. At the time, it seemed like a potentially lonely path.

But as I continued my education and explored different ways of living, my resolution to avoid the need for a private car produced unexpected results. The best way I could see to be free of vehicle dependence was to live and work in the same place—better yet, to seek out ways of living that seamlessly combined living and working in direct relationship with the land. (My drummer had also told me that, despite my suburban roots, revelation was to be found rurally.)

With the ability to be car-free in my daily life as a top priority influencing every decision, I have spent most of my adult years living and working together with others in land-based intentional communities and on small organic family farms. In the modern world, rural survival on one's own or even in a nuclear family can almost require a private motorized vehicle. But joining with others to create a local economy on a piece of land reduces the need to leave it, and makes combined trips and shared vehicles feasible. I did in fact eventually acquire a car, which I use occasionally (hopefully for good causes, including cultivating community connections beyond our 87 acres), but upon which I have never depended for my livelihood.

Now, in addition to gardening and helping develop my community's land as an educational center and nature sanctuary, I also telecommute to my other job (crafting a magazine out of other people's words—except when, as in the current case, my own bubble out in possibly overwhelming abundance). None of these essential activities requires a car. I sometimes go weeks without getting into one—whereas I bicycle every day, both around our own land and into the neighboring forest. I do not miss those hours stuck in traffic—in fact, I never even had to experience them. Instead, I am happy to have spent my life among pedestrians, and discovered community in the process.

"Stop Watching Television!"

My drummer sometimes lacked subtlety, and cast things in black and white that did in fact possess a few shades of gray. By the end of high school, I had identified television as one of the key elements keeping people detached from real life, out of touch with their inner selves, separated from one another, and cut off from the natural world. In my view, it was entirely evil,

and I had fantasies of some kind of cosmic pulse that would simultaneously incinerate all televisions and force people to start actually living again. (Since then, I've decided to relax my judgments and cut Mr. Rogers, at least, a little slack. I know that there is, in fact, some "good stuff" on television, though not enough to make me want to have one in my life.) I resolved to be TV-free once I left home—a resolution I have kept. At the time, this seemed like another lonely-making, solitary choice.

It turned out to be anything but that. Not owning or watching television propelled me into a multitude of television-less experiences among people who were also looking for something more real. Neither my inner nor outer explorations during and after college could have happened in the same way in an environment featuring a television—they were simply incompatible with a mesmerizing image- and noise-making machine being anywhere within sight or earshot. I lived outside, worked with Native Americans, learned to garden, and ultimately settled into a rewarding, TV-free life on farms and in intentional communities. In community, homemade culture and direct personal experience have proven so much more satisfying than manufactured culture and vicarious experience that television has never even tempted me. I've discovered that the world of birds living all around us here in the country, in three dimensions and surround-sound, fascinates me more than could anything on a screen. I've also learned to play the guitar, an almost endless source of do-it-oneself entertainment, often even better when shared with others.

Saying "no" to television made it possible for me to eventually say "yes" to community. As long as I have community in my life, I am staying unplugged (unless, for example, it's for a large-group Inauguration viewing at the local organic eatery, or for a Fred Rogers tribute show watched for old times' sake at my parents' house).

"Eat Low on the Food Chain"

Once again, that nonconformist, earth-minded drummer put a bee in my bonnet during high school, in the form of a vegetarian friend who urged me to read Frances Moore Lappé's *Diet for a Small Planet*. Once I had started thinking about food—its origins, its impacts, its larger implications—I could not retreat back into ignorance or not caring. I became the sole vegetarian

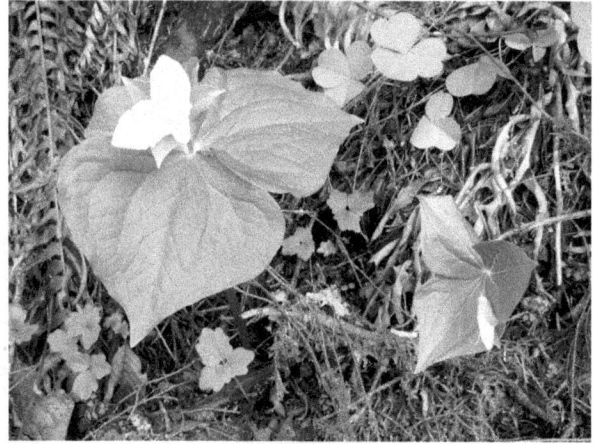

in my family and one of only two I knew in my school. This looked like another surefire path toward social isolation.

Since then, I have gone through a number of different phases, often for many years at a stretch: ovo-lacto-vegetarianism, situationally-dictated omnivory, pure veganism combined with a commitment to organic food, modified veganism, all-organic-mostly-vegetarianism-with-occasional-fish-or-fowl-thrown-in, etc. However, I have never returned to a standard American diet, and my food choices (tending toward the macrobiotic vegan much of the time, and the sustainably grown all of the time) would be considered strange by most people.

In the communities I've lived in, by contrast, my food choices are not strange—sometimes, especially in the presence of raw foodists, they seem downright middle-of-the-road. In these communities, we've eaten a significant portion of our own, homegrown whole foods—especially vegetables and fruits—and seen food as having not only health and spiritual but also political and ecological implications. Eating in ways that minimize our ecological footprints aligns us with the global community, and brings us together as a local community as well. My "small planet" food choices, far from isolating me, have helped me find communities in which I share common values with others.

"Read and Write Consciously or Not at All"

At a certain point in my education, I realized that, even though I'd dispensed with the unreality of television, I was still living mostly vicariously, through words. I had read about many more things than I'd ever experienced. I had learned how to write but felt I had little of substance to write about: I was passionately—and tiresomely—familiar only with the labyrinthine workings of my own mental circuitry. Limited by my academically-bound situation, and out of touch with almost everything outside of it, I realized that I had fled from the world of feeling and experience into a world of word-dominated thinking.

I decided to take a fast from the written word. For an entire summer, I read nothing (except for interpretive signs on Cape

Before reading or writing anything, I tried to gauge whether it would bring me closer to understanding the actual nature of life and the world, or whether it was just human-generated distraction, overintellectualized delusion, or philosophy divorced from the earth.

Cod National Seashore and an American Youth Hostel guidebook) and wrote nothing. I focused instead on my and others' feelings (even if unexpressed) and on the land around me, unmediated by words and without other distractions. I began a process of immersion learning in the language of the natural world, and in my own feelings and relationships within that world. I joined a school that lived, learned, slept, and woke outside every day, exploring the vast areas of wild America to which my suburban upbringing had never exposed me. Before reading or writing anything (once I broke my fast), I tried to gauge whether it would bring me closer to understanding the actual nature of life and the world, or whether it was just human-generated distraction, mass-produced entertainment, overintellectualized delusion, or philosophy divorced from the earth. If it was any of the latter, I skipped it. Like television, irrelevant words would have taken me away from, rather than toward, the kind of integrated ecological life I envisioned. I recognized that words could distract as well as communicate. I returned to reading and writing only cautiously, and, to the best of my ability, consciously.

Since then, my involvement with words has always been a byproduct of my life, rather than something defining my actual reality. In my first few years of college, being wrapped up in words had isolated me. Initially, backing away from words isolated me even more. But it also opened me up to the real world, a prerequisite to finding real community. Like freedom from television, it allowed me to experience new situations more fully, open my senses more completely to the natural world, and make actual connections with people. Rather than creating imaginary situations on paper (or in a computer hard drive, or in cyberspace), I found that I could discover and build real relationships. I was also able to recognize the limitations of human language and tune in more fully to the language of the land and its creatures. I experienced both human and non-human community in ways that most books I'd read had at best only hinted at, and that I could never have described beforehand except in the most general, theoretical terms.

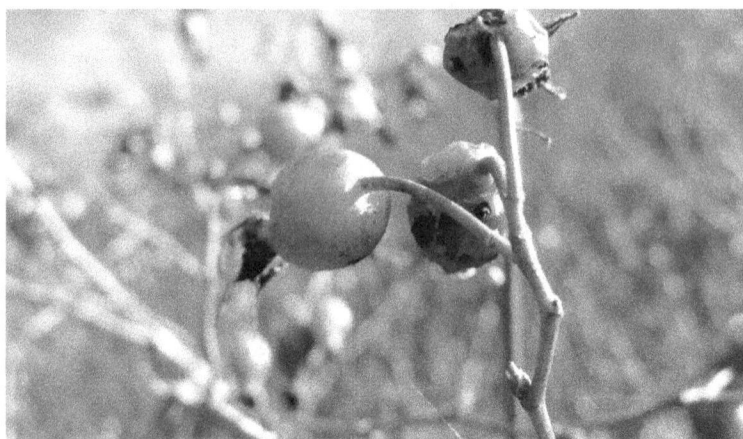

"Get Back to the Land!"

Getting back to the land is not something that most people born and raised in a New York City suburb ever do. That path hadn't even occurred to me during most of my formative years, since I'd had the impression that farmers and rural people were "dumb"—that's why they lived in the country. No, I hadn't actually met anyone fitting this description, or ever lived in the country or on a farm myself, but from what I could gather from the media and from word on the street, rural people talked slowly, did boring physical work, inbred, and chewed tobacco, all sure signs of non-intelligence. In other words, blind prejudice and ignorance kept me from ever aspiring to rural life.

This all changed, in several different phases, as my drummer became more insistent. First, local wild edible weeds caught my interest. Then the notion grabbed me of not only running and bicycling outdoors, but living outdoors. My traveling environmental education program got me used to being outside almost all the time, and also familiarized me with some of this continent's original outdoor livers, whose endangered cultures still survived to a degree. I decided I wanted to live like a Native American, and, when I had a chance, I acted on that desire, moving to a reservation for a year and a half and becoming the only white employee in a center for developmentally disabled Hopis. While there, I received a further marching order (channeled through a Hopi client of the center): I needed to learn to grow my own food. This led me to study organic gardening, which created a role for me to fulfill once I ended up going "back to the land" via organic farms and intentional communities. I also started to study local ecologies, especially plants and birds, allowing me to contribute in other realms of eco-education.

While those voices beckoning me to live in more direct relationship with the land seemed at first to be promising a lonely, socially marginalized existence, the exact opposite turned out to be the case. Each phase of my entry into more integrated ecological living brought me into new kinds of community.

From what I could gather from the media and from word on the street, rural people talked slowly, did boring physical work, inbred, and chewed tobacco. In other words, blind prejudice and ignorance kept me from ever aspiring to rural life.

Some, like the Hopi Center and the organic farms I worked on, were "unintentional" community, but community nonetheless. The intentional communities in which I've settled have been rural and committed to education, thereby developing much larger extended communities beyond their own boundaries. I've never had so little interaction with others as I did in my last couple years in the heart of urban/suburban civilization, and I've never had so much human interaction as I've had way out in the country, becoming rural folk myself, enjoying being connected to the land together with others through organic gardening and other forms of immersion in the landscape. Getting away from human and civilized distractions has helped me discover not only the natural world and how dependent we all are on it, but, surprisingly, the world of people as well.

"Focus on Life, Not on Money"

I grew up in a family that had enough money—not too much, but enough to meet our basic needs. Most of the people in our town, however, had significantly more material wealth than they actually needed. This did not prevent them from striving for more, and transferring that orientation toward money and things to their offspring. My parents instilled different values in me, reinforced as I grew up by poets like William Wordsworth:

The world is too much with us; late and soon,
Getting and spending, we lay waste our powers:
Little we see in Nature that is ours;
We have given our hearts away, a sordid boon!

I recognized that, while money is not necessarily the root of all evil, it is often associated with the squandering of our time and energy in its pursuit, the degradation of the quality of our human relationships, the distraction and demoralization of our spirits, the plundering of the earth's resources to meet manufactured demand for nonessential items, and other forms of

(continued on p. 73)

HOW ECOLOGY LED ME TO COMMUNITY

(continued from p. 33)

destruction of the natural world. As a conscientious objector, I also saw that tax dollars fueled the war machine. I resolved to have as little to do with money as possible: to spend little, and therefore to need to earn little. Aspiring to be "downwardly mobile," to follow Henry David Thoreau's example rather than John D. Rockefeller's, I sensed myself in the distinct minority in my economically privileged town.

Despite its reputedly low survival value (about which I didn't care, since I had my marching orders), I doggedly pursued voluntary poverty. Fresh out of college, I moved into my first house: a tent, pitched on the aforementioned Native American reservation. I spent in the low double-digits per month for food, cooked with free fuel (the sun) in a solar cooker, lived unhooked from the electrical grid (a small solar panel and rechargeable flashlight supplied my lighting needs), traveled on a $50 used bicycle, and had few other expenses. I became a full-time volunteer, knowing that my several thousand dollars of savings could last me quite a while in this situation. Meanwhile, my own unique experience in the heart of Native American country could not have been purchased at any price. I spent all my time with the de-

velopmentally disabled in an ancient culture—taking them for walks on land that their ancestors had known for thousands of years, and helping them cope with daily tasks made challenging by their disabilities (many of which resulted, no doubt, from the uranium mining perpetuated by the white culture for which I could never hope to do full penance). Even after being hired as "direct care staff" several months into my time there, I continued to volunteer during the hours that I wasn't employed. Despite donating 20 percent of my salary back to the Center, I still saved enough money to bridge me through a number of the years which followed, in which I pursued "right ways to live" rather than money. All of my needs were already met, and I was surrounded by the kind of community that most of us from nonindigenous "settler" culture can only envy for its longevity, depth, and cultural richness.

When I felt the call to leave that culture and return to my own, I also knew that I could never in good conscience return to a resource-intensive lifestyle. And as luck would have it, in pursuing organic food-growing and eco-agricultural education, I chose one of the least remunerative, yet most rewarding, paths that modern society has to offer—one in which com-

munity, whether "unintentional" or intentional, is a most essential component. My second organic gardening internship turned out to be in an intentional community and educational center dedicated, among other things, to voluntary simplicity, self-reliance, and "deconsumerizing." Shared efforts and shared resources made many things possible in this setting that no amount of money could have bought—and with negligible or even positive impacts on the natural environment. I have lived in settings with similar ecological orientations (all manifested, of course, slightly differently) ever since.

Over the years, I have relaxed my attitude somewhat toward money: I no longer see it as necessarily a virtue not to earn it or spend it, and I have gradually done more of both. But my cautious attitude and valuing of "life" over money have stayed with me, continued to bring me together with others sharing similar values and similar paths, and made my life "rich" with forms of nonmonetary wealth that can never be owned or horded, but only shared.

I've found that, more than anything we can do (or refrain from doing) as lone individuals, community has an unrivaled ability to lessen the toll we take on the earth, establish new relationships between the human and non-human worlds, and inspire and educate both ourselves and others. This "community" does not need be strictly intentional in structure, but it does need to involve both intention and action: a commitment to sharing that reflects the truth that we are all interdependent parts of the web of life.

Perhaps my drummer wasn't so off-beat after all. ❋

Chris Roth edits COMMUNITIES *and is a long-time resident member, gardener, and nature-trail maintainer at Lost Valley Educational Center (www.lostvalley.org) in Dexter, Oregon.*

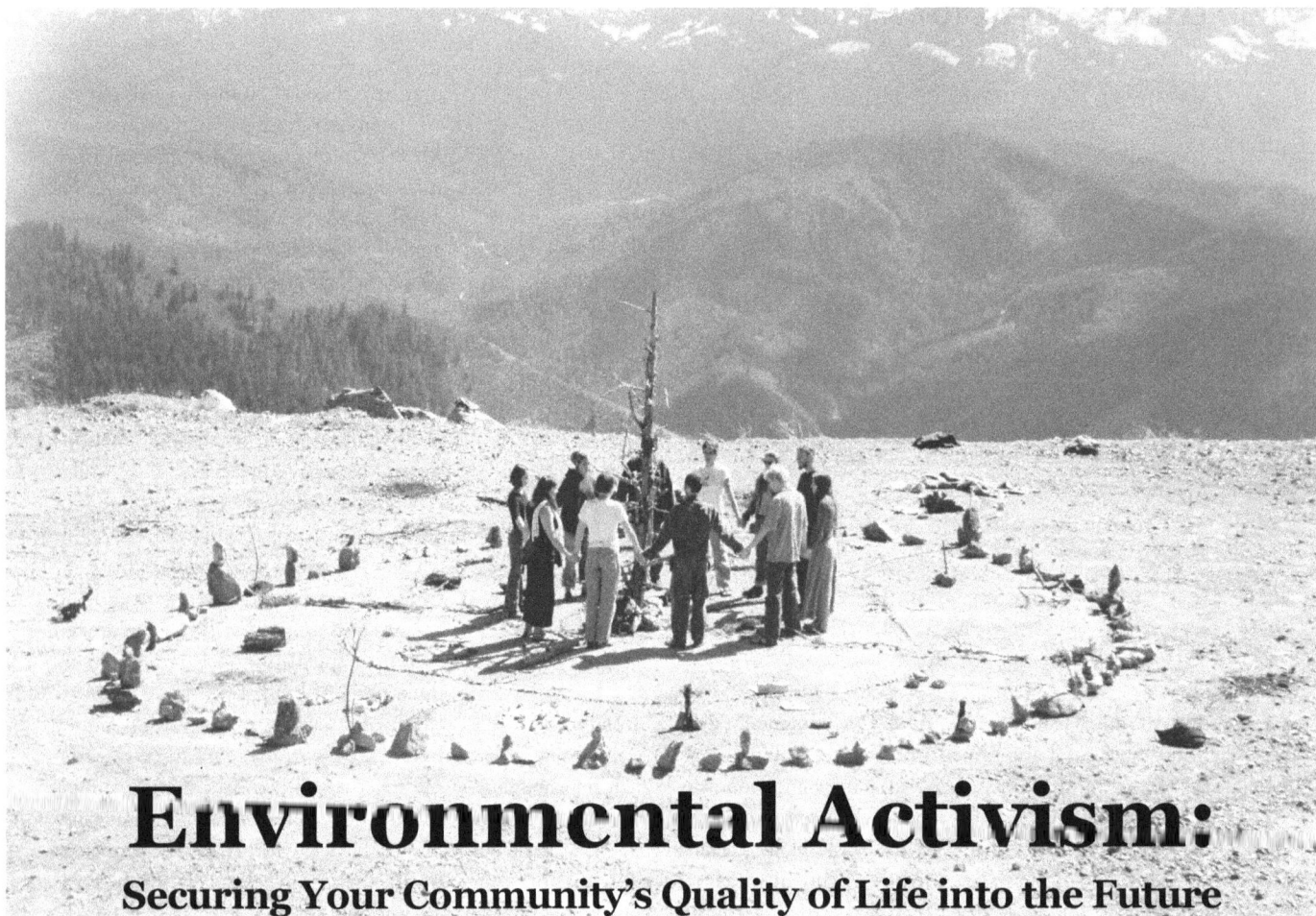

Environmental Activism:
Securing Your Community's Quality of Life into the Future

By Chant Thomas

You might have been there with us…sitting in silent circle, giving thanks for the dinner we were about to eat together. Feeling so *right* in that moment…with a warm current of love coursing though the holding hands of a dozen friends in community. Sweet song of the river rushing over rapids outside the window, savory aromas wafting from pots and oven… A prayer breaks the silence; we laugh and pass the food.

Sounds of footsteps on the kitchen porch announce a visitor at the back door. An acquaintance, who'd been looking to buy land just upriver, opens the door before we could answer. Despite the feast, he declines our joyous invitation to join us for dinner, and with a most serious expression, he tells us he has bad news to share. "I went down to the government office in town today to check on their plans for the canyon. They showed me maps where they plan to clearcut the forest right to the property lines." He continued, "they told me there was nothing we could do. So, I'm not pursuing the land upriver. I'm sorry to bring Trillium this bad news." With that, he was out the door, leaving us with sinking stomachs and appetites that floated on downstream.

Truly shocking news! We were stunned! A few years before buying our Land, I had thoroughly researched land uses, wanting to avoid industrial logging, mining, and similar mischief in the vast forests of southwestern Oregon's Siskiyou Mountains. As several of us were avid backpackers and lovers of wilderness, we knew well the power of wild pristine landscapes to uplift our spirits, helping us feel humbly embedded in the awesome embrace of Nature. We also realized our beautiful wild surroundings would provide both an important amenity for our community residents, and a valuable draw for participants in our planned cultural and educational programs. We wanted our human interplay with a wild and powerful Nature to focus and enhance our spiritual, cultural, and economic life on the Land.

After a lengthy search, we settled on purchasing a remote trout hatchery with several ponds, waterfalls, and meadows along an intimate little creek canyon that then dropped into the much larger canyon of a high mountain river. A towering peak cloaked with old-growth forests rose steeply just across the river, a powerful backdrop to our Gathering Grounds. The creek rose in a wilderness watershed with no roads, logging, or development, providing us with pure gravity-flow water. These natural features enchanted us, despite dozens of junked vehicles, appliances, and equipment. We decided that rather than buying and impacting pristine land elsewhere, we would clean up and restore this special place. Thusly, we became newly minted environmental activists and birthed Trillium Trout Farm during the back-to-the-land movement of the 1970s.

Because our Land came surrounded by wild-lands managed by the federal government, we thoroughly researched the government management plans to see what they had in store. Government managers assured us their management direction for the river canyon focused on recreation, pointing out two existing riverbank campground/picnic areas and several miles of wilderness hiking trails. They told us the forests there did not grow fast enough in the arid climate to manage for commercial timber cutting. These assurances played a major role in deciding to locate our community homestead here, so the news of clearcut logging came totally unexpected.

Back at the dinner table, one of the women guided us through a visualization where we pictured ourselves in the future as elderly people out on the lawn looking up at the forests of Trillium Mountain. We could see that the forests were still uncut, and no logging roads had been built across the mountain. This visualization helped us feel well enough to continue eating dinner while discussing options for action. Turns out the visualization may have done more than just help us feel better! The very next day, a neighbor who I'd been working with on government forest issues called to report that some new neighbors, a famous author and his movie-star wife, had just agreed to get involved in stopping proposed government logging above the stretch of river in their neighborhood, several miles downstream from Trillium.

Imagine getting celebrities involved in your activist campaigns! Turns out their leadership secured victory as we stopped that logging downriver. We next worked *with* the government agency to keep their logging out of the river canyon around Trillium. During that process, we connected with some activists from intentional communities a few valleys to the west, exchanging experiences dealing with logging on federally managed forest lands. We discussed strategies for involving neighbors, fundraising, and publicity. We also shared stories about how well, or not, our various intentional communities had embraced forest activism, and how supportive these communities were of their activist members who had become involved in campaigns to protect forest and wilderness.

We realized that many intentional communities organize around positive activism as a pro-active path toward making the world a better place. Most intentional communities understand that the very act of coming together to live on the Land in community constitutes a powerful statement of ecological and cultural activism. At Trillium, for

Why Vegetarian?

Back in the 1970s, significant numbers of back-to-the-land intentional communities embraced vegetarianism as an essential part of their alternative to the dominant culture, which was characterized by a diet heavy in meat consumption. From a thousand vegans at The Farm in Tennessee to our dozen vegetarians at Trillium in Oregon, a meatless diet flavored much of our Movement. As the negative impacts of industrial meat production on our planet, its people, and its animals have become more apparent during the ensuing decades, our inspirations and reasons for choosing vegetarianism are reinforced.

Back-to-the-land intentional communities have been described as Research and Development Centers for Society. Our research indicates intentional communities owe it to themselves and our larger society to adopt vegetarianism, or at least become aware of what happens to the animals they eat, from birth to plate. Consider you are what you eat:

Vegetarians suffer from far less heart disease, cancer, obesity, and other health problems than do meat eaters. Wouldn't your community function better if your members pursued a diet that favored better health, growing stronger resilient bodies to better enjoy gardening and building, hiking, making music and love? Would there be less sickness to tend and heal?

The Land we've gone back to is so precious, as is the clean air and pure water. Yet, growing animals for human consumption in the US gobbles 80 percent of our farmland, causes more water pollution than all other industrial uses combined, consumes one-third of all the raw materials and fossil fuels we use. Would your community trash its land and resources in this manner?

Eating meat creates a planet of poop! In the US, meat animals produce over 130 times the feces of the human population, with no sewers! These feces constitute the largest source of airborne methane, which traps heat in our atmosphere 20 times more than carbon dioxide. Raising meat animals produces 40 percent more global warming emissions than all transportation combined. Meanwhile, a vegan diet requires 300 gallons of water per day, compared to 5200 daily gallons to support a meat-based diet. Is sustainability an important value for your community? How does your diet reflect your values?

Over 27 billion (that's nearly 20,000 per minute!) animals are slaughtered yearly in the US for human consumption. These intelligent creatures feel pain, and have complex social and psychological lives; most suffer horrible death and torture along the way. Do you really want to be part of this karma?

Mohandas Gandhi said that a nation's moral progress could be judged by the way it treats its animals. That concept expanded to our entire planet indicates that we need a change of consciousness at a planetary level. Heard that before? Be a part of that change now! You'll do more to help solve problems with pollution and global warming by becoming vegetarian than by trading in your SUV on a Prius, with many more ancillary benefits for you and your community. If you're having difficulty considering the change, then take this encouragement from a teenage vegetarian: "Don't be a chicken! Stop being a pig! Don't have a cow! Be the first in your community to eliminate or at least reduce your meat consumption."

For more info, check www.GoVeg.com.

—Chant Thomas

Opposite page: Combining spirituality and art in activism: Ecostery students, Trillium interns, and friends center their energy after constructing a medicine wheel of rubble, spent gun shells, and assorted trash in a gravel quarry built on a nearby mountaintop. This and other photos were printed onto thousands of postcards with a message for federal land managers to stop building logging roads into roadless areas.

All photos courtesy of Chant Thomas

Left: Discussion circles during forest activists conference hosted by Trillium Community Farm. Right: Ecostery students geared and ready for one of Trillium's environmental stewardship programs: litter pick-up along several miles of our unpaved county road.

example, we worked to start or assist in starting a local forest workers coop, a natural foods co-op and gas station, an alternative school, a national women's herbalist conference, and a film festival in town. All these projects combined "positive activism" elements of environmental, social, cultural, economic, and community activism. However, defensive activism became the more difficult and less attractive action necessary to preserve essential components of our quality of life, such as clean water and air, peace and quiet, inspirational wildlands, and spectacular scenery, from looming threats such as logging, mining, off-highway vehicles, cattle grazing, shooters, dam construction, and development. For Trillium, like any land-based community, needed to answer several questions to determine what potential crises, such as government clearcutting, might spur us into defensive activism to secure the environmental amenities that convinced us to homestead on this particular Land: Who are our neighbors? What are the current nearby land uses and how might they change over time? What negative impacts could occur to our local environment? How could our community be affected? What are we going to do about it?

Thousands of acres of government wildlands surround Trillium, quite a behemoth neighbor! As we found out, one manager may favor recreation for our river canyon, while the next manager may see forests to cut. During the last few decades, government timber budgets expanded while their recreation budget shrank to near nothing. The campgrounds were neglected and abandoned; local hikers and equestrians volunteered to maintain the wilderness trails. Meanwhile, government plans for logging thousands of acres surrounding us proceeded beyond the initial clearcutting we'd stopped earlier. Such large-scale logging meant miles of new logging roads punched into the wilderness, providing access to hordes of hunters, shooters, OHV (off-highway vehicle) riders, toxic dumpers, and various other road-related problems. After any clearcutting, the government would spray

Defensive activism became the more difficult and less attractive action necessary to preserve essential components of our quality of life from looming threats.

toxic herbicides like Agent Orange, fouling the water and air. Once the landscape gets developed for industrial logging, the once quiet canyons reverberate with sounds of innumerable forest crews, their traffic and activities: road construction, logging, helicopter spraying, burning, planting, in an endless rotation of perpetual industrial management.

The high stakes convinced us that we needed to succeed! It turned out by default that I became the community's resident activist, as relevant experience gained working in logging and for various government agencies provided me with the necessary confidence to step up to the task. While some community members assisted in the activist campaigns, most were just glad somebody else dealt with it all. Some years saw the community stepping up to support the activism by hosting activist gatherings and training sessions. Other years I had to hustle to keep up with my community work contributions, as the activist work didn't then count toward community work time, even though I considered the activism as protecting the greater wild garden surrounding Trillium.

It has taken years, many years spanning four decades now, to protect our quality of life by working hard to actively influence the planning and implementation of government projects. With sporadic assistance from my community colleagues and some neighbors, I've been able to halt or work to modify most of the huge government logging projects planned for our watershed. Our wilderness drinking watershed that supplies all our gravity-flow domestic and irrigation water still shines in nearly pristine condition since I worked with a local rancher and some sympathetic government specialists to halt cattle grazing in a 28,000 acre area for over 30 years now. Using our natural food co-op/gas station as an outreach base, I was able to gather support to stop a proposed dam on our river before the process got beyond the initial planning stages.

(continued on p. 75)

ENVIRONMENTAL ACTIVISM: SECURING YOUR COMMUNITY'S QUALITY OF LIFE INTO THE FUTURE

(continued from p. 46)

Still, government agencies keep me busy tracking nefarious plans for huge logging projects, road building, mining, and development of vast landscapes dedicated to OHV playgrounds. However, such tasks have become a bit easier lately, even during the reign of W. During the late 1990s Trillium morphed through yet another stage in her evolution as an intentional community. We now focus more than ever before on environmental activism, primarily the education and training of future activists. Some of these new activists have settled in the area; some work as staffers for local and regional environmental activism organizations. Having these wonderful, energetic, younger activists working on similar issues makes my activist work more collegial and less demanding.

Now, when I'm asked what we grow at Trillium Farm, one of my replies is "activists!" Our organic farm intern program exposes participants to activism through growing organic food and assisting with various activist and arts programs we host through Birch Creek Arts and Ecology Center. The interns also learn, and teach us more, about our many efforts to become more sustainable with a smaller ecological footprint as a community, from recycling and buying in bulk to our vegetarian diet.

In our Ecostery program, college students come to Trillium for eight-week residential semesters where they earn 17 university credits in an interdisciplinary curriculum specifically designed to groom and educate future earth activists, land stewards, and communitarians. (See "Wilderness is our Classroom: Growing Education and Community at Trillium Farm," COMMUNITIES #108, Fall 2000,

p. 36). Research conducted by Ecostery participants informs our community as we learn and adopt more innovative ways to be better earth stewards. Ecosterians (as we affectionately call them) introduced us to compact fluorescent lighting, rocket stoves, and some alternative building methods.

Ecostery activist learning opportunities range from monitoring government resource plans to studying a recently burned forest to learning to grow food organically. The Ecosterians form their own intentional learning community embedded within the Trillium Farm Community. They learn to live and work together conducting regular meetings and studying non-violent communication and consensus, all important skills for successful activists.

Well aware of the high numbers of threatened, endangered, and listed species in our local habitats, Ecosterians work in our ongoing collaboration with Oregon Fish and Wildlife to monitor a population of threatened western pond turtles in our old trout ponds. We've also been monitoring the only known Oregon location of endemic birch trees in our watershed. The students work with a Forest Service botanist to identify alien plants that threaten native habitat, putting that knowledge into action by working to eradicate certain alien plants at Trillium and in nearby sensitive locations. The interns and students learn about our community responses to ecological concerns and opportunities, such as our prohibition of dogs at Trillium, our enhancement of anadromous fish habitat along the river, and our environmental stewardship programs

Our environmental stewardship programs present great opportunities for Ecostery students and interns to have fun outside while improving our local transportation routes. We work together to maintain several miles of nearby wilderness hiking trails, a pleasant scenic project despite the poison oak! Our most public such program provides Trillium with an invaluable opportunity to enhance our image within our local community: we pick up litter along four miles of the awesome dirt road that snakes up the canyon from the valley below. Several local folks of the conservative political stripe have expressed gratitude for our work to keep the canyon clean and beautiful.

Operating a teaching/learning center at Trillium brings us the special responsibility to walk our talk. Our interns and Ecostery students keep us on our toes, enriching our environmental sustainability efforts through their previous experiences and their research while here. Participants in our arts and cultural programs can then learn about what we're doing at Trillium Community to lessen our ecological footprint, move toward sustainability, defend our wildland habitat, and enrich our local community. As my beloved partner Susanna Bahaar summarizes, "It all comes down to creating more love, harmony, and beauty—inside and out." ❋

Chant Thomas practices environmental activism as a spiritual path at Trillium Community in the Siskiyou Mountains of southwest Oregon.

Software, Hardware, and Ecology at Ganas

By Tom Reichert with Peggy Wonder

What do you do when the community you choose does not line up behind your most cherished values? I am grappling with this dilemma. To me the environmental crisis is obvious and compelling. I thought for sure the people in my community would want to make the small behavioral changes that could make a big difference—changes that don't require sacrifice, just change of habit (things like turning off fans and lights when you leave a room). But the community I chose did not choose ecology. Although they chose to live frugally, and some of the founders care deeply about the environment, living ecologically has not been a universally shared value.

Yes, we at Ganas community have practices that are ecological, and living communally is eco-friendly by its nature. We share public spaces, refrigerators, laundry facilities, maintenance equipment, and food purchasing and preparation, among other things. We reuse materials in our maintenance and renovation operations. We compost. We recycle. We feed leftovers and yard waste to our chickens. We run a small collection of thrift and vintage stores: Every Thing Goes Clothing, Furniture, and Book Cafe (etgstores.com). Through the stores, we renew and reuse many useful and beautiful things. From some people's point of view, we are a model of urban ecological practice.

The Software/Hardware Choice

Before I moved to Ganas in Staten Island, New York, I was part of the Kerista commune (from 1987-1991) in San Francisco, California. At Kerista, we jokingly and condescendingly referred to the ecologically-oriented communities as being into *Hardware*. We were into *Software*.

There are two basic approaches to changing one's environmental impact. The *hardware* one involves technology: things like insulation, more efficient cars, and energy-efficient appliances. The *software* approach involves behavior change. Changing one's behavior can have the biggest effect on one's environmental impact. Walking or taking public transportation instead of driving is an immediate, low-cost measure you can implement right away. But getting someone to make the software choice can be difficult. Conversely, when you convince someone to insulate their attic, it doesn't mean they have to change their behavior. If they insulate their attic, their fuel bills will go down. They could more easily just lower their thermostat in the

winter. But for many people, this is out of the question. This approach would require that they dress differently in the winter, or that they change other habituated behaviors. So again, we are back to *software—in this case, behavior change.*

When I left Kerista, I wanted another community committed to software. I found one: Ganas.

I chose Ganas because we are committed to communication through dialog. We try to solve problems by talking about them, instead of devising a bunch of rules to apply to the next incident. The former is quite challenging, for it forces us to look at each situation on its own merits. It is much easier to simply refer to the rules and be done with the issue. But because every circumstance is different, each warrants as fresh an evaluation as possible.

As committed as I am to ecology and the environment, I wouldn't want to live in a community that didn't place dialog as priority number one. I wouldn't want to live in one of the "hardware" communities. Sometimes I long for a more homogeneous mixture where it would be easier to promote ecological practices. But I value the openness to diversity that my partners stick to. It has made our community closer to a microcosm of the wider world. So I find in Ganas similar challenges to turning people on to ecology to those I would likely encounter in other places. And I am influenced by ideas I might not hear in a more closed community.

Bringing Ecology Home

My awareness of ecology and the environment started as a young teenager at summer camp in the north woods of Wisconsin. It has never stopped. Although it often wasn't my central focus, caring about the environment and my ecological footprint eventually shaped the ways in which I took showers and washed dishes, shopped for food and supplies for the community, and used paper and computers. This interest developed into a passion for making our buildings more efficient energy users. I sought a way to incorporate my desire to live with minimal impact on the earth and to turn my home into a model of environmentally friendly behaviors and practices.

Going Professional

I felt my way around how to get involved in these issues professionally. I got a lot of help along the way: money, ideas, support, labor. And yet I found that without a partner I wasn't really going to get anywhere. I went from insulating our own

I value the openness to diversity that my partners stick to. It has made our community closer to a microcosm of the wider world.

buildings to starting a Home Performance contracting business, to deciding to work for someone else. Before my first day at the new job, our maintenance and renovation crew joined me for a major push to finish insulating two of our buildings. It was fantastic! We had as many as six of us working at any given moment, together. It was what I had dreamed of. Great workers, interested in doing a good job, partners.

In the new job, I got to advise homeowners on how to make their houses more energy efficient, comfortable, and safe. I could easily respond to customers' energy consumption questions with "set your thermostat temperature lower" or "this will save money and energy." The fact that they were rarely going to follow my advice didn't bother me. I just shared my observations and opinions and that was that; I was on to the next appointment.

Powerful Software to the Rescue

But when issues involving choices that affect energy efficiency came up at home, it was a different story. The issues mattered in a very different way to me. I could not maintain the same level of detachment and even objectivity. When our housekeeping manager presented her proposal to get a top-loading washing machine instead of a front-loader (widely considered to be more efficient and effective), I had a hard time considering her reasons. And time was short. In the initial discussion, there was tension in the air. Did any of it originate anywhere but from me??? She had good reasons: lower initial cost and better expected reliability. My only hope for having it go my way was to do more in-depth research than she had already done—and do it as objectively as possible. I couldn't lie to her and my partners, and I couldn't lie to myself.

So I searched. I used Julie's criteria, by which she had decided that the top-loader was better. She had studied *Consumer Reports* and similar publications. But the reports noted a distinct lack of repair histories. I decided to dig deeper. I found that users of Julie's preferred top loader rated it more poorly for reliability than some more expensive front-loading models. I also noted that recently-published Energy Star® data on clothes washers' ability to extract water from clothes, thereby reducing drying time, favored the front-loaders. My research supported my initial opinion.

There was tension around the discussions, but not as much as there could have been. Knowing that I was being heard, and that I was hearing Julie, helped. But it was easy to see why people simply decide to live in a small nuclear family and not have

all these partners to answer to.

This willingness to go back and forth, to bring up the issue multiple times, and to listen to each others' concerns is why I am into the software approach to community living. All my research means nothing if I cannot incorporate everyone else's wants into mine. I think that the more concerns we can address and the more voices we manage to engage in our decision-making process, the better decisions we can make. Such a process seems to strengthen relationships between members and heighten our awareness of different ways of viewing the issues.

Software—Not an Easy Choice

The point that many people prefer to deal with hardware rather than software was driven home to me as I watched a presentation about intentional communities around the world recently. The depiction of each community described more about the type of building construction than about the group's problem-solving process. How much time each community devotes to meetings, the type of meeting structure, and decision-making process got less emphasis. This is not a criticism of the presentation, which was very well prepared and executed. I think the emphasis didn't necessarily reflect the presenter's bias, but it did reflect the focus of each community.

We at Ganas pride ourselves in having few interpersonal feuds and a well-running community. But we are also legendary in the amount of time we spend in meetings. It appears to take a long time to work issues out. We hope this is because we actually work them out, because we get beyond the surface issues to the underlying ones. And by solving the underlying issues, at least we like to think we really solve the issues.

Many people report having had community-living experiences in college or early adulthood, which they enjoyed. "But nobody did the dishes." Or we have our Ganas alternative: endless meetings, but a well-run community. To many, neither choice is preferable to having the control of a nuclear family or a single person household.

A Combination that Works

If this sounds like I think the *software* is a failure, then right, in some ways I do. As a species, we still fight wars and I don't see the communities movement growing significantly. In fact, we decided to make our own community smaller. Yet I see Ganas getting better at solving problems, and our resulting inner strength (both

individually and collectively) increasing. My personal resolve to address communication issues is as firm as it ever was.

Over the past three or four years, I have found new ways to promote environmentally friendly practices at home. I wrote many articles for our weekly Ganas newsletter, e.g. about how to conserve energy while using fans and while using computers. During this time, our fuel usage dropped. Electricity use appears to be decreasing also, but we don't know whether that's just because the summers have been mild. (Summer appliances that gobble electricity here include fans, air conditioners, and refrigeraters.)

Our communal commitment to learning to listen and to solve problems together has served me well. Along the way, I got lots of help thinking about things as they came up: what I wanted, how I was dissatisfied, what to do differently, how to decide where to work. In November, after checking out possible alternatives, I joined a young promising start-up called Bright Power. It's challenging and offers me lots of room to grow in. This small company offers the kind of full participation I am used to having at Ganas—the opportunity to see the big picture, join in planning future directions, design my job to suit my strengths, weaknesses, needs, and desires.

So, have I resolved the dilemma? Well, yes and no. I certainly would like Ganas to focus more on ecology, but I do love what we do. Because we have such diversity of opinion and because we focus on discussion, I have honed my skills in thinking through and presenting issues well. This software approach has helped me develop my ability to open my ears to my partners, to open my mind with greater agility. The software approach has helped me to make both physical changes and changes in awareness at Ganas over the years. And when I look at other communities, I feel I have made an excellent choice.

But please! Rinse that dish in cold water! ❁

Many people report having had community-living experiences in college or early adulthood, which they enjoyed. "But nobody did the dishes."

A native of Houston, Texas, Thompson Reichert has lived in Ganas Community in Staten Island, New York since 1991. He now works at Bright Power (brightpower.biz) in Manhattan. He loves to answer questions and give advice about energy efficiency. Contact him at Tom@ganas.org.

Peggy Wonder, a California native, has been at Ganas since 1989. There she manages Ganas' Every Thing Goes Vintage and Thrift Clothing store. In her spare time she co-edits Ganas' weekly newsletter.

The Transition Initiative Comes to Cohousing

By Sonja Eriksson

How will the rapid depletion of fossil fuels, especially oil, affect our society, and how can we plan for the inevitable change in lifestyle? The Transition Initiative attempts to find solutions to both climate change and peak oil (defined in Wikipedia as the point in time, likely soon or already passed, when the maximum rate of global petroleum extraction is reached, after which the rate of production enters terminal decline). A Transition Town, which can also mean a village, an island, or even a county, develops methods for a local community to become sustainable through reduced carbon emissions and diminished reliance on fossil fuels.

A group from our cohousing community, Oak Creek Commons in Paso Robles, California, has become active in the Transition Town movement. Even before our cohousing project of 36 households was completed in 2004, we agreed on our strong intention to respect the environment by being sensitive to the interconnections among all things. As a cohousing community, we are already committed to using less energy and to sharing resources, but we have also taken specific steps that lead to a more sustainable future.

Almost three years ago our community sponsored a workshop on climate change. We invited members of the public, including two progressive candidates for City Council. Neither of them thought they would win votes on a platform that included climate change. They told us that change has to come from the bottom up and encouraged us to influence the local government by showing that the public had a genuine desire for the city to consider climate change in its policies and decisions.

Orchard workshop No. 1: "The Rock Brigade."

Our lives will inevitably undergo radical change, but if we plan for this change we can make it smoother. While we recognize the challenges, we also need to envision how attractive living in a sustainable society would be.

These comments inspired community member Jim Cole to establish a nonprofit corporation called The Institute for Sustainable Living. Its purpose is to plan conferences and other events locally to promote sustainable living and business practices in cooperation with business and government leaders. An engineer who has worked in the area of energy efficiency for several decades, Jim is also currently a consultant with the California Energy Commission, where his team works to identify new ways to integrate renewable energy into the California electric system.

As one of its first activities, the Institute brought together members of Oak Creek Commons and of the larger community to form a book discussion group to study sustainability. Jim Cole and his wife, Norma, learned about the Transi-

tion Town initiative at an energy conference at the Findhorn community in Scotland, where they met Rob Hopkins, author of *The Transition Handbook: From oil dependency to local resilience*, and other members of communities involved in the Transition Initiative. The Transition Town movement, which started in England and has spread to other countries, emphasizes building a local economy, reviving lost skills, producing food locally, and even creating local currencies.

Prompted by Jim's enthusiasm about the Transition Initiative, the book discussion group members read *The Transition Handbook* and became active in the Transition Town movement. Carolyn Fergoda, a member of the group from the beginning, describes the Transition Initiative as an exciting opportunity "to plan for major change on all levels—personal,

social, economic, political." I joined the group after reading *The Transition Handbook* on my own. Becoming involved in the challenges of climate change and peak oil on a local level seems manageable when you work with a group. *The Handbook* lays out a sequence of steps to follow for groups that want to promote the Transition Initiative concept in their communities.

The Institute sponsored a Transition Town workshop in January, held at Dancing Deer Ranch, a nearby intentional community. Over 40 people attended, including nine people from our cohousing community and one person from another cohousing community. To prepare for the workshop, we were encouraged to watch videos and read books on related topics.

The workshop and the required reading and videos made it clear that suburbs, big box stores, and industrial agriculture are not sustainable. We will not be able to continue to transport food and other necessities over long distances, but will have to rely more on our local economy and relearn skills that have been lost. I participated in a small-group discussion about using food produced within 100 miles of where you live, except, for now, you are allowed three "cheat foods"—foods that are produced outside of that range. A couple of women in the group, both married with families, said they want to try it.

I used to think that "they" will come up with a replacement when we run out of cheap fossil fuels, but experts say that this is magical thinking and a form of denial. The alternative fuels we have developed so far are not sufficient to replace fossil fuels at current levels of use.

The transition from reliance on fossil fuels may provoke conflicts and even wars to compete for scarce resources. Our lives will inevitably undergo radical change, but if we plan for this change we can make it smoother. While we recognize the challenges, we also need to envision how attractive living in a sustainable society would be. Much of the farm work and other tasks will need to be done cooperatively—fostering social relations, ceremonies, and rituals. James Howard Kunstler, author of *The Long Emergency*, believes that small towns surrounded by agriculture have the best chance of survival. Paso Robles is such a town, although the wine industry will have to change to include other crops.

Our transition town trainers recommended that, in attempting to engage the community, we first contact people who are already moving in the same direction, including other environmental groups. Reaching out to cohousing communities also seems natural to me, because we already do many of the things that make a community sustainable. Sharing resources and working as teams will become the norms in a transition town.

Our cohousing community incorporates many features of a transition town: energy-efficient buildings and appliances, recycling, an organic garden, an orchard, and a workshop we call the Creativity Center.

We planned our buildings at Oak Creek Commons with efficient heating and cooling systems. The temperature in Paso Robles often exceeds 100 degrees F in the summer, but the house I live in is so well insulated that my husband and I did not install air conditioning until last year, and could have been fairly comfortable without it.

We converted three parking spaces in our underground garage into the Creativity Center, used for woodworking and other crafts, which could become even more important in the future when we may need to make our own furniture and other household items.

Our organic garden provides vegetables and herbs all year. Our common meals often include produce from the garden, and we grow enough herbs for everyone to use. On Saturday mornings, we sometimes have our own farmers' market with produce like lettuce, carrots, radishes, and chard laid out on a table in the Common House. People can take what they want and pay what they think is fair. Nancy Scott organizes work parties for the garden and hopes that the money contributions eventually will pay for seeds and other garden supplies.

This past winter, after a year of planning, we planted an organic orchard with 15 fruit trees and a food forest. We published information about three Saturday workshops by word of mouth and through the media. Surprisingly, a dozen or more people who don't live here and who had never visited showed up to help and to learn how to create an orchard—an example of what can happen in a transition town when people get involved in each other's projects.

Whether or not one is convinced that we must "power down" for a new type of economy and lifestyle, I see no downside to being prepared. We have already witnessed a severe downturn in the economy, which could be a signal that our society is not sustainable and that growth on the scale we have been used to can't continue. Cohousing and other intentional communities seem to be ideal partners for the Transition Initiative. We already have a community in place with shared resources and skills to help each other economically as well as emotionally to deal with the challenges that come with climate change and peak oil. ❋

Sonja Eriksson has been a member of Oak Creek Commons Cohousing in Paso Robles, California, since 2000.

For more information about Transition Towns, the following sources are helpful: www.transitiontowns.org; *The Long Emergency: Surviving the End of Oil, Climate Change, and Other Converging Catastrophes of the 21st Century* by James Howard Kunstler; *Peak Everything: Waking Up to the Century of Declines* by Richard Heinberg; *A Crude Awakening: the Oil Crash* (video).

Our cohousing community incorporates many features of a transition town: energy-efficient buildings and appliances, recycling, an organic garden, an orchard, and a workshop we call the Creativity Center.

Above: Orchard workshop No. 1: Joe Brenner and Kayla Wisdom team up.
Opposite page: Orchard workshop No. 1: Cohousers and volunteers work together.

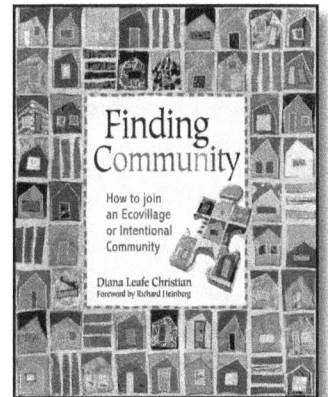

Work Less, Simplify More

By Kim Scheidt

I received a phone call from my mother in the spring of 2009. A high-school teacher in her late 50s, she was overjoyed to tell me that she had just finished her last full day of work for the rest of her life. I congratulated her on her semi-retirement, and in my head a voice said, "I did that five years ago."

Quite a while ago I realized that if I kept a modest cost of living I would not need to work a 40-50 hour a week job for the rest of my life. Instead, I could work part-time and earn enough money to cover my costs. Since then I've found that the more I simplify my life, the less time I need to work to earn money. By reducing my economic impact I believe that I also directly reduce my ecological footprint on the earth, which is important to me too.

This line of thought is slightly different from what mainstream society often tells us. A consumptive lifestyle is still seen as affluent. And a 40-plus hour week is standard. Many people would find it hard to believe that someone could have a happier life by giving up certain creature comforts. But in my experience and those of my community-mates around me, simpler living has led to an increased quality of life.

If you would like to simplify your lifestyle, a good first step is to reanalyze what is perceived as necessary, be it travel, good restaurant meals, movies and theater, or whatever, and put your resources toward what you care most about. Then look to see if there are any "necessities" you pay for that you personally could do without. I recommend spending some period of time living in a third-world country. Learn that everyone in the world does not necessarily have a vehicle, a refrigerator, running water, flush toilets, a washing machine, a telephone, air conditioning...the list goes on.

I spent about four months living in Costa Rica, where the sole fact that I was from the United States traveling for leisure made me seem supremely rich to the locals. The people I was traveling with gave me encouragement to go outside my comfort zone and work on simple living closer to nature using limited resources. Unfortunately,

Kim Scheidt

Kim Scheidt

it seems that a great many people in third-world countries, whose ancestors have excelled at simple living, would do just about anything to live the perceived richness portrayed in Hollywood movies.

When I came back to the United States I was able to figure out for myself what is really important to me. Over time I've realized that I can do without a refrigerator, running water, a flush toilet, a shower, and a washing machine. What I do find necessary are electric lights, high-speed internet, good food, fresh air, strong social connections, and control over my own time.

I live in an intentional community that has a strong focus on permaculture and sustainable living. We aim to have a very small ecological footprint and to be self-sufficient in all the ways we can. We utilize human power for most applications and keep track of the times when we do use fossil fuels, vehicles, and heavy

Kim Scheidt

We aim to have a very small ecological footprint and to be self-sufficient in all the ways we can.

machinery. Our community exists within a larger network of intentional communities in the area that are exploring different approaches toward right livelihood.

Our primary dwelling that I live in is a small passive-solar house with an attached greenhouse space, and this design vastly reduces the amount of fuel we need to provide heat in the winter. We do all our cooking and heating with the sun or with wood, a renewable resource that we harvest from our land using hand tools. To be honest, we have borrowed a chainsaw a couple of times in order to fell some larger trees. But for the most part we keep to our ideals of doing it all by hand.

We are not connected to grid electricity. The power draw of the electric appliances we use is what determines how many thousands of dollars we spend on purchase and upkeep of our power system. For the time being, we have chosen to limit our power load to running very low wattage electric light bulbs, computers, and stereo. The refrigerator-freezer, ubiquitous in households across the U.S., is a power-hog appliance that we've chosen to live without.

It has been over seven years since I've had a refrigerator. In order to do without, I've learned to change the way I cook and eat. During the warmer months the cook is careful to make only so much leftovers that can be eaten up the next day at lunch. And in our climate we have refrigeration roughly half the year just by putting things outside our door. Spoiled food is fed to our animals or composted. Many items commonly kept in a refrigerator actually store just fine at room temperature, and a diet that includes little or no meat makes this easier too. We have plans to build an ice house one day in the future. At that point we will have the luxury of refrigeration, but it will be a very low-tech version.

Our drinking water comes straight from the sky. We collect rain off the metal roof of our main building into a cistern. We use a hand pump to draw water up from the cistern and it goes through a filter before consumption. It is some of the tastiest water

Left photo: Nina pumping water from the cistern into the water filter. This photo: a view of Dandelion. Right photo: the kitchen stove.

on the planet. For other uses such as doing dishes or washing up we use non-potable water that we haul in buckets either from our pond or from a rain catchment barrel. We do not have running water (although we joke that we have "walking water"). Our system is one that requires some physical labor but very little money or infrastructure.

And what about the flush toilet? We are fortunate to live in a part of the country with few zoning laws or building codes and thus have been able to build and use an outhouse that is a mouldering toilet. Human wastes, to which we occasionally add soil and mown grass, decompose over time giving off little odor. Eventually this compost can be spread around trees in our orchard, closing the loop in the fertility cycle.

Cleanliness is an interesting topic. I certainly do not live in a sterile environment, and that makes my life so much richer. My routine used to involve daily hot showers that would dry out my skin, and I frequently shampooed my hair. I would then slather my body in lotion to restore lost moisture and put styling goop in my hair. I was happy to find that when I changed my routine to scrubbing up with just a washcloth and warm water my skin felt pretty amazing. Another interesting discovery is that pond water does wonderful things to my hair that I can't quite get with gel or hair spray.

We wash laundry by hand using water from our pond. When I take our clothes down from the line they always smell nice and clean; however, there are often stains that just don't come out the way they would with a power washer. My solution is that I maintain a set of clothes for when I need to look "nice" and I have another set that is for everyday use. I'm fortunate to live in an environment where appearance is not so important, though I do admit I enjoy fashion. Community-mates often gift clothing that doesn't suit them, and once or twice a year I go to a thrift store to add new items to my wardrobe.

Okay, so what else do people spend money on? One particularly controversial thing that I go without is health insurance. My philosophy is that my right livelihood is my health insurance. If I live in alignment with the universe then I will be taken care of. I understand that this way of thinking does not satisfy all people. I take full responsibility for my health. I hope to embrace death when that time comes. (And living on a low income helps me to qualify for sliding scale rates available from some health practitioners.)

I say that I only work one day a week because that is the amount of time I spend outside my home earning money. However, all my days are filled with physical and mental labor, but those are things I do for myself and for my community, so in many ways I do not consider them work. For the most part I get to choose how I spend my time and only have to do any particular task for as long as feels good to me. I find it really inspiring when there is an obvious connection between the energy I put into a project and the results I get to enjoy, be it in the garden or orchard or in the development of my child.

One of the major roles I play in my life right now is that of being a parent to a youngster. My daughter is being raised in what I consider an almost ideal environment for her. She has both her mother and her father around most of the time. Although she is an only child she is well socialized with peers and has relationships with adults other than her biological parents. She lives rurally but is not isolated. We have clean air for her to breathe, healthy food for her to eat, and pure water for

All my days are filled with physical and mental labor, but those are things I do for myself and for my community, so in many ways I do not consider them work.

Mark Mazziotti

her to drink. She gets plenty of exercise and loves to be outside.

There is a pretty good support network for being a parent around here. I certainly believe that parenting is one of the most challenging things I have taken on in my life. It is so valuable when others make an effort to be an ally to myself and to my child. I believe that in an ideal world there would always be at least three parents to any one child. I don't currently have that situation, but it certainly would be possible to do so

Mark Mazziotti

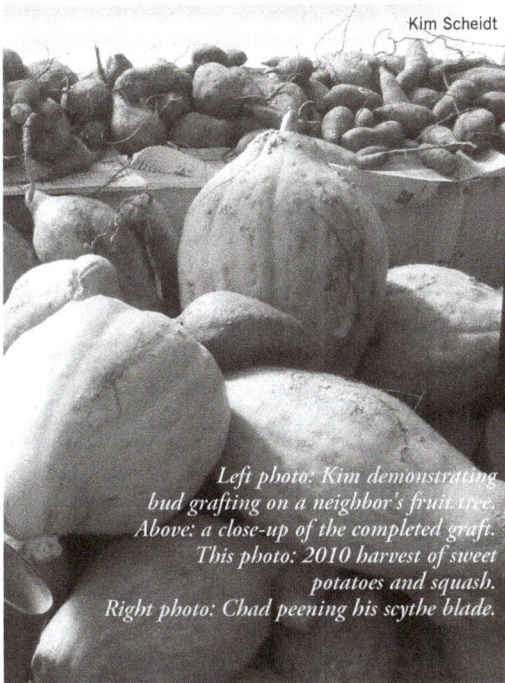

Kim Scheidt

Left photo: Kim demonstrating bud grafting on a neighbor's fruit tree. Above: a close-up of the completed graft. This photo: 2010 harvest of sweet potatoes and squash. Right photo: Chad peening his scythe blade.

Kim Scheidt

within a community setting.

Pioneering a community is another huge project I've taken part in. There are benefits—mainly that my personal vision is incorporated in the shape our community takes. Starting from scratch on raw land is certainly not easy and it is not something I would have ever undertaken alone. A great benefit of settling our community where we did is that members of the other established local intentional communities gave support to us in many and varied ways. So much of our time in the beginning was taken up with satisfying the most basic of our physical needs—a place to sleep, a place to cook, water to drink, etc. All this was done on a pretty tight budget using primarily human power. Phew.

There are certainly ways in which we have fallen short of our ideals. Sometimes we make the choice to spend money on an item rather than taking the extra time and energy to make do with resources we already have at our disposal. When we first moved onto the land six years ago we made choices to build structures that placed values such as speed of construction, comfort, durability, and function over aesthetic beauty and the use of completely local or sustainably harvested building materials.

We also still buy most of the food we eat. However, each year we get closer to being self-reliant in that area. Our fruit and nut orchards will begin bearing soon, and the output from our annual garden continues to increase. It is helpful to keep in mind the long-term goals and vision—the way it is today is not the way it's always going to be. I do finally feel that we are out of the pioneering stage. We have working systems in place and so now we can focus on simply improving our surroundings and quality of life.

I never thought I would be an activist, but I am. I'm proactive in that I am living the change I want to see. I'm demonstrating that there is another way. I never thought I would live in a fishbowl, but I do. Hundreds of people come by each year and we say, "here is our greenhouse, here is our garden, this is how we live." I tend to forget how extreme my life is until I go somewhere out in the mainstream world. Now that's a freaky place. ᕀ

Kim Scheidt is a member of Dandelion, a sub-community of Red Earth Farms in northeast Missouri. She works—part-time—for the Fellowship for Intentional Community.

Social Permaculture

By Starhawk

P atrick Whitefield calls permaculture "the art of designing beneficial relationships." Most permaculturalists are expert at understanding the relationships between land forms and water harvesting, or between soil micro-organisms and plant health. But when it comes to our human relationships, we often founder. Nurturing the vegetables in the garden is a lot easier than nurturing our connections to the people who decide where to plant the vegetables and who will water them. Meeting the needs of chickens or goats is far easier than meeting the needs of your fellow farmers. Many permaculture groups, like many intentional communities, start up with the highest ideals, only to come apart in painful discord and strife.

Diana Leafe Christian, who studied successful ecovillages and intentional communities, found that "No matter how visionary and inspired the founders, only about one out of ten new communities actually get built. The other 90 per cent seemed to go nowhere, occasionally because of lack of money or not finding the right land, but mostly because of conflict. And usually, conflict accompanied by heartbreak. And sometimes, conflict, heartbreak and lawsuits."[1]

Our human relationships are our biggest constraining factor in the work of transforming society. So, is there a way to do them better?

I've been working in collaborative and collective groups of many sorts for more than four decades now, and this question has always been in the forefront of my mind. I've been through many painful learning experiences of my own, and observed many groups struggle with conflict. I've founded one organization, Reclaiming[2], an extended network focused on earth-based spirituality, that is now more than 30 years old. I've worked in hundreds of other groups and facilitated thousands of meetings. I teach permaculture courses called Earth Activist Trainings[3] that include group dynamics and decision-making along with a grounding in spirit and a focus on organizing. Over the last few years I've taught a number of social permaculture courses, several in collaboration with Bill Aal and the late Margo Adair of Tools for Change. I've compiled much of my own learning into a new book, *The Empowerment Manual: A Guide for Collaborative Groups*

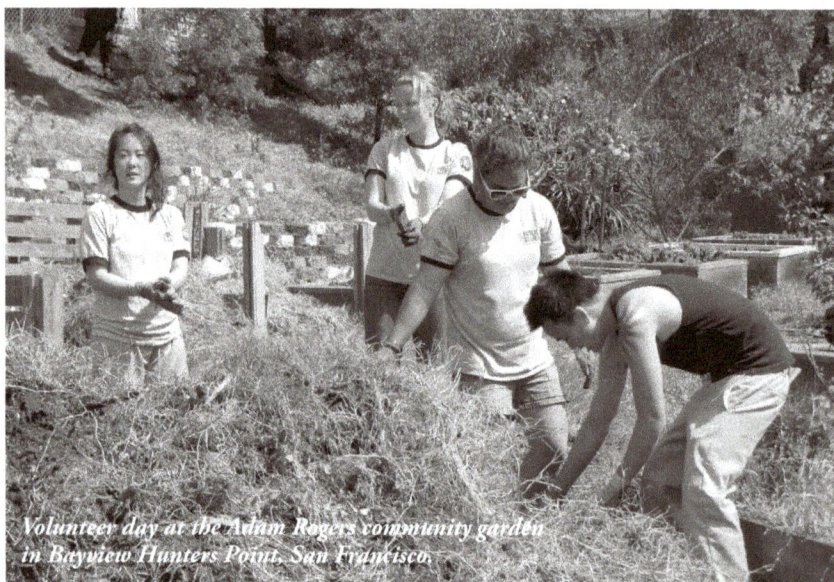

Volunteer day at the Adam Rogers community garden in Bayview Hunters Point, San Francisco.

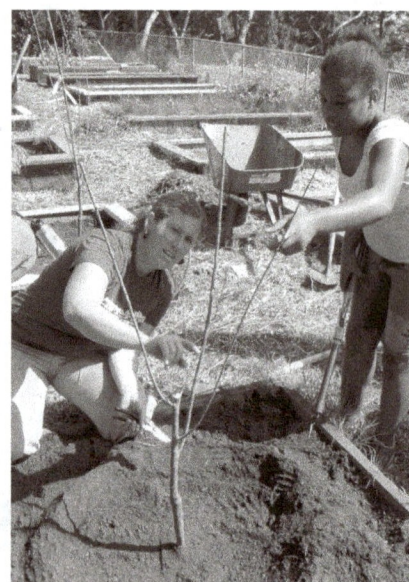

(New Society Publishers, October 2011).

My practice of permaculture informs my approach to group social design and conflict, and my understanding of group dynamics informs my practice of permaculture. Permaculture principles can be translated into guidelines and approaches that will help us to work together more effectively and joyfully as we strive to change the world. Here are a few of my Social Permaculture Principles:

1) Abundance springs from relationships:

True abundance, whether that's measured in garden produce or ecstatic experiences, has little to do with how much stuff we have, but rather, how rich we are in relationships. So—cherish your relationships. Value them. Give them time and attention. Nurture and maintain them. When conflict arises, don't simply discard people, but learn the skills and tools to work things through. Nurture your relationship to your inner self and spirit, as well. As you face your own shadows and develop your own strengths, your relationships with others will be enriched and deepened.

2) Recognize and work with patterns:

Permaculture teaches us to look for patterns in nature and apply that knowledge to our designs. We can also look for social patterns. Hierarchy is a pattern we're all familiar with, but when we try to work collaboratively, outside of a command and control structure, we encounter different challenges. Recognizing them can help us structure our groups more effectively. Collaborative structures differ from hierarchies in many ways:

• *Communication is more complex:* In a hierarchy, we generally know to whom we report and where we are on the chain of command. A collaborative group, however, is more like a web, with many possible pathways for any message to follow to get from person A to person B. People get left out of the loop, often unintentionally, because the loop becomes a knot or a snarl. In a well-run top-down structure, we know who is responsible for carrying out decisions. In a circular structure, we may make a decision but each person in the circle may assume someone else is going to carry it out.

So, pay rigorous attention to communication. Whenever a decision is made, ask, "Who else needs to know about this?" "Who will inform them?" "How will the rest of us know this is done?" When a plan is made, ask "Who will be responsible for making sure this is carried out?" Doing so can forestall much conflict and hurt feelings

• *Mom can't make the kids behave:* In a hierarchy, generally someone at the top can say, "Okay, you two stop fighting and make up." In a collaborative group, there's no Mom, no Dad, but we carry over our family patterns and expect that someone, somehow, can step in and sort things out for us. When they don't, groups often fall apart because they have no way to move conflict out of the system or resolve it.

So, build in conflict resolution systems, mediation, and clear agreements. Develop skills in conflict transformation, and devote group time and resources to training in communication and mediation. Conflict will always arise in groups. Just as you put an overflow on a pond to handle the hundred-year storm, design an "overflow" for group conflict so that it doesn't erode trust and enthusiasm or burst the dam and flood the production fields.

3) Feed what you want to grow:

Industrial agriculture works on the principle: "Kill the pests!" If bugs attack a field, nuke them with chemicals! Organic farmers know that attacking pests with power-ful toxins only breeds resistance. Instead, we create healthy soil that provides what our plants need to repel pests. We plant flowers that attract beneficial insects that keep the chompers in check. We look at insect damage as information—something is out of balance.

In our social relations, too often we revert to "Kill the pests!" Instead of attacking the people whose behavior offends us or trying to drive them out

> Conflict in the group is information. Somehow we've created a habitat that allows destructive behavior to thrive.

of the group, we can look at conflict as information. Something in the group is out of balance. Somehow we've created a habitat that allows destructive behavior to thrive. How do we give a competitive edge to the behaviors that we want?

When we fear conflict, we may resort to gossip and backbiting. Instead of directly confronting Scabiosa Sue when she hurts my feelings, I complain about her to Lennie Legume or post a scathing denunciation on the listserv that goes out to a hundred people around the world, most of whom don't know either of us. The result is a toxic miasma of resentment, rumors, and malicious tattling.

We can clear the air by creating a group culture of direct engagement. When we learn to embrace conflict, to openly argue for our ideas or values without resorting to personal attack, we create an atmosphere that discourages malicious gossip and scapegoating and encourages respect. We can train our group members to respond to a bid for a trash-fest by saying, "How can I support you, Starhawk, in talking directly to Scabiosa about your feelings?" Or perhaps, "Can I be of service to you in helping arrange a mediation?" When one of our friends opens a conversation by saying "I really shouldn't tell you this..." we can learn to say "I'm so glad you recognize that! Now, about that other topic…"

4) Value diversity:

In nature, diversity gives an ecosystem resilience. In groups, a diversity of opinion, backgrounds, ages, ethnic and class backgrounds, and experiences can broaden our perspective and let us see multiple facets of an issue. If we want a diverse group, we must make the extra effort to bring people in who represent that diversity, and to do it in a meaningful way, not as tokens: early in our process so that a wide range of people help form the group and participate in the creative aspects of the project. We can build alliances with diverse communities not just by inviting them to support our work but by sharing information and resources, educating ourselves about their history and current struggles, and showing up in support of their issues.

5) Develop a culture of respect, kindness, and trust:

Trust is built in many ways: by creating opportunities to share something of our lives and feelings, by encouraging people to argue passionately for their ideas and positions while still respecting their opponents' right to differ, by meeting responsibilities and building a track record of dependability, and by sharing risks together.

Kindness, respect, compassion, and encouragement are the compost tea of relationships—they feed all the beneficial impulses. When we respect one another's ideas, think well of one another's motives, and support one another's visions, we create a high-energy atmosphere in which creativity flourishes.

These five principles are merely a sketch of how we might begin to look at our human groups as ecologies. As I said, I've just written a book on the subject—and that is only a bare beginning. Social permaculture is an emerging discipline, and the study of human behavior, in groups and outside of them, is a lifelong pursuit. But as we become more skillful at nurturing our human relations, we will become more effective in every aspect of our work. At this crucial time for the earth, we need the power of creative, effective, loving, and joyful groups to move us forward. When we can be as skillful in our human interactions as we are in our garden designs, we'll become an invincible force of healing for our communities and our earth. ❧

Starhawk is the author of 11 books on Goddess religion, earth-based spirituality, and activism, including The Spiral Dance; *her picture book for young children,* The Last Wild Witch; *and* The Earth Path, *which weaves together permaculture and spirituality. Her twelfth book,* The Empowerment Manual: A Guide for Collaborative Groups *was published in Fall of 2011. She also directs Earth Activist Trainings, offering permaculture design courses with a grounding in spirit and a focus on organizing, and collaborates with community organizations to bring permaculture to the inner city (www.earthactivisttraining.org). Together with director Donna Read Cooper, she created the documentary* Permaculture: The Growing Edge, *released in Fall of 2010 (belili.org). She is currently working with Yerba Buena Films to produce a feature film from her novel,* The Fifth Sacred Thing, *and to build earth-centered ethics and permaculture principles into the production itself (fifthsacredthing.com).*

Starhawk is one of the founders of the Pagan spiritual network Reclaiming, www.reclaiming.org. She has lived collectively and worked collaboratively in many settings for more than three decades. She blogs at www.starhawks-blog.org and her website is www.starhawk.org.

Young gardeners taste wild radish pods in Bayview Hunters Point, San Francisco.

---

1. Diana Leafe Christian, *Creating a Life Together: Practical Tools to Grow Ecovillages and Intentional Communities*, New Society, Gabriola Island, BC, 2003, p. 5.

2. www.reclaiming.org

3. www.earthactivisttraining.org

Wisdom begins with recognizing we are not alone...

www.exemplars.world – a resource for sustainability

There are thousands of organizations engaged with modifying the global society. While they represent a full spectrum of political and special interests, the critical division is between exploitation for short-term gain that ignores long-term consequences, versus respect for the many manifestations of sustainability.

Exemplars.world is a portal to help us understand and organize; a searchable, on-line library of the possible. There is a narrative that ties it all together, and for each organization or community, there is a brief description and a link to their web page. To add Exemplars, or comment, contact pfreundlich@comast.net

EXAMPLE: GREEN AMERICA

Starting point in the '70s and early '80s the lack of efficient links between producers who shared value of social and environmental responsibility.

Organizing strategy: Create marketplace of goods and ideas through a national membership organization (name changed from "Co-op America " to "Green America" in 2009). **Tools:** Retail catalog, quarterly journal, progressive health insurance plan, fair trade and renewable energy initiatives, festivals, campaigns addressing dangerous social and environmental corporate behavior. **Outcomes:** Recognition for pioneering efforts, and continued success. **Primary Resources:** http://www.greenamerica.org/ https://en.wikipedia.org/wiki/Green_America

What Makes Green America Unique: We focus on economic strategies— economic action to solve social and environmental problems. We mobilize people in their economic roles—as consumers, investors, workers, business leaders. We empower people to take personal *and* collective action. We work on issues of social justice *and* environmental responsibility. We see these issues as completely linked in the quest for a sustainable world. It's what we mean when we say "green."

391

Self-Reliance, Right Livelihood, and Economic "Realities": Finding Peace in Compromise

By Abeja Hummel

The dirt road to the valley floor winds its way through oak woodlands and past an enormous corporate vineyard. It bisects our neighbors' small horse farm and a massive overgrazed cattle ranch. If you had told me seven years ago that I'd have a 30-minute commute alone in my car to get to work twice a week, I'd have pointed out that I'd never even owned a car, that I don't need much money, and certainly don't work for "the man."

It's true, I have biked the road many times, and even driven our mule cart to town. Still, I've grown to really appreciate my biodiesel Jetta, and find I actually enjoy the time and space I get driving slowly through the countryside on my way to my bodywork practice in Boonville. Some would say I've grown up, some would say I've sold out. I would say that I have learned to compromise for love and a larger purpose. Having a child and living at Emerald Earth—a small, rural ecovillage in northern California—have taught me a lot about compromise.

We are incredibly blessed in that our land is owned—outright—by a nonprofit, so we aren't pouring money into a mortgage. As this is not currently an income-sharing community, we strive to keep the costs low for residents, and share the values of right livelihood and self-reliance. We are deeply engaged in rediscovering an interconnected, regenerative relationship with our land. We produce or wildcraft much of our own food, and sell or trade the surplus to neighbors for things we don't have. Our kitchen is usually packed with fresh, local, healthy, nutrient-dense foods. Processed, packaged, and sugary foods arrive only with unindoctrinated guests.

The cows and goats produce way more milk than we can consume, which we share with friends and turn into cheese and yogurt—all grass fed and higher quality than almost anything you can buy in a store. The chickens move around, cleaning and fertilizing our gardens and pastures and giving us in return delicious eggs with deep orange yolks. Our gardens pump out amazing organic produce. And on top of that, people from all over (though mostly the San Francisco Bay area) pay us to come to our community to take our workshops in natural building and other land-based practices.

So why is it, then, that I'm getting into my car twice a week and driving to town? Why is it that most residents here find it essential to have a well-paying off-site job, some savings, and little to no debt?

In the mythology of America, families can be completely supported by a successful small farm. Yet we find ourselves walking a line between radical self-sufficiency and the realities of the dominant culture's economic and social systems. We work jobs in town out of fear—must keep health insurance, must have car insurance, must pay debt. We also make money to pay for the fun things we still want from "out there"—a ski trip this winter, a new guitar, a music festival. So we work for someone or something else—taking our time and energy away from the vision we hold for ourselves and this land.

Our plan is to move towards the possibility that all residents can make a living on the land. We believe that a bounty of valuable goods and services can be gleaned in the process of revitalizing degraded topsoil, caring for the forests and creeks, collecting nature's abundance, and bringing life back towards the balance the native Pomo so carefully tended. This bounty includes milk and meat from goats that clear the underbrush from the thrice-logged tinderbox we see as an old-growth forest in the making. Proper management of our cows is rebuilding topsoil in our oak woodlands, as we watch the fertility and biodiversity increase over the years. We can envision a surplus of lumber—or at the very least firewood—resulting from a forestry plan that increases the health of the forest while decreasing the fire load. Mushrooms, acorns, and all sorts of other wild edibles offer themselves to us every year and we believe—as the Pomo have taught us—that wild things WANT to be respectfully gathered and used, and that their life cycles are benefited by that relationship.

I have a lot of time to think about these things, as I drive up and down the hill to work. I have considered abandoning my business in town many times and have experimented with various income sources from the land. Our first year here, my husband and I diligently went to the farmers' market with surplus fruit from ours and our neighbors' land, as well as wildcrafted mushrooms and seaweed. I also did chair massage. It was very socially rewarding and completely in line with our values. We made somewhere around $4 an hour for the harvesting and time at the market—we did not calculate in time spent caring for the fruit trees. The only real income derived from that time is the regular clients I gathered for my bodywork practice.

In America we are accustomed to buying food—as well as every other mass-produced commodity—cheaply. Selling the tastiest eggs you've ever tried at $6 a dozen, I would walk the line between red and black after figuring in the cost of supplemental organic feed. And that would come with a huge amount of work and folks complaining about my eggs being too expensive. Same math for the incredibly delicious fresh bread we bake in our wood-fired cob oven with local, organic, stone-ground wheat. (The saint who is growing the local wheat, I might add, is doing it as a labor of love at $1 a pound.) With time, good marketing, and cultivated relations with neighbors, however, I see examples of folks in our community making a go at it in small-scale, sustainable food production.

It is not only the massive reduction of income that keeps me from making the shift to a land-based cottage industry that is more in line with the goals of Emerald Earth and leads to much greater self-reliance as a community. Another factor is just the effort required. It's easy to go to town and come home with money. More than that, I would say, it's pleasant to do so. I live in a small ecovillage where we share two meals a day, have a dozen community projects going, and are blessed with the presence of kids needing attention. My drive to work is often the only quiet time I get all week, and being at work is the only time I'm not at risk of being distracted or interrupted by children, visitors with questions, or residents with needs or concerns.

Also, I get to make all the decisions about my business by myself, without asking anyone's opinions or permission, and without receiving feedback about how my choices affect each and every person living with me! Save the lecture about how important it is to work collectively, how much better decisions are when made in a group, and the pitfalls of our individualistic culture. I know and I agree—that's why I live in community. I also think it is important for individuals—adults and children alike—to have autonomy in some aspects of their lives. Running a land-based business on a property that you collectively steward with others is like navigating a ship through iceberg-laden waters.

Last year, my fellow resident Liz and I bought two cows, milking equipment, and miles of electric fencing. The goal—to use the cows to build topsoil and restore fertility to the native oak grasslands while producing delicious, nutrient-dense, raw dairy and grass-fed meat for us and to share with others who value that quality of food.

Everyone was supportive. Really, they were. It was hard to remember that, though, as we heard all the concerns—"Is that unsightly fencing going to stay there, where I like to go for a walk every day?" "The cows' hoof prints in the wet soil look like they're tearing up the land!" "It feels disrespectful that you keep having to leave meetings early to go milk." "I don't think you're paying the community enough rent considering the impact you're having on the land and the infrastructure" etc., etc. All valid concerns. All the sorts of concerns I would raise, myself, to someone else starting a business. But, as someone working her butt off trying to make a new project fly—or at least to be worth the money I'd put into it—it was difficult and discouraging.

All that for a project that if we wanted it as a business would make us less than minimum wage while not being quite exactly legal.

Which brings me to what I see as the biggest barrier many small, land-based businesses face—the prohibitive cost of time and money to comply with environmental, food safety, and other laws. I'm not a libertarian, and I fully support the spirit of most of these laws. Giant dairies—whose animals have numbers, not names—really should have a completely sterile environment and a $500,000 bottling facility. They shouldn't sell raw milk, and they do need to be inspected regularly. (I will not get into the debate over raw vs. pasteurized milk except to say that I would strongly warn against raw milk from an animal without a name, provided to you by a person you don't know.)

Some people use the "herd share" shared ownership model, where neighbors buy a "share" of the herd, and therefore get a share of the milk. Then they pay the farmer to care for and milk their animals for them. Everyone signs detailed contracts and understands what they're doing and the risks they are taking, drinking milk from an uncertified dairy. They are welcome to come visit their cows and watch the farmer milk them. They can even participate and muck out the barn! We'd love to do this. The herd has grown to three beautiful jerseys—Blossom, Honey, and Molasses. If any one of them becomes the slightest bit sick, I guarantee we'll notice.

And this is, as far as the feds are concerned, completely illegal. Last year, several herd share operations were busted throughout the state and the country. (Visit www.farmtoconsumer.org for more information.) This crackdown is ostensibly to protect public health, though it oddly seems to do more to protect corporate dairy profits. It is easier here in northern California to legally grow marijuana than it is to sell milk, cheese, pickles, or preserves—all of which require expensive equipment, commercial kitchens, and regular inspections. (Note: I recently learned of a new law passed in California which will make small cottage food production possible—though it excludes dairy.)

Other small business opportunities here are similarly legally dubious. Our work-

Tom makes firewood out of the byproduct of our restoration projects.

Abeja Hummel

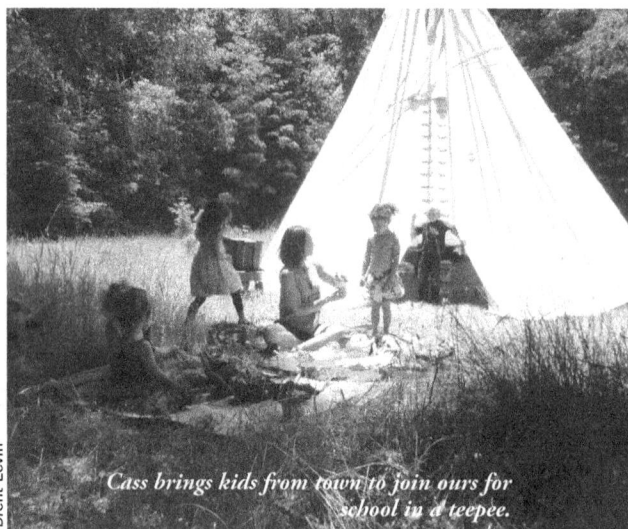

Cass brings kids from town to join ours for school in a teepee.

Brent Levin

shops and classes, for example, involve us feeding folks. We do not have a commercial kitchen, or submit to regular inspections. Any plan to care for our forest through thinning will require an expensive and time-consuming Non-Industrial Timber Harvest Plan (NTHP) prepared by a licensed forester. Only then could we begin selling firewood or lumber legally. Capitalizing any of these ventures legally would take major investment or big debt, which is a part of the system we are trying to escape.

Liz took the plunge. She has taken a break from her eight-year-old acupuncture practice in town to fully engage with her passion. She is now working towards the greater vision, fully embodying the Permaculture principles of care for the land, care for the people, and return the surplus.

I chickened out. I still help milk the cows, and I deliver milk to friends in town on my way to work. But most days I sleep in 'til 6:30 or 7 a.m. (luxurious), spend more time with my family—not with them following me around as I do chores at the barn—and stress less about money.

And so I drive up and down the hill, freshly showered, back seat full of coolers of milk, with most of the dirt dug out from beneath my fingernails. I bridge the worlds, bringing some money back into our community, enjoying the drive and reviewing my decisions. For now, there is peace in the compromise. ❧

Abeja has lived at Emerald Earth with her family for the last six years, and she has lived in intentional community for the better part of the last 18 years. Folks still seem willing to put up with her.

Author and kraut: Since we don't have a commercial kitchen, the world may never know my kraut and kimchi.

The New Membership Challenge

We want (and need) more people here to help us really fulfill the vision we hold for this place. Unfortunately, the last several people in the membership process have struggled and ended up leaving Emerald Earth. Much discussion and reflection on why things haven't worked here has pointed at least one finger at money.

It has become much more difficult to make ends meet here since the financial crisis. Our monthly consumables cost per adult has risen from $180 to $265 in the last four years, while income earning potential in the area has stagnated or even dropped. Our current lack of strong cottage industries means that people arriving need to figure out their own source of income while still plugging into all the great unpaid work we have to do here.

Of course, debt only makes this situation even more tenuous, and, with the cost of education skyrocketing, it is a rare person under 35 who is not burdened with debt. Our current community financial system makes it nearly impossible for the majority of young, intelligent, hard working, educated folks to be able to live here without defaulting on loans.

"Living within our means" (i.e., eschewing debt) is a radical, revolutionary act in this day and age. Most kids today get trapped in the debt cycle as part of getting an "education," so the choice is often made before they can truly understand what that means. I have witnessed that, for many, debt can be a slippery slope. Once you already owe many thousands of dollars, why not add a few hundred more for the latest iPhone or festival?

Interpersonally, I see money—and how people use it—to be a major source of discord. Although we're not income-sharing, we are financially intertwined. Folks often arrive from the outside world with nice cars, clothes, smart phones, laptops, online shopping habits, etc. It can be especially difficult to avoid judgment when these new residents then find they can't meet their minimal financial obligations here due to debt, lack of planning or savings, and/or the difficulties of finding decent paying work in a rural economy. It can also be a big learning curve for folks from the dominant culture to integrate into our current culture of thrift store and craigslist shopping, mending and repairing, creative reuse, and making do with less stuff.

We come to this life with a vision of a new way. This begins with an escape from the parts of the culture that are holding us back, beating us down, keeping us separate, keeping us working jobs that don't serve us. But how do we disentangle ourselves? How do we help others in that process? Can we choose to leave some parts and keep others? How patient can we be with people who share our lives yet make different choices? Can we live our values without succumbing to the fears that are put on us to engage in the the current systems of health insurance, social security, and retirement investment?

The work we're doing is difficult and won't be completed in my lifetime. To keep going, I have to remind myself of the big picture—the future we envision for our children's children.

—A.H.

Communities, Political Empowerment, and Collective Self-Sufficiency

By Mary Wildfire

As an activist concerned about climate change and environmental degradation, as well as peace and social justice, I've gone to countless demonstrations, spoken at many public hearings, had over a dozen op-eds and scores of letters to the editor published, and written hundreds of letters to "my" representatives. None of it, as far as I can see, has done any good.

So what's an activist to do? I've come to think that any effort to challenge the entrenched power structure is doomed—they have amassed such power over the past 30 years that we really can't win by electoral politics, by trying to influence officials, or even by massing in the streets (not without 10 times as many people as we've ever had). Instead, I believe our best course is to ignore that structure and focus on building alternatives ourselves.

We need alternative *livelihoods*, to assist middle-aged people being laid off as jobs are outsourced, and to provide young people an alternative to going deeply into debt for a college degree that likely won't lead to a good job anyway. We need an alternative to *paying taxes* to the IRS, which funnels half of it into the Pentagon for hideously immoral purposes. We need alternatives to *a way of life* that comes with a huge carbon footprint and endless stress, that provides a decent income to the lucky but provides joy and meaning and satisfaction to almost nobody.

Now is the time to work toward finding ways to declare independence from corporations, to provide for our most basic needs ourselves—whether as individuals, families, or communities. Community makes it easier. It takes a lot of time to do for yourself what we in the "developed world" have gotten used to paying others to do—those others now usually faceless and distant corporations. Declaring independence from corporations means no longer being an employee; thus one *has* much more time...for growing food, harvesting rainwater, managing an independent power source, and so forth. Within a community, though, one doesn't have to do everything.

Take my community, the Hickory Ridge Land Trust in West Virginia. Because the land was already paid for when my husband and I joined four years ago, we could get started with building a house at least a year sooner than if we'd had to save money to buy land as well as the building materials. To build a house, we needed a truck, which we still have. The Wilsons, the couple who were already here, need a truck sometimes—now they just use ours. I had some notion of a bicycle-powered washing machine, but they got a super-efficient one, so I just use theirs. They work in a bigger city during the week, so keeping animals would be problematic for them. But we have free-range chickens, so we keep them in eggs part of the year, and our dog patrols their garden some. Meanwhile, they bring us books from the bigger library. They have sandy soil, so I can get sweet potatoes from them.

We put in an off-grid photovoltaic system—my husband Don is an electronics whiz, and he figured out how to do this himself. When the Wilsons put in a grid-tied system the next year, he helped them, and I helped set the posts. There has been a time, in the darkest part of each of the three winters in which we've had our panels, in which we took a little power from the Wilsons' grid-tie (only a total of about 21 kilowatt-hours, though). Then when the derecho came through a few months ago and knocked out power for millions, we were able to pay back a little, keeping the Wilsons' freezer running without the need for a generator. So each couple benefits from the presence of the other—but it would be even better if we had people on the other two leaseholds. Maybe I could share a goat project with someone, for example.

What if more and more people gathered into communities, and built or retrofitted highly efficient housing? What if they began setting up power from solar panels and/or microhydro turbines or windmills, and arranged rainwater col-

Our clearing in winter, which includes an orchard, garden, chicken coop, the house, our solar panels, and the flower/herb bed.

Photos courtesy of Mary Wildfire

The Commons in fall.

This is Mocha Java, HRLT's security chief, official greeter, and animal control officer.

Don making maple syrup.

The author in a "brag shot" in front of this year's field corn.

lection, greywater use, and composting toilets? If they grew increasing amounts of their own food? There would be:

1. less financial support for corporations, and hence they'd have less power
2. less money paid into the IRS and hence less governmental and military power
3. less college debt
4. less greenhouse gas emission, less resource use, less environmental harm
5. a model for the surrounding communities of what is possible, i.e. that one can have one-tenth the income and one-tenth the carbon footprint without "freezing in the dark"
6. protection for the inhabitants in the event of a breakdown, which looks increasingly likely
7. more freedom for activists, supported by their communities
8. last but not least, satisfaction of the repressed hunger for community that I believe to be endemic in America, with its ethic of extreme individualism

And eventually, this alternate economic and social structure would make possible the creation of alternate institutions into which we could transfer the legitimacy we have drained from the oligarchy-controlled old ones. Notably, we could have some equivalent of the IRS, into which communities could pay a surplus to support useful activities like scientific and medical research, maintenance of the internet, and the rescue of climate refugees.

But this leads to the question of whether such a phenomenon, if sufficiently widespread to challenge the current power dynamic, would be tolerated. Exchanging seeds is already illegal in Europe; in the US, a sensible socialized healthcare system was eliminated from discussion but the Supreme Court ruled that citizens can be made to purchase health insurance. With this as precedent, what else can we be made to purchase? However, as of now it's perfectly legal to pool resources to buy land and build efficient housing on it (especially in rural areas where zoning restrictions and building codes are not impediments), set up your own power sources, and grow much of your own food. It seems likely that even if measures are brought to bear to make this more difficult, those of us already thus situated will be free to maintain our independent lifestyles…and we will want to do what we can to assist others.

It's also possible that societal breakdown caused by oil depletion, wars and conflicts, climate change, or some combination of these and other factors will create circumstances in which those of us set up to maintain our own food, water, and heat will be best situated for survival…and threats from the state can be forgotten. In such a scenario, being part of a community would be an enormous advantage. Of course, such a scenario might actually eliminate one of the biggest barriers to growth of self-sufficient communities: the need to buy back our land from the owning class.

A community working to continually reduce what it must purchase from outside (and to source that part locally) is thus best situated to survive catastrophe, to foster activism, to adapt to what may be a permanent recession, to do its part to reduce its environmental impact and to provide a local model for comfortable but low-impact living…as well as meeting the needs of its members for that deep home we all long for. Humans evolved in tribes and I believe we are happiest when part of a group of more than just a few people, with whom we have personal relationships and reciprocal obligations. ❧

Mary Wildfire is a writer, activist, and gardener, living on a ridge in West Virginia. She is part of Hickory Ridge Land Trust. She admits to being a hippie and a tree smoocher, kind of a pinko, who believes subversion to be the highest calling.

CLIMATE CHANGES:
Turn to Face the Strange

By Christopher Kindig

It is a rainy afternoon—the kind I always love for its ability to cool things down and set a calm mood, as if the world is moving at a bit slower or quieter pace. Nature is foremost, apparent, audible. And every drop makes the gardens happy, which allows me to skip watering duty.

This particular late spring in Maryland has seen more heavy rain than in my memory of growing up here. Sipping green tea at my desk, I listen and take it in, and wonder if it is part of the new normal. Melting icecaps and rising temperatures are gradually rearranging weather patterns, which in the mid-Atlantic region is manifesting, among other ways, as increased precipitation. A turning of the handle tells me my lovely fiancee is home from work.

We smile widely at each other. She slumps off her heavy backpack of social work and art therapy gear, pulls her jacket off onto the chair, and plops down onto the bed. Instant savasana. I sense a little something more than just the tired, relieved, after-work bed dive.

Was it something difficult that happened with one of her therapy clients, who face troubling circumstances every day? Was it something existential, say about the "need" for the hustle and bustle of working full time? Was it a resurgent longing for world travel and exploration? I implore sweetly, now lying beside her.

"It's Climate Change." She turns to look at me with honest despair lingering in her usually happy eyes. I sigh deeply. It is the second time this month.

Knowing what I do, how can I console my wife-to-be in the face of this realization of such great magnitude, and of potentially ominous and far-reaching consequence? What can I say when what is happening has been so greatly unmatched by humanity's awareness and action?

How can I protect her, our family, our homestead, and the community we wish to create, from a *freaking changing ecosystem*? As if life isn't complicated enough, just add on the rapid undoing of weather predictability, temperatures, and sea levels. Not to mention the potential disruptions in public health, energy, water, crops, and the economy...just to name a few.

Responding to Climate Change

I start in on a measured answer.

I begin by empathizing that it can be scary to think about, and sad to acknowledge. I have definitely been there (more on this later).

I explain that it is true that we do not know exactly how climate change is going to unfold, and how much clean energy and sequestration technologies will be online fast enough to slow the effects, or possibly even to reverse them. We can, however be certain that some change is already baked into the equation. It does indeed suck, but at least we are aware of it and there is a lot of information to help us respond to it the best we can. We will have to accept what we cannot change, see what we can do to respond, and help others to respond as well. That we are paying attention already is most important.

In terms of safety, I explain that there will not likely be an event which we will not be able to respond to. If there is one that we have absolutely no chance to respond to, that is just our fate.

To feel more confident in this perspective, we launch into a mini research project to determine the patterns of natural disasters in the US, and how it is expected that temperatures, water levels, and storms will change in our part of the world.

What we discover is that where we are planning to settle, near the mountains in the wilderness and farmlands of western Maryland, is going to be a solid place which addresses all of our biggest concerns about climate change, all while being less than two hours from our parents, friends, and families. We couldn't B'more* excited about being able to live our dreams while still being so close to home. *[Editor's Note: this Baltimore pun is intended.]

Also thankfully, many of our existing interests and plans, and likely those of many of the readers of COMMUNITIES, are already lining up with what people can do to effectively respond to Climate Change.

• Practice self-sufficiency via gardening, composting, fermentation, sprouting, etc.

• Learn permaculture so you can work

more effectively with land, plants, and animals, manage water resources, and foster ecological abundance.

• Pick up and use practical DIY skills, such as how to find answers and produce solutions.

• Nurture good relationships and build a stronger sense of community. For us it is not yet through an ecovillage, but through sharing a house with roommates, plus through work, family gatherings, hike clubs, and friends.

• Give back through the work that you do. Make sure that you, other people, and the world are better off and more happy because of the causes to which you dedicate yourself.

• Grow from successes and mistakes, develop your character, stay fit and healthy.

• Enjoy life, stay positive, and laugh, despite the circumstances. What are we alive for, if not to enjoy life!?

After exploring the topic from various angles, Karen and I start to breathe a collective sigh of relief, with cloudy uncertainty replaced by a brighter sense of resolve and creativity about our future. Little smiles around her eyes are a sight I am relieved to witness. She appreciates the talk, and reflects that it is so difficult because of how recent of a realization it is for her, the scope of it all, plus how it is compounded by planning to bring children into the world in a few years.

Through the difficulty of the topic and heaviness of the realization, I am so thankful that she is thinking about all of this, and that we have a plan together of how to respond. I encourage you, your family, and your community to talk about this issue and how you will respond as well.

Community Responses

Intentional communities are in a unique position to respond to climate change. First and foremost if they share strong bonds of respect, teaching, cooperation, and problem solving with their group, they will more likely be able to address new challenges with creative solutions.

Because of the way in which many intentional communities are organized, both ethically and practically, they already share many resources and create less waste. Communities have much smaller environmental footprints and therefore need less than their suburban counterparts.

Many communities also emphasize sustainability and self-sufficiency as core components of their purpose, and have programs that work to produce high quality organic food, harvest clean energy, and nurture a better relationship to the planet. These characteristics give communities the opportunity to thrive through climate changes.

Climate Crusaders

Another reason to be confident that we have a fighting chance against climate change is that there is a small army of exceptionally talented people out there working on this crisis from every different angle. Brilliant and skilled people who are passionate about making a difference are bringing together new energy innovations, multidisciplinary teams, and reimagined strategies to turn innovative potentials into realities today.

Over the last decade the headlines have steadily appeared about new game-changing energy technologies. In laboratories, universities, startups, garages, big companies, accelerator programs, and competitions around the globe, dozens of new ways to produce and store green energy have emerged. For example, using futuristic advancements such as lasers, nanotechnology, or biotechnology, scientists have more than doubled solar cell efficiency from where it has been lingering for close to 40 years, and cut the cost of producing solar power to a fraction of what it has been until now, making it even cheaper than coal-fired power. Tapping into the sun will be a new

Christopher and Karen.

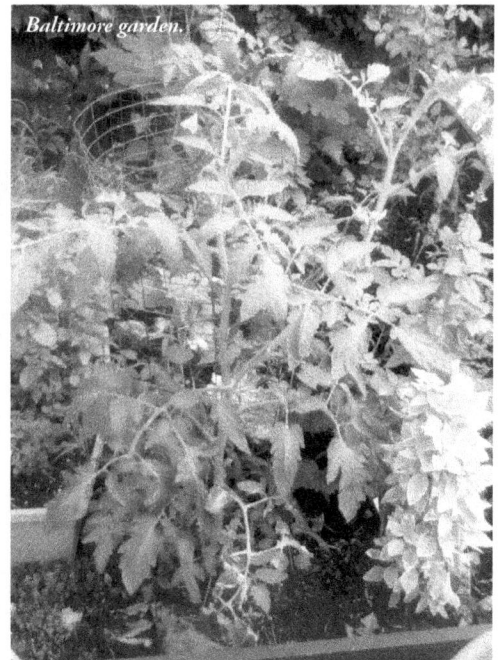
Baltimore garden.

renaissance for humanity.

New biofuel technologies are allowing people to grow high yield, low cost, and low resource-intensive algae for producing biodiesel, ethanol, or biogas. You can find do-it-yourself guides and technology to produce it yourself on OrganicMechanic.com.

Tesla Motors is innovating to bring their $100,000 Roadster down to $35,000 for a pure electric performance plug-in car. They are aiming to further reduce that price by half over the next decade. Most of their charging stations use solar energy and the network is expanding. With the current stations one can now drive from LA to NYC on clean solar electrons alone!

Also promising, and seemingly completely under the radar from the public's attention, the President and his team have laid a legal framework to make carbon pollution officially a dangerous poison that the EPA can regulate. Specifically this means that coal-fired power plants and other large polluters are going to have to reduce their dangerous emissions. This will spawn innovation to create and use energy more efficiently, as well as new sequestration technologies which could even repurpose waste into raw materials.

> **I wrestled with depression about the tragic degradation of our planet and what this means for future generations.**

Nonprofits and other organizations are also bringing their weight to bear, and groups such as 350.org are advancing the cause and deserve much praise for rallying unprecedented support in demonstrations around the globe to bring attention to this issue. Many more initiatives to raise awareness exist, and they could all certainly use your help and support!

Turning Green Torment into Pathways Forward

I was definitely able to empathize with my fiancee's fears and concerns about impending Climate Change. Yet since I have been working in the field of green technology for nearly a decade, and investing my heart, mind, and tears in environmentalism for much longer than that, I have already gone through a lot of torment surrounding the issue.

Christopher fixing the Veggie Pump.

I wrestled with depression about the tragic degradation of our luscious planet Earth, and what this means for animals and future generations. I often worked through the night with chest-thumping anxiety due to the overwhelming feeling: that so few humans seem to care at all about the fate of our planet. I experienced anger at people, companies, institutions, and beliefs that perpetuate problems and stall solutions. I dealt with wrenching toxic guilt over my role in what to personally do about it all.

Through all of this I am now much more accepting and informed of what is happening, how to stay sane despite all of it, and how to play a realistic constructive role in the way forward.

After touring around the US on a biofuel powered school bus, teaching about biofuels to schools, local groups, and media outlets, and developing an easier way to filter vegetable oil along the way, I realized that the world was in need of a go-to place to learn about and to choose smart green solutions. This is why in 2005 I started OrganicMechanic.com, where you can find innovative green technologies, useful information, and friendly support, to help you save money on electricity and fuel. Benefits of green energy also include increasing your energy security, supporting localization, and reducing your carbon footprint.

Earth Tribe on the Bus.

Earth Day 2006: Bus in Corpus Christi.

Photos courtesy of Christopher Kindig

Greasing the Wheels

Before the green business was the green bus. It all started with an adventurous crew, a dream to travel, and a full-sized school bus converted to run on pure vegetable oil.

The five of us were college students in Corpus Christi, Texas who were looking for something exciting to be a part of. We all wanted to travel, and wondered if there was some way to reduce our fuel costs and emissions. After researching and finding out that Rudolf Diesel himself originally advocated vegetable oil to fuel his engine, we decided to pick up a bus from an auction. We then found and worked with a conversion company to install a heated fuel system that would allow us to fuel our journeys with used cooking oil filtered from restaurants.

Earth Tribe became our group name, as we found shared interest in alternative energy, healthy living, and cooperative culture. We decided to launch a campaign to create awareness and support. "Healthy Individual, Healthy Community, Healthy Planet." We developed talking points and gave speeches to local environmental and political organizations, set up demonstrations at Earth Day, and presented at schools from K through College. We organized multiple media appearances, and had a party to raise funds for a great voyage across the country in the veggie-powered bus. Our enthusiasm was well received, and people were amazed learning about how minor vehicle adjustments could provide us with new energy sources today.

Over a few years of off-and-on trips, the bus saw over 20,000 miles of countryside and tight city streets, thanks mostly to recycled grease as fuel. Traveling on biofuels was not always a breeze, however. We did experience multiple breakdowns, and eventually became aware of how poorly constructed and installed our original vegetable oil system was. Far too many times we were stranded on the side of the highway, and in between the thunderous rumbling from trucks storming by, I was dreaming of how an ideal system would operate.

In addition to those trying issues, we also ran into a lot of hassle with collecting and filtering oil, at least at first. Anyone experienced in this will be able to reflect that while you can get it down to a science, it can be a messy learning curve—especially when you are collecting hundreds of gallons at a time for a bus. Waking up every few hours throughout the night to squirt a few more gallons of oil into a sock filter over a barrel was not only annoying, inefficient, and giving me weird dreams, it was also too expensive, and so there just had to be another way.

I started to research and developed an inline filtration system called the GreaseBeast. My business and life partner of that era, Dani Phoenix, now cofounder of the sustainability and education focused nonprofit D.r.e.e.m. Reality (DreemReality.org), took care of the customers, accounting, and taxes, while I guided strategy, improved the technology and access to suppliers, built the online marketing, and assembled filtration equipment in the rooms off of the kitchen.

We both did our share of packaging and hauling giant boxes in shopping carts to the post office. It involved a great deal of literal sweat investment and on-the-go learning, while we also went to school full-time for much of it. Through all of that, I found it very rewarding to run a company that was helping people to get free from the fuel matrix.

Over the years, working with friends and engineers I also designed a diesel conversion kit which solves some of the most challenging issues we faced on the bus. This system knows when to switch between fuels, tells you when to change fuel filters, lets you know if there is water in the fuel, and gives you a reminder to purge the fuel system on diesel fuel when you shut down. You can find these on OrganicMechanic.com/diesel-conversion-kit/ and the Support Manager Bob Karl can help you with any questions about how to convert, and how to find and filter oil.

We eventually decided to sell the bus, as new life chapters presented themselves. I cleaned and tuned her up very nicely, reminiscing all the while, and a beautiful synchronicity occurred when a group of five soon-to-graduate high school students from North Carolina found the veggie bus ad online. It was an opportunity for their dreams of a lifetime to come true, so they became the new caretakers, and the Legend of La Fonda Olive continues on the road today!

—C.K.

If you go to the OM website you can sign up to receive a free guide called "Ways to Go Green" that provides the most high impact ways you can get a grasp on and cut your energy costs. You can also find biofuel equipment, electric bicycles, electric car conversion guides, solar and wind power, efficient heating and cooling, home and vehicle efficiency devices, and more.

Starting Organic Mechanic also addressed a conflict in myself between my passions for the environment and self-sufficiency on the one hand, and my natural interest and inclination for entrepreneurship, marketing, and busi-

Original Earth Tribe Bus crew.

ness on the other. I have grown to see business as a tool, which like any tool can be abused, but which also can be applied constructively to change the world for the better. I am in a similar position now as the Business Manager for FIC, where I am applying business insights to make the organization more sustainable and effective, so that we may support and spread the communities movement even further.

Green businesses, also referred to as B Corps and the like, as with many non-profit organizations, take into account the so called "externalities" that business-as-usual has ignored. The new bottom line measures not only profit, but purpose, including the real impacts on people and the planet. A responsible business or organization, and those running it, realize this truth and decide to be part of that better world.

We Can Change This

"To change something, build a new model that makes the existing model obsolete."
—Richard Buckminster Fuller

To face the climate's change we could sure use a culture change. Companies and industries that are poisoning the earth should be held accountable for their poor decisions. It will also take bet-

ter representation in government to help to set a greener course, and enterprising individuals in nonprofits and businesses to pull people together. Ultimately individuals must seek more responsibility to pay attention to and take care of the world around them.

As harsh as it can be to realize the problems the world is facing, I hope that more people will go through the realization. It is better than ignorance or denial, and it raises hope that it could yield some positive response, for that person and their community, and also for the world at large.

As Greensburg, Kansas showed us (see the movie *Within Reach* or look online for more of that story), people can do breathtakingly incredible and imaginative things when joining together in the face of disaster. If we can show this same tenacity of unity, shared purpose, and creativity to reimagine the way things could be, even before there are disasters to face, we can do nearly anything.

Humanity has been short-sighted in its use of dirty fuels. It turns out that the high energy stuff in the ground was in fact too good to be true. We are collectively awakening to this reality, and to the potential consequences of continued inaction in the not-so-distant future. Will we work together to formulate a strategy big enough to match the challenge?

This has become the new human story. We must learn (remember) to love each other, in order to work together. We must learn (remember) to love our planet, in order to keep it. ❧

Christopher Kindig grew up near and now lives in Baltimore, Maryland. Christopher majored in Psychology at Texas A&M, and founded a green technology company, OrganicMechanic.com, in 2005. He now also serves as the Advertising and Business Manager of the Fellowship for Intentional Community, and is a Sales Representative for Baltimore's first online farmers market by delivery, RelayFoods.com. Christopher loves growing, cooking, and eating fresh food, traveling, yoga, hiking, nature, good people, intellectual inquiry, stimulating conversation, and long walks, especially with his partner.

Baltimore rooftop garden.

Confessions of a Fallen Eco-Warrior

By Chris Roth

Beginning at the End of the Road

AWhen I arrived at my first place-based intentional community, tucked away in the Oregon woods, I wondered if I could feel good ethically about all the compromises I'd be making by living there. In the previous couple years I'd been living mostly in a tent, using just a small solar panel for electricity in my dwelling, cooking only with sunlight, getting around just by foot or bike, eating no animal products or packaged foods, trying to minimize my ecological footprint (including consumption of nonrenewable energy) in all the ways I could think of.

By contrast, this place—named End of the Road, although it turned out to be just the beginning of the road for me in the intentional community world—was, for one, hooked up to the electrical grid. True, our electric bill (for a group that ranged from four to 12 members at a time) was always less than $10 a month. We didn't have a refrigerator (substituting a "draft box" on the back porch instead), but we did have a freezer, which contained, among other indulgences, packaged, nonorganic, milk- and sugar-laden ice cream. Instead of tolerating the ambient temperatures, people here also built fires for warmth (burning trees and adding to pollution and global warming), and also cooked with wood and even propane. A few of them had cars, which they occasionally drove to town. There was even a computer in the office, which some residents used occasionally.

The difficulties in adapting to this collective pact with various civilizational devils were obvious. It was far from ideal for an ardent eco-liver in his early-mid-20s (this was the mid-late 1980s, in an environmental landscape reeling from the policies of Ronald Reagan and James Watt), but it had to do, because it was the place I had chosen to pursue another goal: grow as much of the group's own food as possible by hand, to save all the energy that would otherwise go into growing and transporting the food we'd buy.

I did manage to stay fairly true to my ideals. For the next two years, despite the fact that I had a room available to me, I slept outside, getting my comfort and entertainment from the natural environment instead of pumping it into an indoor space. I don't think I ever actually lit a fire—I always let someone else give in to that weakness. I avoided the ice cream, built a solar cooker, made copious use of the hayboxes (retained-heat cookers) that I learned about there, never obtained a car and usually didn't even step into one, continued to eat a purer-than-thou, unpackaged diet, tried to purchase only "used" (not new) on those rare

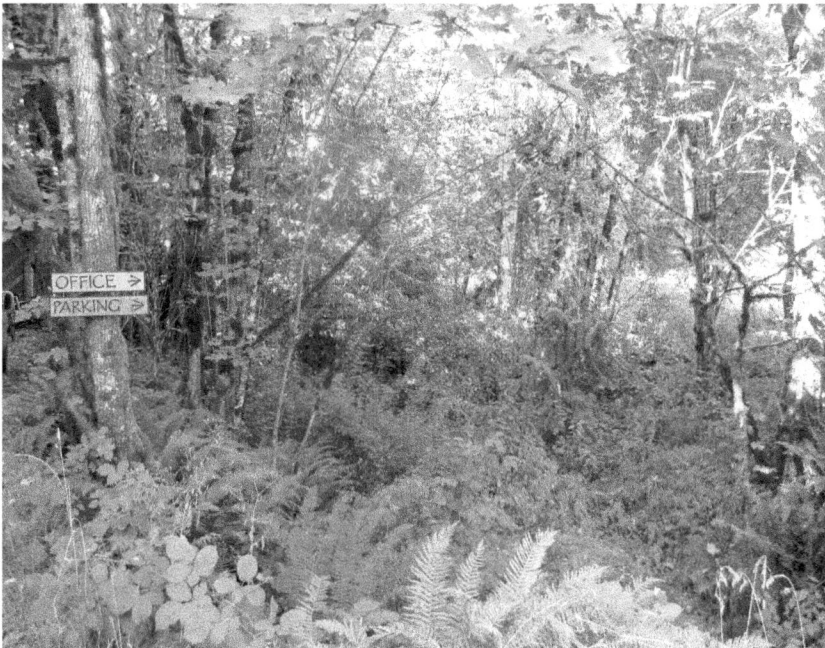

OFFICE →
PARKING →

occasions when I did find myself truly in need of something material, and put together the group's newsletter on a typewriter instead of the computer.

Most visitors to this place were coming from the opposite direction in terms of lifestyle. For them, our way of life seemed hard-core, austere, even severe—aligned with ecological ideals to a fault, often at the expense of comforts to which they were attached. It did fall on the hard-core end of the eco-living spectrum among intentional communities which were open to the public (we offered internships, courses in sustainable living skills, and other opportunities to get involved), but from my perspective it was still a study in compromise, especially compared with how native people had lived in this region for thousands of years preceding the European invasion (of which we were the latest representatives).

We were trying to undo the harm caused by that conquest of the land in whatever ways we could, but it was a long path to that goal, and we knew we had just started on it. We were forever hobbled by our upbringings in western consumer culture, but we hoped to explore and model a different way of doing things. This different way would—must—become the "new normal" if our species were to survive. Eventually, our own bad habits (like that ice cream in the freezer, once we were sufficiently unplugged) would melt away, replaced by the richness of the culture we'd helped create.

The Wisdom of Babes

I'd been following this hard-core path for a while, spanning a couple years with a traveling environmental education school (see "Power and Disempowerment on the Ecobus," issue #148), a year-and-a-half on a Native American reservation, and close to a year immersing myself in solar cooker design and then ecological horticulture, all while living outdoors. Even before the "rebellion" that took me from an east coast suburban liberal arts education to a lifestyle that aspired to out-earthfirst EarthFirst!, I had reduced my nonrenewable energy consumption through an aversion to spending money, a distaste for automobiles and love of foot-powered transport, an ongoing boycott of "canned" entertainment, a dedication to eating low on the food chain, and other strategies. Some of these choices were intellectually and morally driven, stemming from my growing awareness of human impacts on the planet. But some were simply a return to the sensibilities that I'd had as a child before I had any awareness of larger ecological issues or knew much about any world outside my own life and family.

As a young child I was afraid of anything that made a loud noise. Someone else had to flush the toilet for me. Vacuum cleaners caused me great distress. Getting into a car often precipitated crying. Left to my own devices, I would have designed a world without any of those things—and it would have been a world that consumed a lot less (nonrenewable) energy. Gradually I learned to be a "big boy," one who flushed his own toilet, vacuumed his own room, cooperated by getting into the car, and even eventually agreed to get a driver's license (while vowing to use it rarely if ever). I hardened myself to the way modern life is, for survival if nothing else. Only crybabies, I concluded, can't handle the ruckus and commotion that the fossil fuel age has brought—and I didn't want to be a crybaby.

But I wonder:

Did my infantile self know something that our adult selves are just beginning to grasp? Is it possible that using so much energy, and living amidst all the noise created by this energy consumption, is actually bad for our own well-being, not to mention the planet's? Could our energy habits actually be in direct conflict with the biological, spiritual, emotional, and social health of the human animal?

It's Not Easy Being Green

As I mentioned, my arrival at End of the Road involved a lot of apparent compromise. But it was only the beginning of what was either a slippery slide back into being

Photos by Chris Roth

an overconsumer or, looked at another way, a growth out of "energy fundamentalism" into a broader understanding of energy and how it works.

Gradually I realized that even though I couldn't think of myself as being so pure anymore, my participation at End of the Road did probably have a net positive impact on the planet, energy-wise. While not divorced from our culture's bad habits entirely, our group (even when there were up to a dozen of us) likely had a smaller ecological footprint all combined than even just a single typical mainstream American had. And we set out not only to "walk the talk" but to "talk the walk" and expose others directly to some of our practices. Our small nonprofit organization, Aprovecho, was the point from which several influential technologies spread.

Hayboxes, an old technology which can also be constructed with modern materials, result in cooking fuel savings of 70 percent or more. Aprovecho's brochures, newsletters, workshops, and living demonstrations ultimately seeded hayboxes in many places around the world. (I did my small part by later building hayboxes at a few other intentional communities and writing an article touting their benefits in COMMUNITIES #115.) Rocket stoves, highly efficient low-mass stoves with an insulated combustion chamber, able to be constructed from a wide variety of easily available or local materials, originated at Aprovecho, and have spread worldwide (see www.aprovecho.org, www.aprovecho.net).

An ardent advocate of solar cooking, I encountered a mixture of resistance and appreciation as I tried to introduce it at End of the Road and elsewhere. I discovered that others were not necessarily as willing as I to make sacrifices in the interests of cooking with "zero fuel"—inconveniences such as starting the cooking process earlier than they otherwise would, returning to refocus the cooker every few hours, risking uncooked food on potentially cloudy days, etc. The impulse to make a statement and be pure bumped up against the reality that self-nurturance sometimes requires being gentle with oneself and others, using easily-available resources on hand even if they're not perfect, taking one's own reserves of time and energy into account when making choices.

Ultimately, I left End of the Road and Aprovecho for significantly less hard-core situations, as I realized that no amount of energy fundamentalism could substitute for the renewable energy of human connection.

Less Purity, More Renewal

My community-living path took me to varied situations, and in most of them our energy-consumption habits were significantly closer to the American standard than I'd experienced at the end of Hazelton Road. Yet they were still a far cry from the mainstream. Every group I lived with valued energy consciousness, and our per-capita consumption was still well below average as a result of resource sharing, simpler living, ecological values, and a striving for responsible global citizenship.

I often tried to cling to the more extreme, "pure" practices in my personal living space, but found I had to make peace with living with electric heat (for example) in some common spaces, along with refrigeration, computer servers that stayed on all day, and other features of modern life that I could rationalize only through the fact that they were shared among many people, diluting their impact.

But evolving in me simultaneously I discovered a much greater appreciation of a different kind of energy: the energy of love, warmth, and light that human beings themselves can generate for each other, regardless of whether they are on-grid or off-grid. This energy ultimately drew me to the community at which I've stayed the longest (totaling more than a decade-and-a-half now).

When I joined it, this community hosted intensive personal growth workshops and held weekly well-being meetings in which members practiced the

skills and awareness cultivated by those workshops. We consciously worked on creating a culture in which openness, honesty, vulnerability, acceptance, self-acceptance, letting go of attachments, and love could set the tone of our inter-actions. When we dedicated ourselves to these intentions, and prioritized healthy communication and connection in our relationships, the energy we derived from this culture was palpable. In fact, the cul-ture seemed to take on a life of its own, and even became our "default" mode; with our collective energy and daily prac-tice behind it, it brought us along even in times of resistance, and became infec-tious even with visitors and short-term program participants.

It challenged us to see beyond a ten-dency toward judgment and imagined separation. It helped me realize that setting myself apart in a pure world of only "renewable energy" (or none at all) was not only impossible, but based on a false set of assumptions about the world. Without adequate and genuine human connection, the solo renewable energy pioneer may not actually create a model of a sustainable future. In fact, he or she may end up desperately accumu-lating renewable energy toys and gizmos, actually consuming more resources and energy than someone who's learned that the way to a light footprint is to learn to dance with others. This second approach

may involve give-and-take, and compromises of black-and-white worldviews and positions, but it will likely ultimately result in more sharing and more resilience. It reduces the perceived need for more under-inhabited renewable energy mansions or fortresses, and increases the number of people who are happy sleeping on one another's floors, sharing one another's kitchens, and dealing with challenges together.

Solar Power and Soul

Part way through my renewable energy journey, a friend helped me assemble a pho-tovoltaic system to power lights and a cassette player in my otherwise unelectrified cabin. For at least a dozen years, this served as the main or only source of electricity in my living space. Its initial installation cost less than running an electric line to the cabin would have cost, and even when I moved it to another location where grid power was available, I still valued not only the electricity it gave me but the lessons it taught me. As my experiences with solar cooking had done, it helped instill in me a much more acute awareness of weather patterns, and also showed me my own pat-terns of energy usage. I never flipped or left a switch "on" unless I had a good reason for using those electrons. Maintaining my own power system, I was constantly aware

---

If I acted as if the power in my photovoltaic system would never run out, it *would* run out.

---

of the reality of limitations, of the need for conscious use of the earth's "goods." I could not live in a fantasy of limitlessness (at least not physical limitlessness)—if I acted as if the power in my system would never run out, it *would* run out.

Using my own off-grid photovoltaic system, like cooking with the sun, became a way of attuning myself not only to ecological realities, but also ultimately to spiritual realities. It felt like a form of prayer. It didn't always make logical sense—and since for most of that time I also had access to grid power (and used it in our common spaces), it wasn't even a statement of purity or a hard-core activist stance. But it did help me feel more grounded, and was a step back from the less-mindful energy consumption

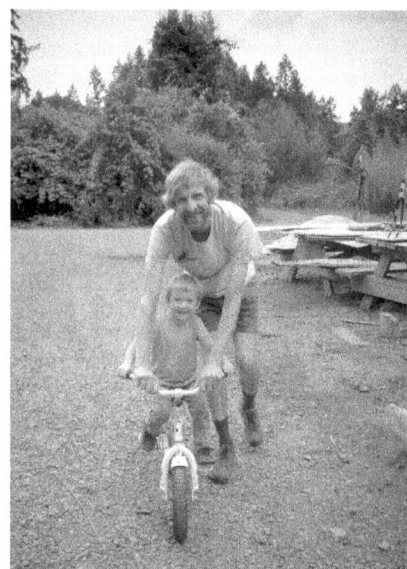

Suzzy Stranger

so easy to fall into without deliberate measures to counteract it.

When, overwhelmed by changes at my home community and convinced that my own path had diverged from it, I set off for what turned out to be a year away, I at first tried to ignore how important my semi-off-grid lifestyle had been to me, and then tried to recreate it even more thoroughly—in two different communities, one of which was entirely on-grid, the other entirely off-grid. In the first case, I ended up partially fixating on misgivings with this on-grid lifestyle; in the second case, even as I was erecting my new panels on the roof of my new cabin rental, I was having grave doubts about whether this place was a good match for me. Sure, I could be "pure" from a renewable energy standpoint (if I ignored that these panels, batteries, and components had been manufactured on-grid and also just been trucked over thousands of miles of highways to reach me here in this remote off-grid location)—but my sense of community, of relation to the land, and of self had not recovered from the many changes I had put them through since leaving my home bioregion of several decades.

Ultimately, I sold my new photovoltaic system, moved back to Oregon to use my old one (with much greater simultaneous use of grid power), prioritized physical healing for a while (which necessitated making lots of car trips and even leaping into the energy footprint of a hospital operating room), stopped imagining that I could be pure, and found myself focusing much more on the kinds of human energy I exchanged than on the forms of physical energy. I did use more energy (whether nonrenewable or renewable) sometimes—but I also used less, since I saw myself as much less separate from others and so participated in a lot more sharing of resources.

A Future

The other night, I followed a link to the video of an interview with Sarah Wilcox-Hughes (www.permaculturedesign-training.com/course/sustainability-interviews, Lecture 255). Sarah interned with me in the Lost Valley gardens a dozen years ago, and afterwards set out on a journey with her now-husband Ethan Hughes which led to their establishment in 2008 of an entirely off-grid homesteading community, now called Still Waters Sanctuary, the headquarters of the Possibility Alliance in La Plata, Missouri. During my recent year in Missouri, I visited their community many times, often staying overnight. In fact, it was the place I tended to feel most at peace. I couldn't have lived there permanently, because not only do they have no electricity but they also forbid computers, and my current job—not to mention chosen work in the world—requires a computer (the one I'm typing on right now).

In the interview, Sarah talks about the richness of life when it is up to us to create more of it—and when there are fewer distractions caused by piped-in power and piped-in culture. For most of human evolution, we have talked with each other face-to-face, created our own music and other entertainment, lived in greater attunement with light and darkness, gotten to know our neighbors and helped one another out partly because working together to meet our needs was a necessity. For most of our evolution, before the advent of fossil fuels and the electric grid, we've lived intimately with our place, with the earth and with one another, with few technological intermediaries and few artificial instant escapes from the moment.

That quality of experience is still accessible to any of us, simply by being present with the earth and with the people around us. It's what makes life in community rich for me. It's what draws me to assist in the four-day workshops that are the current incarnation of those we held "back in the day." It's what I value in my interactions with friends. And yet, unlike the stewards of Still Waters Sanctuary, I am not living that life exclusively most of the time. I make many compromises. I sometimes turn to technology for connection, rather than relying on myself or the people and land around me. I took in Sarah's thoughtful and inspiring words (captured on video more than three years ago) on my computer, imagining that I was back there, once again working in the garden with her, feeling connected to those people and that place instead of to my immediate surroundings. It was a fantasy experience of community and wisdom—but it was also real, in my imagination.

Even these words, typed into the computer, are a bit of a fantasy conversation with you, the reader, and with myself. But in this world of un-purity, in which I am renewed by many kinds of energy, and trying to suspend judgment about what forms it takes, they seem to want to be written. A century from now, many more of us may be living like Sarah, Ethan, and their friends. That life will be good. And this one is too, despite its ironies, compromises, and likely limited shelf-life. Everything evolves, and we're part of that. I'd like to believe that renewable energy—and the energy of renewal—will guide us through, if we keep our eyes open. ❧

> For most of our evolution, before the advent of fossil fuels and the electric grid, we've lived intimately with our place.

Chris Roth (editor@ic.org) lives at Lost Valley Education and Event Center/Meadowsong Ecovillage in Dexter, Oregon (www.lostvalley.org), leads nature walks at Mt. Pisgah Arboretum (www.mountpisgaharboretum.com), assists at Solsara workshops (www.solsara.net), plays guitar, has fun with kids and sometimes even adults, and edits Communities.

Land Management and Lifesharing at Innisfree Village

By Rhonda Miska

A Day in the Life...

At Innisfree Village at 9:00 on a weekday morning—as is the case in so many communities—everyone is beginning the day's work. In the bakery the bakers are tying on their aprons to prepare bread and granola. The weavers are sitting down at their looms to work on scarves and placemats. The kitchen is beginning preparations for lunch, which will feature the greens recently harvested from the garden as well as eggs from the farm. Herb and vegetable gardeners are slathering on sunblock and bug spray before heading out to weed and harvest. In the woodshop you can already hear the whir of machines as wood workers sand and assemble cutting boards. The farm crew heads out to the hen houses to collect eggs, which they will wash, package, and then deliver to several local restaurants and grocery stores.

Each of these work crews are made up of coworkers: adults with intellectual disabilities such as Down syndrome, autism, and cerebral palsy. The term "coworker" was chosen intentionally to emphasize the contributions of community members with disabilities, who in other settings would be referred to in more clinical terms as "clients" or "patients." Coworkers are accompanied by volunteers who range in age from 20 to 70 and come from around the world for one year or more of community living and caregiving experience.

Innisfree was founded in 1971 by a group of parents with children with intellectual disabilities who wanted to create a community, not a facility, and provide a unique alternative to institutions or group homes which were the norm. Inspired in part by the communities movement of the 1960s, the founders dreamed of a place where people with special needs could lead lives of beauty, warmth, and respectfulness. They envisioned creating family-style homes and therapeutic workshops which focused on individuals' abilities, not their limitations. With a bank loan, the founders purchased land outside of Charlottesville, Virginia and chose the name "Innisfree Village" inspired by William Butler Yeats' poem "The Lake Isle of Innisfree." Innisfree's first executive director moved into an old farmhouse on the property along with his family and two adults with disabilities in the fall of 1971.

More than 40 years later, after many ups and downs, joys and growing pains, Innisfree Village now encompasses 550 acres and 15 residential homes. This includes a home with a common house flanked by individual apartments which are designed to give higher-functioning coworkers more independence and autonomy, as well as two houses in the city of Charlottesville for coworkers who hold part-time jobs outside the community.

Hay rolls sit in front of the barn at Innisfree Village, located on 550 acres outside Charlottesville, Virginia.

Residents Cath and Gelly water vegetable starts.

Coworker Tom pulls a wheelbarrow.

An extensive herb garden provides herbs for community use and for CSA members.

Photos courtesy of Rhonda Miska

The Land

From the beginning, the community has been conscious of our relationship with the land. One of the principles outlined in our mission statement is to "promote efforts in the stewardship of our land to acknowledge the reciprocal relationship between our human health and the natural environment." We know that when the world around us is healthy, we feel better. Likewise, the better we feel, the more motivated we are to look around and try to improve the environment.

Currently at Innisfree there are about four acres of gardens which produce all types of vegetables, herbs, and flowers. Their bounty is appreciated both by Innisfree community members and by members of our local CSA (Community Supported Agriculture group). The vegetable garden crew also manages apple, pear, peach, and fig trees—processing much of the fruit through saucing and canning. Beef cattle provide meat to Innisfree community members, and about 300 chickens provide eggs to Innisfree residents as well as to the broader local community. In the past few years we have added a sheep operation, which means the arrival of new baby lambs is one of the most anticipated signs of spring.

Urbanite visitors to Innisfree are often charmed by the farm and gardens described above and we are quick to remind them that there is a lot behind that lovely country scene. Looking out at the flock of clucking chickens, the rows of blooming sunflowers and bright colored vegetables, and the cows on the pasture, one can imagine that Innisfree is a rural utopia. As many communitarians know, it is easy to romanticize living in harmony with the land and with each other...until you actually start doing the work. The days are long, the labor is demanding, and there is no shortage of obstacles to overcome.

Like any agricultural community, we contend with unpredictable weather and natural pests. Here in Virginia's Blue Ridge, we share the land with bears, deer, skunks, snakes, and other creatures. The hot and humid summers bring not only a bounteous vegetable harvest, but also run-ins with poison ivy, as well as ticks and chiggers. And gardening in a community setting—with people with disabilities, no less—means there are challenging relationship dynamics to manage as well. Since the majority of volunteers stay one year, volunteer turnover can impact the productivity of garden and farm workstations. Maintaining consistency is a struggle. Engaging with the land in community is rewarding, and it is also undeniably hard work.

We all reap the benefits of this work—through the delicious and healthy food we enjoy, through the income that is produced by what we sell, through the sense of pride we take in our efforts. There are also less tangible benefits to our engagement with the land. It helps create the rhythm of our common life as we move through the four seasons year after year. We celebrate the spring equinox by painting our vegetable buckets in anticipation of the first harvest of spring onions and greens, and the fall equinox by building a Sukkoth and pressing apple cider. During the colder winter months we enjoy making wreaths with dried flowers and seeds and during the summer many look forward to mowing and haying.

Our setting provides a unique sense of place, and several community members have described the feeling of peace and well-being that is created through being held in the mountains' embrace. Patty Coleman Saul, the daughter of Innisfree's first farmer, Joe Coleman, remembers her childhood fishing in the lake and riding bikes on the paths and reflects that "the land is the core of the idea of Innisfree... it makes us who we are if we are lucky enough to have been a part of it."

The Guiding Principles

Peter and Debra Traverse, farmers and land managers since 2007, articulate their three guiding principles in engaging with the land: "responsible stewardship of assets, meaningful engagement of community members, and financial sustainability." All of our initiatives at Innisfree Village related to land management flow from these three goals.

Responsible stewardship of our assets means, first and foremost, valuing this land and doing what we can to maintain and improve it. "We want to make the moral choice," says Peter Traverse. "We want to make informed decisions about our presence on this land."

We seek to meet the definition of sustainability offered by the United Nations' World Commission on Environment and Development: "development that meets the needs of the present without compromising the ability of future generations to meet their own needs." While much of mainstream agriculture today focuses on producing as much product as possible to create a maximum short-term profit, the approach favored by Innisfree and other ecoagriculturalists seeks to look at the health of the whole ecological system.

A key component of this system is the health of the soil, which is home to a multitude of organisms: earthworms, bacteria, fungi, insects, micro-flora and -fauna. A billion or more organisms may live in a single cubic inch of topsoil. Though "dirt" doesn't often receive much consideration or respect, in truth, soil is the basis of all we do. Healthy soil provides balanced nutrition for plant life, which nourishes us and the animals we raise. Conscious of both human health and soil health, we use no chemicals in our vegetable, fruit, flower, and herb production, and use organic farming practices. We move our chicken coops weekly to provide forage for the birds, and in turn they fertilize the soil. Similarly, we practice intensive rotational grazing for our sheep and cattle.

Meaningful engagement of community members is another guiding principle of land management at Innisfree. The workstations are therapeutic and seek to provide both coworkers and volunteers with meaningful work and the opportunity to learn and refine new skills. Many Innisfree volunteers come here from having been in urban or academic settings, and enjoy the chance to grow food and work with their hands. Coworkers are an integral part of our projects in the gardens and on the farm. Whether through feeding sheep, harvesting tomatoes, cleaning wool, felting soap, or any of many other tasks, they contribute to the good of the community.

Given the diversity of abilities and disabilities among our coworkers, lots of different jobs are needed. One coworker who can't be in the heat because of susceptibility to seizures may work inside helping process vegetables and herbs into pesto or soup mix. Another coworker with a lot of energy to burn off may spend work time pushing wheelbarrows, stacking firewood, or shoveling mulch. Coworkers with good attention to detail and fine motor skills enjoy stemming dried herbs or planting seeds in flats, while others with limited mobility may sift potting soil or grind herbs in a hand grinder.

Finally, financial sustainability guides the way we think about our relationship with our land. Regardless of how lofty our ideals or how spiritual our aims, to endure and grow all communities must think about practical ways to produce income that align with their values. The emerging market of ecosystem services is one area of current exploration. Much of Innisfree's land management efforts in the past years have gone into a stream restoration project, with the goal of producing income through selling wetland

and stream mitigation bank credits. We protect our streams and maintain the health of the ecosystem and are able to create a revenue stream by doing so. Often environmental sustainability and financial growth goals seem to be at odds with each other, so communities who own land like us need to think creatively about ways that both goals can be met simultaneously.

Looking Forward, Looking Back

Much on the land has changed over the last 42 years since the first four community members moved into the Walnut Level farmhouse. Short fences have been replaced by taller ones. Hoop houses have been erected at both the vegetable and herb gardens, allowing us to extend our growing season. A small, unheated potting shed which had been the home base for the vegetable garden was replaced with a much larger structure we call Swallowtail. We have developed relationships with local individuals, stores, and restaurants that purchase what we produce. We have added farm and garden interns to our work teams. We have constructed chicken coops, planted trees, cultivated new garden beds, experimented with new technology.

And we look ahead energized by the possibilities for the future and how our relationship with this land may continue

> We protect our streams and maintain the health of the ecosystem and are able to create a revenue stream by doing so.

to evolve. One current initiative is the creation of an ecological observatory at Innisfree, with an online portal that would be available to scientists, educators, and land managers to access field data. We hope that the observatory will lead to greater sharing of ecoagricultural techniques among farmers and lead to discoveries in land management, as well as create income for the community.

This is just one of many possibilities we are exploring of how to engage with our 550 acres in new and life-giving ways. In brainstorming sessions, we've imagined capturing solar and wind energy, exploring geothermal energy, running our farm equipment on biodiesel, partnering with local schools to provide hands-on environmental educational opportunities to area children, maximizing the energy efficiency of current structures, and building future structures to maximize passive solar energy. Guided by the principles of responsible stewardship of assets, meaningful engagement of community members, and financial sustainability, and with deep gratitude for all that the land gives us, we are hopeful about Innisfree's ongoing relationship to this land and energized when we think of potential new directions we may explore. ❧

Rhonda Miska has served as the Innisfree Village Community Coordinator and been a part of the community since 2008. Originally from Wisconsin, she has lived in Virginia since 2004. She holds an undergraduate degree from the University of Wisconsin-Stevens Point and an M.A. from Boston College. Outside of Innisfree, she is active in local community organizing efforts, immigrants' rights advocacy work, and the Catholic Worker movement.

Chris Roth

Technology, Nature, and Community

What does it mean when a two-and-a-half year old can identify more wildflowers, shrubs, trees, and birds than at least 90 percent of the fourth- and fifth-grade students I took on school nature walks this fall?

The first child's senses seem alert to every sound and sight—he notices every bird call, squirrel scurry, daisy blossom, oak gall, mushroom, animal scat, and celestial body. And he points them out to me.

By contrast, the older children seem almost incapable of being quiet, unable to simply observe and listen—either to the natural world or to each other—except in brief spurts. They seem possessed by noisy internal voices and nervous energy. They are excited to be outdoors, but they know very little about what they are encountering, and they approach it more like bulls in a china shop than like Native American gatherers or hunters.

Why?

One fourth-grader offers a candid explanation, in response to my vain attempt to have even one of them identify our most common conifer, the Douglas fir. "I don't know anything about plants. I stay inside all day and play video games."

The two-and-a-half year old lives in a rural intentional community, mentored by adults for whom ecological literacy is a primary value. Most of his daily life experience is unmediated by technology. The fourth- and fifth-graders live in a small city, their lives shaped much more by the human-created technological artifacts that surround them. They live mostly indoors, and even when they are outside, they are usually not far from a small personal electronic device.

The community-raised toddler interacts with other people in the same spirit he interacts with the natural world—with aware-

ness, sensitivity, curiosity, and caring. Many of the older kids seem to have much less social sensitivity, many fewer of the skills and ways of being that are essential to community living. Apparently high technology and high levels of community skills do not automatically go hand-in-hand (or finger-in-finger—perhaps the digital analog).

We learn the languages and ways of being in which we are immersed. I would never expect myself to learn Spanish without hearing the language spoken, or to learn about gardening without ever doing it. On the other hand, it would be difficult not to absorb and learn these things if they were shared by everyone around me.

I wonder: is the modern technological landscape now immersing us in a kind of language, a way of being, which drowns out some of the awareness, skills, and qualities that are essential to our nature as humans? And if technology has a monopoly on modern attention, can this trend by slowed down or reversed if enough people question it, intentionally divorce themselves from its hold on their lives, and set out to learn *different*, non-technologically-mediated languages and ways of being?

• • •

As always, there is another side to this coin. These words are coming to you via a computer (actually, multiple computers), even if you're reading our print edition. Many people now engaged in community living or other progressive social change movements would not have found their current situations without the internet (including resources like ic.org). And, bucking the trend of "nature deficit disorder," some of the second-graders I guided this year (who were much more nature-attuned and knowledgeable than the older children mentioned earlier) had learned some of what they knew, and stoked some of their interest in the actual living world, via nature documentaries watched via DVDs and computers.

It's no surprise, then, that our articles in this issue span the entire spectrum of attitude and opinion, from the technological optimist to the technological skeptic. Compare Christopher Kindig's "Technology: Our External Thumb" to Ethan Hughes' "Back to Life: Returning from the Virtual to the Real" to get a taste of just how wide the range of sentiment can be. (For additional reading on both ends of the spectrum, check out www.hopedance. org/blog/2747-a-meditation-on-using-facebook-as-a-village-gathering-space by Bob Banner—a greatly shortened version of which almost made it into this issue— and *The Round Table* from Winter 2011 at karenhousecw.org/RT2011Technology. htm, in which an earlier version of Ethan's article appeared.)

In truth, the theme of this edition could have generated several books; this 80-page magazine can hardly do it justice. But we've delved into at least some of the many dimensions of Technology and its relationship to Community. A few that came up but that we didn't explore in depth herein include: technology's ability to help bond together "leavers" from various restrictive religious communal groups (a recent thread on the Communal Studies Association's listserv); the increasing economic viability of rural community living through "techie" telecommuting and "mass digital nomadism" (highlighted by an inquiry from a journalist writing for *Factor* magazine); and the impacts of many non-computer-based modern technologies (we'll explore some of those in more detail in our Summer 2015 "Food and Community" issue).

Thanks again for joining us! 🐛

Chris Roth edits COMMUNITIES *on his laptop computer and also spends as much time as possible with his computer closed, nature guiding at Mt. Pisgah Arboretum, participating in community life at Lost Valley and at Mandala Sanctuary (all outside Eugene, Oregon), and mentoring and being mentored by two preschoolers.*

Back to Life:
Returning from the Virtual to the Real

By Ethan Hughes

Ethan Hughes

Stillwaters Sanctuary, a project of the Possibility Alliance, is an electricity-free, computer-free intentional community located on 110 acres outside La Plata, Missouri. A partner project, the Peace and Permaculture Center, sits on 20 adjoining acres; and another allied group, White Rose Catholic Worker Farm, sits on 30 neighboring acres (both also electricity-free). Here, the group's cofounder reflects on their choices about technology.

In 1999 I declared to my family and friends that I was going to attempt to live car-free. I was already living without personal computer use, emails, airplanes, and movies. Some of the strongest resistance to this new choice came from my grandmother. She feared a disconnect in our relationship as a result of spending less time together.

My first car-free visit to her home required a half-day of bike and train travel instead of a one-and-a-half-hour drive. The lack of an evening train made it necessary for me to spend the night at her home after our dinner together. Had I still been driving, of course, I would have driven home afterward. Instead we enjoyed a wonderful meal together, played some cards, and stayed up late as she told me stories about my dad (her son), who had passed away when I was 13. In the morning, we breakfasted on the second-story back porch while the birds sang. Suddenly, she reached across the table with tears in her eyes, put her hand on mine, and confessed, "I am so happy you do not drive anymore!" It turns out that I had been the first adult grandson to ever spend the night at her house.

As a result of this and similar experiences, I began to learn that often love is most easily nurtured when we slow down and remove everything that can get in the way of two human beings

or a human being and nature interacting. I now believe that movie screens, computer screens, private automobiles, TV screens, cell phones, and other modern technologies simply create a wall between the human-to-human and human-to-nature encounters that can awaken us to love, meaning, and connection.

I also know that another way of living is available to us: a life that emulates the harmonious connection we see in natural ecosystems, a life that lives out the permaculture principles in full integrity. A tree creates zero (unusable) waste, enhances the ecosystem, and supplies a myriad of gifts to hundreds of species. I invite you to believe that humans, you and I, can do the same, that we can shed the trappings of this technological age by conscious choice and once again take our rightful place in the circle of creation.

The Impacts of Modern Technology

Let us evaluate the impacts of modern technology on the earth, creation, society, and our hearts. I believe the greatest conspiracy of our time is the belief that we must kill, enslave, injure, and oppress nature and/or humans to get our needs met. I also invite you to consider that the greater costs of such technology to the living world far outweigh any benefit we may gain from its use. Charles

Eisenstein writes: "All of our systems of technology, money, industry and so forth are built from the perception of separation from nature and from each other."

I propose a movement away from the Age of Information into an Age of Transformation—an age where we are empowered to act on what we have learned and on the calling in our hearts. This great leap and even the thought of it may awaken overwhelming discomfort and turmoil in us. In the face of climate weirding, addiction, species loss, depression, toxicity of the environment, war, and destruction of the last old growth forests, coral reefs, and other climax ecosystems, we must apply an incredible amount of imagination, creativity, love, grace, spirit, and perseverance as we never have before. In fact, to solve such problems, we need a complete paradigm shift.

Some say modern science will catch up and modern technology will become green. It is important to consider that a utopian world through modernization has been promised since the onset of the industrial revolution. In fact, the hard-to-face reality is that no amount of green technology, free energy, or touch screens will heal our disconnection from the natural world; rather they will continue to maintain the barriers that divide us from it. It does not matter if modern technology is clean or has a neutral footprint; it will never bring us back into contact with the earth and universe. We are living in a human-created virtual reality, a technological dreamscape that shelters us from true nature and one another.

As a culture, we are truly frogs in boiling water, indoctrinating each successive generation earlier and earlier into our exponentially accelerating disconnect from nature. According to the *New York Times* there has been a 69 percent decrease in the time children spend outdoors. This is directly linked to the use of social media, with the average child spending eight hours a day on the computer,

watching videos, playing video games, and listening to recorded music. Adults and children are so disconnected from the natural universe that birthed us we do not even consciously miss it. The average American now spends more waking time on a screen than in real life. An infinitesimal amount of people in our society would even *consider* living with their hands, consuming only what their local bioregion provides. Most could not imagine a full, meaningful life without road trips, stereos, digital music dance parties, coconut, chocolate, movie night, electric lights, and Google searches.

But all of these well-accepted forms of entertainment, communication, and transportation are not as benign as we would wish. In fact, they are cumulatively destroying our planet. Even many mainstream publications now recognize humanity's disregard of our planet's natural limits; *USA Today* recently published an article stating that we are in the sixth mass extinction episode to occur in the five billion year history of planet earth, and that the extinction is human-caused.

In his book *The Ascent of Humanity*, Charles Eisenstein defines technology as "the power to manipulate the environment." He goes on to define "progress" as the accumulation of technology. The history of human progress has resulted in our modern industrial society, which Eisenstein states "can remake or destroy our physical environment, control nature's processes, and transcend nature's limitations."

I believe that this kind of progress, essentially an alienation from nature, passed to us through culture, has not only caused the sixth mass extinction and threatened the climate systems of earth but has also jeopardized human beings' physical, spiritual, mental, and emotional health. Can you truly convince yourself that any of your social media, road trips, imported foods, or documentaries are worth this cost?

Photos by Chris Roth

Using Technology Appropriately

We find ourselves in a challenging predicament, because the technologies that negatively impact the living earth are the same devices upon which we currently depend for connection, information, livelihood, transportation, food, shelter, clothing, entertainment...almost everything in our lives. How can we do without them? I say we must find another way, for no matter what noble need they fill, no matter what measurable good they create, their use will always keep us disconnected from life in some way. Audre Lorde writes, "The master's tools will never dismantle the master's house." There must be another way to fulfill these needs, or humanity would never have made it to the current era!

This leads us to another important question: Is there such a thing as an appropriate technology? Our definition of appropriate technology at Possibility Alliance's Stillwaters Sanctuary is:

1. It maintains the health and integrity of the biotic and cultural communities it is made in and/or used in. An appropriate technology can enhance the life, vitality, and diversity of these communities.

2. All people have equal access to the resources and skills to make the appropriate technology, as well as to use and master it.

3. Appropriate technology brings us closer to each other and the ecosystems and species we live with. Appropriate technology promotes relationships with living things.

Here at Stillwaters Sanctuary we live without electricity, use no combustion engines on site, and use no power tools. Even so, almost nothing we use, including most hand tools, beeswax candles, bicycles, and solar cookers, truly meet the criteria of our definition. Yet we know it is indeed possible. Some of us here have visited nearly intact indigenous communities in the Ecuadorian Amazon, islands of Indonesia, and forests of Africa. Almost all their clothing, tools, and shelter qualify under our definition of

appropriate technology. We in the modernized world have a great mountain to climb. Skills have not been passed down to us; most of us are not living in our bioregion of birth nor were we taught how to live bioregionally; ecosystems today are more toxic and compromised; and private ownership and widespread division of land make it difficult for modern-day humans to access enough land to live in full self-sustaining relationship with it.

The Computer Reconsidered

If a tool as simple as a brace-and-bit hand drill does not qualify as appropriate technology, how do we begin to assess the impacts of a more complex technology such as a computer? Jerry Mander, in his book *In the Absence of the Sacred*, proposes a holistic analysis of technology. "The analysis includes political, social, economic, biological, perceptual, informational, epistemological, spiritual impacts; its affect upon children, upon nature, upon power, upon health."

Let us run the computer through a partial holistic analysis as an example:

• It takes 500 pounds of fossil fuels, 47 pounds of chemicals, and 1.5 tons of water to manufacture one computer (in a world where one third of the human population does not have access to clean drinking water).

• 93 percent of the global population does not own a computer and of the poorest one billion, only one percent has access to one.

• The US military is the #1 financial source for computer science research in the world.

• 70 percent of the heavy metals in landfills come from e-waste.

• Paper waste has increased 40 percent with the spread of the personal computer and printer.

• The highest number of Superfund sites (extremely polluted locations) in the US are in Silicon Valley, where computers are manufactured.

• Computer-run systems are cheaper than hiring people, so more money is concentrated in corporate hands, unemployment increases, and the poverty gap widens.

• Computers increase surveillance, used for concentration of power and control by corporations and governments.

• The manufacture of one computer chip contaminates 2,800 gallons of water.

• More than 700 materials and chemicals are used to make a computer. One half of these are known to be hazardous to ecological and human health.

• The entire process from raw materials to the computer in your hands requires minimally 200,000 miles of transportation (almost to the moon) with resources extracted from up to 50 countries.

• Simply by the process of its production, a computer is the antithesis of decentralization and bioregionalism.

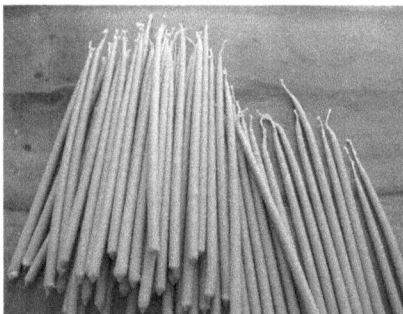

creating psychological patterns of addiction to its use.

• 90 percent of human communication is nonverbal. Thus we use only 10 percent or less of a person's capacity to communicate when we do so through computers.

This is less than five percent of the information on the negative impacts of computers that I have collected in the last decade and a half. Please do your own analysis and research and let me know if you find new or differing information. As Jerry Mander urged us, I am focusing on the negatives in our holistic analysis. We all are familiar with the benefits—they are why many choose to use the computer.

The simple fact that we can exist without a computer seems like an impossibility these days, yet for 100,000 years we have—we did so even just 50 years ago! Wendell Berry quips that "If the use of a computer is a new idea, then a newer idea is not to use one."

Shaking Our Addiction

How can we change our habits, and shake our virtual addiction to modern technology? First we must truly understand, see, and feel the painful costs of the disconnected choices we have made. Bruce Ecker states, "Change occurs through direct experiences of the symptom, not from cognitive insights. Cognitive insight follows from (rather than leads and produces) such experiences." Whenever I meet people who are living electricity-free, not flying, biking everywhere, sharing their home with the homeless, refusing to use the computer, eating locally, giving their money away, or fearlessly risking arrest for a cause, I ask them what led to these choices. Their answers share two common aspects:

They came into direct contact with some form of destruction caused by their lifestyle choices—for example, they witnessed mountaintop removal, met brain-damaged Latino children living downstream from Silicon Valley, visited Black Mesa on the

• Each year between five and seven million tons of e-waste is created. (The majority of this is sent to China, India, South Asia, and Pakistan.)

• The people who build our computers have up to 3,000 times the rate of certain cancers. These workers also have a much higher rate of respiratory diseases, birth defects, miscarriages, and kidney and liver damage.

• 70 percent of all people affected by e-waste (lead, phosphorus, barium, dioxins, furans, etc.) are poor and marginalized people.

• 40 percent of all computers on the planet are owned and operated in the United States.

• Computers are efficient at accelerating consumption, development, advertisement, etc.

• The main Google server in the Columbia River Gorge uses more electricity in one day than the City of San Francisco.

• The computer is a product built for profit. The industry's imperative is growth and profit.

• The computer is rearranging our brain chemistry and functions, in addition to

Navajo Reservation and saw the destruction caused by Peabody Coal, or witnessed families tenting on the Mississippi in zero degree weather.

The exposure was sometimes less than an hour, yet all of these people said their lives changed instantly from the direct experience. There was no thought in the decision to change their lifestyles; it arose naturally from their being.

So this is the good news. When directly exposed to suffering, humans will most often respond and take great risks of which they would not otherwise think themselves capable. I myself began experiencing these shifts when I lost my father to a drunken driver. At age 13 I directly experienced the cost of cars and alcohol. All the facts in the world—like this one: the leading cause

it is also very challenging and difficult. When I recently asked a friend to consider doing his world-impacting, beautiful, personal growth work without the computer or airplane, he said he would be "ripped to shreds." I know from my own experience that such feelings of devastation are real and necessary, *and* I believe we are called to cross this threshold in order to heal ourselves and this earth. We must be ripped to shreds to enter a new paradigm.

Making the Transition

We have very imperfectly begun the transition back to the living world at Stillwaters Sanctuary, at its neighboring Peace and Permaculture Center, and on the adventures of the Bicycling Superheroes, three projects of the Possibility Alliance. We are constantly learning how to embody our individual and collective vision. We have observed during the course of our 7-1/2-year-old experiment at Stillwaters Sanctuary that people must have time, space, love, compassion, inspiration, and support to transition and integrate a new way of being. Heartbreak, grief, tears, joy, disappointment, despair, laughter, gratitude, grace, and fear have been part of each of our transformations. There is also hypocrisy, paradox, and failure daily.

Just in this moment, for example, I realize that what I write by candlelight with pencil on scrap paper someone will soon type into a computer. What can we do? We are not an island of purity. We choose to interface daily with the society that each of us was born and raised in, and of which we are still a part, albeit a dissident part. This interface involves compromise, but we don't want to use this rationale to console ourselves into passivity. Step by imperfect step, we must keep marching toward the goal of transformation—of ourselves, and in tiny increments, of that same society. For example, our last newsletter at Stillwaters Sanctuary was hand-drawn

> I invite you to go expose yourself to a direct experience of the cost of your lifestyle choices. Let the truth of what you see transform you.

of death in the US for 18-25-year-olds is car crashes—would not have changed my behavior or choices. Yet one direct experience of the cost of these things led me to live car-free and substance-free. I also stood on the banks of the Aguarico River in the Ecuadorian rainforest as more oil than spilled from the Exxon Valdez rushed downstream, covering everything. Since witnessing that event, I strive to live without depending on petroleum.

I invite you to go expose yourself to a direct experience of the cost of your lifestyle choices. Let the truth of what you see transform you. For example, go witness the dumping of the elephant-sized amount of toxins, contaminated water, and waste created for your laptop. Visit the poor, marginalized town or village that has to deal with it. What if you visited the Superfund site downstream from Silicon Valley and met children with brain damage from computer industry waste? Could you make the same decisions?

This is not a loaded question. It is an honest question I ask myself if I am imagining a truly just world, with equality and opportunity for all life. I acknowledge that

and photocopied. One step we're taking is to commit to print our next newsletter on an antique printing press, as did our friends at La Borie Noble in France, and as did *Plain* magazine, which printed 5,000 copies each run using typesetting and woodblocks!

With every choice—even if it's to write an article for a magazine or be interviewed for a podcast—we are trying to create a culture and container where it is easier to live with-

418

out industrial society. One successful paradigm shift has come from our choice to burn hand-dipped beeswax candles as our only light source at night. Not only do we create a way to have lighting using resources within a 10-mile radius, but we instantly make obsolete nuclear, coal, wind, solar, or any other industrial power source that requires mining, resource extraction, and the old industrial paradigm to create. Our use of candles also makes us more mindful, both in movement and activity. We must move carefully when using an open flame. We reap the gifts of beauty, calmness, human connection, and connection to nature. What began as an environmental choice has become a spiritual one. Living this way brings us closer to the world: bees, hands, fire, spirit, and life.

Although we celebrate any movement that lessens impact to life, we do not consider "green technology" to be the "end all, be all." For example, shifting from coal power to solar power is a meaningful step, but it may not be enough. As Bill McKibben pointed out in an *Orion* article, hybrid cars, fair trade goods, wind power, and trains only slow down the process of destruction; they do not end it. Our transition must be an unceasing journey toward a fully healed relationship with the Earth.

Lanza del Vasto offers a gauge to know when we have reached the goal: "Find the shortest, simplest way between the earth, the hands, and the mouth. Don't put anything in between—no money, no heavy machinery. Then you know at once what are the true needs and what are fantasies. When you have to sweat to satisfy your needs, you soon know whether or not it's worth your while. But if it's someone else's sweat, there is no end to our needs. We need cigarettes, beer, cars, soft drinks, appliances, electronic devices, and on and on.... Learn to do without.... Learn how to celebrate...prepare the feast from what your own hands have grown and let it be magnificent."

As I continue to simplify and align my life with creation and nature, I am discovering a true and deep wealth: having very little, being happy within the limits of a non-industrial life, remembering that "joy is not in things, it is in us." Joy is also in connecting with each other and nature with nothing in between. No inanimate thing is needed for the human experience of love, justice, equality, joy, aliveness, and meaning.

This change in my own life has taken 30 years of transition and integration...step by

step I am moving toward the goal of living, creating, and enjoying in a way that takes care of and honors everyone and every living thing. My experience with life is increasingly more direct: walking to the orchard composting toilet in a snow storm or under shooting stars; sitting face to face with friends and strangers night after night by candlelight; creating music; storytelling; collecting wild foods; listening to the silence and cricket song that come when there are no combustion machines, no canned music, no white noise; slowing down. In the age of industrial technology it has become a radical act to be completely present with the person or lifeform you are with, with no screens, distractions, intoxicants, or anything else in between.

Many of our friends in communities and projects around the US are shutting off the electricity, shifting to the gift economy, closing email and Facebook accounts. The Downstream Project in Virginia, Be the Change Project in Reno, Loving Earth Sanctuary in California are just a few. This article is an invitation for whoever feels the calling to begin to unplug and plug into What-Is-Alive. We at the Pos-

---

I am discovering a true and deep wealth: having very little, being happy within the limits of a non-industrial life, remembering that "joy is not in things, it is in us."

---

sibility Alliance want to try to support any who would walk this path, by sharing any insights, skills, or resources we have. Let us access more fully the oldest and ultimate technology: community, love, nonviolence, and spirit. It may just blow our minds and hearts wide open. ☙

Ethan Hughes enjoys watching dragonflies, luna moths, and the wonder in the eyes of his two young daughters. He has a long-standing love affair with Gandhian nonviolence and enjoys puddle fights, board games, and jumping into any body of water. He has gotten arrested with nuns three times to resist the war machine (police seem to be much more polite to you when you are with a nun). Contact him at 660-332-4094 or 28408 Frontier Lane, La Plata, Missouri 63549.

CREATING THE IDEAL INTENTIONAL COMMUNITY
(OR REVITALIZING AN EXISTING ONE)

I, Sahmat, grew up in intentional communities and have lived in 10 of them. I have been so dedicated to Community with both humans and Nature that I've been called "The Community Guy". The communities I grew up in shared a fairly strong "sense of community". I call this deep and sustained sense of community "Common-unity" because it's a state of unity we share in common, with the unique individuality of each human and each species still honored. It's this state of Common-unity that I've found most valuable in life and to me it's the main reason for living in an intentional community. When a group is deep in Common-unity together, there's a shared sense of love, joy, and peace that tops any other group experience.

However, I've found that in all the communities I've lived in, the sense of community is not nearly as deep and sustained as it could be. It's precisely this lack of Common-unity that is the root cause of the catastrophic global suffering of racism, wars, child abuse, abuse of women, environmental and species destruction, etc. So the ultimate goal is ending global suffering through "Global Common-unity": the spreading of Common-unity throughout the world by forming a global network of Common-unity-dedicated Communities.

So I've spent my life learning how to create Common-unity-dedicated communities that share true Common-unity: a deeper and more sustained sense of community. There are two keys to starting a Common-unity community (or moving an existing community into deeper Common-unity):

1. The first key to Common-unity is for everyone to be "Common-unity-dedicated" as their top common priority. This doesn't seem to be the case in any existing community, which results in focus and energies being bled off into other priorities. So maintenance of Common-unity doesn't get enough time and energy.

2. The second key to Common-unity is to learn "Common-unity Skills", skills that must be practiced to maintain Common-unity: Speaking from the Heart, Empathetic Listening, Emptying of Ego-attachments, Conflict Resolution, Consensus, Heart Wound Healing, Cooperative Housing, and Cooperative Economics. Modern culture does not teach us these skills.

We at the Alliance for Global Community have developed free workshops that train you in these Common-unity Skills. The workshops contain the Sharing Circle process developed by M. Scott Peck, a Nature connection exercise developed by John Seed and Joanna Macy, healing exercises developed by Byron Katie and Richard Moss, and exercises in creating Cooperative Housing and Cooperative Economics. We've tested various versions of these Common-unity Skill Building workshops over the past 25 years, and we've found them to be quite effective in teaching Common-unity skills that can help maintain Common-unity. If you'd like to start a Common-unity-dedicated community, or if you'd like to bring more Common-unity into an existing community (perhaps through a Common-unity sub-community or "pod"), you need to learn or improve these Common-unity skills as soon as possible.

To find out how to sign up for a free public Common-unity Skills workshop or schedule a free workshop for an existing group or community, please go to my website thecommunityguy.org There you can also find out how to get a free copy of the book "Skill Building for Global Common-unity". You can contact Sahmat directly at info@thecommunityguy.org or at 434-305-4770.

COMMON-UNITY WITH HUMANITY AND NATURE

Technology on the Path to Reality
Snapshots from the Pre-Post-Digital Age

By Chris Roth

My body is aware, before my mind is, that something essential to me is missing. I have the increasingly loud, nagging sense that I've left something behind. The anxiety rises, along with a constricted, empty feeling in my chest. I want to turn around, retrace my steps, get back whatever it is I've lost. I fear I'll be lost, myself, without it.

I've left my cell phone on my friend Suzanne's table, and now we're speeding away from her house, headed to the ferry off Vashon Island. I realize for sure what's happened once we're on the ferry and I'm able to check my daypack pocket, where I usually keep the phone. I'm about to drive five hours south, and Suzanne herself is leaving the island for a few days. In the best-case scenario, I won't have that phone back for a week. What if I have car trouble on the return trip to Eugene? What about my weekly phone call with my parents, with which I'd planned to break up the drive? What will I do back home at Lost Valley, where I often keep in touch with the co-parents of my community "kids" via phone message or text, especially when a change of clothes, a peanut butter sandwich, or comfort from a biological parent after scary encounters with large dogs or knee-scraping gravel patches is in order?

I lived nearly five decades without a cell phone, and never missed it. Now losing it can bring up feelings for me akin to separating from close friends or family. What happened?

• • •

In reality, after a few minutes, I do adapt to the absence of my cell phone. I actually enjoy feeling more independent, less tethered to the world of instant communications, in which everything can seem urgent and nothing is fast enough. I am happy to trust my car's ability to get me back home, and to not cram in a phone call on the way. I slow down internally to a pace more reminiscent of a long hike in the backcountry than of a sprint in a crowded stadium.

Back home, I am happy to not be answering phone calls about how to place ads in COMMUNITIES (not my department; I refer them to Christopher Kindig)—and I find that Terra's and River's parents and I manage to communicate just fine, as we did before I regularly kept my cell phone on, through systems of old-fashioned voice signals, animal hoots, and intuition. In the worst case scenario, I need to sniff out the peanut butter (and whether it's an appropriate choice right now) by relying on my own senses. The following week, I almost don't want my cell phone to arrive in the mail—but it does, and I feel the background stress in my life notch up just a little bit. Its absence was instructive.

•••

More than three decades ago, Suzanne, about 20 others, and I climbed onto a bus to join a traveling experiential-education school, where for nine months we attempted to untether ourselves as much as possible from "Mother Culture." Not only were cell phones unknown to us (or to anyone else at the time), but we were also usually inaccessible by land lines. Ten days or more could pass between encounters with phone booths; our mail pick-up stops ("General Delivery, Homestead, Florida," etc.) occurred every two to four weeks. Our parents would wait for snail-mail letters and occasional phone calls. In the grand scope of history, our communication with our families as we trekked around the country was remarkably frequent and rapid; but by 21st century standards, we were almost as good as lost and unreachable in deep ocean trenches, sometimes for weeks on end.

While our engagement with one another was intense—students and guides typically met and talked as a whole group for several hours every day, in addition to traveling, camping, cooking, hiking, and doing almost everything else together too—we strove also for intense engagement with the natural world and intentional disengagement from technologies that could come between us and it, or us and each other. "Canned" entertainment of all kinds was banned; we entertained ourselves and one another without electronic assistance. This meant that we all learned songs and picked up instruments—many of us for the first time in our lives. We watched no television or movies, and had zero engagement with computers. We spent many hours talking with people directly; many days hiking in the wilderness; many hours on "solos," each in our own spot, directly experiencing the natural world around us, often without mediation of even pen and paper.

We deliberately "did without" and sought experiences that would allow us to explore our relationships with other living beings, with the planet, with the cosmos—rather than solely with the predominantly human-centered, human-created world in which we had been raised, where most choices and experiences were defined and dictated by people. Constant communication with other human beings, constant emphasis on *human* community, constant reliance on tools of comfort and convenience that our species has developed—all of these were seen as interfering with our most primary community, our most important communication, our greatest security and comfort: our connection with Mother Earth.

We learned many things on the bus, but among the most essential were how to slow down, how to be alone (away from not only humans but human artifacts), and the much deeper connections to ourselves, each other, and the earth community that could result from those things.

•••

As I drive away from Vashon, it isn't just my cell phone I am leaving behind: it is the feeling I've had over the past week, first at our Ecobus reunion and then while staying with Suzanne and her housemate for four days. Over that time, Suzanne and I seemed to rekindle that feeling we had on the bus, when (to paraphrase a book title by the program's founder) "our classroom was wild America." Back in those days, we had time to explore neglected cultures and landscapes, disengage from what society expected of us, contemplate the "underbelly of the beast," seek the truth to be found in listening to the earth as best we could. Saying "no" to the dominant culture and the technologies which facilitated it was necessary to say "yes" to everything else.

And we said a lot of "yes"es. Collectively, we learned hundreds of traditional songs and tunes during our time on the bus; many dozens of those songs were shared and known by all of us. Suzanne learned more songs than perhaps anyone else. Thirty-plus years later, she still remembered them—or was able to recall them after (by her own account) having forgotten their existence for decades. We spent evenings on Vashon singing those songs again, remembering the old days, enjoying the shared bond created by the inarguable "reality" that we'd experienced during our years on the bus. Those unmediated experiences still seemed more present to me than any number of movies I might have watched in the interim; and those songs were still more emotionally potent than any recorded music I'd discovered since then.

My missing cell phone, I realize, is not the source of my distress at all. Rather, I am mourning the loss of that shared reality, re-experienced during my time on Vashon, but now becoming subsumed in the onrush of daily life. My cell phone has become a security blanket, a way to hold onto my identity as I re-enter a world in which I feel more alienated (or at least temporarily re-enter it, as I drive down the highway back to the refuge of my home community).

•••

The laptop computer on which I am typing this article is a much more significant security blanket for me these days. Because it is, for all intents and purposes, the "editorial office" of this magazine, it's especially important to me, as it allows me to do the work that I feel is part of my calling. After leaving Vashon, it also allows me to keep in touch with Suzanne, at least initially. And it is an important tool for com-

Photos by Chris Roth

munication within my home intentional community. On all three counts, after returning home, I am thankful to be living in the age of high technology. Mostly.

I also notice that the more emotional weight I give to communications via computer, the more distress it is capable of generating in me. Why didn't so-and-so respond to my email? Where is the article that author promised to send me a week ago? Why hasn't Suzanne either emailed or called in weeks, since our initial nostalgic flurry of messages? Why, instead, am I receiving endless petitions about causes I've already signed petitions for? And why do I have a sinking, off-balance feeling every time we in the Lost Valley community lose our internet signal? Why do I feel I so stymied when I can't get online?

And when I do get online, why do I allow myself to get thrown off-kilter by the occasional inflammatory, emotionally-charged, non-NVC (nonviolent-communication)-compliant email sent to the community email list? (I already know the pattern: despite our group living agreements specifying email etiquette, a resident will either not realize their importance in maintaining healthy communication and community dynamics, or not care. When "things don't work out" with someone in the community, the sending of inappropriate emails is often a key element either leading to or foreshadowing that person's departure.)

Midway through a visit to the midwest later this summer, I leave the internet and cell phone world behind entirely. I enter Stillwaters Sanctuary (the Possibility Alliance's home base in La Plata, Missouri), where community members maintain an environment free of computers, cell phones, and electricity. I am caught up on magazine work, satisfied with the state of my electronic communications with family and friends, and relieved to be taking a vacation from the internet-connected world. I have twinges of apprehension as I power everything down—part of my sense of purpose/identity seems to have become associated with these technologies and how I use them—but I am also excited to simplify, to live more fully in the here and now in a group of people committed to doing the same.

Within a few days, I am so thoroughly comfortable with the less-driven way of life that this disconnection allows that I am convinced I could keep living this way indefinitely, given sufficiently copacetic physical surroundings and a supportive social situation. Come to think of it, I've done that (lived computer- and cell-phone-free, sometimes even grid-electricity-free) for many years of my life; it should come as no surprise that I could do it again. I imagine that it might even feel more fulfilling, at least in the short term, than being on what can seem like an electronic-communications hamster wheel while simultaneously engaging as much as I can in the "real world" as well.

When I reenter internet and cell phone land, I find that Suzanne called me four days ago, just as soon as I went into radio silence, apologizing for letting emails slip and asking me to call her back as soon as possible. She is now kind of wondering why I haven't responded for four days ("You could have waited at least 10 minutes to call me back!" she jokes when she hears my voice). Three weeks later, I am the one wondering why, in the midst of planning a possible mini-expedition—a joint road trip from Chicago to the Pacific Northwest later this year—she has suddenly stopped responding to cell phone or email, and I haven't heard from her for more than two weeks.

It turns out this time *she* has lost her cell phone—also, like mine, in her house. She has also lost my phone number, which was stored in her cell phone but nowhere else.

Ironically, in attempting to recapture and reinvigorate real-life connections cultivated without these technologies, I've put faith in these technologies, and been let down. Good old-fashioned telepathy seems a lot more reliable.

• • •

I feel ambivalent, at best, about these technologies. If it were up to me to create any of them—to acquire the materials that go into them, to put them together, to create the infrastructure that supports their use—I would certainly not do it. I know that the creation, distribution, use, and disposal of these devices have significant environmental and social impacts; they're dependent on rare earth metals and resource-intensive global systems. I need to stay in a certain amount of denial in order to feel good about my use of any of them. But in the world as it stands, in my life as it stands, they are tools I feel I need to use; using them, judiciously, seems a better choice for me, at least for now, than not using them.

At the same time, I don't want to feel attached or addicted to them. One thing protecting me against this is the fact that I do get sick of them—after a certain number of hours, I can't be on the computer any longer, or talk on the phone any longer. To restore my own physical, emotional, psychological, and spiritual equilibrium, I need to do something else.

Also to my advantage in staying in relative balance with these things is the fact that I've lived without them; I know that the realities that they connect me to generally pale in comparison to the reality that I find in present, tactile life, directly experienced. I can live without computers and their kin; but without the more direct reality that feeds me daily, my soul would wither.

• • •

W here do I find that reality, if not in modern technology?

Among other places, I find it in long runs through the woods, which bring me into occasional random encounters with bears, owls, and even cougars, but more commonly just immerse me into ecological communities of plants and animals, rocks, soil, water, and sky that now seem like family to me.

I find it in unstructured play time with young children in my community, whose sense of adventure, imagination, curiosity, and wonder encourage me to keep my eyes constantly open to what is around me, and to trust the beauty and naturalness of all of our feelings.

I find it in intentional community life, where countless daily interactions help us

weave new stories of what groups of people can create together; where conflicts allow us to learn and grow in cooperation; where we each discover how to keep balance between stillness and motion, constancy and change, compassion and "justice," order and productive chaos; and where, if one maintains awareness, there is never a dull moment.

And I find it in personal relationships with friends, family, and others who are also exploring how we can better relate to one another, how we can be authentic and pres-

ent, how we can strip away the impediments to fully experiencing and appreciating life.

Thankfully, nothing in the list above is computer-dependent.

• • •

O ften, "real life" becomes so engaging—or daily activities so involving—that articles like this one, already written in my mind, never make it out of my fingers. I need to discipline myself to disengage, to separate myself—which is what I've done to write this. I'm sitting in a park several miles from my home community, undisturbed by anyone, enjoying a breezy, pleasant, overcast day, visited by myriad birds, surrounded by oak, ash, maple, fir, cedar, with my laptop plugged into the power outlet located conveniently in the middle of the picnic area.

For now, I'm at peace with the world, even as I type into this very manipulated, processed, and rearranged conglomeration of earth elements that came at a cost to both earth and people. I am hoping that I can create some benefit to counterbalance that cost. And ultimately, I also realize that I *can't* know causes and effects, or the ultimate reasons for things—including why I ended up in this park. All I know is that it's beautiful, maybe reason enough in itself for me to tote my laptop here. 🐦

Chris Roth edits COMMUNITIES.

RIDGEWOOD RANCH:
A Mecca For Adaptive Community

By Steve Hellman and Daniel Spiro

The 5,000-acre Ridgewood Ranch includes gardens, pasture land, evergreen forest, and oak woodlands.

In recent years, Ridgewood Ranch in California's Mendocino County has become a mecca for climate-conscious, adaptive community projects. Situated in a lush valley near the headwaters of the Russian and Eel rivers, the 5,000-acre ranch has been home for nearly six decades to the Christ's Church of the Golden Rule (CCGR), which acquired the property in 1961. Through the leadership of the CCGR, the ranch provides fertile ground today for an increasing collection of cooperative, small-scale farming schools, experimental gardens, therapeutic programs, and land preservation efforts. At the heart of this gathering of energies is a shared vision—to do right by the earth and fellow humankind.

According to church elder Tracy Livingston, 75, the path to this coalescence of projects has had its share of bumps and challenges. The CCGR had 100 core members in 1961; that number today has dwindled to only 15. The challenge for the CCGR has been the inevitable passing of long-time members, along with the departure of children of some remaining families, seeking their fortunes in the wider world. To survive financially, Livingston says, the CCGR has needed to sell off considerable portions of what was initially a 16,000-acre property.

In order to achieve its continued viability, the CCGR began inviting a host of like-minded groups and organizations to operate on its unique and beautiful land. The hosting process began in earnest in 2000, when the famed John Jeavons Ecology Action Bio-Intensive Farming Program (EA) came to establish a satellite garden at the ranch. Since then, the CCGR has also welcomed what is now the Grange School of Adaptive Agriculture in 2012, and in 2016 the Wall-to-Wall natural building workshop series saw the construction of a fully functioning natural elements house on the grounds.

Livingston points to numerous other ranch projects that presently contribute to climate-adaptive land stewardship. One is a timber management program that resulted in the planting of 10,000 pines in 1965 on ranch acreage that had been clearcut by previous owners. There is a one-million-dollar, 15-year stream restoration project completed with government funding. Livingston has also been personally instrumental in helping realize the creation of a conservation easement on 1,600 acres at the ranch. The ranch is also home to the Seabiscuit Heritage Foundation, established in 2004, to preserve the history and buildings associated with one of its more famous prior residents—the racehorse Seabiscuit.

In addition, the ranch is presently home to Tequio Gardens, an independent small farming operation; the La Vida Charter School; the Seabiscuit Therapeutic Riding Center, which provides horse rides for children and adults with special needs; and a planned Residential Care Facility for the Elderly. In many ways, Ridgewood Ranch has become a mecca for residents, students, and visitors seeking to cultivate care, growth, and responsible stewardship of the land.

Livingston explains, "None of these programs would be here without the vision of the church." At the same time, he admits, "The Church has been very lucky to survive all these years. Our success has come in part from being here at the right time for certain ideas to take root and come to fruition."

• • •

According to church member Ellen Bartholomew, 56, adaptive practices began showing up on the ranch when the CCGR first installed a corn-mash still to produce sustainable fuel in the face of the 1979 global oil crisis. Their efforts continued when, in the 1980s, they were facing the impact of a seven-year drought.

Ellen says, "Stewardship of the land was always a big thing with us. Back in the '80s, we were working cattle, trying to stay ahead of mob grazing, moving the herd every two weeks, and irrigating, while also trying to keep the rangeland alive. Ultimately we found that rangeland management depended more on how many cattle we could run [sustainably]."

In response to the ecological imperative, they adapted by halving their herd and calving at a different time of year. To this day they continue to run their cattle operation on viable rangeland.

In addition, the CCGR has always grown its own organic fruits, nuts, and vegetables. In 2000, Ellen Bartholomew led the effort to invite the famed Jeavons EA program to establish a training mini-farm at the ranch. Through her guidance as the garden manager, the EA program to this day contributes additional food to the CCGR communal dining room. In turn, this effort has brought the EA interns into the broader CCGR community.

Ellen says, "What our community on the ranch has become is a place for students to dedicate themselves to agriculture, and to live in community and grow as individuals before returning home to grow food for their communities in small-scale local operations the world over."

To that end, the word "adaptive" has taken on a particularly weighted meaning among all the ranch projects.

• • •

For Rachel Britten, being adaptive has meant reconciling her academic background to the real-world situations of training future food-growers through EA. She currently serves as a co-field coordinator for EA and she facilitates the program at the ranch that teaches a dense, closed-loop agriculture system developed by Jeavons over 40 years of design and implementation. Indeed when Rachel, 29, first came upon Jeavons and Ecology Action she was skeptical of his claims.

"I was convinced he was cheating," she says. "I thought he was using human manure, or bringing in nutrients or compost from other places." The issue was key, since EA teaches real-world applications for farming under a variety of severe ecological conditions. The majority of EA's eight-month interns have come from developing countries, including Kenya, Senegal, Cameroon, Ghana, Togo, Sri Lanka, Haiti, Peru, Argentina, Ecuador, and Nicaragua; if the claims of the program were untrue, their teaching would be problematic, to say the least.

Rachel found that the Jeavons system for nutrient recycling and carbon sequestration actually worked. She could measure the result of using the Jeavons practices: the organic matter in the soil truly was increasing. "I realized that he had compiled historically good agricultural practices into a new creative method, which is so vital when we consider the importance of raising food on our planet without negatively affecting climate."

Rachel adds, "We're teaching our students a strategy to reduce inputs and maximize yields, and they're teaching us what subsistence really means." As to how she's adapted to succeed, Rachel describes it as "the cool marriage of academic knowledge and life experience."

• • •

For Cody Bartholomew, Ellen's 31-year-old son, the challenge has been to find his own productive role on the ranch. In 2008, he had completed his B.A. in Construction Management at Chico State University and he returned home to Ridgewood Ranch, planning on staying temporarily before he ventured out into the wider world. At the same time, he began to notice all the abandoned infrastructure and equipment on the property and he started getting big ideas.

He also recognized the potential value in staying at the ranch. Cody says, "Historically, we understood that there were all these intentional communities that got fired up in '60s and '70s, but there wasn't any retention. The question became: how do we adapt and change our view of what a community is and create a new coalition to work together and achieve like goals?"

With highest hopes and a rush of expectant energy, Cody decided to restore the moribund 500-gallon corn-mash alcohol still to operation. He figured he could use the corn alcohol as a viable biofuel for the many pieces of ranch machinery. He refurbished the still, teamed with

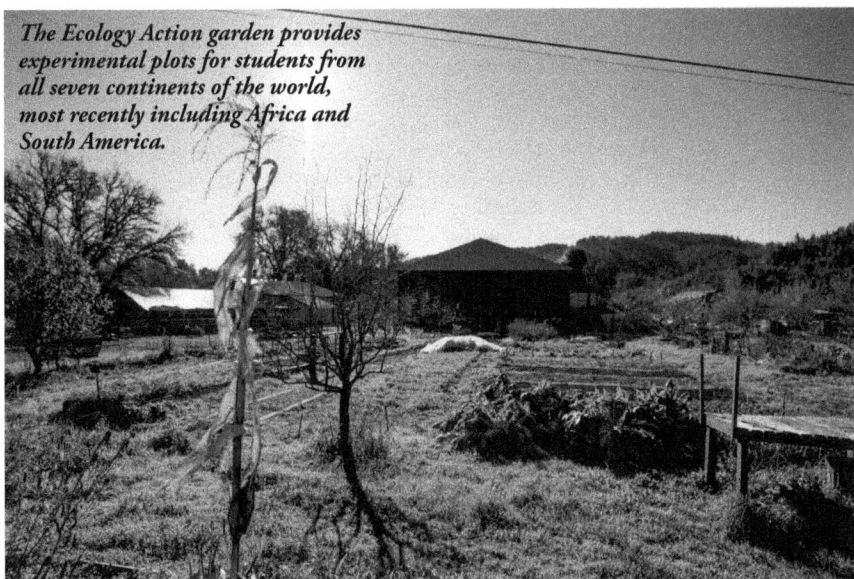

The Ecology Action garden provides experimental plots for students from all seven continents of the world, most recently including Africa and South America.

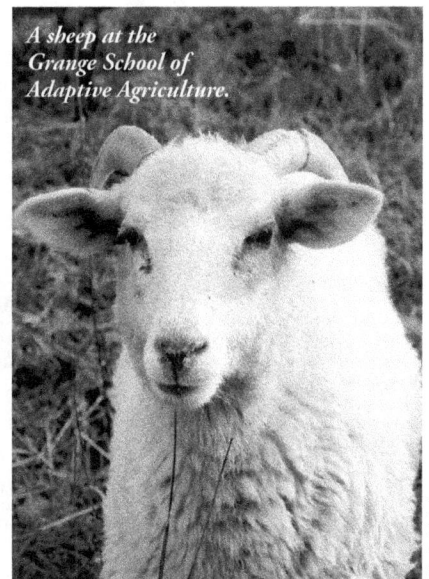

A sheep at the Grange School of Adaptive Agriculture.

Matt Holzhauer

Ruthie King operates the 12-acre Grange School of Adaptive Agriculture that trains students in financially sustainable farming, ecologically conscious food production, animal husbandry, and group conflict resolution.

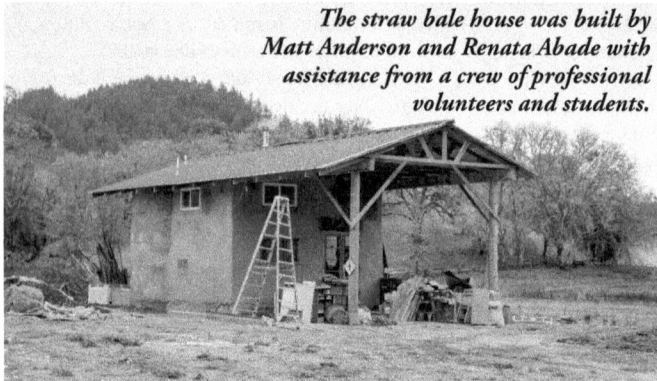

Church Elder Tracy Livingston spearheaded completion of a 1,600-acre conservation easement on the ranch and the creation of the Sea Biscuit Heritage Foundation.

The straw bale house was built by Matt Anderson and Renata Abade with assistance from a crew of professional volunteers and students.

Ridgewood Ranch is located on 5,000 acres along Highway 101 between Ukiah and Willits, California.

the Grange School manager Ruthie King to grow the corn, and organized a symposium for 100 people in 2014 to learn about the fuel program. He also converted one of the ranch tractors to biofuel function.

Unfortunately, when it came to developing sustainable projects within an intentional community, Cody came face to face with two serious obstacles: the corn-alcohol project itself proved financially unfeasible, and despite his hopes to establish a role for himself on the ranch, he found it increasingly hard to work with other members in the community; he was soon arriving at his wit's end. Would he even think to stay on the ranch, given the challenges?

• • •

When Ruthie King took over operations at the Grange School of Adaptive Agriculture in 2012, her goal was to train farmers in ecologically conscious food production. She was going to see, as well, the challenge of sustaining relationships.

"Our current mission is to train new farmers in ecologically responsible and financially viable methods for producing food," says King, 27. "The ranch and its community has provided us with the inspirational and fertile ground."

The Grange School of Adaptive Agriculture, now in its fourth year, operates on 12 acres. The space provides for student housing, a market-vegetable field, an orchard, and a livestock operation that includes sheep and chickens. Its students are immersed in 14-week intensive residential programs, held twice a year. This past summer the school graduated its third class, and nearly all of its graduates have gone on to work in small-scale, climate-conscious agricultural operations.

"Our goal is to teach all the various methods of sustainable food production," says Ruthie. "With the word 'adaptive' we feel like we're shifting the focus from what we want from the land, which is sustainability, to the kind of attitude we want to instill in those stewarding the land in this climate-changing world, which is adaptability."

Along the way, Ruthie says she came to understand, "People are the hardest part of the equation, and it made us realize that communication and community building were actually vital aspects of making our food operations sustainable." In response, Ruthie adapted her curriculum to include lessons in cultivating open, honest, respectful communication and conflict resolution, which in turn encourages students to be adaptive rather than being purely reactive.

Ruthie says, "In all ways, we're in a constant process of adapting."

• • •

Not long ago Matt Anderson and his wife Renata Abbade were by personal choice "nomadic." The couple in their mid-to-late 30s had been traveling the West Coast, visiting intentional communities and observing the work of projects like the Cob Cottage Company in Coquille, Oregon. They began to imagine someday building their own home from naturally sourced materials. The only problem was that neither of them had one ounce of building experience, nor did they have any land to build on.

An opportunity eventually presented itself at Ridgewood Ranch. The couple had learned of EA through the making of their 2013 film, *Fall and Winter: A Survival Guide for the 21st Century.* Their work looked at the current global climate crisis through interviews with a host of experts. After a screening in Bend, Oregon, Matt recalls an audience member confessing to being completely freaked out about climate change, unable to imagine any realistic solutions.

Matt says that one of the panelists calmly explained, "If you have water, food, shelter, and tribe, and figure it out in that order, you will be okay." Renata adds, "We had to become nomadic to find out for ourselves: how do we find our water, our food, our shelter, and our tribe?"

In 2015, the couple arrived at the central EA location on Pine Mountain in Mendocino County. They were excited by the notion of putting up a natural building nearby. They approached CCGR and received approval to build a structure.

With support for construction from key ranch residents like Cody Bartholomew and professional Grange School instructor Takashi Yogi, Matt and Renata witnessed their dream come true in the Wall-to-Wall building project. They used clay and straw harvested from the ranch property; wood recycled from abandoned buildings on-site, as well as wood milled from local timber after a recent fire; and stone they acquired from a local quarry. They hired two experts in natural building practices and invited students to join in the construction and learn the techniques for putting in the foundation, raising the earthen walls, and hammering together the roof trusses. At the center of that project in many ways was Cody Bartholomew, who put his considerable management skills and construction strengths to good use, while he continued to develop his collaborative savvy.

The result is a house made largely from local, natural materials, with a footprint of 288 square feet, plumbing and electricity, a second-story loft, and a covered outdoor kitchen.

Matt says the next step is to help others replicate the process. "It was amazing how it all came together, how we lifted each other up. We realize now, if we can do it here, we can help others do it elsewhere."

Renata adds, "We've learned that it's about adapting to all kinds of people, within the idea of intentional community."

• • •

The adaptive approach at Ridgewood Ranch will likely endure; residents are intent on continuing the ecological work and education while cultivating sustainable relationships. The awareness of climate-conscious adaptation, along with maintaining positive relationships, is at the core of each program.

Rachel Britten has no plans to move on anytime soon. "Staying true to the value of the community means a lot to me," she says.

Ruthie King envisions continued and greater collaboration between the Grange School and the Golden Rule Community. Regarding her own inspirations, she says, "We have a big family here, and we know that being of service to the world is the golden rule that we can all follow and practice."

Matt Anderson swears his vision for the future boils down to one simple lesson: "The adaptability of Ridgewood Ranch, of letting people into the community with a shared value set, is why these projects are here."

Renata Abbade agrees. "Before we arrive at the future, there is always stewardship of the land and the people, which translates into relationships."

Ellen Bartholomew agrees that the challenges will always be to preserve the land, and simultaneously, for people to get along in working toward their common goals, "On the issue of climate, we've adapted here. But the rub is in the relationships with the people."

For the moment, Cody Bartholomew continues working on his people skills and pursuing his myriad projects. He has widened his climate-conscious vision by contacting local wineries in an effort to convince them to use their considerable quantities of "botched wine" to produce fuel in a way that could be financially feasible. He has also initiated a comprehensive solar array project that already has resulted in one five-kilowatt system that runs irrigation pumps for the ranch, and he has planned an even larger 30-kilowatt installation that will power the CCGR's kitchen and dining hall and chapel, and also provide charging for the church's three electric cars.

While uncertainty may loom about the world and a future in flux, at Ridgewood Ranch climate-adaptive projects and intentional community will have a reliable home for the foreseeable future. 🖎

Steve Hellman is a Professor of English at Mendocino College. He has published his writing for more than 40 years. He considers community and climate change among the paramount issues of the day, including how to make a good lentil koshary.

Daniel Spiro is a freelance writer known to wander the country from his base in New Orleans. He's driven to contribute to the movement of ecologically conscientious and sustainable farming practices. He can be reached at www.spiritualfringe.com.

Cody Bartholomew with the solar array he installed to provide power to irrigation pumps for ranch pasture land.

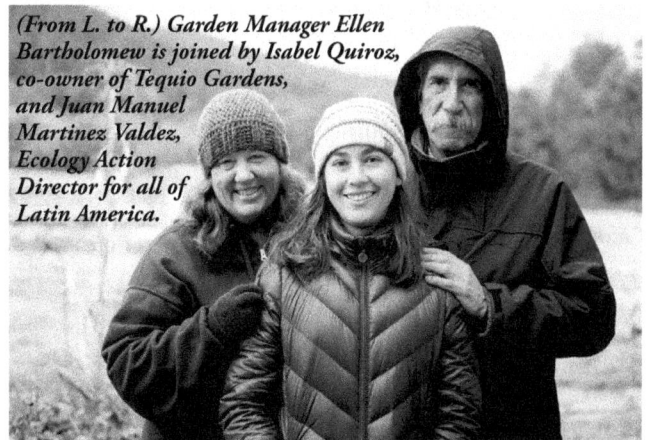
(From L. to R.) Garden Manager Ellen Bartholomew is joined by Isabel Quiroz, co-owner of Tequio Gardens, and Juan Manuel Martinez Valdez, Ecology Action Director for all of Latin America.

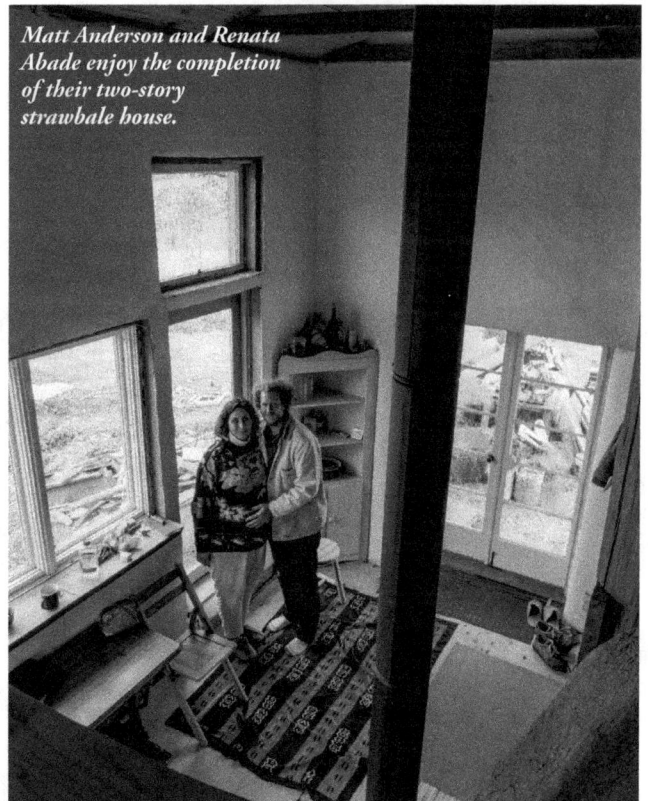
Matt Anderson and Renata Abade enjoy the completion of their two-story strawbale house.

Sustainability in Community

We honor work on the land. We honor physical work – the exertion of muscle and hand – and the craftsman's creativity and precision. We honor the activity of the mind and soul too: the inspired work of the artist, the scholar's exploration of nature and history, the enterprise of the inventor, the skill of the professional. Whatever form our work takes, we are called to do it to the best of our ability in service to others.

We'd love to have you work with us. Go to **bruderhof.com,** then visit us!

Economy, Community, and Place

By Lindsay Hagamen

To last, love must enflesh itself in the materiality of the world—produce food, shelter, warmth or shade, surround itself with careful acts and well-made things.
—Wendell Berry

As a student of nature, I have learned to study the roots, and the linguistic roots of the word "economy" are telling. Far from the anonymity and isolation characteristic of the modern global marketplace, the etymology of "economy" tells the story of the human relationship with community and place. It hints at a place-based identity so powerful that how we cared for our land, our families, and our own bodies were one and the same.

Tracing back the meaning of "economy" leads us to two Greek words: *oikos* and *nomos*. The prefix *eco* stems from the word *oikos*, meaning home or household in ancient Greek. Interpreted narrowly, *oikos* can refer to a house or dwelling. Interpreted more broadly, *oikos* refers to the land—the entire Earth—that is simultaneously our only sustenance and our only home. Hidden in the often academic and disembodied language of "ecosystem," "ecology," and "economics" is a memory of a relationship with our environment that is so personal, so profound, and so integral to our sense of identity and purpose that we know this web of relationships as home: the land is our home, and it is who we are.

Memories of a time when the cycles of Life were deeply ingrained in human culture are embedded in the rich etymological history of *nomos* as well. The earliest accounts of *nomos* refer to a field or pasture. While a field may seem rather insignificant to the modern reader, in a culture where food, clothing, medicines, building materials, fuel, and transportation were all derived directly from fields, pastures, and the hedges that defined them, these intricately connected networks of animals and plants literally embodied one's lifeblood.

Over time, the meaning of *nomos* evolved from the pasture itself to describing the people who tended to the pastures and the customs that provided for its well-being. This linguistic evolution reinforces land not as an isolated entity, but rather as a relationship between the land-tender, their stewardship practices, and the land itself: who we are and how we act are as much a part of the land as the geology or climate. So central was the pasture to ancient Greek society that *nomos* was more broadly used to simultaneously denote steward/manager and custom/rules/laws.

With great irony, we can come to understand the root meaning of

431

"economy" as *stewarding our home*—whether that home is our body, our household, or the Earth itself. Our economy is tending to the intricate web of relationships, processes, and practices that provide for our lifeblood and allow for the flour-

Freedom and security are born from engaging in the natural economy of stewarding body, home, and land.

ishing of the natural cycles that support all Life so abundantly. When we embody this deeply interdependent way of living, when we internalize the fate of the land as the fate of our bodies, then "economy" can simply be understood as the rules we live by— the *house rules*.

• • •

There is a profound power inherent in the relationships with people and place that allow us to provide for our own basic needs and those of our beloveds. As flocks of liberal arts college students and back-to-the-landers alike will attest, provisioning food, water, energy, shelter—the natural economy of stewarding our home—is innately satisfying work. In *The Prophet*, poet philosopher Kahlil Gibran offers a hint as to why: "You work that you may keep pace with the earth and the soul of the earth. For to be idle is to become a stranger unto the seasons, and to step out of life's procession, that marches in majesty and proud submission towards the infinite."

We work so as to keep pace with the soul of the Earth? Gibran's poetic words are reminiscent of the wonder inherent in food tasting good and sex being pleasurable. They speak to a deep knowing in the cells of our bodies that when we are in an intimate relationship with the very places, processes, and people that physically sustain us, we are engaging in the very same patterns that have helped us survive since time immemorial. The intrinsic pleasure, beauty, and fulfillment in these relationships is unparalleled: biting into the juicy flesh of homegrown fruit, placing another log, split by hand, on the fire, caring for a newborn lamb. Biophilia, our inherent love for Life, helps us understand why: our intimate participation in Life's processes is a biological imperative masked as love. As Gibran continues, *"To love life through labour is to be intimate with life's inmost secret."*

Invoking this visceral knowledge of land-tenders around the world, Wendell Berry wrote, "if you are dependent on people who do not know you, who control the value of your necessities, you are not free, and you are not safe." For freedom and security are born not from monetary savings nor political ideology, but rather from engaging in the natural economy of stewarding body, home, and land.

When we intimately participate in meeting our most basic needs—energy, food, water, shel-

ter, clothing—through a relationship with the land and with local networks of others doing the same, we not only come to know the innermost workings of the Earth, we also create abundance and choice. With this comes the true freedom of self-determination. When we love life through provisioning the food we eat, the warmth of our home, the energy that lights up our night, and the clothing on our backs, then freedom and fulfillment are no longer something we seek. They become something we embody.

For freedom, like food, water, or shelter, is a biological imperative. And fulfillment is our hard-won—and hard wired—evolutionary reward for satisfying this imperative. Authority over our own bodies, time, and energy is not a political right, granted or revoked, by the powers of government (or corporations, for that matter). Nor is it a lofty ideal schemed up by lovers of wisdom. Personal choice and freedom of action (and consequences) is inherent to Life's capacity to march in proud submission towards the infinite.

The sovereignty intrinsic to the human condition is what Thomas Jefferson, drawing on a long line of philosophers before him, referenced when he declared "life, liberty and the pursuit of happiness" as our *inalienable* rights, endowed, not by government, but by Nature. Our sovereignty is woven into the very fabric of our being alive. Not only does personal freedom grow out of our participation in the natural economy of stewarding our earthly home, it is our very sovereignty that enables us to steward our home to begin with.

If it is thriving that we truly seek, then reclaiming this natural heritage, and with it our true economy, is a good place to start. For when we align with what the soft animal of our body understands on a visceral level as surviving, evolution has hard wired us to find it full of pleasure, immense joy, and deep satisfaction. Freedom, belonging, and abundance are both foundational to the nature of our being alive and our reward for aligning ourselves with Nature.

This is an excerpt from a longer essay, "Re-Membering the Web of Life: The Biological Imperative for Sovereignty, Interdependence, and a Consent Economy," which can be found online at ic.org/re-membering-the-web-of-life.

Lindsay Hagamen is a lover of Life and a Steward of the Windward Community, located on the southern slopes of Mount Adams in Washington State. She is co-author of Ecosexuality: When Nature Inspires the Arts of Love *and co-creator of the annual EcoSex Convergence and TerraSoma retreats. Lindsay spends her days immersing her hands in rich garden soil, listening intently, and giving belly rubs to her pigs. See www.windward.org.*

Creating Cooperative Culture BY SKY BLUE

TOGETHER RESILIENT:
Why This Book?
Thoughts on Building Community
in the Age of Climate Disruption

Once upon a time, the world was infinite. The edges of the map simply defined what was known, not all that was. Then it became common knowledge that the earth was round, and "the world" started to become something finite. When we were able to see the entire planet, in photos taken from outer space, it really started to set in: this is it. The planet we call home has very clear limits and boundaries, which define the parameters for our survival. We can't take it for granted.

Intentional community is a kind of activism. People who create intentional communities do so because they see problems with the values and principles on which society is based and they want to create something better, and at least in some small way, they hope it will inspire others. But how do we know what's "better"? Whatever it is, toxifying our environment, destabilizing ecosystems, and potentially making the planet uninhabitable for human life are all parts of what needs to change.

Indigenous peoples and utopian visionaries have been warning of the dangers of environmental destruction and depletion for a long time. But humanity has taken a much longer time to recognize it as the existential threat it is. Despite an overwhelming scientific consensus and demonstrable impacts, there is still resistance and denial. How can this be?

Certainly one reason is that climate disruption has not caused enough economic disruption to sufficiently disrupt the lives of those with the most power. But it's more than that. Climate change is terrifying. The factors at play are so monumental, the problems so complex, and the power to effect change on those levels is so beyond the reach of any one of us. Credible predictions about the kind of world we may be creating, one that many of us alive today will have to live through, are enough to make anyone panic. In short, we're overwhelmed.

But most people no longer need convincing that there's a problem, and more than ever people are looking for solutions. Intentional community is part of the solution.

When you're around people and interact with them regularly, and when you have to make important economic decisions with them, you develop intimacy. It's not always easy, but it builds our muscles for empathy and compassion, helping us make choices that are good for all people. This intimacy fills a hole that people usually fill with unsustainable consumerism. And it helps us deal with the overwhelm of being human in today's world. Confronted with the terrifying situation we find ourselves in, facing it together is our only hope.

Whether you're an anti-capitalist or believe in capitalism 2.0, it's clear that our current economic system reinforces the social and political systems that are destroying the planet. Guaranteeing that all people have access to the resources they need to meet their basic needs must be foundational. Intentional community provides a look at how we can take care of everyone, equitably and sustainably.

Intentional community shows us that we can live happy, satisfying lives with less. It shows us that, as the author of *Together Resilient* says, sustainability doesn't have to suck. We're afraid of poverty and deprivation. Sharing is the key. Sharing, on a material level as well as social, is the pathway to benefiting from the earth's resources in a sustainable and enjoyable way.

So, why this book? Because, collectively, humanity has the answers, we have the tools, we have the pieces of the puzzle. We just have to put them together.

Together Resilient: Building Community in the Age of Climate Disruption is available for order at ic.org/community-bookstore/product/together-resilient-building-community.

Sky Blue (sky@ic.org) is Executive Director of the Fellowship for Intentional Community.

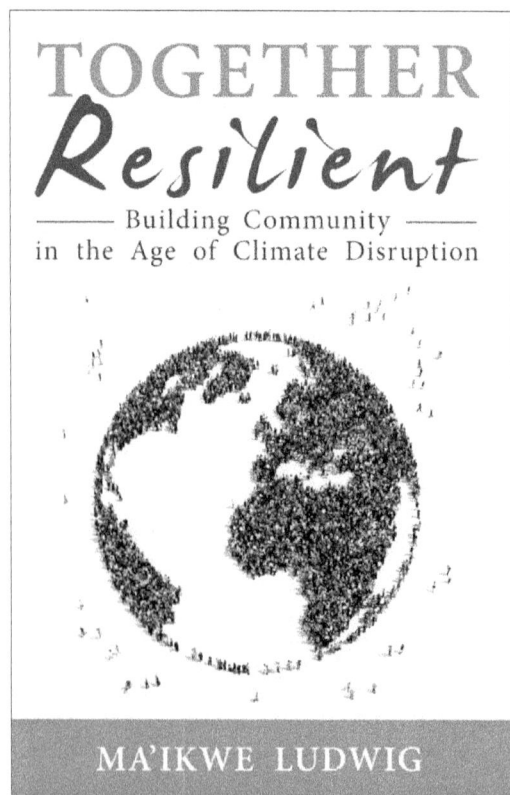

TOGETHER
Resilient
—— Building Community ——
in the Age of Climate Disruption

MA'IKWE LUDWIG

Review BY NANCY ROTH

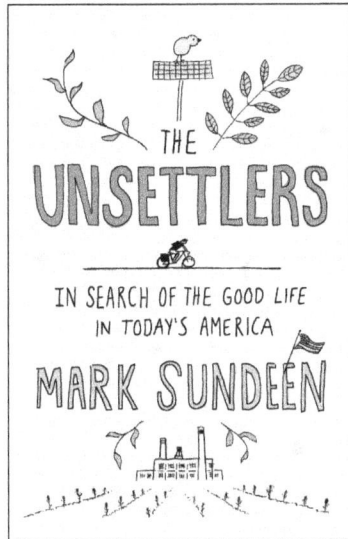

The Virtues of Unsettling

The Unsettlers:
In Search of the Good Life in Today's America
By Mark Sundeen
Riverhead Books, New York, 2017, 336 pages

Reading *The Unsettlers* has been an adventure, the product of the author's search for four American couples who decided to pursue a life of radical simplicity. He helps us make their acquaintance through writing that combines (to quote David James Duncan) "fierce reasoning, romance, impeccable research, the narrative pull of a thriller, and the subliminal magic of some wondrous old myth." The book has given me an opportunity to walk in the footsteps of visionaries for whom the "good life" of the subtitle refers not to a suburban home with a two-car garage, but a radically alternative life, lived lightly on the earth and focused on the well-being of all people, present and future.

Sundeen caught my attention immediately by describing two "unsettlers" alighting from an Amtrak train in La Plata, Missouri in early 2007, each of them wrestling with a large cardboard box. Inside each box are bicycle parts, which Sarah, a classically trained opera singer, five months pregnant, and her husband Ethan, a former marine biologist, manage to piece together—their only transportation since they have vowed to eschew all vehicles whose wheels move because of fossil fuel. Their destination is an old off-grid Amish farmhouse where they hope to conduct their simple life, but they have never been there. In the darkness, with semis speeding by, they soon find themselves lost, but a friendly policeman comes to their rescue and leads them to their new home.

Sarah and Ethan are founders of the Possibility Alliance, an intentional community and activist group, one of whose projects is the Superhero Alliance, a creative venture in which participants dress up as superheroes (with names like CompashMan, Queen Bee, Love Ninja, and Atomic Calm) and ride bicycles, seeking people on their travels who need help, whether it be building a fence or planting a garden. Intentional community is a logical outgrowth of and accompaniment to the work to which Sarah, Ethan, and their friends are called, as it allows them to better embody their goals of more elemental, service-based living. [See articles by Ethan and friends in COMMUNITIES #140, #141, #165, #172, and by Sarah's mother Victoria in #149.]

A scene very different from rural Northeast Missouri awaits us in the next section, entitled "Detroit," where Olivia and Greg, an interracial couple, have a vision of urban farming in the vacant lots of a rough part of town. Some of it is not easy reading: for a while, I felt as if I were struggling along with them. In the end, thankfully, the vision comes to fruition.

In the next chapter, "Montana," Sundeen visits a large farm run by Luci and Steve, for whom sustainable living has become close to a religion. Unfortunately, this does not apply to their finances; they are in debt, struggling to find a market for their crops. What *does* one do with tons of unsold organic potatoes, especially since Missoula, the location of the closest farmers' market, is the the only city within 150 miles? Their son Emmet (who has the distinction of having been born in a tepee on the farm!) is now in New York studying art, rather than contributing to his parents' venture. The influx of Hmong refugees into the area brings new life to the farmers' market and Luci and Steve are finally on the path to recovery.

So how about the author, himself? One reason he undertakes this extensive research is that he himself has felt an increasing attraction to dropping out of the prevailing culture. He is influenced in this by a young woman named Cedar, his partner, who was raised by hippies and knows that world well. One of the key decisions made in this book is his own, as he encourages her to follow her own dreams and to study poetry at a university. His conversations with her are some of several that lead to his own conclusion about his future; he comes to understand that the people he met chose their lives because they wanted to live that way. He, however, is not cut out for it: what seem like "freedoms" to his subjects would be "hardships" for him.

How fortunate that, rather than deciding to be an "unsettler" in the style of those he describes, the author chose to write about them instead. His message is an important contribution to our own knowledge of lives very different from the mainstream.

As Sundeen shares the lives of his subjects, we cannot help but become "unsettled" ourselves. As we come face to face with their values, we can't help but ask some questions of ourselves.

The end result? After closing this book, there is another, as yet unwritten chapter for each reader. It might be entitled "My Own Life." It challenges us with a question: How can I use my *own* particular skills and passions in order to contribute to a healthier, happier, and more sustainable world? Your answers may be similar to those we've read about...or very different choices. Even those already living in intentional community or pursuing a simpler life may be challenged and inspired to make further changes. We need lots of kinds of "unsettlers" these days.

Nancy Roth is a writer, Episcopal priest, retreat and workshop leader, musician, and dancer. She is the author of 13 books (including Grounded in Love: Ecology, Faith, and Action*) and numerous articles, including nine in Lost Valley Educational Center's former publication,* Talking Leaves *(see revnancyroth.com/articles.html) and four previous articles in* COMMUNITIES *(see www.ic.org/communities-index).*